PROGRESS IN BRAIN RESEARCH

VOLUME 61

SEX DIFFERENCES IN THE BRAIN

The Relation Between Structure and Function

Recent volumes in PROGRESS IN BRAIN RESEARCH

PROGRESS IN BRAIN RESEARCH

VOLUME 61

SEX DIFFERENCES
IN THE BRAIN

THE RELATION BETWEEN STRUCTURE AND FUNCTION

Proceedings of the 13th International Summer School of Brain Research, held at the Royal Netherlands
Academy of Arts and Sciences, Amsterdam, The Netherlands, 22–26 August 1983

EDITED BY

G.J. De VRIES, J.P.C. De BRUIN, H.B.M. UYLINGS AND M.A. CORNER

Netherlands Institute for Brain Research,
Meibergdreef 33, 1105 AZ Amsterdam (The Netherlands)

ELSEVIER
AMSTERDAM — NEW YORK — OXFORD
1984

© 1984   ELSEVIER SCIENCE PUBLISHERS B.V.

ISBN FOR THE SERIES 0-444-80104-9
ISBN FOR THE VOLUME 0-444-80532-X

PUBLISHED BY:
ELSEVIER SCIENCE PUBLISHERS B.V.
P.O. BOX 211
1000 AE AMSTERDAM
THE NETHERLANDS

SOLE DISTRIBUTORS FOR THE U.S.A. AND CANADA:
ELSEVIER SCIENCE PUBLISHING COMPANY, INC.
52 VANDERBILT AVENUE
NEW YORK, NY 10017
U.S.A.

Library of Congress Cataloging in Publication Data

Main entry under title:

Sex differences in the brain.

    (Progress in brain research; v. 61)
    "Proceedings of the 13th International Summer School of Brain Research, held at the Royal Netherlands Academy of Arts and Sciences, Amsterdam, The Netherlands, 22–26 August 1983."
    Bibliography: p.
    Includes index.
    1. Brain—Sex differences—Congresses. I. Vries, Gerrit Jacob de. II. International Summer School of Brain Research (13th: 1983: Amsterdam, Netherlands). III. Series. [DNLM: 1. Brain—physiology—congresses. 2. Brain—anatomy & histology—congresses. 3. Sex Factors–congresses. 4. Sex Differentiation–congresses. W1 PR667J v.61 / QS 640 161 1983s]
QP376.P7 vol. 61 612'.82 s[599'.0188]   84-18695
ISBN 0-444-80532-X (v. 61)
ISBN 0-444-80104-9 (set)

PRINTED IN BELGIUM

List of Contributors

D.H. Abbott, Department of Anatomy, University of Cambridge, Cambridge CB2 3DY, U.K. (*Present address:* Institute of Zoology, Regent's Park, London NW1 4RY, U.K.)

J. Balthazart, Laboratoire de Biochimie Générale et Comparée, Université de Liège, place Delcour 17, B-4020 Liège, Belgium.

W.W. Beatty, Department of Psychology, North Dakota State University, Fargo, ND 58105, U.S.A.

C.P. Benbow, Department of Psychology, Johns Hopkins University, Baltimore, MD 21218, U.S.A.

R.M. Benbow, Department of Psychology, Johns Hopkins University, Baltimore, MD 21218, U.S.A.

S.M. Breedlove, Department of Psychology, University of California, Berkeley, CA 94720, U.S.A.

S. Butler, Department of Anatomy, The Medical School, Birmingham University, Vincent Drive, Birmingham B15 2TJ, U.K.

R.M. Buijs, Netherlands Institute for Brain Research, Meibergdreef 33, 1105 AZ Amsterdam, The Netherlands.

M.A. Corner, Netherlands Institute for Brain Research, Meibergdreef 33, 1105 AZ Amsterdam, The Netherlands.

J.P.C. De Bruin, Netherlands Institute for Brain Research, Meibergdreef 33, 1105 AZ Amsterdam, The Netherlands.

F.H. De Jonge, Netherlands Institute for Brain Research, Meibergdreef 33, 1105 AZ Amsterdam, The Netherlands.

T.J. DeVoogd, Cornell University, Department of Psychology, Uris Hall, Ithaca, NY 14853, U.S.A.

G.J. De Vries, Netherlands Institute for Brain Research, Meibergdreef 33, 1105 AZ Amsterdam, The Netherlands.

K.-D. Döhler, Forschungszentrum der Medizinischen Hochschule Hannover, Krankenhaus Oststadt, Podbielskistrasse 380, 3000 Hannover, F.R.G.

C.A. Dudley, Department of Neurology, University of Texas Health Science Center at Dallas, 5323 Harry Hines Boulevard, Dallas. TX 75235, U.S.A.

R.G. Dyer, ARC Institute of Animal Physiology, Babraham, Cambridge CB2 4AT, U.K.

J.A. Eberhart, Department of Anatomy, University of Cambridge, Cambridge CB2 3DY, U.K.

L. Gooren, Division of Endocrinology, Academic Hospital of the Free University, P.O. Box 7057, 1007 MB Amsterdam, The Netherlands.

R.A. Gorski, Department of Anatomy and Laboratory of Neuroendocrinology of the Brain Research Institute, UCLA School of Medicine, Los Angeles, CA 90024, U.S.A.

J.L. Hancke, Department of Clinical Endocrinology, University Medical School, 3000 Hannover, F.R.G.

R.E. Harlan, The Rockefeller University, 1230 York Avenue, New York, NY 10021, U.S.A.

R.A. Harshman, Department of Psychology, University of West Ontario, London, Ontario, Canada.

G. Heister, Universität Konstanz, Fachgruppe Psychologie, D-7750 Konstanz, F.R.G. (*Present address:* Blarestrasse 17, D-7750 Konstanz, F.R.G.)

M.A. Hofman, Netherlands Institute for Brain Research, Meibergdreef 33, 1105 AZ Amsterdam, The Netherlands.

C. Hofmann, Department of Clinical Endocrinology, University Medical School, 3000 Hannover, F.R.G.

J.B. Hutchison, M.R.C. Unit on the Development and Integration of Behaviour, University Sub-Department of Animal Behaviour, Madingley, Cambridge CB3 8AA, U.K.

B. Jarzab, Department of Clinical Endocrinology, University Medical School, 3000 Hannover, F.R.G.

J.M. Juraska, Department of Psychology, Indiana University, Bloomington, IN 47405, U.S.A.

E.B. Keverne, Department of Anatomy, University of Cambridge, Cambridge CB2 3DY, U.K.

D. Kimura, Department of Psychology, University of West Ontario, London, Ontario, Canada.

M.R. Kruk, Department of Pharmacology, Sylvius Laboratories, University of Leiden, Wassenaarseweg 72, 2333 AL Leiden, The Netherlands.

W. Meelis, Department of Pharmacology, Sylvius Laboratories, University of Leiden, Wassenaarseweg 72, 2333 AL Leiden, The Netherlands.

H.F.L. Meyer-Bahlburg, New York State Psychiatric Institute and Department of Psychiatry, College of Physicians and Surgeons of Columbia University, 722 West 168 St., New York, NY 10032, U.S.A.

B.J. Meyerson, Department of Medical Pharmacology, Box 573, Biomedicum, S-75123 Uppsala, Sweden.

J. Mos, Department of Pharmacology, Sylvius Laboratories, University of Leiden, Wassenaarseweg 72, 2333 AL Leiden, The Netherlands.

R.L. Moss, Department of Physiology, University of Texas Health Science Center at Dallas, 5323 Harry Hines Boulevard, Dallas, TX 75235, U.S.A.

H. Nyborg, Institute of Psychology, University of Aarhus, 4 Asylvei, 8240 Risskov, Denmark.

B. Olivier, Department of Pharmacology, Duphar B.V., P.O. Box 2, 1380 AA Weesp, The Netherlands.

D.W. Pfaff, The Rockefeller University, 1230 York Avenue, New York, NY 10021, U.S.A.

J.M. Reinisch, The Kinsey Institute for Research in Sex, Gender, and Reproduction, Indiana University, Morrison Hall 416, Bloomington, IN 47405, U.S.A.

S.A. Sanders, Department of Psychology, Indiana University, Bloomington, IN 47405, U.S.A.

M. Schumacher, Laboratoire de Biochimie Générale et Comparée, Université de Liège, place Delcour 17, B-4020 Liège, Belgium.

B.D. Shivers, The Rockefeller University, 1230 York Avenue, New York, NY 10021, U.S.A.

J.E. Shryne, Department of Anatomy, and Laboratory of Neuroendocrinology of the Brain Research Institute, UCLA School of Medicine, Los Angeles, CA 90024, U.S.A.

F.M.E. Slijper, Sophia Children's Hospital, Department of Infant Psychiatry, Gordelweg 160, Rotterdam, The Netherlands.

P. Södersten, Department of Psychiatry, Karolinska Institutet, S-141 86 Huddinge, Sweden.

S.S. Srivastava, Department of Clinical Endocrinology, University Medical School, 3000 Hannover, F.R.G.

Th. Steimer, Division of Clinical Biology of Growth and Reproduction, University Hospital CH 1211, Geneva 4, Switzerland.

D.F. Swaab, Netherlands Institute for Brain Research, Meibergdreef 33, 1105 AZ Amsterdam, The Netherlands.

C.D. Toran-Allerand, Department of Obstetrics and Gynecology, Columbia University, College of Physicians and Surgeons, 630 West 168th Street, New York, NY 10032, U.S.A.

H.B.M. Uylings, Netherlands Institute for Brain Research, Meibergdreef 33, 1105 AZ Amsterdam, The Netherlands.

C.E. Van der Laan, Department of Pharmacology, Sylvius Laboratories, University of Leiden, Wassenaarseweg 72, 2333 AL Leiden, The Netherlands.

A.M. Van der Poel, Department of Pharmacology, Sylvius Laboratories, University of Leiden, Wassenaarseweg 72, 2333 AL Leiden, The Netherlands.

N.E. Van de Poll, Netherlands Institute for Brain Research, Meibergdreef 33, 1105 AZ Amsterdam, The Netherlands.

C.G. Van Eden, Netherlands Institute for Brain Research, Meibergdreef 33, 1105 AZ Amsterdam, The Netherlands.

F.W. Van Leeuwen, Netherlands Institute for Brain Research, Meibergdreef 33, 1105 AZ Amsterdam, The Netherlands.

R.W.H. Verwer, Netherlands Institute for Brain Research, Meibergdreef 33, 1105 AZ Amsterdam, The Netherlands.

U. Yodyingyuad, Department of Anatomy, University of Cambridge, Cambridge CB2 3DY, U.K.

Preface

Although the notion that brain function is in certain respects sexually differentiated has been accepted for several decades, it was only in the seventies that Raisman and Field demonstrated that brain structure can be sexually dimorphic as well. Since then the number of discoveries of sexually dimorphic structures has risen considerably. The sexually dimorphic nature of the brain appears to be very stimulating for neurobiological research. It led to the exploration of steroid–brain interactions which lead to sexual dimorphism, and further to the study of the developmental processes involved in sexual differentiation of the brain and it offers a unique opportunity to investigate whether functional differences are associated with structural dimorphism. The 13th International Summer School of Brain Research, held in Amsterdam in August 1983 was entirely devoted to the theme of sex differences in the brain and covered the afore-mentioned features.

This book, which contains the proceedings of this Summer School, commences with information on the various ways steroids are known to influence the brain. Not only the classical mechanisms of steroid action (e.g., binding of steroids to cytosolic receptors, translocation into the nucleus and subsequent alteration of genome expression) are discussed but also more recent concepts involving effects of steroids upon the cell membrane, thus directly influencing neurotransmission. In addition, the various pathways via which steroids, in particular testosterone, are converted by the brain, and the importance of this process is evaluated. But also the reverse, i.e., the ways in which steroids mold the brain during development by altering neuronal morphology as revealed by in vitro studies and the possible implications of such changes for further differentiation are.

In the second section most of the recently discovered morphological sex differences in the vertebrate brain are reviewed and discussed. This part of the book shows that sexual dimorphism can be demonstrated in a wide variety of parameters, such as the volumes of certain brain regions, the size and number of specific cells, the extent of dendritic and axonal branching and synapse formation. In addition, sex differences can be found in, e.g., the activity of neurotransmitter systems and the density of steroid receptors in several brain areas. Information is presented about the development of these sex differences and their possible significance.

The following section evaluates the way in which sexual differentiation can become expressed in functional terms. This aspect deals with sex differences not only in reproductive but also in non-reproductive processes (e.g., aggression, play-fighting). Factors such as the time of the day, the position within the group hierarchy, and previous experience, which all influence the expression of the sex differences, are also included in these discussions.

The final part is entirely devoted to studies on human subjects. It begins with a historical review of the research on sex differences in the human brain indicating the changes in the concepts of sexual dimorphism. These range from "proofs of female inferiority", deduced from e.g. differences in brain weight to more recent and substantiated ideas based on data on subtle morphological differences which may underly the various sex differences in brain function described in the following chapters. These contain data on EEG and brain-lesion studies which demonstrate sex differences in the cortical topography of modalities such as speech. Studies are further presented which try to evaluate the factors which underly the development of gender role and gender behavior. In addition, information is included about the influence of the factor sex and of gonadal hormones on parameters such as play, aggression, and cognitive processes e.g. mathematical reasoning both during development and in adulthood. These studies demonstrate that — although in some of these parameters the overlap between the sexes is often more striking than the difference — similar phenomena appear to be involved in sexual dimorphism of the human brain as in "lower" vertebrates, e.g., the presence of morphological sex differences and the influence of gonadal steroids on brain function both during development and adulthood.

This book will therefore be of interest not only for neurobiologists and (developmental) psychologists, but also for medical practitioners working in fields such as neurology, endocrinology and psychiatry.

G.J. De Vries
J.P.C. De Bruin
H.B.M. Uylings
M.A. Corner

Amsterdam, February 1984

Acknowledgements

The 13th International Summer School of Brain Research was made possible by generous financial support from the C.N. van den Houten Fund. We are indebted in addition to all of the following for supplementary contributions:

Duphar B.V., Amsterdam
European Training Programme in Brain and Behaviour Research, Strasbourg (France)
Fidia Research Laboratories, Abano Terme (Italy)
Genootschap ter Bevordering van Natuur-, Genees- en Heelkunde, Amsterdam
I.B.M. Nederland N.V., Amsterdam
Stichting Het Remmert Adriaan Laan-Fonds, Amsterdam
Organon-Nederland B.V., Oss
Sandoz B.V., Uden
Schering Nederland B.V., Weesp
Shell Nederland B.V., Rotterdam

We are also greatly indebted to the members of The Netherlands Institute for Brain Research for their constant support, and in particular, we would like to express our gratitude to Ms. J. Sels for her secretarial assistance. She took care of innumerable organizational details without which neither the Summer School nor the editing of its Proceedings would have been possible.

G.J. De Vries
J.P.C. De Bruin
M.A. Corner
D.F. Swaab
H.H. Swanson
H.B.M. Uylings

Contents

Section 1. — Steroid Actions on the Central Nervous System

Section 2. — Morphological Sex Differences in the Brain

Section 3. — Functional Sex Differences in the Brain

Section 4. — Sex Differences in the Human Brain

STEROID ACTIONS ON THE CENTRAL NERVOUS SYSTEM

G.J. De Vries et al. (Eds.),
Progress in Brain Research, Vol. 61
© 1984 Elsevier Science Publishers B.V., Amsterdam

Molecular Aspects of the Interaction between Estrogen and the Membrane Excitability of Hypothalamic Nerve Cells

ROBERT L. MOSS and CAROL A. DUDLEY

Departments of Physiology and Neurology, University of Texas Health Sciences Center at Dallas, 5323 Harry Hines Boulevard, Dallas, TX 75235 (U.S.A.)

INTRODUCTION

Sexual differentiation of brain structure and function is dependent on the hormonal environment during perinatal life. In the female rat, the model species for the present discussion, the presence of estrogen and the absence of testosterone during perinatal development leads to sexual differentiation of brain structure and function. In the adult female rat, both secretion of the gonadotropins from the anterior pituitary gland and the initiation and maintenance of sexual receptivity are under estrogenic hormonal control (for current review see Feder, 1981a). For instance, if the ovaries are removed, the gonadotropin surge does not occur and the rat fails to come into behavioral heat. However, both hormone secretion and behavior can be induced by the administration of estrogen, either alone or in combination with progesterone (Kobayashi et al., 1969; Swerdoloff et al., 1972; Kow and Pfaff, 1975; Johnston and Davidson, 1979). For the maximum effect in the latter situation, the administration of progesterone must be delayed for a day or more after estrogen treatment (Green et al., 1970; Caligaris et al., 1971).

Investigations into how estrogen regulates reproductive events focused initially on the study of peripheral target tissues such as the uterus. With the use of high specific activity [^{3}H]estradiol, selective retention of estrogen was demonstrated in the uterus, vagina and pituitary (Jensen and Jacobsen, 1962). Since non-target tissues, such as diaphragm, muscle and kidney, did not retain [^{3}H]estradiol, it was assumed that specific molecules binding estradiol must be present only in target tissue; this led to the concept of specific steroid receptors (King et al., 1965). Subsequently, the development of cell fractionation and quantitative binding techniques provided a means of studying subcellular distribution of the steroid. Estrogen receptors were found in the cytoplasm and estrogen receptor complexes were detected inside the cell nucleus in a variety of peripheral target tissues (for review see Baulieu, 1979; Clark and Peck, 1979).

The basic concepts contained in the current theory of steroid hormone action were first proposed by Jensen et al. (1968) and have been amplified by the above demonstrations as well as by experiments involving physiological and biochemical manipulation of the target tissue or the application of anti-estrogens. Current theory proposes that, in the absence of estrogen, the majority of estrogen receptors are located in the cytoplasm. When the target tissue is exposed to estrogen, the hormone readily passes through the cell membrane and binds intracellularly to cytoplasmic receptors. The estrogen–receptor complex then becomes translocated into the cell nucleus. It is presumably at this point that the main hormonal effects occur involving modification of gene transcription and the production of new proteins. The ultimate response produced by estrogen is thus genomic in nature in that estrogen triggers changes in the expression of the genome (Clark and Peck, 1979; McEwen, 1980). The consequences of this estrogen-peripheral target tissue interaction are necessary for reproductive success of the animal (Clark and Peck, 1979).

Although it is apparent that the influence of estrogen on both sexual behavior and gonadotropin release is mediated via the central nervous system (CNS), the study of the mechanisms by which estrogen might exert an action on CNS tissue has lagged behind such investigations in peripheral organs. The brain is anatomically and functionally more complex than peripheral organs and, although certain neural centers have been identified which participate in the modulation of gonadotropin release and/or sexual-behavior, their function may not be confined to the control of reproductive-related events. Nevertheless, since estrogen influences neuroendocrine events controlled by the CNS, it is logical to consider the brain as a target for estrogen action and therefore it becomes important to determine how estrogen is acting at the level of the nerve cell.

ESTROGEN RECEPTORS: THEIR LOCALIZATION IN THE HYPOTHALAMUS AND CORRELATION WITH ENDOCRINE FUNCTION AND REPRODUCTIVE BEHAVIOR

As previously mentioned, exogenous administration of estrogen to ovariectomized female rats has been shown to influence the release of gonadotropins from the anterior pituitary gland and to initiate sexual receptivity (Beach, 1942; Kalra and McCann, 1973; Zemlan and Adler, 1977; Whalen, 1980; Feder, 1981a,b). Gonadotropin release can be both inhibited and stimulated by estrogen. The inhibitory influence of estrogen has been demonstrated by studies in which ovariectomy (i.e., removal of estrogen) resulted in an increase in serum gonadotropin (Gay and Midgley, 1969), whereas administration of estrogen to ovariectomized animals suppressed the high serum levels of gonadotropins (Ramirez and McCann, 1963). Inferences about the stimulatory effect of estrogen on gonadotropin release have been made from studies demonstrating that an increase in plasma estrogen precedes the gonadotropin hormone surge necessary for ovulation (Naftolin et al., 1972; Nequin et al., 1979) whereas administration of anti-estrogen prevents this surge (Shirley et al., 1968; Ferin et al., 1969). Elevations in plasma estrogen also precede sexual heat in the intact animal and the administration of estrogen to ovariectomized animals produces a dose-dependent facilitation of mating behavior (Zemlan and Adler, 1977). Conversely, estrogen-induced receptivity can be negated by the administration of anti-estrogen (Arai and Gorski, 1968). Thus, estrogen "priming" is a prerequisite both for the induction of sexual behavior and for the surge in gonadotropin release.

The brain as a site of integration of estrogenic influences on gonadotropin release and sexual receptivity has been established by utilizing lesion and stimulation techniques as well as by direct implants of the steroid into specific neural centers. Although some controversy exists over the site of action in the brain for the positive and negative feedback effects of estrogen on gonadotropin release (see Feder, 1981a, for review), the suprachiasmatic-medial preoptic area (SCH-MPO) has been implicated in the positive effects of estrogen (Taleisnik and McCann, 1961; Goodman, 1978) and the arcuate-ventromedial area (ARC-VMH) seems to be the target for estrogen inhibition of gonadotropin secretion (Ramirez et al., 1964; Bishop et al., 1972; Everett and Tyrey, 1977). These same two sites are also critically linked to the expression of lordotic behavior. Lesions of the VMH interfere with the ability of estrogen to induce sexual receptivity (Mathews and Edwards, 1977) whereas lesions of the MPO reduce the amount of estrogen required to induce lordotic behavior (Powers and Valenstein, 1972). In addition, direct implants of estrogen into the MPO and VMH have been shown to be effective in the induction of mating behavior (Lisk, 1962; Dörner et al., 1968; Davis et al., 1982). Thus, at least two neural centers in the brain, namely the SCH-MPO and the ARC-VMH, can be considered to be target sites for estrogenic activity.

Early autoradiographic studies demonstrated a preferential accumulation of [³H]estradiol in neural centers of the hypothalamus (Pfaff, 1968; Stumpf, 1968; Pfaff and Keiner, 1973). Although the steroid has been found in a number of brain areas (see Zigmond, 1975; Pfaff, 1980, for review), especially high concentrations have been consistently detected in the MPO and ARC-VMH. Subcellular distribution of estrogen was elucidated in studies employing cell fractionation techniques. Eisenfeld (1969) and Kahwanago et al. (1969) demonstrated the existence of cytoplasmic estrogen receptors in the hypothalamus. Shortly thereafter, high estrogen binding was found in the nuclear fraction of tissue samples from the MPO (Zigmond and McEwen, 1970). Recently, cytoplasmic estrogen receptors in various nuclei and subdivisions of the rat brain were measured using a radioligand binding method (Rainbow et al., 1982); the highest concentration of cytoplasmic estrogen receptors was found in the periventricular-preoptic area, but high concentrations of cytoplasmic estrogen receptors were also detected in the SCH-MPO and ARC-VMH. These results are generally in agreement with autoradiographic and cell fractionation findings. As in peripheral target organs, brain cytoplasmic receptors bound to estrogen have been shown to translocate into the nucleus (Lieberburg et al., 1980). Thus, specific neural sites have been demonstrated both to concentrate estrogen and to contain cytosol receptors which translocate to the nucleus when bound. Furthermore, there is a remarkable overlap between brain sites implicated in gonadotropin release and mating behavior on the one hand, and those which concentrate estrogen, on the other hand.

The overlap between brain sites containing estrogen and controlling reproductive events appears to have physiological significance. The number of cytoplasmic estrogen receptors in the hypothalamus has been found to vary over the estrous cycle in such a way that on the day of proestrus, when circulating estradiol is high, the number of cytoplasmic receptors is at its lowest (Ginsburg et al., 1972). Injection of estradiol has also been shown to decrease the number of estrogen binding sites (Cidlowski and Muldoon, 1974). More recent studies using receptor exchange assays which allow measurement of cell nuclear hormone content have revealed high nuclear concentration of estrogen receptor complexes in the hypothalamus during the proestrus phase of the estrous cycle (McGinnis et al., 1981). In addition, the decrease in cytoplasmic receptors following injections of physiologic doses of estradiol has been shown to be accompanied by an increase in nuclear receptor content (Peck et al., 1979). Furthermore, it has been demonstrated that the degree and duration of estrogen occupation of neural receptors is associated with the influence of the steroid on gonadotropin release and sexual behavior (Parsons et al., 1981; McGinnis et al., 1981; Krey and Parsons, 1982).

The time course for elevation in the number of nuclear estrogen receptor complexes following exposure to the steroid is similar in the uterus and the brain, with maximum nuclear retention occurring within 1 h and remaining above control values for at least 6 h (Clark et al., 1979; Anderson et al., 1973). Despite the relatively rapid process of translocation of the estrogen–receptor complex into the nucleus, most of the effects of estrogen on gonadotropin release and reproductive behavior are slow in onset. The positive feedback effect of estrogen on luteinizing hormone (LH) release in ovariectomized rats cannot be obtained until 16.5–

22.5 h post estrogen administration (Jackson, 1973). Injection of antibodies to 17β-estradiol at 5:00 p.m. on diestrus was effective in blocking the surge of LH and ovulation on the following day (Zigmond, 1975). However, in this same study it was demonstrated that antibody administration at 10:00 p.m. on the day of proestrus did not interfere with either LH release or ovulation. The first signs of an estrogenic facilitation of female sexual behavior were observed at approximately 16 h following an intravenous estradiol injection, while full receptivity occurred 24 h following estrogen administration (Green et al., 1970). When in a later study (McEwen et al., 1975), a behaviorally effective dose of [^{3}H]estradiol was administered i.v., the hormone could be detected in the nucleus 4 h after injection. However, effects on lordosis became apparent only after 20 h, at which time very little nuclear estrogen was left. These results, coupled with findings from anti-estrogen experiments, indicate that nuclear binding of estrogen must precede behavioral and gonadotropic effects but need no longer be present at the time such effects are actually observed. In fact, it has been demonstrated that progesterone facilitated LH release and sexual receptivity can still be elicited 3 days after a brief (30 min) exposure to estrogen (Johnston and Davidson, 1979).

The time course both for estrogenic induction of behavior and for positive feedback of estrogen on LH release is consistent with a genomic mechanism of action. That genomic expression is indeed altered has been shown by inhibiting RNA-dependent DNA synthesis with actinomycin D or inhibiting protein synthesis with cycloheximide, both of which actions block the stimulatory influence of estrogen on LH secretion (Schneider and McCann, 1970;

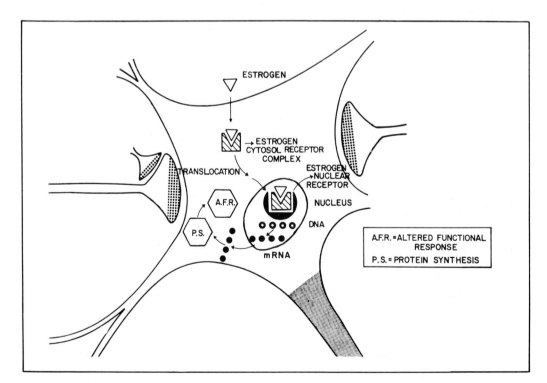

Fig. 1. Diagrammatic representation of the classical or "genomic" mechanism of action of estrogen at the level of a single nerve cell.

Jackson, 1973; Kalra, 1975) and on sexual behavior (Terkel et al., 1973; Quadagno and Ho, 1975). Furthermore, blocking axoplasmic transport by means of colchicine has been demonstrated to delay the induction of lordotic behavior by estrogen, whether administered systemically (Meyerson, 1982) or directly into the medial hypothalamus (Harlan et al., 1982).

The classical model of steroid hormone action derived from studies of peripheral tissues fits the experimental data discussed thus far concerning the brain as a target organ for estrogen action. Fig. 1 depicts this model at the level of the single nerve cell. Estrogen passes through the cell membrane and binds intracellularly to a cytosol receptor. The estrogen–cytosol receptor complex becomes translocated into the nucleus of the cell, which results in modification of gene transcription, new protein synthesis, and ultimately, an altered functional response.

EFFECTS OF ESTROGEN ON THE ELECTROPHYSIOLOGY
OF HYPOTHALAMIC NERVE CELLS

It is possible to draw several conclusions at this point in our discussion of the cellular mechanism underlying the actions of estrogen upon LH release and mating behavior. Firstly, the MPO, SCH, ARC and VMH areas selectively retain estrogen in neurons possessing cytoplasmic and nuclear estrogen receptors and these areas are essential neural links in mediating hormone secretion and behavior. Secondly, there is a positive correlation between the manifestation of secretion and mating on the one hand, and successful cytosol as well as nuclear receptor binding by estrogen in these areas and the transcription of new RNA and subsequent protein synthesis on the other hand. Finally, a minimum period of approximately 24 h appears to be necessary and sufficient to cause the estrogenic signal to initiate its biological actions. Thus, the question arises as to whether the slow estrogenic actions mediated by the CNS can be measured at the level of the nerve cell.

The ability of nerve cells to undergo estrogen-induced biochemical changes that are reflected in the ionic permeability and thus in the electrical conductance of the neuronal membrane has been demonstrated in a wide variety of experiments through the use of electrophysiological recording techniques (for recent review see Dufy et al., 1978; Komisaruk et al., 1981; Kelly, 1982; Pfaff, 1983). These studies have correlated nerve cell activity or membrane excitability of preoptic (PO)-hypothalamic (H) neurons with changes induced by: (1) the variations in plasma levels of estrogen that occur during the estrous cycle in female rats; (2) administration of estrogen, either intravenous (i.v.) or subcutaneous (s.c.); and (3) local application (iontophoresis) of estrogen directly to the neuronal membrane.

The possibility that estrogenic influences on the CNS could be detected at the level of the membrane of PO-H nerve cells was initially investigated in the early 1960s (Barraclough and Cross, 1963; Cross, 1964). These studies demonstrated that more single units in the hypothalamus were inhibited by pain, cold, and cervical stimuli during estrus than during diestrus, and that administration of estrogen to diestrous rats produced similar responses to those occurring on estrous. These results were soon confirmed and extended in studies comparing unit activity recorded from a variety of forebrain regions in persistent estrus, ovariectomized, and ovariectomized estrogen-primed animals (Lincoln, 1967; Lincoln and Cross, 1967). It remained to be determined, however, whether the endogenous variations in plasma estrogen levels during the estrous cycle would be reflected in the spontaneous activity of PO-H neurons. This has been shown to be the case in the MPO and anterior hypothalamic area (AHA), where an increase in unit activity was demonstrated on the afternoon of proestrus in regular 4-day cyclic female rats (Moss and Law, 1971; Cross and Dyer, 1971; Dyer et al., 1972) (Fig. 2). These data suggested that, since the MPO had already been implicated in reproductive functioning, the increased firing of a specific population of neurons could reflect estrogenic regulation of the endocrine system and/or sexual behavior. However, since several steroid and protein hormones vary over the estrous cycle, inferences concerning the exact role of estrogen are difficult to make in this fashion.

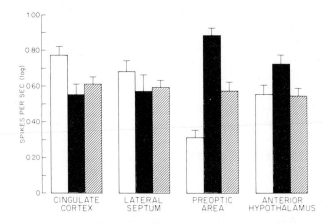

Fig. 2. Effect of the estrous cycle on single cell activity in the cingulate cortex (CC), lateral septal area (LS), preoptic area (POA), and anterior hypothalamic area (AHA). ⊓ = standard error of the mean; open bar = metestrus–diestrus; solid bar = proestrus; hatched bar = estrus. Changes in firing rates as seen in the POA ($P < 0.001$) and AHA ($P < 0.05$) are greater during proestrus than during the metestrous–diestrous or the estrous phases of the estrous cycle. (Modified from Moss and Law, 1971; with permission.)

A series of observations from the laboratory of Yagi and co-workers more clearly demonstrated the relationship between the electrophysiological activity of PO-SCH and ARC neurons and estrogen (Yagi and Sawaki, 1970, 1971, 1973). These authors first confirmed that an increase in firing of PO-SCH and ARC neurons occurs on the afternoon of proestrus. However, they extended previous findings by showing that a decrease in PO-SCH neuronal activity along with a further increase in ARC activity occurred 2 weeks post ovariectomy. Long-term estrogen replacement therapy (daily s.c. injections of estradiol benzoate for 2 weeks) was shown to decrease the number of MPO cells with recordable spontaneous activity while increasing the number of spontaneously active units in the basomedial hypothalamus (Bueno and Pfaff, 1976). However, the firing rate of units in the MPO, ARC, and septal area was shown to increase with similar estrogen treatment when compared to ovariectomized controls (Kubo et al., 1975). Thus the firing rate of MPO and ARC units varies over the estrous cycle, and can be influenced both by removal of endogenous estrogen through ovariectomy and by replacement of estrogen on the basis of repeated systemic injections.

Further evidence for the ability of estrogen to change neural activity was provided by experiments in which changes in spontaneous firing rate were observed in the MPO and ARC of ovariectomized animals following i.v. administration of estrogen (Yagi, 1970, 1973). The mean latency to response in each area was 16 min. These results were confirmed in subsequent studies which demonstrated that PO units which were shown to project to the median eminence were influenced by i.v. administration of estrogen, with latencies ranging from 5 to 30 min (Whitehead and Ruf, 1974; Dufy et al., 1976), while the non-identified PO units responded in 2–3 min (Dufy et al., 1976).

That estrogen can directly affect spontaneous electrical activity at the level of the neuronal membrane was demonstrated in our laboratory in the late 1970s (Kelly et al., 1977a,b) (Fig. 3). Using the technique of iontophoresis it was shown that estrogen (17β-estradiol hemisuccinate; 17β-E$_2$S) applied in minute quantities in the immediate vicinity of PO neurons rapidly (milliseconds to seconds) altered their spontaneous activity. The effect ended when steroid application was terminated and was easily reproducible. The specificity of response was confirmed by showing that application of $17a$-E$_2$S did not affect PO neuronal firing rate. Furthermore, the directionality (i.e., excitation or inhibition) of the response in the PO to 17β-E$_2$S varied over the estrous cycle (Kelly et al., 1976), and ovariectomy resulted in a decrease in the number of neurons responsive to estrogen (Kelly et al., 1978). In order to pursue the investigation into the effects of estrogen on excitable membranes under more controlled conditions, cultured pituitary cells were studied (Dufy and Vincent, 1980). Estrogen application to pituitary cells secreting prolactin resulted in changes in passive membrane properties within 1 sec. A transient depolarization was observed first, followed by a short burst of action potentials. Application of $17a$-E$_2$S had a much weaker effect, leading these authors to suggest that specific recognition sites for estrogen are present on the cellular membrane.

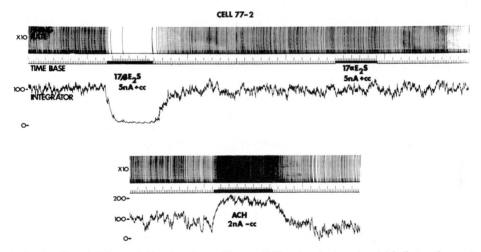

Fig. 3. The effect of 17β-estradiol hemisuccinate, $17a$-estradiol hemisuccinate and acetylcholine on the spontaneous electrical activity of a nerve cell located in the preoptic-septal region. Time base in seconds; ⊔ = 5 sec (2.5 mm = 5 sec). (From Kelly et al., 1977b, with permission.)

How do all these actions of estrogen on the electrophysiology of hypothalamic cells correlate with effects on behavior and gonadotropin release? Facilitation of mating behavior and positive feedback of gonadotropin release, both of which require the presence of estrogen approximately 24 h prior to occurrence, are likely to be the result of a genomic mechanism of action involving changes in protein synthesis as discussed earlier. Electrophysiological correlates of such a mechanism can be inferred from studies demonstrating fluctuation in single unit activity in the MPO and ARC over the estrous cycle, as a consequence of ovariectomy, following systemic estrogen therapy, and as a result of anti-estrogen administration (to be discussed in the next section). Thus, the long-term effects of estrogen can be measured at the neuronal membrane, although it is not known how nuclear binding and subsequent protein synthesis actually change neuronal membrane characteristics. However, the rapid effects of estrogen observed following iontophoresis certainly cannot be accounted for by a genomic mechanism, nor is it clear what the physiological significance of such rapid and short-lasting effects could be.

Electrophysiological investigations aimed at establishing the physiological relevance of the rapid membrane effects of estrogen have been tied to its influence on gonadotropin release. It has been demonstrated that the negative feedback of estrogen on LH release is relatively rapid (McCann, 1974; Legan et al., 1975). Dufy and co-workers (1975, 1976) reported that, following i.v. estrogen administration, a decrease in the firing rate of PO units projecting to the median eminence preceded a dramatic drop in serum LH. In a subsequent study, these investigators observed that actinomycin D or cycloheximide pretreatment did not interfere with the ability of estrogen to inhibit LH release (Dufy et al., 1978). Since RNA and protein synthesis were blocked, these workers proposed that the negative feedback of estrogen may be mediated at the level of the neuronal membrane.

Another in vitro approach used to study estrogenic influences on the neuronal membrane and subsequent effects on gonadotropin release is the hypothalamic slice technique. Drouva et al. (1983) examined the influence of estrogen on the release of luteinizing hormone-releasing hormone (LHRH) from superfused mediobasal hypothalamic slices. Whether estrogen (17β-estradiol) was administered to the animals prior to preparation of the slice or whether it was added directly to the superfusion medium, a significant enhancement of LHRH release was obtained within 30 min in response to depolarization evoked by elevating the K^+ concentration. No such response was observed with addition of 17a-estradiol, nor was somatostatin release affected by 17β-estradiol. Thus, estrogen appeared to act in this case through a process coupling nerve ending depolarization and LHRH release. Furthermore, the estrogen effect was hypothesized to be receptor mediated because LHRH-containing cell bodies are presumably absent from such slice preparation.

Kelly et al. (1980) studied the effects of estrogen on intracellular activity in hypothalamic slices from female guinea pigs presumed to include LHRH-containing neurons. Physiological concentrations of estrogen were shown to hyperpolarize neurons in the ARC-VMH area. The time course of the effect was similar to that reported for putative neurotransmitters. Morphological differences between cells responsive to estrogen and those which were non-responsive came to light through the use of a fluorescent intracellular marker (Kelly, 1982). Furthermore, some of the estrogen-responsive neurons have been demonstrated to contain immunoreactive LHRH (Kelly et al., 1983, submitted). These investigators hypothesized that the negative feedback of estrogen on LH release is mediated at the cellular membrane level via hyperpolarization of LHRH-containing neurons.

The rapid effects of iontophoretically applied estrogen on spontaneous electrical activity, as well as the rapid effects obtained in pituitary cell cultures and hypothalamic slice preparations, suggest that estrogenic influences on nerve cells may occur through a membrane-mediated action in a manner similar to that proposed for certain neurotransmitters and polypeptide hormones. This model of action, as seen in Fig. 4, proposes that hormones alter cell function by interacting with receptors on the cellular membrane. Such interaction stimulates the intracellular production of cyclic AMP. The cyclic AMP then binds to an intracellular receptor, where it stimulates phosphorylation of intracellular proteins to affect intracellular processes. This model does not require that the hormone actually enters the cell nor does it require the relatively long process of translocation to the nucleus and subsequent

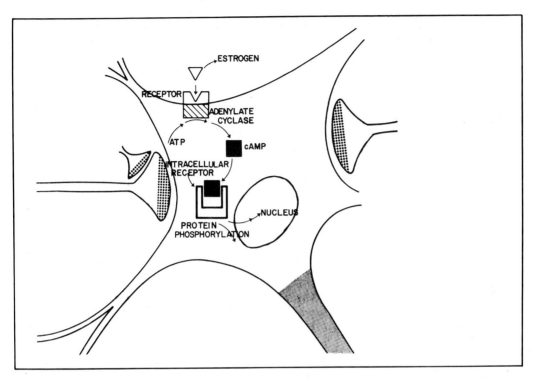

Fig. 4. Diagrammatic representation of a membrane-mediated mechanism of estrogenic action which is similar to that proposed for neurotransmitter action.

DNA-activated transcription of new RNA which results in alterations in protein synthesis that ultimately change cell metabolism. That a steroid hormone is capable of producing effects purely at the membrane level has been demonstrated recently with the *Xenopus laevis* oocyte: a progesterone analog linked to a soluble polymer which could not enter the cell, was nevertheless able to promote oocyte meiosis (Godeau et al., 1978). Similarly, Carette et al. (1979) have demonstrated that iontophoretically applied estradiol-7α-butyric acid, which does not cross the cell membrane, inhibits the firing rate of preoptic neurons within seconds. Thus, it is plausible to suggest that estrogenic influences on nerve cells may occur through a membrane-mediated action in a manner similar to that proposed for certain neurotransmitters and polypeptide hormones.

ACTION OF ANTI-ESTROGEN ON THE ELECTRICAL EXCITABILITY OF HYPOTHALAMIC NEURONS

Electrophysiological experiments conducted in our laboratory over the past few years have provided two lines of evidence which imply that the long-term effects of steroids can be detected at the level of the neuronal membrane. Guided by the well documented hypothesis that estrogenic modulation of sexual receptivity is a long-term, nuclear-mediated process, one approach has been to study the pharmacological responsiveness of the nerve cell membrane under hormonal conditions associated with a sexually receptive state. The other, more direct approach, has been to investigate spontaneous neuronal activity and pharmacological sensitivity in animals treated with anti-estrogens known to block sexual receptivity.

In the first approach neuronal membrane responsiveness to iontophoretic application of hormones, peptides and transmitters was investigated in the MPO and VMH. Hormone-primed ovariectomized female rats were treated with estrogen and progesterone, and electrophysiological recordings were obtained at a time when the animals were presumably sexually receptive, i.e. 4–12 h after progesterone treatment. In hormone-treated animals, more MPO neurons were excited by the iontophoretic application of LHRH than in the untreated rat (Moss and Dudley, 1978). In the VMH, more inhibitory responses were obtained in primed than in untreated animals (Chan et al., 1983). As observed in Fig. 5, alterations in membrane responsiveness in the VMH as a consequence of hormone treatment were somewhat specific as much as responses to prolactin or dopamine were unaffected by the ovarian hormones. The difference in the directionality of the response to LHRH, i.e., more excitatory responses in the MPO in primed animals but more inhibitory effects in the VMH, may be related to functional differences between these two centers in terms of their modulation of gonado-

TREATMENTS	CHEMICAL SENSITIVITY OF VMH NEURONS TO:			SEXUAL BEHAVIOR
	PROLACTIN	DOPAMINE	LHRH	
UNTREATED OVX Ss	↑	↓	↑	–
ESTROGEN-PROGESTERONE TREATED OVX Ss	↑	↓	↓	+

Fig. 5. The responsiveness of VMH neurons to iontophoretically applied prolactin, dopamine and LHRH related to absence (untreated OVX) or presence (estrogen–progesterone OVX) of sexual behavior.

tropin release and mating behavior as reviewed earlier. In an additional study, it was demonstrated that the iontophoresis of 17β-estradiol in intact cyclic animals had its most potent excitatory actions on MPO-septal neurons during the proestrus–estrus phase of the cycle (Haskins and Moss, 1983). Collectively, these experiments confirm that steroidal influences can be detected electrophysiologically by changes in chemical responsiveness of the membrane.

In an attempt to further elucidate the mechanism by which estrogen alters neuronal membrane characteristics, a second line of studies was initiated in collaboration with Dr. Bruce McEwen of The Rockefeller University. These preliminary experiments involved the use of the non-steroidal anti-estrogen, CI-628, which has been shown to be effective in blocking estrogen activation of lordotic behavior (Arai and Gorski, 1968; Whalen and Gorzalka, 1973; Etgen, 1979). Furthermore, the ability of this anti-estrogen to inhibit [^{3}H]estradiol binding by brain cell nuclei has been correlated with its ability to inhibit the display of estrogen-induced sexual receptivity (Etgen, 1979). Although the exact mechanism by which CI-628 antagonizes estrogenic activity is not clear, it has been demonstrated that this anti-estrogen translocates cytoplasmic estrogen receptors to the nucleus where it may be retained for long periods (see Etgen, 1979, for review). In addition, it has been proposed that anti-estrogens induce conformational changes in the nuclear receptor (Etgen and Whalen, 1981–82).

The electrophysiological investigations were designed to determine the effect of anti-estrogen treatment on spontaneous activity and on membrane sensitivity to iontophoretically applied 17β-E_2S of nerve cells in the MPO-septal (MPO-S) region. Ovariectomized female rats received one of the following treatments prior to electrophysiological recording: *controls* — no injection or oil injection at 0 h, *EB* — 4 µg estradiol benzoate at 0 h, *anti-E* — 20 mg/kg CI-628 at 0 h, *EB + anti-E* — 4 µg estradiol benzoate and 20 mg/kg CI-628 at 0 h plus 20 mg/kg CI-628 at 6 h, *EB + vehicle* — 4 µg estradiol benzoate and oil at 0 h plus oil at 6 h. Unit activity was recorded between 20 and 28 h. As seen in Fig. 6, no significant differences were found in the mean firing rate between the two *control* groups. Pretreatment with *EB, anti-E, EB+anti-E* or *EB+vehicle* significantly increased (t test: $P<0.005$) the mean firing rate of MPO-S units above the control level. The firing rate produced by $EB + anti\text{-}E$ was slightly but not significantly higher than that produced by either agent alone (versus EB, $df = 33$, $t = 1.053$; versus anti-E, $df = 19$; $t = 0.821$). These results demonstrate that, in the absence of estrogen, CI-628 can be as effective as estrogen in potentiating the spontaneous firing rate and that combining estrogen and anti-estrogen can further facilitate the effect. In a separate study, the firing rate of MPO-S neurons was recorded between 20 and 28 h in animals treated with EB at 0 h and 2.5 mg progesterone (P) at 18 h. The firing rate obtained as a consequence of EB + P treatment was similar to the *control* and lower than the *EB, anti-E, EB + anti-E* or *EB + vehicle*. Pretreatment with progesterone apparently suppressed the estrogen-induced increase in single cell firing rates, thus demonstrating the well-documented anesthetic-like action of progesterone on hypothalamic electrical activity (see Kelly, 1982, for review).

The results obtained following iontophoretic application of 17β-E_2S are presented in Fig. 7. The percentage of neurons responding to the application of 17β-E_2S was lower in animals treated with CI-628 than in those treated with *EB* or *oil*. A similar difference, although not as large, was observed between animals in the $EB + anti\text{-}E$ group and those treated with $EB + vehicle$. Thus, the administration of CI-628 alone or in combination with EB reduced the membrane responsiveness to iontophoretically applied 17β-E_2S.

CI-628 seems to have acted as an estrogen agonist in terms of elevating the spontaneous firing rate of MPO-S neurons as did EB, whereas its action on membrane sensitivity for 17β-E_2S was opposite to that exerted by EB treatment. CI-628 alone has been demonstrated to exert estrogen-agonistic actions in the uterus (see Clark and Peck, 1979, for review) and to mimic estrogen regulation of eating behavior and body weight (Roy and Wade, 1977). However, a single injection of CI-628 has not been able to facilitate lordotic behavior or to produce an LH surge (Arai and Gorski, 1968; Roy et al., 1979). The ability of CI-628 to antagonize estrogen-induced lordotic behavior depends on the time of administration of the anti-estrogen (Arai and Gorski, 1968; Roy and Wade, 1977; Wade and Blaustein, 1978), the most effective blockade being obtained when CI-628 was administrated 2 h prior to estrogen (Etgen, 1979). However, simultaneous administration of the two agents does inhibit sexual behavior (Landau, 1977). The present results demonstrate the ability of CI-628 to exert two effects on the nerve cell. Dual action of CI-628 was observed when the anti-estrogen was administered either alone or in combination with EB. CI-628 acted as an estrogenic agonist in that it increased the spontaneous unit activity in a manner similar to 17β-E_2S while at the same time and on the same neuron CI-628 reduced or antagonized the membrane responsiveness to 17β-E_2S. It is possible that CI-628 could exert its effect at two different sites or involve two mechanisms at a single membrane site within the same neuron.

As seen in Fig. 8, anti-estrogen may act at the level of the nerve cell membrane in 3 different but not mutually exclusive ways. Firstly, it may bind to a specific postsynaptic estrogen

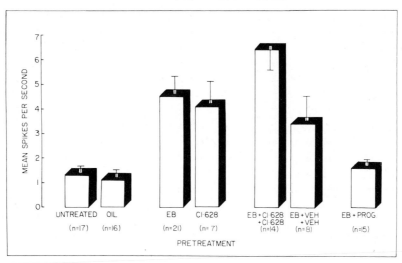

Fig. 6. Mean firing rate of neurons in the preoptic-septal (PO-S) area recorded following various estrogen (EB) and/or anti-estrogen (CI-628) treatments. VEH = vehicle; PROG = progesterone; ⊼ = standard error of the mean. Pretreatment (long term; 24 h prior to recording) with EB, CI-628, EB + CI-628 or EB + vehicle was found to significantly increase ($P < 0.005$) the electrical activity of PO-S neurons as compared to the activity recorded in untreated, oil- and EB + progesterone-treated animals.

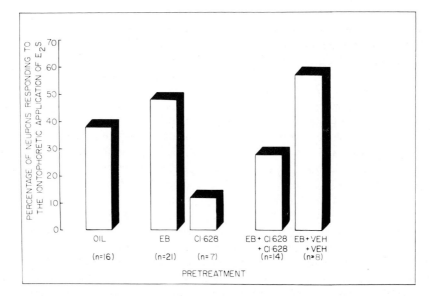

Fig. 7. The influence of various estrogen (EB) and/or anti-estrogen (CI-628) treatments (long term; 24 h prior to recording) on the percentage of preoptic-septal neurons responsive to iontophoretically applied 17β-E_2S (short term).

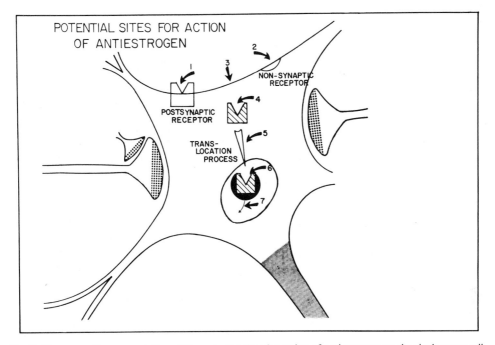

Fig. 8. Diagrammatic representation of the potential sites for action of anti-estrogen on the single nerve cell.

membrane receptor (1); secondly, it may bind to a non-specific membrane receptor (2); and/or thirdly, it may simply pass through the membrane (3) at which point it could block (or mimic) estrogen action at various intracellular sites (4, cytosol receptor; 5, translocation to nucleus; 6, nuclear receptor; 7, modified gene transcription). CI-628 could, for example, bind to specific postsynaptic estrogen receptors as well as pass through the cellular membrane. Further interpretations are difficult to make for several reasons. To begin with, the relationship between increased firing rate and decreased membrane sensitivity to 17β-E_2S in MPO-S neurons, on the one hand, and the expression of lordotic behavior or LH release, on the other hand, is not clear. Nor is it known if the anti-estrogen affects firing rate and membrane responsiveness at the level of the membrane or through an intracellular, nuclear-mediated process. Finally, when an individual neuron is tested, there is usually no evidence that the particular neuron under investigation is involved in a given behavioral or neuroendocrine event, or that it is capable of concentrating EB. Studies are presently in progress to resolve some of these problems.

CONCLUDING REMARKS

One of the most intriguing questions in the field of steroid hormone research is, "what is the mechanism by which estrogen exerts its many actions on the CNS?" The interaction of estrogen with the brain has been demonstrated to occur perinatally as well as in adulthood, and has been shown to modify both brain structure and brain function. However, the mechanism whereby estrogen induces these changes remains ill-defined. Many aspects of this interaction are discussed within this volume: for instance, the fact that estrogen causes an outgrowth of neurites in tissue culture (Toran-Allerand, 1984), is involved in the process of sexual differentiation of the PO-H area (Gorski, 1984; Döhler et al., 1984), and mediates gonadotropin secretion and sexual behavior (Dyer, 1984). The fundamental unit involved in these estrogenic mediated actions is the nerve cell and as such measurement of neuronal activity might provide valuable insight into how estrogen modifies the physiology of the CNS.

The present chapter evaluated the action of estrogen at the level of the nerve cell utilizing the electrophysiological approach. It is clear that estrogen effects on the electrical excitability of nerve cells vary considerably in time of onset, ranging from a few milliseconds to several hours. Presumably these time differences reflect the various ways in which estrogen can influence cell physiology, e.g. from a direct action on the surface of the cell membrane resulting in an immediate change in the spontaneous firing rate to an alteration of the expression of the genome.

The genomic action of estrogen on the nerve cell can be characterized by (1) a slow onset of the estrogenic effect which may take minutes, hours or days following the penetration of the steroid into the cell; (2) a duration of action which may last for many hours; and finally (3) sometimes even persistence of estrogenic action long after estrogen has disappeared. Estrogen acts via this genomic mechanism in order to mediate its positive feedback effects on gonadotropin secretion and on the initiation of sexual behavior. In contrast, the negative feedback effects of estrogen on gonadotropin secretion are probably not mediated via a genomic mechanism. The bulk of the existing evidence supports the notion that estrogenic negative feedback is mediated via a rapid mechanism perhaps at the level of the nerve cell membrane. Electrophysiological correlates of the genomic action of estrogen can be observed as gradual changes in spontaneous firing rate and the membrane responsiveness of PO-H neurons to transmitters and hormones following long-term exposure (24–48 h) to estrogen. Thus single cell activity increases and membrane responsiveness is modified with the long-term exposure to estrogen. On the other hand, when estrogen is applied, in minute quantities directly to the membrane of nerve cells, the effect is: (1) rapid in onset (milliseconds to seconds); (2) short in duration; and (3) present only as long as estrogen is available. This short-term action of estrogen is considered to be non-genomic, and presumably involves a membrane-mediated process. Interestingly, pretreatment with the anti-estrogen CI-628 enhanced the genomic action of estrogen by further increasing the spontaneous firing rate of PO-H neurons. At the same time, pretreatment with CI-628 diminished the membrane-mediated process of estrogen presumably by reducing the number of sites in which direct application of estrogen to the neuronal membrane can elicit an electrophysiological response. Thus is seems that specific binding of CI-628 with the membrane receptor site and the intracellular cytosol receptor complex may determine whether it antagonizes, mimics or facilitates a specific estrogen response. The full significance of such findings remains to be established.

The aforementioned data may be indicative of the fact that the individual neuron is elastic or pliable and thus can mediate relatively rapid turnover of macromolecules as well as regulate the slower process of synthesis and thus can maintain for a duration a memory or engram of the estrogenic-functional properties that need to be executed. It is generally thought that the nerve cell membrane poses no barrier to lipid-soluble estrogen. Thus estrogen can initiate a membrane-mediated process that is associated with changes in ion permeability and subsequently interact with a specific cytoplasmic receptor for translocation into the cell nucleus. The latter is a critical step in hormone action while the physiological significance of the former remains to be defined.

ACKNOWLEDGEMENTS

The authors wish to acknowledge Sue Sauter for her expert assistance in the preparation of this manuscript.

Research conducted in the authors' laboratory was supported by NIH grants NS10434 and HD11814.

In addition, the authors would like to thank Debbie Aldridge and June Roman for their technical assistance.

REFERENCES

Anderson, J.N., Peck, Jr., E.J. and Clark, J.H. (1973) Nuclear estrogen receptor complex: accumulation, retention and localization in the hypothalamus and pituitary. *Endocrinology*, 93: 711–717.

Arai, Y. and Gorski, R.A. (1968) Effect of an antiestrogen on steroid induced sexual receptivity in ovariectomized rats. *Physiol. Behav.*, 3: 351–353.

Baulieu, E.-E. (1979) Aspects of steroid hormone-target cell interactions. In: W.W. Leavitt and J.H. Clark (Eds.), *Steroid Hormone Receptor Systems*, Plenum, New York, pp. 377–399.

Barraclough, C.A. and Cross, B.A. (1963) Unit activity in the hypothalamus of the cyclic female rat: effect of genital stimuli and progesterone. *J. Endocrinol.*, 26: 339–359.

Beach, F.A. (1942) The importance of progesterone to the induction of sexual receptivity in spayed female rats. *Proc. Soc. Exp. Biol. Med.*, 51: 369–371.

Bishop, W., Kalra, P.S., Fawcett, C.P., Krulich, L. and McCann, S.M. (1972) The effects of hypothalamic lesions on the release of gonadotropins and prolactin in response to estrogen and progesterone treatment in female rats. *Endocrinology*, 91: 1404–1410.

Bueno, J. and Pfaff, D.W. (1976) Single unit recording in hypothalamus and preoptic area of estrogen-treated and untreated ovariectomized female rats. *Brain Res.*, 101: 67–78.

Caligaris, L., Astrada, J. and Taleisnik, S. (1971) Biphasic effect of progesterone on the release of gonadotropin in rats. *Endocrinology*, 89: 331–337.

Carette, B., Barry, J., Linkie, D., Ferin, M., Mester, J. and Beaulieu, E.E. (1979) Effets de l'œstradiol-7-α-acide butyrique au niveau de cellules hypothalamiques. *C.R. Acad. Sci. (Paris), Ser. D*, 288: 631–634.

Chan, A., Dudley, C.A. and Moss, R.L. (1983) Action of prolactin, dopamine and LHRH on ventromedial hypothalamic neurons as a function of ovarian hormones. *Neuroendocrinology*, 36: 397–403.

Cidlowski, J.A. and Muldoon, T.G. (1974) Estrogenic regulation of cytoplasmic receptor populations in estrogen-responsive tissues of the rat. *Endocrinology*, 95: 1621–1629.

Clark, J.H. and Peck, E.J. (1979) *Female Sex Steroids: Receptors and Function*, Springer, New York.

Clark, J.H., Markaverich, B., Upchurch, S., Eriksson, H. and Hardin, J.W. (1979) Nuclear binding of estrogen receptor: heterogeneity of sites and uterotropic response. In: W.W. Leavitt and J.H. Clark (Eds.), *Steroid Hormone Receptor Systems*, Plenum, New York, pp. 17–46.

Cross, B.A. (1964) The hypothalamus in mammalian homeostasis. In: G.M. Hughes (Ed.), *Symp. Soc. Exp. Biol., No. 18*, Cambridge University Press, pp. 157–193.

Cross, B.A. and Dyer, R.G. (1971) Cyclic changes in neurons of the anterior hypothalamus during the rat estrous cycle and the effect of anaesthesia. In: C.H. Sawyer and R. Gorski (Eds.), *Steroid Hormones and Brain Function*, University of California Press, Los Angeles, CA, pp. 95–102.

Davis, P.G., Kruger, M.S., Barfield, R.J., McEwen, B.S. and Pfaff, D.W. (1982) The site of action of intrahypothalamic estrogen implants in feminine sexual behavior: an autoradiographic analysis. *Endocrinology*, 111: 1581–1586.

Döhler, K.D., Hancke, J.L., Srivastava, S.S., Hofmann, C., Shrine, J.E. and Gorski, R.A. (1984) Participation of estrogens in female sexual differentiation of the brain; neuroanatomical, neuroendocrine and behavioral evidence. In: G.J. De Vries, J.P.C. De Bruin, H.B.M. Uylings and M.A. Corner (Eds.), *Sex Differences in the Brain. The Relation between Structure and Function. Progress in Brain Research*, this volume, Ch. 5.

Dörner, G., Döcke, F. and Moustafa, S. (1968) Differential localization of male and female hypothalamic mating center. *J. Reprod. Fertil.*, 17: 583–586.

Drouva, S.V., LaPlante, E. and Kordon, C. (1983) Effects of ovarian steroids on in vitro release of LHRH from mediobasal hypothalamus. *Neuroendocrinol.*, 37: 336–341.

Dufy, B. and Vincent, J.D. (1980) Effects of sex steroids on cell membrane excitability: a new concept for the action of steroids on the brain. In: D. deWeid and P.A. van Keep (Eds.), *Hormones and the Brain*, University Park Press, Baltimore, MD, pp. 29–41.

Dufy, B., Partouche, C., Dufy-Barbe, L. and Vincent, J.D. (1975) Effects of estrogen on the electrical activity of hypothalamic units: correlations with gonadotrophic hormone levels. *Int. Congr. Psychoneuroendocrinol.*, Budapest, pp. 303–312.

Dufy, B., Partouche, C., Poulain, D., Dufy-Barbe, L. and Vincent, J.D. (1976) Effects of estrogen on the electrical activity of identified and unidentified hypothalamic units. *Neuroendocrinology*, 22: 38–47.

Dufy, B., Dufy-Barbe, L. and Vincent, J.D. (1978) Effects of protein synthesis inhibitors on the negative feedback effect of estrogen on LH release. *Hormone Res.*, 9: 279–291.

Dyer, R.G. (1984) Sexual differentiation of the forebrain — relationship to gonadotrophin secretion. In: G.J. De Vries, J.P.C. De Bruin, H.B.M. Uylings and M.A. Corner (Eds.), *Sex Differences in the Brain. The Relation between Structure and Function. Progress in Brain Research*, this volume, Ch. 13.

Dyer, R.G., Pritchett, C.J. and Cross, B.A. (1972) Unit activity in the diencephalon of female rats during the estrous cycle. *J. Endocrinol.*, 53: 151–160.

Eisenfeld, A.J. (1969) Hypothalamic estradiol binding molecules. *Nature (London)*, 224: 1202–1203.

Etgen, A.M. (1979) Antiestrogens: Effects of tamoxifen, nafoxidine, and CI-628 on sexual behavior, cytoplasmic receptors, and nuclear binding of estrogen. *Hormone Behav.*, 13: 97–112.

Etgen, A.M. and Whalen, R.E. (1981–82) Kinetic analysis of estrogen and antiestrogen competition for hypothalamic cytosol estrogen receptors. Evidence for noncompetitive ligand-receptor interactions. *J. Recept. Res.*, 2: 531–553.

Everett, J.W. and Tyrey, L. (1977) Induction of LH release and ovulation in rats by radiofrequency lesions of the medial basal tuber cinereum. *Anat. Rec.*, 197: 575.

Feder, H.H. (1981a) Experimental analysis of hormone actions on the hypothalamus, anterior pituitary, and ovary. In: N.T. Adler (Ed.), *Neuroendocrinology of Reproduction, Physiology and Behavior*, Plenum, New York, pp. 243–278.

Feder, H.H. (1981b) Estrous cyclicity in mammals. In: N.T. Adler (Ed.), *Neuroendocrinology of Reproduction*, Plenum, New York, pp. 279–348.

Ferin, M., Tempone, A., Zimmering, P.E. and Van Wiek, R.L. (1969) Effect of anti-bodies to 17β-estradiol and progesterone on the estrous cycle of the rat. *Endocrinology*, 85: 1070–1078.

Gay, V.L. and Midgley, Jr., A.R. (1969) Response of adult rat to orchidectomy and ovariectomy as determined by LH radioimmunoassay. *Endocrinology*, 84: 1359–1364.

Ginsburg, M., MacLusky, N.J., Morris, I.D. and Thomas, P.J. (1972) Cyclical fluctuation of estradiol receptors in hypothalamus and pituitary. *J. Physiol. (London)*, 244: 72P.

Godeau, F., Schorderst-Slatkine, S., Hubert, P. and Baulieu, E.E. (1978) Induction of maturation in *Xenopus laevis* oocytes by a steroid linked to a polymer. *Proc. Natl. Acad. Sci. (U.S.A.)*, 75: 2353–2357.

Goodman, R.L. (1978) The site of the positive feedback action of estradiol in the rat. *Endocrinology*, 102: 151–159.

Gorski, R.A. (1984) Critical role for the medial preoptic area in the sexual differentiation of the brain. In: G.J. De Vries, J.P.C. De Bruin, H.B.M. Uylings and M.A. Corner (Eds.), *Sex Differences in the Brain. The Relation between Structure and Function. Progress in Brain Research*, this volume, Ch. 7.

Green, R., Luttge, W. and Whalen, R. (1970) Induction of receptivity in ovariectomized female rats by a single intravenous injection of estradiol-17β. *Physiol. Behav.*, 5: 137–141.

Harlan, R.E., Shivers, B.D., Kow, L.-M. and Pfaff, D.W. (1982) Intrahypothalamic colchicine infusions disrupt lordotic responsiveness in estrogen-treated female rats. *Brain Res.*, 238: 153–167.

Haskins, J.T. and Moss, R.L. (1983) Action of estrogen and mechanical vaginocervical stimulation on the membrane excitability of hypothalamic and midbrain neurons. *Brain Res. Bull.*, 10: 489–496.

Jackson, G.L. (1973) Time interval between injection of estradiol benzoate and LH release in the rat and effect of actinomycin D or cycloheximide. *Endocrinology*, 93: 887–892.

Jensen, E.V. and Jacobsen, H.I. (1962) Basic guides to the mechanism of estrogen action. *Recent Progr. Hormone Res.*, 18: 387–414.

Jensen, E.V., Suzuki, T., Kawashima, T., Stumpf, W.E., Jungblut, P. and DeSombre, E.R. (1968) A two-step mechanism for the interaction of estradiol with rat uterus. *Proc. Natl. Acad. Sci. (U.S.A.)*, 59: 632–638.

Johnston, P.G. and Davidson, J.M. (1979) Priming action of estrogen: minimum duration of exposure for feedback and behavioral effects. *Neuroendocrinology*, 28: 155–159.

Kahwanago, I., Heinrichs, W.L. and Hermann, W.L. (1969) Isolation of oestradiol receptors from bovine hypothalamus and anterior pituitary gland. *Nature (London)*, 223: 313–314.

Kalra, S.P. (1975) Studies on the site(s) of blockade by actinomycin D of estrogen induced LH release. *Neuroendocrinology*, 18: 333–344.

Kalra, S.P. and McCann, S.M. (1973) Effects of drugs modifying catecholamine synthesis on LH release induced by preoptic stimulation in the rat. *Endocrinology*, 93: 356–362.

Kelly, M.J. (1982) Electrical effects of steroids in neurons. In: K.W. McKerns and V. Pantic (Eds.), *Brain Peptides: Structure and Function*, Plenum, New York, pp. 253–277.

Kelly, M.J., Moss, R.L. and Dudley, C.A. (1976) Differential sensitivity of preoptic-septal neurons to microelectrophoresed estrogen during the estrous cycle. *Brain Res.*, 114: 152–157.

Kelly, M.J., Moss, R.L. and Dudley, C.A. (1977a) The effects of microelectrophoretically applied estrogen, cortisol, and acetylcholine on medial preoptic septal unit activity throughout the estrous cycle of the female rat. *Exp. Brain Res.*, 30: 53–64.

Kelly, M.J., Moss, R.L., Dudley, C.A. and Fawcett, C.P. (1977b) The specificity of the response of preoptic septal neurons to estrogen: 17α-estradiol versus 17β-estradiol and the response of extrahypothalamic neurons. *Exp. Brain Res.*, 30: 43–52.

Kelly, M.J., Moss, R.L. and Dudley, C.A. (1978) The effect of ovariectomy on responsiveness of preoptic-septal neurons to microelectrophoresed estrogen. *Neuroendocrinology*, 25: 204–211.

Kelly, M.J., Kuhnt, U. and Wuttke, W. (1980) Hyperpolarization of hypothalamic parvocellular neurons by 17β-estradiol and their identification through intracellular staining with procion yellow. *Exp. Brain Res.*, 40: 440–447.

King, R.J.B., Gordon, J. and Inman, D.R. (1965) The intracellular localization of oestrogen in rat tissues. *J. Endocrinol.*, 32: 9–15.

Kobayashi, F., Hara, K. and Miyake, T. (1969) Effects of steroids on the release of luteinizing hormone in the rat. *Endocr. Jpn.*, 16: 251–260.

Komisaruk, B.R., Terasawa, E. and Rodriquez-Sierra, J.F. (1981) How the brain mediates ovarian responses to environmental stimuli: neuroanatomy and neurophysiology. In: N.T. Adler (Ed.), *Neuroendocrinology of Reproduction*, Plenum, New York, pp. 349–376.

Kow, L. and Pfaff, D. (1975) Induction of lordosis in female rats: two modes of estrogen action and the effect of adrenalectomy. *Hormone Behav.*, 6: 259–276.

Krey, L.C. and Parsons, B. (1982) Characterization of estrogen stimuli sufficient to initiate cyclic luteinizing hormone release in acutely ovariectomized rats. *Neuroendocrinology*, 34: 315–322.

Kubo, K., Gorski, R.A. and Kawakami, M. (1975) Effects of estrogen on neuronal excitability in the hippocampal–septal–hypothalamic system. *Neuroendocrinology*, 18: 176–191.

Landau, I.T. (1977) Relationships between the effects of the antiestrogen, CI-628, on sexual behavior, uterine growth, and cellular nuclear estrogen retention after estradiol 17β-benzoate administration in the ovariectomized rat. *Brain Res.*, 133: 119–138.

Legan, S.J., Coon, G.A. and Karsch, F.J. (1975) Role of estrogen as initiation of daily LH surges in the ovariectomized rat. *Endocrinology*, 96: 50–56.

Lieberburg, I., MacLusky, N.J. and McEwen, B.S. (1980) Cytoplasmic and nuclear estradiol 17β binding in male and female rat brain: regional distribution, temporal aspects, and metabolism. *Brain Res.*, 193: 487–503.

Lincoln, D.W. (1967) Unit activity in the hypothalamus, septum, and preoptic area of the rat: characteristics of spontaneous activity and the effect of oestrogen. *J. Endocrinol.*, 37: 177–189.

Lincoln, D.W. and Cross, B.A. (1967) Effect of oestrogen on the responsiveness of neurones in the hypothalamus, septum and preoptic area of rats with light-induced persistent oestrus. *J. Endocrinol.*, 37: 191–203.

Lisk, R.D. (1962) Diencephalic placement of estradiol and sexual receptivity in the female rat. *Am. J. Physiol.*, 203: 493–496.

Mathews, D. and Edwards, D.A. (1977) The ventromedial nucleus of the hypothalamus and hormonal arousal of sexual behaviors in the female rat. *Hormone Behav.*, 8: 40–51.

McCann, S.M. (1974) Regulation of secretion of follicle stimulating hormone and luteinizing hormone. In: R.O. Greys and E.B. Astwood (Eds.), *Handbook of Physiology, Section 7, Endocrinology, Vol. 5(2)*, American Physiological Society, Washington, DC, pp. 498–517.

McEwen, B.S. (1980) The brain as a target organ of endocrine hormones. In: D.T. Krieger and J.C. Hughes (Eds.), *Neuroendocrinology*, Sinauer Associates, Sunderland, MA, pp. 33–42.

McEwen, B.S., Pfaff, D.W., Chaptal, C. and Luine, U.N. (1975) Brain cell nuclear retention of [³H]estradiol doses able to promote lordosis: temporal and regional aspects. *Brain Res.*, 86: 155–161.

McGinnis, M.Y., Krey, L.C., MacLusky, N.J. and McEwen, B.S. (1981) Characterization of steroid receptor levels in intact and ovariectomized estrogen-treated rats: an examination of the quantitative, temporal, and endocrine factors which influence efficacy of an estradiol stimulus. *Neuroendocrinology*, 33: 157–161.

Meyerson, B.J. (1982) Colchicine delays the estrogen-induced copulatory response in the ovariectomized female rat. *Brain Res.*, 253: 281–286.

Moss, R.L. and Dudley, C.A. (1978) Changes in responsiveness of medial preoptic neurons to the microelectrophoresis of releasing hormones as a function of ovarian hormones. *Brain Res.*, 149: 511–515.

Moss, R.L. and Law, O.T. (1971) The estrous cycle: its influence on single unit activity in the forebrain. *Brain Res.*, 30: 435–438.

Naftolin, F., Brown-Grant, K. and Corker, C.S. (1972) Plasma and pituitary luteinizing hormone and peripheral plasma oestradiol concentrations in the normal oestrus cycle of the rat and after experimental manipulation of the cycle. *J. Endocrinol.*, 53: 17–30.

Nequin, L.G., Alvarez, J. and Schwartz, N.B. (1979) Measurement of serum steroid and gonadotropin levels and uterine and ovarian variables throughout the 4-day and 5-day estrous cycles in the rat. *Biol. Reprod.*, 20: 659–670.

Parsons, B., Rainbow, T.C., Pfaff, D.W. and McEwen, B.S. (1981) A discontinuous schedule of oestradiol binding in rat hypothalamus is sufficient to activate lordosis behavior and to increase cytosol progestin receptors. *Nature (London)*, 292: 58–59.

Peck, Jr., E.J., Miller, A.L. and Kelner, K. (1979) Estrogen receptors and activation of RNA polymerases by estrogens in the central nervous system. In: T.H. Hamilton, J.H. Clark and W.A. Sadler (Eds.), *Ontogeny of Receptors and Reproductive Hormone Action*, Raven, New York, pp. 403–410.

Pfaff, D.W. (1968) Autoradiographic localization of radioactivity in the rat brain after injection of tritiated sex hormones. *Science*, 161: 1355–1356.

Pfaff, D.W. (1980) *Estrogens and Brain Function*, Springer, New York.

Pfaff, D.W. (1983) Actions of estrogens and progestins on nerve cells. *Science*, 219: 808–814.

Pfaff, D.W. and Keiner, M. (1973) Atlas of estradiol-concentrating cells in the central nervous system of the female rat. *J. Comp. Neurol.*, 151: 121–158.

Powers, B. and Valenstein, E.S. (1972) Sexual receptivity: facilitation by medial preoptic lesions in female rats. *Science*, 175: 1003–1005.

Quadagno, D.M. and Ho, G.K.W. (1975) The reversible inhibition of steroid-induced sexual behavior by intracranial cycloheximide. *Hormone Behav.*, 6: 19–26.

Rainbow, T.C., Parsons, B., MacLusky, N.J. and McEwen, B.S. (1982) Estradiol receptor levels in rat hypothalamic and limbic nuclei. *J. Neurosci.*, 2: 1439–1445.

Ramirez, V.D. and McCann, S.M. (1963) Comparison of the regulation of luteinizing hormone (LH) secretion in immature and adult rats. *Endocrinology*, 72: 452–462.

Ramirez, V.D., Abrams, R.M. and McCann, S.M. (1964) Effect of estradiol implants in the hypothalamohypophysial region of the rat on the secretion of luteinizing hormone. *Endocrinology*, 75: 243–248.

Roy, E.J. and Wade, G.N. (1977) Role of food intake in estradiol-induced body weight changes in female rats. *Hormone Behav.*, 8: 265–274.

Roy, E.J., Schmit, E., McEwen, B.S. and Wade, G.N. (1979) Antiestrogens in the central nervous system. In: M.K. Agarwal (Ed.), *Antihormones*, Elsevier, Amsterdam, pp. 181–197.

Schneider, H.P.G. and McCann, S.M. (1970) Estradiol and the neuroendocrine control of LH release in vitro. *Endocrinology*, 87: 330–338.

Shirley, B., Wolinsky, J. and Schwartz, N.B. (1968) Effects of a single injection of an estrogen antagonist on the estrous cycle of the rat. *Endocrinology*, 82: 959–968.

Stumpf, W.E. (1968) Estradiol concentrating neurons: topography in the hypothalamus by dry-mount autoradiography. *Science*, 162: 1001-1003.

Swerdoloff, R.S., Jacobs, H.S. and Odell, W.D. (1972) Synergistic role of progesterone in estrogen induction of LH and FSH surge. *Endocrinology*, 90: 1529–1536.

Taleisnik, S. and McCann, S.M. (1961) Effects of hypothalamic lesions on the secretion and storage of hypophysial luteinizing hormone. *Endocrinology*, 68: 263–272.

Terkel, A.A., Shryne, J. and Gorski, R.A. (1973) Inhibition of estrogen facilitation of sexual behavior by the intra-cerebral infusion of actinomycin-D. *Hormone Behav.*, 4: 377–386.

Toran-Allerand, C.D. (1984) On the genesis of sexual differentiation of the central nervous system: morpho-genetic consequences of steroidal exposure and possible role of α-fetoprotein. In: G.J. De Vries, J.P.C. De Bruin, H.B.M. Uylings and M.A. Corners (Eds.), *Sex Differences in the Brain. The Relation between Structure and Function. Progress in Brain Research*, this volume, Ch. 4.

Wade, G.M. and Blaustein, J.D. (1978) Effects of an antiestrogen on neural estradiol binding and on behaviors in female rats. *Endocrinology*, 102: 245–251.

Whalen, R.E. (1980) Hormone receptors in the brain. In: D. deWard and P.A. van Keep (Eds.), *Hormones and the Brain*, University Park Press, Baltimore, MD, pp. 3–10.

Whalen, R.E. and Gorzalka, B.B. (1973) Effects of an estrogen antagonist on behavior and on estrogen retention in neural and peripheral target tissues. *Physiol. Behav.*, 10: 35–40.

Whitehead, S.A. and Ruf, K.B. (1974) Responses of antidromically identified preoptic neurons in the rat to neuro-transmitters and to estrogen. *Brain Res.*, 79: 185–198.

Yagi, K. (1970) Effects of estrogen on unit activity of rat hypothalamus. *J. Physiol. Soc. Jpn.*, 32: 692–693.

Yagi, K. (1973) Changes in firing rates of single preoptic and hypothalamic units following an intravenous administration of estrogen in the castrated female rat. *Brain Res.*, 53: 343–352.

Yagi, K. and Sawaki, Y. (1970) Neural mechanism in the rat hypothalamus. *J. Physiol. Soc. Jpn.*, 32: 496.

Yagi, K. and Sawaki, Y. (1971) Changes in the electrical activity of the hypothalamus during sexual cycle and the effect of castration on it in the female rat. *J. Physiol. Soc. Jpn.*, 33: 546–547.

Yagi, K. and Sawaki, Y. (1973) Feedback of estrogen in the hypothalamic control of gonadotropin secretion. In: K. Yagi and S. Yoshida (Eds.), *Neuroendocrine Control*, University of Tokyo Press, Tokyo, pp. 297–325.

Zemlan, F.P. and Adler, N.T. (1977) Hormonal control of female sexual behavior in the rat. *Hormone Behav.*, 9: 345–377.

Zigmond, R.E. (1975) Binding, metabolism, and action of steroid hormones in the central nervous system. In: L.L. Iverson, S.D. Iverson and S.H. Snyder (Eds.), *Handbook of Psychopharmacology, Vol. 5*, Plenum, New York, pp. 239–328.

Zigmond, R.E. and McEwen, B.S. (1970) Selective retention of estradiol by brain cell nuclei in specific regions of the ovariectomized rat. *J. Neurochem.*, 17: 889–899.

DISCUSSION

E. FRIDE: Do you know of any evidence for a similar action on the cell membrane for other steroids, such as corticosterone?

R.L. MOSS: There are a number of investigators that have iontophoretically applied the adrenocortical steroids to nerve cells, namely Drs. Fedman, Ruf, Steiner, and Mandelbrod. In general, the application of corticosteroid, a potent inhibitor of ACTH secretion, can either excite or inhibit neuronal spontaneous activity. Some of the corticosteroid-induced effects persisted for 20–30 sec after steroid application.

E. FRIDE: If the assumption is correct that the short-term action of estrogen may be through membrane or cytosol receptors (which are presumably proteins), don't you think that inhibition of protein synthesis (with e.g. cycloheximide) — if given well before your measurements — should interfere with these short-term actions too?

R.L. MOSS: What my data suggest is that a single steroid-containing neuron or a non-steroid-containing neuron may also have an estrogen-sensitive receptor on the surface membrane. Evidence has been published indicating that protein synthesis inhibitors do block estrogen nuclear-mediated events but I do not know the effect of such substances on the membrane activity of neurons.

R.G. DYER: The circumstantial evidence for a membrane receptor for estrogen is now quite strong. However, there is no reason to locate this receptor upon postsynaptic sites. All of the known short-term effects of estrogen upon the electrical activity of the neurons can be explained equally well if the steroid occupies a presynaptic receptor. If this is indeed the case, the cell bodies of neurons with presynaptic membrane receptors for estrogen may be distant from the postsynaptic neurons. Since the electrophysiological evidence suggests that occupation of the membrane receptor is a transient process, and therefore unlikely to be detected with autoradiographic techniques, should we now consider the maps showing the distribution of estrogen-receptive cells to be out of date.

R.L. MOSS: Estrogen membrane receptors can be located on the postsynaptic membrane as well as pre-synaptic terminals. The existence of presynaptic estrogen receptors is not entirely new, since Dr. Kordon and co-workers have demonstrated that in the mediobasal hypothalamic slice, K^+-induced release of LHRH can be enhanced by estrogen and blocked by tamoxifen. Since this preparation has mainly fibers, a presynaptic system must be involved to explain the data.

D.W. PFAFF: If the immediate effect of estradiol is behaviorally important, why does it take reproductive behavior 24–48 h or more after estrogen to appear?

R.L. MOSS: I believe that the action of estrogen in sexual behavior is nuclear mediated (genomic). However, I also feel that estrogen can also modulate the membrane activity of neurons involved in sexual behavior to "fine tune" the many overt and covert aspects of the behavior.

J. RODRIGUEZ-SIERRA: What is the response of cells to iontophoretically applied 17β-estradiol nemisuccinate after treatment with estradiol and progesterone?

R.L. MOSS: That specific experiment has not been completed.

J. RODRIGUEZ-SIERRA: If the lordosis response is a genomic response, why is it present in ovariectomized animals? Could it be that estrogen activated sexual behavior via a non-genomic mechanism?

R.L. MOSS: Here again, the main mechanism of estrogen in sexual behavior appears to be genomic. However, under certain extreme, non-physiological conditions the modification of the "sex behavior neurons" can result in the display of a lordotic-like posture.

G.J. De Vries et al. (Eds.),
Progress in Brain Research, Vol. 61
© 1984 Elsevier Science Publishers B.V., Amsterdam

Androgen Metabolism in the Brain: Behavioural Correlates

J.B. HUTCHISON and Th. STEIMER *

M.R.C. Unit on the Development and Integration of Behaviour, University Sub-Department of Animal Behaviour, Madingley, Cambridge CB3 8AA (Great Britain)

INTRODUCTION

The view that behaviour can be related directly to hormone-sensitive cellular events in the brain has received support over the past decade. This is a result of increasing knowledge of the way in which hormonal steroids influence target cells. Studies of the fate of radioactively labelled sex steroids in peripheral target tissues, such as the chick oviduct for oestrogen (O'Malley and Means, 1974) and the rat prostate for androgen (Mainwaring, 1977), have shown that steroids enter the target cell, and bind to high-affinity, low-capacity "receptor" proteins in the cytoplasm. The steroid–receptor complex is translocated to the cell nucleus where initiated genomic events modify the physiological characteristics of the target cell. Biochemical studies have now raised the possibility that this classical cellular model of the action of steroid hormones may be applicable to brain cells associated with reproductive behaviour.

Correlations between the localization of oestrogen or progestin receptors in the ventromedial hypothalamic nuclei and brain areas known to be responsive to the behavioural effects of locally acting hormone implants have been established in the female rat (reviewed by Pfaff, 1980; Pfaff and McEwen, 1983; Harlan et al., 1984). Although less is known about hormone-sensitive brain mechanisms underlying male sexual behaviour, there is evidence that androgenic hormones influence preoptic and hypothalamic loci associated with masculine copulatory behaviour in many vertebrate groups. These loci, which appear to be stable, irrespective of phylogenetic status (reviewed by Kelley and Pfaff, 1978; J.B. Hutchison, 1978; McEwen, 1981), take up [³H]testosterone. Since cytosolic androgen receptor molecules have been identified in hypothalamic cells (Kato, 1976; Sheridan, 1981, 1983), it can be argued that, as in the female rat, the classical model of steroid action also applies to male sexual behaviour. Steroid receptors within the cytoplasm and nucleus, in particular, have attracted attention as possible intracellular regulators of steroid action in both the neuroendocrine (McEwen, 1981) and psychiatric literature (Rubin, 1982). However, other cellular mechanisms are clearly implicated in the action of steroid hormones on brain function. For example, oestradiol increases electrical activity in individual hypothalamic neurones within seconds of electrophoretic application to the cell membrane, suggesting that this hormone directly affects membrane excitability (Kelly et al., 1977; Dufy and Vincent,

---

* Present address: Division of Clinical Biology of Growth and Reproduction, University Hospital CH 1211, Geneva 4, Switzerland.

1980; Moss and Dudley, 1984). The question arises, therefore, whether the classical model of steroid action, applied successfully to simple reflexive patterns of lordosis (Pfaff and McEwen, 1983), has any alternatives. Can other cellular mechanisms be related to more complex patterns of sexual behaviour where environment influences the rapidly changing interaction between male and female?

With the development of radioimmunoassay methods for the accurate measurement of sex hormones in blood plasma, there is now a wealth of information indicating that circulating gonadotrophic and steroid hormone levels show not only daily rhythms, but also rapid responses to social stimulation (Coquelin and Bronson, 1980) or stressful events in the environment. In many mammals (Bronson, 1979) and birds (Wingfield, 1983) there is a strong correlation between male sexual behaviour and elevated plasma sex hormones. The conclusion that there is a causal relationship between increased androgen secretion, activated protein synthesis in hypothalamic target cells and male behaviour is attractively simple. But in practice, relationships between male sexual behaviour and plasma androgen levels are notoriously difficult to unravel. For example, the male rhesus monkey, interacting with a female after a period of isolation, shows an increase in plasma testosterone and a correlated increase in sexual behaviour. However, in a social situation where dominance rank of the male is important in determining the type of behavioural interaction with the female, plasma testosterone level and male sexual behaviour become dissociated, suggesting that individual behavioural responsiveness to endogenous androgen is affected by environmental factors (Rose, 1980; Keverne et al., 1984).

The major question to be considered in this paper is whether cellular mechanisms associated with the action of androgen in the brain have a role in mediating the effects of environment on behaviour. A second, and related question, is whether such mechanisms are specific to the male brain and do not occur in the female. The gap between behavioural and biochemical levels of analysis is obviously wide, but there are indications that the beginnings of an answer to these questions may be found in cellular events in the brain that do not initially involve the cell nucleus. Studies of steroid metabolism, mainly in the rat brain (reviewed by Martini, 1982), have established that androgens are extensively converted to biologically active metabolites. Unlike peripheral target tissues such as the prostate and seminal vesicles (Mainwaring, 1977; Hamilton and Ofner, 1982), where the major metabolites are 5α-reduced androgens, the brain also has the capacity to convert androgens to oestrogens. The existence of two physiologically important metabolic pathways within the same brain areas (Selmanoff et al., 1977), and possibly even in the same cells, appears to be a unique feature of brain tissue (Martini, 1982). This capacity of brain cells to convert androgens to physiologically active metabolites such as oestrogens is widespread in vertebrates (Callard et al., 1978) and is thought to be a phylogenetically "primitive" characteristic. In contrast to androgens, circulating oestrogens do not appear to be converted to physiologically active steroids in brain target areas. Although the catechol oestrogens may represent active metabolites (reviewed by Naftolin et al., 1975; Goy and McEwen, 1980; Parvisi et al., 1981) their role in both lordosis behaviour and gonadotrophin release is difficult to substantiate (Krey et al., 1983). There is, therefore, a difference in the fate of the major sex hormones within the brain where rapid metabolic "activation", relatively unimportant in 17β-oestradiol action, is crucial to the action of testosterone. Given the fact that androgens circulate at higher concentrations in males of most vertebrate species, it follows that pathways of androgen metabolism are likely to be associated more with hormone action in the male brain than in the female. As will be discussed later, this does not necessarily mean that there are inherent sex differences in androgen-metabolizing enzymes or their activity.

In view of the complexity of mammalian hormone–behaviour relationships (e.g. Holman and Hutchison, 1982), discussion of the role of androgen metabolism in the brain cannot be restricted to mammals alone. Submammalian vertebrates, particularly species of birds, are proving valuable in the study of androgen action, because male sexual behaviour is strictly hormone-dependent. The components are stereotyped and easily identified. Moreover, all of the enzymatic pathways for androgen metabolism in mammals are also found in the avian brain (Massa, 1980; Steimer and Hutchison, 1981), and the presumed metabolites of testosterone directly affect-target brain nuclei (Nottebohm, 1980) and individual neurones (DeVoogd and Nottebohm, 1981; DeVoogd, 1984) identified as being associated with behaviour. Bearing in mind these advantages of using the avian brain as a model for studying androgen action, the purposes of this paper are to discuss: (a) pathways of androgen metabolism in the brain relevant to behaviour; (b) recent data suggesting that brain enzyme activity, influenced by environmental stimuli, may act as a regulatory step in behavioural changes during the reproductive cycle; (c) the hypothesis that the sensitivity of brain mechanisms of behaviour to androgen may be determined in part by metabolic processes involved in the inactivation of this hormone; and (d) the role of androgen-metabolizing enzymes in developmental changes within the brain leading to sex differences in behaviour.

MOLECULAR ASPECTS OF ANDROGEN METABOLISM

Pathways of androgen metabolism in the brain

Studies of androgen metabolism in the brain and measurement of the relevant enzymatic activities are now possible using radiolabelled tracers of high specific activity which are usually tritiated steroids. Brain slices or tissue homogenates can be incubated in vitro under controlled conditions and the steroid products identified in terms of type, quantity and rate of production. Metabolic activity can also be examined in discrete areas, such as identified brain nuclei associated with androgenic effects on behaviour by means of microdissection procedures. A direct correlation can be made between molecular mechanisms, such as enzymatic conversions and receptor binding, and the behavioural effects of hormones. The influence of peripheral metabolism of androgens including catabolism in liver cells is eliminated using these in vitro methods. But complementary studies in vivo are required to assess the physiological significance of such findings. Systemic administration of tritiated hormones to castrated animals is commonly used for the estimation of steroid uptake in the brain and localization of hormone-sensitive areas. Application of this method to the study of brain metabolism has limitations, because brain cells are exposed to a wide range of steroid substrates arising from peripheral metabolism. Interpretation of the observed metabolic patterns is only possible if additional data from in vitro experiments are available. This problem can be solved by injecting, or stereotaxically implanting, radiolabelled androgens into the brain (Steimer and Hutchison, in preparation). Diffusion of the tracer is limited, metabolism can be studied in vivo in specific brain areas under more physiological conditions, and interference from peripheral metabolism is negligible.

The main pathways of androgen metabolism in the vertebrate brain (for reviews see Naftolin et al., 1975; McEwen et al., 1979; Martini, 1982), based on data derived from in vitro experiments in birds and mammals, show a general pattern (Fig. 1) which appears to be common to all brain regions. Aromatization presents an exception in that this pathway appears to occur only in limited areas of the brain, including the hypothalamus and

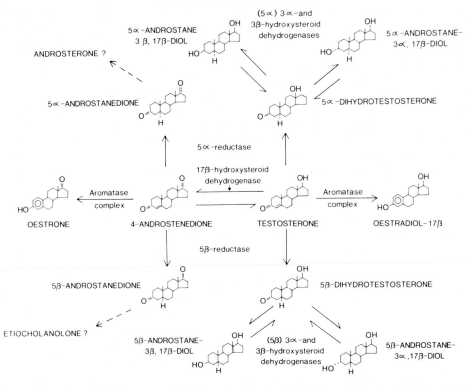

Fig. 1. Major pathways of androgen metabolim determined from in vitro studies carried out principally on limbic areas of the avian and mammalian brain (see Naftolin et al., 1975; Massa et al., 1977; Callard et al., 1978; Steimer and Hutchison, 1981a; Martini, 1982, for reviews).

amygdala (Selmanoff et al., 1977; Callard et al., 1978). However, there are pronounced quantitative differences in enzyme activities between, for example, hypothalamic and cortical regions (Denef et al., 1973). The two main androgens found in the plasma, testosterone and androstenedione, are interconvertible through a reversible reaction involving 17β-hydroxysteroid dehydrogenase (17β-HSD). The 5a-reduction pathway leading to the formation of 5a-dihydrotestosterone (DHT) via 5a-reductase and 3a- or 3β,17β-diols (via 3a- and 3β-hydroxysteroid dehydrogenase (3a-, 3β-HSD), respectively), is common to most male target tissues including the brain (Hamilton and Ofner, 1982). Aromatization of testosterone to 17β-oestradiol or of androstenedione to oestrone is, however, unusual in male peripheral target organs and appears to be a specific feature of the central nervous system (Martini, 1982). The coexistence of 5a-reduction and aromatization in the same brain areas seems paradoxical, because 5a-reduced metabolites, including DHT, are well known inhibitors of the aromatization reaction in other systems such as the human placenta (Siiteri and Thompson, 1975). However, it is not known whether these two enzymatic pathways occur in the same cells. If this is the case, differences in subcellular localization of the enzymes or other intracellular mechanisms may limit their interaction. An interesting aspect of the aromatization pathway in the adult avian brain, which is shared with lower vertebrates and juvenile mammals, is that it is highly active. Thus, at physiological testosterone levels (in the nanomolar range) concentrations of oestrogenic products formed in the preoptic area of the male dove (*Streptopelia risoria*) are comparable quantitatively to 5a-reduced metabolites

(Steimer and Hutchison, 1980). Such a relationship has not been shown to exist in adult mammals (Jenkins and Hall, 1977; Selmanoff et al., 1977). Therefore, the dove appears to be a particularly attractive model for the study of the effects of interaction between metabolic pathways on male behaviour at the molecular level.

The 5β-reduction pathway (lower part of Fig. 1) has been discovered in the brain recently, and has so far only been described fully in avian species (Nakamura and Tanabe, 1974; Massa et al., 1977, 1979, 1983; Steimer and Hutchison, 1981a). But, it is also present in the brain of mammalian species, notably the adult hamster (Callard et al., 1979) and foetal human (Lisboa et al., 1976). The 5β-reduced metabolites are also formed in the immature hamster (Terada et al., 1980) and avian (reviewed in Kime, 1980) testes. The major metabolites formed in this pathway are the 5β-androstanes, 5β-dihydrotestosterone (5β-DHT) and the two corresponding 5β-androstane 3α- and 3β,17β-diols (Fig. 1). Although 5β-reduction is a major catabolic pathway for androgens in the liver (Stylianou et al., 1961), its occurrence in an androgen target tissue is quite unique. Whether there are sex differences in brain metabolism of androgen is still open to question. The pattern of metabolism in the hypothalamus and other areas of the female rat brain following systemic injection of [3H]testosterone differs from that in the male. Thus epitestosterone and 5β-dihydroepitestosterone have been found specifically in areas of the female brain (Gustafsson et al., 1976). Other androgenic metabolites, 5α-androstane-3α/β,17β-diols also occur predominately in the female brain. By contrast, androstenedione and unmetabolized testosterone are the major androgens in the male brain. Gustafsson et al. (1976) have suggested that (1) testosterone is metabolized more rapidly to inactive compounds in the brain of the female than in the male, (2) testosterone is protected from metabolism in the male brain by being bound to specific high affinity, protein binding sites which are not detectable in the female brain. However, the relative importance of peripheral and central metabolism is difficult to estimate when [3H]testosterone is administered systemically. There are known sex differences in the hepatic metabolism of testosterone (Mode et al., 1981) which complicate interpretation of steroid uptake by the brain.

Aromatase activity measured by in vitro methods in limbic and hypothalamic areas of intact, adult male rabbits (Naftolin et al., 1975) and rats (Naftolin et al., 1972; Reddy et al., 1974; Selmanoff et al., 1977) is higher than that of females. This sex difference is greater when nuclei with the highest aromatase activity (e.g. preoptic and anterior hypothalamic nuclei) in the male rat brain are compared with those of the female (Kobayashi and Reed, 1977; reviewed in Goy and McEwen, 1980). However, interpretation is complicated by possible effects of endocrine condition on these apparent sex differences. Gonadectomy increases hypothalamic aromatase activity in both male and female rabbits and this eliminates the sex difference (Naftolin et al., 1975). In the absence of endogenous adrenal and gonadal steroids, the difference in hypothalamic aromatase activity between male and female rats is also much reduced (Selmanoff et al., 1977). Circulating steroids evidently contribute to sex differences in brain aromatase activity. No reliable differences between male and female 5α- or 5β-reductase have yet been demonstrated in mammals and birds (see Balthazart and Schumacher, 1983, for review). At present, it is premature to speculate on sex differences in brain metabolism of androgen until the molecular characteristics of these enzymes and their regulation have been taken into account. These aspects are considered in subsequent sections of this paper where enzyme activity is related to functional changes in the action of androgen on behaviour.

Metabolic activation and inactivation of androgens

All pathways of androgen metabolism shown in Fig. 1 are present in the avian brain (Massa et al., 1979; Steimer and Hutchison, 1981a), but pronounced differences in enzyme activity may exist between specific areas (Fig. 2). Enzyme-catalyzing reactions which result in the formation of biologically active metabolites, such as DHT and oestradiol, are part of *activation pathways*. The initial reaction in both the 5α-reduction and the aromatization pathways is irreversible. In the case of aromatization it is also a limiting step, because the low activity of the enzyme concerned will effectively control the availability of active metabolites for further cellular actions, including binding to specific receptors. Further conversions to other products which are less potent than DHT (e.g. the 5α-diols, MacLusky and Naftolin, 1981) are mainly inactivating, but may be reversible. The 5β-reduction of androgens, however, is irreversible and represents a major *inactivation pathway* in brain target cells. The 5β-reduction of androgens is likely to occur at an early stage of their cellular action in brain target areas. Due to the high capacity for conversion of testosterone to inactive metabolites, 5β-reductase is likely to interfere both with further metabolism and binding of active steroids to their specific intracellular receptors. Therefore, 5β-reduction can be considered a mecha-

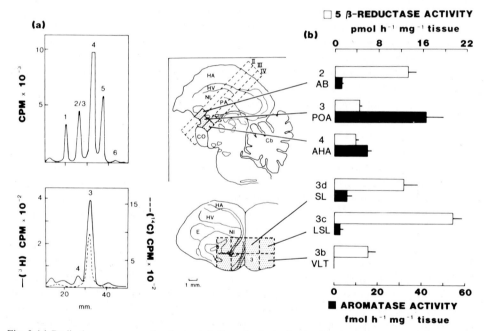

Fig. 2 (a) Radiochromatograms showing metabolites obtained after in vitro incubation of dove hypothalamic tissue with [³H]testosterone at physiological concentrations (1–10 nM). Upper panel: neutral steroids; 1, 5β-androstane-3α,17β-diol; 2, 5α-androstanediols; 3, 17β-oestradiol; 4, testosterone; 5, 5α-DHT; 6, 4-androstenedione. Thin-layer chromatography on silica gel, chloroform/methanol, 98/2 (v/v). Lower panel: thin-layer chromatography of 17β-oestradiol (silica gel, dichloromethane/diethyl ether, 85/15) after ion-exchange chromatography on QAE-Sephadex (recovery standard: [¹⁴C]oestradiol). Centre panel shows sagittal (upper) and coronal (lower) views of the brain giving planes of section and location of samples. (b) Distribution of aromatase and 5β-reductase activity in preoptic and adjacent areas of the dove brain (sexually active males). Area basalis (AB, sample 2); preoptic area (POA, sample 3), anterior hypothalamus (AHA, sample 4), septal nuclei (SL, sample 3d), lateral septal area (LSL, sample 3c), ventrolateral thalamic n. (VLT, sample 3b). (Modified from Steimer and Hutchison, 1981a, and unpublished data.)

nism of *primary inactivation*. This can be distinguished from *secondary inactivation* which occurs after the receptor–steroid complex has influenced genomic transcription. At this stage, specific pathways, notably terminal hydroxylation reactions affecting positions 6 and 7 of the steroid nucleus, appear to terminate the hormonal response by converting androgens to more polar metabolites that can be easily eliminated from the cell (Hamilton and Ofner, 1982).

Anatomical localization of enzymes

The anatomical distribution of the various enzymatic activities in the dove brain has been studied using a topographical micro-dissection procedure. The results of these studies show that 5β-reduction occurs in most parts of the adult brain, but is markedly lower in known androgen target areas, including the basal hypothalamus (see samples 3 and 4 of Fig. 2b, and Steimer and Hutchison, 1981). This distribution of 5β-reductase activity is consistent with its presumed role as an inactivating enzyme: androgens are eliminated rapidly in non-target areas, but must be available for a minimum period of time in areas where their action is required. In vitro experiments carried out at physiological substrate concentrations (in the nanomolar range) show that the half-life of testosterone in the dove brain, due to rapid inactivation by 5β-reduction, is approximately 7–8 min in non-target areas. In specific target areas such as the preoptic area (J.B. Hutchison and Steimer, 1981), it is prolonged by a factor of 5–10.

Aromatization of testosterone occurs only in limited areas of the dove brain, mainly the anterior hypothalamus-preoptic area and the posterior hypothalamus (see samples 3 and 4 of Fig. 2b, and J.B. Hutchison et al., 1981). These well-known androgen target areas are involved in the control of sexual behaviour and neuroendocrine activity (Davies et al., 1980). In mammals, aromatase activity also seems to be restricted to the hypothalamus and the limbic system (Naftolin et al., 1975; Jouan and Samperez, 1980). The data available on 5α-reductase in the dove brain indicate that the distribution of this enzyme is probably similar to that of 5β-reductase. This is surprising in view of the fact that it is supposed to play a part in androgen activation (Adkins-Regan, 1981), and it also contrasts with the situation in the mammalian brain (Denef et al., 1973). On the other hand, circulating levels of DHT are higher in birds (Feder et al., 1977) than in mammals. Central 5α-reduction of androgens in the former group may well be of limited physiological significance.

The subcellular distribution of 5β-reductase in the male dove brain has been established using cell fractionation. This enzymatic activity is, as in the liver (Stylianou et al., 1961), entirely localized in the cytosol ($105\,000 \times g$ supernatant of cell homogenates). It is probable that 5β-reductase interacts preferentially with substrate entering the cell and competes effectively with enzymes involved in alternative pathways, as well as with cytosolic receptors. The subcellular distribution of other enzymes in the dove brain has not been studied in detail yet, but it is likely to be similar to that found in other groups, where most enzymes of steroid metabolism are present in either the microsomal fraction (Noma et al., 1975) or the nuclear membrane (Verhoeven et al., 1974).

Enzyme kinetics

Knowledge of the kinetic characteristics of key enzymes will be required to establish a valid model of androgen metabolism in the brain and its regulation. Kinetic data can be useful in understanding the mechanism of action, control of isolated enzymes and the role of enzymes in the cell (Price and Stevens, 1982). There is some kinetic information concerning aromatase, 5α- and 5β-reductase in the dove brain. The aromatase complex found in the dove hypothalamus has a limited capacity for testosterone conversion to oestrogen, with a maximum velocity lower than 1 pmole/h/mg protein (Steimer and Hutchison, 1981b). The Michaelis constant (K_m), which can be considered as an index of the affinity of the enzyme for its substrate, is in the nanomolar range (approximately 2×10^{-8} M). Therefore, this enzyme will be most efficient at a low substrate concentration. But it is rapidly saturated when substrate concentration is increased, so that other pathways will then predominate. The same applies to 5α-reductase (unpublished data). In contrast, 5β-reductase appears to have a much higher capacity (Steimer and Hutchison, 1981a), but its affinity is also lower. Clearly, this latter pathway will be favoured at higher substrate concentrations. Taken together, the kinetic data available at present on enzymes in the dove preoptic area suggest that the formation of oestrogenic metabolites and 5α-reduced metabolites may predominate at testosterone concentrations in the lower range (plasma concentrations of 1–3 ng/ml), whereas at higher concentrations androgenic and inactive 5β-reduced metabolites may be formed preferentially.

Control of metabolic pathways

An important feature of pathways of androgen metabolism in the brain is that they share common substrates (see Fig. 1). Consequently, alternative pathways are in competition, and the overall orientation of metabolism will depend on modulation of particular enzyme activities. Two modes of control are probably involved. First, enzyme synthesis can be regulated by hormonal factors, an action which is likely to involve the classical receptor system and specific gene transcription. The control of aromatase activity by gonadal steroids in the dove hypothalamus may illustrate this type of regulation (see next section). Second, enzyme activity can be directly affected by regulatory molecules, including steroids. These small molecules can either compete with the substrate for active sites or they can act by inducing changes in the conformation of the enzyme which reversibly alters its affinity for the substrate (true enzyme regulators, Price and Stevens, 1982). For example, 5α-DHT is a well-known inhibitor of aromatization. In addition, 5β-DHT and androgen precursors, such as progesterone and 17β-hydroxyprogesterone, also affect aromatase activity in the dove brain in vitro (Steimer and Hutchison, unpublished results). These regulatory steroids can either be products of competing pathways (such as 5α- and 5β-DHT) or derived from circulating steroids reaching the brain. The complexity of the system becomes formidable when competition between enzymes and receptor-binding proteins for intracellular steroids is also taken into account. This type of interaction, which has been shown to occur in a mammalian peripheral target tissue (Nozu and Tamaoki, 1975), has not yet been studied in the brain.

METABOLIC ACTIVATION OF ANDROGEN

Testosterone as a pre-hormone for behaviour

Behavioural evidence for the apparent lack of specificity of either testosterone or oestradiol in inducing male sexual behaviour assumed importance with the discovery in vitro of the capacity of the brain for aromatization (Naftolin et al., 1975). Although the original studies (Reddy et al., 1974) indicated that level of androgen conversion is extremely low ($< 1\%$ in male rat hypothalamus), it can be argued that hypothalamic areas implicated in male sexual behaviour contain aromatase activity and cytosolic receptors for the oestrogen derived from androgen. Two types of behavioural evidence, mainly from the rat, have been used to substantiate this "aromatization hypothesis". First, oestradiol can replicate the effect of testosterone when injected into a castrated rat providing that DHT (the other major metabolite of testosterone in both brain and peripheral target tissues) is also administered (Baum and Vreeburg, 1973). Second, a pharmacologically active compound that blocks aromatization in vitro (androst-1,4,6-triene-3,17-dione, ATD) is effective in preventing testosterone-induced male copulatory behaviour (Christensen and Clemens, 1975). Since DHT is effective in androgen target tissues such as the penis (see Hart, 1978), this hormone is thought to act peripherally while oestradiol influences target neurones in the brain.

Behavioural action of the two hormones at different sites can also be postulated. Support for the dual nature of sex hormone action in the male rat has also been obtained from studies in which oestradiol, implanted into the anterior hypothalamus and presumably acting locally, is highly effective in inducing male copulatory behaviour providing that DHT is administered systemically at the same time (Davis and Barfield, 1979). A similar effect has been obtained in the hamster (Lisk and Greenwald, 1983). DHT itself appears to have little effect in promoting male copulatory behaviour. More recently, however, doubt has been raised (Södersten, 1980) as to whether or not the postulated dual hormonal action in the male rat is correct. The synthetic steroid methyltrienolone (17β-OH-17α-methyl-estra-4,9,11-triene-3-one, R1881), which is not metabolized to oestrogens in vitro, restores complete copulatory behaviour in male rats (Baum, 1979) as effectively as testosterone (Södersten and Gustafsson, 1980). Therefore DHT may also have a primary effect in the brain. However, the interesting suggestion has been made (Södersten, 1980) that oestradiol acts not by binding to cytosolic receptors, but by inhibiting the catabolism of DHT to inactive metabolites (3α- and 3β-diols). This allows more unmetabolized DHT to bind to androgen receptors in target neurones and thus induces male copulatory behaviour. The apparent synergism between oestradiol and DHT actions might well be explicable in terms of an inhibitory effect of oestradiol on the 3α- and 3β-hydroxysteroid dehydrogenases involved in the formation of $3\alpha/\beta$-diols.

The role of active metabolites of testosterone in other mammalian species is unclear, difficulties of interpretation being compounded by species differences in the effectiveness of DHT on copulatory behaviour. Unlike the rat, where DHT has little effect, male sexual behaviour has been induced after castration by DHT in rhesus monkeys (Phoenix, 1974), rabbits (Beyer and Rivaud, 1973), hamsters (DeBold and Clemens, 1978), guinea pigs (Alsum and Goy, 1974) and mice (Luttge and Hall, 1973), suggesting a central role for this metabolite of testosterone in the brain. In contrast, oestradiol is as potent as testosterone in restoring sexual activity in the red deer stag, indicating that DHT is probably not involved (Fletcher and Short, 1974). Similarly in avian species (notably the Japanese quail) oestradiol mimics the effects of testosterone on male copulatory behaviour (Adkins and Adler, 1972; R.E. Hutchison, 1978). A different approach based on the premise that both oestradiol and DHT act centrally has been employed by Clemens and Pomerantz (1982). In separate experiments injection of the 5α-reductase inhibitor, 17β-C (5-androstene-3-one-17β-carboxylic acid) and the aromatase inhibitor ATD (1,4,6-androstatriene-3,17-dione) blocked induction of copulatory behaviour by testosterone in male deer mouse, suggesting that both 5α-reduction and aromatization of testosterone are required for the behavioural effect. This is one of the first indications that more than one pathway of androgen metabolism in the brain may be involved in masculine copulatory behaviour at least in some rodents.

A major difficulty in the interpretation of all studies of the actions of presumed metabolites of androgen on copulatory behaviour is the relative importance of the brain and peripheral target sites. Male copulatory behaviour depends on androgen-sensitive sensory input from the penis and genital area (Hart, 1978). Therefore, androgen influences copulatory behaviour by central and peripheral routes. A second difficulty, which applies generally to studies of the behavioural effects of presumed testosterone metabolites in mammals, is that the metabolic pathways have largely been established by biochemical work which has not been designed with behavioural questions in mind. Description of the metabolic pathways directly relevant for specific behaviour patterns may not have used the same species or type of tissue. However, with increasing interest in the problem of androgen metabolism in the brain, attempts are being made to correlate changes in steroid metabolism directly with behavioural alterations. To take a lower vertebrate example where rhombencephalic mechanisms associated with male sexual behaviour have been identified (J.B. Hutchison, 1964), 5α-reductase activity has been detected in vitro in the spinal cord and medulla of *Xenopus laevis* males. Comparison of 5α-reductase activity in spinal cord segments which innervate brachial muscles used in sexual clasping have revealed both elevated production of DHT in the sexually active males as compared with castrated males, and uptake of this hormone by spinal neurones (Erulkar et al., 1981). Therefore, higher reductase activity and local action of DHT in the spinal cord may be required to facilitate the performance of clasping behaviour. As will be discussed in detail below, there is increasing evidence that interactions among several androgen-metabolizing enzymes are likely to be involved in the control of male behaviour.

Separable hormone-sensitive systems

A limitation of many physiological studies concerned with the action of testosterone on brain mechanisms underlying male copulatory behaviour is that they often suggest a unitary mechanism of "sexual behaviour", which is "activated" in some way by specific hormones (for discussion, see J.B. Hutchison, 1978). The central issue has been to determine which metabolite or combination of metabolites substitute for testosterone circulating as a pre-hormone. However, in view of the diversity of motivational mechanisms involved in sexual behaviour (Hinde, 1970), and the rapidity with which social and other environmental stimuli (e.g. photoperiod) influence short-term changes in behaviour, it is likely that distinct hormone-sensitive control systems operate in the brain at different stages of the male reproductive cycle. Environmental factors might, therefore, directly affect changing hormone action in the brain over time. This possibility has been considered in our studies on the hormonal control of courtship behaviour of the Barbary dove *Streptopelia risoria*.

The initial courtship behaviour of the male dove consists of a rapid alternation between two types of behaviour which elicit different female responses (J.B. Hutchison, 1970). First, the male's *aggressive courtship* patterns induce the female to retreat. Second, *nest-orientated behaviour* attracts the female to a potential nest-site. Over time, there is a highly predictable transition from behaviour characterized mainly by aggressive courtship to predominantly nest-orientated activity. Male courtship, therefore, consists of the expression of two motivational systems, one associated with aggressive courtship and the other with nest-orientated courtship. This provides a unique model for studying both the effects of hormones on two linked behavioural systems and changes in hormone action on the brain which accompany the behavioural transition.

Courtship in the male dove depends upon testicular androgen acting directly on the preoptic-anterior hypothalamic areas of the brain (J.B. Hutchison, 1971, 1976). Several lines of work indicate, however, that a distinct oestrogen-sensitive mechanism in the dove brain is associated with nest-orientated behaviour. First, although intrahypothalamic oestradiol is effective for nest-orientated behaviour, it is virtually ineffective for eliciting aggressive courtship (Fig. 3a). Second, diethylstilboestrol (DES) which binds specifically to high-affinity, low-capacity oestrogen receptors, but has no affinity for androgen receptors (Chamness et al., 1979), replicates the effects of oestradiol on nest-orientated behaviour in castrated doves. Third, specificity differences between the behavioural effects of oestradiol and testosterone increase in the prolonged absence of gonadal hormones (Fig. 3b, and J.B. Hutchison et al., 1981). There is good evidence, therefore, that activation of oestrogen-sensitive target cells in the brain is important in determining when, and to what degree, the male will show nest-orientated behaviour. These differences in the specificity of action of oestrogen and androgen in the dove offer a contrast to findings in other species of birds (J.B. Hutchison, 1978), in reptiles (Crews and Morgentaler, 1979) and in mammals (Fletcher and Short, 1974), where oestradiol treatment replicates the effects of testosterone on male sexual behaviour.

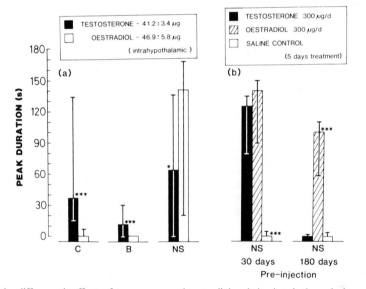

Fig. 3. Specificity difference in effects of testosterone and oestradiol on behaviour in the male dove. (a) Action of intrahypothalamic hormones on chasing (C), bowing (B) and nest soliciting (NS) in short-term (30-day) castrated doves. (b) Effects of daily hormone treatments (300 μg × 10) compared to saline-treated controls on nest soliciting in short-term (30-day) and long-term (180-day) castrated birds. Comparisons (median and ranges) are between testosterone and oestradiol in (a) and saline and hormone treatments in (b). *P <0.05, ***P <0.01 (Mann–Whitney U test, 2-tailed). (Data from J.B. Hutchison, 1971; J.B. Hutchison et al., 1981.)

Originally it was proposed that the separable components of courtship, aggressive and nest-orientated behaviour, differed in their sensitivity to testosterone, with a "threshold mechanism" in the brain distinguishing between them (J.B. Hutchison, 1970). Behavioural evidence for this idea was obtained from a study in which castrated doves received intrahypothalamic testosterone propionate (TP) implants differing in surface area and, therefore, in the rate of hormone diffusion to surrounding brain tissue. The "low-diffusion" implants resulted in nest-orientated behaviour, whereas castrated males with "high-diffusion" implants showed both aggressive and nest-orientated components. This finding led to the hypothesis that the different components of courtship behaviour may depend both on effective testosterone concentration in the hypothalamus and on differing "sensitivity" thresholds of their underlying brain mechanisms to androgen (see J.B. Hutchison, 1976, for discussion, and Fig. 4a). This model, although highly speculative, is compatible with recent in vitro data on enzyme kinetics showing that substrate concentrations differentially affect pathways of androgen metabolism and, therefore, the type of metabolites formed in the preoptic area. At low concentrations of testosterone, metabolism is biased towards oestradiol production optimal for nest-orientated behaviour (Fig. 4b–d). At higher concentrations, the aromatase becomes saturated by substrate so that more testosterone remains unmetabolized and available for effects on the aggressive components of courtship. This suggests that a threshold model of androgen action on separate components of behaviour may be explained physiologically in terms of differences in capacity of intracellular enzymes for conversion of androgen to active and inactive metabolites.

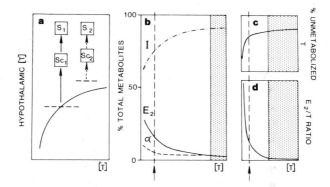

Fig. 4. (a) Hypothetical threshold mechanism underlying units of sexual behaviour with different levels of responsiveness to androgen. Hypothalamic testosterone [T] level, which is assumed to increase with elevation in plasma concentration, activates specified androgen-sensitive cell populations Sc_1, Sc_2 with differing thresholds of sensitivity (dotted lines) to androgen concentration specifically associated with brain systems S_1, S_2 integrating units of sexual behaviour. In the example, hypothalamic T is assumed to rise to concentrations below Sc_2 (further details from J.B. Hutchison, 1978). The possible physiological basis for sensitivity differences based on kinetic studies of enzymes involved in androgen metabolism is shown in b, c, and d. (b) Changes in the distribution of testosterone metabolites (expressed as % of all metabolites formed) when testosterone concentration [T] is increased in the male dove preoptic area (diagram based on unpublished experimental data obtained in vitro using [T] varying from 1 to 80 nM). I, total inactive metabolites, i.e. 5β-androstanes and $5a$-androstanediols; E_2, 17β-oestradiol; a, $5a$-DHT. Arrow indicates the average [T] in the plasma of sexually active males and [T] outside the stippled area are assumed to be within the physiological range for hypothalamic cells (up to 5 times plasma concentration). Maximal production of active metabolites, i.e. oestradiol and $5a$-DHT, occurs at [T] in the lower range, whereas inactive metabolites predominate when [T] increases. (c) Unmetabolized testosterone as a function of [T] over the same range of substrate concentration as in b. Under in vitro experimental conditions where enzymes, but not substrate, are rate-limiting, unmetabolized T varies from 65 to 90%. However, enzyme concentrations in intact cells are much higher than in experimental systems in vitro and most of the substrate would be metabolized. Despite less unmetabolized testosterone, kinetic relationships between enzymes are likely to be the same as those measured in vitro. The curve plotted for percentage of unmetabolized testosterone shows that, as a result of cellular metabolic activity, [T] in preoptic cells is not linearly related to substrate concentration in vitro. Therefore, preoptic [T] is unlikely to be directly related to plasma concentration (compare to original threshold model). (d) Oestradiol/testosterone ratio as a function of substrate (T) concentration in vitro. At high [T] outside the physiological range, the ratio is very low (0.01). But at lower concentrations, the ratio increases. Where substrate availability is limiting in intact cells, the ratio is likely to be much higher. The dramatic change in androgen/oestrogen ratio which occurs at lower [T] may well form the molecular basis for the theoretical threshold model proposed in (a) (see text for further details).

Brain aromatase in hormone-mediated behavioural transitions

Interaction with the female results in a surge of circulating testosterone in adult males of many mammalian species including humans (Lincoln, 1974). A massive rise in plasma testosterone accompanies male territorial behaviour and courtship in some species of birds (Wingfield, 1983). In the male dove, interaction with the female results in a surge of testosterone within 30 min of pairing (O'Connell et al., 1981). The immediate question arising from this finding is whether or not the change in peripheral androgen concentration bears any relation to behavioural transitions which are known to occur during the early part of the reproductive cycle. In view of the finding that conversion of testosterone to oestradiol occurs in the preoptic area, and that nest-orientated activity in the male is specifically oestradiol-dependent, it can be suggested that social stimuli from the female and/or changing testosterone level influence brain aromatase activity.

What evidence is there that the activity of preoptic aromatase can be modified? Behavioural experiments provide an initial clue as to the mechanism involved. In contrast to the action of testosterone on nest-orientated behaviour in short-term castrated birds, this hormone has little effect in long-term castrates (Fig. 3b). But oestradiol is highly effective in both groups, suggesting that the capacity for aromatization declines in the course of a prolonged androgen deficit (J.B. Hutchison et al., 1981). The conclusion can be drawn that brain aromatase activity varies according to the hormonal status and, perhaps, the behavioural state of the male. The importance of hormonal factors is indicated by the additional observation that testosterone, at high doses, is marginally effective for nest-orientated behaviour following prolonged treatment in long-term castrated birds. This suggests that the production of behaviourally effective oestradiol increases as a consequence of higher brain aromatase activity (J.B. Hutchison et al., 1981). Therefore, the preoptic aromatase may require "priming" by testosterone over time, a possibility which can be examined directly by comparing aromatase activity in hormone- and saline-treated castrated birds. Androgen treatment has a striking effect. On average the activity is increased 3–5-fold by doses of testosterone which are in the same range as those used for behavioural experiments (Steimer and Hutchison, 1981b; J.B. Hutchison and Steimer, 1983). However, activity of this enzyme is unaffected in the area basalis, which is not an androgen target area and shows much lower rates of testosterone conversion. Kinetic studies indicate that the observed increase in activity in the preoptic area is probably due to induction of the enzyme. The maximum velocity V_{max} of the conversion is markedly increased (5-fold, 250 vs. 48 fmoles/h/mg protein) by TP treatment. But the Michaelis constant K_m is not significantly altered (2.1×10^{-8} M, controls; 2.7×10^{-8} M, TP). These results indicate a specific inductive action of androgen on the preoptic aromatase. The effect is likely to involve both binding of the active steroid to a specific "receptor" in preoptic cells and genomic activation resulting in de novo synthesis of the aromatase complex. Evidently, the inductive process does not occur in non-target cells, such as those in the area basalis, despite the presence of the enzyme in low concentrations. This may be due to the absence of androgen receptors in these cells.

The importance of aromatase activity is also emphasized by in vivo studies. Oestrogen is not only formed by conversion of testosterone in the preoptic area, but it is also taken up by cell nuclei in the same brain region (Steimer and Hutchison, 1983). In the male dove, capacity for oestradiol uptake by preoptic cell nuclei following [³H]oestradiol administration in vivo (19.0 ± 2.0 dpm/mg tissue) is approximately twice as high as that for testosterone following [³H]testosterone injection (7.4 ± 2.1 dpm/mg tissue). The amount of oestradiol bound to nuclear sites is much lower (3.2 ± 0.3 dpm/mg tissue) when the hormone is formed locally in the preoptic area from testosterone. This suggests that the limiting step in oestrogen action on preoptic cells is its local formation by the aromatase complex and not the binding capacity of oestrogen-sensitive cells.

The behavioural significance of preoptic aromatase induction in the male dove still remains to be established. However, plasma testosterone reaches a peak (Feder et al., 1977) 1–2 days after the initial interaction which coincides with the transition from aggressive to nest-orientated phases of courtship. The surge in testosterone could set in motion events which increase preoptic aromatase activity, the formation of behaviourally effective oestradiol and, ultimately, the behavioural transition (J.B. Hutchison and Steimer, 1983). The time course of the induction effect is obviously crucial and this is being studied at present. We already have evidence that the conversion rate of testosterone to oestradiol increases in the preoptic area of intact males following 2–4 days of interaction with females, and even in males that are observing such interactions (Hutchison and Steimer, in preparation). Whether induction of brain aromatase activity plays any part in mammalian sexual behaviour has not been studied yet. However, long-term exposure of male rats to "female odour" from weaning to sexual maturity increases plasma testosterone and also appears to elevate hypothalamic aromatase activity significantly (Dessi-Fulgheri and Lupo, 1982). Replication of the latter result has proved difficult (Dessi-Fulgheri et al., 1983). But there is a possibility that elevated plasma T may be related to an increase in aromatase activity.

Regulation of brain aromatase

The finding that androgen can induce preoptic aromatase activity in the dove brain raises a number of questions of general interest concerning the types of cellular mechanism involved. These are largely unanswered as yet, and have not been explored in other species of birds or in mammals. (a) Is the inductive effect due to a direct action of testosterone itself or via behavioural changes which accompany hormone action? This issue is difficult to resolve, because male behaviour is extremely sensitive to testosterone, and behavioural and hormonal actions are almost impossible to separate as experimental variables. However, brief interaction with the female in TP-treated males does not enhance preoptic aromatase activity (Hutchison and Steimer, in preparation), suggesting that a direct effect of the hormone itself is involved in aromatase induction rather than the behavioural change brought about by the hormone. (b) Does testosterone induce aromatase activity or is a metabolite responsible? The evidence available so far suggests that the inductive effect is not due to DHT, but may largely be due to oestradiol. This raises the intriguing possibility that preoptic aromatase activity becomes autocatalytically increased by the product of the reaction. Testosterone treatment appears to set in motion a positive feedback system. (c) Does testosterone or its metabolite, oestradiol, act directly by local effect in the brain on preoptic aromatase? Intracerebral implantation of TP into an area immediately adjacent to the preoptic nuclei enhances aromatase activity, indicating a direct effect on cells in this area (Hutchison and Steimer, in preparation). However, FSH and cyclic AMP (Callard, 1981) are known to be regulators of gonadal aromatase, while the adrenergic agonists, L-isoprenalin and noradrenalin stimulate the conversion of testosterone to oestradiol (Verhoeven et al., 1979). Neurotransmitters or hormones could, therefore, be acting as intermediaries in the induction effect.

METABOLIC INACTIVATION OF ANDROGEN

Differences in behavioural effectiveness of androgen

Androgens affect male sexual behaviour by direct action on the brain. Theoretically, their action can be influenced in two ways: (1) the hormone itself changes in amount and availability within specific areas of the brain or (2) the sensitivity of the tissues mediating the behaviour can change. In the early fifties, Young and his co-workers (Grunt and Young, 1952, 1953) put forward the hypothesis that individual difference in male sexual responsiveness to androgen was due to differences between individuals in the "reactivity" of underlying brain mechanisms to androgen. Surprisingly, little mammalian evidence has come to light in the intervening years to support this hypothesis. The problem has been approached in a few instances by examining the effects of gonadectomy and photoperiod on the behavioural effectiveness of androgen. Thus, ejaculatory behaviour can be maintained in castrated rats at precastration levels only by using a much higher dose of TP than that required for initiating behaviour, suggesting a decline in behavioural responsiveness to hormone after castration (Davidson and Bloch, 1969). Photoperiod also influences responsiveness to androgens. Thus, in the hamster, males maintained on a short daily photoperiod are less responsive to androgen in terms of induced level of copulatory behaviour than are males on a long-day cycle (Morin et al., 1977; Campbell et al., 1978). A seasonal decline in responsiveness of rutting behaviour in the red deer stag (*Cervus elaphus*) to TP (Lincoln et al., 1972 suggests a similar phenomenon. These studies all employed systemic androgen administration, and were not addressed to the question of whether the decline in behavioural effectiveness specifically involved the brain. Changes in effectiveness of hormone could equally well be due to alterations in peripheral transport or metabolism, or to a change in afferent input from androgen-dependent sensory structures.

Evidence for a change in brain sensitivity to testosterone which can be directly related to a decline in behavioural responsiveness to the hormone has been obtained in the male dove (J.B. Hutchison, 1974). The effectiveness of TP implants in the anterior hypothalamic-preoptic area declines with time after the male dove is castrated, suggesting that local sensitivity to androgen changes according to hormonal status, and that target cells within this brain area participate in the change. Social stimuli (e.g. vocalizations) reduce the decline in brain sensitivity to testosterone (J.B. Hutchison, 1978). It is likely, therefore, that both specific environmental factors and long-term androgen deficit directly affect androgen target cells in the brain. The question arising from this finding is whether or not factors associated with the cellular action of androgen are involved. Following the classical model of steroid hormone action on brain cells, likely candidates for change in intracellular effects would be receptor binding, translocation of testosterone and, ultimately, protein synthesis. But there appears to be no post-castration decrease in nuclear uptake of testosterone that could account for behavioural insensitivity to androgen (J.B. Hutchison, 1978). Similarly, differences in the effectiveness of TP on copulatory behaviour between guinea pig males could not be related to intracellular uptake of testosterone (Harding and Feder, 1976).

5β-Reduction as a metabolic inactivation pathway

In view of the importance of steroid metabolites in the action of androgen on the brain, we have been examining the possibility that metabolism in target cells can determine behaviourally effective androgen levels in the brain. Several lines of evidence suggest that 5β-reduction of testosterone in the brain is part of a steroid inactivation mechanism. Apart from specifically inducing haem synthesis in erythropoietic systems (Mainwaring, 1977), the 5β-androstanes appear to be biologically inactive. The 5β-isomer of DHT does not compete for androgen-binding sites in the prostate and is generally devoid of androgenic activity in mammals (Martini, 1982). This is probably due to the extremely angular orientation of the A ring of 5β-reduced steroids, because it has been demonstrated that the steric but not the electronic characteristics of the A ring are essential for androgen activity (Liao et al., 1973).

Experimental evidence supports the view that 5β-reduced metabolites have no androgenic properties in birds. Thus, 5β-DHT has no effect on the rooster comb (Mori et al., 1974), a classical androgen-sensitive tissue, nor is there any negative feedback action on plasma LH or FSH levels or effect on copulatory behaviour (Adkins and Pniewski, 1978; Davies et al., 1980) in Japanese quail. We have shown that intrahypothalamic 5β-DHT is ineffective for eliciting male courtship in doves. The 5β-reduced metabolites are also major products of hepatic catabolism of testosterone in the dove (Steimer and Hutchison, 1981a) as well as in other mammalian species, including the human (Stylianou et al., 1961). In vivo study of the uptake and metabolism of [³H]testosterone in the brain after systemic injection shows that 5β-reduced metabolites form only a minor part of the radioactive content of brain cells, and they are not detected in hypothalamic cell nuclei (Steimer and Hutchison, 1983). This suggests that these metabolites are rapidly eliminated from the brain under physiological conditions. Testosterone inactivation by 5β-reduction is potentially a very efficient process (see section: Metabolic activation and inactivation of androgens). Because 5β-reductase and the other enzymes (notably aromatase and 5α-reductase) which are involved in the production of active metabolites of testosterone share a common substrate, the overall effect of changes in 5β-reductase activity is likely to be great.

Regulation of brain sensitivity to androgen

Study of the role of metabolic inactivation of testosterone in relation to male behaviour requires manipulation of hormonal state, assessment of behavioural responsiveness to testosterone during the post-castration period, and measurement of enzyme activity in the brain. Since interaction with females could influence both behavioural responsiveness to hormone and activity of metabolic enzymes, it is also necessary to assess the behavioural effects of testosterone without using conventional test situations for male sexual behaviour. The behaviour of the male dove offers an opportunity for doing this, because the effects of testosterone on a specifically androgen-dependent vocal behaviour (perch calling) can be measured without the necessity of male interaction with a test female. Preoptic 5β-reductase activity increases over time after castration (Fig. 5a) suggesting an effect of long-term androgen deficit. Behavioural data indicate an inverse relationship with the level of 5β-reduction in the preoptic area. Thus the effectiveness of TP on vocal behaviour decreases with rising preoptic 5β-reductase activity (Fig. 5b). Enzymatic activity in the anterior hypothalamus is not affected, indicating the specificity of the enzymatic change. This also demonstrates an anatomical separation in level of 5β-reduction between the preoptic and anterior hypothalamic areas of long-term castrates which is not present in intact males. The activity of the enzyme is clearly responsive to hormonal condition, because both testosterone and oestradiol decrease 5β-reductase activity when administered systematically (J.B. Hutchison and Steimer, 1981) under conditions of androgen deficit.

An intriguing question raised by these findings is whether oestradiol derived from testosterone, in addition to its specific effects on nest-orientated courtship, may also play a part

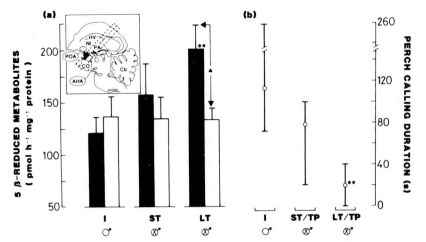

Fig. 5. (a) Total 5β-reduced metabolites ($\bar{x} \pm$ S.E.M.) in the preoptic area (POA, shaded bars) and anterior hypothalamus (AHA, open bars). I, intact, sexually active male doves; ST, short-term 30-day castrated birds; LT, long-term (200-day) castrates. Comparison between intact castrated birds, ** $P < 0.001$ (ANOVA); and between POA and AHA samples, ▲ $P = 0.025$ (paired t test, 2-tailed). (b) Durations of perch calling (medians and ranges) of intact males (I), short-term (ST) and long-term (LT) castrated doves. Intact group compared with castrated birds, ** $P < 0.01$ (Mann–Whitney U test, 2-tailed). Insert shows coronal views of brain areas from which samples, area basalis (2) and preoptic (3) were taken. (Modified from J.B. Hutchison and Steimer, 1981.)

in the regulation of testosterone-dependent brain mechanisms of behaviour. Both oestradiol and DES suppress 5β-reduction, thus indicating that 5β-reductase is oestrogen-sensitive (J.B. Hutchison and Steimer, 1981). The suppressive effect of oestrogen does not appear to be due to a direct action on the enzyme, because in vitro incubation of preoptic tissue with 10 nM [³H]testosterone and a 100-fold excess of oestradiol or DES does not diminish the amount of testosterone (approximately 20%) which is converted to 5β-reduced metabolites (J.B. Hutchison and Steimer, 1981). Evidently, aromatization products have an indirect influence on the synthesis or degradation of 5β-reductase and testosterone inactivation.

Work on other species, notably the starling, have supported the view that inactivation of testosterone by 5β-reduction has a physiological role. Massa et al. (1983) have suggested that the 5β-reduction pathway acts as an "inactivation shunt" modulating the conversion of circulating testosterone to active androgens. This in turn could modify the inhibitory feedback effects of testosterone on gonadotrophin secretion. Seasonal changes in 5β-reduction may be related to this effect. Thus levels of 5β-reductase activity in the hypothalamus are lower during the starling breeding season than at the end of the photorefractory period (Bottoni and Massa, 1981). Whether seasonal changes in 5β-reduction also occur in the preoptic target sites associated with sexual behaviour is not known. Although 5β-reduction of testosterone in the brain has not been studied to any extent yet in mammals, the presence of a 5β-reduced metabolite (5β-androstane-3,17-dione) has been detected in hypothalamic and limbic areas of the male hamster (Callard et al., 1979). As both the starling and the hamster are photoperiodic, it could be suggested that 5β-reduction occurs in photoperiodic species. However, as pointed out by Martini (1982), this attractive hypothesis cannot be substantiated at present.

ANDROGEN-METABOLIZING ENZYMES AND DEVELOPMENT

Active brain metabolites of androgen

Androgens are implicated in sexual differentiation of both the neuroendrocrine system and behaviour in mammals during "critical" sensitive periods in early development (MacLusky and Naftolin, 1981). Testosterone appears to "organize" brain mechanisms of male sexual behaviour by a direct action in the brain. Studies of the developing rat brain have established that sexual dimorphism in brain structure can be related to the action of androgen both at the level of light microscopy (Gorski et al., 1978; Gorski, 1984) and neuronal structure demonstrated by electron microscopy (Ayoub and Greenough, 1983). Moreover, cytosolic oestrogen and androgen receptors occur in hypothalamic cells at the relevant perinatal period (Vito and Fox, 1979; Vito et al., 1979), indicating that the brain is a steroid target site early in development. The differentiating effects of androgen on male sexual behaviour in mammals have been extensively reviewed elsewhere (e.g. Goy and McEwen, 1980). The main consideration here will be to assess briefly the role of androgen-metabolizing enzymes in the brain during early development in relation to behaviour.

Steroid hormones effective in mammalian development are thought to act in two ways to differentiate the neural substrate of sexual behaviour in the male. First, androgens "masculinize" by enhancement of systems underlying male behaviour, and, second, "defeminize" by suppression of behavioural systems underlying female behaviour. Whether these processes operate independently or as a consequence of the action of different hormones, is still uncertain (Goy and McEwen, 1980). There are, however, a number of lines of evidence suggesting that brain aromatase activity and the production of oestrogen may be crucial for the sexual differentiation of male behaviour in rodent species, particularly the rat (reviewed by Plapinger and McEwen, 1978; Martini, 1982). Thus, oestradiol as well as synthetic oestrogens (e.g. DES) are more potent organizers than is testosterone in the neonatal rat brain (MacLusky and Naftolin, 1981). Androgen-insensitive (Tfm) mice which have fewer receptors for androgens, nevertheless become differentiated sexually by the action of testicular hormones (Olsen, 1979). In this case, androgens are presumably being converted to oestrogens which directly affect oestrogen-sensitive brain mechanisms crucial for the differentiating action of the hormone. Additional evidence has been obtained by administration either of an anti-oestrogen or inhibitors of aromatase, which block the organizing action of testicular androgen during the perinatal period (McDonald and Doughty, 1974). An intermediary in the conversion of testosterone to oestradiol, 19-hydroxytestosterone, is also more potent than testosterone as a differentiating agent in the rat (Parrott, 1975). More recently, oestradiol has been found to stimulate neurite growth in organotype cultures of mice hypothalamus, suggesting that oestradiol has potent effects on developing neurones (Toran-Allerand, 1978, 1984).

Not all mammals, however, become differentiated sexually by the action of oestrogens. In male guinea pigs and rhesus monkeys (Goy and McEwen, 1980), non-aromatizable DHT is effective in masculinizing mechanisms of sexual behaviour. Despite species differences, there is agreement that brain aromatase is important in behavioural differentiation of the male. Receptors for oestradiol have been located in the hypothalamus at the relevant sensitive period of hormone action after birth in the rat (Vito and Fox, 1979). Oestradiol has also been localized in hypothalamic cell nuclei of neonatal male rats in vivo (MacLusky et al., 1976), strongly supporting the view that both oestrogen and aromatase activity are important in the early organization of male behaviour. There is, however, a discrepancy between the peak of aromatase activity, measured during gestation and after birth in the rat (George and Ojeda, 1982), and the sensitive neonatal period for brain differentiation. The former occurs on days 18–20 of gestation, whereas the latter is during the first 5 days after birth. Male and female rats have detectable brain aromatase activity and aromatizable serum androgen, indicating that both sexes have the capacity for oestrogen formation in the brain and the necessary androgenic precursors. Therefore, factors associated with male hypothalamic cell development are likely to determine when differentiation to the male type occurs in the rat. Similarly, there are no sex differences in diencephalic aromatase activity measured in rabbit embryos (George et al., 1978). Although development of aromatase activity has been studied in only a few species, it is becoming clear that there are marked species differences in the functional role of this pathway with respect to behaviour. When both $5a$-reductase and aromatase pathways are blocked by 17β-C and ATD respectively in the male ferret during the sensitive period (days 5–15 after birth) normal sexual differentiation still occurs, indicating that testosterone itself is the important androgen in this species (Baum et al., 1983).

The processes of sexual differentiation in birds were thought to be the reverse of those in mammals (Adkins, 1975). In agreement with this view, the brain of the female Japanese quail was found to be differentiated (or "demasculinized") by oestrogen acting during a sensitive embryonic period (Adkins, 1975; Adkins-Regan, 1983); the male develops without hormonal intervention. This observation has led to the widely quoted hypothesis (Adkins, 1975) that the brain of the homogametic sex is "neutral" and does not require the differentiating effects of hormones. However, this hypothesis is now seen as an oversimplification (see Konishi and Gurney, 1982, for discussion). In quail, the differentiating effects of oestrogen are not necessarily restricted to embryonic development (R.E. Hutchison, 1978; Schumacher and Balthazart, 1983). Furthermore, in at least one avian species, the zebra finch (*Peophila guttata*), brain mechanisms of male behaviour are differentiated by steroid hormones (Konishi and Gurney, 1982).

Although oestrogens appear to act during the perinatal period in the rat and all other mammalian species studied so far the actual neurone groups involved have not been identified. The zebra finch provides the only example known where oestrogen has an early differentiating effect on brain neurones which are unequivocally involved in behaviour. In this species, only the male sings and there is marked sexual dimorphism in the volumes of telencephalic nuclei (n. robustus archistriatais, RA, n. hyperstriatum ventrale, HVc) known to be involved in the control of song (Nottebohm and Arnold, 1976). The ontogeny of this dimorphism of the song control system appears, at first hand, to show a remarkable similarity to corresponding processes in male rodents (e.g. the rat) in that oestrogens are the determining hormones in the male. Oestradiol, administered systemically to female zebra finch chicks soon after hatching, acts not only to "masculinize" the volume of neuronal soma and size of dendritic fields, but also to induce them as adults to respond to androgen treatment with the production of song. The non-aromatizable androgen, DHT, is not effective, and it has been suggested that the masculinizing effects of testosterone are mediated through its aromatization in the brain to oestradiol during the sensitive period immediately after hatching (Gurney, 1982; Konishi and Gurney, 1982). Following this hypothesis brain aromatase activity would be crucial for the differentiating effects of testosterone in male zebra finches. But as there is no sex difference in circulating testosterone level during the sensitive period (Hutchison et al., in preparation) between male and female chicks, aromatase must, following the aromatization hypothesis, be selectively active in the male brain. So far, no study has been made of aromatase activity in zebra finches. But in chicks of two other avian species (doves (Fig. 6b) and quail, Hutchison and Steimer, in preparation) aromatase activity, although detectable within the hypothalamus, shows no sex difference. It is more likely that a large pulse of circulating oestradiol, detected only in male plasma on days 3 and 4 after hatching, is the crucial factor in the differentiation of the male song control system in the brain (Hutchison et al., in preparation). This example serves to illustrate the complexity of brain–hormone relationships during early development. The brain aromatase system is not necessarily involved. Oestradiol, presumed to be the effective brain metabolite of testosterone, is produced peripherally during the sensitive period of development.

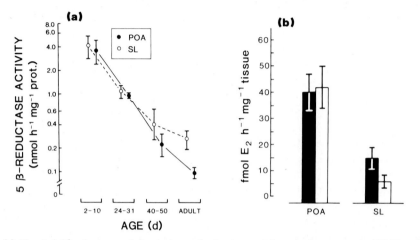

Fig. 6. (a) Elevated 5β-reductase activity during early development in male dove preoptic (POA) and septal areas (SL). Samples were taken from squabs of the age ranges shown and compared to adult (>1 year) sexually active males. The anatomical differences in enzyme activity (mean ± S.E.M.) between POA and SL areas do not appear until adulthood. (b) Aromatase activity of male squabs (2–10 days of age, shaded bars) and adult sexually active males (unshaded bars) in preoptic and septal areas. (Data from Hutchison et al., in preparation.)

Inactive brain metabolites of androgen

In view of the evidence presented above that 5β-reduction may act in the adult as an androgen inactivation pathway, the question arises as to whether similar metabolic pathways in young animals have any regulatory effect on androgen action during development. Two questions arising from work on 5β-reductase in adult doves are relevant: (a) Are there regional differences in 5β-reductase activity during development? In the adult male dove, preoptic target areas for testosterone and other hypothalamic areas associated with the neuroendocrine function have markedly less 5β-reductase activity than non-target areas (Fig. 2). (b) Does the level of 5β-reductase, and testosterone inactivation, change during development? In view of the high activity of brain 5β-reductase, this enzymatic pathway could have a regulatory influence on the production of active metabolites. Answers to both questions have been obtained in the male dove. Unlike the adult (Fig. 2), there are no obvious regional differences in 5β-reductase activity early in development. The marked anatomical difference in enzyme activity between brain areas (e.g. the area basalis and septal area as compared to the preoptic area) of adult males, are not seen in squabs taken immediately after hatching nor 24–30 days later in development (Fig. 6a). The activity of 5β-reductase in male squabs is far higher than in adult males by an order of magnitude. Therefore, the half-life of testosterone in the preoptic area of the post-hatching male is considerably shorter in the juvenile than in the adult bird. That 5β-reduction of testosterone changes during development has also been shown by measuring enzyme activity in brain areas sampled from groups of males at various stages of growth. The activity of 5β-reductase declines progressively until adulthood (Fig. 6a). Whether this decline is a function of increasing testicular output of testosterone during later stages of development is not yet known. Although precise neuro-anatomical information is not available for other avian species, it would appear that brain 5β-reductase activity is also elevated in quail (Balthazart and Schumacher, 1984) and cockerel (Massa and Sharp, 1981) after hatching. Sex differences in 5β-reduced metabolites have not yet been detected in either the dove or quail during early development (Hutchison and Steimer, unpublished observations). High 5β-reductase activity, as found in avian brain during early post-hatching development, appears to be paralleled by high 5α-reductase activity in neonatal male rats (Massa et al., 1975; Denef et al., 1974).

Is there any evidence that 5β-reductase activity acts as part of an inactivation pathway relevant to behavioural development in young birds? Contrary to this view, 5β-reduced androgen, 5β-DHT, given alone or in combination with oestradiol stimulates juvenile copulatory activity in male domesticated chicks, suggesting that 5β-DHT is an active metabolite in the developing chick brain (Balthazart and Hirschberg, 1979; see also Martini, 1982). However, 5β-DHT is generally a biologically inactive steroid and has no behavioural effect in the adult dove or in adults of other avian species (Steimer and Hutchison, 1981a). This latter observation together with the fact that excessively high does of testosterone are often required for producing behavioural effects in young birds (Schleidt, 1970), suggests an inactivating role for the 5β-reduction pathway.

Recently, the applicability of the inactivation hypothesis has been tested in quail (Balthazart et al., 1984) by comparing the effects of testosterone with those of its metabolite, DHT. Both of these androgens have similar effects on peripheral target organs (e.g. cloacal gland), but testosterone is much less effective behaviourally (induction of crowing) than DHT in male chicks. The latter cannot be 5β-reduced and is, therefore, protected from inactivation. Whether the activity of the 5β-reduction pathway is determined by aromatization products, as it appears to be in the adult dove brain, and whether similar inactivation processes occur in other vertebrate groups (including mammals) during development remains to be established. The 5β-reduction pathway is known to be active in the human foetal brain (Lisboa et al., 1976). The position as regards the role of 5β-reduced androstanes in mammalian development is not clear. Recent findings in mice (Yanai et al., 1977) and rats (Arai et al., 1981) suggest that 5β-DHT can masculinize the female neuroendocrine system. This apparent masculinizing action may be due to pharmacological interaction of 5β-DHT with oestrogen receptors in the brain, rather than being a true physiological effect. Although species difference complicate the picture, there are indications that steroid inactivation may have a role in determining effective androgen levels and the differentiating effects of these androgens during development.

SUMMARY AND CONCLUSIONS

One of the challenging problems facing neuroendocrine research is to establish the way in which hormone-sensitive cellular events in the brain relate to behaviour. Evidence mainly from mammalian and avian species indicates that sex steroids directly influence preoptic and hypothalamic cells. Biochemical studies are now being directed to a more detailed analysis of the cellular action of steroids at the molecular level. A widely accepted model of steroid action derived from this work postulates that the active hormone binds to a specific cytosolic receptor which is subsequently translocated to the cell nucleus. According to this model, behaviourally active steroids are involved in the regulation of gene expression in target brain cells. This has been shown to apply to oestrogen-sensitive mechanisms associated with reflex patterns of female sexual behaviour. But it is not known whether events of this type mediate the action of androgen on male behaviour. There is little evidence so far for a direct correlation between steroid–receptor binding and androgenic effects.

Recent data, notably from the avian brain, have suggested that additional cellular mechanisms need to be considered. Intracellular conversion of androgens to active metabolites is known to be a prerequisite for hormone action in peripheral target organs. However, production of both active and inactive metabolites occurs in the brain. This production can be influenced by changes in environment which affect behaviour. The enzymes involved in metabolic activation and inactivation may be crucial in controlling the behavioural effectiveness of circulating androgen. Thus aromatase, which converts testosterone to 17β-oestradiol in the dove brain, is induced specifically in the preoptic area by elevated androgen concentration. This induction process appears to be influenced by social stimuli relevant to behaviour. The 5β-reductase activity involved in the conversion of androgen to biologically inactive metabolites is correlated with behavioural insensitivity to androgen in adult seasonally breeding males and males subject to prolonged androgen deficit. Moreover, in the adult avian brain there are neuroanatomical differences in which androgen target areas have lower 5β-reductase activity than non-target areas. In young animals, these differences are minimal and 5β-reductase activity is considerably higher. An important question arising from this finding is whether inactivation also regulates effective androgen levels in the developing brain. Factors which influence 5β-reduction and other pathways of androgen metabolism may be crucial in determining phasic effects of hormones during early development.

Whether these processes relating to androgen metabolism in the brain are specific to the male is not yet known. Examination of sex differences in enzymes converting androgen to active metabolites in both mammalian and avian species indicates similarities in enzyme activity rather than differences between the sexes. The same appears to be true for inactivating enzymes. To resolve this question, further studies of metabolic activation and inactivation of androgen will be required using selective enzyme inhibitors and anti-hormones which, in many cases, are not available at present. It should be emphasized that enzymes involved in central androgen metabolism cannot be studied realistically as isolated systems, as is currently done. Since many different pathways and receptor systems are likely to occur in the same cells, a better understanding of their interactions will be required before the role of metabolism in modulating androgen action can be fully understood.

Although peaks in circulating steroid sex hormones are associated in time with behavioural changes in the male during development and in the adult reproductive cycle, enzymes which metabolize androgen in brain cells are likely to influence when and to what extent these hormones have their behavioural effects. Steroid metabolizing enzymes in the male brain provide, therefore, a degree of plasticity in the action of hormones on brain mechanisms of behaviour.

ACKNOWLEDGEMENTS

Support was received from an E.T.P. Twinning Grant awarded by the European Science Foundation.

The technical assistance of L. Barden, R. Duncan, T. Goss, P. Jaggard, L. Innes and Ch. Steimer in various aspects of work carried out in this laboratory is gratefully acknowledged.

T.S. was supported by a post-doctoral fellowship from the Swiss National Fund (European Science Exchange Programme, Royal Society).

We thank Prof. R.E. Offord for facilities made available in the Department of Medical Biochemistry, University of Geneva (Switzerland). We are also indebted to Prof. R.A. Hinde and Dr. R.E. Hutchison for their comments on the manuscript.

REFERENCES

Adkins, E.K. (1975) Hormonal basis of sexual differentiation in the Japanese quail. *J. Comp. Physiol. Psychol.*, 89: 61–71.

Adkins, E.K. and Adler, N.T. (1972) Hormonal control of behavior in the Japanese quail. *J. Comp. Physiol. Psychol.*, 81: 27–36.

Adkins, E.K. and Pniewski, E.E. (1978) Control of reproductive behavior by sex steroids in male quail. *J. Comp. Physiol. Psychol.*, 92: 1168–1169.

Adkins-Regan, E.K. (1981) Effect of sex steroids on the reproductive behavior of castrated male ring doves (*Streptopelic risoria*). *Physiol. Behav.*, 26: 561–565.

Adkins-Regan, E.K. (1983) Sex steroids and the differentiation and activation of avian reproductive behaviour. In: J. Balthazart, E. Pröve and R. Gilles (Eds.), *Hormones and Behaviour in Higher Vertebrates*, Springer, Berlin, pp. 218–230.

Alsum, P. and Goy, R.W. (1974) Actions of esters of testosterone dihydro-testosterone or estradiol on sexual behavior in castrated male guinea pigs. *Hormone Behav.*, 5: 207–217.

Arai, Y., Yamanouchi, K., Mizoukami, S., Yanai, R., Shibita, K. and Nagasawa, H. (1981) Induction of anovulatory sterility by neonatal treatment with 5β-dihydrotestosterone in female rats. *Acta Endocrinol.*, 96: 439–443.

Ayoub, D.M. and Greenough, W. T. (1983) Sex differences in dendritic structure in the preoptic area of the juvenile Macaque monkey brain. *Science*, 219: 197–198.

Balthazart, J. and Hirschberg, D. (1979) Testosterone metabolism and sexual behavior in the chick. *Hormone Behav.*, 12: 253–263.

Balthazart, J. and Schumacher, M. (1983) Testosterone metabolism and sexual differentiation in quail. In: J. Balthazart, E. Pröve and R. Gilles (Eds.), *Hormones and Behaviour in Higher Vertebrates*, Springer, Berlin, pp. 261–274.

Balthazart, J. and Schumacher, M. (1984) Changes in testosterone metabolism by the brain and cloacal gland growth during sexual maturation in the Japanese quail (*Coturnix coturnix japonica*). *J. Endocrinol.*, 100: 13–18.

Balthazart, J., Schumacher, M. and Malacarne, G. (1984) Relative potencies of testosterone and $5a$-dihydrotestosterone on crowing and cloacal gland growth in the Japanese quail (*Coturnix coturnix japonica*). *J. Endocrinol.*, 100: 19–23.

Baum, M.J. (1979) A comparison of the effects of methyltrienolone (R1881) and $5a$-dihydrotestosterone on sexual behaviour of castrated male rats. *Hormone Behav.*, 13: 165–174.

Baum, M.J. and Vreeburg, J.T.M. (1973) Copulation in castrated male rats following combined treatment with estradiol and dihydrotestosterone. *Science*, 182: 283–285.

Baum, M.J., Carrick, J.A., Erskine, M.S., Gallagher, C.A. and Shim, J.H. (1983) Normal differentiation of masculine sexual behavior in male ferrets despite neonatal inhibition of brain aromatase or $5a$-reductase activity. *Neuroendocrinology*, 36: 277–284.

Beyer, C. and Rivaud, N. (1973) Differential effects of testosterone and dihydrotestosterone on the sexual behavior of prepuberally castrated male rabbits. *Hormone Behav.*, 4: 175–180.

Bottoni, L. and Massa, R. (1981) Seasonal changes in testosterone metabolism in the pituitary gland and central nervous system of the European starling (*Sturnus vulgaris*). *Gen. Comp. Endocrinol.*, 43: 532–536.

Bronson, F.H. (1979) The reproductive ecology of the house mouse. *Quart. Rev. Biol.*, 54: 265–299.

Callard, G.V. (1981) Aromatization is cyclic-AMP dependent in cultured brain cells. *Brain Res.*, 204: 461–464.

Callard, G.V., Petro, Z. and Ryan, K.J. (1978) Phylogenetic distribution of aromatase and other androgen-converting enzymes in the central nervous system. *Endocrinology*, 103: 2283–2290.

Callard, G.V., Hoffman, R.A., Petro, Z. and Ryan, K.J. (1979) In vitro aromatization and other androgen transformations in the brain of the hamster (*Mesocricetus auratus*). *Biol. Reprod.*, 21: 33–38.

Campbell, C.S., Finkelstein, J.S. and Turek, W. (1978) The interaction of photoperiod and testosterone on the development of the copulatory behaviour in castrated male hamsters. *Physiol. Behav.*, 21: 409–415.

Chamness, G.C., King, T.W. and Sheridan, P.J. (1979) Androgen receptor in the rat brain — assays and properties. *Brain Res.*, 161: 267–276.

Christensen, L.W. and Clemens, L.G. (1975) Blockade of testosterone-induced mounting behaviour in the male rat with the application of the aromatization inhibitor androst-1,4,6-triene-3,17-dione. *Endocrinology*, 97: 1545–1551.

Clemens, L.G. and Pomerantz, S.M. (1982) Testosterone acts as a prohormone to stimulate male copulatory behavior in male Deer mice (*Peromyscus maniculatus bairdi*). *J. Comp. Physiol. Psychol.*, 6: 114–122.

Coquelin, A. and Bronson, F.H. (1980) Secretion of luteinizing hormones in male mice: Factors that influence release during sexual encounters. *Endocrinology*, 106: 1224–1229.

Crews, D. and Morgentaler, A. (1979) Effects of intracranial implantation of oestradiol and dihydrotestosterone on the sexual behaviour of the lizard (*Anolis carolinensis*). *J. Endocrinol.*, 82: 373–381.

Davidson, J.M. and Bloch, G.J. (1969) Neuroendocrine aspects of male reproduction. *Biol. Reprod.*, 1: 67–92.

Davies, D.T., Massa, R. and James, R. (1980) Role of testosterone and its metabolites in regulating gonadotrophin secretion in the Japanese quail. *J. Endocrinol.*, 84: 211–222.

Davis, P.G. and Barfield, R.J. (1979) Activation of masculine sexual behaviour by intracranial estradiol benzoate implants in male rats. *Neuroendocrinology*, 28: 217–227.

DeBold, J.F. and Clemens, L.G. (1978) Aromatization and the induction of male sexual behavior in male, female and androgenized female hamsters. *Hormone Behav.*, 11: 401–413.

Denef, C., Magnus, C. and McEwen, B.S. (1973) Sex differences and hormonal control of testosterone metabolism in rat pituitary and brain. *J. Endocrinol.*, 59: 605–621.

Denef, C., Magnus, C. and McEwen, B.S. (1974) Sex-dependent changes in pituitary 5α-dihydrotestosterone and 3-androstenediol formation during post-natal development and puberty in the rat. *Endocrinology*, 94: 1265–1274.

Dessi-Fulgheri, F. and Lupo C. (1982) Odour of male and female rats changes hypothalamic aromatase and 5α-reductase activity and plasma sex steroid levels in unisexually reared male rats. *Physiol. Behav.*, 28: 231–235.

Dessi-Fulgheri, F., Lupo, C., Ciampi, G.M., Canonaco, M. and Larsson, K. (1983) Exposure to odour during development and hypothalamic metabolism of testosterone. In: J. Balthazart, E. Pröve and R. Gilles (Eds.), *Hormones and Behaviour in Higher Vertebrates*, Springer, Berlin, pp. 305–312.

DeVoogd, T. (1984) The avian song system: relating sex differences in behavior to dimorphism in the central nervous system. In: G.J. De Vries, J.P.C. De Bruin, H.B.M. Uylings and M.A. Corner (Eds.), *Sex Differences in the Brain. The Relation between Structure and Function. Progress in Brain Research*, this volume, Ch. 9.

DeVoogd, T. and Nottebohm, F. (1981) Gonadal hormones induce dendritic growth in the adult avian brain. *Science*, 214: 202–204.

Dufy, B. and Vincent, J.D. (1980) Effects of sex steroids on cell membrane excitability: a new concept for the action of steroids on the brain. In: D. deWied and P.A. vanKeep (Eds.), *Hormones and the Brain*, MTP Press, Lancaster, pp. 29–43.

Erulkar, S.D., Kelley, D.B., Jurman, M.E., Zemlan, F.P., Schneider, G.T. and Krieger, N.R. (1981) Modulation of the neural control of the clasp reflex in male *Xenopus laevis* by androgens: A multidisciplinary study. *Proc. Natl. Acad. Sci. (U.S.A.)*, 78: 5876–5880.

Feder, H.H., Storey, A., Goodwin, D. and Reboulleau, C. (1977) Testosterone and "5α-dihydrotestosterone" levels in peripheral plasma of male and female ring doves (*Streptopelia risoria*) during the reproductive cycle. *Biol. Reprod.*, 16: 666–667.

Fletcher, T.J. and Short, R.V. (1974) Restoration of libido in castrated red deer stag (*Cervus elaphus*) with oestradiol-17β. *Nature (London)*, 216: 616–618.

George, F.W. and Ojeda, S.R. (1982) Changes in aromatase activity in the rat brain during embryonic, neonatal and infantile development. *Endocrinology*, 92: 589–594.

George, F.W., Tobleman, W.T., Milewich, L. and Wilson, J.D. (1978) Aromatase activity in the developing rabbit brain. *Endocrinology*, 102: 86–91.

Gorski, R.A. (1984) Critical role for the medial preoptic area in the sexual differentiation of the brain. In: G.J. De Vries, J.P.C. De Bruin, H.B.M. Uylings and M.A. Corner (Eds.), *Sex Differences in the Brain. The Relation between Structure and Function. Progress in Brain Research*, this volume, Ch. 7.

Gorski, R.A., Gordon, J.H., Shryne, J.E. and Southern, A.M. (1978) Evidence for a morphological sex difference within the preoptic area of the rat brain. *Brain Res.*, 148: 333–346.

Goy, R.W. and McEwen, B.S. (1980) *Sexual Differentiation of the Brain.* MIT Press, Cambridge, MA.

Grunt, J.A. and Young, W.C. (1952) Differential reactivity of individuals and the response of the male guinea pig to testosterone propionate. *Endocrinology*, 51: 237–248.

Grunt, J.A. and Young, W.C. (1953) Consistency of sexual behavior patterns in individual male guinea pigs following castration and androgen therapy. *J. Comp. Physiol. Psychol.*, 46: 138–144.

Gurney, M.E. (1982) Behavioural correlates of sexual differentiation in the zebra finch song. *Brain Res.*, 231: 153–172.

Gustafsson, J.-Å., Pousette, Å. and Svensson, E. (1976) Sex specific occurrence of androgen receptors in the rat. *J. Biol. Chem.*, 247: 4047–4054.

Hamilton, D.W. and Ofner, P. (1982) Androgen action and target-organ androgen metabolism. In: D.W. Hamilton and F. Naftolin (Eds.), *Basic Reproductive Medicine, Vol. 2, Reproductive Function in Man*, MIT Press, Cambridge, MA.

Harding, C.F. and Feder, H.H. (1976) Relation of uptake and metabolism of [1,2,6,7-^{3}H]testosterone to individual differences in sexual behaviour in male guinea pigs. *Brain Res.*, 105: 137–149.

Harlan, R.E., Shrivers, B.D. and Pfaff, D.W. (1984) Lordosis as a sexually dimorphic neural function. In: G.J. De Vries, J.P.C. De Bruin, H.B.M. Uylings and M.A. Corner (Eds.), *Sex Differences in the Brain. The Relation between Structure and Function. Progress in Brain Research*, this volume, Ch. 14.

Hart, B.L. (1978) Hormones, spinal reflexes and sexual behaviour. In: J.B. Hutchison (Ed.), *Biological Determinants of Sexual Behaviour*, Wiley, Chichester, pp. 316–347.

Hinde, R.A. (1970) *Animal Behaviour. A Synthesis of Ethology and Comparative Psychology*, McGraw-Hill, New York.

Holman, S.D. and Hutchison, J.B. (1982) Pre-copulatory behaviour in the male Mongolian gerbil. 1. Differences in dependence on androgen of component patterns. *Anim. Behav.*, 30: 221–230.

Hutchison, J.B. (1964) Investigations on the neural control of clasping and feeding in *Xenopus laevis* (Daudin). *Behaviour*, 24: 47–65.

Hutchison, J.B. (1970) Influence of gonadal hormones on the hypothalamic integration of courtship behaviour in the Barbary dove (*Streptopelia risoria*). *J. Reprod. Fertil.*, Suppl., 11: 15–41.

Hutchison, J.B. (1971) Effects of hypothalamic implants of gonadal steroids on courtship behaviour in Barbary doves (*Streptopelia risoria*). *J. Endocrinol.*, 50: 97–113.

Hutchison, J.B. (1974) Post-castration decline in behavioural responsiveness to intrahypothalamic androgen in doves. *Brain Res.*, 81: 169–181.

Hutchison, J.B. (1976) Hypothalamic mechanism of sexual behavior, with special references to birds. In: J.F. Rosenblatt, R.A. Hinde, F. Shaw and C. Beer (Eds.), *Advances in the Study of Behavior, Vol. 6*, Academic Press, New York, pp. 159–200.

Hutchison, J.B. (1978) Hypothalamic regulation of male sexual responsiveness to androgen. In: J.B. Hutchison (Ed.), *Biological Determinants of Sexual Behaviour*, Wiley, Chichester, pp. 277–317.

Hutchison, J.B. and Steimer, Th. (1981) Brain 5β-reductase: A correlation of behavioral sensitivity to androgen. *Science*, 213: 244–246.

Hutchison, J.B. and Steimer, Th. (1983) Hormone-mediated behavioural transitions: A role for brain aromatase. In: J. Balthazart, E. Pröve and R. Gilles (Eds.), *Hormones and Behaviour in Higher Vertebrates*, Springer, Berlin, pp. 161–174.

Hutchison, J.B., Steimer, Th. and Duncan, R. (1981) Behavioural action of androgen in the dove: effects of long-term castration on response specificity and brain aromatization. *J. Endocrinol.*, 90: 167–178.

Hutchison, R.E. (1978) Hormonal differentiation of sexual behavior in Japanese quail. *Hormone Behav.*, 11: 363–387.

Jenkins, J.S. and Hall, C.J. (1977) Metabolism of [^{14}C]-testosterone by human foetal and adult brain tissue. *J. Endocrinol.*, 74: 425–429.

Jouan, P. and Samperez, S. (1980) Metabolism of steroid hormones in the brain. In: M. Motta (Ed.), *The Endocrine Functions of the Brain*, Raven, New York, pp. 95–115.

Kato, J. (1976) Cytosol and nuclear receptors for 5α-dihydrotestosterone and testosterone in the hypothalamus and hypophysis, and testosterone receptors isolated from neonatal female rat hypothalamus. *J. Steroid. Biochem.*, 7: 1179–1187.

Kelley, D.B. and Pfaff, D.W. (1978) Generalizations from comparative studies on neuroanatomical and endocrine mechanisms of sexual behaviour. In: J.B. Hutchison (Ed.), *Biological Determinants of Sexual Behaviour*, Wiley, Chichester, pp. 225–255.

Kelly, M.J., Moss, R. and Dudley, C.A. (1977) The effects of microelectrophoretically applied oestrogen, cortisol and acetylcholine on medial preoptic-septal unit activity throughout the oestrus cycle of the female rat. *Exp. Brain Res.* , 30: 53–64.

Keverne, E.D., Eberhart, J.A., Yodyingyuad, U. and Abbott, D.H. (1984) Social influences on sex differences in the behaviour and endocrine state of talapoin monkeys. In: G.J. De Vries, J.P.C. De Bruin, H.B.M. Uylings and M.A. Corner (Eds.), *Sex Differences in the Brain. The Relation between Structure and Function. Progress in Brain Research*, this volume, Ch. 19.

Kime, D.E. (1980) Comparative aspects of testicular androgen biosynthesis in nonmammalian vertebrates. In: G. Delrio and J. Brachet (Eds.), *Steroids and their Mechanism of Action in Nonmammalian Vertebrates*, Raven, New York, pp. 17–31.

Kobayashi, R.M. and Reed, K.C. (1977) Conversion of androgens to estrogens (aromatization) in discrete regions of the rat brain: sexual differences and effects of castration. In: *Neuroscience Abstracts, Vol. III, Seventh Annual Meeting of the Society for Neuroscience, Anaheim, CA, November 6–10, 1977*, p. 348.

Konishi, M. and Gurney, M.E. (1982) Sexual differentiation of brain and behavior, *Neurosciences*, 5: 20–23.

Krey, C.L., MacLusky, N.J., Pfeiffer, D.G., Parsons, B., Merriam, G.R. and Naftolin, F. (1983) Role of catechol estrogens in estrogen-induced lordosis behavior in the female rat. In: G.R. Merriam and M.B. Lipsett (Eds.), *Catechol Estrogens*, Raven, New York, pp. 249–263.

Liao, S., Liang, T., Fang, S., Casteneda, E. and Shao, T. (1973) Steroid structure and androgenic activity. Specificities involved in the receptor binding and nuclear retention of various androgens. *J. Biol. Chem.*, 248: 6154–6162.

Lincoln, G.A. (1974) Luteinizing hormone and testosterone in man. *Nature (London)*, 252: 232–233.

Lincoln, G.A., Guinness, F. and Short, R.V. (1972) The way in which testosterone controls the social and sexual behavior of the red deer stag (*Cervus elaphus*). *Hormone Behav.*, 3: 375–396.

Lisboa, B.F., Srassner, M., Wulff, C. and Hoffmann, U. (1976) 5β-reductase in the human foetal brain. *Acta Endocrinol.*, Suppl., 184: 156.

Lisk, R.D. and Greenwald, D.P. (1983) Central plus peripheral stimulation by androgen is necessary for complete restoration of copulatory behavior in the male hamster. *Neuroendocrinology*, 36: 211–217.

Luttge, W.G. and Hall, N.R. (1973) Differential effectiveness of testosterone and its metabolites in the induction of male sexual behavior in two strains of albino mice. *Hormone Behav.*, 4: 31–43.

MacLusky, N.J. and Naftolin, F. (1981) Sexual differentiation of the central nervous system. *Science*, 211: 1294–1303.

MacLusky, N.J., Chaptal, C., Lieberburg, I. and McEwen, B.S. (1976) Properties and subcellular interrelationships of presumptive estrogen receptor macromolecules in the brains of neonatal and prepubertal female rats. *Brain Res.*, 114: 158–165.

Mainwaring, W.I.P. (1977) The mechanism of action of androgens. In: *Monographs on Endocrinology, Vol. 10*, Springer, New York, pp. 1–178.

Martini, L. (1982) The 5α-reduction of testosterone in the neuroendocrine structures. Biochemical and biophysiological implications. *Endocrine Rev.*, 3: 1–25.

Massa, R. (1980) The role of androgens in male birds reproduction. In: G. Delrio and J. Brachet (Eds.), *Steroids and their Mechanisms of Action in the Nonmammalian Vertebrates*, Raven, New York, pp. 148–159.

Massa, R. and Sharp, J. (1981) Conversion of testosterone to 5β-reduced metabolites in the neuroendocrine tissues of the maturing cockerel. *J. Endocrinol.*, 88: 263–269.

Massa, R., Justo, S. and Martini, L. (1975) Conversion of testosterone into 5α-reduced metabolites in the anterior pituitary and in the brain of maturing rats. *J. Steroid Biochem.*, 6: 567–571.

Massa, R., Cresti, L. and Martini, L. (1977) Metabolism of testosterone in the anterior pituitary gland and the central nervous system of the European starling (*Sturnus vulgaris*). *J. Endocrinol.*, 75: 347–354.

Massa, R., Davies, D.T., Bottoni, L. and Martini, L. (1979) Photoperiodic control of testosterone metabolism in the central and peripheral structures of avian species. *J. Steroid Biochem.*, 11: 937–944.

Massa, R., Bottoni, L. and Lucini, V. (1983) Brain testosterone metabolism and sexual behaviour in birds. In: J. Balthazart, E. Pröve and R. Gilles (Eds.), *Hormones and Behaviour in Higher Vertebrates*, Springer, Berlin, pp. 261–274.

McDonald, P.G. and Doughty, C. (1974) Effects of neonatal administration of different androgens in the female rat: correlation between aromatization and the induction of sterilization. *J. Endocrinol.*, 61: 95–103.

McEwen, B.S. (1981) Neural gonadal steroid actions. *Science*, 211: 1303–1311.

McEwen, B.S., Davis, P.G., Parsons, B. and Pfaff, D.W. (1979) The brain as a target for steroid hormone action. *Annu. Rev. Neurosci.*, 2: 65–112.

Mode, A., Norstedt, G., Simic, B., Eneroth, P and Gustafsson, J.-Å. (1981) Continuous infusion of growth hormone feminizes hepatic steroid metabolism in the rat. *Endocrinology*, 108: 2103–2108.

Mori, M., Suzuki, K. and Tamaoki, B.I. (1974) Testosterone metabolism in the rooster comb. *Biochim. Biophys. Acta*, 337L: 118–128.

Morin, L.P., Fitzgerald, K.M., Rusak, B. and Zucker, I. (1977) Circadian organization and neural mediation of hamster reproductive rhythms. *Psychoneuroendocrinology*, 2: 73–98.

Moss, R.L. and Dudley, C.A. (1984) Molecular aspects of the interaction between estrogen and the membrane excitability of hypothalamic nerve cells. In: G.J. De Vries, J.P.C. De Bruin, H.B.M. Uylings and M.A. Corner (Eds.), *Sex Differences in the Brain. The Relation between Structure and Function. Progress in Brain Research*, this volume, Ch. 1.

Naftolin, F., Ryan, K.J. and Petro, Z. (1972) Aromatization of androstenedione by the anterior hypothalamus of adult male and female rats. *Endocrinology*, 90: 295–298.

Naftolin, F., Ryan, K.J., Davies, I.J., Reddy, V.V., Flores, F., Petro, D., Kuhn, M., White, R.J., Takaota, Y. and Wolin, L. (1975) The formation of estrogens by central neuroendocrine tissue. *Recent Progr. Hormone Res.*, 31: 295–316.

Nakamura, T. and Tanabe, Y. (1974) In vitro metabolism of steroid hormones by chicken brain. *Acta Endocrinol.*, 75: 410–416.

Noma, K., Sato, B., Yano, S. and Yamamura, Y. (1975) Metabolism of testosterone in the hypothalamus of male rat. *J. Steroid Biochem.*, 6: 1261–1266.

Nottebohm, F. (1980) Testosterone triggers growth of brain vocal control nuclei in adult female canaries. *Brain Res.*, 189: 429–436.

Nottebohm, F. and Arnold, A.P. (1976) Sexual dimorphism in vocal control areas of the song bird brain. *Science*, 194: 211–213.

Nozu, K. and Tamaoki, B. (1975) Formation, nuclear incorporation and enzymatic decomposition of androgen–receptor complex of rat prostate. *J. Steroid Biochem.*, 6: 1319–1323.

O'Connell, M.E., Reboulleau, C., Feder, H.H. and Silver, R. (1968) Social interactions and androgen levels in birds. 1. Female characteristics associated with increased plasma androgen levels in the male ring dove (*Streptopelia risoria*). *Gen. Comp. Endocrinol.*, 44: 454–464.

Olsen, K.L. (1979) Androgen insensitive rats are defeminized by their testes. *Nature (London)*, 279: 238–239.

O'Malley, B.W. and Means, A.R. (1974) Female steroid hormones and target cell nuclei. *Science*, 183: 610–620.

Parrott, R.F. (1975) Aromatizable and 5α-reduced androgens: differentiation between central and peripheral effects on male rat sexual behavior. *Hormone Behav.*, 6: 99–108.

Parvisi, N., Ellendorf, F. and Wuttke, W. (1981) Catecholestrogens in the brain: action on pituitary hormone secretion and catecholamine turnover. In: K. Fuxe, J.A. Gustaffson and L. Wetterberg (Eds.), *Steroid Hormone Regulation of the Brain*, Pergamon, New York, p. 107.

Pfaff, D.W. (1980) *Estrogens and Brain Function*, Springer, New York, pp. 1–275.

Pfaff, D.W. and McEwen, B.S. (1983) Actions of estrogens and progestins on nerve cells. *Science*, 219: 808–814.

Phoenix, C.H. (1974) Effects of dihydrotestosterone on sexual behavior of castrated male rhesus monkeys. *Physiol. Behav.*, 12: 1045–1055.

Plapinger, L. and McEwen, B.S. (1978) Gonadal steroid and brain interaction in sexual differentiation. In: J.B. Hutchison (Ed.), *Biological Determinants of Sexual Behaviour*, Wiley, Chichester, pp. 153–219.

Price, N.C. and Stevens, L. (1982) *Fundamentals of Enzymology*, Oxford University Press, Oxford, p. 454.

Reddy, V.V.R., Naftolin, F. and Ryan, K.J. (1973) Aromatization in the central nervous system of rabbits: effects of castration and hormone treatment. *Endocrinology*, 92: 589–594.

Reddy, V.V.R., Naftolin, F. and Ryan, K.J. (1974) Conversion of androstenedione to estrone by neural tissues from fetal and neonatal rat. *Endocrinology*, 94: 117–121.

Rose, R.M. (1980) Androgens and behaviour. In: D. deWied and P.A. vanKeep (Eds.), *Hormones and the Brain*, MTP Press, Lancaster, pp. 175–189.

Rubin, R.T. (1982) Testosterone and aggression in men. In: P.C. Beumont and G. Burrows (Eds.), *Handbook of Psychiatry and Endocrinology*, Elsevier, Amsterdam, pp. 355–366.

Schleidt, W.M. (1970) Precocial sexual behaviour in turkeys (*Meleagris gallopauo* L.). *Anim. Behav.*, 18: 760–761.

Schumacher, M. and Balthazart, J. (1983) Effects of castration on postnatal differentiation in the Japanese quail (*Coturnix coturnix japonica*), *I.R.C.S. Med. Sci.*, 11: 102–103.

Selmanoff, M.K., Brodkin, L.D., Weiner, R.I. and Siiteri, P.K. (1977) Aromatization and 5α-reduction of androgens in discrete hypothalamic and limbic regions of the male and female rat. *Endocrinology*, 101: 841–848.

Sheridan, P.J. (1981) Unaromatised androgen is taken up by the neonatal rat brain: Two receptor systems for androgen. *Develop. Neurosci.*, 4: 46–54.

Sheridan, P.J. (1983) Androgen receptors in the brain: What are we measuring? *Endocrine Rev.*, 4: 171–178.

Siiteri, P.K. and Thompson, E.A. (1975) Studies of human placental aromatase. *J. Steroid Biochem.*, 6: 317–322.

Södersten, P. (1980) A way in which estradiol might play a role in the sexual behavior of male rats. *Hormone Behav.*, 14: 271–274.

Södersten, P. and Gustafsson, J.A. (1980) Activation of sexual behavior in castrated male rats with the synthetic androgen 17β-hydroxyl-17a-methyl-estra-4,9,11-triene-3-one (methyltrienolone R1881). *J. Endocrinol.*, 87: 279–283.

Steimer, Th. and Hutchison, J.B. (1980) Aromatization of testosterone within a discrete hypothalamic area associated with the behavioural action of androgen in the male dove. *Brain Res.*, 192: 586–591.

Steimer, Th. and Hutchison, J.B. (1981a) Metabolic control of the behavioural action of androgens in the dove brain: testosterone inactivation by 5β-reduction. *Brain Res.*, 209: 189–591.

Steimer, Th. and Hutchison, J.B. (1981b) Androgen increases formation of behaviourally effective oestrogen in dove brain. *Nature (London)*, 292: 345–347.

Steimer, Th. and Hutchison, J.B. (1983) Nuclear uptake of testosterone in the dove preoptic area. *Brain Res.*, 274: 193–196.

Stylianou, M., Forchielli, E., Tummillo, M. and Dorfman, R.I. (1961) Metabolism in vitro of [4-^{14}C]-testosterone by a human liver homogenate. *J. Biol. Chem.*, 236: 692–694.

Terada, N., Sato, B. and Matsumoto, K. (1980) Formation of 5a- and 5β-products as major C_{19}-steroids from progesterone in vitro in immature golden hamster testis. *Endocrinology*, 106: 1554–1561.

Toran-Allerand, C.D. (1978) Gonadal hormones and brain development: cellular aspects of sexual differentiation. *Am. Zool.*, 18: 553–565.

Toran-Allerand, C.D. (1984) On the genesis of sexual differentiation of the central nervous system: morphogenetic consequences of steroidal exposure and possible role of a-fetoprotein. In: G.J. De Vries, J.P.C. De Bruin, H.B.M. Uylings and M.A. Corner (Eds.), *Sex Differences in the Brain. The Relation between Structure and Function. Progress in Brain Research*, this volume, Ch. 4.

Verhoeven, G., Lamberigts, G. and DeMoor, P. (1974) Nucleus-associated 5a-reductase activity and androgen responsiveness. A study of various organs and brain regions of rats. *J. Steroid Biochem.*, 5: 93–100.

Verhoeven, G., Dierickx, P. and DeMoor, P. (1979) Stimulation effect of neurotransmitters on the aromatization of testosterone by Sertoli cell enriched cultures. *Mol. Cell. Endocrinol.*, 13: 241–253.

Vito, C.C. and Fox, T.O. (1979) Embryonic rodent brain contains estrogen receptors. *Science*, 204: 517–519.

Vito, C.C., Wieland, S.J. and Fox, T.O. (1979) Androgen receptors exist throughout the 'critical period' of brain sexual differentiation. *Nature (London)*, 282: 308–319.

Wingfield, J.C. (1983) Influences of environmental stress on reproduction in birds. In: B. Lofts (Ed.), *Proc. IXth Int. Symp. Comp. Endocrinol.*, Hong Kong Press, in press.

Yanai, R., Mori, T. and Nagasawa, H. (1977) Long-term effects of prenatal and neonatal administration of 5β-dihydrotestosterone on normal and neoplastic mammary development in mice. *Cancer Res.*, 37: 4456–4459.

DISCUSSION

M.A. CORNER: To what extent do the studies on birds with respect to the brain mechanisms underlying sexually dimorphic behaviour, seem to be in line with the picture emerging for mammals?

J.B. HUTCHISON: Work on quail (Adkins-Regan, 1983) suggests that oestrogens demasculinize the developing brain in genetic females during embryonic life. The suggestion can be made that sexual differentiation in birds is the reverse of that seen in mammals in that it occurs in the female rather than the male. However, recent studies of the sexually dimorphic vocal control system in the zebra finch indicate that oestrogen or aromatizable androgen acting soon after hatching differentiates the male song control system in the brain (Gurney, 1982) and the capacity of the male to sing in adulthood. This appears to be essentially similar to rodent species, particularly the male rat. Therefore, quite different hormonal mechanisms underly the sexual differentiation of vocal and sexual behaviour in birds. As in mammals, the limits of the sensitive period for the organizational effects of hormones on behaviour have not been established. But in quail, it has been shown experimentally that the female brain is responsive to the differentiating effects of oestradiol in adulthood, suggesting that plasticity for organization of sexual mechanisms is not restricted to a limited period in very early development (Hutchison, 1978). This capacity for sexual differentiation in adulthood does not appear to have been demonstrated in mammals yet.

D.H. ABBOTT: Since you have associated elevated 5β-reductase activity with low testosterone levels in adult male doves (i.e. following castration), are the elevated 5β-reductase activity levels in 1–5-day-old male doves also associated with low testosterone levels?

J.B. HUTCHISON: This question raises an interesting point, because it emphasizes the complex relationship between brain 5β-reductase activity and oestrogenic steroids. In the adult male preoptic area, 5β-reductase activity is suppressed by exogenous 17β-oestradiol (E_2). We have suggested that levels of 5β-reduced metabolites are normally lower in the preoptic nuclei and ventromedial hypothalamus of intact males, because of the suppressive effects of E_2 formed from testosterone in the preoptic area. We have no idea yet whether E_2 has a comparable suppressive effect on 5β-reduction in the early post-hatching male. Levels of aromatizable androgens are likely to be low in male squabs after hatching, therefore it is conceivable that high 5β-reductase activity in the preoptic area of squabs is due to a lack of oestrogenic suppression. However, this does not explain the contrast between the marked difference in 5β-reductase activity seen in the preoptic and adjacent brain areas of the adult, and the lack of a difference in activity of the squab "brain". Differentiation of enzyme activity is presumably due to factors other than oestrogen action, because levels of E_2 in the preoptic area after hatching match those seen in adult males.

D.H. ABBOTT: When does sexual differentiation occur in doves? Is it before or after hatching?

J.B. HUTCHISON: We have no data on when sexual differentiation occurs in doves.

K.M. KENDRICK: Do you have any evidence that sexual experience alters aromatase or reductase activity? In particular, does sexual experience alter the long-term effects of castration on aromatase activity?

J.B. HUTCHISON: We have studied the effects of short interactions on the induction of preoptic aromatase activity in the male dove. So far, we have not been able to find an effect of this short-term (<10 min) sexual experience on aromatase induction. However, it does seem likely that longer experience of interaction with the female over a number of hours may well be a significant factor. We have some indication that males that have been interacting with females for at least 24 h have higher preoptic aromatase activity than controls.

C.D. TORAN-ALLERAND: Is there any sex difference in aromatase activity in doves of the type described for a brief post-natal period in the rat?

J.B. HUTCHISON: Our data suggest that there is no sex difference in aromatase activity in the developing dove brain. However, we have only looked at the preoptic area and posterior hypothalamus which have high aromatase activity in the adult. Distribution of aromatase activity may be different in young doves. Possibly, examination of other brain areas may reveal sex differences.

G.J. DE VRIES: Does metabolic activity differ between brain areas and is it possible that one area, for example high in aromatase activity, switches to another metabolic activity under different physiological conditions?

J.B. HUTCHISON: It is quite clear that there are pronounced differences between brain areas in enzyme activity. Non-target areas for androgen have higher 5β-reductase activity than target areas. Similarly, aromatase activity is restricted largely to hypothalamic target areas. The other major androgen-metabolizing enzyme is 5α-reductase. This is active in both target and non-target areas. Our preliminary data suggest that its activity matches that of 5β-reductase to some extent. However, it must be emphasized that the activity of all metabolic pathways depends on substrate (T) concentrations. We have found, for example, that preoptic 5β-reductase predominates at high testosterone concentrations. But at physiological levels, aromatase and 5α-reductase are relatively more active. Therefore, if testosterone levels change within a particular brain area it is likely that the relative activity of the pathways will change.

REFERENCES

Adkins-Regan, E.K. (1983) Sex steroids and the differentiation and activation of avian reproductive behaviour. In: J. Balthazart, E. Pröve and R. Gilles (Eds.), *Hormones and Behaviour in Higher Vertebrates*, Springer, Berlin, pp. 218–230.

Gurney, M.E. (1982) Behavioural correlates of sexual differentiation in the zebra finch song. *Brain Res.*, 231: 153–172.

Hutchison, R.E. (1978) Hormonal differentiation of sexual behavior in the Japanese quail. *Hormone Behav.*, 11: 363–387.

G.J. De Vries et al. (Eds.),
Progress in Brain Research, Vol. 61
© 1984 Elsevier Science Publishers B.V., Amsterdam

53

Sexual Dimorphism
in the Hypothalamic Metabolism of Testosterone
in the Japanese Quail (*Coturnix coturnix japonica*)

MICHAEL SCHUMACHER * and JAQUES BALTHAZART

Laboratoire de Biochimie Générale et Comparée, Université de Liège, Liège (Belgium)

INTRODUCTION

In Japanese quail, males are bisexual and show mounts and copulation in response to androgens as well as sexual crouch after injections of oestrogens (Adkins and Adler, 1972). Females, in contrast, never show male sexual behaviour in response to testosterone (T) treatment (Adkins and Adler, 1972; Balthazart et al., 1983), even if ovariectomized or photoregressed.

The insensitivity of female quail to the activating effects of T might be due to an incapacity to transform sufficient amounts of T into active metabolites like 17β-oestradiol (E_2) and 5α-dihydrotestosterone (5α-DHT). Indeed, intracellular T metabolism is crucial for the activation of sexual behaviour. In quail, as in other vertebrates, it is probably through its metabolites that T activates the copulation mechanism, since E_2 in combination with 5α-DHT restores reproductive behaviour in castrated males (Schumacher and Balthazart, 1983a). The fact that T fails to activate copulation in ovariectomized female quail could also be related to a more rapid inactivation of T in its target organs. There is an enzymatic system in the avian brain (5β-reductase; Balthazart et al., 1979; Massa et al., 1977), which is considered to be an inactivation pathway of T, since injections of 5β-dihydrotestosterone (5β-DHT) neither activate sexual behaviour nor stimulate the differentiation of secondary sexual characteristics (Adkins, 1977; Massa et al., 1980; Mori et al., 1974; Steimer and Hutchison, 1981a; see, however, Balthazart and Hirschberg, 1979). Moreover, 5β-reduced metabolites of T could not be detected in hypothalamic cell nuclei following intramuscular injection of tritiated T, since they are believed to be rapidly eliminated from brain cells (Steimer and Hutchison, 1981a; Hutchison and Steimer, 1984). Over the past 2 years, we have been testing the hypothesis that hypothalamic metabolism of T may control sexual dimorphism of reproductive behaviour in Japanese quail. For this reason, we have studied the in vitro metabolism of labelled T in hypothalamic tissues from males and females, using 3 different approaches.

---

* Address all correspondence and reprint requests to Michael Schumacher, Laboratoire de Biochimie Générale et Comparée, Université de Liège, 17, place Delcour, B-4020 Liège, Belgium.

TESTOSTERONE METABOLISM IN THE WHOLE HYPOTHALAMUS OF MALES AND FEMALES

In a first experiment, we incubated the hypothalamus, the pituitary glands, pieces of the hyperstriatum, the cloacal glands (an epithelial, sexually dimorphic glandular tissue behind the cloaca) and the syrinx in the presence of $[4\text{-}^{14}C]$testosterone to analyse the intracellular metabolism of T (Balthazart et al., 1983). Samples were incubated in a Krebs–Ringer solution for birds (5 mg of fresh tissue/ml of solution, containing about 100 000 dpm/ml of $[4\text{-}^{14}C]$testosterone, specific activity: 58 mCi/mmole). This large excess of labelled T precluded any interference of endogenous T or with steroid receptors. The metabolites were separated by thin-layer chromatography and quantified by liquid scintillation (see Balthazart et al., 1979; Davies et al., 1980, for details). Five androgens were quantified in the samples: androstenedione (D4), 5β-DHT, $5a$-DHT, 5β-androstane-$3a$,17β-diol (5β,$3a$-diol) and $5a$-androstane-$3a$,17β-diol ($5a$,$3a$-diol) (for major testosterone-metabolizing pathways, see Fig. 1 in Hutchison and Steimer, 1984).

In this incubation medium, $5a$-reduced metabolites were produced in very small amounts by the hypothalamic samples and their specific identity could not be confirmed. Moreover, we failed to detect the conversion of T into E_2. Whereas in samples of the cloacal gland and syringeal muscles all 5 metabolites were found in sufficient quantities to conclude that intact males and females differ, such sex differences were not found in brain tissue samples encompassing the whole hypothalamus. This was true for intact, gonadectomized and T-treated gonadectomized birds.

In a second experiment, whole hypothalamic samples were collected in quail of various ages (between 1 day and 5 weeks). Again, no sex-related differences could be detected whereas they were observed in samples of the cloacal gland taken at the same ages (Balthazart and Schumacher, 1984).

Our failure to demonstrate a sexual dimorphism for T metabolism in the hypothalamus could be due to the heterogenity of this structure. A metabolic dimorphism specific to a limited group of neurones would be obscured in a mass of sexually non-differentiated tissue. Indeed, Steimer and Hutchison (1981a) demonstrated important local differences in T metabolism within specific parts of the dove hypothalamus. Furthermore, they showed that T metabolism in different hypothalamic areas does not respond in the same way to experimental treatments such as castration or steroid injections (Hutchison et al., 1981; Hutchison and Steimer, 1981, 1984; Steimer and Hutchison, 1981b).

THE 5β-REDUCTASE ACTIVITY IN DISCRETE SUBAREAS OF THE HYPOTHALAMUS

In a following experiment (Schumacher and Balthazart, 1983b), we studied the in vitro metabolism of T in homogenates from different regions of the hypothalamus and the adjacent lobus paraolfactorius (which is photosensitive and implicated in the control of gonadotrophin secretion; Sicard et al., 1983) of intact sexually mature male and female quail using a microdissection procedure and a slightly modified enzymatic radioassay similar to that described by Steimer and Hutchison (1981a).

The brains were rapidly removed, frozen on dry ice and six 1.2-mm coronal sections were used to dissect the median lower parts as illustrated in Fig. 1. These were then homogenized and incubated with a large excess (2.10^{-6} M) of $[4\text{-}^{14}C]$testosterone and the same metabolites as before were quantified. Like in the previous experiment, only very small amounts of 5α-reduced metabolites could be detected and were not quantified. 5β-Reductase activity (measured by the accumulation of 5β-DHT and 5β,3α-diol) appeared to be unevenly distributed. In both sexes, this enzymatic activity was higher in the samples anterior (A) than in those posterior (P) to the tractus septomesencephalicus (Fig. 1). Although the anatomical distribution of 5β-reduction was similar in the samples of each individual animal, great interindividual variability was witnessed in the absolute production of 5β-reduced metabolites. Therefore, the results in Fig. 1 are expressed as the percentage of the mean of the individual animals for each individual, the mean production of 5β-DHT + 5β,3α-diol for the 6 brain samples was set at 100% and results in separate samples are expressed accordingly.

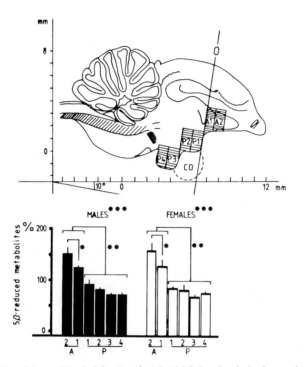

Fig. 1. Top: Sagittal view of the quail brain (after Baylé et al., 1974) showing the brain samples taken (A2–A1 and P1–P4). The O axis passes through the tractus septomesencephalicus and represents the frame of reference for the A and P samples. CO = chiasma opticum. Bottom: Production of 5β-reduced metabolites (5β-DHT and 5β,3α-diol) in 6 different hypothalamic samples (A2–A1, P1–P4) from intact male ($n = 6$) and female ($n = 6$) quail. The mean of 6 individual values was set at 100% and levels (± S.E.M.) are expressed accordingly. Overall differences between either male or female samples were analysed by one-way analysis of variance (ANOVA) (indicated above the figures beside the males or females headings), while differences between samples were tested with the Newman–Keuls test. *** $P \leq 0.001$; ** $P \leq 0.01$; * $P \leq 0.05$; ns, not significant.

Sex differences in the absolute levels of 5β-reductase activity were obscured by the large individual variability, but some differences could be demonstrated for 5β,3α-diol accumulation: females produced significantly more 5β,3α-diol than did males in the samples A2, A1 and P4 (Fig. 1). In view of the uneven distribution of 5β-reductase as shown in the above samples, it is probable that in certain hypothalamic nuclei sexual differences in 5β-reduction could be more important than what has been shown here.

Another problem which may be obscuring the detection of sex differences in intracellular metabolism of T, concerns the incubation conditions in these experiments. We used a large excess of substrate (labelled T) in order to preclude either interference with cold endogenous T or specific and non-specific binding (2.10^{-6} M of T, whereas serum concentrations of T do not exceed 6.10^{-8} M; Balthazart et al., 1983). Although the conversion of T into 5β-DHT and $5\beta,3\alpha$-diol is linear for substrate concentrations up to 3.10^{-6} M (Balthazart and Schumacher, 1983b), it is possible that such high T concentrations can induce T-metabolizing enzymes (Steimer and Hutchison, 1982). Thus, a sexual dimorphism in the 5β-reductase activity might appear only when physiological concentrations of substrate are used. Moreover, the low specific activity of [4-^{14}C]testosterone did not allow us to quantify and differentiate the 5α-reduced metabolites and oestrogens produced in vitro by the hypothalamic samples. For these reasons, we incubated small hypothalamic samples in the presence of physiological concentration of [1,2-α-^{3}H]T which has a high specific activity (60 Ci/mmole).

AROMATIZATION, 5β- AND 5α-REDUCTION OF TESTOSTERONE IN DISCRETE AREAS OF THE HYPOTHALAMUS

We first tested whether or not the enzymatic conversion of T (aromatization, 5β- and 5α-reduction) shows a linear pattern as a function of time and/or substrate concentration. All reactions were linear during the first 15 min of incubation. The enzyme kinetics were different for the aromatase and for the 5α- and 5β-reductase. Maximal velocity was achieved for aromatase at 1.8×10^{-8} M, for 5α-reductase at 2.5×10^{-7} M and for 5β-reductase at 3.10^{-6} M. In view of these results, we decided to incubate homogenates from small brain samples with 1.7×10^{-8} M of [1,2-α-^{3}H]T for 15 min. The dissection procedure of the hypothalamic samples was the same as in the previous experiment (Fig. 1). The enzymatic radioassay was similar to that described by Hutchison et al. (1981) (for more details: Schumacher and Balthazart, in preparation). In this experiment, we found clear sex differences in the production of 5β- and 5α-reduced metabolites as well as of oestradiol.

5β-Reduced metabolites

The anatomical distribution of 5β-reductase activity was the same as in the experiment in which a large excess of substrate was used (see above), viz., a rostral to caudal decrease of activity of 5β-reductase in both males and females. Male brains, however, formed less 5β-DHT than did female brains in the rostral samples (A1, P1). No sample differences were found in the levels of $5\beta,3\alpha$-diol in either sex, but its formation was less in males than in females, especially in the two most rostral samples (Fig. 2).

5α-Reduced metabolites

Although Fig. 3 suggests that 5α-reductase activity in the samples increases in a rostro-caudal direction, this is statistically significant only in females. The production of both 5α-reduced metabolites was similar in both male and female samples, with the exception of the P4 sample (Fig. 3).

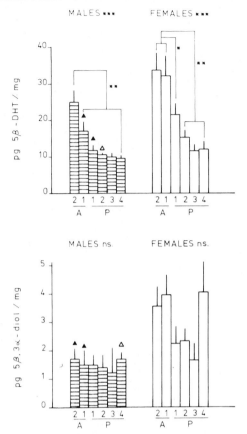

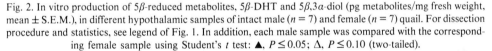

Fig. 2. In vitro production of 5β-reduced metabolites, 5β-DHT and 5β,3α-diol (pg metabolites/mg fresh weight, mean $\pm$ S.E.M.), in different hypothalamic samples of intact male ($n = 7$) and female ($n = 7$) quail. For dissection procedure and statistics, see legend of Fig. 1. In addition, each male sample was compared with the corresponding female sample using Student's t test: ▲, $P \leq 0.05$; Δ, $P \leq 0.10$ (two-tailed).

Oestradiol

The largest sex difference in testosterone metabolism is found in the aromatase activity. Whereas in male brain samples there is a significant increase in the rostro-caudal direction, the samples from female brains did not differ significantly from each other. The production of oestradiol in the two most caudal samples is higher in males than in females (Fig. 4).

GENERAL DISCUSSION

Steroid metabolism is an important step in the control of gonadal steroid action and thus is possibly involved in the appearance and the expression of sexual dimorphism (Balthazart and Schumacher, 1983b). In mammalian brains, some of the T-metabolizing enzymes are sexually differentiated. Aromatase activity is higher in the anterior hypothalamus and in other parts of the limbic system in intact males (Jouan and Samperez, 1980; Reddy et al.,

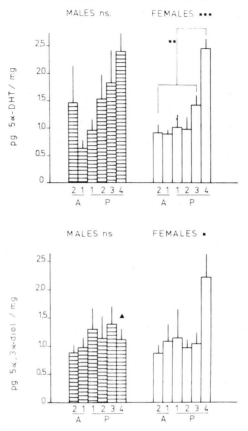

Fig. 3. In vitro production of 5a-reduced metabolites, 5a-DHT and 5a,3a-diol ($\bar{x} \pm$ S.E.M.), in different hypothalamic samples of intact male ($n = 7$) and female ($n = 7$) quail. For dissection procedure and statistics, see legends of Figs. 1 and 2.

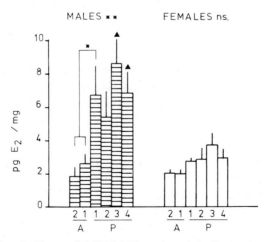

Fig. 4. In vitro production of 17β-oestradiol (E$_2$) in different hypothalamic samples of intact male ($n = 7$) and female ($n = 7$) quail. For dissection procedure and statistics, see legends of Figs. 1 and 2.

1973), whereas 5α-reductase activity is higher in the hypothalamus and the pituitary gland of intact females, albeit only at certain developmental stages (Degtiar et al., 1981).

The results presented above show that, in the Japanese quail, the activities of different enzymes metabolizing testosterone are unevenly distributed in the hypothalamus and that sexual dimorphism of T metabolism is limited to specific subregions of the hypothalamus. These studies also illustrate that sex differences in 5β-reductase activity appear more clearly when physiological concentrations of substrate are used, competition with "cold" endogenous T and interactions with binding molecules perhaps being important for this effect. Indeed, male quail tend to have higher T levels than females (Balthazart et al., 1983) and endogenous T might compete more with labelled T in brain samples from intact males. However, when we used high concentrations of labelled substrate, females still tended to have a higher 5β-reductase in some brain regions.

Competition with "cold" T cannot, however, explain the higher aromatase activity in the P3 and P4 samples of intact males. These results support our working hypothesis that the insensitivity of the female quail to the activating effects of T might be due to a greater inactivation of T (production of 5β-reduced metabolites) in their target neurones and/or to their incapacity to produce sufficient amounts of behaviourally active metabolites of T (oestradiol) (see Introduction).

In rodents, as in quail, females are also less sensitive to the behaviour-activating effects of T although the process of sexual differentiation during ontogeny seems to be different (for review in mammals: McEwen, 1982; Dörner, 1980; in birds: Adkins, 1978). In mammals, sexual dimorphism might also be partly related to the incapacity of the females to produce sufficient amounts of behaviourally active metabolites like 17β-oestradiol (see above) which facilitate copulation also in this group (Larsson, 1979). Although gonadectomy seems to abolish the dimorphism for aromatase activity in mammals (Vangala et al., 1973; Jouan and Samperez, 1980), one study reports a higher aromatization in discrete hypothalamic and limbic regions of gonadectomized and adrenalectomized male rats when compared to females, although the number of samples was too small for definitive conclusions (Selmanoff et al., 1977).

We are now planning to investigate whether or not these differences in the metabolism of T between intact male and female quail are maintained in gonadectomized birds and in birds treated with T. If this proves to be the case, we will then have isolated a biochemical mechanism which could explain the behavioural dimorphism in quail. It would then make sense to carry out additional experiments for the purpose of localizing the specific brain areas showing the postulated dimorphism.

ACKNOWLEDGEMENTS

We are indebted to Prof. E. Schoffeniels for his continued interest in our research.

This study was supported by grant 2.4518.80 from the Fonds de Recherche Fondamentale Collective to Prof. E. Schoffeniels and a grant from the Belgian Fonds National de la Recherche Scientifique (crédit aux chercheurs) to J. Balthazart. M. Schumacher is supported by a grant from the Institut pour l'Encouragement de la Recherche Scientifique dans l'Industrie et l'Agriculture.

REFERENCES

Adkins, E.K. (1977) Effects of diverse androgens on sexual behavior and morphology of castrated male quail. *Hormone Behav.*, 8: 201–207.

Adkins, E.K. (1978) Sex steroids and the differentiation of avian reproductive behavior. *Am. Zool.*, 18: 501–509.

Adkins, E.K. and Adler, N.T. (1972) Hormonal control of behavior in the Japanese quail. *J. Comp. Physiol. Psychol.*, 81: 27–36.

Balthazart, J. and Hirschberg, D. (1979) Testosterone metabolism and sexual behavior in the chick. *Hormone Behav.*, 12: 253–263.

Balthazart, J. and Schumacher, M. (1984) Changes in testosterone metabolism by the brain and the cloacal gland during sexual maturation in the Japanese quail (*Coturnix coturnix japonica*). *J. Endocrinol.*, 100, 13–18.

Balthazart, J. and Schumacher, M. (1983b) Testosterone metabolism and sexual differentiation in quail. In: J. Balthazart, E. Pröve and R. Gilles (Eds.), *Hormones and Behaviour in Higher Vertebrates*, Springer, Berlin, pp. 237–260.

Balthazart, J., Massa, R. and Negri-Cesi, P. (1979) Photoperiodic control of testosterone metabolism, plasma gonadotrophins, cloacal gland growth and reproductive behavior in the Japanese quail. *Gen. Comp. Endocrinol.*, 39: 222–235.

Balthazart, J., Schumacher, M. and Ottinger, M.A. (1983) Sexual differences in the Japanese quail: behavior, morphology, and intracellular metabolism of testosterone. *Gen. Comp. Endocrinol.*, 51: 191–207.

Baylé, J.D., Ramade, E. and Oliver, J. (1974) Stereotaxic topography of the brain of the quail. *J. Physiol. (Paris)*, 68: 219–241.

Davies, D.T., Massa, R. and James, M. (1980) Role of testosterone and of its metabolites in regulating gonadotrophin secretion in the Japanese quail. *J. Endocrinol.*, 84: 211–222.

Degtiar, V.G., Loserva, L.A. and Isatchenkov, B.A. (1981) In vitro metabolism of androgens in hypothalamus and pituitary from infantile and adolescent rats of both sexes. *Endocrinol. Exp.*, 15: 181–190.

Dörner, G. (1980) Sexual differentiation of the brain. *Vitam. Hormone*, 38: 325–381.

Hutchison, J.B. and Steimer, Th. (1981) Brain 5β-reductase. A correlate of behavioral sensitivity to androgen. *Science*, 213: 244–246.

Hutchison, J.B. and Steimer, Th. (1984) Androgen metabolism in the brain: behavioural correlates. In: G.J. De Vries, J.P.C. De Bruin, H.B.M. Uylings and M.A. Corner (Eds.), *Sex Differences in the Brain. The Relation between Structure and Function. Progress in Brain Research*, this volume, Ch. 2.

Hutchison, J.B., Steimer, Th. and Duncan, R. (1981) Behavioural action of androgen in the dove: Effects of long-term castration on response specificity and brain aromatisation. *J. Endocrinol.*, 90: 167–178.

Jouan, P. and Samperez, S. (1980) Metabolism of steroid hormones in the brain. In: M. Motta (Ed.), *The Endocrine Functions of the Brain*, Raven, New York, pp. 95–115.

Larsson, K. (1979) Features of the neuroendocrine regulation of masculine sexual behavior. In: C. Beyer (Ed.), *Endocrine Control of Sexual Behavior*, Raven, New York, pp. 77–163.

Massa, R., Cresti, L. and Martini, L. (1977) Metabolism of testosterone in the anterior pituitary gland and the central nervous system of the European starling (*Sturnus vulgaris*). *J. Endocrinol.*, 75: 347–354.

Massa, R., Davies, D.T. and Bottoni, L. (1980) Cloacal gland of the Japanese quail: androgen dependence and metabolism of testosterone. *J. Endocrinol.*, 84: 223–230.

McEwen, B.S. (1982) Sexual differentiation of the brain: Gonadal hormone action and current concepts of neuronal differentiation. In: I.R. Brown (Ed.), *Molecular Approaches to Neurobiology*, Academic Press, New York, pp. 195–219.

Mori, M., Suzuki, K. and Tamaoki, B. (1974) Testosterone metabolism in rooster comb. *Biochim. Biophys. Acta*, 337: 118–128.

Palkovits, M. (1975) Isolated removal of hypothalamic nuclei for neuroendocrinological and neurochemical studies. In: W.E. Stumpf and L.D. Grant (Eds.), *Anatomical Neuroendocrinology*, Karger, Basel, pp. 72–80.

Reddy, V.V.R., Naftolin, F. and Ryan, K.J. (1973) Aromatisation in the central nervous system of rabbits: Effects of castration and hormone treatment. *Endocrinology*, 92: 589–594.

Schumacher, M. and Balthazart, J. (1983a) The effects of testosterone and its metabolites on sexual behavior and morphology in male and female Japanese quail. *Physiol. Behav.*, 30: 335–339.

Schumacher, M. and Balthazart, J. (1983b) Testosterone metabolism in discrete areas of the hypothalamus and adjacent brains regions of male and female Japanese quail (*Coturnix coturnix japonica*). *Brain Res.*, 278, 337–340.

Selmanoff, M.K., Brodkin, L.D., Weiner, R.I. and Siiteri, K. (1977) Aromatization and 5α-reduction of androgens in discrete hypothalamic and limbic regions of the male and female rat. *Endocrinology*, 101: 841–848.

Sicard, B., Oliver, J. and Bayle, J.D. (1983) Gonadotropic and photosensitive abilities of the lobus paraolfactorius: Electrophysiological study in quail. *Neuroendocrinology*, 36: 81–87.

Steimer, Th. and Hutchison, J.B. (1981a) Metabolic control of the behavioural action of androgen in the dove brain: testosterone inactivation by 5β-reduction. *Brain Res.*, 207: 9–16.

Steimer, Th. and Hutchison, J.B. (1981b) Androgen increases formation of behaviourally effective oestrogen in dove brain. *Nature (London)*, 292: 345–347.

Steimer, Th. and Hutchison, J.B. (1982) Testosterone metabolism in the avian brain: 5β-reduction and the inactivation hypothesis. In: *Abstracts of the Symposium on Hormones and Behaviour in Higher Vertebrates, 4th ESCPB Conference, Bielefeld*, pp. 259–260.

G.J. De Vries et al. (Eds.),
Progress in Brain Research, Vol. 61
© 1984   Elsevier Science Publishers B.V., Amsterdam

On the Genesis of Sexual Differentiation of the Central Nervous System: Morphogenetic Consequences of Steroidal Exposure and Possible Role of α-Fetoprotein

C. DOMINIQUE TORAN-ALLERAND

Center for Reproductive Sciences (IISHR) and Departments of Neurology, and Anatomy and Cell Biology, Columbia University, College of Physicians and Surgeons, New York, NY 10032 (U.S.A.)

INTRODUCTION

Many vertebrate species exhibit marked sex differences in the neural control of reproductive endocrine function and of a wide variety of sexual and non-reproductive behaviors. Sex differences in such central nervous system (CNS) functions represent the consequence of developmental interactions between several different factors among which in birds and mammals, for example, the hormones secreted by the gonads are paramount (for recent reviews see MacLusky and Naftolin, 1981; McEwen, 1983). It is generally believed that testicular androgens exert an inductive, or "organizational", influence on the developing CNS during restricted ("critical"), late fetal or early postnatal periods of neural differentiation, at which time the tissue is sufficiently plastic to respond permanently and irreversibly to these hormones. In many developing mammals, for example, plasma concentrations of androgens are higher in males than females only during such "critical" periods (Weisz and Ward, 1980). In older animals, on the other hand, the CNS is either refractory or exhibits the characteristically reversible and excitatory, or "activational", effects of the gonadal hormones which characterize steroid-sensitive regions in the adult.

Developmental exposure of the sexually undifferentiated and bipotential developing CNS to these apparent differences in androgen levels results in the phenotypic differentiation of a broad spectrum of neuroendocrine and behavioral responses which are congruent with the genotype. Depending upon the species, moreover, sexual differentiation consists of one or two independent processes, both dependent on androgens but involving differential hormonal sensitivities, different CNS regions and temporally different "critical" periods. "Masculinization" refers to the development and potentiation of the behavioral and neuroendocrine patterns characteristic of the adult male and is universally present. "Defeminization", which is typical of only certain species such as the rodent, relates to the additional suppression or elimination of such female characteristics as cyclical LH secretion (resulting in anovulatory sterility in androgenized females) and a decrease in the expression of female sexual behavior. While masculinization with or without defeminization of CNS function follows exposure to androgens in both sexes, feminization (in mammals at least) whether normally derived or following neonatal castration of the male is poorly understood and has generally been considered to emerge passively in the absence of any specific hormonal induction and to represent the expression of the brain's presumed intrinsic or unmodified pattern of neural organization.

POSSIBLE MODES OF STEROID ACTION

The fundamental biochemical and molecular mechanisms by which testicular androgens mediate their irreversible effects are not fully known (see MacLusky and Naftolin, 1981; McEwen, 1983; for review). A requisite event for the masculinization of many neural functions in many species appears to involve local intraneuronal metabolic conversion of the major testicular hormonal product, testosterone, by aromatization to the estrogen, 17β-estradiol, and the subsequent binding of 17β-estradiol to high-affinity, distinct estrogen-binding macromolecules or "receptors", located intracellularly in relatively small neuronal subpopulations of the aromatase-rich hypothalamus, preoptic area (POA) and the amygdala. While local estrogen formation appears to be crucial for sexual differentiation in the rat and mouse, for example, there is a great deal of species variability and even differences between regions and between types of sexually differentiated functions within a given species with respect to the extent to which estrogen is required for sexual differentiation of the CNS. In other species, such as the guinea pig, ferret and rhesus monkey, and to a much lesser extent in the rodent, behavioral masculinization appears to be mediated by both testosterone and 5α-dihydrotestosterone (DHT), acting directly as androgens through binding to specific intraneuronal androgen receptors which may or may not be localized to many of the same loci as those for estrogen. In rats and mice, on the other hand, which depend, for the most part, on aromatization, intrahypothalamic implants of testosterone or 17β-estradiol have been found to be equally effective in eliciting masculinization of reproductive function and sexual behavior (Christensen and Gorski, 1978). Anti-estrogens have been shown to block testosterone-induced and estradiol-induced masculinization, and aromatase inhibitors to attenuate the masculinizing effects of both endogenous and exogenous testosterone, whereas non-aromatizable androgens such as DHT appear to be largely ineffective (Luttge and Whalen, 1970; McDonald and Doughty, 1974). Androgens, however, may also elicit direct effects in the rodent (Breedlove et al., 1982), which can be inhibited by androgen antagonists (Breedlove and Arnold, 1983), and even interactions between estrogens and such non-aromatizable androgens as DHT appear to potentiate the masculinizing effects of 17β-estradiol given concurrently to male rats castrated at birth at doses ineffective when used alone (Booth, 1977; Hart, 1979; Van der Schoot, 1980).

SEXUAL DIMORPHISM OF CNS STRUCTURE

The cellular basis for the permanent differentiating effects of steroids on the developing CNS is also poorly understood. Since it is generally believed that steroids mediate their effects through the intermediary of specific nuclear receptors and to act at the level of the genome (see O'Malley and Birnbaumer, 1978, for review), changes may be visible at both molecular and structural levels. Various experiments suggest that testosterone may permanently alter such chemical features of target neurons as receptor or neurotransmitter phenotype, and/or may alter neuronal responsiveness to afferent inputs elicited by hormones or other chemical signals. Testosterone may elicit its effects through (i) hormonal modulations of the levels of neurotransmitter receptors (Arimatsu et al., 1981) or of enzymes controlling synaptic transmission (McEwen, 1983, for review); (ii) by interference with maturational or metabolic aspects of the receptor system (Vertés and King, 1971) or (iii) by alterations in membrane properties.

It is reasonable, however, to consider that sex differences in neurally controlled functions might also be expressed as structural differences of the relevant neural substrate. That gonadal hormones influence and alter the direction of cellular differentiation in the CNS has been supported by increasingly numerous examples of hormone-dependent structural dimorphism in such physiologically significant, steroid receptor-containing regions as the hypothalamus, POA, amygdala, cerebral cortex, hippocampus, habenula and spinal cord in mammals such as the rat, mouse, hamster, monkey and human as well as in the vocal control centers of the frog (*Xenopus laevis*) and songbird (canary and zebra finch). Structural sexual dimorphism has also been observed in such non-CNS neural centers as the autonomic ganglia of the cat, mouse and rat (Calaresu and Henry, 1971; Suzuki et al., 1982; Wright and Smolen, 1983).

The morphological consequences of perinatal exposure of the CNS to endogenous or exogenous hormones have been summarized in Table I and are characterized by such cytological parameters as: (1) an increase in neuronal cell numbers (Gorski et al., 1978;

TABLE I

STEROID-DEPENDENT STRUCTURAL DIMORPHISM IN THE VERTEBRATE CNS*

Cytological difference	Region	Animal
Neuronal numbers	POA, amygdala, spinal cord, vocal centers	Rat, mouse, songbird, frog
Neuronal size	POA, ventromedial, amygdala, habenula, hippocampus cerebral cortex, vocal centers	Rat, mouse, monkey, songbird, frog
Dendritic length/branching	POA, suprachiasmatic, vocal centers	Rat, hamster, monkey, frog, songbird
Dendritic spines	POA, hippocampus, vocal centers	Rat, monkey, songbird
Numbers of synapses	Arcuate, suprachiasmatic	Rat
Type of synapses	Suprachiasmatic	Rat
Synaptic organization	POA, arcuate, amygdala	Rat
Synaptic organelles	Arcuate, suprachiasmatic, amygdala	Rat
Axonal density	Hippocampus (sympathetic); septum and habenula (vasopressinergic)	Rat
Regional nuclear volume	POA, spinal cord, amygdala, vocal centers	Rat, mouse, frog, songbird
Volume of neural structures	Cerebral cortex	Rat
	?Corpus callosum	Human

* For references cf. text.

Breedlove and Arnold, 1980, 1983; Gurney and Konishi, 1980; Gurney, 1981; Hannigan and Kelley, 1981; Jordan et al., 1982); (2) an increase in neuronal size — including the soma, nucleus and nucleolus (Ifft, 1964; Pfaff, 1966; Dörner and Staudt, 1968, 1969a,b; Bubenik and Brown, 1973; Gregory, 1975; Hellman et al., 1976; Staudt and Dörner, 1976; Breedlove and Arnold, 1980, 1983; Gurney, 1981; Hannigan and Kelley, 1981; Jordan et al., 1982); (3) differences in neuronal organelles (Güldner, 1976); (4) an increase in the length and branching of dendrites (Greenough et al., 1977; DeVoogd and Nottebohm, 1981a; Gurney, 1981; Ayoub et al., 1982; Kelley and Fenstemaker, 1983); (5) a change in dendritic fields (Greenough et al., 1977); (6) an increase in the overall numbers and density of dendritic spines (Meyer et al., 1978; Gurney, 1981; Ayoub et al., 1982); (7) an increase in the numbers of different types of synapses (i.e., asymmetrical vs.

symmetrical) (Güldner, 1982); (8) a change in the topographic distribution of synapses (shaft vs. spine) (Raisman and Field, 1973; Matsumoto and Arai, 1980, 1981b; Nichizuka and Arai, 1981a,b); (9) an increase in synaptic organelles (postsynaptic density material, receptors, vesicles and terminals) (Ratner and Adamo, 1971; King, 1972; Arimatsu et al., 1981; Güldner, 1982; LeBlond et al., 1982); (10) an increase in the regional density of axonal innervation (DeVries et al., 1981, 1983; Milner and Loy, 1980, 1982; Loy and Milner, 1980); and (11) an increase in the gross volume of defined neuronal groups (Nottebohm and Arnold, 1976; Gorski et al., 1978, 1980; Breedlove and Arnold, 1980; Mizukami et al., 1983) and of certain neural structures, including the corpus callosum (DeLacoste-Utamsing and Holloway, 1982) and the cerebral cortex (Pappas et al., 1978; Diamond et al., 1981).

With the possible exception of frog and songbird vocal control centers and of the rodent sexually dimorphic spinal nucleus of the bulbo-cavernosus, which innervates the penile musculature, the precise sexually dimorphic functions subserved by these cellular differences or even subserved by the regional localization of these differences is largely unknown (Lawrence and Raisman, 1980; Arendash and Gorski, 1983). Inferential evidence based on the cytological characteristics of the dimorphic features, as well as on the direct electro-physiological demonstration of sexual dimorphism in the synaptic connections between the amygdala and POA/anterior hypothalamic regions (Dyer et al., 1976), have suggested that sex-specific differences in neural pathways or circuits may form the substrate for sexual differentiation of function. All of the examples of sexual dimorphism of the adult CNS, however, merely represent the final or ultimate response to steroidal exposure during development and, as such, provide little information about the underlying morphogenetic or cellular mechanisms which produced them.

GONADAL HORMONES AND BRAIN DEVELOPMENT IN VITRO

Organotypic culture of the CNS has offered a useful approach to understanding the manner of action of gonadal steroids (testosterone and 17β-estradiol during the early stages of sexual differentiation of the brain (Toran-Allerand, 1976, 1980a; Toran-Allerand et al., 1980, 1983). These studies have dealt with the cellular expression of the hormonal effects in steroid receptor-containing regions of the developing mouse CNS in vitro as an attempt at elucidating the cellular mechanisms underlying the genesis of sexual differentiation.

Morphological concomitants of the hormonal effect

In the above-mentioned experiments it was shown that, regardless of genetic sex, continuous exposure of explants of the 17-day fetal or newborn mouse hypothalamus and POA to either testosterone or estradiol selectively enhances growth and arborization of neuronal processes (neurites) from specific explant regions (Fig. 1A and B). These include the MPOA,

---

Fig. 1. Steroid-responsive neuritic outgrowth. Homologous pair of explants from the POA, 13 days in vitro. (A) Control (horse serum, endogenous estradiol 200 pg/ml); (B) 50 ng/ml in horse serum. Morphological concomitant of a dose–response effect. The surface areas of the neuritic arborizations do not differ significantly but the differences in unit density are striking, suggesting steroidal induction of neuritic branching. The localization of the relatively small number of fibers contributing to the arborization is correlated with the topographic distribution of [^{3}H]estradiol-labeled cells in that region. Holme's silver impregnation. Darkfield ($\times$16). (From Toran-Allerand et al., 1980.)

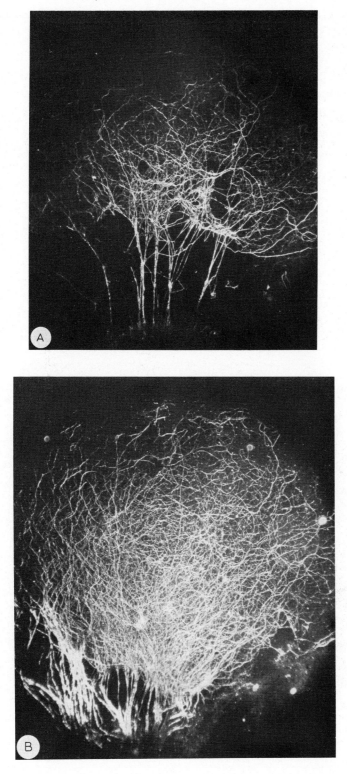

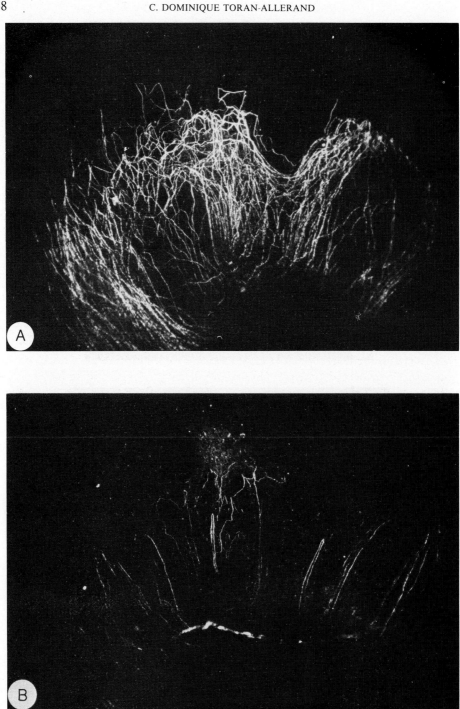

Fig. 2. The importance of estradiol per se. Homologous pair of explants from the POA, 22 days in vitro, exposed to serum containing either (A) antibodies to bovine serum albumin (BSA) or (B) antibodies to 17β-estradiol/BSA. Note the striking reduction in neuritic outgrowth following physiological inactivation of the estradiol. Holme's, Darkfield (×15.8). (From Toran-Allerand, 1980a.)

the bed nucleus of the stria terminalis, and the infundibular and ventral premamillary nuclei. This regional specificity, moreover, can be correlated with the presence and topographic distribution of the [³H]estradiol-concentrating neurons (Toran-Allerand et al., 1980) whose topography in the explants is comparable to the distribution of the estrogen receptor-containing neurons in the developing rodent brain in vivo (Sheridan et al., 1974; Stumpf et al., 1980). This regional localization of the neuritic response, the relatively small number of fibers contributing to the neuritic arborizations and the focal increase of fiber density within the arborizations all suggest that steroids may induce neuritic branching only in specific neuronal subpopulations, viz., those which contain steroid receptors (Toran-Allerand, 1980a).

The hormonal specificity of the in vitro response is comparable to that seen during sexual differentiation of the rodent brain (Toran-Allerand, 1980a), in that estrogen appears to be of primary importance. The effect seems to be dose-dependent (Fig. 1A and B). Reducing the availability of estrogen, by exposure to serum which has been pretreated by either pharmacological (the anti-estrogen, CI-628) or immunochemical (antibodies to estradiol) means, reduces and retards neuritic development only in the steroid responsive regions (Fig. 2A and B). Unlike testosterone, moreover, the non-aromatizable DHT failed to elicit a visible neuritic response. This emphasizes the developmental importance of estrogens derived from aromatization as a component of the androgen effect, as does the enhanced neuritic outgrowth which is elicited by testosterone in hypothalamus/POA cultures, derived from the androgen-insensitive, androgen receptor-deficient, but normally aromatizing Tfm/y mutant mouse (Toran-Allerand, unpublished). That testosterone's action requires more than local aromatization alone, however, and that there may exist an additional requirement for estradiol other than that derived from aromatization is suggested by the observation that previously stimulatory levels of testosterone fail to elicit a neuritic response, if the serum estrogen levels are reduced concurrently.

Aromatization in vitro

The above-mentioned hypothesis is predicated on the assumption that aromatase activity itself is normally present in the cultures. That aromatization does occur in steroid-responsive culture regions has been demonstrated in more recent studies (MacLusky and Toran-Allerand, in preparation) which show the intactness of all the metabolic pathways for androgen in the CNS (POA). This includes very high levels of aromatase activity, as measured by the recovery of [³H]crystalline estrogens from ³H-aromatizable androgens which were fed to the cultures.

Since conventional in vitro homogenate assays typically give conversions of 0.1%/g/h (MacLusky, personal communication), the failure of testosterone alone to induce neuritic enhancement in an estrogen-deficient medium despite the presence of a remarkable degree of aromatase activity (the percent conversion of the substrate with the intact cultures is in the order of 1%), is of considerable interest. Such findings further support the earlier formulated hypothesis concerning the additional importance of estrogen per se in the mechanisms underlying aromatase-dependent androgenization (Toran-Allerand, 1976, 1980a). Estrogen may exert its effects on neuronal differentiation by acting either through synergism with androgen or by a priming effect, including the possible very induction or augmentation of aromatase enzymatic activity itself; much like estradiol's reported influence on choline acetyltransferase and acetylcholinesterase activity in vivo (Amenta et al., 1979; Luine and McEwen,

1983). This possibility is especially interesting in view of the fact that estrogens have been shown to increase follicle-stimulating hormone (FSH)-induced ovarian aromatase activity (Adashi and Hsueh, 1982) in rat granulosa cells in vitro.

POSSIBLE CELLULAR AND MORPHOGENETIC MECHANISMS OF STEROIDAL EFFECTS

It appears, therefore, that explant regions containing estrogen receptors respond to varying levels of estrogen by variations in both the rate and extent of their neuritic outgrowth. This apparently regionally specific stimulation may result from one or more of several possible cellular mechanisms. On the other hand, one may be dealing with an inductive phenomenon resulting from steroidal effects either on selective neuronal proliferation, i.e. more neurons produced, therefore more neurites formed, or on neuritic growth itself (i.e. more processes formed from the branching or sprouting of neurites in an essentially postmitotic neuronal population). The mitogenic property of estrogen in another target tissue, the uterus, is well known (Pietras and Szego, 1979) and Jacobson and Gorski (1981) as well as Seress (1978) have suggested that androgens may be mitogenic in the developing rat CNS.

Alternatively or in addition, like the many neural growth and trophic factors which have been reported in a variety of "conditioned" tissue culture media, and like nerve growth factor (NGF), the gonadal steroids may be neuronotrophic ("survival-promoting") (Fig. 3) as distinct from neurite-promoting ("growth-promoting") (Varon et al., 1983). By acting either directly on steroid receptor-containing neurons or indirectly, via the intermediary of other neurons and/or neuroglial cells in their immediate vicinity, which might themselves secrete neuronotrophic factor(s), they might support neuronal survival, thereby reducing or selectively stabilizing naturally occurring neuronal death (see Oppenheim, 1981, for review). This would not only result in more neurons, and hence more neurites observed, but would also lead to the differentiation of the various sexually dimorphic nuclei of the POA, amygdala, spinal cord and vocal control centers described in various species (see above). In this regard,

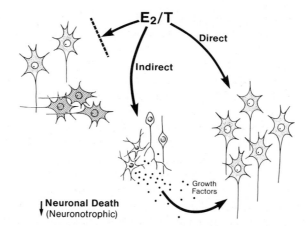

Fig. 3. Diagrammatic representation of the hypothesized neuronotrophic effect of estradiol (E_2) and testosterone (T). In their absence, a certain number of steroid receptor-containing neurons may die (hatched cells); whereas in their presence, more of these neurons survive whether by direct effects on these neurons themselves or by indirect effects via the intermediary of other neurons or even neuroglial cells, which might themselves secrete the neuronotrophic factors to selectively stabilize the steroid receptor-containing subpopulations.

Perez-Polo et al. (1977) have suggested that C-6 glioma cells, a glial-derived cell line, respond to estradiol by increased synthesis and secretion of NGF, a trophic factor critical for the survival of dorsal root and sympathetic ganglia neurons at a certain "critical" period of their development both in vivo and in vitro (Levi-Montalcini and Angeletti, 1968).

Aspects of dendritic differentiation

That the induction of neuritic branching or sprouting may be an important aspect of the steroidal effect in brain cultures, however, is supported not only by the observed pattern of the focal outgrowth of proportionately few fibers arborizing extensively, but also by recent Golgi–Cox impregnations of paired, homologous cultures of the newborn mouse POA (Toran-Allerand et al., 1983). Computer quantification of estrogen effects on dendritic differentiation of the impregnated neurons within the explant reveals a highly significant steroidal effect ($P < 0.005$), with a 31% increase in the number of complete first-order dendritic branches emanating directly from the cell body of the estrogen-treated homologues. This complements the earlier observations (Toran-Allerand, 1976, 1980a) which, after all, represent an uncontrollable (and obviously biased) selection of only those neurites which not only grow preferentially into the visible outgrowth but which manage to become impregnated with silver as well.

The preferential involvement of first-order dendritic branching as a consequence of exposure to estrogen seems particularly germane, especially when considered in terms of certain aspects of dendritic differentiation. The process of dendritic differentiation may be viewed as consisting of two components: a primary pattern, exemplified by first-order branching which contributes to the basic dendritic phenotype for each neuronal category and a secondary pattern which defines the complexity of the ultimate dendritic arborization and involves the subsequent stages of higher-order branching. Whereas primary dendritic differentiation is probably "intrinsically" (genomically) determined, secondary differentiation appears to be highly dependent on neuronal interactions, being considerably influenced by the afferent axonal innervation. A striking example is the difference in the patterns of dendritic differentiation of the cerebellar Purkinje cell in vivo and in vitro. Its distinctive single, apical first-order dendrite and flattened dendritic tree are phenotypic, but the complexity of the higher-order dendritic arborization depends to a considerable degree on the extent of its afferentation. While the classical dendritic phenotype does develop in vitro (Allerand, 1971), dendritic complexity never approaches that in vivo, as a result of the significant reduction in the (afferent) granule cell population and the essential absence of climbing fibers (Allerand, 1971). If, therefore, estrogen is believed to act upon the genome in its other target tissues (see O'Malley and Birnbaumer, 1978, for review), then this selective involvement of first-order branching in the estrogen-treated cultures would provide evidence supporting such a postulated genomic effect for estrogen in the CNS as well.

Other cellular aspects

What still is not clear, as illustrated in Fig. 4, is whether or not the neuritic response, elicited by estrogen in the cultures, results from a direct (i.e., genomic) effect on receptor-containing neurons or from an indirect one, acting via the intermediary of other hormone-sensitive cells (neurons and/or neuroglia). These might themselves secrete "neurite-promoting" growth factors (instead of, or in addition to the postulated "neuronotrophic" ones in Fig. 3), that would act upon the visibly responsive ones. This is all the more germane,

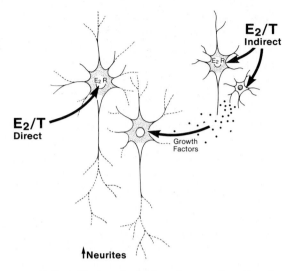

Fig. 4. Diagrammatic representation of the hypothesized neurite-promoting effect of estradiol (E_2) and testoster-one (T). The gonadal steroids may exert their effects directly on the genome via the intranuclear estrogen receptor (E_2R) or indirectly via the intermediary of other hormone-sensitive neurons and/or neuroglia which might themselves secrete neurite-promoting growth factors whose targets need not necessarily be estrogen receptor-containing.

since technical limitations currently prevent correlating the estrogen-induced arborizations with their cell bodies of origin. Although responsive regions contain estrogen receptors, it is still not known whether or not the responsive neurons themselves are receptor-containing.

It should be pointed out that whereas the estrogen-induced focal arborizations of neurites appear to represent a response which is intrinsic to neurons localized within the explant proper, the very pattern of the response (i.e. the extensive arborizations themselves) may also be influenced by the absence of suitable targets, as well as by the deafferented and non-afferented culture situation itself. That steroid-sensitive local circuit neurons (in which the hypothalamus and POA abound) can respond intrinsically to steroidal exposure by enhanced neuritic development is suggested by recent observations of the significant enhancement of synapse formation on dendritic shafts within medial amygdaloid anterior chamber transplants exposed to masculinizing levels of estrogen in oculo (Nichizuka and Arai, 1982). The response of this ectopic amygdaloid tissue was comparable to the specific and permanent increase in shaft synapses reported in the medial amygdaloid nuclei of neonatal male rats exposed to gonadal steroids in vivo (Nichizuka and Arai, 1981a,b).

TEMPORAL FACTORS IN NEURAL DEVELOPMENT

Differentiation and development of the CNS proceed in well-ordered sequences of inter-locking phenomena whose timing is critical. Temporal alterations, moreover, may have profound physiological consequences which may be expressed morphologically, however, in only such subtle ways as by alterations in the patterns of axonal growth, of dentritic differen-tiation and of synaptic organization which need not otherwise be abnormal in themselves. The morphogenetic and temporal importance of the afferent axonal input to subsequent dendritic differentiation and synaptic organization of target neurons has been shown in many studies on the ontogeny of neural circuits throughout the CNS (Ramon y Cajal, 1909–1911; Morest, 1969; Kornguth and Scott, 1972); the spatial distribution of synapses as well as dendritic morphology apparently ultimately reflecting the numbers and differential growth rates of the specified axons present during synaptogenesis (Gottlieb and Cowan, 1972). Even dendrites, moreover, appear to compete for their afferents (Perry and Linden, 1982). In addition, the site of termination of a particular axon may also depend on the rate of maturation of its target, since different regions of receptive surfaces appear to differentiate at different times (Schwartz et al., 1968).

The "cascade hypothesis" of sexual dimorphism

The tissue culture studies suggest that differences in neuronal responsiveness to steroid may result in differences in the growth and development of target axons and dendrites and in the organization and stability of their synapses, thus enhancing neuronal survival and resulting in fundamentally different, sex-specific neural circuits with sexually dimorphic cytologic constituents (Fig. 5). If one were to consider that the stimulation of neuritic growth may

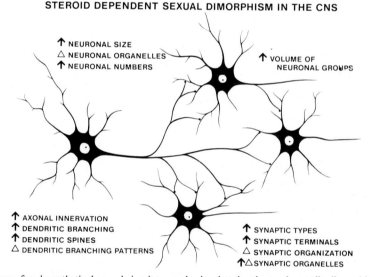

Fig. 5. Diagram of an hypothetical neural circuit to emphasize that the observed sexually dimorphic cytological features of the CNS are all constituents of such circuits.

represent an early or initial response of steroid-sensitive neurons to estrogens or aromatizable androgens, then the morphogenetic consequences would necessarily influence all subsequent aspects of target neural differentiation, including circuit organization. This cascading type of effect and its far-reaching implications for the genesis of all the steroid-dependent, structural dimorphisms observed in the adult brain are summarized in Fig. 6.

With more neurites present, the potential numbers of both axons and dendrites would presumably be increased. If more axons, then their growth patterns and the density of their innervation within a region as well as their terminal arborizations would be affected. This, in turn, would influence dendritic differentiation and thus increase the potential for synaptic contact, thereby affecting the numbers of synapses as well as their topographic distribution.

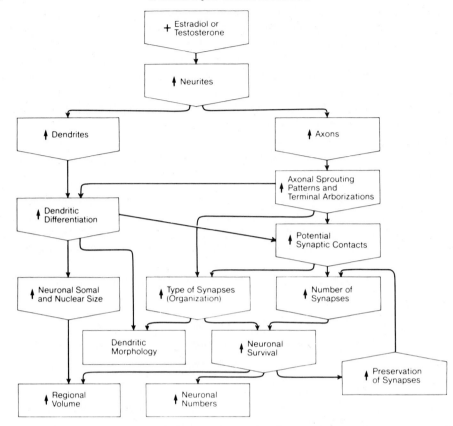

Fig. 6. Diagrammatic representation of the "cascade hypothesis". The morphogenetic consequences of early stimulation of neuritic growth by steroid could elicit a cascade of cellular events affecting subsequent aspects of target neural differentiation to result in the sexual dimorphism of brain structures.

This increased formation of synaptic contacts would also result in enhanced neuronal survival, augmenting the numbers of neurons and thus contributing to the size or volume of regional nuclei such as the sexually dimorphic nuclei of the POA, spinal cord and the amygdala (Gorski et al., 1978; Breedlove and Arnold, 1980; Mizukami et al., 1983) and of the avian vocal control centers (Nottebohm and Arnold, 1976).

If more dendrites, on the other hand, their number, morphology, branching patterns and fields would be affected which, in turn, would also influence synaptogenesis, synaptic organization, neuronal survival and neuronal numbers. In addition, the resultant increase in overall axonal and dendritic cytoplasmic mass would require augmented neuronal metabolic activity for its maintenance which might be reflected cytologically by enlargement of the neuronal cell body, nucleus and nucleolus. This increase in neuronal size, in neuronal numbers and in neuropil would all contribute as well to the observed increase in regional nuclear volumes.

As is suggested by the tissue culture studies, therefore, an early, hormonally induced regulation of neuritic growth and its presumed consequences, synapse formation, would initiate a cascade of morphogenetic events which probably enhance neuronal survival and specify the nature and extent of the synaptic inputs and outputs. In this manner, the organizational effects exerted by the gonadal hormones on axonal and/or dendritic differentiation may well determine the subsequent sexually dimorphic structural and functional properties of target neural pathways.

Relevance of in vitro studies

The hypothesis that the responses of the cultures to the gonadal hormones do have physiological relevance and that experimental exposure of the developing CNS to steroids does influence the morphogenetic consequences of neuritic interactions in situ (as proposed in Fig. 6) is heightened by a growing number of recently published experiments in both the developing and adult CNS. Estrogen- or androgen-induced enhancement of neuronal numbers, neuronal development, axonal growth, dendritic differentiation, neuropil complexity, synaptogenesis, synaptic organization and of regional nuclear volumes has, in fact, been shown in the hypothalamus, POA, septum and the amygdala of the developing rat and mouse (Raisman and Field, 1973; Arai and Matsumoto, 1978; Matsumoto and Arai, 1976, 1980, 1981a; Nichizuka, 1978; Breedlove and Arnold, 1983; Breedlove et al., 1982; Jacobson and Gorski, 1981; Nichizuka and Arai, 1980, 1981a,b; DeVries et al., 1983; Mizukami et al., 1983) and in the vocal control nuclei of the developing frog and songbird (Hannigan and Kelley, 1981; Gurney, 1981).

Similar phenomena have also been reported in experimental situations involving the steroid receptor-containing regions of the adult rodent and avian brain. These experiments include the deafferented mediobasal hypothalamus of the adult female rat (Matsumoto and Arai, 1981b); the regenerating hypoglossal nerve of the adult rat of both sexes (Yu and Srinivasan, 1981); the vocal control nuclei of the ovariectomized adult female canary (DeVoogd and Nottebohm, 1981b) and perhaps also in the septal-lesioned adult male rat (Nance et al., 1975). Of particular note is that in the adult rat, at least, all of these situations first require trauma to the CNS for the subsequent expression of the stimulatory effect of estrogen on neurites. This suggests that the potential for responses that may normally be characteristic of developing neurons can also be expressed in adult mammalian neurons but only in abnormal situations such as regeneration which, to a certain extent, recapitulates certain aspects of the developmental process. The responses of the adult female bird, on the other hand, appear to be an expression of the extreme plasticity which has already been shown (Nottebohm, 1981) in the normal adult male vocal control centers.

ESTROGEN AND FEMINIZATION OF THE CNS

The tissue culture studies described above also suggest that the absence of androgen imprinting may not be sufficient for the emergence of the female pattern of neural organization. Masculinization and feminization of neural development may both be hormone-mediated and require active induction by estrogen (Shapiro et al., 1976; Toran-Allerand, 1976, 1980a; Döhler, 1978). The source of such estrogen in the developing rodent is intriguing.

The importance of ovarian secretions

The possible importance of ovarian secretions for feminization of the patterns of neural differentiation has been suggested by a variety of studies in the rat. The presence of ovaries during postnatal and prepubertal periods has been shown to influence feminization of both reproductive (sexual receptivity) (Gerall et al., 1973; Hendricks and Duffy, 1974; Hendricks and Weltin, 1976) and non-reproductive (open-field activity) (Stewart and Cygan, 1980) behaviors. Moreover, exposure of neonatally gonadectomized males or females to low (submasculinizing) levels of estradiol has been shown to lead to the development of the high levels of open-field activity, characteristic of the adult female (Stewart and Cygan, 1980). On the other hand, ovariectomy has also been shown to influence the development of the sex differences in the thickness of the rat cerebral cortex (Diamond et al., 1981). The cerebral asymmetry in cortical thickness (R > L in males; L > R in females) changed to the masculine pattern following postnatal but not adult ovariectomy.

That estrogen may have a positive developmental role in sexual differentiation of the female rodent brain is further suggested by studies in which postnatal exposure to the estrogen antagonist, tamoxifen, was reported to result in defeminization of both gonado-tropin regulation and female sexual behavior (without the concomitant development of masculine behavior), as well as an inhibition of the feminine structure of the sexually dimor-phic nucleus of the POA (Hancke and Döhler, 1980; Döhler et al., 1984). Concurrent administration of "low" doses of estradiol prevented the effects of tamoxifen, which was reported to be more effective than its partly estrogenic cis-isomer, ICI 47699 (Döhler et al., 1984). One might also consider the possibility, however, that the absence of masculinization in the above experiments may also reflect the known differences between the "critical" periods for many aspects of masculinization (largely prenatal), and for defeminization, which is a largely postnatal phenomenon (see McEwen, 1983, for discussion).

THE BIOLOGY OF a-FETOPROTEIN (AFP)

The apparent availability of circulating estrogens to the developing female rodent brain has, until recently, been at variance with the generally held concept that feminization results merely from lack of exposure to androgen. Extracellular sequestration of maternal and placental estrogens through binding to the feto-neonatal estrogen binding-protein of the rodent, a-fetoprotein (AFP), is generally assumed to completely protect the developing rodent brain (particularly that of the female) from excessive exposure to estrogens, which could result from the normally high circulating levels during the critical period for sexual differentiation (McEwen et al., 1975; Vannier and Raynaud, 1975).

Natural history of AFP

AFP is a major fetal plasma protein which is present in most developing vertebrate species, including the human. It is the first a-globulin to appear in the plasma of embryonic mammals. Its preservation throughout evolution tends to support its functional importance, although what those development functions are is largely unknown. AFP is synthesized transiently in great quantities (mg/ml) by the endodermal cells of the visceral yolk sac, fetal liver (hepatocytes), and gastrointestinal tract (Gitlin and Boesman, 1967; Gitlin and Perri-celli, 1970; Gitlin et al., 1972), normally only during gestation and the immediate postnatal period. AFP is distributed via the circulation into the cerebrospinal fluid (CSF), extracellular space and amniotic fluid. The massive synthesis of AFP is short-lived. Its half-life in the rodent, for example, is 24 h (Raynaud, 1971; Olsson et al., 1977). In the rodent, moreover, AFP decreases linearly from its very high concentration at birth (1–6 mg/ml) to trace levels

(0.01% of fetal levels) at weaning (Raynaud, 1971; Vannier and Raynaud, 1975; Olsson et al., 1977), where it persists unless its synthesis is restimulated by such conditions as hepatic malignancy, teratocarcinoma or liver damage in the adult (Ruoslahti and Engvall, 1978).

Depending upon the species, AFP binds a variety of hormones (natural but not synthetic estrogens) and other biologically active ligands (the non-esterified polyunsaturated long-chain free fatty acids; bilirubin; dyes, copper (Ruoslahti and Engvall, 1978; Ruoslahti and Seppälä, 1979). Unlike that of most other species, rat and mouse AFP alone binds estrogens with a high affinity (Nunez et al., 1976); the lower affinity of estradiol for AFP (K_D 10^{-8} M) than for its own receptor (K_D 10^{-11} M) being offset by the extremely high concentration of AFP in fetal and newborn plasma (Aussel and Masseyeff, 1978). A small fraction of AFP from human cord serum, however, has also been reported to bind to estradiol (Arnon et al., 1973; Uriel et al., 1976). AFP does not bind androgen, however, presumably leaving testosterone free to enter the rodent brain.

Possible functions of AFP

Increasing evidence suggests that plasma-binding proteins may subserve multiple complex functions: extracellular ligand sequestration either as carriers, reservoirs or to prevent ligand metabolism by conjugation or enzymatic degradation; modulators and regulators of the cellular uptake and metabolism of ligands; and transplacental transfers of ligands (Friend, 1977; Payne and Katzenellenbogen, 1979; LeGuern et al., 1982; Savu et al., 1981). Some investigators have proposed that AFP may serve as a fetal counterpart to albumin, fulfilling the same transport role in the fetus as the later-developing albumin does in the adult (Ruoslahti and Terry, 1976; Grigorova et al., 1977). The ligand specificities of AFP, however, are quite different from those of albumin (Hervé et al., 1982). A protein-mediated step has been proposed to regulate cellular entry of low levels of estrogens into the immature rat uterine cell (Milgrom et al., 1973); whereas high levels enter mainly by diffusion. The modulation by AFP of estrogen binding to specific uterine cytoplasmic estrogen receptors has been shown (Benassayag et al., 1981) and studies (Raynaud, 1971; Germain et al., 1978) suggest that AFP may control uterine uptake and tissue levels of estradiol. Other studies (Nunez et al., 1979) have shown the opposite, however. Finally, it is not even clear whether or not estrogen enters the cell alone or bound to AFP.

The intraovarian, immunocytochemical localization of rat AFP has been postulated to regulate postnatal ovarian activity (follicular maturation) by decreasing the local free estrogen levels (Castelli et al., 1982). Injection of pure AFP into adult cycling female rats results in a decrease in ovarian activity (Aussel et al., 1981), and adult female rats with AFP-secreting hepatomas or following hepatocarcinogenesis similarly exhibit a blockade of ovarian activity (Pool et al., 1978; Aussel et al., 1979). It has also been suggested that AFP may have an immunoregulatory (immunosuppressive) role during gestation, but there are contradictory data on the effect of AFP on immune responses in vitro and in vivo (Ruoslahti and Seppälä, 1979, for review). Still other studies have proposed that AFP may be mitogenic for a variety of cells including adult rat neurons (Page, 1974; Lundberg and Møllgård, 1979). Rat AFP, moreover, has been shown to inhibit estrogen metabolism by rat liver microsomes in vitro (Aussel and Masseyeff, 1978).

Inhibition of AFP synthesis or activity by injection of antibodies to AFP into pregnant female rats and rabbits early in gestation has been reported to be associated with a high fetal mortality rate (Slade, 1973; Smith, 1973; Mizejewski and Grimley, 1976; Chandra, 1979) and frequent congenital defects — most commonly spina bifida (meningomyelocele) and omphalocele (Chandra, 1979) — or else to have no effect at all (Leung et al., 1977). Intracerebral injections of antibodies to AFP into neonatal mice, moreover, have been reported to induce an anovulatory syndrome (polyfollicular ovaries without corpora lutea), attributable to the accumulation of excess unbound estrogen in the brain ("masculinization") as a consequence, of antibody blockage of the estradiol-binding sites on the AFP molecule (Mizejewski et al., 1980). The possible contributory roles of trauma and of AFP per se, were not considered alternatively, however, even though the same workers demonstrated earlier that the formation of the AFP antigen/anti-AFP antibody complex does *not* prevent the binding of estradiol (Mizejewski et al., 1979).

AFP in the developing CNS

In the mouse the elevated circulating levels of AFP span the entire period of neural development, from embryonic (E) day 7 (neural plate formation) to postnatal (P) day 25 (the end of cerebral cortical differentiation). Although this may be merely an epiphenomenon, it is nonetheless worth considering. There is an intracellular pool of AFP of unknown function in brain cytosol of a large variety of developing avian and mammalian species such as the fetal and neonatal rat (Plapinger and McEwen, 1973), mouse (Attardi and Ruoslahti, 1976), sheep (Saunders and Møllgård, 1981), pig (Saunders and Møllgård, 1981), and human fetus (Ali et al., 1981). Its specifically intraneuronal (intracytoplasmic) localization has been confirmed within the developing nervous system of these same species as well as in the chick (Moro and Uriel, 1981) and the baboon (Uriel et al., 1982) by means of immunocytochemistry (Benno and Williams, 1978; Møllgård et al., 1979; Trojan and Uriel, 1979; Toran-Allerand, 1980b; Dziegielewska et al., 1981; Saunders and Møllgård, 1981; Mareš et al., 1982). Other plasma-binding proteins, such as albumin (Møllgård et al., 1979; Trojan and Uriel, 1979; Toran-Allerand, 1980b), prealbumin (Møllgård et al., 1979), transferrin (Toran-Allerand, 1980b), fetuin (Saunders and Møllgård, 1981), androgen-binding protein (Carreau et al., 1983), and α-1-anti-trypsin (Saunders and Møllgård, 1981) have similarly been localized within the developing brain.

The autoradiographic observation of a discrete [³H]estradiol label in the cytoplasm but not the nucleus of a number of cells within our cultures (Toran-Allerand et al., 1980) led to our interest in the possible neurobiological role of AFP during neural development. While this cytoplasmic binding might represent a class of cytoplasmic receptors that does not normally interact with the nucleus (Clark et al., 1978), more intriguing was the possibility that the observed labeling pattern might represent the binding of estradiol by intraneuronal AFP. This was shown to be at least partly true in a subsequent in vivo immunocytochemical study on the localization and topographic distribution of intraneuronal AFP in the same strain of developing mouse (RIII) (Toran-Allerand, 1980b) and also in the postnatal rat (Sprague–Dawley) (Toran-Allerand, 1982).

AFP is present within the neurons of both sexes and at all stages of CNS development in the rodent from the postmitotic neuroblast to more differentiated neurons (Fig. 7). The degree of immunoreactivity and the number of immunoreactive cells appear to increase with the extent of neuronal differentiation within a given region. AFP is not present in the normal adult mouse brain nor is it present in the brain of adult rats bearing the Morris hepatoma, a liver tumor which secretes AFP at high levels comparable to those found during development (mg/ml) (Toran-Allerand and Linkie, unpublished). This observation is important, and while maturational differences including the presence of the blood/brain barrier and/or the adult stage of neuronal differentiation may explain its absence in the normal and hepatoma-

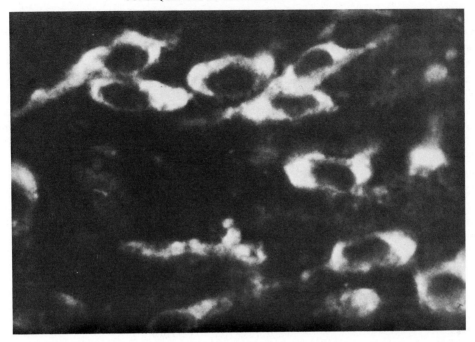

Fig. 7. Localization of immunoreactive mouse AFP in neurons of the newborn male mouse hypothalamus. Rhodamine immunofluorescence (×200).

bearing adult brain, the intraneuronal presence of AFP only in the *developing* CNS suggests that this protein might indeed subserve important developmental functions within the CNS.

The origins of intraneuronal AFP

The presence during development of very high levels of AFP in the blood, CSF and extracellular fluid suggests that this intraneuronal protein is derived from these extracellular sources rather than being synthesized locally. Reports to the contrary notwithstanding (Mackiewicz et al., 1978; Ali et al., 1983), there is, in fact, no good evidence that intraneuronal AFP can be synthesized locally. This hypothesis was recently confirmed by studies using recombinant DNA methods and a cloned cDNA probe specific for mouse AFP (Schachter and Toran-Allerand, 1982); and subsequently supported by Andrews et al. (1982). The absence of messenger RNA for AFP in the fetal, newborn and adult mouse brain is clearly demonstrated in Fig. 8 (lanes 5, 6 and 7), with two different concentrations of input RNA from newborn and adult liver, serving as positive (lanes 1 and 2) and negative (lanes 3 and 4) controls, respectively. In a correlative fashion, moreover, fetal CNS cultures were also shown to be unable to synthesize AFP from radiolabeled precursors (Schachter and Toran-Allerand, 1982), with fetal liver cultures serving as positive controls.

The above-mentioned studies confirm earlier ones (Gitlin and Boesman, 1967) about the inability of the rat and human fetal brain to synthesize AFP. Moreover, they demonstrate that since the observed high levels of intraneuronal immunoreactive AFP cannot be accounted for by local synthesis, they must be derived from external sources — perhaps by receptor-mediated endocytosis, a mechanism by which many plasma proteins appear to be taken up by cells (Pastan and Willingham, 1981). The ability of developing neurons to internalize exogenous AFP has been demonstrated by the specific uptake of purified AFP by primary cultures of fetal mouse brain (Uriel et al., 1981) and in fetal mouse hypothalamic explants co-cultured in juxtaposition with fetal hepatocyte cultures (Toran-Allerand, unpublished).

Reports of synthesis and secretion of AFP by cultures of human embryonic (Mackiewicz et al., 1978) and neonatal rat brain (Ali et al., 1983) probably do not represent endogenous synthesis but rather secretion and/or leakage from cells containing AFP prior to being placed in culture. Despite ostensible inhibition by cyclohexamide (Ali and Sahib, 1983), the biochemical methods used in their studies are not adequate to remove unequivocally all proteins or other substances that might bind covalently to the AFP molecule. Were such molecules being actively synthesized by the cultures, they would readily co-precipitate with antibodies specific to AFP, be inhibited by cyclohexamide, and thus give the spurious impression of active biosynthesis of AFP (MacLusky, personal communication; Roberts, personal communication).

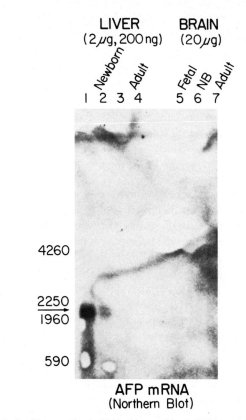

Fig. 8. Northern blot analysis of liver and brain RNA. Liver and brain RNA samples were fractionated on formamide agarose gels, transferred to nitrocellulose sheets, then hybridized with [^{32}P]AFP DNA probes. Positions of ECORI cut lambda DNA size markers are indicated on the side of the figure. The arrow indicates AFP mRNA. (Relabeled from Schachter and Toran-Allerand, 1982.)

NEUROBIOLOGICAL ROLES OF AFP

These observations discussed above suggest that AFP may have more than its attributed "protective" role (McEwen et al., 1975) and may subserve multiple extra- and intraneuronal functions which may be essential for normal CNS development — including sexual differentiation. These possibilities have been summarized in Table II. For example, AFP may well serve as the postulated extracellular source and reservoir of estrogen and its other biologically active ligands (Levina et al., 1975; McEwen et al., 1975; Döhler, 1978). This would be important in the immediate postnatal period not only for protecting the neonatal CNS from excessive estrogen exposure, but also by prolonging the half-life of maternal/placental estrogens (estradiol and estrone) for perhaps critical estrogen-dependent developmental functions until the neonatal ovaries are capable of producing estrogens on their own; all the more so, since AFP has been shown to specifically inhibit the microsomal enzymes responsible for the metabolism of estrogens (Aussel and Masseyeff, 1978).

The discrete intracytoplasmic localization of the estrophilic rodent AFP suggests its possible active involvement in estrogen-sensitive neurons during "critical" periods of neural development especially with respect to sexual differentiation of the brain. For one thing, its intracellular presence forces one to reconsider the degree to which the developing rodent brain is actually protected from exposure to estrogens by the extracellular AFP. As hypothesized in Fig. 9, neuronal uptake of such an estrogen-binding protein as AFP, which is present only during neural development and at a concentration calculated to bind all circulating estrogen, must perforce bring estradiol into the cell. Since there is a difference of several orders of magnitude between the affinity constants for estradiol binding by AFP (K_D 10^{-8} M) (Savu et al., 1981) and by the estrogen receptor (K_D 10^{-11} M) the subsequent intracytoplasmic dissociation or breakdown of the AFP/estradiol complexes in estrogen receptor-containing neurons could liberate the internalized steroid and lead to receptor binding. Such a series of events might serve as an intracellular mechanism for regulating the equilibrium between free and bound estrogens. By controlling the level of estrogen interacting with its receptor, the intraneuronal AFP could thus provide target neurons of both sexes with the low levels of estrogen of non-androgen-derived origin which were postulated earlier (Toran-Allerand, 1976, 1980a). The modulation by AFP of estrogen binding to specific cytoplasmic receptors in the uterus has in fact been demonstrated (Benassayag et al., 1981).

While the estrogen-binding property of AFP in the rodent emphasizes its potential importance for rodent sexual differentiation, its possible role with respect to the other ligands —

TABLE II
NEUROBIOLOGICAL FUNCTIONS OF EXTRA-/INTRANEURONAL AFP?

1. Transplacental transport of maternal/placental estradiol (E_2)
2. Extracellular source and reservoir of E_2 and other ligands
3. Extracellular sequestration of E_2: "protection" from estrogen
4. Mediator and/or modulator of the intraneuronal transport of E_2 and other ligands, including teratogens
5. Regulator of intracellular concentrations of E_2 and other ligands
6. Inhibitor of the rapid intra- and extracellular metabolism of E_2
7. Intracellular reservoir, providing low level source of E_2 for:
   a. Neurons with both receptors and aromatase activity (hypothalamus/POA, amygdala)
   b. Neurons that have no aromatase activity but have E_2 receptors (cerebral cortex)
   c. Neurons that have no receptors but in which E_2 may have non-receptor-mediated functions
8. Trophic factor per se

including teratogens but particularly polyunsaturated free fatty acids such as arachidonic, docosahexaenoic and docosatetraenoic acids, which behave as true competitive ligands with estrogens (Nunez et al. 1979; Vallette et al., 1980) and whose critical importance to neural development in mammals, including the human has been shown as well (Crawford and Sinclair, 1972; Sinclair and Crawford, 1972; Pineiro et al., 1979) — must not be neglected. This is all the more crucial since, unlike estrogen, such ligands are bound by AFP in all species (Vallette et al., 1980). AFP may also serve in the rodent as an intracellular reservoir of estrogen, providing low levels of estrogen to: (1) neurons involved in sexual differentiation and containing both estrogen receptors and aromatase activity (hypothalamus/POA and the amygdala); (2) neurons that lack aromatase activity (Lieberburg and McEwen, 1975; MacLusky and Toran-Allerand, in preparation) but have estrogen receptors (vide infra) (Friedman et al., 1983; Gerlach et al., 1983) (cerebral cortex); and (3) neurons without demonstrable estrogen receptors but in which estrogen may have non-receptor-mediated (non-genomic) functions either on the pre- or postsynaptic membrane or on neurotransmitter receptors (McEwen, 1980; Moss and Dudley, 1984). Finally, although it remains purely speculative at present, we must consider the possibility that AFP may be important developmentally in its own right and not solely by virtue of its bound ligands. AFP per se, for example, has been reported to be a specific inhibitor of cell multiplication in an estrogen-sensitive pituitary cell line, quite independent of any estrogen-binding properties (Soto and Sonnenschein, 1980).

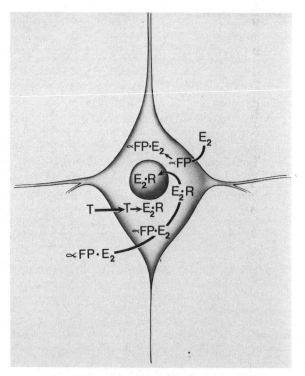

Fig. 9. Diagrammatic representation of the postulated neurobiological role of AFP in sexual differentiation of the rodent brain. Neuronal uptake of the estrophilic AFP must bring estradiol into the cell, where it can modulate the levels of estrogen interacting with the estrogen receptor and thus provide target neurons of both sexes with low levels of estrogen of non-androgen origin. Such a transport mechanism could also mediate and modulate neuronal uptake of the other ligands, including teratogens.

The topographic distribution of intraneuronal AFP

Matters have become complicated by recent observations (Toran-Allerand, 1982) that, although widespread intraneuronal localization of immunoreactive AFP is observed in neuronal groups throughout the rodent brain of both sexes, within the estrogen receptor-containing regions of the developing septum, POA, hypothalamus, and amygdala certain nuclei such as the nuclei of the diagonal band, the medial POA, the suprachiasmatic, the arcuate, and the ventral premammillary nuclei of the hypothalamus and the medial and cortical amygdaloid nuclei are anatomically distinctive by virtue of their almost complete absence of immunoreactivity (e.g., Fig. 10).

The significance of this striking absence of immunoreactivity specifically with the presumed target regions of estrogen during the "critical period" for sexual differentiation is not known. It is conceivable that estrogen-sensitive regions may be "protected" by the specific inability of their neurons to take up AFP. Regional differences in immunofluorescence may represent a conformational change in the internalized AFP consequent to the shift of estrogen to its receptors and be manifested by the loss of immunoreactivity. Uriel et al. (1976) have suggested that when AFP enters the uterus it undergoes a conformational change and can no longer be detected immunologically. Other studies (Bayard et al., 1978; Smalley and Sarcione, 1980) have shown the existence of a masked intracellular form of AFP in the uterus which becomes immunoreactive only after treatment with 0.4 M KCl. This does not appear to apply to the developing brain however (Toran-Allerand, 1982). Finally, the absence of fluorescence could represent a corresponding absence of AFP following the possible augmentation in the destruction of the protein molecule, perhaps due to enhanced (estrogen-induced) proteolytic activity of the type reported in another estrogen target, the endometrial cell (Pietras and Szego, 1979).

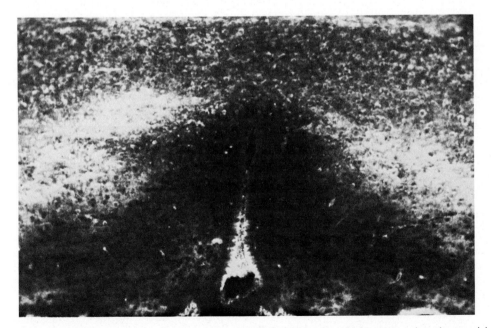

Fig. 10. Topographic distribution of mouse AFP in the POA of the newborn male mouse to show the essential absence of immunofluorescence in the medial POA. Rhodamine immunofluorescence ($\times$ 25).

Although the developmental functions of AFP remain largely unknown, its preservation throughout evolution implies a functional importance, especially since congenital absence of AFP is also unknown. Of note, however, are some recently reported cases in the human of an association of low to "undetectable" maternal serum AFP levels with various fetal chromosome abnormalities (Rubin, personal communication), associated with severe congenital neurological defects (mental retardation, seizures, microcephaly and meningomyelocele). Since maternal AFP levels are fetally derived, the possibly crucial importance of AFP for neural development is further heightened by such observations, especially since such CNS defects may all be viewed as failures of various aspects of neural differentiation.

SEXUAL DIFFERENTIATION IN MALES *AND* FEMALES IS HORMONE-MEDIATED

The potential importance of AFP as a modulator of the access of estrogen to the developing rodent brain suggests that feminization, like masculinization, may be an estrogen-dependent active process. Sexual differentiation of the female neural phenotype appears to depend on more than simply a female genotype plus the absence of excessive androgen exposure. Thus, in the genetic female or neonatally castrated male rodent, for example, exposure of the perinatal developing brain only to low (submasculinizing), "priming" levels of estradiol, derived from the intraneuronal dissociation of the AFP/estrogen complexes, might elicit neuronal growth and differentiation in a specific or "female" pattern. The additional superimposition of intraneuronal aromatization of androgen to estrogen, on the other hand, could produce a more concentrated estrogenic effect, perhaps additively or synergistically or even through a change in the balance or ratio of testosterone to estradiol (Fox, 1975), and thus induce different or what could be termed "male" patterns of neural differentiation. The possibility that estrogen can exhibit biphasic effects on growth and can elicit quite different, even antagonistic, developmental responses, depending on the levels present, is further supported by the observation (Levine et al., 1983) that whereas high levels of estrogen inhibit bone growth, low levels, in contrast, increase its growth significantly. Moreover, studies on the relationship of intrauterine positioning and proximity of male and female fetuses (Vom Saal and Bronson, 1980; Vom Saal et al., 1983; Meisel and Ward, 1981) have suggested that circulating estrogens and androgens may interact during the prenatal period to regulate sexual differentiation of both the male and female brain and influence the range of phenotypes seen in each sex.

The importance of estrogen per se

It is currently unknown whether the response of neurons to estrogen is solely related to the process of sexual differentiation, or whether estrogen may have a more fundamental role in the development of the CNS of both sexes. The possible fundamental importance of estrogen to vertebrate CNS differentiation is underlined by the absence of known genetic defects of its receptor, suggesting that such defects would be incompatible with life. In contrast, many genetic deficiencies of the androgen receptor, such as the Tfm mutation, are well described in the rodent CNS (MacLusky and Naftolin, 1981).

Puymirat et al. (1982) have reported that estradiol (10^{-12} M) is an absolute prerequisite for the successful culture of dissociated hypothalamic neurons in the absence of serum. While neuronal survival was significantly enhanced, estrogen-induced neuritic arborization

(Toran-Allerand, 1976, 1980a) was not observed. Although such methodological aspects as differences in culture method (organotypic vs. cell dissociates), in nutrient medium (serum vs. serum-free) and in added estrogen levels (10^{-9}–10^{-7} M vs. 10^{-12} M) undoubtedly play an important etiologic role in the dissimilarity in the observed responses, it is tempting to speculate that this might also represent the expression of the postulated dual neuronotrophic and neurite-promoting roles of estrogen (see Figs. 3 and 4) which may well be dose-dependent.

THE MORPHOGENETIC IMPORTANCE OF ESTROGEN

The potential importance of estrogen for neural development is considerably heightened by the demonstration that in the developing rodent of both sexes certain regions of the CNS (such as the cerebral cortex) contain large numbers of estrogen-concentrating neurons (Presl et al., 1971; Sheridan, 1976). Such neurons are found primarily in layers V and VI of the frontal and anterior cingulate cortex (Gerlach et al., 1983). High (adult) levels of estrogen receptors (Barley et al., 1974; MacLusky et al., 1979; Friedman et al., 1983) have been demonstrated in these same regions during the first 2 weeks of postnatal life only — a period which can probably be considered as "critical" with respect to neuronal differentiation in the cerebral cortex. Estrogen binding by the developing rodent cerebral cortex is maximal around days P-7–10, with the number of cortical binding sites declining precipitously (5-fold/mg of DNA) to significantly lower levels thereafter (McEwen et al., 1975; MacLusky et al., 1976, 1979; Friedman et al., 1983). The reason for their disappearance is unknown. Does this represent receptor loss resulting secondarily from naturally occurring neuronal death? Is it a transient stage of cytological differentiation which features receptor loss but no neuronal death; or is it merely dilution secondary to the marked increase in cerebral cortical mass which occurs during the second and third postnatal weeks? The time course for the cortical estrogen receptors, which at their peak attain levels comparable to those seen in the adult female rodent hypothalamus (Friedman et al., 1983; Gerlach et al., 1983), coincides with the onset of several important aspects of morphological, biochemical and functional differentiation within the cerebral cortex (Bass et al., 1969a,b), characterized by the growth and development of neurons, the intense sprouting of neurites and the onset of myelinogenesis.

In the postnatal murine cerebellar cortex of both sexes, estrogen receptors appear to be restricted largely to the granule cells during the third week (Fox, 1977). The presence of estrogen receptors in this region coincides with the onset of an obviously crucial period of granule cell differentiation: the end of their mitotic phase and migration from external to internal granular layer, and the period of active neuritic (parallel fiber) development.

The significance of the estrogen receptors within the cerebral cortex and cerebellum is unknown. The absence of aromatizing enzymes in these CNS regions of the rat and mouse (Lieberburg and McEwen, 1975; MacLusky and Toran-Allerand, in preparation) would appear to preclude any androgen-derived estrogen effect. It has, therefore, been suggested (Barley et al., 1974; Toran-Allerand, 1978, 1981) that, since the estrogen receptors of the neonatal rodent cerebral cortex are unlikely to be involved in sexual differentiation (masculinization), they may mediate instead more generalized developmental effects attributable to the circulating estrogens. In neonatal rats of both sexes elevated serum estrogen levels (maternal/placental) have been reported to fall rapidly after the first 2 postnatal days, only to increase abruptly again during the second and third postnatal weeks (with a peak around day 10) to levels which are never subsequently observed during life (Döhler and Wüttke, 1975).

While the origin of this estrogen in unknown (?ovarian; ?adrenal; Weisz and Gunsalus, 1973), the concurrent rapidly falling postnatal levels of the estrogen-binding AFP might liberate significant levels of free estrogens for developmental interactions with the "short-lived" estrogen receptors of the postnatal cerebral cortex and cerebellum. This postulated role of estrogen in cerebral cortical development finds support in observations of estrogen-induced enhancement of cortical myelinogenesis (Curry and Heim, 1966), of functional cortical maturation (Heim and Timiras, 1963; Heim, 1966) and of behavioral feminization (Stewart and Cygan, 1980) as well as of both stimulatory and inhibitory effects on cerebral amino acid concentrations (Hudson et al., 1970; Litteria and Thorner, 1976; Litteria, 1977). Diamond et al. (1971) have suggested moreover, that estrogen might protect the cerebral cortex from the developmental retardation which usually accompanies environmental impoverishment.

ESTROGEN AND THE CEREBRAL CORTEX IN VITRO

It is not known whether or not the estrogen receptors of the cerebral cortex are at all functional, since their occupancy by endogenous estrogen has not been shown (MacLusky et al., 1979). This negative finding has been attributed to AFPs preventing estrogen entry into the cell (MacLusky et al., 1979) but may also represent limitations in the sensitivity of the assay used. That the cortical estrogen receptors are in fact functional and that estradiol might exert a direct effect on the developing cerebral cortex, is suggested by recent studies from the author's laboratory. Organotypic cultures of the perinatal mouse anterior cingu-

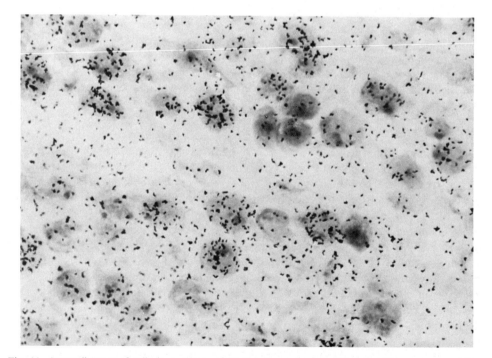

Fig. 11. Autoradiogram of cells in a culture of the newborn mouse anterior cingulate cortex exposed to [³H]estradiol on the 8th day in vitro. Radioactivity is seen as silver grains concentrated over the nuclei of large cells which are presumably neurons. (×252.)

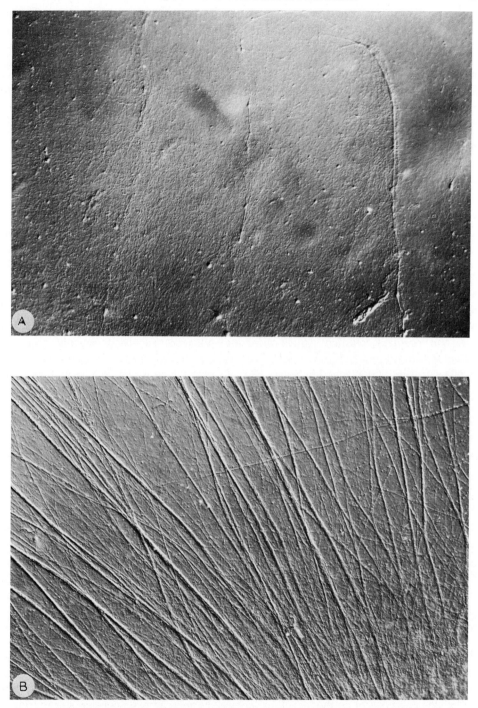

Fig. 12. Estrogen-induced enhancement of neuritic growth in living homologous cultures of the newborn mouse anterior cingulate cortex, 9 days in vitro. (A) Control (horse serum; estradiol 200 pg/ml); (B) Estradiol 50 ng/ml in horse serum. Note that unlike the response in the POA (Fig. 1B) the responsive cortical neurites are radial and very long, with little or no tendency to arborize extensively. Nomarski (×25.2).

late/frontal cortex have been shown by means of [³H]estradiol autoradiography to contain estrogen receptors (Fig. 11) and to respond to estradiol by (i) a marked enhancement of radial neuritic growth, with little tendency to arborize (Fig. 12A and B) and (ii) by a significant incorporation of [³H]leucine into trichloroacetic acid (TCA)-precipitable proteins (MacLusky and Toran-Allerand, unpublished). The predominant localization of the estrogen receptors to the layers which contribute to the cortical outflow (layers V and VI) and the non-arborizing, radial enhancement of the cortical neuritic outgrowth in vitro suggest that estradiol may specifically mediate the differentiation and development of both inter- and extracortical interconnections.

CONCLUSIONS AND GENERAL IMPLICATIONS

Although this paper has focused on cellular aspects in the ontogeny of sexual differentiation of the rodent CNS, the nature or expression of these cellular responses of developing nervous tissue to the gonadal hormones is not peculiar to sexual differentiation. The characteristics of these responses represent yet another facet of the much broader question of the factors and cellular mechanisms contributing to neural plasticity in both the developing and adult CNS. Patterns of axonal growth, dendritic differentiation, dendritic spine density and of synaptogenesis, for example, are cytological features which have not only been shown to be gonadal hormone-dependent and sexually dimorphic but which also exhibit considerable pre- and postnatal plasticity. Such disparate influences as vision (Ruiz-Marcos and Valverde, 1969; Lund and Lund, 1972; Parnavelas et al., 1973) environmental enrichment (Holloway, 1966; Globus and Scheibel, 1967; Greenough et al., 1973), pre- and postnatal injury (Goldman et al., 1974; Goldman-Rakic, 1981a,b) as well as other hormones such as thyroxine (Rebière and Legrand, 1972), all acting during restricted, "critical" periods of neural development can also permanently modify these patterns. Moreover, even the responses to certain of these very influences, such as injury may also be modified differentially by sex differences and by exposure to exogenous androgen as well (Goldman et al., 1974; Beatty, 1979; Yu, 1982).

That the nature of the morphological response to estrogen which was observed in vitro may be a universal response of undifferentiated, steroid receptor-containing nerve cells to steroids is suggested by the studies of Cherbas et al. (1982) on a hormone-dependent cell line of probable neural origin (Kc and Kc-H) derived from embryos of the fruit fly, *Drosophila melanogaster*. Exposure of Kc and Kc-H cells from clones of undifferentiated imaginal disk cells in culture to the insect steroid molting hormone, 20-hydroxyecdysone (which transforms the larva to the adult) results in cessation of cell division and subsequent cytologic transformation or differentiation, characterized morphologically by the extension of long and elaborate cell processes which arborize extensively. The effect is specific to ecdysteroid hormones and is mediated by ecdysteroid receptors which appear to be very similar to vertebrate steroid receptors (Cherbas et al., 1982).

Finally, although there is considerable variability in the types of neural functions which may be sexually dimorphic, in the CNS regions involved, in the timing of the hormone-sensitive periods and even in the very hormones responsible for the developmental effects, the underlying principles of hormonal action may well be valid across a considerable portion of the animal kingdom.

NOTE ADDED IN PROOF

A recent study by Stumpf et al. (1983), using dissociated cell cultures of E-18 rat hypothalamus and gonadal steroids at dose levels comparable to those of the author's, found a marked increase in the length of neuronal processes elicited by both 17β-estradiol and testosterone but not by 5a-dihydrotestosterone. Their results thus far support the author's findings described above. In addition, Stumpf et al. observed different responses to the two steroids as expressed by an early enhancement of cell numbers by testosterone only and a reduction in dense-core vesicles after long-term exposure to estradiol.

ACKNOWLEDGEMENTS

The skilled technical assistance of Messrs. Hubert Cummins and Manuel Urena is gratefully acknowledged in various aspects of the author's investigations. The depicted [³H]estradiol autoradiography of the cortical cultures was carried out in collaboration with Dr. Bruce S. McEwen and Mr. John L. Gerlach (Rockefeller University). The expert graphic assistance of Dr. Edward Toran and Mr. Robert Demarest and the skilled typing assistance of Ms. Christine Wade are also gratefully acknowledged.

The author's research was supported in part by the National Institutes of Health (HD-08364); the National Science Foundation (BNS 77-0859); the Whitehall Foundation; the W.T. Grant Foundation; the March of Dimes Birth Defects Foundation and a National Institute of Mental Health Research Scientist Development Award (MH-00192) and by institutional funds from the Rockefeller Foundation and the Mellon Foundation.

REFERENCES

Adashi, E.Y. and Hsueh, A.J.W. (1982) Estrogens augment the stimulation of ovarian aromatase activity by follicle-stimulating hormone in cultured rat granulosa cells. *J. Biol. Chem.*, 257: 6077–6083.

Ali, M. and Sahib, M.K. (1983) Changes in alpha-fetoprotein and albumin synthesis rates and their levels during fetal and neonatal development of rat brain. *Develop. Brain Res.*, 6: 314–317.

Ali, M., Balapure, A.K., Singh, D.R., Shukla, R.N. and Sahib, M.K. (1981) Ontogeny of alpha-fetoprotein in human fetal brain. *Brain Res.*, 207: 459–464.

Ali, M., Mujoo, K. and Sahib, M.K. (1983) Synthesis and secretion of alpha-fetoprotein and albumin by newborn rat brain cells in culture. *Develop. Brain Res.*, 6: 47–55.

Allerand, C.D. (1971) Patterns of neuronal differentiation in developing cultures of neonatal mouse cerebellum: a living and silver impregnation study. *J. Comp. Neurol.*, 142: 167–204.

Amenta, F., Cavallotti, C. and Porcelli, F. (1979) Influence of estradiol-17β on the postnatal development of cholinergic neurons in rat brain. *Verh. Anat. Ges.*, 73: 675.

Andrews, G.K., Dziadek, M. and Tamaoki, T. (1982) Expression and methylation of the mouse a-fetoprotein gene in embryonic, adult and neoplastic tissues. *J. Biol. Chem.*, 257: 5148–5153.

Arai, Y. and Matsumoto, A. (1978) Synapse formation of the hypothalamus arcuate nucleus during post-natal development in the female rat and its modification by neonatal estrogen treatment. *Psychoneuroendocrinology*, 3: 31–45.

Arendash, G.W. and Gorski, R.A. (1983) Effects of discrete lesions of the sexually dimorphic nucleus of the preoptic area or other medial preoptic regions on the sexual behavior of male rats. *Brain Res. Bull.*, 10: 147–154.

Arimatsu, Y., Seto, A. and Amano, T. (1981) Sexual dimorphism in a-bungarotoxin binding capacity in the mouse amygdala. *Brain Res.*, 213: 432–437.

Arnon, R., Teicher, E., Bustin, M. and Sela, M. (1973) Preparation of antisera to a-fetoprotein making use of estradiol affinity column. *FEBS Lett.*, 32: 335–338.

Attardi, B. and Ruoslahti, E. (1976) Foetoneonatal oestradiol-binding protein in mouse brain cytosol is α-fetoprotein. *Nature (London)*, 263: 685–687.

Aussel, C. and Masseyeff, R. (1978) Alpha-fetoprotein and estrogen metabolism. *Biochimie*, 58: 737–741.

Aussel, C., Lafaurie, M. and Stora, C. (1981) Rôle physiologique de l'alpha-fœtoprotéine: Effet d'injection d'AFP purifiée sur l'activité ovarienne du rat femelle. *C.R. Acad. Sci. (Paris)*, 292: 553–556.

Ayoub, D.M., Greenough, W.T. and Juraska, J.M. (1982) Sex differences in dendritic structure in the preoptic area of the juvenile macaque monkey brain. *Science*, 219: 197–198.

Barley, J., Ginsburg, M., Greenstein, B.D., MacLusky, N.J. and Thomas, P.J. (1974) A receptor-mediating sexual differentiation? *Nature (London)*, 252: 259–260.

Bass, H., Netsky, M.G. and Young, E. (1969a) Microchemical studies of postnatal development in rat cerebrum. I. Migration and differentiation of cells. *Neurology*, 19: 258–268.

Bass, N.H., Netsky, M.G. and Young, E. (1969b) Microchemical studies of postnatal development in rat cerebrum. II. Formation of myelin. *Neurology*, 19: 405–414.

Bayard, B., Kerckaert, J.P. and Biserte, G. (1978) Differences in the molecular heterogeneity of alpha-fetoprotein from uterus and serum of immature rats. *Biochem. Biophys. Res. Commun.*, 85: 47–54.

Beatty, W.W. (1979) Gonadal hormones and sex differences in non-reproductive behaviors in rodents: Organizational and activational influences. *Hormone Behav.*, 12: 112–163.

Benassayag, C., Vallette, G., Savu, L., Clerc-Hofmann, F., Christeff, N., Muller, F., Delorme, J. and Nunez, E.A. (1981) Relations between serum a_1-foetoprotein (AFP) and uterine cytosol receptors in the immature rat: Importance of fatty acid ligands. In: H. Peeters (Ed.), *Protides of the Biological Fluids, Vol. 29*, Pergamon, London, pp. 369–372.

Benno, R.H. and Williams, T.H. (1978) Evidence for intracellular localization of alpha-fetoprotein in the developing rat brain. *Brain Res.* 142: 182–186.

Booth, J.E. (1977) Sexual behavior of neonatally castrated rats injected during infancy with oestrogen and dihydrotestosterone. *J. Endocrinol.*, 72: 135–141.

Breedlove, S.M. and Arnold, A.P. (1980) Hormone accumulation in a sexually dimorphic motor nucleus of the rat spinal cord. *Science*, 210: 564–566.

Breedlove, S.M. and Arnold, A.P. (1983) Hormonal control of a developing neuromuscular system. I. Complete demasculinization of the male rat spinal nucleus of the bulbocavernosus using the anti-androgen flutamide. *J. Neurosci.*, 3: 417–423.

Breedlove, S.M., Jordan, C.L. and Arnold, A.P. (1982) Masculinization of the female rat spinal cord following a single neonatal injection of testosterone propionate but not estradiol benzoate. *Brain Res.*, 237: 173–181.

Bubenik, G.A. and Brown, G.M. (1973) Morphologic sex differences in primate brain areas involved in regulation of reproductive activity. *Experientia*, 26: 619–621.

Calaresu, F.R. and Henry, J.L. (1971) Sex differences in the number of sympathetic neurons in the spinal cord of the cat. *Science*, 173: 343–344.

Carreau, S., Musto, N.A. and Gunsalus, G.L. (1983) In fetal rats androgen binding protein (rABP) is synthesized by liver and testis. *Endocr. Soc. Abstracts, 65th Annual Meeting*, p. 238.

Castelli, D., Aussel, C., Lafaurie, M., Ayraud, N. and Stora, C. (1982) Immunolocalization of alpha-fetoprotein in the ovary and hypophysis of immature female rats. *Histochem. J.*, 14: 879–887.

Chandra, R.K. (1979) Functional significance of alpha-fetoprotein during pregnancy: immunosuppression, estrogen binding and morphogenesis. In: W.A. Hemmings (Ed.), *Protein Transmission through Living Membranes*, Elsevier/North-Holland, Amsterdam, pp. 423–427.

Cherbas, P., Savakis, C., Cherbas, L. and Koehler, M.M.D. (1982) Steroid-controlled gene expression in a Drosophila cell line. In: F.O. Schmitt, S.J. Bird and F.E. Bloom (Eds.), *Molecular Genetic Neuroscience*, Raven, New York, pp. 277–288.

Christensen, L.W. and Gorski, R.A. (1978) Independent masculinization of neuroendocrine systems by intracerebral implants of testosterone or estradiol in the neonatal female rat. *Brain Res.*, 146: 325–340.

Clark, J.H., Hardin, J.W., Upchurch, S. and Eriksson, H. (1978) Heterogeneity of estrogen binding sites in the cytosol of the rat uterus. *J. Biol. Chem.*, 253: 7630–7634.

Crawford, M.A. and Sinclair, A.J. (1972) Nutritional influences in the evolution of the mammalian brain. In: *Lipids, Malnutrition and the Developing Brain*, Ciba Found. Symp., Churchill, London, pp. 267–287.

Curry, J.J. and Heim, L. (1966) Brain myelination after neonatal administration of oestradiol. *Nature (London)*, 209: 915–916.

DeLacoste-Utamsing, C. and Holloway, R.L. (1982) Sexual dimorphism in the human corpus callosum. *Science*, 216: 1431–1432.

DeVoogd, T.J. and Nottebohm, F. (1981a) Sex differences in dendritic morphology of a song control nucleus in the canary: A quantitative Golgi study. *J. Comp. Neurol.*, 196: 309–316.

DeVoogd, T.J. and Nottebohm, F. (1981b) Gonadal hormones induce dendritic growth in the adult avian brain. *Science*, 214: 202–204.

DeVries, G.J., Buijs, R.M. and Swaab, D.F. (1981) Ontogeny of the vasopressinergic neurons of the suprachiasmatic nucleus and their extrahypothalamic projections in the rat brain — presence of a sex difference in the lateral septum. *Brain Res.*, 218: 67–78.

DeVries, G.J., Best, W. and Sluiter, A.A. (1983) The influence of androgens on the development of a sex difference in the vasopressinergic innervation of the rat lateral septum. *Develop. Brain Res.*, 8: 377–380.

Diamond, M.C., Johnson, R.E. and Ingham, C. (1971) Brain plasticity induced by environment and pregnancy. *Int. J. Neurosci.*, 2: 171–178.

Diamond, M.C., Young, D., Sukhwinder, S. and Johnson, R.E. (1981) Morphological differences between the cerebral hemispheres in the female rat. *Soc. Neurosci. Abstr.*, 7: 286.

Döhler, K.D. (1978) Is female sexual differentiation hormone-mediated? *Trends Neurosci.*, 1: 138–140.

Döhler, K.D. and Wüttke, W. (1975) Changes with age in levels of serum gonadotropins, prolactin and gonadal steroids in prepubertal male and female rats. *Endocrinology*, 97: 898–907.

Döhler, K.D., Hancke, J.C., Srivastava, S.S., Shryne, J.E. and Gorski, R.A. (1983) Evidences for estrogenic influence on female sexual brain differentiation. In: *Third European Winter Conference on Brain Research*, Abstracts.

Döhler, K.D., Hancke, J.L., Srivastava, S.S., Hofmann, C., Shrine, J.E. and Gorski, R.A. (1984) Participation of estrogens in female sexual differentiation of the brain; neuroanatomical, neuroendocrine and behavioral evidence. In: G.J. De Vries, J.P.C. De Bruin, H.B.M. Uylings and M.A. Corner (Eds.), *Sex Differences in the Brain. The Relation between Structure and Function. Progress in Brain Research*, this volume, Ch. 5.

Dörner, G. and Staudt, J. (1968) Structural changes in the preoptic anterior hypothalamic area of the male rat, following neonatal castration and androgen substitution. *Neuroendocrinology*, 3: 136–140.

Dörner, G. and Staudt, J. (1969a) Perinatal structural sex differentiation of the hypothalamus in rats. *Neuroendocrinology*, 5: 103–106.

Dörner, G. and Staudt, J. (1969b) Structural changes in the hypothalamic ventromedial nucleus of the male rat, following neonatal castration and androgen treatment. *Neuroendocrinology*, 4: 278–281.

Dyer, R.G., MacLeod, N.K. and Ellendorf, F. (1976) Electrophysiological evidence for sexual dimorphism and synaptic convergence in the preoptic area and anterior hypothalamic areas of the rat. *Proc. R. Soc. Lond. (Biol.)*, 193: 421–440.

Dziegielewska, K.M., Evans, C.A.N., Lorscheider, F.L., Malinowska, D.H., Møllgård, K., Reynolds, M.L. and Saunders, N.R. (1981) Plasma proteins in fetal sheep brain: blood–brain barrier and intracerebral distribution. *J. Physiol. (London)*, 318: 239–250.

Fox, T.O. (1975) Androgen- and estrogen-binding macromolecules in developing brain: Biochemical and genetic evidence. *Proc. Natl. Acad. Sci. (U.S.A.)*, 72: 4303–4307.

Fox, T.O. (1977) Estradiol and testosterone binding in normal and mutant mouse cerebellum. Cytochemical and cellular specificity. *Brain Res.*, 128: 263–273.

Friedman, W.J., McEwen, B.S., Toran-Allerand, C.D. and Gerlach, J.L. (1983) Perinatal development of hypothalamic and cortical estrogen receptors in mouse brain: methodological aspects. *Develop. Brain Res.*, 11: 19–27.

Friend, J.P. (1977) Persistence of maternally derived ^{3}H-estradiol in fetal and neonatal rats. *Experientia*, 33: 1235–1236.

Gerall, A.A., Dunlap, J.L. and Hendricks, S.E. (1973) Effect of ovarian secretions on female behavioral potentiality in the rat. *J. Comp. Physiol. Psychol.*, 82: 449–465.

Gerlach, J.L., McEwen, B.S., Toran-Allerand, C.D. and Friedman, W.J. (1983) Perinatal development of estrogen receptors in mouse brain assessed by radioautography, nuclear isolation and receptor assay. *Develop. Brain Res.*, 11: 7–18.

Germain, B.J., Campbell, P.S. and Anderson, J.N. (1978) Role of the serum estrogen-binding protein in the control of tissue estradiol levels during postnatal development in the female rat. *Endocrinology*, 103: 1401–1410.

Gitlin, D. and Boesman, M. (1967) Sites of serum fetoprotein synthesis in the human and in the rat. *J. Clin. Invest.*, 46: 1010–1016.

Gitlin, D. and Perricelli, A. (1970) Synthesis of serum albumin, prealbumin, a-foetoprotein, a_1-anti-trypsin and transferrin by the human yolk sac. *Nature (London)*, 228: 995–997.

Gitlin, D., Perricelli, A. and Gitlin, G.M. (1972) Synthesis of alphafetoprotein by liver yolk sac and gastrointestinal tract of the human conceptus. *Cancer Res.*, 32: 979–982.

Globus, A. and Scheibel, A.B. (1967) The effect of deprivation on cortical neurons: a Golgi study. *Exp. Neurol.*, 19: 331–345.

Goldman, P.S., Crawford, H.T., Stokes, L.P., Galkin, T.W. and Rosvold, H.E. (1974) Sex dependent behavioral effects of cerebral cortical lesions in developing rhesus monkey. *Science*, 186: 540–542.

Goldman-Rakic, P.S. (1981a) Development and plasticity of primate frontal association cortex. In: F.O. Schmitt, F.G. Worden, S.G. Dennis and G. Adelman (Eds.), *The Organization of the Cerebral Cortex*, MIT Press, Boston, MA, pp. 69–97.

Goldman-Rakic, P.S. (1981b) Morphological consequence of prenatal injury to the primate brain. In: McConnell, Boer Ronijn, van de Poll and Corner (Eds.), *Adaptive Capabilities of the Nervous System, Progress in Brain Research, Vol. 53*, Elsevier/North-Holland, Amsterdam, pp. 3–19.

Gorski, R.A., Gordon, J., Shryne, J.E. and Southam, A. (1978) Evidence for a morphological sex difference within the medial preoptic area of the rat brain. *Brain Res.*, 148: 333–346.

Gorski, R.A., Harlan, R.E., Jacobson, C.D., Shryne, J.E. and Southam, A.M. (1980) Evidence for the existence of a sexually dimorphic nucleus in the preoptic area of the rat. *J. Comp. Neurol.*, 193: 529–539.

Gottlieb, D.I. and W.M. Cowan (1972) Evidence for a temporal factor in the occupation of available synaptic sites during the development of the dentate gyrus. *Brain Res.*, 41: 452–456.

Greenough, W.T., Volkmar, F.R. and Juraska, J.M. (1973) Effects of rearing complexity on dendritic branching in frontolateral and temporal cortex of the rat. *Exp. Neurol.*, 41: 371–378.

Greenough, W.T., Carter, C.S., Steerman, C. and DeVoogd, T.J. (1977) Sex differences in dendritic patterns in hamster preoptic area. *Brain Res.*, 126: 63–72.

Gregory, E. (1975) Comparison of postnatal CNS development between male and female rats. *Brain Res.*, 99: 152–156.

Grigorova, A.M., Cittanova, N. and Jayle, M.F. (1977) Physico-chemical analogues of rat alpha-fetoprotein and rat serum albumin. *Biochimie*, 59: 217–220.

Güldner, F.H. (1976) Synaptology of the rat suprachiasmatic nucleus. *Cell Tissue Res.*, 165: 509–544.

Güldner, F.H. (1982) Sexual dimorphisms of axo-synapses and postsynaptic density material in the suprachiasmatic nucleus of the rat. *Neurosci. Lett.*, 28: 145–150.

Gurney, M.E. (1981) Hormonal control of cell form and number in zebra finch song system. *J. Neurosci.*, 1: 658–673.

Gurney, M.E. and Konishi, M. (1980) Hormone induced sexual differentiation of brain and behavior in zebra finches. *Science*, 208: 1380–1382.

Hancke, J.C. and Döhler, K.-D. (1980) Postnatal estradiol treatment prevents tamoxifen induced defeminization of the female rat brain. *Acta Endocrinol.*, 94, Suppl. 234: 102.

Hannigan, P.C. and Kelley, D.B. (1981) Male and female laryngeal motoneurons in *Xenopus laevis. Soc. Neurosci. Abstr.*, 7: 269.

Hart, B.L. (1979) Sexual behavior and penile reflexes of neonatally castrated male rats treated in infancy with estrogen and dihydrotestosterone. *Hormone Behav.*, 13: 256–268.

Heim, L.M. (1966) Effect of estradiol on brain maturation: dose and time response relationships. *Endocrinology*, 78: 1130–1134.

Heim, L.M. and Timiras, P.S. (1963) Gonad–brain relationship: Precocious brain maturation after estradiol in rats. *Endocrinology*, 72: 598–606.

Hellman, R.E., Ford, D.H. and Rhines, R.K. (1976) Growth in hypothalamic neurons as reflected by nuclear size and labelling with ^{3}H-uridine. *Psychoendocrinology*, 1: 389–397.

Hendricks, S.E. and Duffy, J.A. (1974) Ovarian influence on the development of sexual behavior in neonatally androgenized rats. *Develop. Psychobiol.*, 7: 297–303.

Hendricks, S.E. and Weltin, M. (1976) Effect of estrogen given during various periods of prepubertal life on the sexual behavior of rats. *Physiol. Psychol.*, 4: 105–110.

Hervé, F., Grigorova, A.M., Rajkowski, K. and Cittanova, N. (1982) Differences in the binding of thyroid hormones and indoles by rat α_1-fetoprotein and serum albumin. *Eur. J. Biochem.*, 122: 609–612.

Holloway Jr., R. (1966) Dendritic branching: some preliminary results of training and complexity in rat visual cortex. *Brain Res.*, 2: 393–396.

Hudson, D.B., Vernadakis, A. and Timiras, P.S. (1970) Regional changes in amino acid concentration in the developing brain and the effects of neonatal administration of estradiol. *Brain Res.*, 23: 213–222.

Ifft, J.D. (1964) The effect of endocrine gland extirpation on the size of nucleoli in the rat hypothalamic neurons. *Anat. Rec.*, 148: 599–604.

Jacobson, C.D. and Gorski, R.A. (1981) Neurogenesis of the sexually dimorphic nucleus of the preoptic area in the rat. *J. Comp. Neurol.*, 196: 519–529.

Jordan, C.L., Breedlove, S.M. and Arnold, A.P. (1982) Sex dimorphism and the influence of neonatal androgen in the dorsolateral motor nucleus of the rat lumbar spinal cord. *Brain Res.*, 309–314.

Kelley, D.B. and Fenstemaker, S.B. (1983) Sexually dimorphic neurons of the vocal production nucleus in *Xenopus laevis*. *Soc. Neurosci. Abstr.*, 9: 1094.

King, J.C. (1972) *Ultrastructure Analysis of Arcuate Neurons in Normal and Androgenized Female Rats*. Ph. D. Thesis, Tulane University.

Kornguth, S.E. and Scott, G. (1972) The role of climbing fibers in the formation of Purkinje cell dendrites. *J. Comp. Neurol.*, 146: 61–82.

Lawrence, J.M. and Raisman, G. (1980) Ontogeny of synapses in a sexual dimorphic part of the preoptic area in the rat. *Brain Res.*, 183: 466–471.

LeBlond, C.B., Morris, S., Karakiulakis, G., Powell, R. and Thomas, P.J. (1982) Development of sexual dimorphism in the suprachiasmatic nucleus of the rat. *J. Endocrinol.*, 95: 137–145.

LeGuern, A., Benassayag, C. and Nunez, E.A. (1982) Role of alpha-fetoprotein in the transplacental transfer of natural and synthetic estrogen in the rat. *Develop. Pharm. Ther.*, 4, Suppl. 1: 79–87.

Leung, C.C.K., Watabe, H. and Brent, R.L. (1977) Lack of effect of antisera to alpha fetoprotein. *Am. J. Anat.*, 148: 457–462.

Levi-Montalcini, R. and Angeletti, P.U. (1968) Nerve growth factor. *Physiol. Rev.*, 48: 534–569.

Levina, S.E., Gyevai, A. and Horvath, E. (1975) Responsiveness of the ovary to gonadotrophins in pre- and perinatal life: oestrogen secretion in tissue and organ culture. *J. Endocrinol.*, 65: 219–223.

Levine, J.A., Cassorla, F., Skerda, M. and Valk, I.M. (1983) The effect of estrogen dose on ulnar growth rate in patients with Turner's syndrome. *Endocr. Soc. Abstracts, 65th Annual Meeting*, p. 83.

Lieberburg, I. and McEwen, B.S. (1975) Estradiol-17β: A metabolite of testosterone recovered in cell nuclei from limbic areas of neonatal rat brains. *Brain Res.*, 85: 165–170.

Litteria, M. (1977) Inhibitory action of neonatal estrogenization on the incorporation of ^{3}H-lysine into proteins of specific limbic and paralimbic neurons of the adult rat. *Brain Res.*, 127: 164–167.

Litteria, M. and Thorner, M.W. (1976) Inhibitory action of neonatal estrogenization on the incorporation of ^{3}H-lysine into corticol neuroproteins. *Brain Res.*, 103: 584–587.

Loy, R. and Milner, T.A. (1980) Sexual dimorphism in extent of axonal sprouting in hippocampus. *Science*, 208: 1282–1284.

Luine, V.N. and McEwen, B.S. (1983) Sex differences in cholinergic enzymes of diagonal band nuclei in the rat preoptic area. *Neuroendocrinology*, 36: 475–482.

Lund, J.S. and Lund, R. (1972) The effects of varying periods of visual deprivation on synaptogenesis in the superior colliculi of the rat. *Brain Res.*, 42: 21–32.

Lundberg, J.J. and Møllgård, K. (1979) Mitotic activity in adult brain induced by implantation of pieces of fetal rat brain and liver. *Neurosci. Lett.*, 13: 265–270.

Luttge, W.G. and Whalen, R.E. (1970) Dihydrotestosterone, androstenedione, testosterone: Comparative effectiveness in masculinizing and defeminizing reproductive systems in male and female rats. *Hormone Behav.*, 1: 265–281.

Mackiewicz, A., Hejduk, W. and Breborowicz, J. (1978) The in vitro production of alpha-fetoprotein by human embryonic brain. *Scand. J. Immunol.*, 8, Suppl. 8: 231–233.

MacLusky, N.J. and Naftolin, F. (1981) Sexual differentiation of the central nervous system. *Science*, 211: 1294–1303.

MacLusky, N.J., Chaptal, C., Lieberburg, I. and McEwen, B.S. (1976) Properties and subcellular interrelationship of presumptive estrogen receptor macromolecules in the brains of neonatal and prepubertal female rats. *Brain Res.*, 114: 158–165.

Mareš, V., Kovářů, F. and Kovářů, H. (1982) Alpha-fetoprotein in the brain of developing rats and pigs. An immunofluorescence study of cell- and tissue-differentiation. *Bas. Appl. Histochem.*, 26: 53–63.

Matsumoto, A. and Arai, Y. (1976) Effect of estrogen on early postnatal development of synaptic formation in the hypothalamic arcuate nucleus of female rats. *Neurosci. Lett.*, 2: 79–82.

Matsumoto, A. and Arai, Y. (1980) Sexual dimorphism in "wiring pattern" in the hypothalamic arcuate nucleus and its modification by neonatal hormonal environment. *Brain Res.*, 190: 238–242.

Matsumoto, A. and Arai, Y. (1981a) Neuronal plasticity in the deafferented hypothalamic arcuate nucleus of adult female rats and its enhancement by treatment with estrogen. *J. Comp. Neurol.*, 197: 197–206.

Matsumoto, A. and Arai, Y. (1981b) Effect of androgen on sexual differentiation of synaptic organization in the hypothalamic arcuate nucleus: an ontogenetic study. *Neuroendocrinology*, 33: 166–169.

McDonald, P.G. and Doughty, C. (1974) Effect of neonatal administration of different androgens in the female rat: Correlation between aromatization and the induction of sterilization. *J. Endocrinol.*, 61: 95–103.

McEwen, B.S. (1980) Gonadal steroids: humoral modulators of nerve-cell function. *Moll. Cell Endocrinol.*, 18: 151–164.

McEwen, B.S. (1983) Gonadal steroid influences on brain development and sexual differentiation. In: R.O. Greep (Ed.), *International Review of Physiology, Vol. 27*, University Park Press, Baltimore, MD, pp. 99–145.

McEwen, B.S., Plapinger, L., Chaptal, C., Gerlach, J. and Wallach, G. (1975) The role of fetoneonatal estrogen binding proteins in the association of estrogen with neonatal brain cell nuclear receptors. *Brain Res.,* 96: 400–407.

Meisel, R.L. and Ward, I.L. (1981) Fetal female rats are masculinized by male littermates located caudally in the uterus. *Science,* 213: 239–241.

Meyer, G., Ferres-Torres, R. and Mas, M. (1978) The effects of puberty and castration on hippocampal dendritic spines of mice. A Golgi study. *Brain Res.,* 155: 108–112.

Milgrom, E., Atger, M. and Baulieu, E.E. (1973) Studies on estrogen-entry into uterine cells and on estradiol-receptor complex attachment to the nucleus — is the entry of estrogen into uterine cells a protein mediated process? *Biochim. Biophys. Acta,* 320: 267–283.

Milner, T.A. and Loy, R. (1980) Interaction of age and sex in sympathetic axon ingrowth into the hippocampus following septal afferent damage. *Anat. Embryol.,* 161: 159–168.

Milner, T.A. and Loy, R. (1982) Hormonal regulation of axonal sprouting in the hippocampus. *Brain Res.,* 243: 180–185.

Mizejewski, G.M. and Grimley, P.M. (1976) Abortogenic activity of antiserum to alpha-fetoprotein. *Nature (London),* 259: 222–224.

Mizejewski, G.J., Plummer, J.H., Blanchett, K.A., Vonnegut, M. and Jacobson, H.I. (1979) α-Fetoprotein immunoreactivity of the major oestrogen-binding component in mouse amniotic fluid. *Immunology,* 36: 685–690.

Mizejewski, G.J., Vonnegut, M. and Simon, R. (1980) Neonatal androgenization using antibodies to alpha-fetoprotein. *Brain Res.,* 188: 273–277.

Mizukami, S., Nichizuka, M. and Arai, Y. (1983) Sexual difference in nuclear volume and its ontogeny in the rat amygdala. *Exp. Neurol.,* 79: 569–575.

Møllgård, K., Jacobsen, M., Jacobsen, G.K., Clausen, P.P. and Saunders, N.R. (1979) Immunohistochemical evidence for an intracellular localization of plasma proteins in human foetal choroid plexus and brain. *Neurosci. Lett.,* 14: 85–90.

Morest, D.K. (1969) The growth of dendrites in the mammalian brain. *Z. Anat. Entwickl.-Gesch.,* 128: 290–317.

Moro, R. and Uriel, J. (1981) Early localization of alpha-fetoprotein in the developing nervous system of the chicken. *Oncodevelop. Biol. Med.,* 2: 391–398.

Moss, R.L. and Dudley, C.A. (1984) Molecular aspects of the interaction between estrogen and the membrane excitability of hypothalamic nerve cells. In: G.J. De Vries, J.P.C. De Bruin, H.B.M. Uylings and M.A. Corner (Eds.), *Sex Differences in the Brain. The Relation between Structure and Function. Progress in Brain Research,* this volume, Ch. 1.

Nance, D.M., Shryne, J. and Gorski, R.A. (1975) Facilitation of female sexual behavior in male rats by septal lesions: An interaction with estrogen. *Hormone Behav.,* 6: 289–299.

Nichizuka, M. (1978) Topography of the neurons responding to estrogen in the hypothalamic arcuate nucleus of immature female mice. *Brain Res.,* 152: 31–40.

Nichizuka, M. and Arai, Y. (1980) Possible role of sex steroids in synaptogenesis in the medial amygdala of the rat. *Neurosci. Lett.,* Suppl. 4: S80.

Nichizuka, M. and Arai, Y. (1981a) Sexual dimorphism in synaptic organization in the amygdala and its dependence on neonatal hormone environment. *Brain Res.,* 212: 31–38.

Nichizuka, M. and Arai, Y. (1981b) Organizational action of estrogen on synaptic pattern in the amygdala: implications for sexual differentiation of the brain. *Brain Res.,* 213: 422–426.

Nichizuka, M. and Arai, Y. (1982) Synapse formation in response to estrogen in the medial amygdala developing in the eye. *Proc. Natl. Acad. Sci. (U.S.A.),* 79: 7024–7026.

Nottebohm, F. (1981) A brain for all seasons: Clinical anatomical changes in song control nuclei of the canary brain. *Science,* 214: 1368–1370.

Nottebohm, F. and Arnold, A. (1976) Sexual dimorphism in vocal control areas of the songbird brain. *Science,* 194: 211–213.

Nunez, E.A., Benassayag, C., Savu, L., Vallette, G. and Jayle, M.F. (1976) Serum binding of some steroid hormones during development in different animal species. Discussion of the biological significance of this binding. *Ann. Biol. Anim. Biochem. Biophys.,* 16: 491–501.

Nunez, E.A., Benassayag, C., Savu, L., Vallette, G. and Delorme, J. (1979) Biological functions of rat alpha-fetoprotein in relation to the endocrine system: experimental facts and hypotheses. In: F.G. Lehmann (Ed.), *Carcino-Embryonic Proteins. Chemistry, Biology, Clinical Application, Vol. I,* Elsevier, Amsterdam, pp. 171–180.

Olsson, M., Lindahl, G. and Ruoslahti, E. (1977) Genetic control of alpha-fetoprotein synthesis in the mouse. *J. Exp. Med.*, 145: 819–827.

O'Malley, B.W. and Birnbaumer, L. (Eds.) (1978) *Receptor and Hormone Action II*, Academic Press, New York.

Oppenheim, R.W. (1981) Neuronal cell death and some related regressive phenomena during neurogenesis: A selective historical review and progress report. In: W.M. Cowan (Ed.), *Studies in Developmental Neurobiology: Essay in Honor of Viktor Hamburger*, Oxford, pp. 74–133.

Page, M. (1974) Activité des protéines fœto-embryonnaires sur la prolifération cellulaire in vitro. In: R. Masseyeff (Ed.), *Alpha-Fetoprotein*, INSERM, Paris, pp. 457–466.

Pappas, C.T., Diamond, M.C. and Johnson, R.E. (1978) Effects of ovariectomy and differential experience on rat cerebral cortical morphology. *Brain Res.*, 154: 53–60.

Parnavelas, J.G., Globus, A. and Kaups, P. (1973) Changes in lateral geniculate neurons of rats as a result of continuous exposure to light. *Nature New Biol.*, 245: 287–288.

Pastan, I.H. and Willingham, M.C. (1981) Receptor-mediated endocytosis of hormones in cultured cells. *Annu. Rev. Physiol.*, 43: 239–250.

Payne, D.W. and Katzenellenbogen, J.A. (1979) Binding specificity of rat alpha-fetoprotein for a series of estrogen derivatives: studies using equilibrium and non-equilibrium binding. *Endocrinology*, 105: 745–753.

Perez-Polo, J.R., Hall, K., Livingston, K. and Westlund, K. (1977) Steroid-induction of nerve growth factor synthesis in cell culture. *Life Sci.*, 21: 1535–1543.

Perry, V.H. and Linden, R. (1982) Evidence for dendritic competition in the developing retina. *Nature (London)*, 297: 683–685.

Pfaff, D.W. (1966) Morphological changes in the brains of adult male rats after neonatal castration. *Endocrinology*, 36: 415–416.

Pietras, R.J. and Szego, C.M. (1979) Estrogen-induced membrane alterations and growths associated with proteinase activity in endometrial cells. *J. Cell Biol.*, 81: 649–663.

Pineiro, A., Olivito, A.-M. and Uriel, J. (1979) Fixation d'acides gras polyinsaturés par l'alphafœtoprotéine et la sérum albumine de rat. Comparaison avec l'accumulation de ces acides au cours du développement postnatal. *C.R. Acad. Sci. (Paris) D*, 289: 1053–1056.

Plapinger, L. and McEwen, B.S. (1973) Ontogeny of estradiol-binding sites in rat brain. Appearance of presumptive adult receptors in cytosol and nuclei. *Endocrinology*, 93: 1119–1128.

Pool, T.B., Hagino, N. and Cameron, I.L. (1978) Relationship between functional castration and alphafetoprotein produced by hepatoma-bearing female rats. *J. Reprod. Fertil.*, 53: 39–44.

Presl, J., Pospisil, J. and Horsky, J. (1971) Autoradiographic localization of radioactivity in female rat neocortex after injection of tritiated estradiol. *Experientia*, 27: 465–467.

Puymirat, J., Loudes, C., Faivre-Bauman, A., Tixier-Vidal, A. and Bourre, J.M. (1982) Expression of neuronal function by mouse fetal hypothalamic cells cultured in hormonally defined medium. In: G.H. Sato, A.B. Pardee and D.A. Sirbasky (Eds.), *Growth of Cells in Hormonally Defined Media, Cold Spring Harbor Conferences on Cell Proliferation, Vol. 9*, Cold Spring Harbor Laboratory, Cold Spring Harbor, NY, pp. 1033–1052.

Raisman, G. and Field, P.M. (1973) Sexual dimorphism in the neuropil of the preoptic area of the rat and its dependence on neonatal androgen. *Brain Res.*, 54: 1–29.

Ramon y Cajal, S. (1909–1911) *Histologie du Système Nerveux de l'Homme et des Vertébrés, Vol. II*, L. Azoulay (Transl.), CSIC, Madrid (1952), pp. 80–106.

Ratner, A. and Adamo, N.J. (1971) Arcuate nucleus region in androgen-sterilized female rats: ultrastructural observations. *Neuroendocrinology*, 8: 26–35.

Raynaud, P. (1971) Influence of rat estradiol binding plasma protein (EBP) on uterotrophic activity. *Steroids*, 21: 249–258.

Rebière, A. and Legrand, J. (1972) Données quantitatives sur la synaptogenèse dans le cervelet du rat normal et rendu hypothyroïdien par le propylthiouracile. *C.R. Acad. Sci. (Paris)*, 274: 3581–3584.

Ruiz-Marcos, A. and Valverde, F. (1969) The temporal evolution of the distribution of dendritic spines in the visual cortex of normal and dark raised mice. *Exp. Brain Res.*, 8: 284–294.

Ruoslahti, E. and Engvall, E. (1978) Alpha-fetoprotein. *Scand. J. Immunol.*, 7, Suppl. 6: 1–17.

Ruoslahti, E. and Seppälä, M. (1979) α-Fetoprotein in cancer and fetal development. *Adv. Cancer Res.*, 29: 275–346.

Ruoslahti, E. and Terry, W.D. (1976) α-Foetoprotein and albumin show sequence homology. *Nature (London)*, 260: 804–805.

Saunders, N.R. and Møllgård, K. (1981) The natural internal environment of the developing brain: beyond the barrier. *Trends Neurosci.*, 4: 56–60.

Savu, L., Benassayag, C., Vallette, G., Christeff, N. and Nunez, E.A. (1981) Mouse α-foetoprotein and albumin. A comparison of their binding properties with estrogen and fatty acid ligands. *J. Biol. Chem.*, 256: 9414–9418.

Schachter, B.S. and Toran-Allerand, C.D. (1982) Intraneuronal α-fetoprotein and albumin are not synthesized locally in developing brain. *Develop. Brain Res.*, 5: 93–98.

Schwartz, I.R., Pappas, G.D. and Purpura, D.P. (1968) Fine structure of neurons and synapses in the feline hippocampus during postnatal ontogenesis. *Exp. Neurol.*, 22: 394–407.

Seress, L. (1978) The effect of neonatal testosterone treatment on the postnatal cell formation of the rat brain. *Med. J. Osaka*, 28: 285–289.

Shapiro, B.H., Goldman, A.S., Steinbeck, H.F. and Neumann, F. (1976) Is feminine differentiation of the brain hormonally determined? *Experientia*, 32: 650–651.

Sheridan, P.J. (1976) Estrogen binding in the neonatal neocortex. *Brain Res.*, 178: 201–206.

Sheridan, P.J., Sar, M. and Stumpf, W.E. (1974) Autoradiographic localization of ³H-estradiol or its metabolites in the central nervous system of the developing rat. *Endocrinology*, 93: 1386–1390.

Sinclair, A.J. and Crawford, M.A. (1972) The accumulation of arachidonate and docosahexaenoate in the developing rat brain. *J. Neurochem.*, 19: 1753–1758.

Slade, B. (1973) Antibodies to α-fetoprotein cause fetal mortality in rabbits. *Nature (London)*, 246: 493–494.

Slade, B. and Milne, J. (1977) Localization and synthesis of α-fetoprotein in the chicken. *J. Cell Tissue Res.*, 180: 411–419.

Smalley, J.R. and Sarcione, E.J. (1980) Synthesis of alpha-fetoprotein by immature rat uterus. *Biochem. Biophys. Res. Commun.*, 92: 1429–1434.

Smith, J.A. (1973) Effect of antibody to α-fetoprotein on the development of chicken and rat embryos. *Arch. Immunol. Ther. Exp.*, 21: 163–173.

Soto, A.M. and Sonnenschein, C. (1980) Control of growth of estrogen-sensitive cells: Role of α-fetoprotein. *Proc. Natl. Acad. Sci. (U.S.A.)*, 77: 2084–2087.

Staudt, J. and Dörner, G. (1976) Structural changes in the medial and central amygdala of the male rat, following neonatal castration and androgen treatment. *Endokrinologie*, 67: 296–300.

Stewart, J. and Cygan, D. (1980) Ovarian hormones act early in development to feminize adult open-field behavior in the rat. *Hormone Behav.*, 14: 20–32.

Stumpf, E., Narbaitz, R. and Sar, M. (1980) Estrogen receptors in the fetal mouse. *J. Steroid Biochem.*, 12: 55–64.

Stumpf, W.E., Sar, M., Reisdert, I. and Pilgrim, Ch. (1983) Estrogen receptor sites in the developing central nervous system and their relationships to catecholamine systems. *Monogr. Neural Sci.*, 9: 205–212.

Suzuki, Y., Ishii, H., Furuya, H. and Arai, Y. (1982) Developmental changes of the hypogastric ganglion associated with the differentiation of the reproductive tracts in the mouse. *Neurosci. Lett.*, 32: 271–276.

Taylor, R.N. and Smith, R.G. (1982) Identification of a novel sex steroid binding protein. *Proc. Natl. Acad. Sci. (U.S.A.)*, 79: 1742–1746.

Toran-Allerand, C.D. (1976) Sex steroids and the development of the newborn mouse hypothalamus and preoptic area in vitro: Implications for sexual differentiation. *Brain Res.*, 106: 407–412.

Toran-Allerand, C.D. (1978) Gonadal hormones and brain development: Cellular aspects of sexual differentiation. *Am. Zool.*, 18: 553–565.

Toran-Allerand, C.D. (1980a) Sex steroids and the development of the newborn mouse hypothalamus and preoptic area in vitro. II. Morphological correlates and hormonal specificity. *Brain Res.*, 189: 413–427.

Toran-Allerand, C.D. (1980b) Coexistence of α-fetoprotein, albumin and transferrin immunoreactivity in neurones of the developing mouse brain. *Nature (London)*, 286: 733–735.

Toran-Allerand, C.D. (1981) Cellular aspects of sexual differentiation of the brain. In: H. Vogel and G.M. Jagiello (Eds.), *Bioregulators of Reproduction, P&S Symposium Series, Vol. 5*, Academic Press, New York, pp. 43–52.

Toran-Allerand, C.D. (1982) Regional differences in intraneuronal localization of alpha-fetoprotein in developing mouse brain. *Develop. Brain Res.*, 5: 213–217.

Toran-Allerand, C.D., Gerlach, J.L. and McEwen, B.S. (1980) Autoradiographic localization of ³H-estradiol related to steroid responsiveness in cultures of the hypothalamus and preoptic area. *Brain Res.*, 184: 517–522.

Toran-Allerand, C.D., Hashimoto, K., Greenough, W.T. and Saltarelli, M. (1983) Sex steroids and the development of the newborn mouse hypothalamus and preoptic area in vitro. III. Effects of estrogen on dendritic differentiation. *Develop. Brain Res.*, 7: 97–101.

Uriel, J., deNechaud, B. and Dupiers, M. (1972) Estrogen-binding properties of rat, mouse, man fetospecific serum proteins. Demonstration by immuno-autoradiographic methods. *Biochem. Biophys. Res. Commun.*, 46: 1175–1180.

Uriel, J., Bouillon, D., Aussel, C. and Dupiers, M. (1976) Alpha-fetoprotein: the major high affinity estrogen binder in rat uterine cytosols. *Proc. Natl. Acad. Sci. (U.S.A.)*, 73: 1452–1456.

Uriel, J., Faivre-Bauman, A., Trojan, J. and Foiret, D. (1981) Immunocytochemical demonstration of alpha-fetoprotein uptake by primary cultures of fetal hemisphere cells from mouse brain. *Neurosci. Lett.*, 27: 171–175.

Uriel, J., Trojan, J., Dubouch, P. and Pineiro, A. (1982) Intracellular alphafetoprotein and albumin in the developing nervous system of the baboon. *Pathol. Biol.*, 30: 79–83.

Vallette, G., Benassayag, C., Savu, L., Delorme, J., Nunez, E.A., Doumas, J., Maume, G. and Maume, B.F. (1980) The serum competitor of estrogen rat alpha$_1$-fetoprotein interactions. Identification as a mixture of non-esterified fatty acids. *Biochem. J.*, 187: 851–856.

Van der Schoot, P. (1980) Effects of dihydrotestosterone and oestradiol on sexual differentiation in male rats. *J. Endocrinol.*, 84: 397–407.

Varon, S., Adler, R., Manthorpe, M. and Skaper, S.D. (1983) Culture strategies for trophic and other factors directed to nerve cells. In: S. Pfeiffer (Ed.), *Neuroscience Approached through Cell Culture, Vol. II*, CRC Press, Boca Raton, FL, pp. 53–77.

Vertés, M. and King, R.J.B. (1971) The mechanisms of oestradiol binding in rat hypothalamus: effect of androgenization. *J. Endocrinol.*, 51: 271–282.

Vom Saal, F.S. and Bronson, F.H. (1980) Sexual characteristics of adult female mice are correlated with their blood testosterone levels during prenatal development. *Science*, 108: 597–599.

Vom Saal, F.S., Grant, W.M., McMullen, C.W. and Laves, K.S. (1983) High fetal estrogen concentrations: Correlation with increased adult sexual activity and decreased aggression in male mice. *Science*, 220: 1306–1308.

Weisz, J. and Gunsalus, G. (1973) Estrogen levels in immature rats. True or spurious-ovarian or adrenal? *Endocrinology*, 93: 1059–1065.

Weisz, J. and Ward, I.L. (1980) Plasma testosterone and progesterone titers of pregnant rats, their male and female fetuses, and neonatal offspring. *Endocrinology*, 106: 306–316.

Wright, L.L. and Smolen, A.J. (1983) Effects of 17β-estradiol on developing superior cervical ganglion neurons and synapses. *Develop. Brain Res.*, 6: 299–303.

Yu, W.-H.A. (1982) Sex differences in the regeneration of the hypoglossal nerve in rats. *Brain Res.*, 238: 404–406.

Yu, W.-H.A. and Srinivasan, R. (1981) Effect of testosterone and 5-alpha-dihydrotestosterone on regeneration of the hypoglossal nerve in rats. *Exp. Neurol.*, 71: 431–435.

DISCUSSION

D.F. SWAAB: You mentioned all possible cellular mechanisms which could be influenced by steroids (i.e. mitosis, fiber formation, synapse formation, cell death) except cell migration. Has this process been excluded for steroid effects?

C.D. TORAN-ALLERAND: That is a good point. No, I certainly would not exclude steroidal effects on migration. We are currently looking into this question. The only person who has looked into this in culture is Vernadakis who suggested that estradiol may enhance migration from cerebellar explants.

G.J. DE VRIES: From your presentation I have understood that you are comparing the effects of steroids on homologous pairs of tissue, that is, you compare tissue from the left with tissue from the right side of the brain. Recently Nordeen and Yahr (1982) have demonstrated that there is a left–right difference in the sensitivity of hypothalamic areas for gonadal hormones. Could this interfere with your results?

C.D. TORAND-ALLERAND: Originally the explants were randomly assigned to their treatment groups without regard for their right- or left-sided origin. But since the Nordeen paper we have started keeping tract which side the explants come from. In general the right and left side of coronal sections develop quite comparably in organotypic culture.

E.B. KEVERNE: The spectacular outgrowth of neurites appears to lack any distinct organization. Bearing in mind the strategy of neurite "overkill" to target tissues followed by "die-back" in neural morphogenesis, to what extent would the incorporation of a target tissue, e.g. periaqueductal grey, retain this outgrowth?

C.D. TORAN-ALLERAND: It is likely that the luxuriant outgrowth is quite influenced by the artificiality of the culture situation. If one grew the explants with proper target explants the patterns would be quite different, especially with respect to the deafferented or non-afferented state of the culture. We are currently studying the effect of co-culturing target regions.

T. DEVOOGD: Do you have evidence from your explants for (1) normal cell death, and (2) cell death inhibition with steroid administration?

C.D. TORAN-ALLERAND: Not yet, although we are currently looking at this question. This is made difficult by the fact that cells normally die in culture and it is difficult to ascertain whether this is physiological or due to the culture situation.

REFERENCE

Nordeen, E.J. and Yahr, P. (1982) Hemispheric asymmetries in the behavioral and hormonal effects of sexually differentiating mammalian brain. *Science*, 218: 391–394.

G.J. De Vries et al. (Eds.),
Progress in Brain Research, Vol. 61
© 1984 Elsevier Science Publishers B.V., Amsterdam

Participation of Estrogens in Female Sexual Differentiation of the Brain; Neuroanatomical, Neuroendocrine and Behavioral Evidence

K.D. DÖHLER [1,2], J.L. HANCKE [1], S.S. SRIVASTAVA [1], C. HOFMANN [1],
J.E. SHRYNE [2] and R.A. GORSKI [2]

[1] *Department of Clinical Endocrinology, University Medical School, 3000 Hannover (F.R.G.) and*
[2] *Department of Anatomy, and Laboratory of Neuroendocrinology of the Brain Research Institute, UCLA School of Medicine, Los Angeles, CA 90024 (U.S.A.)*

INTRODUCTION

The brain controls a variety of functions that are different in males and females. Some of these functional differences may exist simply because the endogenous hormonal environment of adult male animals is different from that of adult females. Other brain functions, however, may be sexually dimorphic regardless of diversities in adult hormonal environment. In the former case a given identical neural substrate or circuit responds differentially according to the nature of the hormonal activation. In the latter case, the neural substrate or circuit has developed divergently in the two sexes, so as to react to one and the same hormone in quite different ways.

We shall limit the present account to the study of those brain structures and functions which have developed differentially in male and female animals, and we shall investigate some of the biological causes which induce such developmental disparities.

"Activation" of sexually dimorphic brain functions

The most obvious functional differences between male and female animals are those involved in reproductive physiology and reproductive behavior. The best-studied animal model in this respect is the rat. In the female rat, rising plasma titers of estrogens trigger a cyclic neural stimulus which activates the release of gonadotropin-releasing hormone(s) (GnRH) from the hypothalamus (positive feedback). GnRH, in turn, stimulates the release of luteinizing hormone (LH) and follicle-stimulating hormone (FSH) from the pituitary gland. The gonadotropins FSH and LH stimulate follicular maturation in the ovaries and trigger ovulation. In the male rat, rising plasma titers either of estrogens or of androgens are unable to stimulate the release of GnRH. The neural substrate which controls GnRH release has apparently developed differently in males and females.

The neural substrate which controls sexual behavior has also developed along different lines in males and females. Under the influence of estrogens and progesterone, adult female rats will respond to the mounting attempts of a sexually active male by an arching of the back, the so-called lordosis reflex. Adult male rats will hardly show any lordosis behavior, even if given the same hormone treatment. Under the influence of testosterone, adult male rats will show vigorous mounting, intromission and ejaculatory behavior towards a receptive female, whereas female rats will show little or no such responses when so treated with testosterone.

"Organization" of sexually dimorphic brain functions

Present knowledge of hormonal influences on the development of sexually dimorphic brain functions is based on a great number of studies, most of which have been carried out in the last 25 years. The individual contributions to the field of sexual brain differentiation have been discussed in several excellent reviews (Plapinger and McEwen, 1978; Booth, 1979; Goy and McEwen, 1980; Dörner, 1981; Gorski and Jacobson, 1981). In summary, there is a sensitive developmental period during which sexual differentiation of neural substrates proceeds irreversibly under the influence of gonadal hormones. In the rat this period starts a few days before birth and ends approximately 10 days after birth. Female rats treated during this sensitive period with testosterone or estradiol will permanently lose the capacity to release GnRH in response to estrogenic stimulation, and apparently the capacity to show lordosis behavior: *"defeminization"*. Instead, they will develop the capacity to show the complete masculine sexual behavior pattern following administration of testosterone in adulthood: *"masculinization"*. If castrated perinatally, male rats become unable to display male sexual behavior patterns after treatment with testosterone in adulthood: *"demasculinization"*. Instead, they will develop the capacity to show lordosis behavior, and to respond in adulthood with a positive GnRH feedback to estrogen treatment: *"feminization"*.

These studies indicate that androgens and/or estrogens, whether released by the testis or applied exogenously during the perinatal period, will permanently defeminize and masculinize neural substrates controlling sexually dimorphic brain functions (Fig. 1). Since inhibitors of aromatase activity, as well as estrogen antagonists prevent the testosterone-induced defeminization of the brain (McDonald and Doughty, 1973/74; McEwen et al., 1977; Södersten, 1978; Davis et al., 1979), the organizational effects of androgenic hormones appear, in reality, to depend upon the aromatization of these hormones to estrogens within specific brain areas (Naftolin et al., 1975).

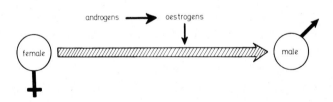

Fig. 1. Diagram summarizing contemporary thinking on the mechanism of sexual brain differentiation. The genetic program for brain development is thought to be inherently female. It will remain female unless male differentiation tendencies are epigenetically triggered by androgens or estrogens during a sensitive period. The organizational effects of androgens are thought to be mediated by intracellular conversion of these hormones in certain brain areas to estrogens (aromatization hypothesis). Diagram from Döhler and Hancke (1978) after modification.

Sexually dimorphic structures in the brain

Despite the well-known sex differences in brain functions, brain structure was for a long time believed to be essentially the same in males and females. The first anatomical sex differences observed in the mammalian brain were rather subtle. In rats Pfaff (1966) as well as Dörner and Staudt (1968, 1969) observed differences between the sexes in the size of nerve cell nuclei. Sex-linked differences in the pattern of neuronal connections were observed in rodents by Raisman and Field (1973), Dyer et al. (1976), Dyer (1984), Greenough et al. (1977), Nishizuka and Arai (1981) and De Vries et al. (1981, 1984). In all these cases the sex differences proved to be dependent upon the degree of androgen exposure during the perinatal period.

The first discovery of a gross sexual dimorphism of the brain was made by Nottebohm and Arnold (1976) on two species of song birds. During a reinvestigation of the male and female rat brain Gorski et al. (1978) and Gorski (1984) observed a striking sexual dimorphism in gross morphology of the medial preoptic area. The volume of an intensely staining area, now called the sexually dimorphic nucleus of the preoptic area (SDN-POA), is several times larger in adult male rats than in females (Gorski et al., 1978, 1980). The development of this nucleus starts during late fetal life (Jacobson and Gorski, 1981; Jacobson et al., 1980; Hsü et al., 1980) and depends on the hormonal environment during the critical period of sexual differentiation (Gorski et al., 1978; Jacobson et al., 1981; Döhler et al., 1982a,b, 1983a,b).

FEMALE BRAIN DIFFERENTIATION — A CLOSE LOOK AT SOME UNSUPPORTED ASSUMPTIONS

Sexual organization of the brain is thought to be inherently female unless male differentiation is superimposed by androgens or estrogens during a critical period of development. The organizational effects of androgens are thought to be mediated by intracellular conversion of these hormones in certain brain areas to estrogens. In other words, female differentiation is thought to proceed in the absence of specific hormonal influences, whereas male differentiation requires estrogenic stimulation (Fig. 1).

Although the concept on male differentiation of the brain is based on the results of a large number of studies (for reviews see Plapinger and McEwen, 1978; Booth, 1979; Goy and McEwen, 1980; Dörner, 1981; Gorski and Jacobson, 1981), the situation is probably more complex than is generally thought (see Döhler et al., 1983a; Vom Saal, 1983; Vom Saal et al., 1983, for discussion). The purpose of the present survey, however, was to re-examine the concept of female sexual differentiation, a concept which in fact is based more on certain assumptions than on solid experimental evidence. Before we plunge into the actual experimental studies, however, we will do well to take a close look at the most important of these assumptions.

Does fetal ovariectomy really clear the fetus of ovarian hormones?

The assumption that female sexual differentiation proceeds normally in the absence of gonadal hormones is based upon the early observation by Jost (1950) that gonadectomy of female rabbit fetuses does not interfere with female differentiation. Estrogen concentrations in mammalian fetuses are known to be very high, often higher than during later reproductive life (Reyes et al., 1974; Strott et al., 1974; Resko et al., 1975; Belisle and Tulchinsky, 1980;

Vom Saal, 1983; Vom Saal et al., 1983), and fetal ovariectomy was assumed to clear the fetal blood circulation of estrogens. Recently it was shown, however, that the fetal ovaries are in fact not the major source of the estrogens found in the fetal circulation (Kime et al., 1980; Gibori and Sridaran, 1981). In the best studied species, the human, the primary source of estrogens during pregnancy are the fetal and, to a lesser degree, the maternal adrenals. The adrenals secrete aromatizable androgens (mainly dehydroepiandrosterone sulfate) which are aromatized to estrogens in the placenta (Kime et al., 1980). There is, therefore, no reason to believe that fetal gonadectomy renders the fetus free from estrogens.

Does postnatal ovariectomy really clear the newborn rat of ovarian hormones?

In the rat, the determination of sexually dimorphic brain development occurs mostly after birth. The assumption that female sexual differentiation of the rat brain would proceed in the absence of gonadal hormones is based on the early observation by Pfeiffer (1936), that ovariectomy of newborn female rats did not interfere with female differentiation of the brain. Neonatal ovariectomy was assumed to clear the blood circulation of ovarian hormones. It was later shown, however, that the ovaries of newborn rats do not secrete any estrogens before day 7 of life (Lamprecht et al., 1976). Nevertheless, estrogen concentrations in postnatal rats are extremely high (Meijs-Roelofs et al., 1973; Weisz and Gunsalus, 1973; Döhler and Wuttke, 1975), and they remain elevated (for several days) even after adreno-ovariectomy (Weisz and Gunsalus, 1973; Kronibus and Wuttke, 1977). Although it was speculated that at least some of this material may not really be of estrogenic nature, Kronibus and Wuttke (1977) could demonstrate that when chromatographed, this material displayed an elution pattern similar to estradiol. The presence of estradiol in the circulation for several days after adreno-ovariectomy seemed unreasonable at the time, leading the authors (Kronibus and Wuttke, 1977) to regard their data as artefacts. However, it is well known that the elimination rate of estrogens from the blood circulation is much slower in immature than in adult rats (Woolley et al., 1969; De Hertogh et al., 1970; Ojeda et al., 1975; Rabh and Ganong, 1976) due to the presence of high levels of estrogen-binding a-fetoprotein (AFP) in immature rats (Nunez et al., 1971; Raynaud et al., 1971), which protect circulating estrogens from metabolism. Because of binding of estrogens to AFP, newborn rats will not be cleared from circulating estrogens, regardless of whether or not the ovaries secrete estrogens during the immediate postnatal period.

Although we may now be aware that neonatal ovariectomy fails to clear estrogens from the blood circulation, we still do not know the origin of estrogens in the neonatal rodent. Since the ovaries of newborn rats start to release estrogens only after the first week of life (Lamprecht et al., 1976) the high levels of estradiol observed in the serum of newborn rats (Döhler and Wuttke, 1975) have to originate from extraovarian sources. In the pregnant rat a great portion of circulating estrogens might originate from the fetus itself, since fetectomy was shown to reduce estrogen levels in the maternal circulation significantly (Gibori and Sridaran, 1981). In the mouse estrogen levels are higher in the fetuses than in their mothers (Vom Saal and Bronson, 1980). Alternatively, estrogens can be taken up by fetuses from the maternal circulation, where they are known to increase immensely in concentration during the last week of pregnancy (Yoshinaga et al., 1969; Shaikh, 1971). When pregnant rats were treated with [^{3}H]estradiol, the radioactivity was taken up wholly by the fetuses within 15 min and could still be detected in the newborns 5 days after birth (Friend, 1977).

It might well be that, due to the presence of estrogen-binding AFP, estrogens are preferentially retained in the fetuses and are carried over into the postnatal period. By these means animals with a short gestation (such as the rat, mouse and hamster) possess the unique ability to extend the prenatal intrauterine hormonal milieu into the postnatal period, where it is retained for at least several days, until the postnatal ovaries are able to produce their own estrogens. There is no good reason, therefore, to believe that gonadectomy of newborn rats would result in clearance of estrogens from the circulation and would render the developing organism unexposed to circulating estrogens.

Does α-fetoprotein prevent circulating estrogens from interaction with brain cells?

It may be difficult at first to imagine that male and female differentiation of the brain could be directly controlled by one and the same hormone. Since estrogens had been shown to stimulate masculinization of the brain (for review see Naftolin et al., 1975), the subsequent observations of high estrogen levels in neonatal female rats (Weisz and Gunsalus, 1973; Meijs-Roelofs et al., 1973; Döhler and Wuttke, 1975) raised the question of why female rats did not become masculinized. The proposed answer to this question was not grounded in experimental evidence. Biological activity of perinatally circulating estradiol was denied on the assumption that it was bound by AFP, which supposedly prevented estrogens from interacting with brain cells (Lieberburg and McEwen, 1975; McEwen et al., 1975).

The presence of steroid-binding proteins in the serum, however, does not seem to prevent interaction of steroids with tissue target cells. Steroid-binding proteins, including AFP, transport the steroids in a biologically inactive form, so that relatively large amounts can be continuously circulated without producing effects of hyperfunction (i.e., masculinization in females). However, such hormones are always "on call" and can be made immediately available at the target site by rapid dissociation of the steroid–protein complexes (Westphal, 1980).

The assumption that AFP prevents estrogens from interacting with brain cells becomes highly dubious in view of the presence of AFP also within brain cells (Benno and Williams, 1978; Toran-Allerand, 1980). As AFP does not appear to be synthesized within the brain (Schachter and Toran-Allerand, 1982) it must have been transported there, possibly due to active endocytosis (Mollgard et al., 1979; Dziegielewska et al., 1980). On the basis of these findings, there is no longer any reason to suppose that AFP prevents circulating estrogens from interaction with brain cells. It may even be possible that estrogens are actively transported by AFP into brain cells. By such a mechanism AFP could control the level of interaction of estrogen with brain cells.

Steroid-binding proteins (such as AFP) protect steroids from being attacked by enzymes or chemical reagents such as oxygen. They counteract adsorption to blood vessel walls or other structural elements, and they inhibit steroid uptake by the liver, thus precluding metabolism and excretion (Westphal, 1980). They might even act as carriers for the transport of estrogen into the cell (Toran-Allerand, 1984). In the case of AFP, the overall result would be the conservation of vital estrogens, which (as the following paragraph will demonstrate) are crucial not only for female differentiation of the brain but also for certain aspects of brain development.

NEW APPROACHES TO THE STUDY OF FEMALE SEXUAL DIFFERENTIATION OF THE BRAIN

The key question during the reinvestigation of female sexual differentiation was "how to get rid of estrogenic influences in fetal and neonatal organisms". Placentectomy would obviously lead to abortion, while fetal or neonatal ovariectomy or adrenalectomy would not seriously remove estrogens from the circulation (see above). We therefore decided to adopt the approach of inactivating the endogenous estrogens by treating newborn rats with the estrogen antagonist tamoxifen. Tamoxifen is known to inhibit the biological effects of estrogens (Harper and Walpole, 1967), both by competing with estrogens for intracellular estrogen receptor-binding sites and by inhibiting cytosol receptor replenishment (Nicholson et al., 1976; Jordan et al., 1977).

It has previously been shown that permanent anovulatory sterility (PAS) can be induced by postnatal treatment of female rats with a variety of estrogen antagonists, e.g. clomiphen (Gellert et al., 1971), tamoxifen (Döhler et al., 1976), nafoxidine (Clark and McCormack, 1977), MER-25 (Doughty and Booth, unpublished; Döhler, unpublished) and CI 628 (McEwen et al., 1977). If female differentiation of the brain really occurs in the absence of estrogens, perinatal treatment of female rats with estrogen antagonists should produce no lasting central effects. Therefore the effects of tamoxifen and other estrogen antagonists on induction of PAS and on permanent inhibition of female sexual receptivity appear, at least at first glance, to be similar to the effects of perinatal treatment of female rats with estrogens or aromatizable androgens, which are known to induce PAS and to reduce the capacity for the expression of female sexual behavior patterns, as mentioned above. In addition, the intracellular "behavior" of tamoxifen resembles that of estrogen. Tamoxifen is known to bind to intracellular estrogen receptors and to translocate these receptors into the nucleus in an apparently similar fashion as is done by estradiol and other estrogens (Nicholson et al., 1976; Jordan et al., 1977). The initial step in estrogen receptor movement is thought to initiate a series of activational events at the genome which eventually will result in an estrogenic biological response, viz. induction of PAS and interference with differentiation of female sexual behavior. On the basis of such similarities between tamoxifen and estrogens one is tempted to consider the possibility that the defeminizing effects of tamoxifen on the developing female brain may actually be due to estrogenic effects, rather than to estrogen antagonism.

Although the initial step of intracellular estrogen receptor translocation, induced by either tamoxifen or by estrogenic hormones, may be similar in certain respects, this fact does not provide a basis for concluding that there must be similarities in other biological effects. MacLusky et al. (1983) have shown that the ability of a compound to translocate estrogen receptors into brain cell nuclei is not necessarily related with the ability to evoke biological effects. Estradiol, for example, is more efficient than 4-hydroxyestradiol (4-OH-E$_2$) to translocate estrogen receptors into brain cell nuclei, but is less efficient than 4-OH-E$_2$ in inducing PAS. An indication that tamoxifen and estrogenic hormones act differently at the receptor or post-receptor level is the observation that tamoxifen inhibits, whereas estradiol stimulates, resynthesis of estrogen receptors in the cytosol (Nicholson et al., 1976; Jordan et al., 1977).

Action of tamoxifen on defeminization and masculinization

If the induction of PAS by tamoxifen would be caused by estrogenic activity, then treatment of newborn female rats with tamoxifen should not only result in defeminization but also in masculinization of the brain, since postnatal estrogen exposure is known to not only defeminize the brain but also to stimulate the differentiation of masculine sexual behavior patterns (Plapinger and McEwen, 1978; Booth, 1979; Goy and McEwen, 1980; Dörner 1981; Gorski and Jacobson, 1981). To test this possibility, we injected newborn female Sprague-Dawley rats subcutaneously (s.c.) with different amounts of tamoxifen, dissolved in oil (Table I). The drug was always stored in the dark and the injection solutions were freshly prepared, since tamoxifen dissociates, under the influence of light, into an isomer with a moderate estrogenic potency. This fact is not universally known and may explain some scattered reports in which tamoxifen seemed to have actually exhibited some estrogenic activity. In our hands tamoxifen never displayed any signs of estrogenic activity on the hypothalamo-pituitary axis when administered in threshold doses (Döhler et al., 1977) and when handled in the above-mentioned fashion.

TABLE I

DEFEMINIZATION BUT NO MASCULINIZATION AFTER POSTNATAL TREATMENT OF FEMALE RATS WITH TAMOXIFEN

Influence of early tamoxifen treatment (postnatal days 1–5) of female rats on the expression of male and female sexual behavior in adulthood.

Sex	Tamoxifen (μg/day)	N	Percent of animals		Number/min of	
			ovulating	showing female sexual receptivity	mounts and intromissions	intromissions
M	–	6	–	–	1.50 ± 0.05	1.33 ± 0.13
F	–	7	100	100	1.37 ± 0.32	0.61 ± 0.20
F	0.4	16	100	87.5	0.95 ± 0.42	0.56 ± 0.40
F	4	8	0	37.5	0.41 ± 0.23*	0.11 ± 0.10*
F	20	8	0	12.5	0.19 ± 0.15**	0.03 ± 0.02**

* $P = 0.05$; ** $P = 0.001$; compared with untreated females (Student's t test).

At 90 days of age all animals were ovariectomized and the ovaries inspected for the presence of corpora lutea. For the purpose of testing female sexual receptivity the animals were primed with a single injection of 5 μg estradiol benzoate (EB), followed 48 h later by a single injection of 0.5 mg progesterone (P). They were housed individually but in the company of sexually active male rats. Vaginal smears were taken on the following morning and were inspected for the presence of spermatozoa. It appeared that postnatal treatment with either 4 or 20 μg tamoxifen per day induced PAS in all animals and reduced female sexual receptivity (Table I).

Subsequently, all rats were implanted with a silastic capsule containing 1 mg testosterone propionate (TP). 3 weeks later each experimental animal was placed with a receptive female. During a test period of 20 min both the number of mounts with pelvic thrusts and the number of intromission-like behavior sequences were recorded. All tests were performed during the early dark period and were repeated 1 week later. The results of these tests make it evident that postnatal treatment of female rats with tamoxifen fails to result in an increase of male sexual behavior. On the contrary, a dose-dependent decrease was observed in the capacity for showing male patterns of mounting and intromission (see Table I).

Sexual brain functions of female rats, which had been treated postnatally with tamoxifen, were thus defeminized but not masculinized. It seems unlikely, therefore, that tamoxifen acts postnatally like an estrogen.

Comparison of the defeminizing capacity of tamoxifen and ICI 47699

There is a flaw in this conclusion, however. It may be argued that defeminization by postnatal tamoxifen was induced through estrogenic activity, whereas masculinization was prevented by estrogenic antagonism. Still, if we suppose that defeminization of developing brain functions was controlled exclusively by estrogenic influences, then compounds with strong estrogenic potency should obviously be more efficient in defeminizing the brain than are compounds with low estrogenic potency. ICI 47699 is the *cis*-isomer of tamoxifen and is known to behave in the rat like a conventional estrogen with moderate potency (Harper and Walpole, 1967). This estrogenic compound should be more potent than the, at best, weakly estrogenic isomer tamoxifen in defeminizing the brain of newborn rats. This, however, was not the case.

On an equimolar basis tamoxifen was more than 4 times as potent as ICI 47699 in inducing PAS when administered neonatally (Table II). Tamoxifen was also more potent than ICI 47699 in permanently reducing the tendency for exhibiting lordosis when primed with estradiol and progesterone as described above (Table II). These results indicate that efficiency in postnatally inducing defeminization of brain functions is not correlated with the estrogenic potency of a compound. Our results suggest instead that postnatal antagonism of estrogenic activity, rather than estrogen agonism, is the more probable explanation for the defeminizing activity of tamoxifen.

TABLE II

COMPARISON OF THE EFFECTS OF ICI 47699 AND TAMOXIFEN ON FEMALE SEXUALITY

Efects of administration of oil or equimolar doses of tamoxifen and ICI 47699 from postnatal days 1 to 5 on adult female sexuality. Lordosis quotient represents the percentage of mounts which evoke lordosis.

Postnatal treatment	Dose (μg/day)	N	Number of animals ovulating	Lordosis quotient
Oil	–	7	7	100
ICI 47699	0.5	9	9	100
	1	11	11	100
	2	8	8	100
	4	10	2	100
Tamoxifen	0.5	7	7	84.0
	1	7	0	82.7
	2	7	0	75.6
	4	10	0	70

Interference of estrogen and tamoxifen action on defeminization

Another argument in favor of the conclusion that tamoxifen causes defeminization via estrogen antagonism is found in the results of an experiment in which tamoxifen and estrogen were given simultaneously. If tamoxifen should act as an estrogen antagonist, concomitant postnatal treatment with an effective dose of estradiol would attenuate the defeminizing effect of tamoxifen. Conversely, if the defeminizing effect of tamoxifen were based on an intrinsic estrogenic action, concomitant postnatal treatment with estradiol might be expected to reinforce the effect of tamoxifen. Of course, the treatment doses of estrogen are of critical importance since at high concentrations, estradiol can itself cause a defeminization of brain functions.

Treatment of newborn female rats with 1 μg tamoxifen per day induced PAS in all animals. Concomitant postnatal treatment with 0.1 μg estradiol prevented PAS in 6 out of 10 animals (Table III). However, all animals which had been treated daily with either 1 μg tamoxifen or with 0.1 μg estradiol, or with both compounds, showed female sexual receptivity, when primed with estradiol and progesterone as described above. Treatment of newborn female rats with 4 μg tamoxifen per day induced PAS in all animals, and only 3 out of 8 animals showed female sexual receptivity. Concomitant daily treatment with either 0.05, 0.2 or 0.5 μg estradiol failed to prevent PAS, but all 3 doses prevented the defeminizing effect of tamoxifen on female sexual receptivity (Table III).

These results indicate that the defeminizing effects of tamoxifen on sexual brain functions in newborn female rats can be attenuated by concomitant treatment with appropriate doses of estradiol.

TABLE III

INTERFERENCE OF EARLY ADMINISTRATION OF ESTROGEN AND TAMOXIFEN ACTION ON FEMALE SEXUALITY

Influence of administration of tamoxifen, either alone or in combination with estradiol, to female rats from postnatal days 1 to 5 on adult female sexuality.

Postnatal treatment		N	Percentage of animals	
Tamoxifen (μg/day)	Estradiol (μg/day)		ovulating	showing female sexual receptivity
–	–	10	100	100
–	0.1	9	88.9	100
1	–	7	0	100
1	0.1	10	60	100
4	–	8	0	37.5
4	0.05	8	0	100
4	0.2	7	0	85.7
4	0.5	6	0	100

Morphological evidence for the necessity of estrogens for the development of the female brain

The data obtained from the first 3 experiments demonstrate that the defeminizing effects of tamoxifen on differentiation of sexual brain functions are the result of estrogen antagonism rather than estrogen agonism. Neuroanatomical support for this mechanism is still lacking.

We mentioned in the Introduction that the sexually dimorphic nucleus of the preoptic area (SDN-POA) in the rat brain becomes permanently enlarged when treated during the perinatal period with either estrogens (Döhler et al., 1982b, 1983a,b; Jacobson et al., unpublished) or aromatizable androgens (Gorski et al., 1978; Jacobson et al., 1981; Döhler et al., 1982a, 1983a,b). Perinatal treatment of male rats with tamoxifen inhibited SDN-POA

TABLE IV

MORPHOLOGICAL EFFECTS OF TAMOXIFEN TREATMENT ON NEWBORN FEMALE RATS

Effects of a single injection of tamoxifen on body and brain weights, formation of corpora lutea and on the volume of the sexually dimorphic nucleus of the preoptic area (SDN-POA) in adulthood. Means ± S.E.M. are listed.

Treatment (µg tamoxifen)	N	Body weight (g)	Brain weight (g)	SDN-POA volume (10^{-3} mm^3)	Animals with corpora lutea
–	8	199 ± 6	1.85 ± 0.03	6.0 ± 0.6	8
10	12	202 ± 4	1.82 ± 0.02	2.9 ± 0.3*	1
100	14	202 ± 2	1.81 ± 0.02	3.4 ± 0.4*	0

* $P = 0.01$; compared with oil control females (Duncan's multiple range test).

differentiation (Döhler et al., 1983a,b). Since administration of tamoxifen leads to behavioral and physiological defeminization it was of interest to see, whether or not tamoxifen also influences the morphological development of the SDN-POA in the female rat.

To be able to answer this question newborn female rats of the Lewis strain were injected subcutaneously with 10 or 100 µg tamoxifen in 0.05 ml vegetable oil, or with the vehicle only. Following the intraperitoneal injection of sodium pentobarbital (30 mg/kg), all animals were sacrificed at 3 months of age by intracardiac perfusion with 0.9% saline (37°C), followed by 10% formalin (37°C). The ovaries were inspected for the presence of corpora lutea. The brains were removed, weighed after comparable trimming and stored in 10 formalin for a minimum of 2 weeks. The brains were then embedded in gelatin and frozen-sectioned at 60 µm using the De Groot plane (De Groot, 1959) and stained with thionine. Using a blind procedure, 3 investigators independently estimated the boundaries of the SDN-POA on the left side of the brain in successive histological sections, with the aid of a microprojector. The 3 individual drawings were then averaged and the nuclear area was determined using

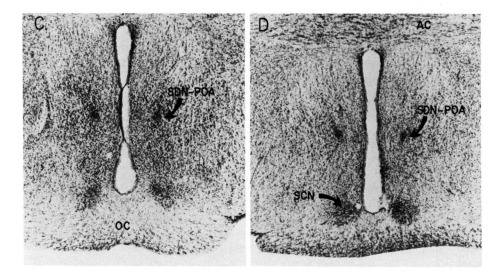

Fig. 2. The sexually dimorphic nucleus of the preoptic area (SDN-POA) as viewed in coronal sections of brains from adult female rats, treated postnatally either with oil (left) or with 100 µg tamoxifen (right). Abbreviations: AC, anterior commissure; OC, optic chiasm; SCN, suprachiasmatic nucleus; V, third ventricle.

a calibrated planimeter (see Jacobson et al., 1980, for further details). Statistical analysis of all data was performed with computer assistance and involved one-way analysis of variance (ANOVA) and Duncan's multiple range test.

Postnatal treatment with 10 or 100 μg tamoxifen did not significantly influence either body or brain weights, but reduced the volume of the SDN-POA by 52 and 43% respectively (Table IV). PAS was induced in 25 out of 26 of these animals. Representative coronal sections through the area of the SDN-POA of female rats, treated postnatally either with oil or with 100 μg tamoxifen, are shown in Fig. 2.

The fact that postnatal treatment of female rats with tamoxifen did not stimulate the maturation of the SDN-POA again indicates that tamoxifen did not act on this brain area in the manner of an estrogen. The observed inhibition of SDN-POA differentiation gives rise to the likelihood that tamoxifen may rather have inhibited estrogenic influences postnatally. Whether the observed inhibition of SDN-POA differentiation and the appearance of PAS may causally be related or may denote separate kinds of action of tamoxifen cannot be clarified at present.

Summary of results

The combined results of our 4 experiments lead to the following conclusions:

(A) Tamoxifen interferes postnatally with the process of feminization of brain functions.

(B) Tamoxifen does not masculinize brain functions when administered postnatally.

(C) Tamoxifen does not act postnatally like an estrogen agonist, but rather as an antagonist, since the defeminizing activity of tamoxifen postnatally was stronger than that of the more estrogenic ICI 47699. Furthermore, its defeminizing action was attenuated by concomitant treatment with estradiol.

(D) Tamoxifen inhibits the differentiation of the SDN-PAO in male as well as in female rats.

Abundant evidence was thus obtained supporting the hypothesis that female sexual differentiation of the brain along feminine lines does not proceed normally under estrogen-free conditions. Not only male, but also female sexual differentiation of the brain appears, therefore, to be under the influence of estrogenic hormones.

IMPORTANCE OF ESTROGEN FOR FEMALE BRAIN DEVELOPMENT

This conclusion is supported by the results from several other studies. Toran-Allerand (1976) demonstrated that hypothalamic neurons of newborn mice did not develop neurite processes in vitro when the culture medium was devoid of estrogens. Vom Saal (1983) and Vom Saal et al. (1983) observed that male and female mice, which were located in utero between two other females had higher levels of estradiol in their amniotic fluid and showed better adult sexual performance (male or female, as the case might be) but less aggressiveness than did their male or female littermates which had been located in utero between two male fetuses.

Within the framework of these and other observations (Toran-Allerand, 1980; Benno and Williams, 1978; Schachter and Toran-Allerand, 1982; MacLusky et al., 1983) our data suggest that female sexual brain differentiation, or even brain development per se may require perinatal estrogenic stimulation for its full expression. Therefore the capacity for the normal display of female sexual behavior and for the cyclic release of gonadotropins is not, as has been assumed, inherent to central nervous tissue, but depends on active hormonal induction during a sensitive period of development. Perinatal antagonism of estrogenic activity thus produces animals which are neither male nor female, behaviorally and physiologically speaking. In adulthood they respond neither to estradiol nor to testosterone, at least under the experimental conditions so far tested. Requirements for estrogenic influences on male and female brain differentiation, functional and structural, may then be quantitative rather than qualitative (Döhler, 1978; Döhler and Hancke, 1978).

FEMINIZATION VERSUS MASCULINIZATION OF THE BRAIN AS A PROCESS OF QUANTITATIVE INDUCTION BY ESTROGEN EXPOSURE

The question now arises, "how can differentiation of two such different biological mechanisms as feminization and masculinization of the brain be induced by one and the same hormone?".

Female differentiation of the brain

Our results and those of Toran-Allerand (1976) suggest that the embryonic brain is as yet undetermined for either a masculine or feminine course of development. Under the influence of moderate levels of estrogens, the embryonic sex centers in the brain differentiate into neural substrates and circuitries which will be able, in adulthood, to respond to female sex hormones (i.e. estrogens and gestagens) with a display of characteristic female sexual functions. During the period of determination of the sexual differentiation of the brain moderate levels of estrogens in the fetal blood circulation are provided by the placenta. In rodents with a short gestation period, such as the rat, mouse, and hamster, this process proceeds for the most part shortly after birth, at a time when the immature ovaries are still inactive. In these animals prenatal estrogens of maternal or placental origin are carried over into the postnatal period, probably by AFP which protects them from metabolic degradation. Although the majority of these estrogens circulate in a biologically inactive form, they are always "on-call" and are immediately available at the target site by rapid dissociation of the estrogen–AFP complex.

Male differentiation of the brain

Under the influence of sufficiently high levels of estrogens, on the other hand, the embryonic sex centers in the brain will develop and differentiate into neural substrates and circuitries which are able, in adulthood, to respond physiologically in a *male* fashion to estrogens and to aromatizable androgens. High levels of estrogens are delivered for local action on the brain by means of aromatizable androgens, released from the developing testes. Since androgens are not bound by AFP, they can reach the brain fairly rapidly, and be aromatized intracellularly into estrogens within certain brain areas. Via this mechanism, estrogens can act specifically and at high concentrations on selective brain regions without influencing other estrogen-sensitive target tissues. The question of whether or not androgens as such may, in addition, also be involved in masculinization of certain brain functions cannot be handled in the present review, but has been extensively discussed elsewhere (Döhler et al., 1983b; Vom Saal, 1983; Vom Saal et al., 1983).

Variability in sexual differentiation of the brain

The quantitative "model" of estrogenic induction of both male and female patterns of brain differentiation is illustrated in Fig. 3. This model is not only compatible with all of the presently available experimental data, but it also accounts for the seemingly confusing observations that postnatal treatment of rats with estrogen antagonists can prevent feminization as discussed above, or masculinization of the brain (McDonald and Doughty, 1973/74;

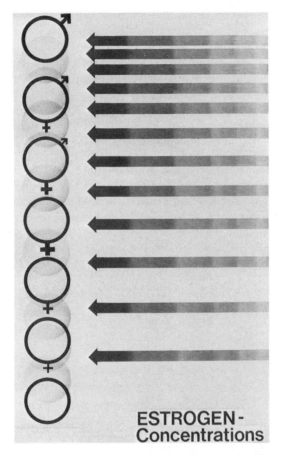

Fig. 3. Diagram summarizing the concept of quantitative induction of sexual brain differentiation. The embryonic brain (represented by the circular symbol at the bottom) is as yet undetermined for either male or female development. Under the influence of *moderate* levels of estrogens (of placental origin), represented by the widely spaced arrows, the embryonic brain elaborates neural substrates and circuitries which will be able, in adulthood, to respond to estrogens with *female* sexual functions (represented by the female symbol in the center). In contrast, under the influence of *high* levels of estrogens (represented by the closely spaced arrows) from locally acting, aromatizable androgens, which are provided by the developing testes, the embryonic brain elaborates neural substrates and circuitries which will be able, in adulthood, to respond to estrogens or to aromatizable androgens with *male* sexual functions (represented by the male symbol on top). Individual differences in the quantitative interaction of estrogens with the developing brain will lead to corresponding individual differences in sexual brain organization. This variability in sexual brain organization within a given population will be expressed in adulthood as variability in sexual functions and sexual orientation (represented by the intermediary symbols), with the extremes being hypo- and bisexuality. (Not included in the diagram is the possibility that androgens may act synergistically with estrogens during masculinization of the brain.)

McEwen et al., 1977; Södersten, 1978; Davis et al., 1979), under the appropriate respective conditions. This hypothesis can also explain the regularly observed variability in sexual functions within apparently normal populations of male or female animals. It was recently shown that an important source of variability in sexual functions within a population of rats and mice of the same sex is the intrauterine positioning of the fetuses, an effect which is directly related to the concentrations of estrogens in the fetuses (Vom Saal, 1983; Vom Saal et al., 1983). Since masculinization is established before defeminization takes place (Vreeburg et al., 1977) the model of quantitative induction of sexual brain differentiation can also explain occasional observations that males or females from an apparently normal population may also show female receptivity when mounted by a male, and may show male sexual behavior patterns in the presence of receptive females. In these cases estrogenic interaction with the developing brain may have been strong enough to cause masculinization, but not high enough to induce defeminization. The result is an animal with (demonstrable) bisexual potentialities.

ACKNOWLEDGEMENTS

This work was supported by NIH grant HD 01182 and through fellowships to K.D.D. by the Heisenberg Program, to J.L.H. by the World Health Organization, and to S.S.S. by the German Academic Exchange Service.

The authors wish to thank Mrs. E. Freiberg (Los Angeles) and Miss M. König (Hannover) for expert technical assistance, and Mr. A. Kloppenburg, Mr. S. Sekat and Mr. H. Wycenti (Studio für Werbung, Hannover) for graphic design. Tamoxifen and ICI 47699 were generously supplied by Imperial Chemical Industries (Macclesfield, Great Britain).

REFERENCES

Belisle, S. and Tulchinsky, D. (1980) Amnionic fluid hormones. In: D. Tulchinsky and K. Ryan (Eds.), *Maternal-Fetal Endocrinology*, Saunders, Philadelphia, PA, pp. 169–195.

Benno, R. and Williams, T. (1978) Evidence for intracellular localization of alpha-fetoprotein in the developing rat brain. *Brain Res.*, 142: 182–186.

Booth, J.E. (1979) Sexual differentiation of the brain. In: C.A. Finn (Ed.), *Oxford Reviews of Reproductive Biology, Vol. I*, Clarendon Press, Oxford, pp. 58–158.

Clark, J.H. and McCormack, S. (1977) Clomid or nafoxidine administered to neonatal rats causes reproductive tract abnormalities. *Science*, 197: 164–165.

Davis, P.G., Chaptal, C.V. and McEwen, B.S. (1979) Independence of the differentiation of masculine and feminine sexual behavior in rats. *Hormone Behav.*, 12: 12–19.

De Groot, J. (1959) The rat forebrain in stereotaxic coordinates. *Verh. Kon. Ned. Akad. Wet.*, 52: 1–40.

De Hertogh, R., Ekka, E., Van der Heijden, I. and Hoet, J.J. (1970) Metabolic clearance rates and the interconversion factors of estrogen and estradiol-17β in the immature and adult female rat. *Endocrinology*, 87: 874–880.

De Vries, G.J., Buijs, R.M. and Swaab, D.F. (1981) Ontogeny of the vasopressinergic neurons of the suprachiasmatic nucleus and their extrahypothalamic projection in the rat brain — presence of a sex difference in the lateral septum. *Brain Res.*, 218: 67–78.

De Vries, G.J., Buijs, R.M. and Van Leeuwen, F.W. (1984) Sex differences in vasopressin and other neurotransmitter systems in the brain. In: G.J. De Vries, J.P.C. De Bruin, H.B.M. Uylings and M.A. Corner (Eds.), *Sex Differences in the Brain. The Relation between Structure and Function. Progress in Brain Research*, this volume, Ch. 10, pp. 185–203.

Döhler, K.-D. (1978) Is female sexual differentiation hormone mediated? *Trends Neurosci.*, 1: 138–140.

Döhler K.-D. and Hancke, J.L. (1978) Thoughts on the mechanism of sexual brain differentiation. In: G. Dörner and M. Kawakami (Eds.), *Hormones and Brain Development*, Elsevier/North-Holland Biomedical Press, Amsterdam, pp. 153–158.

Döhler, K.-D. and Wuttke, W. (1975) Changes with age in levels of serum gonadotropins, prolactin, and gonadal steroids in prepubertal male and female rats. *Endocrinology*, 97: 898–907.

Döhler, K.-D., Von zur Mühlen, A. and Döhler, U. (1976) Estrogen–gonadotropin interaction in postnatal female rats, and the induction of anovulatory sterility by treatment with an estrogen antagonist. *Ann. Biol. Anim. Biochem. Biophys.*, 16: 363–372.

Döhler, K.-D., Von zur Mühlen, A. and Döhler, U. (1977) ICI 46,474 — lack of estrogenic activity in the rat. *IRCS Med. Sci.*, 5: 185.

Döhler, K.-D., Coquelin, A., Davis, F., Hines, M., Shryne, J.E. and Gorski, R.A. (1982a) Differentiation of the sexually dimorphic nucleus in the preoptic area of the rat brain is determined by the perinatal hormone environment. *Neurosci. Lett.*, 33: 295–298.

Döhler, K.-D., Hines, M., Coquelin, A., Davis, F., Shryne, J.E. and Gorski, R.A. (1982b) Pre- and postnatal influence of diethylstilboestrol on differentiation of the sexually dimorphic nucleus in the preoptic area of the female rat brain. *Neuroendocrinol. Lett.*, 4: 361–365.

Döhler, K.D., Coquelin, A., Davis, F., Hines, M., Shryne, J.E. and Gorski, R.A. (1983a) Geschlechtsunterschiede in der Grobstruktur des Rattenhirns und ihre Prägung durch Sexualhormone. *Tierärztl. Prax.*, 11: 543–550.

Döhler, K.-D., Coquelin, A., Hines, M., Davis, F., Shryne, J.E. and Gorski, R.A. (1983b) Hormonal influence on sexual differentiation of rat brain anatomy. In: J. Balthazart, E. Pröve and R. Gilles (Eds.), *Hormones and Behaviour in Higher Vertebrates*, Springer, Berlin, pp. 194–203.

Dörner, G. (1981) Sexual differentiation of the brain. *Vitam. Hormones*, 38: 325–381.

Dörner, G. and Staudt, J. (1968) Structural changes in the preoptic anterior hypothalamic area of the male rat, following neonatal castration and androgen substitution. *Neuroendocrinology*, 3: 136–140.

Dörner, G. and Staudt, J. (1969) Structural changes in the hypothalamic ventromedial nucleus of the male rat, following neonatal castration and androgen treatment. *Neuroendrocrinology*, 4: 278–281.

Dyer, R.G. (1984) Sexual differentiation of the forebrain — relationship to gonadotrophin secretion. In: G.J. De Vries, J.P.C. De Bruin, H.B.M. Uylings and M.A. Corner (Eds.), *Sex Differences in the Brain. The relation between Structure and Function. Progress in Brain Research*, this volume, Ch. 13, pp. 225–236.

Dyer, R.G., MacLeod, N.K. and Ellendorf, F. (1976) Electrophysiological evidence for sexual dimorphism and synaptic convergence in the preoptic and anterior hypothalamic areas of the rat. *Proc. R. Soc. London (Biol.)*, 193: 421–440.

Dziegielewska, K., Evans, C., Malinowska, D., Mollgard, K., Reynolds, M. and Saunders, N. (1980) Blood–cerebrospinal fluid transfer of plasma proteins during fetal development in the sheep. *J. Physiol. (London)*, 300: 457–465.

Friend, J.P. (1977) Persistance of maternally derived ^{3}H-estradiol in fetal and neonatal rats. *Experientia*, 33: 1235–1236.

Gellert, R.J., Bakke, J.L. and Lawrence, N.L. (1971) Persistent estrus and altered estrogen sensitivity in rats treated neonatally with clomiphene citrate. *Fertil. Steril.*, 22: 244–250.

Gibori, G. and Sridaran, R. (1981) Sites of androgen and estradiol production in the second half of pregnancy in the rat. *Biol. Reprod.*, 24: 249–256.

Gorski, R.A. (1984) Critical role for the medial preoptic area in the sexual differentiation of the brain. In: G.J. De Vries, J.P.C. De Bruin, H.B.M. Uylings and M.A. Corner (Eds.), *Sex Differences in the Brain. The relation between Structure and Function. Progress in Brain Research*, this volume, Ch. 7, pp. 129–146.

Gorski, R.A. and Jacobson, C.D. (1981) Sexual differentiation of the brain. In: S.J. Kogan and E.S.E. Hafez (Eds.), *Pediatric Andrology*, Martinus Nijhoff, The Hague, pp. 109–134.

Gorski, R.A., Gordon, J.H., Shryne, J.E. and Southam, A.M. (1978) Evidence for a morphological sex difference within the medial preoptic area of the rat brain. *Brain Res.*, 148: 333–346.

Gorski, R.A., Harlan, R.E., Jacobson, C.D., Shryne, J.E. and Southam, A.M. (1980) Evidence for the existence of a sexually dimorphic nucleus in the preoptic area of the rat. *J. Comp. Neurol.*, 193: 529–539.

Goy, R.W. and McEwen, B.S. (1980) *Sexual Differentiation of the Brain*, Massachusetts Institute of Technology Press, Cambridge, MA.

Greenough, W.T., Carter, C.S., Steerman, C. and De Voogt, T.J. (1977) Sex differences in dendritic patterns in hamster preoptic area. *Brain Res.*, 126: 63–72.

Harper, M.J.K. and Walpole, A.L. (1967) A new derivative of triphenyl-ethylene: effect on implantation and mode of action in rats. *J. Reprod. Fertil.*, 13: 101–119.

Hsü, H.K., Chen, F.N. and Peng, M.T. (1980) Some characteristics of the darkly stained area of the medial preoptic area of rats. *Neuroendocrinology*, 31: 327–330.

Jacobson, C.D. and Gorski, R.A. (1981) Neurogenesis of the sexually dimorphic nucleus of the preoptic area in the rat. *J. Comp. Neurol.*, 196: 519–529.

Jacobson, C.D., Shryne, J.E., Shapiro, F. and Gorski, R.A. (1980) Ontogeny of the sexually dimorphic nucleus of the preoptic area. *J. Comp. Neurol.*, 193: 541–548.

Jacobson, C.D., Csernus, V.J., Shryne, J.E. and Gorski, R.A. (1981) The influence of gonadectomy, androgen exposure, or a gonadal graft in the neonatal rat on the volume of the sexually dimorphic nucleus of the preoptic area. *J. Neurosci.*, 1: 1142–1147.

Jordan, V.C., Dix, C.J., Rowsby, L. and Prestwich, G. (1977) Studies on the mechanism of action of the non-steroidal antioestrogen tamoxifen in the rat. *Mol. Cell. Endocrinol.*, 7: 177–192.

Jost, A. (1950) Sur le contrôle hormonal de différenciation sexuelle du lapin. *Arch. Anat. Microscop. Morphol. Exp.*, 39: 577–598.

Kime, D., Vinson, G., Major, P. and Kilpatrick, R. (1980) Adrenal-gonad relationships. In: I. Jones and I. Henderson (Eds.), *General, Comparative and Clinical Endocrinology of the Adrenal Cortex, Vol. 3*, Academic Press, New York, pp. 183–264.

Kronibus, J. and Wuttke, W. (1977) Positive feedback action of oestradiol on gonadotrophin release in 15 day old female rats. *Acta Endocrinol.*, 86: 263–272.

Lamprecht, S.A., Kohen, F., Ausher, J., Zor, U. and Lindner, H. (1976) Hormonal stimulation of estradiol-17β release from the rat ovary during early postnatal development. *J. Endocrinol.*, 68: 343–344.

Lieberburg, I. and McEwen, B.S. (1975) Estradiol-17β metabolite of testosterone recovered in cell nuclei from limbic areas of neonatal rat brains. *Brain Res.*, 85: 165–170.

MacLusky, N.J., Riskalla, M., Krey, L., Parvizi, N. and Naftolin, F. (1983) Anovulation in female rats induced by neonatal administration of the catechol estrogens, 2-hydroxy-estradiol and 4-hydroxy-estradiol. *Neuroendocrinology*, 37: 321–327.

McDonald, P.G. and Doughty, C. (1973/74) Androgen sterilization in the neonatal female rat and its inhibition by an estrogen antagonist. *Neuroendocrinology*, 13: 182–188.

McEwen, B.S., Chaptal, C., Gerlach, J., and Wallach, G. (1975) The role of fetoneonatal estrogen binding proteins in the associations of estrogen with neonatal brain cell nuclear receptors. *Brain Res.*, 96: 400–406.

McEwen, B.S., Lieberburg, I., Chaptal, C. and Krey, L.C. (1977) Aromatization: important for sexual differentiation of the neonatal rat brain. *Hormone Behav.*, 9: 249–263.

Meijs-Roelofs, H.M.A., Uilenbroek, J.Th., de Jong, F.H. and Welschen, R. (1973) Plasma oestradiol-17β and its relationship to serum follicle-stimulating hormone in immature female rats. *J. Endocrinol.*, 59: 295–304.

Mollgard, K., Jacobson, M., Praetorius-Clausen, P. and Saunders, N. (1979) Immunochemical evidence for and intracellular localization of plasma proteins in human fetal choroid plexus and brain. *Neurosci. Lett.*, 14: 85–90.

Naftolin, F., Ryan, K.J., Davies, I.J., Reddy, V.V., Flores, F., Pedro, Z., Kuhn, M., White, R.J., Takaoko, J. and Wolin, L. (1975) The formation of oestrogens by central neuroendocrine tissue. *Recent Progr. Hormone Res.*, 31: 259–319.

Nicholson, R.I., Golder, M.P., Davies, P. and Griffiths, K. (1976) Effects of oestradiol-17β and tamoxifen on total and accessible cytoplasmic oestradiol-17β-receptors in DMBA-induced rat mammary tumours. *Eur. J. Cancer*, 12: 711–717.

Nishizuka, M. and Arai, Y. (1981) Sexual dimorphism in synaptic organization in the amygdala and its dependence on neonatal hormone environment. *Brain Res.*, 212: 31–38.

Nottebohm, F. and Arnold, A.P. (1976) Sexual dimorphism in vocal control areas of the songbird brain. *Science*, 194: 211–213.

Nunez, E.A., Engelmann, F., Benassayag, C., Savu, L., Crepy, O. and Jayle, M.F. (1971) Mise en évidence d'une fraction protéique liant les œstrogènes dans le sérum de rats impubères. *C.R. Acad. Sci. (Paris) D*, 272: 2396–2399.

Ojeda, S.R., Kalra, P.S. and McCann, S.M. (1975) Further studies on the maturation of the estrogen negative feedback on gonadotropin release in the female rat. *Neuroendocrinology*, 18: 242–255.

Pfaff, D.W. (1966) Morphological changes in the brains of adult male rats after neonatal castration. *J. Endocrinol.*, 36: 415–416.

Pfeiffer, C.A. (1936) Sexual differences in the hypophyses and their determination by the gonads. *Am. J. Anat.*, 58: 195–226.

Plapinger, L. and McEwen, B.S. (1978) Gonadal steroid–brain interactions in sexual differentiation. In: J.B. Hutchison (Ed.), *Biological Determinants of Sexual Behaviour*, John Wiley, Chichester, NY, pp. 153–218.

Rabh, J. and Ganong, W.F. (1976) Responses of plasma estradiol and plasma LH to ovariectomy, ovariectomy plus adrenalectomy, and estrogen injection at various ages. *Neuroendocrinology*, 20: 270–281.

Raisman, G. and Field, P.M. (1973) Sexual dimorphism in neuropil of the preoptic area of the rat and its dependence on neonatal androgen. *Brain Res.*, 54: 1–29.

Raynaud, J.P., Mercier-Bodard, C. and Baulieu, E.E. (1971) Rat estradiol binding plasma protein. *Steroids*, 18: 767–787.

Resko, J.A., Ploem, J.G. and Stadelman, H.L. (1975) Estrogens in fetal and maternal plasma of the rhesus monkey. *Endocrinology*, 97: 425–430.

Reyes, F.I., Boroditsky, R.S., Winter, J.S.D. and Faiman, C. (1974) Studies on human sexual development. II. Fetal and maternal serum gonadotropin and sex steroid concentrations. *J. Clin. Endocrinol. Metab.*, 38: 612–617.

Schachter, B. and Toran-Allerand, C.D. (1982) Intraneural alpha-fetoprotein and albumin are not synthesized locally in developing brain. *Develop. Brain Res.*, 5: 93–98.

Shaikh, A.A. (1971) Estrone and estradiol levels in the ovarian venous blood from rats during the estrous cycle and pregnancy. *Biol. Reprod.*, 5: 297–307.

Södersten, P. (1978) Effects of anti-oestrogen treatment of neonatal male rats on lordosis behaviour and mounting behaviour in the adult. *J. Endocrinol.*, 76: 241–249.

Strott, C.A., Sundrel, H. and Stahlman, M.L. (1974) Maternal and fetal plasma progesterone, cortisol, testosterone and 17β-estradiol in preparturient sheep: response to fetal ACTH infusion. *Endocrinology*, 95: 1327–1339.

Toran-Allerand, C.D. (1976) Sex steroids and the development of the newborn mouse hypothalamus and preoptic area in vitro: Implications for sexual differentiation. *Brain Res.*, 106: 407–412.

Toran-Allerand, C.D. (1980) Coexistence of alpha-fetoprotein, albumin and transferrin immunoreactivity in neurons of the developing mouse brain. *Nature (London)*, 286: 733–735.

Toran-Allerand, C.D. (1984) On the genesis of sexual differentiation of the central nervous system: morphogenetic consequences of steroidal exposure and possible role of α-fetoprotein. In: G.J. De Vries, J.P.C. De Bruin, H.B.M. Uylings and M.A. Corner (Eds.), *Sex Differences in the Brain. The Relation between Structure and Function. Progress in Brain Research*, this volume, Ch. 4, pp. 63–98.

Vom Saal, F.S. (1983) The interaction of circulating estrogens and androgens in regulating mammalian sexual differentiation. In: J. Balthazart, E. Pröve and R. Giles (Eds.), *Hormones and Behaviour in Higher Vertebrates*, Springer, Berlin, pp. 194–203.

Vom Saal, F.S. and Bronson, F.H. (1980) Sexual characteristics of adult female mice are correlated with their blood testosterone levels during prenatal development. *Science*, 208: 597–599.

Vom Saal, F.S., Grant, W.M., McMullen, C.W. and Laves, K.S. (1983) High fetal estrogen concentrations: correlation with increased adult sexual performace and decreased aggression in male mice. *Science*, 220: 1306–1309.

Vreeburg, J.T.M., Van der Vaart, P.D.M. and Van der Schoot, P. (1977) Prevention of central defeminization but not masculinization in male rats by inhibition neonatally of oestrogen biosynthesis. *J. Endocrinol.*, 74: 375–382.

Weisz, J. and Gunsalus, P. (1973) Estrogen levels in immature female rats: true or spurious — ovarian or adrenal? *Endocrinology*, 93: 1057–1065.

Westphal, U. (1980) Mechanism of steroid binding to transport proteins. In: E. Genazzani, F. Di Carlo and W.I.P. Mainwaring (Eds.), *Pharmacological Modulation of Steroid Action*, Raven, New York, pp. 33–47.

Woolley, D.E., Holinka, C.F. and Timiras, P.S. (1969) Changes in ^{3}H-estradiol distribution with development in the rat. *Endocrinology*, 84: 157–161.

Yoshinaga, K., Hawkins, R.A. and Stocker, J.F. (1969) Estrogen secretion by the rat ovary in vivo during the estrous cycle and pregnancy. *Endocrinology*, 85: 103–112.

DISCUSSION

G.J. de VRIES: You have mentioned tamoxifen as a substance that binds to a cytosolic estrogen receptor and then is translocated into the nucleus but that, in that stage, blocks further estrogenic effects. Did you consider a direct action of tamoxifen on other sites, e.g. as has been demonstrated for estrogen, on membranes?

K.-D. DÖHLER: There are still many questions about intracellular and extracellular actions of estrogens and their possible participation in sexual differentiation. Moss and Dudley (1984) and others have shown that estrogens may exert actions on cell membranes for which penetration and nuclear translocation are not required. Moss and Dudley (1984) have also demonstrated a membrane effect of estrogen antagonists, in particular tamoxifen. Other research groups have suggested the presence of intracellular binding sites which are specific for estrogen antagonists, but do not bind estrogens. I have discussed our data only in traditional terms, i.e. tamoxifen inhibits binding of estrogens. I do not want to exclude the possibility that tamoxifen may influence sexual differentiation via action on cell membranes or via interaction with a specific intracellular receptor for estrogen antagonists. Your question actually raises some interesting points for future research. The mechanism of sexual differentiation is so complex; why should different components within this complex not be induced or controlled by different cellular modes of estrogenic action?

D.H. ABBOTT: In view of your behavioral findings, do you think we should re-name "feminization" as "incomplete masculinization", or "masculinization" as "supra-feminization"?

K.-D. DÖHLER: The adjectives "incomplete" or "supra" would add a measure of value to the process of sexual differentiation. Although terminologies are helpful in communication, terminologies per se rarely explain biological mechanisms. If I have a choice, I would prefer to consider "masculinization" and "feminization" as a mode of variability of "sexuality" in general.

H.J. ROMIJN: Is it indeed fully excluded, as you suggested, that not any gene located on the Y-chromosome plays a role in the maturation of the male brain?

K.-D. DÖHLER: "Sex reversal" of the volume of the sexually dimorphic nucleus (SDN-POA) was achieved by treating female rats perinatally which testosterone propionate (Döhler et al., 1982a) or with diethylstilbestrol (Döhler et al., 1982b) and by treating male rats perinatally with tamoxifen (Döhler et al., 1983). These findings may indicate that the sex chromosomes may have little or no influence on differentiation of the SDN-POA. It can all be done by hormones. We even can reduce the volume of the SDN-POA by treating female rats postnatally with tamoxifen (this paper). However, even with prolonged treatment with tamoxifen we could never eliminate development of this nucleus totally. This finding leaves room for a possible involvement of chromosomal influences. The appropriate genes would, however, not necessarily have to be located on a sex chromosome, they could be located on an autosome, since a basic development of the SDN-POA (without apparent influence of hormones) can be seen in both sexes.

J.M. REINISCH: How would you argue against the possibility that tamoxifen is toxic, rather than acting as an antagonist?

K.-D. DÖHLER: If tamoxifen were toxic, we should have observed other functional deficiencies or degenerative influences on other brain nuclei than the sexually dimorphic nucleus. At least in the vicinity of the preoptic area and anterior hypothalamus we did not observe other degenerative influences after perinatal treatment with tamoxifen.

S.M. BREEDLOVE: Another argument against tamoxifen acting in a toxic fashion is the result that simultaneous injection of estradiol blocks the defeminization effect of tamoxifen. One would expect these results only if tamoxifen is competitively, but reversibly acting via an estrogen-receptor-mediated mechanism rather than some general, poisoning effect.

C.D. TORAN-ALLERAND: Tamoxifen effect is probably not due to toxicity since other studies (Stewart and Cygan, 1980) favor estrogen in low, non-masculinizing levels as having a feminizing effect in castrated male or female neonatal rats.

REFERENCES

Döhler, K.-D., Coquelin, A., Davis, F., Hines, M., Shryne, J.E. and Gorski, R.A. (1982a) Differentiation of the sexually dimorphic nucleus in the preoptic area of the rat brain is determined by the perinatal hormone environment. *Neurosci. Lett.*, 33: 295–298.
Döhler, K.-D., Hines, M., Coquelin, A., Davis, F., Shryne, J.E. and Gorski, R.A. (1982b) Pre- and postnatal influence of diethylstilboestrol on differentiation of the sexually dimorphic nucleus in the preoptic area of the female rat brain. *Neuroendocrinol. Lett.*, 4: 361–365.

Döhler, K.-D., Coquelin, A., Hines, M., Davis, F., Shryne, J.E. and Gorski, R.A. (1983) Hormonal influence on sexual differentiation of rat brain anatomy. In: J. Balthazart, E. Pröve and R. Gilles (Eds.), *Hormones and Behaviour in Higher Vertebrates*, Springer, Berlin, pp. 194–203.

Moss, R.L. and Dudley, C.A. (1984) Molecular aspects of the interaction between estrogen and the membrane excitability of hypothalamic nerve cells. In: G.J. De Vries, J.P.C. De Bruin, H.B.M. Uylings and M.A. Corner (Eds.), *Sex Differences in the Brain. The Relation between Structure and Function. Progress in Brain Research*, this volume, Ch. 1, pp. 3–22.

Stewart, J. and Cygan, D. (1980) Ovarian hormones act early in development to feminize adult open-field behavior in the rat. *Hormone Behav.*, 14: 20–32.

G.J. De Vries et al. (Eds.),
Progress in Brain Research, Vol. 61
© 1984 Elsevier Science Publishers B.V., Amsterdam

Serotoninergic Influences
on Sexual Differentiation of the Rat Brain

BARBARA JARZAB* and KLAUS D. DÖHLER**

Department of Clinical Endocrinology, University Medical School, 3000 Hannover (F.R.G.)

INTRODUCTION

Although the influence of gonadal steroids on sexual differentiation of the brain has extensively been studied (Döhler et al., 1984; Gorski, 1984), very little is known yet about the detailed physiological and molecular mechanisms of steroid-induced sexual differentiation. There are some indications that biogenic amines may be involved in this process, since a number of tranquilizers and psychotrophic drugs known to influence biogenic amine activity have been shown to influence sexual differentiation of the brain (for review see Booth, 1979; Dörner, 1981). These drugs were demonstrated to permanently change, when administered postnatally, not only the pattern of gonadotropic hormone release and sexual behavior but also the structure and chemistry of specific brain areas (Dörner et al., 1977; Staudt et al., 1978).

DOES SEROTONIN MEDIATE THE INFLUENCE OF SEX STEROIDS ON SEXUAL DIFFERENTIATION OF THE BRAIN?

A prime candidate for mediation of sex hormone activity during sexual differentiation of the brain seems to be the serotoninergic system. Serotonin levels in the brains of 12-day-old rats were shown to be higher in females than in males (Ladosky and Gaziri, 1972; Giulian et al., 1973). Castration of newborn males gave rise to increased serotonin levels in the brain (Ladosky and Gaziri, 1972), whereas treatment of newborn females with androgens resulted in reduced brain serotonin content on days 12 and 14 (Giulian et al., 1973).

Although these studies suggest a relationship between masculinization of the brain and reduced brain serotonin levels during development, they fail to indicate whether the reduced serotonin levels are a cause for, or a consequence of masculinization. The fact that the critical period for steroid-induced masculinization of the brain is limited to the first 10 days of life, whereas the sex differences in brain serotonin levels were observed only after this period, favors the latter assumption, viz., that reduced serotonin levels in 10–14-day-old male and in androgenized female rat brains are a consequence rather than a cause of masculinization. On the other hand, there are a variety of experimental data which suggest the active partici-

---

* Research fellow of the German Academic Exchange Service.
** Heisenberg fellow.

pation of the serotoninergic system in sexual differentiation of the brain immediately after birth. Shirama et al. (1975) observed that postnatal treatment of female rats with the serotonin precursor 5-hydroxytryptophan delayed the permanent anovulatory sterility (PAS)-inducing effect of postnatal testosterone proprionate (TP). An even stronger protective effect on androgen-induced PAS was observed when rats were treated postnatally with the serotonin synthesis inhibitor *para*-chlorophenylalanine (pCPA) (Reznikov et al., 1979). Hyyppä et al. (1972), however, reported that postnatal treatment of rats with pCPA had no influence on cyclicity, but that it reduced ear-wiggling behavior in females and stimulated male sexual behavior in males.

Since these data are rather contradictory, and do not provide conclusive answers on how serotonin may influence sexual differentiation, we tried to re-examine these data by using a different approach. We studied not only the possible influence of the serotonin synthesis inhibitor pCPA on defeminization and masculinization of brain functions, but also the influence of the serotonin precursor L-tryptophan. In addition, we wanted to eliminate possible direct effects of the drugs on testicular function, which could mask direct effects of drugs on the developing brain. Therefore, we induced defeminization and masculinization by treating newborn female rats with TP.

EXPERIMENTAL PROCEDURES

Newborn female Sprague–Dawley rats were injected subcutaneously (s.c.), daily during the first 5 days of life, either with 20 μg TP dissolved in 0.025 ml sesame oil or with the oil vehicle only. All TP-treated animals received additional s.c. injections either of pCPA (0.1 mg daily on days 1–3, and 0.5 mg daily on days 4–7) or of L-tryptophan (0.5 mg daily on days 1–7) or of 0.025 ml of the solvent. The solvent consisted of 10% gum acacia and 1 mM ascorbic acid, dissolved in 0.9% NaCl (pH 5.5). The first injections were given 2 h after birth (day 1). TP was injected approximately 5 min after pCPA or L-tryptophan had been administered. The injection sites were sealed with Novecutan (Astra, F.R.G.).

All animals were born and raised under identical specific pathogen-free, temperature-controlled ($21 \pm 1\,^\circ$C) and light-controlled conditions (light period from 5.00 to 17.00 h).

OVULATION AND GONADOTROPIN RELEASE

At 80 days of age all animals were ovariectomized and the ovaries were inspected for the presence or absence of corpora lutea. The ovaries of control rats, which had been treated with sesame oil postnatally, contained corpora lutea (Table I), which indicates that ovulation had occurred. The ovaries of all rats which had been treated with TP, with or without pCPA or L-tryptophan, contained large follicles but no corpora lutea (Table I).

At 90 days of age, the animals received a single injection of 20 μg estradiol benzoate (EB) at 10.00 h, dissolved in 0.05 ml sesame oil, which was followed 48 h later by a single injection of 2.5 mg progesterone (P) in the same vehicle. Blood samples were withdrawn from the retro-bulbar venous plexus under ether anesthesia 1 h before, as well as 48, 54 and 72 h after EB injection. The serum samples were stored temporarily at $-20\,^\circ$C, and serum levels of luteinizing hormone (LH) were determined by RIA (NIAMDD-kit), as described previously (Döhler et al., 1977).

TABLE I

EFFECTS OF pCPA AND L-TRYPTOPHAN ON FEMALE SEXUALITY

Sex	Postnatal treatment	N	Animals with corpora lutea	Lordosis quotient	
				After priming with EB + P	After priming with EB + oil
M	Oil	12	–	13.0 ± 9.0**	Not tested
F	Oil	11	11	67.8 ± 8.2	7.2 ± 2.8***
F	TP + solvent	10	0	61.5 ± 11.8	47.0 ± 9.2
F	TP + pCPA	8	0	46.3 ± 9.8	42.5 ± 13.3
F	TP + L-tryptophan	9	0	12.1 ± 8.1**	18.0 ± 6.8*

* $P < 0.05$; ** $P < 0.01$; *** $P < 0.001$, significantly different from females treated postnatally with TP + solvent. Statistical analysis by analysis of variance (ANOVA).

Lordosis quotients in adult gonadectomized male (M) and female rats (F) after priming with 20 μg estradiol benzoate (EB) followed by 2.5 mg progesterone (P) or 0.05 ml sesame oil. All animals had been treated postnatally (days 1–5) either with 20 μg testosterone propionate (TP) daily or with 0.025 ml of sesame oil. All TP-treated animals received additional treatment postnatally either with para-chlorophenylalanine (pCPA: 0.1 mg days 1–3, 0.5 mg days 4–7), or with L-tryptophan (0.5 mg days 1–7) or with the solvent (0.025 ml days 1–7). Means ± S.E.M. are listed.

Serum levels of LH after gonadectomy were significantly higher in control rats (male and female) than in the rats which had been treated postnatally with ($P < 0.05$). Additional postnatal treatment with pCPA or with L-tryptophan did not alter serum levels of LH in comparison to postnatal treatment with TP only (Fig. 1). Treatment of gonadectomized rats with EB resulted in an initial decrease in serum LH levels in all groups. However, a subsequent rise in serum LH levels, as a result of a positive feedback mechanism of EB + P on LH release, was observed only in control females (Fig. 1).

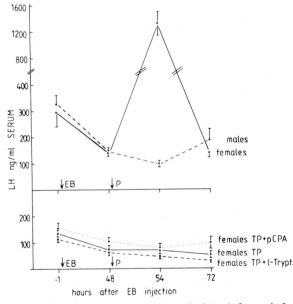

Fig. 1. Serum levels of luteinizing hormone (LH) in gonadectomized rats before and after treatment with 20 μg estradiol benzoate (EB), followed 48 h later by a single injection of 2.5 mg progesterone (P). Top: Control male and female rats which had been treated postnatally with sesame oil. Bottom: Female rats which had been treated postnatally either with testosterone propionate (TP), or with TP and para-chlorophenylalanine (pCPA), or with TP and L-tryptophan (l-Trypt.) daily. Means ± S.E.M. are listed.

Our own data, therefore, fail to confirm the protective effect either of postnatal serotonin synthesis inhibition by pCPA on testosterone-induced anovulation reported by Reznikov et al. (1979) or of elevated brain serotonin levels on TP-induced anovulation (cf. Shirama et al., 1975). Instead, we demonstrated that postnatal treatment of female rats with TP permanently abolished the positive feedback effect of EB on LH release, nor was concomitant postnatal treatment with either pCPA or L-tryptophan able to restore this mechanism (Fig. 1).

FEMALE SEXUAL BEHAVIOR

All animals received a single injection of 20 μg EB (at 11.00 h) at approximately 100 days of age, followed 48 h later by a single injection of 2.5 mg P. During the early dark period of the same day, the animals were placed individually with 2 sexually active male rats. The total number of lordosis responses by the test animals was counted in response to 20 mounting attempts from the stud males, and a lordosis quotient (LQ) was calculated (number of lordoses : number of mounts × 100). The entire procedure for lordosis testing was repeated 1 week later, but this time with EB and without P priming.

The LQ in female control rats was significantly higher after EB + P priming than after priming with EB only (Table I). Postnatal treatment with TP or with TP + pCPA did not significantly change the LQ after EB + P priming. Postnatal treatment with TP + L-tryptophan, however, resulted in significantly lower lordosis scores after EB + P priming than in any other group of female rats. Lordosis quotients after EB priming were significantly lower both in control rats and in rats treated postnatally with TP + L-tryptophan than in rats treated postnatally either with TP or with TP + pCPA (Table I). Clemens et al. (1969) had previously described the same phenomenon, viz. that, after priming with EB only, normal control rats showed less lordosis responsiveness than did rats treated postnatally with TP. This phenomenon may indicate increased responsiveness to estradiol in rats treated postnatally with TP.

Since lordosis behavior in female rats which had been treated postnatally with TP + pCPA was similar to the lordosis behavior of rats treated postnatally with TP only, there is no indication that pCPA may have either promoted or prevented the postnatal effect of TP on lordosis behavior. In contrast, postnatal stimulation of serotonin synthesis by L-tryptophan significantly influenced the expression of female sexual behavior patterns in TP-treated rats. Female rats treated postnatally with TP plus L-tryptophan showed very little lordosis behavior after priming with either EB or EB + P.

MALE SEXUAL BEHAVIOR

At 120 days of age, all animals received s.c. implants of silastic tubing (30 mm length, 2.5 mm outer diameter, 1.5 mm inner diameter) which contained 25–30 mg of TP. The animals were then housed individually in order to avoid the establishment of dominance hierarchies, which have been shown to influence the sexual behavior pattern of male rats (Swanson and Van de Poll, 1983). At 21, 25, 28 and 35 days after application of the TP implant, the animals were placed individually in a test arena where they were allowed to adapt for 2 h. Subsequently, an ovariectomized female rat which had been brought into heat by priming with EB and P was placed in the arena for 20 min. Sexual encounters were not recorded on days 21 and 25 after implantation of TP, since the animals were only supposed to get familiar with the test situation. Only on day 28 and day 35 were the total number of mounts and intromission approaches counted for each test animal during the test period. All animals were subsequently checked for the presence of the TP implants.

As indicators of male type sexual activities, the behavioral approach patterns of the test animals toward receptive females were observed. We recorded the frequency of mounts with pelvic thrusting, including those showing the characteristic intromission pattern ("mount frequency"), and the frequency of intromission patterns ("intromission frequency") separately. Since female rats of course cannot achieve a physical intromission, we regarded those behavioral approach patterns as intromission patterns which were similar to the behavioral patterns of intact males during and after successful intromission. The frequency both of mounts and of intromission patterns was significantly higher in intact male rats than in any group of females (Table II). Female rats which had been treated with TP postnatally, exhibited a higher frequency of mounts than did control females, but there was no difference in intromission frequency between the two groups. The frequency of mounts and of intromissions was not significantly different in animals treated postnatally with TP + pCPA, when compared to the animals treated with TP only. Postnatal treatment with L-tryptophan, however, significantly reduced the stimulatory effect of postnatal TP on mount frequency, while reducing the frequency of intromissions below the frequency observed in any other group of females.

TABLE II

EFFECTS OF pCPA AND L-TRYPTOPHAN ON MALE SEXUALITY

Sex	Postnatal treatment	N	Frequency/min of	
			mounts	intromissions
M	None	12	2.26 ± 0.15**	1.95 ± 0.14**
F	Oil	11	0.73 ± 0.10**	0.63 ± 0.05
F	TP + solvent	10	1.41 ± 0.11	0.59 ± 0.10
F	TP + pCPA	8	1.20 ± 0.13	0.48 ± 0.13
F	TP + L-tryptophan	9	0.68 ± 0.22*	0.11 ± 0.04**

* $P < 0.01$; ** $P < 0.001$, significantly different from females treated postnatally with TP + solvent. Statistical analysis by analysis of variance (ANOVA).
Male sexual behavior patterns (mounts and intromission patterns) in adult gonadectomized female rats (F) after priming with testosterone propionate (TP). All animals had been treated postnatally either with 20 μg TP daily (days 1–5) or with 0.025 ml of sesame oil. All animals, which had been treated with TP postnatally, received additional treatment either with *para*-chlorophenylalanine (pCPA: 0.1 mg days 1–3, 0.5 mg days 4–7), or with L-tryptophan (0.5 mg days 1–7) or with the solvent (0.025 ml days 1–7). Intact adult male rats (M) were included for comparison. Means ± S.E.M. are listed.

CONCLUDING REMARKS

In summary, our results indicate that postnatal inhibition of serotonin synthesis neither stimulates nor inhibits the effects of postnatal TP on either the pattern of gonadotropin release or the expression of male and female sexual behavior. Postnatal stimulation of serotonin synthesis, however, significantly inhibited the expression of male and female sexual behavior patterns, but it had no influence on the pattern of gonadotropin release. Our results do not allow for an indubitable conclusion about the possible influence of serotonin in sexual differentiation of gonadotropic hormone release. Re-examination of this question using threshold levels of TP may provide more conclusive data, since our rats had received rather high doses of TP during 5 consecutive days.

In contrast to the inconclusive data about the possible influence of serotonin on differentiation of the gonadotropin release pattern, the available data about the possible influence of serotonin on differentiation of sexual behavior patterns are less problematic. Increased availability of serotonin in TP-treated rats, due to the administration of L-tryptophan, interfered significantly with the differentiation both of male and female sexual behavior patterns. Thus, serotonin seems to have a similar inhibitory effect on postnatal "organization" of male and female sexual behavior patterns as it has on "activation" in adulthood. Treatment of adult rats with a serotonin precursor or with serotonin agonists has been shown to inhibit the expression of female and male sexual behavior (Meyerson, 1954; Malmnäs, 1973; Michanek and Meyerson, 1977). The extent to which serotonin and testosterone interact during sexual differentiation of the brain remains uncertain. It is also not clear whether this interaction takes place before or after testosterone has been converted into estradiol within the brain (e.g., Naftolin et al., 1975).

Döhler and Hancke (1978), Vom Saal et al. (1983), and Döhler et al. (1984) have all suggested that the differentiation of both male and female sexual behavior might be controlled by estrogens. Rats and mice which had been exposed to high levels of estrogens during intrauterine development were more efficient in the expression of male or female sexual behavior in adulthood than were rats which had been exposed to low levels (Vom Saal et al., 1983). Treatment of newborn rats with the estrogen antagonist tamoxifen interfered with the differentiation of both male and female sexual behavior patterns (Döhler et al., 1984). The fact that postnatal treatment of rats either with TP + L-tryptophan or with tamoxifen had similar defeminizing and demasculinizing effects on differentiation of sexual behavior patterns may point to a similar mechanism of action in the two experiments, possibly via interference with the activity of circulating estrogens. The question of participation of serotonin in sexual differentiation of the brain leaves two additional questions unanswered. First of all, what is the biological purpose for the elevation of serotonin levels in female rats 12–14 days after birth, at a time when steroid-induced sexual differentiation is already completed? If this elevation of serotonin levels in female rats is indeed involved in sexual differentiation of the brain (demasculinization?), then the search for an answer to the second question may result in a reconsideration of the thinking on the mechanism of sexual brain differentiation: how can postnatal treatment of rats with TP or EB have opposite effects on subsequent serotonin levels in the brain (see Giulian et al., 1973), when they seem to have similar effects on masculinization and defeminization of brain function (see Plapinger and McEwen, 1978; Booth, 1979; Goy and McEwen, 1980; Dörner, 1981; Gorski and Jacobson, 1981)?

ACKNOWLEDGMENTS

The authors wish to thank Miss M. König, Mrs. S. Hanssen and Miss P. Sickmöller (Hannover) for invaluable assistance.

REFERENCES

Booth, J.E. (1979) Sexual differentiation of the brain. In: C.A. Finn (Ed.), *Oxford Reviews of Reproductive Biology, Vol. I*, Clarendon Press, Oxford, pp. 58–158.

Clemens, L.G., Hiroi, M. and Gorski, R.A. (1969) Induction and facilitation of female mating behavior in rats treated neonatally with low doses of testosterone propionate. *Endocrinology*, 84: 1430–1438.

Döhler, K.-D. and Hancke, J.L. (1978) Thoughts on the mechanism of sexual brain differentiation. In: G. Dörner and M. Kawakami (Eds.), *Hormones and Brain Development*, Elsevier/North-Holland Biomedical Press, Amsterdam, pp. 153–158.

Döhler, K.-D., Gärtner, K., Von zur Mühlen, A. and Döhler, U. (1977) Activation of anterior pituitary, thyroid and adrenal gland in rats after disturbance stress. *Acta Endocrinol.*, 86: 489–497.

Döhler, K.-D., Hancke, J.L., Srivastava, S.S., Hofmann, C., Shryne, J.E. and Gorski, R.A. (1984) Participation of estrogens in female sexual differentiation of the brain; neuroanatomical, neuroendocrine and behavioral evidence. In: G.J. De Vries, J.P.C. De Bruin, H.B.M. Uylings and M.A. Corner (Eds.), *Sex Differences in the Brain. The Relation between Structure and Function. Progress in Brain Research*, this volume, Ch. 5, pp. 99–117.

Dörner, G. (1981) Sexual differentiation of the brain. *Vitam. Hormone*, 38: 325–381.

Dörner, G., Staudt, J., Wenzel, J., Kvetnansky, R. and Murgas, K. (1977) Further evidence of teratogenic effects apparently produced by neurotransmitters during brain differentiation. *Endokrinologie*, 70: 326–330.

Giulian, D., Pohorecky, L.A. and McEwen, B.S. (1973) Effects of gonadal steroids upon brain 5-hydroxytryptamine levels in the neonatal rat. *Endocrinology*, 93: 1329–1335.

Gorski, R.A. (1984) Critical role for the medial preoptic area in the sexual differentiation of the brain. In: G.J. De Vries, J.P.C. De Bruin, H.B.M. Uylings and M.A. Corner (Eds.), *Sex Differences in the Brain. The Relation between Structure and Function. Progress in Brain Research*, this volume, Ch. 7.

Gorski, R.A. and Jacobson, C.D. (1981) Sexual differentiation of the brain. In: S.J. Kogan and E.S.E. Hafez (Eds.), *Pediatric Andrology*, Martinus Nijhoff, The Hague, pp. 109–134.

Goy, R.W. and McEwen, B.S. (1980) *Sexual Differentiation of the Brain*, Massachusetts Institute of Technology Press, Cambridge, MA.

Hyyppä, M., Lampinen, P. and Lehtinen, P. (1972) Alteration in the sexual behavior of male and female rats after neonatal administration of *p*-chlorophenylalanine. *Psychopharmacologia*, 25: 152–161.

Ladosky, W. and Gaziri, L.C.J. (1972) Brain serotonin and sexual differentiation of the nervous system. *Neuroendocrinology*, 6: 168–174.

Malmnäs, C.O. (1973) Monoaminergic influence on testosterone activated copulatory behavior in the castrated male rat. *Acta Physiol. Scand.*, Suppl. 395: 1–128.

Meyerson, B.J. (1964) Central nervous monoamines and hormone induced estrus behavior in the spayed rat. *Acta Physiol. Scand.*, Suppl. 241: 1–32.

Michanek, A. and Meyerson, B.J. (1977) A comparative study of different amphetamines on copulatory behavior and stereotype activity in the female rat. *Psychopharmacologia*, 53: 175–183.

Naftolin, F., Ryan, K.J., Davies, I.J., Reddy, V.V., Flores, F., Petro, Z., Kuhn, M., White, R.J., Takaoko, J. and Wolin, L. (1975) The formation of oestrogen by central neuroendocrine tissue. *Recent Progr. Hormone Res.*, 31: 259–319.

Plapinger, L. and McEwen, B.S. (1978) Gonadal steroid–brain interactions in sexual differentiation. In: J.B. Hutchison (Ed.), *Biological Determinations of Sexual Behavior*, John Wiley, Chichester, NY, pp. 153–218.

Reznikov, A.G., Nosenko, N.D. and Demkiv, L.P. (1979) New evidences for participation of monoamines in androgen-dependent sexual differentiation of hypothalamic control of gonadotropin secretion in rats. *Endokrinologie*, 73: 11–19.

Shirama, K., Takeo, Y., Shimizu, K. and Maekawa, K. (1975) Inhibitory effect of 5-hydroxytryptophane on the induction of persistent estrus by androgen in the rat. *Endocrinol. Jpn.*, 22: 575–579.

Staudt, J., Stüber, P. and Dörner, G. (1978) Permanent changes of sexual dimorphism in the rat brain following neonatal treatment with psychotrophic drugs. In: G. Dörner and M. Kawakami (Eds.), *Hormones and Brain Development*, Elsevier/North-Holland, Amsterdam, pp. 35–41.

Swanson, H.H. and Van de Poll, N.E. (1983) Sex differences in dominance relationships in rats. Abstract presented at the Third European Winter Conference on Brain Research, Les Arcs.

Vom Saal, F.S., Grant, W.M., McMullen, C.W. and Laves, K.S. (1983) High fetal estrogen concentrations: correlation with increased adult sexual performance and decreased aggression in male mice. *Science*, 220: 1306–1309.

BARBARA JARZAB, KLAUS D. DÖHLER

DISCUSSION

G.J. de VRIES: Could it be that when you manipulate the serotoninergic innervation of the brain, predominantly those sites are influenced that are innervated by serotoninergic fibers and, if so, that this is the reason why you cannot get a complete inhibition of the action of TP on defeminization and masculinization when you administer a serotonin precursor simultaneously?

B. JARZAB: To be honest, we do not know where the serotonin precursors act in the developing brain. It may be assumed that they act only on those sites which are innervated by serotonin fibers. Thus, in some areas they may interact with testosterone, in other areas they may not. Incidentally, Gorski (1984) has mentioned that the central part of the sexually dimorphic nucleus of the preoptic area is devoid of serotoninergic fibers. This nucleus, however, is definitely a target for testosterone (Gorski, 1984; Döhler et al., 1982). On the other hand, postnatal treatment with serotonin precursors may also result in excess availability of serotonin in brain areas which are normally devoid of this transmitter during development. Thus, the interference of L-tryptophan with male and female behavioral differentiation might as well be the result of a false imprinting effect of serotonin, or the result of serotonin interference with the imprinting activity of other transmitters.

REFERENCES

Döhler, K.-D., Coquelin, A., Davis, F., Hines, M., Shryne, J.E. and Gorski, R.A. (1982) Differentiation of the sexually dimorphic nucleus in the preoptic area of the rat brain is determined by the perinatal hormone environment. *Neurosci. Lett.*, 33: 295–298.
Gorski, R.A. (1984) Critical role for the medical preoptic area in the sexual differentiation of the brain. In: G.J. De Vries, J.P.C. De Bruin, H.B.M. Uylings and M.A. Corner (Eds.), *Sex Differences in the Brain. The Relation between Structure and Function. Progress in Brain Research*, this volume, Ch. 7, pp. 129–146.

MORPHOLOGICAL SEX DIFFERENCES IN THE BRAIN

G.J. De Vries et al. (Eds.),
Progress in Brain Research, Vol. 61
© 1984   Elsevier Science Publishers B.V., Amsterdam

Critical Role for the Medial Preoptic Area in the Sexual Differentiation of the Brain

ROGER A. GORSKI

*Department of Anatomy and Laboratory of Neuroendocrinology of the Brain,
Research Institute, UCLA School of Medicine, Los Angeles, CA (U.S.A.)*

INTRODUCTION

The sexual differentiation of the mammalian brain is now firmly established in functional terms for a large number of species (for reviews see Gorski, 1983a,b; Gorski and Jacobson, 1982; Goy and McEwen, 1980; Harlan et al., 1979; McEwen, 1983). In fact, for a relatively wide range of neural functions across many species the following generalizations appear to apply: for many of its functions the brain is neuter or fundamentally female in its potential at some point during development. Exposure to the organizational action of testicular hormones is necessary both to establish those neural functions recognized as typical of the male of a given species (masculinization), and in many cases, to suppress those functions characteristic of the female sex (defeminization). It may also be that exposure to similar hormones at much lower concentrations is necessary for the development of the normal functional potential of the female (see Döhler et al., 1984; Gorski, 1983b).

The specific period of sexual differentiation of the brain may be pre-, post-, or perhaps perinatal depending both upon the species and the specific functional parameter under study (see Gorski, 1983a,b). Even the precise molecular form of gonadal hormone which causes masculinization and/or defeminization of a given functional system may be different. In the rat, for example, testosterone may act in the brain as estradiol after its intraneuronal aromatization (see Gorski, 1983b), but an androgenic steroid is responsible for the masculinization of penile musculature and/or the companion masculinization of the spinal motor neurons of those muscles (Breedlove, 1984). Although the sexual differentiation of the brain clearly occurs, one must remain aware of the probability that each functional system undergoes sexual differentiation independently of the other. Although sexual differentiation is dependent upon gonadal activity, most importantly that of the testes, differences in (i) the rate of development of a specific neural system, (ii) regional or local differences in steroid metabolism, and (iii) differences in neuronal sensitivity to a given hormonal species each may contribute a degree of independence to the sexual differentiation of different functional systems. It is unlikely that there is a single mechanism of sexual differentiation of the brain.

In one sense most studies of the sexual differentiation of the mammalian brain have been relatively descriptive in nature. The general approach has been to manipulate the hormonal environment during critical periods of development, which have had to be determined empirically, and then to describe the resultant alterations in function, usually in the adult. Few studies have been performed at the mechanistic level. These include attempts to inhibit the masculinizing or defeminizing action of testosterone by antibiotics (Gorski and Shryne,

1972; Kobayashi and Gorski, 1970; Salaman and Birkett, 1974), neuroactive drugs (Arai and Gorski, 1968a; Ladosky et al., 1970) and barbiturates (Arai and Gorski, 1968a,b). In some studies attempts were made to detect alterations in metabolic processes (Litteria, 1973, 1977) or in the uptake and processing of steroid hormonal signals in adulthood (DeBold, 1978; Olsen and Whalen, 1980; Rainbow et al., 1982; Vértes et al., 1978). Two important contributions of this level of research have been the observation that in the rat hypothalamus the aromatization of testosterone to estrogen appears to be a prerequisite for at least some of its organizational actions (Gorski, 1983b; Lieberburg et al., 1977; Södersten, 1978), and that in the perinatal rat a-fetoprotein serves as an important estrogen-binding molecule (Nunez et al., 1971; Plapinger et al., 1973; Raynaud et al., 1971), the full significance of which remains unknown (see Döhler et al., 1984; Gorski, 1983b; Toran-Allerand, 1984).

PROBABLE SITES OF SEXUAL DIFFERENTIATION

One factor which has contributed to the relative lack of mechanistic studies, in addition to the real need to define the full extent of the process of the functional sexual differentiation of the brain, is the question of the site of the organizational action of gonadal hormones during development. A reasonable approach to this question involved the direct application of hormones to specific regions of the brain of the perinatal animal (Christensen and Gorski, 1978; Hayashi and Gorski, 1974; Lobl and Gorski, 1974; Nadler, 1968; Wagner et al., 1966). Because of the possibility of diffusion away from such implants, results from this type of approach cannot stand alone. However, when the results of these studies are evaluated in conjunction with those from the study of hormonal uptake, electrolytic lesioning and even the recording of electrophysiological activity, conceptual progress is possible.

From the results of such studies the medial preoptic area (MPOA) has become generally accepted as at least one site of hormone action during development (see Gorski, 1971, 1983b). The MPOA in general is clearly important in the control of gonadotropin release and sexual behavior, especially masculine behavior. It has even been shown that in the male rat that is gonadectomized on postnatal day 1 and thus can support the ovulatory discharge of gonadotropin, experimental manipulations such as electrolytic destruction of the MPOA or the placement of a knife cut just posterior to this region, will disrupt ovulatory function in these genetic males just as they do in females. The MPOA of the neonatally castrated male clearly is feminine in its functional activity.

In spite of the identification of the MPOA as a probable site of sexual differentiation, mechanistic studies involving this specific neural site have also been very limited. The MPOA is a relatively large and complex area of the hypothalamus and is implicated in the control of many functional processes. Thus, one might expect (or hope for) a much more discrete locus of hormone action during development, in fact, one might require a more discrete locus in order to perform meaningful mechanistic studies. In addition, it is likely that the MPOA is not the only locus of hormone action during development. The ventromedial arcuate region (Christensen and Gorski, 1978; Hayashi and Gorski, 1974), amygdala (Nishizuka and Arai, 1981) and brain stem (Lookingland et al., 1982) have also been suggested as possible loci. Moreover, the present proceedings include several reports of functional and structural sex differences which involve regions of the brain other than the aforementioned areas. It is difficult to carry out mechanistic studies without knowledge of the major site of sexual differentiation.

STRUCTURAL SEX DIFFERENCES IN THE RAT BRAIN

Recent studies of structural sex differences reinforce the importance of the MPOA in the sexual differentiation of the rat brain. This statement does not imply that the MPOA is the only, the principal, or even the most critical site of sexual differentiation. However, the MPOA, or more precisely, a smaller component of this area, does represent a major site of hormone action (presumably direct, although this is yet to be established) and offers a model system for mechanistic studies which heretofore have been impossible.

The earliest reports of possible structural sex differences in the rat brain involved the size of individual cell nuclei and nucleoli (Dörner and Staudt, 1968, 1969; Pfaff, 1966). However, such size differences could reflect different metabolic demands due to the size and configuration of the dendritic field (i.e., a real structural difference) or perhaps just metabolic state in general (i.e., a physiological difference). In 1973, however, Raisman and Field published a study of great importance. They reported that at the ultrastructural level there was a significant sex difference in terms of the number of dendritic spine synapses of non-strial origin in the MPOA; females have significantly more of such synapses. Importantly, they demonstrated that the number of these synapses followed the "rules of sexual differentiation". That is, males castrated at birth, or females exposed to androgen after the period of sexual differentiation had a large (female-like) number of such synapses, whereas androgenized females or males castrated after the period of sexual differentiation had fewer (i.e., the masculine pattern) synapses of this type.

Although a relatively subtle difference, this report clearly indicated that morphological sex difference did exist in the rat brain. This represented an important conceptual advance since it was possible, before these observations, to suggest that neural circuitry was equivalent in both the male and female. The male rat, for example, although rarely displaying lordosis behavior can do so on occasion. Therefore, he must have the neural circuitry that subserves this reflexive behavior. Perhaps sex differences merely reside in the accessibility (presumably hormonally controlled) of this circuitry, not in the circuitry itself.

The pioneering observation of Raisman and Field (1973) has been followed by several observations of sex differences in connectivity in terms of dendritic arborization in the hamster (Greenough et al., 1977) and the rhesus monkey (Ayoub et al., 1983), and synaptology in the rat in the arcuate (Matsumoto and Arai, 1980) and amygdaloid nuclei (Nishizuka and Arai, 1981). Although these results are very important in demonstrating the existence of structural sex differences, their subtle nature limits their use as potential model systems for experimental study of the mechanisms of hormone action. The problem of adequate sampling at the ultrastructural level is one obvious limitation to this as a model system.

Fortunately, the report of Nottebohm and Arnold (1976) opened a new chapter in sexual differentiation research. These investigators discovered the existence of relatively marked structural sex differences at the level of regional nuclear volume in the neural substrate of song production in the songbird. This demonstration of surprisingly large structural sex differences in the avian brain led Dr. L.W. Christensen in my laboratory simply to compare female and male rat brains side by side. Had earlier investigators missed an obvious sex difference in the brain of this species?

The sexually dimorphic nucleus of the preoptic area

As illustrated in Fig. 1A and B, the answer is yes. Within the MPOA is an area of darkly staining neurons which is approximately 5-fold larger in volume in the male (Gorski et al.,

1978). Because the density of neurons per unit area within this region is greater than that of the surrounding tissue (Gorski et al., 1978; Jacobson and Gorski, 1981), we have labeled this region a nucleus, specifically the sexually dimorphic nucleus of the preoptic area (SDN-POA; Gorski et al., 1980). Moreover, since neuronal density within the SDN-POA is equivalent in both male and female, the larger volume of this structure in the male means that his SDN-POA contains more neurons than that of the female. It is important in the context of the present discussion of possible model systems, that the SDN-POA and its sex difference in volume is readily apparent even by analysis of the appropriate brain sections with the unaided eye. Thus, the SDN-POA is one example of a relatively gross sex difference which might provide a useful model system, that is, if SDN-POA volume is indeed a parameter of sexual differentiation.

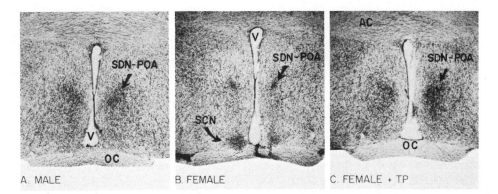

Fig. 1. Photomicrographs (at same magnification) of coronal sections through the rat brain at the level of the center of the sexually dimorphic nucleus of the preoptic area (SDN-POA) of the male (A), female (B), and the female exposed to testosterone propionate (TP) for a prolonged period during perinatal development (C). Abbreviations: AC, anterior commissure; OC, optic chiasm; SCN, suprachiasmatic nucleus; V, third ventricle. Reprinted with permission from Gorski (1983c).

To verify this possibility we have performed two types of experiments. In one we asked when does the SDN-POA and more importantly, the sex difference in its volume, develop (Jacobson et al., 1980). Rats were sacrificed beginning at 18 days post fertilization and the volume of the SDN-POA, as it appears in the adult, determined. On day 18 post fertilization the SDN-POA could not be identified; on day 20 the nucleus is present but not sexually dimorphic. In fact, no significant sex difference in SDN-POA volume was detected until the day of birth, but essentially thereafter a sex difference in volume was maintained. Over approximately the first week of postnatal development, the period of the determination of the functional sexual differentiation of the brain, SDN-POA volume gradually increased in the male while that of the female showed no statistically significant change with time (Fig. 2). Thus, the morphological development of the SDN-POA in terms of volume, closely parallels the period of the organization by androgens of adult functional potential.

Our second approach was to determine the effects of both endogenous and exogenous hormones on the volume of the SDN-POA. Although the SDN-POA of the adult rat contains a high percentage of neurons which take up and retain radiolabeled steroids (Jacobson et al., 1982), and is thus presumably responsive to gonadal hormones, we did not observe significant changes in the volume of the SDN-POA in adult gonadectomized males or females treated with exogenous steroids in doses effective in facilitating masculine or

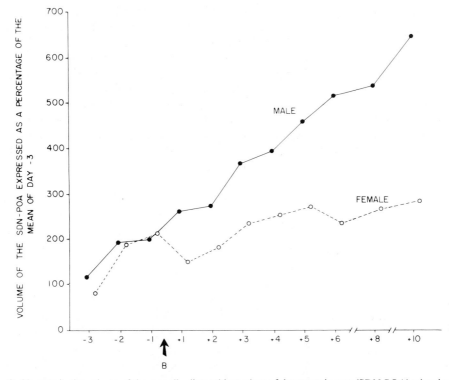

Fig. 2. Changes in the volume of the sexually dimorphic nucleus of the preoptic area (SDN-POA) related to the day of birth. Data are expressed as a percentage of the mean volume observed in males and females sacrificed at − 3 days (20 days post fertilization) before birth (B). The day of birth (23 days post fertilization) is called day + 1. Reprinted with permission from Gorski (1983d).

feminine reproductive behavior (Gorski et al., 1978). However, the possible responsiveness of the SDN-POA to gonadal steroids during development is much more important in terms of sexual differentiation.

In this regard, the developing SDN-POA is clearly sensitive to gonadal hormones (Fig. 3). Castration of the male rat on postnatal day 1 reduces SDN-POA volume by more than 50% when measured in adulthood (Gorski et al., 1978; Jacobson et al., 1981a,b). In addition, the injection of 100 μg testosterone propionate (TP) on the day after castration on day 1, restores the volume of the SDN-POA in the adult to that of the normal male (Jacobson et al., 1981a). In the female, the administration of a single injection of TP (Gorski et al., 1978; Jacobson et al., 1981a,b) or estradiol benzoate (EB) (Jacobson and Gorski, unpublished observation) significantly increases SDN-POA volume when measured in adulthood.

Although these results indicate that gonadal hormones can influence final SDN-POA volume, note that these procedures did not sex-reverse nuclear volume (see Fig. 3). There are several possible explanations for this observation. First, testosterone levels have been shown to surge at birth (Corbier et al., 1978); is this testosterone surge critical for SDN-POA development in the male? Second, perhaps exposure to gonadal hormones is required both pre- and postnatally. Finally, it may be assumed that in addition to hormonal effects, genetic factors do play a role in the development of the SDN-POA.

The first explanation appears incorrect. With the assistance of Dr. P. Corbier, who castrated male rats just before, or 6, 12 or 24 h after natural birth, we found that castration at each of these 4 times reduced SDN-POA volume in the adult by approximately 50% (Handa et al., 1982). There was no difference, however, among the 4 groups of perinatally castrated animals; castration just before natural birth is not more effective than castration 24 h later.

The precise design of experiments to challenge the second possible explanation requires information that is not presently available. If prenatal exposure to testicular hormones also plays a role in determining the volume of the SDN-POA of the adult, one might expect a greater sensitivity at one time or another, perhaps during the period of neurogenesis, or perhaps on day 17 (the time of an endogenous surge of testosterone (Weisz and Ward, 1980)), or perhaps a few hours before birth. Without any basis to select one period over another, our initial approach to this problem was to maximize the period of hormonal exposure. Thus, pregnant dams were injected daily with 2 mg TP beginning on day 16 post conception. After spontaneous parturition individual pups (of both sexes since it was impossible to distinguish male from female from the external genitalia) were injected with 100 μg TP daily for the first 10 days of postnatal life. These animals were sacrificed at 30 days of age, sexed according to gonadal structure, and SDN-POA volume determined (Döhler et al., 1982a). Such prolonged exposure to TP did not alter SDN-POA volume in males, but completely sex-reversed SDN-POA volume in the females (see Figs. 1C and 3). Fig. 1C provides visual

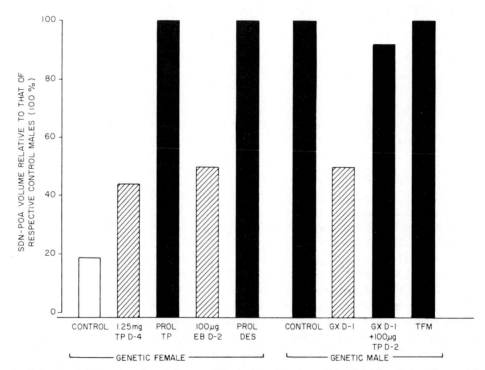

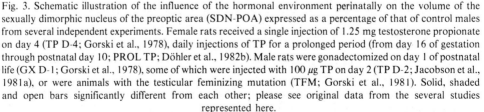

Fig. 3. Schematic illustration of the influence of the hormonal environment perinatally on the volume of the sexually dimorphic nucleus of the preoptic area (SDN-POA) expressed as a percentage of that of control males from several independent experiments. Female rats received a single injection of 1.25 mg testosterone propionate on day 4 (TP D-4; Gorski et al., 1978), daily injections of TP for a prolonged period (from day 16 of gestation through postnatal day 10; PROL TP; Döhler et al., 1982b). Male rats were gonadectomized on day 1 of postnatal life (GX D-1; Gorski et al., 1978), some of which were injected with 100 μg TP on day 2 (TP D-2; Jacobson et al., 1981a), or were animals with the testicular feminizing mutation (TFM; Gorski et al., 1981). Solid, shaded and open bars significantly different from each other; please see original data from the several studies represented here.

evidence that the increase in SDN-POA volume in the sex-reversed female is due, at least in part, to an increase in the number of neurons which comprise the nucleus.

Although this observation of the sex reversal of SDN-POA does not rule out the importance of possible genetic factors under physiological conditions, it clearly demonstrates that gonadal steroids alone can completely determine SDN-POA volume. In this regard, note that similarly prolonged exposure to diethylstilbestrol, a synthetic estrogen which is not bound to α-fetoprotein, also sex-reverses SDN-POA volume in females (see Fig. 3) (Döhler et al., 1982b). As indicated above, certain parameters of sexual differentiation of the brain, at least in the rat, appear to be dependent upon estrogen, not androgen. The SDN-POA appears to be one such parameter. Also in support of this view is the observation that in the androgen-insensitive male rat with the feminizing testis mutation (Naess et al., 1976), SDN-POA volume is equivalent to that of the normal male (Gorski et al., 1981). However, the spinal nucleus of the bulbocavernosus is completely feminine in the same animals (Breedlove and Arnold, 1981). This observation that the morphological differentiation of the central nervous system is determined in the same animal apparently by estrogens in one locus (the SDN-POA) and androgens in another (the spinal cord) strongly supports the earlier mentioned concept of independence among the various neural parameters, presumably both structural and functional, which undergo sexual differentiation.

POSSIBLE MECHANISMS OF THE SEXUAL DIFFERENTIATION OF BRAIN STRUCTURE

At this stage it is useful to summarize the data we have just reviewed. Within the MPOA of the rat, a region of the brain which has been implicated in the control of numerous neuro-endocrine functions and which has been considered one site of hormone-induced sexual differentiation, there exists a marked structural sex difference, viz. in the volume of the SDN-POA. Moreover, this sex difference develops over the first week or so of postnatal life, the period of the functional differentiation of the brain. Importantly, the volume of the SDN-POA and the number of neurons which comprise it are modified by manipulations of the hormonal environment. In fact, prolonged exposure to gonadal hormones perinatally completely sex-reverses SDN-POA volume. We thus submit that the SDN-POA is a morphological signature of the organizational effects of gonadal hormones on the developing brain. Because of the magnitude of the sex difference in SDN-POA volume, we believe this nucleus can serve as a model system to investigate possible mechanisms by which gonadal hormones act to differentiate the brain sexually.

If we first focus our attention on the fact that exposure to gonadal steroids appears to increase the number of neurons which ultimately comprise the SDN-POA of the adult, it is possible to suggest several possible mechanisms of hormone action. The steroid environment (1) may promote or prolong neurogenesis; (2) may influence the migration of neurons from their origin in the ventricular ependyma to the region of the SDN-POA; (3) may influence unknown cell–cell recognition processes which lead to the aggregation of these neurons into a recognizable, if not discrete, nucleus and/or (4) may promote cell survival during a developmental period of neuronal death.

The results of previous studies of the temporal origin of the neurons of the MPOA do not support the hypothesis that testicular hormones influence the mitotic formation of the neurons of the SDN-POA. The technique of dating the birth of neurons with tritiated thymidine autoradiography led to the conclusion that the neurons of the MPOA become postmitotic by about day 16 of gestation (Altman and Bayer, 1978; Anderson, 1978; Ifft, 1972). Since SDN-POA volume can be changed significantly by hormonal manipulations postnatally, a major effect on neurogenesis per se seemed unlikely. Nevertheless, we decided to apply the thymidine autoradiographic technique to the SDN-POA, arguing that if we permanently labeled a high percentage of the neurons of the MPOA, in general, we might be able to quantify by focusing on the SDN-POA itself, possible sex (or hormonal) differences in cell death which might contribute to its sex dimorphism.

As shown in Fig. 4 our results both confirmed and extended previous data. In accord with the literature, neurons of the MPOA become postmitotic by about day 16 of gestation (Fig. 4A). However, to our surprise, mitotic activity of those cells which eventually formed the neurons of the SDN-POA was still occurring on day 18 of gestation (Fig. 4B; Jacobson and Gorski, 1981). As seen in Fig. 5B, this fact permits us to label very specifically and permanently the cells of the SDN-POA. As will be indicated below, this gives us a unique opportunity to investigate a possible influence of sex or the hormonal environment on the migration of SDN-POA neurons during development. First, however, note that there was a statistically significant effect of sex on the labeling index following prenatal exposure to tritiated thymidine (Fig. 4B).

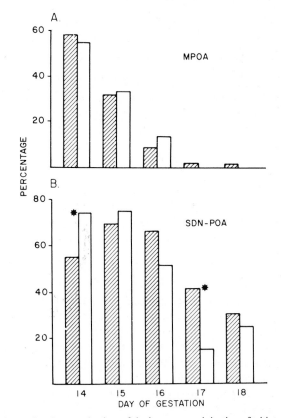

Fig. 4. The influence of gestational age at the time of the intravenous injection of tritiated thymidine to pregnant rats on the mean percentage of labeled neurons in (A) the medial preoptic area (MPOA) just lateral to (B) the sexually dimorphic nucleus of the preoptic area (SDN-POA) for male (hatched bars) and female (open bars) rats from these pregnancies. The offspring were sacrificed on postnatal day 30. Asterisks indicate a significant sex difference. Reprinted with permission from Gorski et al. (1981).

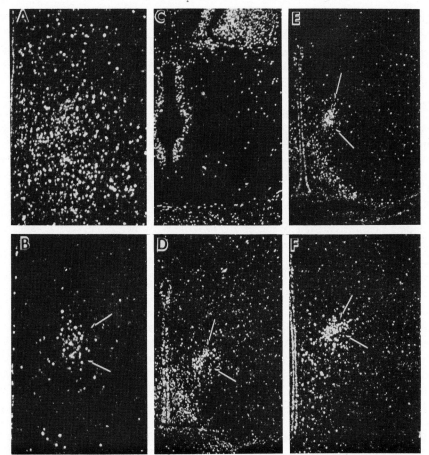

Fig. 5. Dark-field photomicrographs of coronal sections through the sexually dimorphic nucleus of the preoptic area (SDN-POA; arrows) d monstrating the prolongation of apparent genesis of the neurons of the SDN-POA (compare A and B), and the change in position of labeled cells over time following exposure to tritiated thymidine on day 18 of gestation (compare C–F). In A and B (both at the same magnification), pregnant rats were exposed to tritiated thymidine on days 15 and 18 post conception, respectively, and the offspring sacrificed on postnatal day 30. For C–F (all at same magnification), all rat embryos were exposed to tritiated thymidine at the same time (day 18 of gestation), but these rats were sacrificed at different times: (C) 18 days plus 2 h; (D) 22 days, (E) 26 days, or (F) 32 days post conception. In each panel the ependymal lining of the third ventricle is to the left. A and B from Jacobson and Gorski (1981); C–F from Jacobson et al. (1981b). Reprinted with permission from Gorski (1983e).

When thymidine is administered on day 14 of gestation, the labeling index in females is significantly higher than that in males, but upon thymidine exposure on day 17 the sex difference is reversed. The latter sex difference might be related to the testosterone surge reported to occur in the male rat on day 18 of gestation (Weisz and Ward, 1980), but there is no known hormonal explanation of the opposite sex difference in labeling index observed upon exposure to tritiated thymidine on day 14 of gestation. It must be emphasized, however, that the labeling index was evaluated on postnatal day 30. Thus, the sex differences after exposure to thymidine on day 14 or day 17 post fertilization, could be due to a difference in neurogenesis, or in any process which takes place before day 30 postnatally including migration, aggregation and/or survival. Nevertheless, these statistically significant sex differences in labeling index demand further study.

The fact that exposure to tritiated thymidine on day 18 of gestation eventually specifically labels neurons of the SDN-POA offers an opportunity to identify the pathway of their migration and possibly, sex or hormonally induced differences. As shown in Fig. 5C, when embryonic animals are sacrificed 2 h after the injection of tritiated thymidine to pregnant dams 18 days post conception, labeled cells are restricted to the ependymal lining of the third ventricle (Jacobson et al., 1981b). If additional pregnant animals are exposed to tritiated thymidine on day 18 of gestation and their pups sacrificed at different intervals following thymidine exposure, it should be possible to follow the fate of those cells synthesizing DNA on day 18 throughout the perinatal period and the formation of the SDN-POA of the adult.

As shown in Fig. 5E–F, this is indeed the case. Cells labeled with tritiated thymidine on day 18 of gestation appear to migrate over time to the base of the third ventricle and into the surrounding neural tissue (Jacobson et al., 1981b). With increasing age the labeled cells appear to migrate dorso-laterally to the SDN-POA. Over time there is a clear decrease in the number of labeled cells between the base of the third ventricle and the SDN-POA. We are currently in the process of evaluating these data for possible sex differences, either qualitative or quantitative, in this migratory process.

Even though we cannot answer this important question at this time, these data already add a new dimension to our thoughts on the possible mechanisms of steroid action in influencing the formation of the SDN-POA. Current opinion favors an action of testicular hormones which promotes neuronal survival during a period of cell death. Two basic arguments can be offered to support this view: (1) the general acceptance by developmental neurobiologists of the concept that more neurons are produced than actually survive development (Cowan, 1978; Purves, 1977; Silver, 1978). In fact, it is generally believed that neuronal survival requires the establishment of appropriate connections which provide such successful neurons access to an unknown neuronotropic substance (Hamburger and Oppenheim, 1982). Competition for this substance(s) may mold the final histological organization of the nervous system. (2) The demonstrations that estrogen can stimulate the growth of neuronal processes in some systems. There are several examples of this: hormone-dependent synaptogenesis in both the rat (Clough and Rodriguez-Sierra, 1982; Matsumoto and Arai, 1976) and songbird (Nottebohm, 1981; DeVoogd, 1984) in vivo, and the stimulation of neurite outgrowth by estrogen in explant cultures of mouse hypothalamus (Toran-Allerand, 1981, 1984; Toran-Allerand et al., 1980, 1983). In the latter case, estrogen may actually be required for such outgrowth.

Although this hypothesis of the promotion of neuronal survival by hormone action is an attractive one to explain the development of the sex difference in the SDN-POA, it clearly has not been proven. Fig. 5 suggests an additional possibility. Note that it appears that far more neurons are labeled by exposure to tritiated thymidine on day 18 than actually form the SDN-POA. What happens to these cells? Note especially the region of the brain between the base of the third ventricle and the SDN-POA. Although these cells over time could merely migrate into the SDN-POA of an adjacent and non-analyzed section, or perhaps beyond the MPOA itself, it is tempting to consider that many of these neurons die before reaching the SDN-POA, that is, before they enter the theoretical competition for a neuronotropic substance. Thus, is it possible that steroid hormones act *directly* as a neurotrophic substance during the migration process, i.e., during morphogenesis, before these cells arrive at the SDN-POA and extend processes which could be expected to reach the hypothetical source of a neural (or glial) neuronotropic substance. Thus, steroids may play a role in morphogenic and/or histogenic cell death.

Although much additional research is obviously required, the value of the SDN-POA as a model system to elucidate the nature of the morphological actions of gonadal hormones on the developing brain seems clear. Gonadal hormones may play an important role in regulating or modifying neurogenesis, neuronal migration and neuronal survival during morphogenesis and/or after the neurons reach their appropriate location and begin to establish connections necessary for their survival. At the same time, however, it must be emphasized that current studies of the SDN-POA are actually relatively crude. The volume of a nucleus such as the SDN-POA is a complex parameter which includes the number and size of neurons and glia, as well as their internal ultrastructure and the development of fields and configurations of synaptic contact. In the case of the MPOA in general, for example, synaptogenesis appears to take place over the first several weeks of postnatal development (Lawrence and Raisman, 1980; Reier et al., 1977), and may actually change near the time of puberty (Clough and Rodriguez-Sierra, 1982). Which of these parameters: nuclear volume, number of neurons, neuronal ultrastructure, or neuronal connectivity, is the primary site of hormone action? Which is of primary importance in the etiology of sex differences in brain function? These problems are important but clearly very complex. Hopefully the study of model systems such as the SDN-POA at all levels of analysis will provide guidance for future experiments and/or new understanding.

Towards this end we have not restricted our studies of the SDN-POA to the use of tritiated thymidine, to the developing animal, or even to the rat. Although they are still in progress, a brief description of these studies may serve at least to indicate the approaches that are possible.

THE ONTOGENY OF STEROID RESPONSIVENESS

The preceding discussion is based on a fundamental assumption: the development of the SDN-POA is modified by hormone action. There is, however, no proof that any of the proposed actions of estrogen are direct. Although we know that a high percentage of the cells of the SDN-POA of the adult take up and retain radiolabeled steroids (Jacobson et al., 1982), is this true during development? If it is, when do the neurons of the SDN-POA acquire the ability to take up and retain steroids, presumptive evidence of hormone responsiveness? Do migrating cells take up steroids? Do presumptive neuroblasts in the ependyma take up steroids?

We are currently attempting to answer questions of this type and have started by evaluating the uptake of tritiated moxestrol (a synthetic estrogen which is not bound by a-fetoprotein) and tritiated methyltrienolone (a synthetic non-aromatizable androgen) in the 2-day-old rat. Although we have not seen labeled cells following androgen administration, cells of the SDN-POA are labeled in both sexes by tritiated moxestrol (Schoonmaker et al., 1983). However, these results also suggest that there may be an antero-posterior gradient in this respect. Anteriorly, the cells of the SDN-POA are labeled while those of the immediate surround are not; posteriorly the situation is the reverse: labeled cells are restricted to the immediate surround of the unlabeled SDN-POA. Whether this represents a temporal gradient, as has been observed in terms of neurogenesis (Jacobson and Gorski, 1981), or a more complex organization of the SDN-POA in terms of the direct responsiveness of its neurons to steroids remains unknown at this time.

THE RELATIONSHIP BETWEEN THE SDN-POA AND THE MEDIAL PREOPTIC NUCLEUS

We have also evaluated the MPOA cytoarchitectonically in parallel with immunohisto-chemistry utilizing an antibody to serotonin (Simerly et al., 1984). This analysis permits us to divide the classical medial preoptic nucleus (MPN) into 3 subdivisions each of which may be

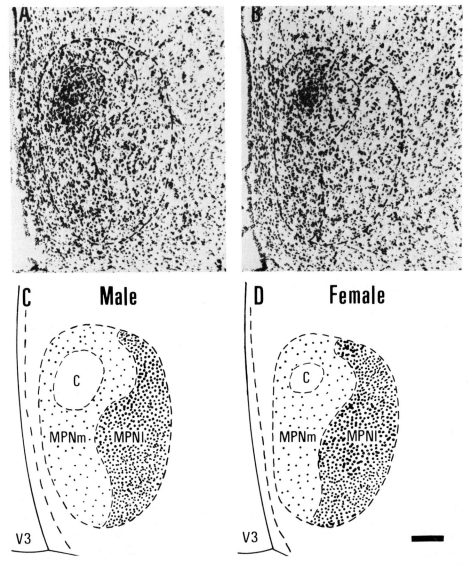

Fig. 6. (A and B) Photomicrographs (at same magnification) of thionine-stained 30-μm-thick sections through the medial preoptic nucleus (MPN) on which the boundaries of the 3 subdivisions of the MPN in the male (A) and female (B) are outlined. (C and D) The same outlines of subdivisions of the MPN are reproduced and the relative intensity of immunoreactive serotonin fibers for each subdivision are indicated by the intensity of stippling. Abbreviations: C, the central component of the MPN which is equivalent to the sexually dimorphic nucleus of the preoptic area; MPNl, the lateral component of the MPN; MPNm, the medial component of the MPN; V3, third ventricle. Data from Simerly et al. (1984).

sexually dimorphic (Fig. 6). The lateral division is very rich in serotoninergic fibers, while the medial component has far fewer serotoninergic fibers. Imbedded within this medial component is an area of dense cellular concentration which is essentially devoid of serotoninergic fibers. This central component of the MPN appears to be the equivalent of the SDN-POA. This classification of the SDN-POA as one component of a more complex MPN will be of value in the interpretation of connectivity studies which are currently underway. Moreover, the exclusion of serotoninergic fibers from the SDN-POA may be expected to have functional significance although unknown at this time. Clearly, the identification of the neurotransmitter input to the SDN-POA, the chemical specificity of its neurons, and their relationship with other components of the MPN, will be of importance in identifying the function(s) of the SDN-POA and in understanding its development.

THE FUNCTION OF THE SDN-POA

Although we have put forth the SDN-POA as a model system for the study of sexual differentiation irrespective of the specific function(s) subserved by its neurons, knowledge of this function(s) would be critical information. To date, however, we have no clear idea of the function of the SDN-POA. The absolute volume of the nucleus does not correlate with ovulatory function, nor with lordosis responsiveness (Gorski et al., 1978). Lesions of the SDN-POA do not disrupt masculine copulatory behavior, although small lesions just dorsal to the nucleus do (Arendash and Gorski, 1983a). We have also approached the functional potential of the SDN-POA in a rather unusual way. We have punched out tissue from the MPOA including the SDN-POA of newborn male rats and transplanted this neural tissue stereotaxically into the MPOA of female littermates. When adult, these females bearing transplants of male brain tissue, displayed enhanced behavioral responsiveness, both in terms of masculine and feminine copulatory behavior (Arendash and Gorski, 1982). Although these results are quite intriguing in terms of the possible functional incorporation of neuronal grafts into the host brain, they currently do not identify the specific function(s) of the SDN-POA, if any. Recent studies, however, have shown that transplant volume is increased by treatment of the recipient with exogenous TP (Arendash and Gorski, 1983b). Thus, even in this unusual experimental paradigm, a trophic influence of gonadal hormones on neuronal tissue can be demonstrated.

THE SPECIES SPECIFICITY OF THE SDN-POA

A final question relative to the SDN-POA relates to species specificity. The concept of the functional sexual differentiation of the brain applies to many mammalian species. Is this true for the SDN-POA? Without knowledge of the function of the neurons of the SDN-POA, their connectivity or neurochemical characteristics, it is difficult to accept the absence of a distinct SDN-POA, as in the mouse (Young, 1982), as indicative of a true absence of a comparable structural sexual dimorphism. However, it is also difficult to accept that the presence of an apparent homologue of the rat SDN-POA in a given species indicates that this is an absolutely equivalent structure. Nevertheless, such a homologue has been identified in the gerbil (Yahr and Commins, 1983), ferret (Tobet et al., 1983) and the guinea pig (Hines et al., 1982). In the latter species, there is also a clear sexual dimorphism in the volume of a darkly staining component of the bed nucleus of the stria terminalis, which is significantly larger in males than in females (Hines et al., 1983).

It appears to be a safe prediction to suggest that numerous structural sex differences will be identified in the mammalian brain, perhaps as components of a complex sexually dimorphic neural system as exists in the songbird brain (Arnold, 1980; Gurney, 1981). At present, however, the SDN-POA of the rat represents the most well characterized and most prominent structural sex difference in the mammalian brain. As a model system it offers significant opportunities to investigate possible mechanisms of steroid action in bringing about the structural and presumably functional sexual differentiation of the brain. Whether future studies of the SDN-POA will reveal principles of hormone action of general applicability to the sexual differentiation of the brain remains to be determined.

ACKNOWLEDGEMENTS

The research of the author has been supported by NIH Grant HD-01182, and by grants from the Ford, Grant and Kroc Foundations and the Tejon Ranch.

REFERENCES

Altman, J. and Bayer, S.A. (1978) Development of the diencephalon in the rat. I. Autoradiographic study of the time of origin and settling patterns of neurons of the hypothalamus. *J. Comp. Neurol.*, 182: 945–972.

Anderson, C.H. (1978) Time of neuron origin in the anterior hypothalamus of the rat. *Brain Res.*, 154: 119–122.

Arai, Y. and Gorski, R.A. (1968a) Protection against the neural organizing effects of exogenous androgen in the neonatal female rat. *Endocrinology*, 82: 1005–1009.

Arai, Y. and Gorski, R.A. (1968b) The critical exposure time for androgenization of the developing hypothalamus in the female rat. *Endocrinology*, 82: 1010–1014.

Arendash, G.W. and Gorski, R.A. (1982) Enhancement of sexual behavior in female rats by neonatal transplantation of brain tissue from males. *Science*, 217: 1276–1278.

Arendash, G.W. and Gorski, R.A. (1983a) Effects of discrete lesions of the sexually dimorphic nucleus of the preoptic area or other medial preoptic regions on the sexual behavior of male rats. *Brain Res. Bull.*, 10: 147–154.

Arendash, G.W. and Gorski, R.A. (1983b) Testosterone-induced enhancement of male medial preoptic tissue transplant volumes in female recipients: a "neuronotrophic" action of testosterone. *Soc. Neurosci. Abstr.*, 9:307.

Arnold, A.P. (1980) Sexual differences in the brain. *Am. Scient.*, 68: 165–173.

Ayoub, D.M., Greenough, W.T. and Juraska, J.M. (1983) Sex differences in dendritic structure in the preoptic area of the juvenile macaque monkey brain. *Science*, 219: 197–198.

Breedlove, S.M. (1984) Steroid influences on the development and function of a neuromuscular system. In: G.J. De Vries, J.P.C. De Bruin, H.B.M. Uylings and M.A. Corner (Eds.), *Sex Differences in the Brain. The Relation between Structure and Function. Progress in Brain Research*, this volume, Ch. 8.

Breedlove, S.M. and Arnold, A.P. (1981) Sexually dimorphic motor nucleus in the rat lumbar spinal cord: Response to adult hormone manipulation, absence of androgen-insensitive rats. *Brain Res.*, 225: 297–307.

Christensen, L.W. and Gorski, R.A. (1978) Independent masculinization of neuroendocrine systems by intracerebral implants of testosterone or estradiol in the neonatal female rat. *Brain Res.*, 146: 325–340.

Clough, R.W. and Rodriguez-Sierra, J.F. (1982) Puberty associated neural synaptic changes in female rats administered estrogen. *Soc. Neurosci. Abstr.*, 8: 196.

Corbier, P., Kerdelhue, B., Picon, R. and Roffi, J. (1978) Changes in testicular weight and serum gonadotropin and testosterone levels before, during and after birth in the perinatal rat. *Endocrinology*, 103: 1985–1991.

Cowan, W.M. (1978) Aspects of neural development. In: R. Porter (Ed.), *International Review of Physiology and Neurophysiology III, Vol. 17*, University Park Press, Baltimore, MD, pp. 149–191.

DeBold, J.F. (1978) Modification of nuclear retention of [^{3}H]estradiol by cells of the hypothalamus as a function of early hormone experience. *Brain Res.*, 159: 416–420.

DeVoogd, T. (1984) The avian song system: relating sex differences in behavior to dimorphism in the central nervous system. In: G.J. De Vries, J.P.C. De Bruin, H.B.M. Uylings and M.A. Corner (Eds.), *Sex Differences in the Brain. The Relation between Structure and Function. Progress in Brain Research*, this volume, Ch. 9.

Döhler, K.D., Coquelin, A., Davis, F., Hines, M., Shryne, J.E. and Gorski, R.A. (1982a) Differentiation of the sexually dimorphic nucleus in the preoptic area of the rat is determined by the perinatal hormone environment. *Neurosci. Lett.*, 33: 295–298.

Döhler, K.D., Hines, M., Coquelin, A., Davis, F., Shryne, J.E. and Gorski, R.A. (1982b) Pre- and postnatal influence of diethylstilboestrol on differentiation of the sexually dimorphic nucleus in the preoptic area of the female rat brain. *Neuroendocrinol. Lett.*, 4: 361–365.

Döhler, K.D., Hancke, J.L., Srivastava, S.S., Hofmann, C., Shryne, J.E. and Gorski, R.A. (1984) Participation of estrogens in female sexual differentiation of the brain; neuroanatomical, neuroendocrine and behavioral evidence. In: G.J. De Vries, J.P.C. De Bruin, H.B.M. Uylings and M.A. Corner (Eds.), *Sex Differences in the Brain. The Relation between Structure and Function. Progress in Brain Research*, this volume, Ch. 5.

Dörner, G. and Staudt, J. (1968) Structural changes in the preoptic anterior hypothalamic area of the male rat, following neonatal castration and androgen substitution. *Neuroendocrinology*, 3: 136–140.

Dörner, G. and Staudt, J. (1969) Structural changes in the hypothalamic ventro-medial nucleus of the male rat, following neonatal castration and androgen treatment. *Neuroendocrinology*, 4: 278–281.

Gorski, R.A. (1967) Localization of the neural control of luteinization in the feminine male rat (FALE). *Anat. Rec.*, 157: 63–69.

Gorski, R.A. (1971) Gonadal hormones and the perinatal development of neuroendocrine function. In: L. Martini and W.F. Ganong (Eds.), *Frontiers in Neuroendocrinology, 1971*, Oxford University Press, New York, pp. 237–290.

Gorski, R.A. (1983a) Comparative aspects of sexual differentiation of the brain. In: M.M. Grumbach, P.C. Sizonenko and M.L. Aubert (Eds.), *The Control of the Onset of Puberty, Vol. II*, Academic Press, New York, in press.

Gorski, R.A. (1983b) Sexual dimorphisms of the brain. *J. Anim. Sci.*, in press.

Gorski, R.A. (1983c) Steroid-induced sexual characteristics in the brain. In: E.E. Muller and R.M. MacLeod (Eds.), *Neuroendocrine Perspectives, Vol. 2*, Elsevier, Amsterdam, in press.

Gorski, R.A. (1983d) Sexual differentiation of brain structure in rodents. In: L. Martini and F. Naftolin (Eds.), *Sexual Differentiation Basic and Clinical Aspects*, Raven Press, New York, in press.

Gorski, R.A. (1983e) Gonadal hormones as putative neuronotropic substances. In: C.W. Cotman (Ed.), *Synaptic Plasticity and Remodeling*, Guilford Press, New York, in press.

Gorski, R.A. and Jacobson, C.D. (1982) Sexual differentiation of the brain. *Frontiers in Hormone Research, Vol. 10*, pp. 1–14.

Gorski, R.A. and Shryne, J. (1972) Intracerebral antibiotics and androgenization of the neonatal female rat. *Neuroendocrinology*, 10: 109–120.

Gorski, R.A., Gordon, J.H., Shryne, J.E. and Southam, A.M. (1978) Evidence for a morphological sex difference within the medial preoptic area of the rat brain. *Brain Res.*, 148: 333–346.

Gorski, R.A., Harlan, R.E., Jacobson, C.D., Shryne, J.E. and Southam, A.M. (1980) Evidence for the existence of a sexually dimorphic nucleus in the preoptic area of the rat. *J. Comp. Neurol.*, 193: 529–539.

Gorski, R.A., Csernus, V.J. and Jacobson, C.D. (1981) Sexual dimorphism in the preoptic area. In: B. Flerkó, G. Sétáló and L. Tima (Eds.), *Advances in Physiological Sciences, Vol. 15, Reproduction and Development*, Pergamon, London and Akadémiai Kiadó, Budapest, pp. 121–130.

Goy, R.W. and McEwen, B.S. (1980) *Sexual Differentiation of the Brain.* MIT Press, Cambridge, MA, 223 pp.

Greenough, W.T., Carter, C.S., Steerman, C. and DeVoogd, T.J. (1977) Sex differences in dendritic patterns in hamster preoptic area. *Brain Res.*, 126: 63–72.

Gurney, M.E. (1981) Hormonal control of cell form and number in the zebra finch song system. *J. Neurosci.*, 1: 658–673.

Hamburger, V. and Oppenheim, R.S. (1982) Naturally-occurring neuronal death in vertebrates. *Neurosci. Comment.*, 1: 39–55.

Handa, R.J., Shryne, J.E., Schoonmaker, J.N., Corbier, P. and Gorski, R.A. (1982) Differential effects of the perinatal steroid environment on two parameters of sexual differentiation. *Soc. Neurosci. Abstr.*, 8: 197.

Harlan, R.E., Gordon, J.H. and Gorski, R.A. (1979) Sexual differentiation of the brain: Implications for neuroscience. *Rev. Neurosci.*, 4: 31–71.

Hayashi, S. and Gorski, R.A. (1974) Critical exposure time for androgenization by intracranial crystals of testosterone propionate in neonatal female rats. *Endocrinology*, 94: 1161–1167.

Hines, M., Davis, F.C., Goy, R.W. and Gorski, R.A. (1982) The existence of a sexually dimorphic nucleus in the preoptic area of the guinea pig brain. *Biol. Reprod.*, 26, Suppl. 1: 49A.

144   ROGER A. GORSKI

Hines, M., Coquelin, A., Davis, F.C., Goy, R.W. and Gorski, R.A. (1983) Sex differences in the preoptic area and the bed nucleus of the stria terminalis in the guinea pig are not a function of the adult hormonal environment. *Soc. Neurosci. Abstr.*, 9: 1094.

Ifft, J.D. (1972) An autoradiographic study of the time of final division of neurons in rat hypothalamic nuclei. *J. Comp. Neurol.*, 144: 193–204.

Jacobson, C.D. and Gorski, R.A. (1981) Neurogenesis of the sexually dimorphic nucleus of the preoptic area of the rat. *J. Comp. Neurol.*, 196: 519–529.

Jacobson, C.D., Shryne, J.E., Shapiro, F. and Gorski, R.A. (1980) Ontogeny of the sexually dimorphic nucleus of the preoptic area. *J. Comp. Neurol.*, 193: 541–548.

Jacobson, C.D., Csernus, V.J., Shryne, J.E. and Gorski, R.A. (1981a) The influence of gonadectomy, androgen exposure, or a gonadal graft in the neonatal rat on the volume of the sexually dimorphic nucleus of the preoptic area. *J. Neurosci.*, 1: 1142–1147.

Jacobson, C.D., Davis, F.C., Freiberg, E. and Gorski, R.A. (1981b) Formation of the sexually dimorphic nucleus of the preoptic area of the male rat. *Soc. Neurosci. Abstr.*, 7 : 286.

Jacobson, C.D., Arnold, A.P. and Gorski, R.A. (1982) Steroid accumulation in the sexually dimorphic nucleus of the preoptic area (SDN-POA). *Anat. Rec.*, 202: 88A.

Kobayashi, F. and Gorski, R.A. (1970) Effects of antibiotics on androgenization of the neonatal female rat. *Endocrinology*, 86: 285–289.

Ladosky, W., Kesikowski, W.M. and Gaziri, I.F. (1970) Effect of a single injection of chlorpromazine into infant male rats on subsequent gonadotrophin secretion. *J. Endocrinol.*, 48: 151–156.

Lawrence, J.M. and Raisman, G. (1980) Ontogeny of synapses in a sexually dimorphic part of the preoptic area in the rat. *Brain Res.*, 183: 466–471.

Lieberburg, I., Wallach, G. and McEwen, B.S. (1977) The effects of an inhibitor of aromatization (1,4,6-androstatriene-3,17-dione) and an antiestrogen (CI-628) on in vivo formed testosterone metabolites recovered from neonatal rat brain tissues and purified cell nuclei. Implications for sexual differentiation of the rat brain. *Brain Res.*, 128: 176–181.

Litteria, M. (1973) Inhibitory action of neonatal androgenization on the incorporation of [^{3}H]lysine in specific hypothalamic nuclei of the adult female rat. *Exp. Neurol.*, 41: 395–401.

Litteria, M. (1977) Effect of neonatal estrogen on in vivo transport of α-aminoiso-butyric acid into rat brain. *Exp. Neurol.*, 57: 817–827.

Lobl, R.T. and Gorski, R.A. (1974) Neonatal intrahypothalamic androgen administration: The influence of dose and age on androgenization of female rats. *Endocrinology*, 94: 1325–1330.

Lookingland, K.J., Wise, P.M. and Barraclough, C.A. (1982) Failure of the hypothalamic noradrenergic system to function in adult androgen-sterilized rats. *Biol. Reprod.*, 27: 268.

Matsumoto, A. and Arai, Y. (1976) Effect of estrogen on early postnatal development of synaptic formation in the hypothalamic arcuate nucleus of female rats. *Neurosci. Lett.*, 2: 79–82.

Matsumoto, A. and Arai, Y. (1980) Sexual dimorphism in "wiring pattern" in the hypothalamic arcuate nucleus and its modification by neonatal hormonal environment. *Brain Res.*, 190: 238–242.

McEwen, B.S. (1983) Gonadal steroid influences on brain development and sexual differentiation. In: R.O. Greep (Ed.), *International Review of Physiology*, University Park Press, Baltimore, MD, pp. 99–145.

Nadler, R.D. (1968) Masculinization of female rats by intracranial implantation of androgen in infancy. *J. Comp. Physiol. Psychol.*, 66: 157–167.

Naess, O., Haug, E., Attramadal, A., Aadvaag, A., Hansson, V. and French, F. (1976) Androgen receptors in the anterior pituitary and central nervous system of the androgen "insensitive" (Tfm) rat: correlation between receptor binding and effects of androgens on gonadotropic secretion. *Endocrinology*, 99: 1295–1303.

Nishizuka, M. and Arai, Y. (1981) Organizational action of estrogen on synaptic pattern in the amygdala: implications for sexual differentiation of the brain. *Brain Res.*, 213: 422–426.

Nottebohm, F. (1981) A brain for all seasons: cyclical anatomical changes in song control nuclei of the canary brain. *Science*, 214: 1368–1370.

Nottebohm, F. and Arnold, A.P. (1976) Sexual dimorphism in vocal control areas of the songbird brain. *Science*, 194: 211–213.

Nunez, E., Savu, L., Engelmann, F., Benassayag, C., Crepy, O. and Jayle, M.F. (1971) Origine embryonnaire de la protéine sérique fixant l'œstrone et l'œstradiol chez la ratte impubère. *C.R. Acad. Sci. (Paris)*, 273: 242–245.

Olsen, K.L. and Whalen, R.E. (1980) Sexual differentiation of the brain: Effects on mating behavior and ^{3}H-estradiol binding by hypothalamic chromatin in rats. *Biol. Reprod.*, 22: 1068–1072.

Pfaff, D.W. (1966) Morphological changes in the brains of adult male rats after neonatal castration. *J. Endocrinol.*, 36: 415–416.

Plapinger, L., McEwen, B.S. and Clemens, L.E. (1973) Ontogeny of estradiol-binding sites in rat brain. II. Characteristics of a neonatal binding macromolecule. *Endocrinology*, 93: 1129–1139.

Purves, D. (1977) The formation and maintenance of synaptic connections. In: G.S. Stent (Ed.), *Function and Formation of Neural Systems*, Dahlem Konferenzen, Berlin, pp. 21–49.

Rainbow, T.C., Parsons, B. and McEwen, B.S. (1982) Sex differences in rat brain oestrogen and progestin receptors. *Nature (London)*, 300: 648–649.

Raisman, G. and Field, P.M. (1973) Sexual dimorphism in the neuropil of the preoptic area of the rat and its dependence on neonatal androgen. *Brain Res.*, 54: 1–29.

Raynaud, J.P., Mercier-Bodard, C. and Baulieu, E.E. (1971) Rat estradiol binding plasma protein (EBP). *Steroids*, 18: 767–788.

Reier, P.J., Cullen, M.J., Froelich, J.S. and Rothchild, I. (1977) The ultrastructure of the developing medial preoptic nucleus in the postnatal rat. *Brain Res.*, 122: 415–436.

Salaman, D.F. and Birkett, S. (1974) Androgen-induced sexual differentiation of the brain is blocked by inhibitors of DNA and RNA synthesis. *Nature (London)*, 247: 109.

Schoonmaker, J.N., Breedlove, S.M., Arnold, A.P. and Gorski, R.A. (1983) Accumulation of steroid in the sexually dimorphic nucleus of the preoptic area in the neonatal rat hypothalamus. *Soc. Neurosci. Abstr.*, 9: 1094.

Silver, J. (1978) Cell death during development of the nervous system. In: M. Jacobson (Ed.), *Handbook of Sensory Physiology, Vol. IX, Development of Sensory Systems*, Springer, Berlin, pp. 429–436.

Simerly, R.B., Swanson, L.W. and Gorski, R.A. (1984) Demonstration of a sexual dimorphism in the distribution of serotonin immunoreactive fibers in the medial preoptic nucleus of the rat. *J. Comp. Neurol.*, 225: 151–166.

Södersten, P. (1978) Lordosis behaviour in male, female and androgenized female rats. *J. Endocrinol.*, 70: 409–420.

Tobet, S.A., Gallagher, C.A., Zahniser, D.J., Cohen, M.H. and Baum, M.J. (1983) Sexual dimorphism in the preoptic/anterior hypothalamic area of adult ferrets. *Endocrinology*, 112, Suppl.: 240.

Toran-Allerand, C.D. (1981) Gonadal steroids and brain development. *Trends Neurosci.*, 4: 118–121.

Toran-Allerand, C.D. (1984) On the genesis of sexual differentiation of the central nervous system: Morphogenetic consequences of steroidal exposure and possible role of α-fetoprotein. In: G.J. De Vries, J.P.C. De Bruin, H.B.M. Uylings and M.A. Corner (Eds.), *Sex Differences in the Brain. The Relation between Structure and Function. Progress in Brain Research*, this volume, Ch. 4.

Toran-Allerand, C.D., Gerlach, J.L. and McEwen, B.S. (1980) Autoradiographic localization of ^{3}H-estradiol related to steroid responsiveness in cultures of the hypothalamus and preoptic area. *Brain Res.*, 184: 517–522.

Toran-Allerand, C.D., Hashimoto, K., Greenough, W.T. and Saltarelli, M. (1983) Sex steroids and the development of the newborn mouse hypothalamus and preoptic area in vitro. III. Effects of estrogen on dendritic differentiation. *Develop. Brain Res.*, 7: 97–101.

Vértes, M., Vértes, Z. and Kovács, S. (1978) Analysis of the hypothalamic mechanism of action of oestradiol in developing and adult rats. In: K. Lissák (Ed.), *Recent Developments of Neurobiology in Hungary, Vol. 7*, Hungarian Academy of Sciences, Budapest, pp. 99–143.

Wagner, J.W., Erwin, W. and Critchlow, V. (1966) Androgen sterilization produced by intracerebral inplants of testosterone in neonatal female rats. *Endocrinology*, 79: 1135–1142.

Weisz, J. and Ward, I.L. (1980) Plasma testosterone and progesterone titers of pregnant rats, their male and female fetuses, and neonatal offspring. *Endocrinology*, 106: 306–316.

Yahr, P. and Commins, D. (1983) The neuroendocrinology of scent marking. In: R.M. Silverstein and D. Muller-Schwarze (Eds.), *Chemical Signals in Vertebrates, Vol. 2*, Plenum, New York, in press.

Young, J.K. (1982) A comparison of hypothalami of rats and mice: lack of gross sexual dimorphism in the mouse. *Brain Res.*, 239: 233–239.

DISCUSSION

K.-D. DÖHLER: You demonstrated that female rats which had received SDN-POA implants from male rats postnatally not only showed more mounting behavior in adulthood than normal control females, but they also showed more lordosis behavior after priming with estradiol. Lordosis behavior after priming with estradiol was even more intense when these animals were treated postnatally with small amounts of testosterone. We also observed that androgenized female rats showed more intense lordosis behavior after priming with estradiol in adulthood, than normal females (Jarzab and Döhler, 1984). The same phenomenon was observed already in 1969 by Clemens, Gorski and Hiroi. It seems to me that postnatal treatment of female rats with small amounts of an aromatizable androgen actually increases, not decreases, lordosis responsiveness to estradiol.

R.A. GORSKI: This is true. Lightly androgenized females can be behaviorally more responsive to estrogen. It may be that this is related to your suggestion and that of Dr. Toran-Allerand that some hormone exposure may be necessary for the development of the female brain; at least the observation that female behavior is "improved" by exposure to small doses of testosterone is consistent with that hypothesis.

C.D. TORAN-ALLERAND: I am not sure why one need postulate a steroidal effect on migration since steroidal effects on neurogenesis or cell survival would of necessity influence the patterns of migration, since increased cell numbers would of necessity influence their migratory patterns.

R.A. GORSKI: In thinking about possible mechanisms, I thought it possible that gonadal hormones might modify the process of migration independent of other developmental parameters. Changes in migration might, as you say, be dependent on other factors such as neurogenesis, and perhaps not influenced by hormones at all. Until we have conclusive data, however, I feel we should entertain all possibilities.

E.B. KEVERNE: From the slide you showed of early neurogenesis it appeared that from the population of migrating neuroblasts from the ependyma, some were also passing down to the SCN. Bearing in mind the dimorphic functioning of SCN and its rich 5-HT innervation, was there any evidence for either a dimorphic appearance of this nucleus or its innervation?

R.A. GORSKI: We have not analyzed other regions carefully but we do think that there are other neuronal populations arising at this time, which may form a structurally dimorphic system but this still has to be proven. We do not believe the SCN will be part of that system.

H.H. SWANSON: 200 μg TP for 5 consecutive days after birth is sufficient to cause functional masculinization. If you found that this dose increased the size of transplants from male tissue, how do you know that residual female tissue might not have similarly increased in size and have had similar behavioral consequences?

R.A. GORSKI: This is certainly true, but in this study we were trying to determine an effect of TP on graft survival and/or growth. These animals were not studied behaviorally. In our initial study we used a low dose of TP (8 μg) which had no, or only minimal effects on the females without, or with control grafts.

E. FRIDE: If I understood you correctly, you noted for the first time a significant sex difference in thymidine labeling when you injected it on day 17 of gestation. This fits well with the T surge in male rats on this day. Now, after prenatal stress, which feminizes the male, this peak is delayed by 1 day. In view of these data, do you think that you could detect a reversal of the sex difference in the size of the SDN (i.e. a decrease) after (the same form of) prenatal stress?

R.A. GORSKI: Rhees had reported that prenatal stress does reduce the size of the SDN-POA of the male. Although it is tempting to relate the apparent sex difference in neurogenesis on day 17 of pregnancy to the testosterone surge, two points are important. First, we see another sex difference on day 14 (female greater than male) but no known hormonal basis; our results on day 17 may be only related to testosterone by coincidence. Second, and more important, since the animals were not sacrificed until day 30 postnatally, other developmental processes (e.g. migration, neuronal death; even postnatal hormone action) could also be involved.

D.F. SWAAB: Since you mentioned immunocytochemical work being in progress on the sexually dimorphic nucleus, can you tell us anything on the transmitter content of the cell bodies of this nucleus?

R.A. GORSKI: In many cases the SDN-POA appears to be devoid of transmitters and neuropeptides. There is evidence for cholecystokinin-positive terminals within the SDN-POA, as well as opiate receptors.

REFERENCES

Clemens, L.G., Hiroi, H. and Gorski, R.A. (1969) Induction and facilitation of female mating behavior in rats treated neonatally with low doses of testosterone propionate. *Endocrinology*, 84: 1430–1438.

Jarzab, B. and Döhler K.D. (1984) Serotoninergic influences on sexual differentiation of the rat brain. In: G.J. De Vries, J.P.C. De Bruin, H.B.M. Uylings and M.A. Corner (Eds.), *Sex Differences in the Brain. The Relation between Structure and Function. Progress in Brain Research*, this volume, Ch. 6.

G.J. De Vries et al. (Eds.),
Progress in Brain Research, Vol. 61
© 1984   Elsevier Science Publishers B.V., Amsterdam

Steroid Influences on the Development and Function of a Neuromuscular System

S. MARC BREEDLOVE

Department of Psychology, University of California, Berkeley, CA 94720 (U.S.A.)

INTRODUCTION

Among the many recent discoveries of sexual dimorphism in the CNS of various species (Arnold, 1980) are examples of sex differences in neuronal number (Calaresu and Henry, 1971; Nottebohm and Arnold, 1976; Gorski et al., 1978; Hannigan and Kelley, 1981), size (Pfaff, 1966; Bubenik and Brown, 1973; Nottebohm and DeVoogd, 1981) and pattern of connectivity (Raisman and Field, 1973; Greenough et al., 1977). For all of the sexual dimorphisms which have been investigated thus far, steroid hormone exposure during early development has proven responsible for male neural structures differing from those of females. But research has only begun to elucidate the mechanisms by which hormones alter development, and often the functional significance of such alterations is not understood. This chapter focuses upon a sexually dimorphic neuromuscular system in the rat: the spinal nucleus of the bulbocavernosus (SNB) and its target musculature (Breedlove and Arnold, 1980). The SNB system is readily studied and therefore provides a model for the elucidation of steroidal mechanisms which shape the developing nervous system. Steroids have both long- and short-term effects on this neuromuscular system throughout ontogeny, and the function of these neurons is now well established. In discussing the SNB system I will describe: (1) sex differences in the morphology of muscles and motoneurons, (2) the hormone sensitivity of neurons and target in adulthood, (3) the crucial function of this neuromuscular system in reproduction, and (4) the ontogenetic role of steroid hormones in determining the number, size and connectivity of these neurons.

SEXUAL DIMORPHISM IN THE RODENT SPINAL CORD AND PERINEUM: THE SNB SYSTEM

Sexual dimorphism of perineal musculature

Most mammals, such as cats, dogs and primates possess striated perineal muscles which, while differing in form in males and females, are nonetheless recognizably the same muscle in both sexes. In rodents however, there are 4 striated perineal muscles which are present only in males (Greene, 1963). These muscles are the medial and lateral bulbocavernosus (BC), the levator ani (LA) and the ischiocavernosus (IC). The IC attaches to the base of the penis and the ischium, while the other muscles attach exclusively to the penis (see Fig. 1). Although in

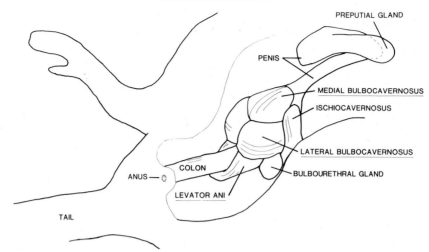

Fig. 1. Schematic dissection of the perineal region of a male rat. The muscles bulbocavernosus (BC) and levator ani (LA) are innervated by the spinal nucleus of the bulbocavernosus. The LA is sometimes called the dorsal bulbocavernosus. The ischiocavernosus (IC) is innervated by a subpopulation of the dorsolateral nucleus of the fifth and sixth lumbar spinal segments. The striated muscles BC, LA and IC are absent from adult female rats (Wainman and Shipounoff, 1941). (From Breedlove, 1981.)

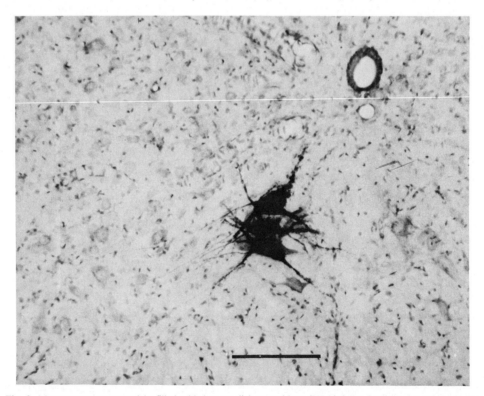

Fig. 2. Motoneurons retrogradely filled with horseradish peroxidase (HRP) following injection of the bulbo-cavernosus muscle of a male rat. The HRP was stained by the *o*-dianisidine method of DeOlmos, then counterstained with carbol-fuchsin. The central canal is visible in the upper right. Scale bar equals 200 μm. (From Breedlove, 1981.)

terms of homology and function it would be more appropriate to name the LA the dorsal bulbocavernosus (Hayes, 1965), there is a considerable literature calling this muscle the LA, and therefore that designation will be used here.

Sexual dimorphism in the spinal cord

While I was a graduate student with Dr. Arthur P. Arnold at UCLA, we injected horseradish peroxidase (HRP) into the perineal muscles of male rats in order to retrogradely fill and thereby locate the motoneurons innervating them (Fig. 2). Those motoneurons innervating the muscles BC and LA form a distinctive nucleus in the dorso-medial aspect of the ventral horn in lumbar segments 5 and 6 (Breedlove and Arnold, 1980) (see Fig. 3). We named this nucleus the spinal nucleus of the bulbocavernosus, or SNB. The SNB is strikingly dimorphic in the two sexes, as it is visible to the naked eye in Nissl-stained sections from male but not female rats (Fig. 4). The BC/LA muscles and the SNB of mice, hamsters, golden-mantled ground squirrels and white-footed mice are also present exclusively in males (S.M. Breedlove, unpublished observations). Detailed analysis of the SNB region of the spinal cord in both sexes revealed that female rats had only one-third as many densely staining neurons in this area, and those few neurons present were only one-half as large as in males (Breedlove and Arnold, 1981). The scarcity and small size of motoneurons in the SNB region results in females lacking a coherent nucleus there. For ease of quantification, however, motoneurons present in that region of the spinal cord are designated as SNB cells. The function of these "remnant" SNB cells in normal females is presently unknown, but obviously they do not innervate the BC or LA, since female rats lack these muscles.

The fifth and sixth lumbar spinal segments of rats contain 3 motoneuronal nuclei representing a range of sexual dimorphism. The SNB, which innervates the masculine musculature BC and LA, is quite dimorphic in the number and size of neurons. The retrodorsolateral nucleus (RDLN, see Fig. 3) innervates leg muscles (Schroder, 1980) via the sciatic nerve (Navaratnam and Lewis, 1970) and there is no significant sex difference in the number or size of RDLN neurons (Jordan et al., 1982). The dorsolateral nucleus (DLN, see Fig. 3) displays an intermediate degree of sexual dimorphism. Most DLN motoneurons innervate leg

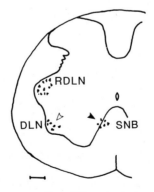

Fig. 3. Schematic drawing of a transverse section of the rat spinal cord showing the location of dorsolateral nucleus (DLN) motoneurons innervating the ischiocavernosus, and the spinal nucleus of the bulbocavernosus (SNB) innervating the bulbocavernosus and levator ani. Motoneurons of the retrodorsolateral nucleus (RDLN) innervate leg muscles via the sciatic nerve. Scale bar equals 200 μm. (From Breedlove, 1981.)

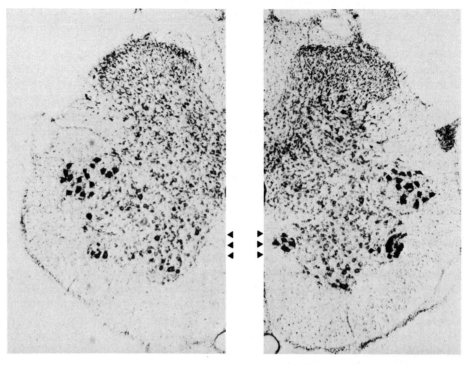

FEMALE   MALE

Fig. 4. Photomicrographs of the fifth lumbar segment of the spinal cord of a female (left) and male rat. The spinal nucleus of the bulbocavernosus (SNB) is an easily recognized, discrete nucleus in the male only. The arrows indicate the anatomical limits of the SNB in males (right). This region, 200–400 μm ventral to the central canal and within 250 μm of the midline, was examined in male and female fifth and sixth lumbar spinal segments, within which all densely staining cells were designated as SNB cells for comparison between treatment groups and the two sexes. (Modified from Breedlove and Arnold, 1981.)

muscles of both sexes (Schroder, 1980), but a subpopulation of the DLN innervates the IC (Breedlove and Arnold, 1980) which is present only in males. Consequently, although both sexes possess a coherent DLN, there are significantly more motoneurons in the DLN of male than of female rats (Jordan et al., 1982).

HORMONE SENSITIVITY OF THE SNB SYSTEM

SNB cells accumulate androgens but not estrogens

The sexually dimorphic character of both the SNB and its target muscles suggests that they play a role in androgen-sensitive masculine behavior, therefore the hormone accumulation of these motoneurons was investigated. Using autoradiographic criteria, we found that virtually every lumbar motoneuron accumulates the androgen dihydrotestosterone (DHT) or its metabolites and essentially none accumulate estradiol (Breedlove and Arnold, 1980, 1983c). For example, more than 90% of the SNB cells accumulate DHT or its metabolites, but less than 4% reach the criterion for accumulation of estrogen (Fig. 5).

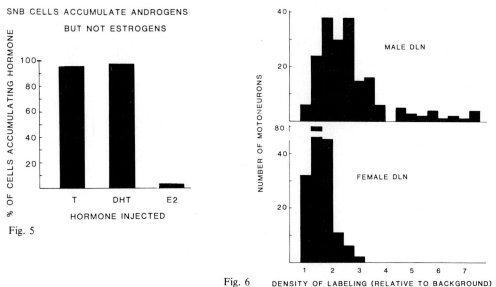

Fig. 5

Fig. 6   DENSITY OF LABELING (RELATIVE TO BACKGROUND)

Fig. 5. Motoneurons of the SNB accumulate significant quantities of radioactivity into their nuclei following the injection of tritiated testosterone (T) or dihydrotestosterone (DHT), but not estradiol (E2). The Poisson criterion (Arnold, 1981) for determination of accumulation was used. (Modified from Breedlove and Arnold, 1980.)

Fig. 6. Histograms comparing the relative density of silver grains over the motoneuronal nuclei in the dorsolateral nucleus (DLN) in autoradiograms from male (upper) and female rats following the injection of tritiated testosterone. Note that in addition to an overall greater density of labeling of DLN cells in males, some cells are very densely labeled (upper right). The morphology and anatomical location of these heavily labeled cells suggest they are that subpopulation of the DLN which innervates the sexually dimorphic ischiocavernosus muscle.

Regional differences in hormone accumulation by motoneurons

When tritiated testosterone (T) is injected, the various motoneuronal nuclei accumulate steroid to different extents. While more than 95% of the SNB cells significantly accumulate T or its metabolites, only 72% of the RDLN cells do. Furthermore, the SNB cells accumulate more radioactivity per cell than do RDLN motoneurons. Thus SNB motoneurons innervating muscles with a distinctly masculine function (see The reproductive function of SNB cells) accumulate more androgen more often than RDLN motoneurons innervating the non-sexually related leg muscles. The DLN motoneuronal group provides an interesting intermediate condition. Following T injection, most DLN cells show a moderately dense accumulation of radioactivity, comparable to that of RDLN cells. However, a subpopulation of DLN cells accumulate hormone much more heavily than the others (see Fig. 6, top right). The elongate morphology of these labeled cells, and their anatomical position within the DLN are reminiscent of IC motoneurons identified in HRP studies. It may be that, within the DLN, IC motoneurons with masculine functions accumulate androgen more efficiently than their non-sexually related neighbors.

Sex differences in hormone accumulation by motoneurons

The autoradiographic study by Breedlove and Arnold (1983c) revealed that following tritiated T injection, about twice as many DLN or RDLN motoneurons are labeled in males

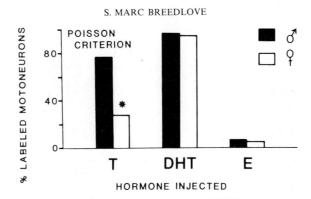

Fig. 7. Histograms displaying the percentage of dorsolateral nucleus (DLN) motoneurons accumulating radioactivity after the injection of tritiated T, or its metabolites DHT or E. The number of hormone-accumulating cells was determined by the Poisson criterion (Arnold, 1981). DLN cells in male rats accumulate hormone more often than those of females following the injection of T ($P < 0.01$), but not DHT or E. (From Breedlove and Arnold, 1983c.)

as in females, indicating a sex difference in hormone accumulation (Fig. 7). This sex difference in hormone accumulation by motoneurons is not observed following the injection of DHT or estradiol (E), both of which are normal metabolites of T. Virtually no motoneurons accumulate E or its metabolites, while nearly every motoneuron from either sex accumulates hormone after DHT injection. There are now several reports of subtle but demonstrable sex differences in hormone accumulation in the CNS (Breedlove, 1983a). In some cases, these sex differences are in regions known to be dimorphic in neuronal number, such as the dorsolateral nucleus (DLN) motoneurons in Breedlove and Arnold (1983c). There is no sex difference in the number of retrodorsolateral nucleus (RDLN) cells (Jordan et al., 1982) and yet more of these motoneurons accumulate T or its metabolites in males than in females (Breedlove and Arnold, 1983c). Although the functional significance of the sex difference in hormone accumulation by motoneurons is unknown, the generalized function of the RDLN-innervated leg muscles suggests that the sex difference in hormone accumulation may be a general characteristic of motoneurons in rats.

The sex difference in accumulation of T or its metabolites by motoneurons may be of functional significance since T is the normally occurring form of androgen in rats. How does this sex difference in hormone accumulation arise during ontogeny? The rats in the aforementioned study (Breedlove and Arnold, 1983c) were gonadectomized and adrenalectomized 3 days prior to hormone injection, and therefore the hormonal environments should have been equalized in the two sexes. It may be that the sex difference in the hormonal milieu a few days prior to T injection is responsible for the observed sex difference in accumulation, or perhaps the sex difference in hormone accumulation is a more permanent distinction caused by the different perinatal hormonal environments of the two sexes. For example, the perinatal presence of androgen in males may favor the survival of androgen-accumulating motoneurons, or may augment the number of androgen receptors or the activity of enzymes in those motoneurons present. Such sex differences in hormone accumulation may contribute to sex differences in behavioral response to hormone and may represent an important dimension of the sexual differentiation of the nervous system.

Evidence for regional variation in 5α-reductase

Thus there are both regional differences and sex differences in the accumulation of radioactivity by motoneurons after injection of T but not DHT or E. Two general mechanisms could account for these variations. If rat spinal motoneurons contain two androgen receptors, one with a high affinity for T and the other for DHT, then the present results might indicate a sex difference in the number of motoneurons with T receptors, but no sex difference in DHT receptors. Similarly, the various motoneuronal nuclei might vary in the concentration of T but not DHT receptors. Since there has yet to be a conclusive demonstration of the existence of separate T and DHT receptors (McEwen, 1981), this interesting hypothesis remains dubious.

Alternatively, it may be that monotypic androgen receptors in motoneurons of male and female rats differ in their functional access to hormone. The following 5 propositions provide the most parsimonious explanation for region and sex differences in androgen accumulation by these motoneurons. (1) Virtually all the motoneurons have androgen receptors because they heavily accumulate DHT or its metabolites. (2) These androgen receptors, like those found elsewhere (Krieg et al., 1974), have a greater affinity for DHT than T, since all motoneurons accumulate hormone more densely following the injection of DHT than T (Breedlove and Arnold, 1983c). (3) Among males, SNB cells may have more 5α-reductase than RDLN cells and therefore accumulate more androgen in their nuclei after T injection. (4) IC motoneurons within the DLN of males have more reductase available than the leg motoneuron neighbors within the same nucleus. (5) The RDLN cells of female rats have less reductase available than do those of males. There is such a sex difference in 5α-reductase activity in the frog cervical spinal cord (Jurman et al., 1982).

Steroid receptors in rat perineal muscles

Many researchers tried to detect androgen receptors in striated muscle and, until 1972 they all failed (e.g. Mainwaring, 1972). The first successful detection of androgen receptors in striated muscle was in the LA (Jung and Baulieu, 1972), which shows the greatest physiological responsiveness to androgen in rats (Kochakian, 1975). Eventually androgen receptors were found in other striated muscles (Michel and Baulieu, 1974). LA/BC muscles also contain a protein which preferentially binds estradiol (Dube et al., 1976) and apparently the estrogenic metabolites of T mediate androgen's augmentation of enzyme activity in rat LA (Knudsen and Max, 1980). Therefore considerations of steroid influence upon the SNB system must include the musculature itself as a potential site of action, via either androgenic or estrogenic metabolites.

Motoneurons may mediate androgen's anabolic effect

It has long been known that androgens exert an "anabolic" effect, i.e. increase muscle protein content (Kochakian, 1975). It has been generally assumed that androgens act directly upon the muscle to increase its weight. This assumption was supported by the eventual discovery of androgen receptors in muscle (Jung and Baulieu, 1972) and the report that T increased mitotic activity in pure muscle cell culture (Powers and Florini, 1975). These findings together are offered as proof that androgen acts directly on muscles to increase their weight (Bardin and Catterall, 1981). However, there are several reasons to doubt this assertion. (1) The weight of LA is increased 50–500% more effectively by DHT than by T

(Dorfman and Kincl, 1963; Edgren, 1963). This greater effectiveness of DHT is puzzling if the muscle itself is the only site of androgen action because several laboratories have shown that the LA muscle rapidly converts systemically administered DHT to inactive compounds, and binds much more radioactivity after T injection than after DHT injection (Krieg et al., 1974; Dionne et al., 1979). Furthermore, there is virtually no 5a-reductase activity in the LA/BC muscle complex (Gloyna and Wilson, 1969). If the muscle is the sole site of action, T would be expected to be a more effective anabolic agent than DHT, but quite the opposite is true. (2) The concentration of androgen receptors measured in muscle by in vitro techniques is much lower than for classic androgen targets such as the prostate (e.g. Krieg et al., 1974). Similarly, autoradiographic analysis fails to show any accumulation of androgen over LA/BC muscle nuclei (Breedlove and Arnold, unpublished observations). In fact, there is no evidence that the biochemically detected androgen receptors in LA/BC are translocated into muscle fiber nuclei. (3) T treatment is ineffective in increasing the weight of adult LA muscles that are denervated (Buresova et al., 1972), although admittedly this lack of responsiveness could be due to a general debilitation of the LA. (4) The report of increased mitosis in muscle cultures treated with T (Powers and Florini, 1975) may be of little relevance to the adult muscle's response to androgen, because in rats and mice the anabolic response is mediated by an increase in muscle fiber size, not an increase in the number of fibers (Venable, 1966). In short, myogenesis is not relevant to androgen's anabolic effect in vivo.

The subsequent discovery that motoneurons at various CNS levels readily accumulate androgen (Sar and Stumpf, 1977) suggests that there may be a neural site of androgen's anabolic action in addition to or instead of the muscular site. If so, then the finding that motoneurons accumulate hormone much more effectively after DHT than T injection (Breedlove and Arnold, 1983c) correlates well with the greater anabolic effect of DHT. Similarly, the lack of effect of androgen in denervated muscle may be due to the loss of motoneuronally mediated influences. Finally, the greater androgen sensitivity of LA and BC muscles may be due to the fact that their motoneurons in the SNB accumulate T or its metabolites more frequently and more densely than other motoneurons (Breedlove and Arnold, 1983c).

THE REPRODUCTIVE FUNCTION OF SNB CELLS

Briefly, SNB motoneurons control BC muscles mediating penile reflexes which accomplish several tasks: (1) help form a proper copulatory plug over the female's cervix and thereby facilitate sperm transport through the uterus, (2) remove any copulatory plug presently covering the cervix, and (3) possibly provide some of the vagino-cervical stimulation which is essential for the maintenance of pregnancy in rats. Obviously, these functions are crucial to male reproductive success.

Androgen-sensitive genital reflexes in male rats

In an extensive series of studies, Hart described a pattern of reflexive flips and erections of the penis in male rats. These reflexes were elicited by simply holding back the preputial sheath of male rats whose spinal cord had been transected at the mid-thoracic level (Hart, 1968). Hart (1967) found that castration results in a decrease in the frequency of these reflexes, while testosterone replacement therapy restores them. The spinal cord itself may be the site at which androgen potentiates the reflexes, since Hart and Haugen (1968) found that local implants of androgen into the spinal cord could augment the reflexes. These implants did not affect male secondary sex organ weight, which indicates that the implant was resulting in little systemic androgen exposure. Hart (1979) also found that of the two major metabolites of T, only dihydrotestosterone propionate (DHTP) and not estradiol benzoate (EB) potentiated the flips.

The next logical step was to determine the relevance of these reflexes in spinally transected males to the normal course of male copulatory behavior. However, this determination proved difficult. Only a minority of intact males could be made to display the reflexes (Sachs and Garinello, 1978), therefore the reflexes might have been a mere artifact of the spinal transection. Furthermore, since spinally transected males do not copulate, it would be impossible to correlate manipulations of the reflexes with effects on copulatory behavior. Of those intact males which displayed the reflexes, there was no clear correlation of reflex intensity with the traditional measures of rodent male copulatory behavior (Sachs and Garinello, 1978; Kurtz and Santos, 1979). Finally, the relevance of the flips was called into question by the types of hormones to which they responded. Because the aromatized metabolites of T were known to be much more effective for restoring masculine behavior in castrates than the 5a-reduced metabolites, the insensitivity of the flips to EB (Hart, 1979) indicated to some researchers that the flips could not be important to normal male copulatory behavior.

Perineal muscles mediate genital reflexes

SNB cells control the BC muscles which in dogs (Hart and Kitchell, 1966; Purohit and Beckett, 1976), goats (Beckett et al., 1972), horses (Beckett et al., 1973), cows (Beckett et al., 1974) and humans (Kollberg et al., 1962; Karacan et al., 1983) are known to be active during erection and/or ejaculation. However, the function of these muscles in rats has been studied only very recently. After examining the anatomy of the BC/LA/IC musculature, Breedlove and Arnold (1980) simply asserted that these perineal muscles must mediate the genital reflexes described by Hart (1968). Later research from two independent laboratories (Sachs, 1982; Hart and Melese-d'Hospital, 1983) confirmed this assertion and provided considerable detail about the individual contributions of the different muscles.

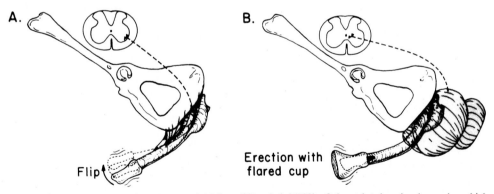

Fig. 8. Schematic diagram from Hart and Melese-d'Hospital (1983) of the striated perineal muscles which mediate penile reflexes in male rats. (A) Penile flips appear to be caused by contraction of the ischiocavernosus muscle which is innervated by dorsolateral nucleus motoneurons. (B) Contraction of the bulbocavernosus produces a flared, cup-like erection of the glans penis. As indicated in the figure, the bulbocavernosus is innervated by motoneurons of the SNB.

Hart and Melese-d'Hospital (1983) recorded electromyographic activity of the striated perineal musculature and found that the BC is active during erections and the IC is active during flips of the penis (Fig. 8). These authors also reported that surgical removal of the BC eliminates the type of erection that produces a flaring of the distal glans penis, resulting in a cup-like appearance. Surgical removal of the IC reduces penile flips, virtually eliminating the more vigorous types of flips (Hart and Melese-d'Hospital, 1983). Sachs (1982) had earlier reported very similar findings based on ablation of the muscles: i.e. removal of the IC eliminates flips but not erections, while removal of the BC eliminates cup-like erections but not flips. Because the SNB mediates these penile reflexes and receives enkephalinergic afferents (Moskowitz et al., 1982), it is possible that naloxone inhibits penile reflexes (Sachs et al., 1981) by acting upon the motoneurons themselves.

Perineal muscles are important for male reproductive success

Once the muscles mediating the penile reflexes had been identified, it was possible for the first time to relate the reflexes observed in transected males to normal male copulation. Manipulation of these muscles in spinally intact males revealed that the same muscles which were necessary for the reflexes were also necessary for successful reproduction. Sachs (1982) reported that in spinally intact males, removal of the IC greatly reduced the number of literal intromissions. Males in which the BC and LA muscles were removed showed normal male copulatory behavior as measured by the postural correlates of copulation, but this apparent normality is deceiving. Sachs found that the females mated to such males only rarely became pregnant and he concluded that the infertility of males without BC/LA muscles was caused by the failure to form proper copulatory plugs over the cervix. These seminal plugs are known to be important for sperm transport (Matthews and Adler, 1978). Wallach and Hart (1983) likewise concluded that animals with excised BC muscles failed to form normal copulatory plugs. These authors also concluded that intact BC musculature was necessary for the removal of previously deposited copulatory plugs. In wild rats, the ability to remove previously deposited plugs, which may have been implanted by another male, is probably vital to successful reproduction (McClintock et al., 1982). Because the perineal muscles mediate the penile reflexes, and because these same muscles are necessary for the successful deposition of seminal plugs, it may be inferred that the muscles deposit the plug via activation of the reflexes. This inference has not been tested directly, and it is possible that the reflexes do not occur during copulation, but are simply a convenient measure of neuromuscular condition. In either case, the perineal muscles themselves are indisputably important for male copulation and reproduction.

Because there had been no clear correlations of the penile reflexes with normal male copulatory behavior, it might have been expected that removal of the BC/LA/IC musculature would have little or no effect on traditional measures of such behavior. This expectation was in fact confirmed (Sachs, 1982). However, this does not mean that the reflexes are not important to male reproduction. On the contrary, the traditional measures of male copulatory behavior were insensitive to movements of the phallus. These behavioral measures rely upon careful descriptions of normal male rats (Beach and Holz-Tucker, 1949), in which the postural patterns during mounts and dismounts correlate with intromission and ejaculation. Specifically, mature male rats achieve literal intromission of the penis into the vagina with almost every mount of a receptive female. Immediately following each mount with an intromission, the male displays an unmistakable springing dismount. In the behavioral literature, such a springing dismount provides a convenient indicator of intromission. Unfortunately, these measures are often reported as "intromissions" and not "postural indications of intro-mission", and one is left with the impression that actions of the penis have been observed. Thus adult female rats who are given androgen very occasionally show an intromission-type of dismount when presented with a receptive female (Breedlove, 1981). This behavior is measured and reported as an "intromission", but since the female has only a clitoris rather than a penis, this intromission is obviously not equivalent to that displayed by a normal male. Movements of the penis during copulation provide an additional dimension of sexual behavior in male rats beyond simple mounting and dismounting. These penile reflexes play a vital but previously unsuspected role in the reproductive behavior of rats.

SNB cells respond morphologically to androgen manipulation in adulthood

Androgens have marked morphological effects on the motoneurons of the SNB (Breedlove and Arnold, 1981). While hormone manipulation in adulthood did not alter the number of SNB cells in either sex, the cross-sectional area of Nissl-stained SNB somas shrank following castration of adult males, and this shrinkage could be partially avoided with testosterone propionate (TP) therapy (Fig. 9). This change in soma size may reflect changes in motoneuronal physiology and/or dendritic morphology. Since SNB cells accumulate androgens (Breedlove and Arnold, 1980), it may be that the waxing and waning of neuronal size is due to direct androgen action upon the neurons. There are two pieces of evidence which hint that the steroid-dependent waxing and waning of SNB soma size may be related to the steroid-dependent penile reflexes which, after all, are mediated by SNB target muscles in male rats. Firstly, Hart and Haugen (1968) demonstrated that spinal implants of T augmented the penile reflexes, even though male accessory glands showed no response. This

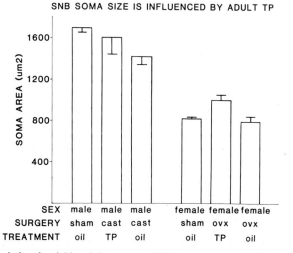

Fig. 9. Hormonal manipulations in adulthood alter the size of SNB somas as seen in Nissl stain. Histograms represent the mean cross-sectional area of neuronal somas in the SNB region. Castrated males (male/cast/oil) have smaller somas than sham-operated males (male/sham/oil). Castrated males given TP (male/cast/TP) have SNB somas of intermediate size. Ovariectomized female rats treated with TP (female/ovx/TP) have larger motoneuronal somas in this region than either sham-operated (female/sham/oil) or ovariectomized controls (female/ovx/oil). The brackets represent standard errors of the mean. (From Breedlove and Arnold, 1981.)

result indicates that androgen augments the reflexes by action upon the spinal cord itself. Secondly, the reflexes are sensitive to T or DHT, but not E. Thus the behaviorally active steroids are exactly those which SNB cells accumulate (Breedlove and Arnold, 1980, 1983c). Therefore, androgen's action in the spinal cord may be mediated by the swelling of SNB somas, causing physiological or morphological changes which augment the reflexes.

Perineal muscles respond morphologically to androgen manipulation in adulthood

Androgen action upon the perineal muscles themselves may affect the penile reflexes. The weight of these muscles is very sensitive to androgenic manipulations (Wainman and Shipounoff, 1941). Perhaps the anabolic response of the muscles to androgens results in variation in their ability to accomplish the reflexes. Because the muscles contain androgen receptors (Jung and Baulieu, 1972), androgen may act upon the muscles themselves to potentiate penile reflexes. However, since androgen treatment can augment penile erections in as little as 12 h (Gray et al., 1980), there may be additional or alternative sites of action capable of responding more quickly than the muscles, e.g. the nervous system.

HORMONAL CONTROL OF THE DEVELOPING SNB SYSTEM

SNB morphology is hormonally determined

The sexually dimorphic character of the SNB cells, their hormone accumulation and morphological response to androgen, together suggest that the dimorphic development of the SNB might be controlled by perinatal androgens. This suggestion has been supported through a wide range of experimental approaches. For example, examination of the androgen-insensitive rat mutant, the testicular feminized (*tfm*) male suggests that androgens direct the masculine development of the SNB system. The *tfm* males have an Y chromosome

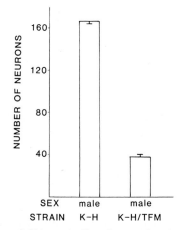

Fig. 10. Genetically normal male rats (left) have significantly more densely staining neurons in the region of the SNB than their male littermates with the *tfm* mutation rendering them insensitive to androgens. The spinal cord morphology of *tfm* males is completely feminine in terms of the number and size of SNB cells. These males, like females, also lack the perineal muscles bulbocavernosus, levator ani and ischiocavernosus. The bars represent means ± S.E.M. (From Breedlove and Arnold, 1981.)

and therefore develop testes which secrete testosterone during development, but the tissues of the affected animal fail to respond to the T, and therefore the external genitalia develop a feminine phenotype, including a clitoral-like phallus and a patent vagina (Stanley et al., 1973). These animals fail to respond to androgen because they have much fewer androgen receptors than normal males (Naess et al., 1976). These *tfm* males have drastically feminine SNBs (Fig. 10) and lack the target muscles BC/LA (Breedlove and Arnold, 1981), indicating that the interaction of androgens with their receptors plays a crucial role in the masculine development of this neuromuscular system.

Pharmacological blockade of androgen receptors prevents the masculine development of the SNB system

It is possible that the *tfm* mutants have an additional, as yet undetected defect, and this undetected defect may be responsible for the feminine SNB system in these males. Therefore Breedlove and Arnold (1983a) directly manipulated the androgen system of genetically normal rats during development by exposing males to the anti-androgen, flutamide (FL), prenatally. These males were castrated on the day of birth, and their SNB system was completely sex-reversed in adulthood (Fig. 11, left). They had as few motoneurons in the

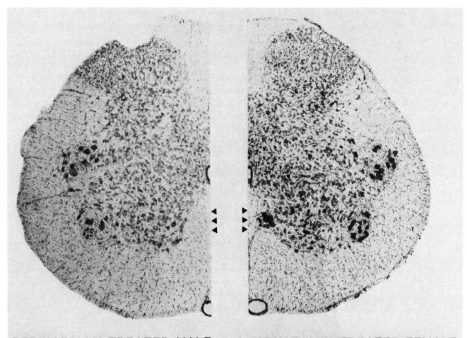

PERINATALLY TREATED MALE   NEONATALLY TREATED FEMALE

Fig. 11. Photomicrographs of transverse sections of the fifth lumbar spinal segment from a male (left) and female rat. The arrows point out the anatomical region occupied by the SNB in normal male rats. The spinal cord on the left lacks a coherent nucleus because this male was treated with an anti-androgen prenatally and was then castrated at birth. The spinal morphology is within the range of normal female rats in this male which, like females, does not possess the SNB target muscles BC/LA (Breedlove and Arnold, 1983a). The spinal cord on the right is from a female which was injected with 1 mg DHTP on days 1, 3 and 5 of life. In adulthood, this female possesses an SNB (Breedlove and Arnold, 1983b) which innervates the muscles BC/LA (Breedlove, unpublished observations).

SNB region as normal females, and the cells present were no larger than in normal females. Furthermore, 9 of 10 such males had no trace of the SNB target muscles, even after weeks of androgen treatment in adulthood. Since flutamide or its metabolites are known to block androgen receptor activation (Neri et al., 1972), the morphological demasculinization caused by this agent affirms that the interaction of androgens with their receptors is important to the dimorphic development of the SNB system in males. Interestingly, the FL treatment which completely demasculinized the SNB system had no effect on traditional postural correlates of intromission or mounting behavior. This finding represents an additional dissociation of the BC/LA musculature and the postural measures, and emphasizes the limitations of these measures of male copulatory behavior in rodents.

Perinatal testosterone masculinizes SNB system morphology

Perinatal androgen treatment of female rats was used to directly manipulate all 3 masculine characters of the SNB system: the number of SNB cells, the size of SNB cells, and the number of target muscle fibers. Injection of pregnant dams with TP during the last week of gestation, or injection of pups either early (days 1–5) or late (days 7–11) postnatally, revealed that the adult number of SNB neurons in females can be increased by treatment during either the pre- or postnatal period (Breedlove and Arnold, 1983b), and such treatments cause females to retain the BC/LA muscles into adulthood (Cihak et al., 1970). The number of SNB cells could be significantly increased by androgen treatment during the early (days 1–5) but not the late (days 7–11) postnatal period (Fig. 12). Thus the critical period for the androgen-induced increase in SNB cell number appears to be over before day 7 of life.

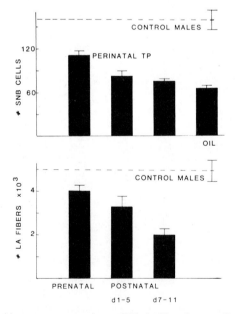

Fig. 12. Perinatal treatment with testosterone propionate (TP) significantly masculinized the adult morphology of the spinal cord (upper histograms) and perineum (lower histograms) of female rats. Exposure during the week immediately before birth (left most column) induced the most masculinization. Exposure during the second week of life significantly increased the number of levator ani (LA) muscle fibers, but not the number of SNB cells. The broken lines indicate the mean values for male controls. (Redrawn from Breedlove and Arnold, 1983b.)

Perinatal androgen treatment also had permanent enlarging effects on the individual size of SNB motoneurons. In fact, there appear to be two separate critical periods for the masculinization of SNB cell size and number, since late postnatal treatment with androgen resulted in significantly larger SNB neurons, but not significantly more SNB motoneurons in adulthood (Breedlove and Arnold, 1983b).

Estradiol is neither sufficient nor necessary for SNB masculinization

The "aromatization hypothesis" suggests that the aromatized metabolites of T such as E mediate masculinization of the nervous system (e.g. McEwen et al., 1977). While this hypothesis is valid for some systems, there is now a good deal of evidence that it does not apply to the SNB system of rats. Three experiments indicate that estrogens alone cannot effect the masculine development of the SNB system. Firstly, *tfm* mutant males produce ample supplies of T, normal levels of aromatization to produce E, and normal levels of neural estrogen receptors (Olsen and Fox, 1981), and yet they have a completely feminine SNB system (Breedlove and Arnold, 1981). These mutants demonstrate that normal male levels of estrogen receptor stimulation are insufficient to masculinize the SNB in the absence of androgen action. Similarly, pharmacological blockade of androgen receptors in male fetuses can completely demasculinize the SNB system (Breedlove and Arnold, 1981) even though FL has no known effect on estrogen receptors; therefore presumably these rats too, were exposed to normal male levels of estrogen stimulation. Finally, administration of 100 μg of estradiol benzoate (EB) to 2-day-old female rats had no measurable effect on the SNB in adulthood (Fig. 13), even though a 1-mg dose of TP did (Breedlove et al., 1982). Estrogenic stimulation alone is quite insufficient to masculinize the SNB system.

There is also evidence that estrogens are unnecessary for at least partial masculinization of the SNB, since neonatal treatment with the non-aromatizable androgen, dihydrotestosterone propionate (DHTP), significantly masculinized all measures of the SNB system in female rats (Fig. 11, right). There is one remaining possibility whereby estrogen may play a role in SNB development. Although estrogen stimulation alone has no masculinizing effects, and

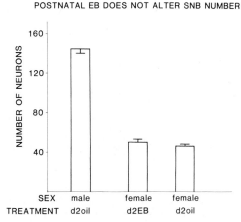

Fig. 13. The mean number of SNB cells in adult female rats is not significantly altered by injection of 100 μg estradiol benzoate on the day after birth. On the other hand, injection of testosterone propionate on day 2 increased the number of SNB cells in females. (From Breedlove et al., 1982.)

purely androgenic manipulations have marked effects on SNB morphology, estrogens *in the presence of androgen* may yet contribute to the masculine development of this system. However, aromatized metabolites of T may not play even a contributory role in SNB development, since neonatal exposure of female rats to non-aromatizable DHTP resulted in a slightly more masculinized spinal morphology than did an equivalent regimen of TP (Breedlove and Arnold, 1983b). Because systemically injected DHT is rapidly metabolized to inactive compounds in rats (McEwen, 1981), the greater effectiveness of DHTP treatment indicates that aromatized products from TP have no influence on SNB morphology. An attempt to test directly the hypothesized contribution of estrogen in the presence of androgen by perinatally treating male rats with the anti-estrogen tamoxifen was unsuccessful because the tamoxifen apparently influenced endogenous androgen production (Breedlove et al., 1983a).

Mechanism of hormonal determination of neuronal number

How do androgens bring about a greater number of SNB cells in males than females? The 3 possible mechanisms are: (1) androgens may increase neurogenesis in males, thereby providing extra cells for the SNB, or (2) androgens may direct the differentiation of cells into motoneurons to make up the SNB, or (3) androgens may rescue SNB motoneurons in males from the programmed cell death which normally occurs during development (Hamburger and Oppenheim, 1982). At present we can refute the first two possibilities and have indirect evidence to support the third.

Androgen does not alter SNB neurogenesis

Injection of tritiated thymidine, a specific precursor of DNA, on the 12th day of gestation resulted in concentration of radioactivity in the nuclei of more than 90% of SNB cells in

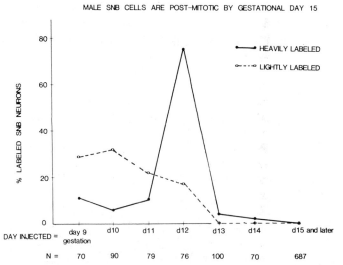

Fig. 14. A single exposure of male fetuses to tritiated thymidine on the 12th day of gestation results in radioactive labeling of more than 90% of the SNB cells seen in adulthood. More than 70% of the SNB cells are heavily labeled (solid line), indicating that these cells were near the final division on the 12th day of gestation. Although there is still some SNB neurogenesis on the 13th and 14th days, single injections of thymidine on the 15th day of gestation until the 3rd day of life all failed to result in any labeled SNB cells in adulthood. Thus SNB neurogenesis is complete before the 15th day of gestation. (From Breedlove et al., 1983b.)

adulthood. But no SNB cell nuclei were ever heavily labeled with thymidine if it was injected on the 15th day of gestation or later, indicating the completion of neurogenesis by day 14 (Fig. 14). All lumbar motoneurons in either sex were postmitotic by day 15 of gestation (Breedlove et al., 1983b). In male rats, T production does not commence until day 16 (Warren et al., 1973; Feldman and Bloch, 1978) or perhaps day 15 (Picon, 1976), and measurable sex differences in plasma T levels do not occur until even later on day 18 of gestation (Weisz and Ward, 1980). Therefore, androgen determination of the sex difference in the adult number of SNB cells (Breedlove and Arnold, 1983a,b) does not involve a sex difference in the proliferation of these cells, because androgens are not present in males until after neurogenesis is complete. Indeed, the number of SNB cells can be increased or decreased by appropriate androgen manipulations more than a week after neurogenesis is completed (Breedlove et al., 1982; Breedlove and Arnold, 1983a,b).

Androgen does not redifferentiate cells into motoneurons for the SNB

In female rats given a single exposure to tritiated thymidine on day 12 of gestation, almost every motoneuron's nucleus contains radioactivity on the day of birth, 11 days later. In fact, by the day of birth most of the heavily labeled cells are motoneurons (Breedlove, unpublished observations). If instead of being sacrificed at birth for autoradiography, such females are neonatally treated with TP, they retain all 3 perineal muscles and have more SNB cells in adulthood. These "androgen-induced" SNB cells are also heavily labeled with the thymidine injected on day 12 of gestation (Breedlove, in preparation). Since at the time of TP treatment, all motoneurons were heavily labeled, the heavily labeled SNB cells in androgenized females probably had already differentiated into motoneurons *before* androgen treatment. Apparently the androgen treatment of neonatal females adds SNB cells, not be redifferentiating cells into motoneurons, but rather by utilizing pre-existing motoneurons to construct the SNB. Presumably these motoneurons in the absence of androgen would have either died during the perinatal period of motoneuronal death (Nurcombe et al., 1981), or joined other motoneuronal groups. Since androgenized females do not have a deficit in cell number in any motoneuronal group in this region (Jordan et al., 1982), this latter hypothesis seems unlikely. By elimination, the androgen-induced SNB cells must have been spared from programmed death by the intervention of androgen.

Androgens probably spare motoneurons from programmed death

There is an additional piece of evidence to support the view that androgen forms the SNB by sparing developing motoneurons from programmed death. Nurcombe et al. (1981) report that 45% of rat brachial motoneurons die between birth and day 6 of life. This completion of cell death by day 6 correlates remarkably well with the results of neonatal androgenization of females. If females are given androgen on days 1, 3 and 5 of life, more SNB cells are seen in adulthood. However, if the androgen is given on days 7, 9 and 11, there is no significant increase in adult SNB numbers (Breedlove and Arnold, 1983b). It may be that androgen treatment after day 7 fails to increase SNB numbers because motoneuronal death is already complete, and there are no locally available cells to be rescued. While the time course of death may be slightly different for lumbar motoneurons, this correlation between the end of cell death and the end of the critical period for altering SNB numbers suggests that androgens act by preventing the death of motoneurons. Counts of dying (pyknotic) and living motoneurons during development are presently under way to test this hypothesis.

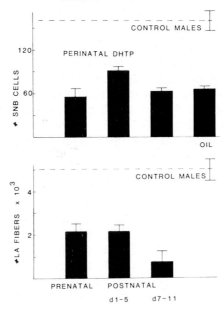

Fig. 15. Perinatal treatment of female rats with dihydrotestosterone propionate (DHTP) significantly masculinized the spinal cord (upper histograms) and perineal muscles as seen in adulthood. The number of SNB cells
(upper) was significantly increased by treatment in the first week of life (postnatal d1–5), and the number of
levator ani (LA) muscle fibers was increased by each of the perinatal treatments. It is intriguing that the prenatal
treatment with DHTP (left columns) greatly increased the number of LA fibers, but resulted in no more SNB cells
than in female controls (upper right bar). (Redrawn from Breedlove and Arnold, 1983b.)

The specificity of motoneuron to muscle innervation can be manipulated hormonally

Unexpectedly, prenatal treatment of females with DHTP masculinizes the SNB target
muscles but not the SNB motoneurons themselves (Fig. 15). There are 4 possible explanations for this independent masculinization of the muscles (Breedlove and Arnold, 1983b).
Either (1) the muscle fibers are not innervated, (2) the muscle fibers are innervated by
neurons which are not recognizable because, unlike all other known CNS motoneurons, they
are small and lightly Nissl-staining, (3) the number of muscle fibers innervated per
motoneuron is greatly increased, thereby eliminating the need for additional motoneurons, or
(4) muscle fibers are innervated by additional motoneurons which are outside their normal
anatomical locus in the SNB, and therefore are missed by SNB counts. The correct possibility can be determined by HRP experiments. When HRP is injected into the LA/BC
muscles of females prenatally treated with DHTP, retrogradely labeled cells are found in the
ventral horn of the spinal cord, contradicting the first possibility. Neutral red staining of these
cells reveals all the structural characteristics of motoneurons, i.e. they are large, multipolar,
densely Nissl-staining neurons (Breedlove, 1983b). This finding rules out the second possibility. Thus the induced LA/BC muscles are indeed innervated, and by cells which are morphologically normal motoneurons.

There remain two possible explanations of how prenatal DHTP masculinizes the perineal
muscles but not the SNB region: (3) each motoneuron innervates many more muscle fibers,
or (4) the muscles are innervated by motoneurons outside the SNB region. The HRP studies
indicate that the latter explanation is correct (Breedlove, 1983b). A small volume (0.5–1.0 μl)

of HRP was injected into the BC/LA of 7 adult females which had received prenatal TP treatment and 7 adult females which had received prenatal DHTP treatment. The injections were done in yoked pairs of one prenatal TP female and one DHTP female in order to equalize experimental conditions as much as possible. The number of HRP-filled cells was not different in prenatal TP- and DHTP-treated females ($P > 0.20$, matched-pairs t test), therefore the ratio of motoneuron to muscle fiber innervation is not different in the two groups, as would be expected if the third possibility were correct. However, the *anatomical location* of the motoneurons innervating the BC was drastically different. In females prenatally treated with TP, the HRP-filled cells were primarily located in the medial motoneuron column, which includes the SNB region (Fig. 16, middle). But in adult females prenatally treated with DHTP, most of the HRP-filled cells were in the lateral, DLN motoneuronal column, more than 500 μm away (Fig. 16, upper). In normal males, these small HRP injections virtually never label lateral column motoneurons (Fig. 16, bottom). In other words, prenatal TP produces females with BC/LA muscles primarily innervated by the same motoneuron pools as in males, i.e. the medial, SNB pool. But prenatal DHTP produces females with muscles innervated by a different and, relative to males, abnormal motoneuronal pool (Breedlove, 1983b). Of course, these results raise additional questions about how prenatal DHTP treatment accomplishes this anomalous innervation pattern. Do DHTP and TP differentially affect the outgrowth, migration or death of motoneurons?

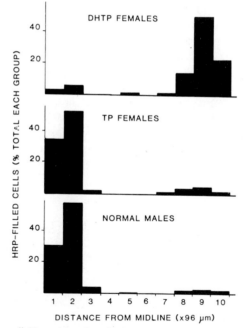

Fig. 16. Distributions of the medial-lateral location of motoneurons innervating the bulbocavernosus (BC) muscle were revealed by retrograde HRP labeling. In normal males (bottom) the vast majority of motoneurons innervating the BC are within 288 μm (3 × 96 μm) of the midline, in the region of the SNB. Female rats given TP before birth (middle histograms) show an identical distribution of motoneurons innervating BC, but females treated with DHTP before birth (upper) show a quite different arrangement. In these females, the motoneurons innervating the BC are in the *most lateral* portion of the spinal cord. The number of HRP-filled motoneurons per volume of injected HRP was not different in the two groups of females. The lateral position of motoneurons in the DHTP females explains the absence of cells in the SNB region in such females, despite the presence of BC and LA muscles. (From data presented in Breedlove, 1983b.)

Possible site(s) of androgen action

There are 3 candidates for the site at which androgen acts to masculinize the developing SNB system: (1) androgen may preserve the muscles which then maintain the motoneurons, or (2) androgen may maintain the motoneurons which then maintain the muscles, or (3) androgen may maintain supraspinal afferents to the SNB, and these afferents maintain the SNB and thereby maintain the muscles. Preliminary results of work done by Renata Fishman indicate that the last possibility is incorrect. Fishman has found that neonatal TP treatment of female rats masculinizes perineal muscles and spinal cord, even if the spinal cord is transected at mid-thoracic levels before androgen treatment (Fishman and Breedlove, in preparation). Further experiments are necessary to distinguish between the other two loci: i.e. does androgen act upon the motoneurons, the muscles or both. Both the neurons and their targets bind androgen and morphologically respond to androgen manipulations in adulthood.

In summary, the mechanisms by which gonadal hormones dictate the development and function of sexually dimorphic neural regions have been studied in a model neuromuscular system. Both the development and adult function of the SNB system are controlled by steroid hormones. Perinatal secretions of androgen in male rats induce the persistence of the BC muscles and probably prevent the programmed cell death of the SNB motoneurons innervating them. Perinatal exposure of female rats to androgen mimics the masculine pattern of preservation of SNB motoneurons and BC musculature. The perinatal hormonal milieu is also important for the anatomical specificity of motoneuron to muscle innervation in this system. Unlike other examples of sexual differentiation in rodents, the development of the SNB system seems to be independent of the estrogenic metabolites of testosterone. At maturity, both the SNB motoneurons and BC muscles bind androgen and respond morphologically to hormonal manipulations. The BC musculature plays a crucial role in male fertility, probably by aiding copulatory plug formation and therefore sperm transport. The morphological responsiveness of motoneurons and muscles to steroids may mediate the androgen sensitivity of the neuromuscular system as measured by spinal reflexes and fertility. In short, the SNB is a relatively simple neural system which promises to elucidate the mechanisms by which steroid hormones direct morphology and behavioral function of the nervous system throughout ontogeny.

ACKNOWLEDGEMENTS

I thank Sue Breedlove for her encouragement and valuable comments.

This research was supported by NIH grants HD 15021 to A.P. Arnold and NS 19790 to S.M.B. and BRSG 2-S07-RR07006 to S.M.B.

REFERENCES

Arnold, A.P. (1980) Sexual differences in the brain. *Am. Scient.*, 68: 165–173.
Arnold, A.P. (1981) Quantitative analysis of steroid autoradiograms. *J. Histochem. Cytochem.*, 29: 207–211.
Bardin, C.W. and Catterall, J.F. (1981) Testosterone: a major determinant of extragenital sexual dimorphism. *Science*, 211: 1285–1293.
Beach, F.A. and Holz-Tucker, A.M. (1949) Effects of different concentrations of androgen upon sexual behavior in castrated male rats. *J. Comp. Physiol. Psychol.*, 42: 433–453.

Beckett, S.D., Hudson, R.S., Walker, D.F., Vachon, R.I. and Reynolds, T.M. (1972) Corpus cavernosum penis pressure and external penile muscle activity during erection in the goat. *Biol. Reprod.*, 7: 359–364.

Beckett, S.D., Hudson, R.S., Walker, D.F., Reynolds, T.M. and Vachon, R.I. (1973) Blood pressure and penile muscle activity in the stallion during coitus. *Am. J. Physiol.*, 225: 1072–1075.

Beckett, S.D., Walker, D.F., Hudson, R.S., Reynolds, T.M. and Vachon, R.I. (1974) Corpus cavernosum penis pressure and penile activity in the bull during coitus. *Am. J. Vet. Res.*, 35: 761–764.

Breedlove, S.M. (1981) *Hormonal Influences on a Sexually Dimorphic Motor Nucleus in the Rat Spinal Cord.* Ph.D. dissertation, University of California, Los Angeles, CA.

Breedlove, S.M. (1983a) Regional sex differences in steroid accumulation in vertebrate nervous systems. *Trends Neurosci.*, 6: 403–406.

Breedlove, S.M. (1983b) The specificity of motoneuron to muscle innervation can be manipulated hormonally in the rat. *Soc. Neurosci. Abstr.*, 9: 307.

Breedlove, S.M. and Arnold, A.P. (1980) Hormone accumulation in a sexually dimorphic motor nucleus in the rat spinal cord. *Science*, 210: 564–566.

Breedlove, S.M. and Arnold, A.P. (1981) Sexually dimorphic motor nucleus in the rat lumbar spinal cord: response to adult hormone manipulation, absence in androgen-insensitive rats. *Brain Res.*, 225: 297–307.

Breedlove, S.M. and Arnold, A.P. (1983a) Hormonal control of a developing neuromuscular system. I. Complete demasculinization of the spinal nucleus of the bulbocavernosus in male rats using the anti-androgen, flutamide. *J. Neurosci.*, 3: 417–423.

Breedlove, S.M. and Arnold, A.P. (1983b) Hormonal control of a developing neuromuscular system. II. Sensitive periods for the androgen induced masculinization of the rat spinal nucleus of the bulbocavernosus. *J. Neurosci.*. 3: 424–432.

Breedlove, S.M. and Arnold, A.P. (1983c) Sex differences in the pattern of steroid accumulation by motoneurons of the rat lumbar spinal cord. *J. Comp. Neurol.*, 215: 211–216.

Breedlove, S.M., Jacobson, C.D., Gorski, R.A. and Arnold, A.P. (1982) Masculinization of the female rat spinal cord following a single injection of testosterone propionate but not estradiol benzoate. *Brain Res.*, 237: 173–181.

Breedlove, S.M., Döhler, K.D., Coquelin, A., Gorski, R.A. and Arnold, A.P. (1983a) Effects of perinatal tamoxifen treatment on the spinal nucleus of the bulbocavernosus in male rats. *Conf. reprod. Behav. Abstr.*, p. 75.

Breedlove, S.M., Jordan, C.L. and Arnold, A.P. (1983b) Neurogenesis of motoneurons in the sexually dimorphic spinal nucleus of the bulbocavernosus in rats. *Develop. Brain Res.*, 9: 39–43.

Bubenik, G.A. and Brown, G.M. (1973) Morphologic sex differences in primate brain areas involved in regulation of reproductive activity. *Experientia*, 26: 619–621.

Buresova, M., Gutmann. E. and Hanzlikova, V. (1972) Differential effects of castration and denervation on protein synthesis in the levator ani muscle of the rat. *J. Endocrinol.*, 54: 3–14.

Calaresu, F.R. and Henry, J.L. (1971) Sex difference in the number of sympathetic neurons in the spinal cord of the cat. *Science*, 173: 343–344.

Cihak, R., Gutmann, E. and Hanzlikova, V. (1970) Involution and hormone-induced persistence of the muscle sphincter (levator) ani in female rats. *J. Anat.*, 106:93–110.

Dionne, F.T., Dube, J.Y., Lesage, R.L. and Tremblay, R.R. (1979) In vivo androgen binding in rat skeletal and perineal muscles. *Acta Endocrinol.*, 91: 362–372.

Dorfman, R.I. and Kincl, F.A. (1963) Relative potency of various steroids in an anabolic-androgenic assay using the castrated rat. *Endocrinology*, 72: 259–266.

Dube, J.Y., Lesage, R. and Tremblay, R.R. (1976) Androgen and estrogen binding in rat skeletal and perineal muscles. *Can. J. Biochem.*, 54: 50–55.

Edgren, R.A. (1963) A comparative study of the anabolic and androgenic effects of various steroids. *Acta Endocrinol.*, suppl. 87:3–21.

Feldman, S.C. and Bloch, E. (1978) Developmental pattern of testosterone synthesis by fetal rat testes in response to luteinizing hormone. *Endocrinology*, 102: 999–1007.

Gloyna, R.E. and Wilson, J.D. (1969) A comparative study of the conversion of testosterone to 17-hydroxy-5-alpha-androstan-3-one (dihydrotestosterone) by prostate and epididymis. *J. Clin. Endocrinol.*, 29: 970–977.

Gorski, R.A., Gordon, J.H., Shryne, J.E. and Southam, A.M. (1978) Evidence for a morphological sex difference within the medial preoptic area of the rat brain. *Brain Res.*, 148: 333–346.

Gray, G.D., Smith, E.R. and Davidson, J.M. (1980) Hormonal regulation of penile erection in castrated male rats. *Physiol. Behav.*, 24: 463–468.

Greene, E.C. (1963) *The Anatomy of the Rat*, Hafner, New York.

Greenough, W.T., Carter, C.S., Steerman, C. and DeVoogd, T.J. (1977) Sex differences in dendritic patterns in hamster preoptic area. *Brain Res.*, 126: 63–72.

Hamburger, V. and Oppenheim, R.W. (1982) Naturally occurring neuronal death in vertebrates. *Neurosci. Comment.*, 1: 39–55.

Hannigan, P.C. and Kelley, D.B. (1981) Male and female laryngeal motoneurons in *Xenopus laevis*. *Soc. Neurosci. Abstr.*, 7: 269.

Hart, B.L. (1967) Testosterone regulation of sexual reflexes in spinal male rats. *Science*, 155: 1282–1284.

Hart, B.L. (1968) Sexual reflexes and mating behavior in the male rat. *J. Comp. Physiol. Psychol.*, 65: 453–460.

Hart, B.L. (1979) Activation of sexual reflexes of male rats by dihydrotestosterone but not estrogen. *Physiol. Behav.*, 23: 107–109.

Hart, B.L. and Haugen, C.M. (1968) Activation of sexual reflexes in male rats by spinal implantation of testosterone. *Physiol. Behav.*, 3: 735–738.

Hart, B.L. and Kitchell, R.L. (1966) Penile erection and contraction of penile muscles in the spinal and intact dog. *Am. J. Physiol.*, 210: 257–261.

Hart, B.L. and Melese-d'Hospital, Y. (1983) Penile mechanisms and the role of the striated penile muscles in penile reflexes. *Physiol. Behav.*, 31: 807–813.

Hayes, K.J. (1965) The so-called "levator ani" of the rat. *Acta. Endocrinol.*, 48: 337–347.

Jordan, C.L., Breedlove, S.M. and Arnold, A.P. (1982) Sexual dimorphism in the dorsolateral motor nucleus of the rat lumbar spinal cord and its response to neonatal androgen. *Brain Res.*, 249: 309–314.

Jung, I. and Baulieu, E.E. (1972) Testosterone cytosol "receptor" in the rat levator ani muscle. *Nature (London)*, 237: 24–26.

Jurman, M.E., Erulkar, S.D. and Krieger, N.R. (1982) Testosterone 5-alpha-reductase in spinal cord of *Xenopus laevis*. *J. Neurochem.*, 38: 657–661.

Karacan, I., Aslan, C. and Hirshkowitz, M. (1983) Erectile mechanisms in man. *Science*, 220: 1080–1082.

Knudsen, J.F. and Max, S.R. (1980) Aromatization of androgens to estrogens mediates increased activity of glucose 6-phosphate dehydrogenase in rat levator ani muscle. *Endocrinology*, 106: 440–443.

Kochakian, C.D. (1975) Definition of androgens and protein anabolic steroids. *Pharmacol. Ther. B*, 1: 149–177.

Kollberg, S., Petersen, I. and Stener, I. (1962) Preliminary results of an electromyographic study of ejaculation. *Acta Chir. Scand.*, 123: 478–483.

Krieg, M., Szalay, R. and Voigt, K.D. (1974) Binding and metabolism of testosterone and of 5-alpha-dihydrotestosterone in bulbocavernosus/levator ani (BC/LA) of male rats: in vivo and in vitro studies. *J. Steroid Biochem.*, 5: 453–459.

Kurtz, R.G. and Santos, R. (1979) Supraspinal influences on the penile reflexes of the male rat: A comparison of the effects of copulation, spinal transection and cortical spreading depression. *Hormone Behav.*, 12: 73–94.

Mainwaring, W.I.P. (1972) The distribution of specific androgen receptor proteins. *J. Endocrinol.*, 52: iv–v.

Matthews, M.K. and Adler, N.T. (1978) Systematic interrelationship of mating, vaginal plug position and sperm transport in the rat. *Physiol. Behav.*, 20: 303–309.

McClintock, M.K., Ansiko, J.J. and Adler, N.T. (1982) Group mating among Norway rats. II. Social dynamics of copulation: competition, cooperation and mate choice. *Anim. Behav.*, 30: 410–425.

McEwen, B.S. (1981) Neural gonadal steroid actions. *Science*, 211: 1303–1311.

McEwen, B.S., Lieberburg, I., Chaptal, C. and Krey, L.C. (1977) Aromatization: Important for sexual differentiation of the neonatal rat brain. *Hormone Behav.*, 9: 249–263.

Michel, G. and Baulieu, E. (1974) Récepteur cytosoluble des androgènes dans un muscle strié squelettique. *C.R. Acad. Sci. (Paris)*, 279: 421–424.

Moskowitz, A.S., Breedlove, S.M., Arnold, A.P. and Liebeskind, J.C. (1982) Distribution of enkephalin-like immunoreactivity in the rat spinal cord: An immunohistochemical study. *Soc. Neurosci. Abstr.*, 8: 100.

Naess, O., Haug, E., Ahramadal, A., Aakvaag, A., Hansson, V. and French, F. (1976) Androgen receptors in the anterior pituitary and central nervous system of the androgen "insensitive" (Tfm) rat: correlation between receptor binding and effects of androgens on gonadotropin secretion. *Endocrinology*, 99: 1295–1303.

Navaratnam, V. and Lewis, P.R. (1970) Cholinesterase-containing neurones in the spinal cord of the rat. *Brain Res.*, 18: 411–425.

Neri, R.O., Florence, K., Koiziol, P. and VanCleave, C. (1972) A biological profile of a non-steroidal anti-androgen, SCH 13521 (4'-nitro-3'-trifluoromethylyisobutyranilide). *Endocrinology*, 91: 427–437.

Nottebohm, F. and Arnold, A.P. (1976) Sexual dimorphism in vocal control areas of the songbird brain. *Science*, 194: 211–213.

Nottebohm, F. and DeVoogd, T. (1981) Gonadal hormones induce dendritic growth in the adult avian brain. *Science*, 214: 202–204.

Nurcombe, V., McGrath, P.A. and Bennett, M.R. (1981) Postnatal death of motor neurons during the development of the brachial spinal cord of the rat. *Neurosci. Lett.*, 27: 249–254.

Olsen, K.L. and Fox, T.O. (1981) Differences between androgen-resistant rat and mouse mutants. *Soc. Neurosci. Abstr.*, 7: 219.

Pfaff, D.W. (1966) Morphological changes in the brains of adult male rats after neonatal castration. *J. Endocrinol.*, 36: 415–416.

Picon, F. (1976) Testosterone secretion by fetal rat testes in vitro. *J. Endocrinol.*, 71: 231–237.

Powers, M.L. and Florini, J.R. (1975) A direct effect of testosterone on muscle cells in tissue culture. *Endocrinology*, 97: 1043–1047.

Purohit, R.C. and Beckett, S.D. (1976) Penile pressures and muscle activity associated with erection and ejaculation in the dog. *Am. J. Physiol.*, 231: 1343–1348.

Raisman, G. and Field, P.M. (1973) Sexual dimorphism in the neuropil of the preoptic area of the rat and its dependence on neonatal androgen. *Brain Res.*, 54: 1–29.

Sachs, B.D. (1982) Role of the rat's striated penile muscles in penile reflexes, copulation and the induction of pregnancy. *J. Reprod. Fertil.*, 66: 433–443.

Sachs, B.D. and Garinello, L.D. (1978) Interaction between penile reflexes and copulation in male rats. *J. Comp. Physiol. Psychol.*, 92: 759–767.

Sachs, B.D., Valcourt, R.J. and Flagg, H.C. (1981) Copulatory behavior and sexual reflexes of male rats treated with naloxone. *Pharmacol. Biochem. Behav.*, 14: 251–253.

Sar, M. and Stumpf, W.E. (1977) Androgen concentration in motor neurons of cranial nerves and spinal cord. *Science*, 197: 77–79.

Schroder, H.D. (1980) Organization of the motoneurons innervating the pelvic muscles of the male rat. *J. Comp. Neurol.*, 192: 567–587.

Stanley, A.J., Gumbreck, L.G. and Allison, J.E. (1973) Male pseudohermaphroditism in the laboratory Norway rat. *Recent Progr. Hormone Res.*, 29: 43–64.

Venable, J.H. (1966) Morphology of the cells of normal, testosterone deprived and testosterone stimulated levator ani muscles. *Am. J. Anat.*, 119: 271–302.

Wainman, P. and Shipounoff, G.C. (1941) The effects of castration and testosterone propionate on the striated perineal musculature of the rat. *Endocrinology*, 29: 955–978.

Wallach, S.J.R. and Hart, B.L. (1983) The role of the striated penile muscles of the male rat in seminal plug dislodgement and deposition. *Physiol. Behav.*, 31: 815–821.

Warren, D.W., Haltmeyer, G.C. and Eik-nes, K.B. (1973) Testosterone in the fetal rat testes. *Biol. Reprod.*, 8: 560–565.

Weisz, J. and Ward, I.L. (1980) Plasma testosterone and progesterone titers of pregnant rats, their male and female fetuses, and neonatal offspring. *Endocrinology*, 106: 306–316.

DISCUSSION

J.C. KING: You have not told us about the possible common origin of the 3 motor nuclei innervating muscles of the penis in the rat. Have you looked at this in the thymidine-injected animals examined during development?

S.M. BREEDLOVE: All the lumbar motoneuron groups in either sex show the same time course of neurogenesis as seen in thymidine studies (Breedlove et al., 1983). I do not believe that neurogenesis is involved in the sex differences seen in the spinal cord.

W.W. BEATTY: Are there any functional differences (e.g., in neuromuscular activity) between the TP- and the DHTP-treated females which are apparently different in patterns of connectivity?

S.M. BREEDLOVE: I have not measured genital reflexes in any androgenized females. Ben Sachs and David Thomas have done such a study, but I do not know what their conclusions are.

C.D. TORAN-ALLERAND: In view of increasing evidence of trophic effect of muscle factors on anterior horn cell survival, do you have any evidence as to whether or not androgens act on muscle rather than neurons directly to enhance neuron survival?

S.M. BREEDLOVE: I think this is a terribly important question, and I regret that we do not yet know whether the hormone accumulation is important for the sexual differentiation, or is a secondary *result* of the sexual differentiation. In other words, we do not yet know the site of androgen action for the development of any sexual dimorphism.

K. DÖHLER: Could you increase the size of the SNB up to the size of normal males by giving females an extended pre- and postnatal treatment with testosterone propionate?

S.M. BREEDLOVE: I have not examined the SNB system in females given both prenatal and postnatal androgen, but I would expect them to be more masculinized than females receiving only prenatal or only postnatal treatment. However, I do not attach much theoretical importance to the ability to completely sex-reverse characters with pharmacological doses of hormone. In such cases it is always possible that a large enough dose of hormone could compensate for the absence of some unidentified influence.

REFERENCE

Breedlove, S.M., Jordan, C.L. and Arnold, A.P. (1983) Neurogenesis of motoneurons in the sexually dimorphic spinal nucleus of the bulbocavernosus in rats. *Develop. Brain Res.*, 9: 39–43.

G.J. De Vries et al. (Eds.),
Progress in Brain Research, Vol. 61
© 1984 Elsevier Science Publishers B.V., Amsterdam

The Avian Song System:
Relating Sex Differences in Behavior to Dimorphism in the Central Nervous System

TIMOTHY DeVOOGD

Department of Psychology, Cornell University, Ithaca, NY (U.S.A.)

INTRODUCTION

Over the last 15 years, sex differences within the brain have moved from being a subject of speculation (see Swaab and Hofman, 1984) to being a focus of intense research and widespread interest. Research on the avian song system has been central during this time in demonstrating neural dimorphisms and in provoking allied study in other systems and animals. This review will survey these initial findings and will delineate the status of current research. It focuses on those aspects of the neurobiology of the song system which have been related to sex dimorphisms or hormone action. Nottebohm (1980b) and Arnold (1980a, 1982) have recently reviewed all aspects of the song system, including laterality and recovery of function which topics will not be considered here. This review emphasizes canaries and zebra finches, since most of the neurobiological research to date has been done on these species. Steroid influences on behavior, neurochemistry, and neuroanatomy will be discussed separately. A final section will speculate about unanswered questions within this system.

STEROID EFFECTS ON SONG

Most bird species show sex differences in the pattern or frequency of vocalizations. Males either use unique vocalizations or use particular vocalizations more frequently than do females. In many song birds, only the males sing. Song is used for territory definition and for attracting females (Thorpe, 1961; Immelmann, 1969). It can also serve to indicate group membership for those species in which local dialects occur. In song bird species studied to date, both sexes make begging calls in the nest. These may be modified or elaborated in subsong where both sexes produce variable, subdued sounds which have been compared to babbling (Marler, 1970). In males, this is succeeded by plastic song in which recurring patterns of sound elements ("syllables") can first be discerned. Many syllables may occur, including ones which will not be used as an adult (Marler and Peters, 1982). Adult full song is characterized by loud vigorous singing of highly stereotyped syllables. Birds differ widely in the number of stereotyped syllables used in song: a canary may use 25–35 while a marsh wren may use more than 100 (reviewed by Nottebohm, 1980b; Kroodsma, 1982). In many songbirds, the song heard as a juvenile is stored as a "template" which the bird will later try to match when he in turn begins to sing (Konishi, 1965; Marler, 1970; Marler and Sherman, 1983).

The acquisition of singing and its adult expression are affected by gonadal steroids. Male canaries castrated in infancy show some plastic song but never full song (Nottebohm, 1981). If castrated as adults, zebra finches will decrease their singing (Prove, 1974; Arnold, 1975), and canaries gradually cease singing (Nottebohm, 1969). Soon after testosterone (T) was first synthesized, it was given to adult female canaries. Within 10–14 days, they began to sing, and over the next several weeks, the song syllables became highly stereotyped (Leonard, 1939; Shoemaker, 1939; Baldwin et al., 1940). However, while individual syllables are indistinguishable from those sung by males, the females produce only 8–12 syllables, about one-third the male repertoire size. Recently, Greenspon (1983) has shown that song in hormone-treated females tends to match an auditory template as it does in normal males. If a female is exposed to a song model during the first 30 days of life, most of the syllables of the hormone-induced song will be derived from that model. In contrast, testosterone does not induce singing in adult female zebra finches unless they had also received a source of estrogen as an infant (Gurney and Konishi, 1980; Gurney, 1982). Thus, song for this species seems to follow the classical mammalian pattern of neonatal estrogen-induced organization followed by adult androgen-induced activation. Both female canaries and female zebra finches stop singing when the androgens are removed (Gurney, 1982; Greenspon and Stein, 1983).

In many bird species, especially those in temperate zones, all phases of reproductive activity including song are seasonal (reviewed by Farner and Wingfield, 1980). Male canaries, for example, begin singing in late winter. They continue singing as they pair and assist in building nests and raising clutches of young. They gradually stop singing in the late summer or early fall (Nottebohm and Nottebohm, 1978; Nottebohm, 1981). Gonad size and level of plasma steroids go in phase with these behavioral changes in both males and females. Increasing day length appears to signal gonadal growth and steroid resurgence (Follett et al., 1973; Nottebohm, 1981). Eventually the birds become photorefractory and a period of short days is necessary before they can once again become reproductive (Hinde and Steel, 1966).

Song is very important to females. Song accelerates ovarian development and egg laying in female budgerigars (reviewed by Brockway, 1969) and ring doves (Lehrman, 1965). Exposure to singing male canaries causes increased estrogen production in females (Warren and Hinde, 1961). Females show reproductive responses differentially to different examples of male song. Canaries build nests more quickly and lay more eggs in response to a highly varied song than to a simpler song (Kroodsma, 1976). White-crowned sparrows solicit copulation in response to songs heard as juveniles and not to songs sung by this species in other areas (Baker et al., 1981). Female zebra finches lay eggs close to a source of male song rather than in a nest box away from the song (Sheridan and Harding, personal communication).

Several laboratories are currently determining which particular steroids modulate avian song. Birds, like mammals, produce enzymes which can metabolize testosterone into either dihydrotestosterone (DHT), or estradiol (E_2). DHT, however, cannot be aromatized into E_2 (Naftolin et al., 1975; Callard et al., 1978). Thus, the central effects of testosterone may result from stimulating androgen receptors, estrogen receptors or a combination of both (see discussion by Toran-Allerand, 1984). Singing in female canaries appears to require both androgenic and estrogenic actions since DHT causes singing in intact but not in ovariecto-mized birds (DeVoogd and Nottebohm, 1981b). Harding et al. (1983) have shown that several androgens can restore singing in castrated male zebra finches. Somewhat surprisingly, androstenedione induces reproductive behavior levels above those seen in intact males.

In summary, song in male songbirds is closely related to the level of gonadal steroids. Both sexes learn many song features as juveniles although females of many species never normally sing. However, the appropriate song will release or accelerate many female reproductive behaviors.

STEROID EFFECTS ON THE NEURAL NETWORK FOR SONG

Avian song is controlled by several discrete brain nuclei (Nottebohm et al., 1976), including the hyperstriatum ventrate, pars caudale (HVc), which projects to robustus archistriatalis (RA), which in turn projects to the nucleus intercollicularis (ICo) and to the caudal part of the hypoglossal motor nucleus (nXIIts). The dorsomedial (DM) part of ICo also projects to nXIIts which in turn projects to the syrinx, the avian vocal organ (see Fig. 1). Lesions in this system produce dramatic song deficits. After bilateral HVc lesion, a canary may hold the song posture but produce virtually no sounds, a phenomenon Nottebohm has called "silent song" (Nottebohm et al., 1976). After RA lesions, individual syllables making up song are virtually unrecognizable. The bird produces harsh clicks and hisses but still appears to use phrase structure similar to that seen in intact birds (Nottebohm et al., 1976).

Several other structures have also been implicated in the song system (see Fig. 2). Field L, a high auditory relay nucleus (Leppelsack, 1974), projects to the borders of HVc and RA (Kelley and Nottebohm, 1979; Katz and Gurney, 1981). The magnocellular nucleus of the neostriatum (MAN) projects to both HVc and RA (Nottebohm et al., 1982). There is a substantial projection from HVc to area X, a large nucleus in the lobus parolfactorius. However, mature birds lesioned in field L, area X or MAN have few if any immediate deficits in song (Nottebohm et al., 1976). Recently, Nottebohm et al. (1982) have shown that nucleus interface (NIF) near field L and nucleus uva in the midbrain also project to HVc. It is not yet known whether these two small nuclei are directly involved in song production.

Early work by Nottebohm and Arnold (1976) showed the song system to be an ideal system in which to study sex differences in the nervous system. HVc and RA are 2–6 times larger in male canaries and zebra finches than in females. nXIIts is consistently about 30% larger in males than in females. Area X cannot even be distinguished in female zebra finches.

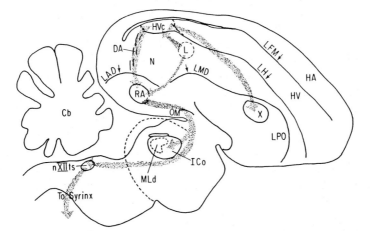

Fig. 1. Motor pathways for song control in the canary. HVc projects to RA, which projects to ICo and the tracheosyringeal motor neurons of the hypoglossal nucleus (nXIIts). The hypoglossal nucleus, in turn projects to the syrinx, the avian vocal organ.

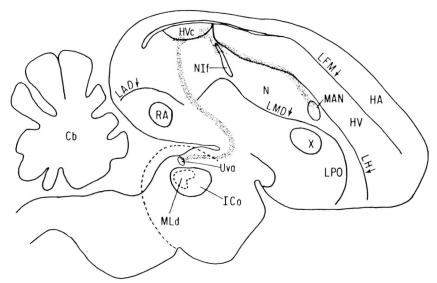

Fig. 2. Nuclei which are afferent to HVc. MAN projects to RA as well as to HVc.

These areas are sensitive to gonadal steroids. Radioactive testosterone, when given to adult birds, concentrates heavily in nXIIts, moderately in HVc, MAN, and ICo, and lightly in RA (Zigmond et al., 1973, 1980; Arnold et al., 1976; Arnold, 1980b; Arnold and Saltiel, 1979). There is a sex difference in the degree of labeling which occurs: a significantly greater proportion of the neurons in HVc and MAN are labeled in male than in female zebra finches (Arnold and Saltiel, 1979). Thus, although the sexes are similar in gross connectivity pattern between song control regions, particular regions differ in size and probably also in number of steroid-sensitive cells.

The fine structure of song control nuclei is also dimorphic. Both males and females have neurons of all the classes found in RA (DeVoogd and Nottebohm, 1981a; Gurney, 1981). The sexes differ in various aspects of the morphometry of these cells. Neurons from male zebra finches have more primary dendrites and longer branch segments than do neurons from females (Gurney, 1981). This results in the male neurons having more dendritic segments per unit RA volume than the female neurons as well as a larger dendritic field volume. In canaries, male and female RA neurons have equal numbers of primary dendritic branches (DeVoogd and Nottebohm, 1981a), but the distal dendritic segments are longer in the male, resulting here too in greater field volume for the male (Fig. 3).

The canary song system remains responsive to gonadal steroids in adulthood. Giving testosterone to adult female canaries causes HVc, RA and nXIIts to grow larger although never to the size typical of males (Nottebohm, 1980a; DeVoogd and Nottebohm, unpublished observations). Castrating a male canary causes HVc and RA to decrease in size although not to size seen in females (Nottebohm, 1980a). Indeed, the bird's seasonal cycles form a natural neuroendocrine experiment. During the fall, the gonads regress, steroid levels drop — and RA and HVc shrink to less than 60% of their size during reproduction (Nottebohm, 1981). Ovariectomizing a female canary neonatally results in neurons within RA having smaller dendritic fields than those seen in intact females (Fig. 4) (DeVoogd and Nottebohm, 1981b). However, exposing neonatally ovariectomized females to estradiol or dihydrotestosterone for 1 month as adults results in dendritic patterns similar to intact

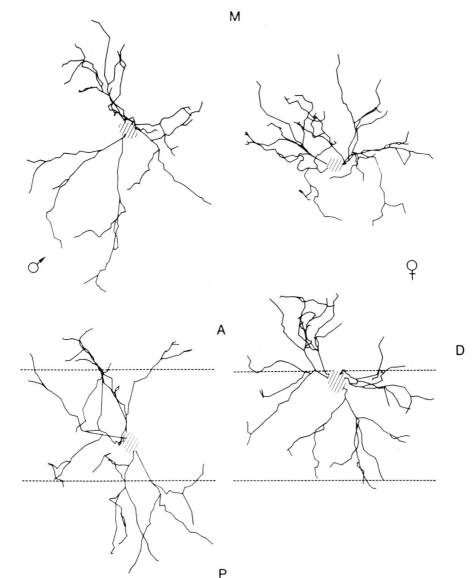

Fig. 3. Computer-generated plots of RA neurons from a male (left) and from a female (right) canary. The computer acquired and analyzed coordinate information in 3 dimensions; the bottom plots show the same neurons as the top plots after a 90° rotation. Notice how the male cell tends to have longer terminal dendritic segments than does the female cell, leading to a larger dendritic field. (From DeVoogd and Nottebohm, 1981a.)

females. Giving testosterone to ovariectomized females results in dendritic growth to levels similar to those seen in normal males. As mentioned above, only the females treated with testosterone begin to sing.

The effects of testosterone treatment can also be seen at the ultrastructural level. In RA, synaptic density in testosterone-treated females is maintained at only slightly less than the level seen in control females as the size of the nucleus doubles (DeVoogd et al., 1983). This

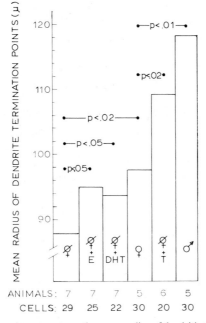
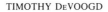

Fig. 4. Effects of various hormonal treatments on the mean radius of dendritic termination points for a sample of neurons from RA. E_2 and DHT cause dendrites from ovariectomized females to grow to the size seen in intact females; T causes growth to the size seen in normal males. (From DeVoogd and Nottebohm, 1981b.)

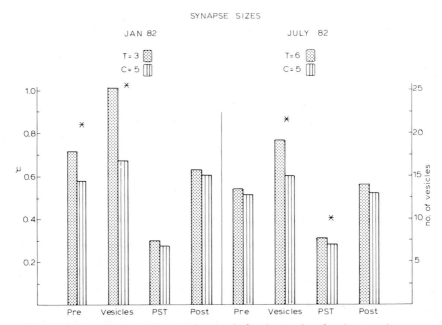

Fig. 5. Several aspects of synaptic morphology increase in female canaries after they are given testosterone. These include vesicle number, presynaptic process profile and postsynaptic thickening.

results in a 50% increase in the total number of synapses within the nucleus. Associated with the increase in synaptic number are changes in synaptic morphology: synapses from T-treated females have more vesicles, larger presynaptic profiles and a slightly larger post-synaptic thickening than do synapses from untreated females (Fig. 5). Each of these testosterone-induced changes is consistent with increased synaptic efficacy. These gross and microanatomical studies indicate that substantial neuronal rewiring can be induced in adulthood in this species.

In contrast, no comparable plasticity is seen in the adult zebra finch. Castrating adult males or giving androgens to adult females does not result in significant changes in the volume of HVc or RA. DM and nXIIts grow slightly in females in response to androgens (Gurney and Konishi, 1980; Arnold, 1980c). The neonatal hormonal milieu of the song control nuclei appears to determine their adult morphology in this species; only when hormonal state is altered in the neonate can the morphology be changed by steroid treatment in adulthood. Gurney (1981) reports that both androgenic and estrogenic influences must be present neonatally for male-like song nuclei to develop. Early E_2 treatment increases the size of cells within RA and HVc while early DHT treatment increases the number of cells found in these nuclei. If early E_2 treatment has occurred, administration of androgens to the adult bird will result in growth of HVc, RA, MAN and area X — and the onset of song. In fact, Pohl-Apel (1983) has found that the quality of the song elicited by these treatments is significantly correlated with the degree to which RA size is masculinized.

Little research to date has attempted to link template formation or juvenile song crystallization to neural changes. Nottebohm (personal communication) indicates that HVc and RA can be distinguished in 30-day-old canaries; thus these nuclei could play a role in the development of song. Bottjer et al. (1983) have just reported that bilateral lesions in MAN in juvenile zebra finches severely disrupt later song. Thus this nucleus may have functions during the period of vocal learning which it does not have later on when song is crystallized.

Many of the studies cited above explicitly make the assumption that morphological differences between the sexes are tightly related to behavioral differences. Several lines of evidence are converging to make this assumption more plausible. A certain degree of anatomical masculinization of the song system appears necessary before song can occur (Arnold et al., 1976; Nottebohm, 1980b; DeVoogd and Nottebohm, 1981b; Gurney, 1981). Within birds, there is a significant correlation between the size of RA or HVc and the complexity (Nottebohm et al., 1981) or quality of song (Pohl-Apel, 1983). Indeed, the regression line associating song repertoire size and size of song nuclei in male canaries can be used to predict this relation in testosterone-treated females as well (Nottebohm, unpublished observations).

NEUROCHEMISTRY OF THE AVIAN SONG SYSTEM

Any hormone action in a tissue is contingent on that tissue being able to detect the presence of the hormone. Siegel et al. (1983) report that male zebra finches have higher levels of androgen receptors than do females in a forebrain zone which includes HVc, RA and MAN. Estrogen receptor levels are very low in both sexes. Autoradiographic studies give similar results. More cells in HVc and MAN concentrate androgens in males than in females (Arnold and Saltiel, 1979). No neurons in these nuclei appear to concentrate estrogens in either sex (Arnold, 1979, 1980b). Thus, androgens may regulate their own receptors during development. A female finch may not respond to androgens with male-like behavior or neuroanatomy at least in part because her brain cannot register the presence of the androgens. In contrast female white-crowned sparrows, like canaries, respond to adult androgens by beginning to sing (Konishi, 1965). They show elevated protein synthesis in HVc, RA and area X within 2 days of receiving testosterone (Konishi and Akutagawa, 1981). The nature of the proteins synthesized and their relation to changes in song system morphology and function have not yet been studied.

Perhaps the most fascinating information so far discovered on the neurochemistry of the song system concerns the ubiquity of cholinergic transmission throughout the system. There are high levels of muscarinic cholinergic receptors present in zebra finch HVc and area X (Rainbow et al., 1982; Ryan and Arnold, 1981). Acetyl cholinesterase (AChE) is found in HVc, RA, area X, MAN, NIf, uva, DM, and nXIIts — virtually every nucleus implicated in the song system to date (Ryan and Arnold, 1981). A large proportion of the neurons in each of these nuclei except area X appear to synthesize AChE, while in area X AChE staining is concentrated only in the neuropil. In males this staining highlights area X while in females it appears light and diffuse (Ryan and Arnold, 1981). The authors suggest that males may have a cholinergic input to area X which is missing in females. The neurons of nXIIts are also cholinergic, in common with central motor neurons in general. There are sex differences both in ACh turnover and in ACh reception. Choline acetyltransferase (CAT), a cholinergic synthetic enzyme, and AChE have higher specific activities in male canaries and zebra finches than females in nXIIts, in the syringeal part of the hypoglossal nerve and in the syrinx (Luine et al., 1980). There are almost 4 times as many ACh receptors in the syrinx of a male zebra finch as in a female (Bleisch et al., 1983).

Each of these features is dynamically responsive to changes in androgen level. Castration causes AChE and CAT to drop rapidly in nXIIts, the hypoglossal nerve, and the syrinx (Luine et al., 1980; Bleisch et al., 1983). The number of ACh receptors drops slowly and progressively, suggesting that the loss of androgens prevents receptor replacement rather than actively eliminating receptors (Bleisch et al., 1983). Androgen replacement for 1 week causes complete recovery of intact AChE levels and substantial recovery of intact CAT levels (Luine et al., 1980). The drop and subsequent recovery of enzyme activity in the syrinx is associated with comparable changes in the weight of the syringeal muscles: specific enzyme activity does not change. Similarly, muscle weight, AChE activity and ACh receptor number go up in females when they are given testosterone (Luine et al., 1980; Bleisch et al., 1983). The rise in AChE exceeds the rise in muscle weight. Androgen effects on the syrinx require the integrity of the hypoglossal nerve. In denervated syrinxes, testosterone no longer causes the elevation in muscle protein or ACh receptor levels. However, AChE levels still rise after denervation (Bleisch et al., 1983), suggesting that the androgen receptors known to be present in this muscle (Lieberburg and Nottebohm, 1979) can affect this enzyme.

Much less research has been done on the roles of other neurotransmitters or neuromodulators in the song system. Lewis et al. (1981) have shown that there is a catecholaminergic projection from the area ventralis of Tsai (AVT) into area X in male zebra finches. This projection is sexually dimorphic: it is much less discrete and less intense in females. Little is known of the function of AVT. Also, it is not yet known whether this projection is sensitive to adult hormonal changes. Enkephalin-like immunoreactivity occurs in MAN, HVc, NIf, RA, and ICo, and sets these areas off from surrounding tissue (Ryan et al., 1981). These pathways exist in both sexes but have not yet been quantified.

In summary, research on the neurochemistry of the avian song system is just beginning. The song system appears to be characterized by steroid receptors and by particular neurotransmitters and neuromodulators. The distribution of these receptors and chemicals is very similar between the sexes but their levels are often dimorphic. It appears likely that testosterone can cause increased levels of androgen receptors, thus increasing the sensitivity of the system, and also can cause increased ACh receptors, so as to magnify the effects of any activity within the system.

UNANSWERED QUESTIONS

The avian song system continues to be a provocative and exciting system in which to study the effects of gonadal steroids on central nervous system development and functioning. Major facets of this system remain to be explored, however.

Very little research has been done on the electrophysiology of neurons in song control regions, while no research has been done on whether steroids might modulate this function. Katz and Gurney (1981) report that units in the zebra finch HVc may show weak, long-latency auditory responses. Katz (1982) has recently shown that there are also auditory units in the neostriatal shelf under HVc and in RA. Margoliash (1983) finds that occasional auditory units in HVc of male white-crowned sparrows may be highly selective for the bird's own song or for the song heard as a juvenile.

The function of the song control nuclei in female birds remains unknown. Females appear to form a song template (Konishi, 1965; Miller, 1979a) and use song in mate selection and recognition (Thorpe, 1961; Immelmann, 1969; Miller, 1979b). HVc and RA could contribute to such functions. If so, one would predict the presence of song-specific neurons in females like those Margoliash (1983) finds in males. In females of many species, reproductive behaviors occur seasonally in phase with elevated levels of gonadal steroids. Since these include behaviors facilitated by song, it is possible that song-specific neurons in HVc or RA would vary in selectivity or sensitivity according to the hormonal state.

The research reviewed above suggests that one reason for the size difference between male and female nuclei is the addition of a major function, namely song. One would predict, therefore, that these differences would be much less extreme in bird species where both sexes sing. However, in robin chats, one such species, MAN, HVc, RA and area X are between 2 and 3 times larger in males than in females (Brenowitz and Arnold, 1983) — a difference nearly as large as in those species where females never sing.

Since song appears to have a different meaning for females than for males, it is possible that it is perceived and processed differently in the two sexes. Indeed, it is plausible that in brain regions involved in fine discrimination of songs, female synapses or neurons may be even more developed than those of males. One reasonable site for such differences would be forebrain auditory regions, but no microanatomical comparisons of the sexes in these areas have yet been done.

What are the functions of the brain nuclei that do not appear to participate in singing? Area X, for example, is a large nucleus which responds to testosterone with sharply increased protein synthesis (Konishi and Akutagawa, 1981). Why should the nucleus persist as a major component of the lobus parolfactorius unless it retains important functions in adulthood?

What neurobiological processes occur in the instances where plastic change is observed? What occurs, for example, when song control nuclei in female canaries appear larger after testosterone treatment? Possibilities include alteration of cells from adjacent striatum so that the nucleus boundary is now seen as including them, or an "explosion" in which all the constituents of the nucleus are pushed apart. If the latter is true, as would appear to be the case in RA (DeVoogd and Nottebohm, 1981b), synaptic relations will be distorted. Do synapses stretch to accommodate the new geometry, slide to a more comfortable position or simply break and reform?

How do steroids affect or interact with new neurons within HVc? Neurons continue to be generated along the telencephalic venticular zone in adult canaries from which they migrate into many regions of the forebrain (Goldman and Nottebohm, 1983; Nottebohm and Kasparian, 1983). While no direct effect of gonadal steroids on neurogenesis or migration has been observed, some effect must occur. It is unlikely that the new neurons simply go into HVc and die there — they appear healthy, in any case, at least 5 weeks after neurogenesis. If they contribute toward "a constant rebuilding of adult forebrain networks", as Nottebohm and Kasparian (1983) suggest, then the new neurons must end up looking and acting like other HVc neurons. They should have androgen receptors and be sensitive to steroid levels. They should also help to maintain the anatomical dimorphisms within HVc.

The actions of gonadal steroids on the avian song system are multifaceted. Hormone-induced dimorphisms appear at every nucleus in this system. They appear at every level of analysis used to date, from brain volume involved in song to estimates of hormone receptors per cell. Indeed, in the canary, effects of adult administration of testosterone appear to cascade down the system. Thus, many moderate increases in transmission efficiency throughout the system result in a huge overall increase in transmission capacity. As Arnold (1982) notes, there is no single switching point at which hormonal status and experience are integrated in deciding to produce song. Rather, this "switch" is distributed, perhaps, to incorporate a variety of functions into song (Arnold, 1982), or to provide this very important system with redundancy.

In either case, how general a model is the avian song system for steroid actions in the vertebrate brain? Over the past 10 years, the avian song system has predicted the presence and ubiquity of large dimorphic brain regions. Function-specific regions of the central nervous system which have high androgen affinities have been shown in birds as well as many other systems (see e.g. Breedlove, 1984). While the major reorganization of adult nervous system structure and function which occurs in the response to steroids in the canary (DeVoogd and Nottebohm, 1981b; DeVoogd et al., 1983) has not yet been shown in mammals, its existence is provocative and should encourage the search for the combination which will unlock similar change in other systems.

ACKNOWLEDGEMENTS

This work was supported by NIH Grant No. 08-R3HD17746A and by a grant from the Alfred P. Sloan Foundation.

REFERENCES

Arnold, A.P. (1975) The effects of castration and androgen replacement on song, courtship, and aggression in zebra finches (*Poephila guttata*). *J. Exp. Zool.*, 191: 309–326.

Arnold, A.P. (1979) Hormone accumulation in the brain of the zebra finch after injection of various steroids and steroid competitors. *Soc. Neurosci. Abstr.*, 5: 437.

Arnold, A.P. (1980a) Sexual differences in the brain. *Am. Scient.*, 68: 165–173.

Arnold, A.P. (1980b) Quantitative analysis of sex differences in hormone accumulation in the zebra finch brain: Methodological and theoretical issues. *J. Comp. Neurol.*, 189: 421–436.

Arnold, A.P. (1980c) Effects of androgens on volumes of sexually dimorphic brain regions in the zebra finch. *Brain Res.*, 185: 441–444.

Arnold, A.P. (1982) Neural control of passerine song. In: D.E. Kroodsma and E.H. Miller (Eds.), *Acoustic Communication in Birds, Vol. 1*, Academic Press, New York, pp. 75–94.

Arnold, A.P. and Saltiel, A. (1979) Sexual difference in pattern of hormone accumulation in the brain of a songbird. *Science*, 205: 702–705.

Arnold, A.P., Nottebohm, F. and Pfaff, D.W. (1976) Hormone accumulating cells in vocal control and other brain regions of the zebra finch (*Poephila guttata*). *J. Comp. Neurol.*, 165: 487–512.

Baker, M.C., Spitler-Nabors, K.J. and Bradley, D.C. (1981) Early experience determines song dialect responsiveness of female sparrows. *Science*, 214: 819–821.

Baldwin, F.M., Goldin, H.S. and Metfessel, M. (1940) Effects of testosterone proprionate on female roller canaries under complete song isolation. *Proc. Soc. Exp. Biol. Med.*, 44: 373–375.

Bleisch, W.V., Luine, V.N. and Nottebohm, F. (1983) Modification of synapses in androgen-sensitive muscle. I. Hormonal regulation of acetylcholine receptor number in the songbird syrinx. *J. Neurosci.*, in press.

Bottjer, S.W., Miesner, E. and Arnold, A.P. (1983) Developmental changes in effects of lesions in forebrain song control nuclei of passerine birds. *Soc. Neurosci. Abstr.*, 9: 537.

Breedlove S.M. (1984) Steroid influences on the development and function of a neuromuscular system. In: G.J. De Vries, J.P. De Bruin, H.B.M. Uylings and M.A. Corner (Eds.), *Sex Differences in the Brain. The Relation between Stucture and Function. Progress in Brain Research*, this volume, Ch. 8.

Brenowitz, E. and Arnold, A. (1983) Neural correlates of avian song duetting. *Soc. Neurosci. Abstr.*, 9: 538.

Brockway, B. (1969) Roles of budgerigar vocalization in the integration of breeding behavior. In: R. Hinde (Ed.), *Bird Vocalizations*, Cambridge University Press, London, pp. 131–158.

Callard, G.V., Petro, Z. and Ryan, K.J. (1978) Conversion of androgen to estrogen and other steroids in the vertebrate brain. *Am. Zool.*, 18: 511–523.

DeVoogd, T.J. and Nottebohm, F. (1981a) Sex differences in dendritic morphology of a song control nucleus in the canary: A quantitative Golgi study. *J. Comp. Neurol.* 196: 309–316.

DeVoogd, T. and Nottebohm, F. (1981b) Gonadal hormones induce dendritic growth in the adult avian brain. *Science*, 214: 202–204.

DeVoogd, T.J., Nixdorf, B. and Nottebohm, F. (1983) Formation of new synapses related to acquisition of a new behavior. Submitted.

Farner, D.S. and Wingfield, J.C. (1980) Reproductive endocrinology of birds. *Am. Rev. Physiol.*, 42: 457–472.

Follett, B.K., Hinde, R.A., Steel, E. and Nicholls, T.J. (1973) The influence of photoperiod on nest building, ovarian development and luteinizing hormone secretion in canaries (*Serinus canarius*). *J. Endocrinol.*, 59: 151–162.

Goldman, S. and Nottebohm, F. (1983) Neuronal production, migration, and differentiation in a vocal control nucleus of the adult female canary brain. *Proc. Natl. Acad. Sci. (U.S.A.)*, 80: 2390–2394.

Greenspon, J.M. (1983) An analysis of the origin and parameters of testosterone-induced song in adult female canaries (*Serinus canarius*). *East. Psychol. Assoc. Abstr.*, 54: 75.

Greenspon, J.M. and Stein, D.G. (1983) Functional asymmetry of the song bird brain: Effects of testosterone on song control in adult female canaries. *Neurosci. Lett.*, in press.

Gurney, M.E. (1981) Hormonal control of cell form and number in the zebra finch song system. *J. Neurosci.*, 1: 658–673.

Gurney, M.E. (1982) Behavioral correlates of sexual differentiation in the zebra finch brain. *Brain Res.*, 231: 153–172.

Gurney, M.E. and Konishi, M. (1980) Hormone-induced sexual differentiation of brain and behavior in zebra finches. *Science*, 208: 1380–1383.

Harding, C.F., Sheridan, K. and Walters, M.T. (1983a) Hormonal specificity and activation of sexual behavior in male zebra finches. *Hormone Behav.*, 17: 111–133.

Hinde, R.A. and Steel, E. (1966) Integration of the reproductive behaviour of female canaries. *Symp. Soc. Exp. Biol.*, 20: 401–426.

Immelmann, K. (1969) Song development in the zebra finch and other Estrildid finches. In: R.A. Hinde (Ed.), *Bird Vocalizations*, Cambridge University Press, London, pp. 61–74.

Katz, L.C. and Gurney, M.E. (1981) Auditory responses in the zebra finch's motor system for song. *Brain Res.*, 211: 192–197.

Kelley, D.B. and Nottebohm, F. (1979) Projections of a telencephalic auditory nucleus — field L — in the canary. *J. Comp. Neurol.*, 183: 455–470.

Konishi, M. (1965) The role of auditory feedback in the control of vocalization in the white-crowned sparrow. *Z. Tierpsychol.*, 22: 770–773.

Konishi, M. and Akutagawa, E. (1981) Androgen increases protein synthesis within the avian brain vocal control system. *Brain Res.*, 222: 442–446.

Kroodsma, D.E. (1976) Reproductive development in a female songbird: Differential stimulation by quality of male song. *Science*, 192: 574–575.

Kroodsma, D.E. (1982) Song repertoires: Problems in their definition and use. In: D.E. Kroodsma and E.H. Miller (Eds.), *Acoustic Communication in Birds, Vol. 1*, Academic Press, New York, pp. 125–146.

Lehrman, D.S. (1965) Interaction between internal and external environments in the regulation of the reproductive cycle of the ring dove. In: F.A. Beach (Ed.), *Sex and Behavior*, Wiley, New York.

Leonard, S.L. (1939) Induction of singing in female canaries by injections of male hormone. *Proc. Soc. Exp. Biol. Med.*, 41: 229–230.

Leppelsack, H.-J. (1974) Funktionelle Eigenschaften der Horbahn im Field L des Neostriatum caudale des Staren (*Sturnus vulgaris* L., Aves). *J. Comp. Physiol.*, 88: 271–320.

Lewis, J.W., Ryan, S.M., Arnold, A.P. and Butcher, L.L. (1981) Evidence for a catecholaminergic projection to area X in the zebra finch. *J. Comp. Neurol.*, 196: 347–354.

Lieberburg, I. and Nottebohm, F. (1979) High-affinity androgen binding proteins in syringeal tissues of song birds. *Gen. Comp. Endocrinol.*, 37: 286–293.

Luine, V., Nottebohm, F., Harding, C. and McEwen, B.S. (1980) Androgen affects cholinergic enzymes in syringeal motor neurons and muscle. *Brain Res.*, 192: 89–107.

Margoliash, D. (1983) Acoustic parameters underlying the responses of song specific neurons in the white-crowned sparrow. *J. Neurosci.*, 3: 1039–1057.

Marler, P. (1970) A comparative approach to vocal learning: Song development in white-crowned sparrows. *J. Comp. Physiol. Psychol.*, 71: 1–25.

Marler, P. and Peters, S. (1982) Developmental overproduction and selective attrition: New processes in the epigenesis of birdsong. *Develop. Psychobiol.*, 15: 369–378.

Marler, P. and Sherman, V. (1983) Song structure without auditory feedback: Emendations of the auditory template hypothesis. *J. Neurosci.*, 3: 517–531.

Miller, D.B. (1979a) Long-term recognition of father's song by female zebra finches. *Nature (London)*, 280: 389–391.

Miller, D.B. (1979b) The acoustic basis of mate recognition by female zebra finches (*Taeniopygia guttata*). *Anim. Behav.*, 27: 376–380.

Naftolin, F., Ryan, J. Davies, I.J., Reddy, V.V., Flores, F., Petro, Z., White, R.J., Takaoka, Y. and Wolin, L. (1975) The formation of estrogen by central neuroendocrine tissues. *Recent Progr. Hormone Res.*, 31: 295–319.

Nottebohm, F. (1969) The critical period for song learning. *Ibis*, 111: 386–387.

Nottebohm, F. (1980a) Testosterone triggers growth of brain vocal control nuclei in adult female canaries. *Brain Res.*, 189: 429–436.

Nottebohm, F. (1980b) Brain pathways for vocal learning in birds: A review of the first ten years. *Progr. Psychobiol. Physiol. Psychol.*, 9: 85–124.

Nottebohm, F. (1981) A brain for all seasons: cyclical anatomical changes in song control nuclei of the canary brain. *Science*, 214: 1368–1370.

Nottebohm, F. and Arnold, A.P. (1976) Sexual dimorphism in vocal control areas of the songbird brain. *Science*, 194: 211–213.

Nottebohm, F. and Kasparian, S. (1983) Widespread labeling of avian forebrain neurons after systematic injections of ^{3}H-thymidine in adulthood. *Soc. Neurosci. Abstr.*, 9: 380.

Nottebohm, F. and Nottebohm, M.E. (1978) Relationship between song repertoire and age in the canary, *Serinus canarius*. *Z. Tierpsychol.*, 46: 298–305.

Nottebohm, F., Stokes, T.M. and Leonard, C.M. (1976) Central control of song in the canary, *Serinus canarius*, *Z. Tierpsychol.*, 46: 298–305.

Nottebohm, F., Kasparian, S. and Pandazis, C. (1981) Brain space for a learned task. *Brain Res.*, 213: 99–109.

Nottebohm, F., Kelley, D.B. and Paton, J.A. (1982) Connections of vocal control nuclei in the canary telencephalon. *J. Comp. Neurol.*, 207: 344–357.

Pohl-Apel, G. (1983) Quality of song and degree of masculinization of the brain in female zebra finches. *Soc. Neurosci. Abstr.*, 9: 537.

Pröve, E. (1974) Der Einfluss von Kastration and Testosteronsubtitution auf das Sexualverhalten mannlicher Zebrafinken (*Taeniopygia guttata castanotis* Gould). *J. Ornithol.*, 115: 338–347.

Rainbow, T.C., Bleisch, W.V., Biegon, A. and McEwen, B.S. (1982) Quantitative densitometry of neurotransmitter receptors. *J. Neurosci. Meth.*, 5: 127–138.

Ryan, S.M. and Arnold, A.P. (1981) Evidence for cholinergic participation in the control of bird song: Acetylcholinesterase distribution and muscarinic receptor autoradiography in the zebra finch brain. *J. Comp. Neurol.*, 202: 211–219.

Ryan, S.M., Elde, R.P. and Arnold, A.P. (1981) Enkephalin-like immunoreactivity in vocal control regions of the zebra finch brain. *Brain Res.*, 229: 236–240.

Shoemaker, H.H. (1939) Effect of testosterone propionate on the behavior of the female canary. *Proc. Soc. Exp. Biol. Med.*, 41: 299–302.

Siegel, L.I., Fox, T.O. and Konishi, M. (1983) Androgen and estrogen receptors in zebra finch brain. *Soc. Neurosci. Abstr.*, 9: 1078.

Swaab, D.F. and Hofman, M.A. (1984) Sexual differentiation of the human brain. A historical perspective. In: G.J. De Vries, J.P.C. De Bruin, H.B.M. Uylings and M.A. Corner (Eds.), *Sex Differences in the Brain. Relation between Structure and Function. Progress in Brain Research*, this volume, Ch. 21.

Thorpe, W.H. (1961) *Bird Song*, Cambridge University Press, London.

Toran-Allerand, C.D. (1984) On the genesis of sexual differentiation of the central nervous system: morphogenetic consequences of steroidal exposure and possible role of α-fetoprotein. In: G.J. De Vries, J.P.C. De Bruin, H.B.M. Uylings and M.A. Corner (Eds.), *Sex Differences in the Brain. Relation between Structure and Function. Progress in Brain Research*, this volume, Ch. 4.

Warren, R.P. and Hinde, R.A. (1961) Does the male stimulate oestrogen secretion in female canaries? *Science*, 133: 1354–1355.

Zigmond, R.E., Nottebohm, F. and Pfaff, D.W. (1973) Androgen-concentrating cells in the midbrain of a songbird. *Science*, 179: 1005–1007.

Zigmond, R.E., Detrick, R.A. and Pfaff, D.W. (1980) An autoradiographic study of the localization of androgen concentrating cells in the chaffinch. *Brain Res.*, 182: 369–381.

DISCUSSION

H.B.M. UYLINGS: Do you have data on the presence of lateralization in the male and female brain (related to season)?

T. DeVOOGD: To date, anatomical correlates for lateralization of song control have not been found in RA or HVc of the canary. The hypoglossal nucleus is larger on the left than on the right (Nottebohm and Arnold, 1976). This difference is present in intact females and androgen-treated females (DeVoogd, unpublished data) but has not yet been studied across seasons.

H.B.M. UYLINGS: When the size of the nuclei is reduced, is the number of neurons within these nuclei reduced too?

T. DeVOOGD: This has not yet been measured.

R.A. GORSKI: Would you comment on the possible relationship between testosterone, neuronal anatomy and the learning of song?

T. DeVOOGD: Testosterone seems to induce neuroanatomical growth which is necessary for singing. When testosterone drops, singing stops. It is possible that the relearning of song with the addition of new syllables which happens every spring in canaries, is only possible because a preceding drop in testosterone had resulted in neuroanatomical regression and forgetting.

C.D. TORAN-ALLERAND: Have you been able to sex-reverse the female brain by androgenizing at an earlier age? The basic substrate is well differentiated in the adult and even though there is a certain amount of plasticity a more undifferentiated substrate might allow for complete sex reversal.

T. DeVOOGD: Your point is a good one. Anatomical consequences of early hormone treatments have not yet been studied in canaries.

D. KIMURA: Do you know how specific the dendritic growth you have described for RA is, i.e., is this a general phenomenon throughout the brain, either between male and female canaries or in testosterone-treated females? Or is it specific to some structures such as RA and HVc?

T. DeVOOGD: Dendritic growth has not been measured elsewhere. However, the volumes of nucleus spiriformis and nucleus rotundus do not differ between sexes (Nottebohm and Arnold, 1976) and show only minor seasonal variations (Nottebohm, 1981), suggesting that the sex differences and steroid-induced plasticity may be quite specific.

REFERENCES

Nottebohm, F. (1981) A brain for all seasons: cyclical anatomical changes in song control nuclei of the canary brain. *Science*, 214: 1368–1370.

Nottebohm, F. and Arnold, A.P. (1976) Sexual dimorphism in vocal control areas of the songbird brain. *Science*, 194: 211–213.

G.J. De Vries et al. (Eds.),
Progress in Brain Research, Vol. 61
© 1984 Elsevier Science Publishers B.V., Amsterdam

Sex Differences in Vasopressin and Other Neurotransmitter Systems in the Brain

G.J. DE VRIES, R.M. BUIJS and F.W. VAN LEEUWEN

Netherlands Institute for Brain Research, Meibergdreef 33, 1105 AZ, Amsterdam (The Netherlands)

INTRODUCTION

In 1971 Raisman and Field demonstrated that sex differences exist in the structure of the brain. To be precise, they found more spine synapses of non-strial origin in the medial preoptic area (MPOA) of female than of male rats. The years to follow yielded an ever growing list of morphological sex differences, e.g. in the size of specific brain regions, in dendritic and axonal branching patterns, and in the distribution of synapses. Most of these differences were shown to be dependent on the presence of androgens during a restricted period during development (for recent reviews see Gorski, 1984; Toran-Allerand, 1984). The functional meaning of some of these sex differences seems very clear, as for instance the presence or absence of the spinal motor nucleus of the bulbocavernosus in respectively male and female rats (Breedlove and Arnold, 1980): in male rats this nucleus contains motoneurons innervating the striated muscles of the penis, which are absent or vestigial in females. In most cases, however, it appears to be very difficult to elucidate the significance of a particular morphological sex difference. Several experimental procedures have been used in this respect, e.g. lesion studies, implantation of steroids, or attempts to find electrophysiological correlates (Dyer et al., 1976; Christensen and Gorski, 1978; Arendash and Gorski, 1983; Dyer, 1984). Up till now, such studies have made the topological correlation stronger of the site where sexually dimorphic functions are being regulated and the presence of morphological sex differences. For example, the MPOA — which shows sexual dimorphism with respect to synaptic patterns (Raisman and Field, 1971) and the size of the "sexually dimorphic nucleus of the preoptic area" (SDN-POA; Gorski et al., 1978) — has been further implicated in the regulation of gonadotropin release and male sexual behavior (e.g. Gorski, 1984). The functional implications of this structural dimorphism remain unclear.

An approach that might prove to be fruitful in obtaining a deeper insight into the nature and significance of the sex differences, is the study of the various neurotransmitter systems which form part of a given morphological sex difference. Especially the use of immunocytochemistry might be of great help in this respect. Such a technique would not only facilitate the identification of the various components of a particular sexually dimorphic area, it can also be used to study the influence of various hormonal conditions on a specific neurotransmitter system. This chapter will first give a brief survey about various aspects of the study of sex differences in neurotransmitter systems. Then, as an example of the use of immunocytochemistry in studying sex differences, the vasopressin innervation of the brain will be discussed.

SEX DIFFERENCES IN NEUROTRANSMITTER SYSTEMS

Chemical assays

The sex differences which are found in neuronal connectivity (for review see Toran-Allerand, 1984) suggest that such differences may also be expected with respect to the neurotransmitter content measured within sexually dimorphic areas. Knowledge about the neurotransmitter content, however, gives no information about the ongoing activity of the system being studied. The state of activity can be inferred from information about (i) the concentrations of the neurotransmitter and (ii) of its precursors and metabolites, (iii) the activities of synthesizing and degrative enzymes, and (iv) the receptor content. The presumed involvement of, e.g., monoaminergic and cholinergic systems in sexually dimorphic functions such as gonadotropin release and sexual behavior (Everitt et al., 1975; Hery et al., 1976; Clemens et al., 1981; Meyerson, 1984), suggests that in any case sex differences in the activity of these systems can be expected.

Sex differences have indeed been found in neurotransmitter content and enzyme activities of the cholinergic, noradrenergic, dopaminergic and serotoninergic systems (Libertun et al., 1973; Gordon and Shellenberger, 1974; Vaccari, 1980; Luine and McEwen, 1983). Similar differences have been reported in the number of adrenergic, cholinergic and serotoninergic receptors (Arimatsu et al., 1981; Avissar et al., 1981; Orensanz et al., 1982; Arimatsu, 1983; Fischette et al., 1983). Sex differences in neurotransmitter systems were in fact known even before any structural sex difference in the brain had been demonstrated. To our knowledge, the earliest report is that of Kato, who demonstrated in 1960 that from the 68th day of life onward the serotonin content of the entire brain is higher in the female than in the male rat. This study has been repeated by various authors with more refined techniques, resulting in the description of sex differences in the content of serotonin, of its precursors and metabolites, and in the activity of the enzymes implicated in its metabolic pathways in a variety of rat brain areas (for review see Vaccari, 1980). Furthermore, elevated serotonin levels in the female brain have been reported to be present as early as the 12th postnatal day (Ladosky and Gaziri, 1970; Giulian et al., 1973). The early appearance of this sex difference is dependent on the neonatal presence of androgens in the male rat and, in turn, has been thought to be responsible for further sexual differentiation of the brain (Ladosky and Gaziri, 1970). This hypothesis would explain why it is that certain psychotropic drugs which interfere with the serotoninergic activity of the brain, when given during pregnancy, can interfere with processes such as "defeminization" and "masculinization" of the brain (Jarzab and Döhler, 1984; a similar involvement in sexual differentiation has been claimed for the catecholaminergic system: Reznikov, 1978).

In addition to its use for tracing sex differences in neurotransmitter systems, chemical assays may give an indication about the influence of gonadal hormones on the activity of a certain neurotransmitter system. It therefore enables one to relate the neurotransmitter system in question to sexually dimorphic functions which vary consistently. For example, the administration of the dopamine agonist apomorphine reverses the decline in the display of male copulatory behavior which usually follows castration (Malmnas, 1977), whereas the neurotoxic destruction of the dopaminergic forebrain innervation in non-castrated male rats has detrimental effects on male sexual behavior (Caggiula et al., 1976). In addition, the administration of dopamine antagonists blocks copulatory behavior of castrated male rats, whether or not metabolites of testosterone — which normally stimulate this behavior (Baum and Starr, 1979) — had been simultaneously administered. These results suggest that under normal conditions testosterone facilitates male sexual behavior by stimulating the activity of dopaminergic neurons. This idea was corroborated by the fact that castration resulted in a decrease of dopamine concentrations in the septum and the nucleus accumbens septi, which could be reversed by administration of testosterone or of its metabolites estrogen and 5-dihydrotestosterone (Alderson and Baum, 1981; for similar studies see Muth et al., 1980; Luine and Rhodes, 1983; Luine and McEwen, 1983).

Although this research on the dopaminergic innervation of the brain shows the value of chemical assays, one should bear in mind that most of the aforementioned methods are at present only applicable to a small number of monoaminergic, cholinergic and amino acid neurotransmitters, which probably forms only the top of the iceberg of the neurotransmitter population present in the brain. In addition, the chemical techniques do not allow a detailed morphological insight into the observed differences, and therefore are only of limited usefulness for clarifying the significance of a given morphological sex difference.

Anatomical studies

The study of the connectivity of a given sexually dimorphic brain structure may be of help for clarifying the function of this dimorphism. Examples of neuronal systems where such knowledge has indeed been indispensable in this respect are the previously mentioned spinal nucleus of the bulbocavernosus (Breedlove, 1984) and the vocal control areas in the bird brain (see e.g. DeVoogd, 1984). The anatomy of the latter system was originally studied by making lesions followed by a combination of behavioral and anatomical techniques (recording of song and detection of degenerating fibers, respectively; Nottebohm et al., 1976). These studies have demonstrated that this system was built of a series of interconnected forebrain and midbrain nuclei, which are connected to a medullar nucleus, which in turn contains motoneurons innervating the vocal organ: the syrinx. Some of these nuclei are much larger in male than in female birds, which is consistent with the fact that males sing, while females do not (Nottebohm and Arnold, 1976; DeVoogd, 1984). Although these examples demonstrate that unspecific methods such as anterograde and retrograde tracing techniques are of great value for determining the connections between specific brain areas, there are limitations to their usefulness. Difficulties arise, for instance, when one wishes to establish the source of the sexually dimorphic terminals in the MPOA, about which the only thing known is that they are of non-strial origin (Raisman and Field, 1971), or when one wants to describe the afferents and efferents of a relatively small area, such as the SDN-POA (Gorski et al., 1978). In such cases an approach which reveals the neurotransmitter systems present in the neuronal elements might be more appropriate since it might enable more refined anatomical studies.

Several methods have been developed for studying the anatomy of neurotransmitter systems (see e.g., Palay and Chan-Palay, 1982): (i) the histofluorescent demonstration of the indolamines and catecholamines, (ii) enzymes histochemical procedures for cholinergic neurotransmitter pathways and (iii) immunocytochemistry, which is potentially the most versatile method, since it does not depend on detailed knowledge of either the chemical nature or the metabolizing enzymes for a given neurotransmitter. Moreover, it can be used for demonstrating an extremely wide variety of substances. The introduction of these methods has led to the discovery of many anatomical pathways in the brain which were not previously known (for review see e.g. Livett, 1978).

Recently these methods have been introduced in the study of sexually dimorphic vocal control nuclei in the zebra finch brain (Lewis et al., 1981; Ryan and Arnold, 1981; Ryan et al., 1981; DeVoogd, 1984), and a start has been made in exploring the various neurotransmitter systems which are present in the SDN-POA of the rat. Sladek et al. (1983) have demonstrated with histofluorescence that the catecholaminergic innervation of this structure appears denser in the female than in the male. Watson and Hoffman (1983) identified peptidergic components of the SDN-POA using immunocytochemical techniques. They found, for instance, that cholecystokinin-containing perikarya are present in the SDN-POA of both sexes, whereas substance P and neurotensin could be demonstrated only in males. Simerly et al. (1983), combining immunocytochemistry with a cytoarchitectonic study, demonstrated that the SDN-POA is virtually void of serotoninergic innervation. In addition, they reported that the part of the MPOA immediately adjacent to the SDN-POA, contains a low density of serotoninergic innervation (this part was larger in males than in females), while the remaining lateral part of the MPOA receives a relatively dense innervation (this latter part was smaller in males than in females). This study therefore shows that besides its use in clarifying the various components of known sexually dimorphic areas immunocytochemistry can reveal new morphological sex differences.

The aforementioned studies, which identify the various neurotransmitter components of a sexually dimorphic area, form only the onset to get a deeper insight in the anatomy and function of the sexually dimorphic areas. One way in which research on this topic might be pursued is exemplified by the study of the vasopressinergic innervation within the brain, to be discussed in the next section.

SEXUALLY DIMORPHIC VASOPRESSIN PATHWAYS IN THE BRAIN

The vasopressinergic innervation of the brain

One decade ago vasopressin (VP) was only known to be present in the hypothalamo-neurohypophyseal system. VP was believed to be synthesized exclusively in the hypothalamic paraventricular (PVN) and supraoptic nuclei (SON), from where fibers ran via the median eminence towards the posterior pituitary, where VP was released into the blood stream (Bargman and Scharrer, 1951). Immunocytochemical staining of sections of the rat brain for the presence of VP, however, revealed that also the parvocellular suprachiasmatic nucleus (SCN) contained VP (Swaab and Pool, 1975; Vandesande et al., 1975). Furthermore, VP fibers appeared not to be confined to the known neurosecretory pathways. In fact, they were found to innervate many areas throughout the brain, ranging from the olfactory bulb down to the spinal cord (Buijs, 1978; Sofroniew and Weindl, 1978). Limbic brain structures such as the lateral septum, lateral habenular nucleus and medial amygdaloid nucleus, appeared to be especially densely innervated by VP-containing fibers.

Several findings suggest that VP acts as a neurotransmitter in these areas. To begin with, VP fibers have been demonstrated to terminate synaptically on other neuronal elements in, e.g., the lateral septum and the nucleus of the solitary tract (Buijs and Swaab, 1979; Voorn and Buijs, 1983), from which areas VP can be released following physiological (Cooper et al., 1979) or depolarizing stimuli (Buijs and Van Heerikhuijze, 1982). When applied locally to these areas VP is able to change unit activity (e.g. Hywiler and Felix, 1980; Joëls and Urban, 1982; Mühlethaler et al., 1982) which effect can be blocked by vasopressin antagonists (Mühlethaler et al., 1982). VP-binding sites could in fact be demonstrated autoradiographically in several areas, notably in the lateral septum (Baskin et al., 1983; Van Leeuwen and

Wolters, 1983). Since, finally, also VP-degrading mechanisms have been found in the brain (Burbach et al., 1983), VP has already met many of the established criteria for neurotransmitter identification (Barchas et al., 1978).

Sex differences and influence of gonadal steroids

As this peptide was suggested to be of possible importance for brain development (Boer et al., 1980), the ontogeny of the VP pathways in the brain was studied (Buijs et al., 1980; De Vries et al., 1981). In these studies no distinction was made at first between the two sexes. When studying the lateral septum and the lateral habenular nucleus, the first VP fibers were found on the 10th postnatal day. From the 12th postnatal day onwards large individual differences were found in the density of the innervation in these areas. In some animals the density remained very low while other animals developed a high VP fiber density. When, in a second experiment, the rats were separated according to their sex, this variation turned out to be due to a sex difference, the VP fiber density in the lateral septum and, to a lesser extent, in the lateral habenular nucleus being higher in male than in female rats from the 12th postnatal day onwards (Fig. 1) (De Vries et al., 1981). To determine whether or not this sex difference was dependent on the neonatal presence of androgens, a series of castration and testosterone supplementation experiments was performed, after which the rats were examined on the 26th postnatal day (De Vries et al., 1983). At this age the normal difference between male and female rats is most pronounced. All of the male rats which had been castrated on the first day of life showed a VP fiber density in the lateral septum which was as low as in control females,

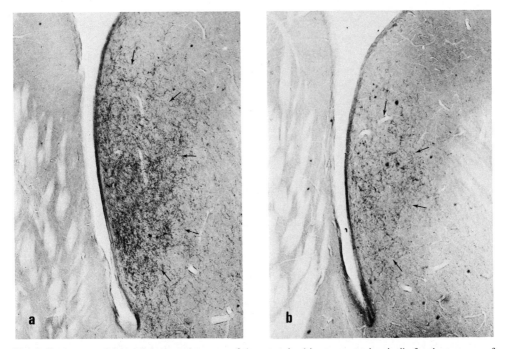

Fig. 1. Transverse sections of the lateral septum of the rat stained immunocytochemically for the presence of vasopressin. Note that the density of the vasopressin fiber network (arrows) is higher in the male (a) than in the female rat (b). (Modified from De Vries et al., 1981.)

i.e., hardly any fibers were found. In male rats castrated on the 7th postnatal day, a fiber density intermediate to that of control males and females was detected. When the rats were castrated on the 14th day of life, a fiber density was found which was equal to that in control males. These results suggested that in males the presence of androgens during the first 2 postnatal weeks caused the VP innervation to become denser than in females. The administration of testosterone proprionate either to female or to neonatally castrated male rats, however, yielded results that pointed to another possibility. Although high doses stimulated the VP network in the lateral septum to become as dense as in normal males, it did not make any difference whether the testosterone was administered in the first, second or third week of life. This suggested that the plasticity of the system is great enough to permit an influence of testosterone even at later stages of life.

This has been recently confirmed in an experiment showing that in male rats which were castrated at 3 months of age, the fiber density in the lateral septum decreased gradually within a period of 15 weeks from very high to a level at which almost no fibers were found. When, at this point, the castrated rats received an implant of silastic tubing packed with testosterone, fiber density returned to the original level within 5 weeks (Table I). Ovariectomy of female rats appeared to have the same effect as castration in male rats (De Vries et al., 1984). Therefore, gonadal steroids seem to be of general importance for the maintenance as well as for the development of the VP fibers in the lateral septum.

TABLE I

VP FIBER DENSITY IN THE LATERAL SEPTUM AT SEVERAL WEEKS AFTER CASTRATION AND SUBSEQUENT TESTOSTERONE SUPPLEMENTATION IN MALE RATS

Weeks	Male rats	Fiber density						
1	Control	++++	++++	++++	++++	++++		
	Castrated	++++	++++	++++	++++	++++		
3	Control	++++	++++	++++	++++	++++		
	Castrated	++++	+++	+++	+++	+++		
8	Control	++++	++++	++++	++++	++++		
	Castrated	+++	++	++	++	++		
15	Control	++++	++++	++++	++++	++++		
	Castrated	+	+	+	+	+		
25	Control	++++	++++	++++	++++	++++		
	Castrated	+	+	+				
	Castrated plus testosterone	++++	++++	++++	++++	++++	+++	+++

Each entry in the table represents 1 rat: +, almost no fibers; ++, a low fiber density; +++, a high fiber density; ++++, a very high fiber density.

The question of the origin of the sexually dimorphic VP innervation of the lateral septum

The source of all extrahypothalamic VP fibers was originally thought to be the PVN and SCN (Buijs, 1978; Sofroniew and Weindl, 1978). The SON seemed an unlikely candidate, since virtually all its efferents appear to run towards the neurohypophysis (Troiano and

Siegel, 1975; Swanson and Sawchenko, 1983). However, lesioning the SCN or the PVN did not affect the VP fiber density in the lateral septum although these lesions eliminated the VP innervation of areas bordering the third ventricle and of areas in the hind brain (Hoorneman and Buijs, 1982; De Vries and Buijs, 1983). Retrograde studies confirmed these findings, because no retrogradely labeled cells were found in the SCN, PVN and SON after placement of various tracers in the lateral septum (De Vries and Buijs, 1983). At that point all known VP-containing nuclei had been eliminated as plausible sites for the origin of the VP fibers in the lateral septum. Recently, however, VP-containing cells were found in still other places in the brains of rats which had been pretreated with colchicine (Caffe and Van Leeuwen, 1983; Van Leeuwen and Caffe, 1983). The site where most of the additional VP cells were detected was the bed nucleus of the stria terminalis (BST; Fig. 2). Some other groups were found in the medial amygdaloid nucleus, the locus coeruleus, and the dorsomedial hypothalamus. When the BST was lesioned a strong reduction in the density of the VP innervation of the lateral septum was indeed found. Other areas where the fiber density was affected, were the diagonal band of Broca, the lateral habenular nucleus, the medial amygdaloid nucleus, the periventricular grey and the locus coeruleus (De Vries and Buijs, 1983).

Because these lesions might also have destroyed fibers of passage, ultimate proof for the VP projections of the BST can only be obtained after retrograde tracing in combination with the demonstration of VP in the labeled neuron (cf. Sawchenko and Swanson, 1982). Several findings, however, support the candidacy of the BST as source of the VP fibers in those areas where fibers were seen to disappear; (i) after injection of tracers in the lateral septum, retro-

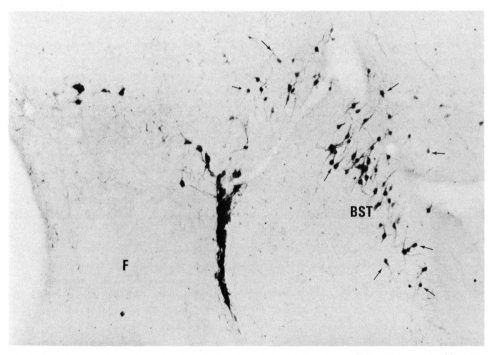

Fig. 2. Transverse section of the region of the bed nucleus of the stria terminalis (BST) of the rat stained immunocytochemically for the presence of vasopressin (VP). Arrows indicate the VP cells which became visible after colchicine pretreatment. The magnocellular VP cells immediately adjacent to the fornix (F) are neurosecretory neurons which project to the neurohypophysis (Kelly and Swanson, 1980).

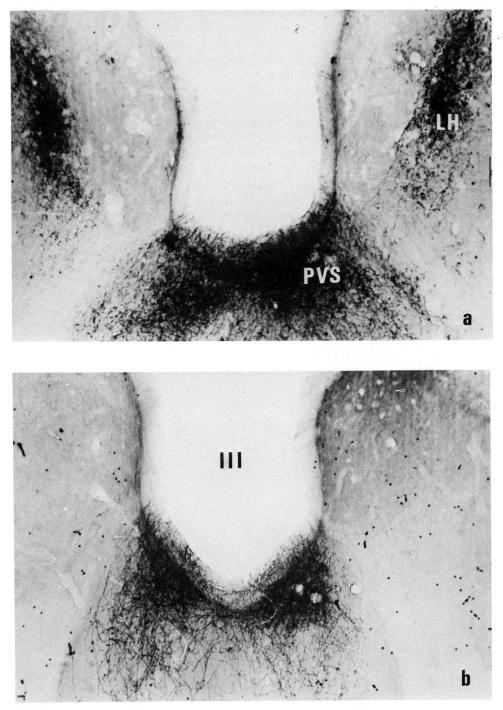

Fig. 3. Transverse sections of the area around the third ventricle (III) stained immunocytochemically for the presence of vasopressin (VP), showing a dense VP fiber network in the lateral habenular nucleus (LH) of a control rat (a), in contrast to the absence of fiber staining in a rat at 15 weeks after castration (b). Note that this difference is not present in the periventricular nucleus (PVS).

gradely labeled cells were found in the same regions of the BST where VP cells were found in colchicine-treated rats (De Vries and Buijs, 1983; Van Leeuwen and Caffe, 1983), in addition (ii) anterograde tracing studies have shown that the BST sends projections to all areas where VP fibers were affected after BST lesions (Conrad and Pfaff, 1976), and (iii) the

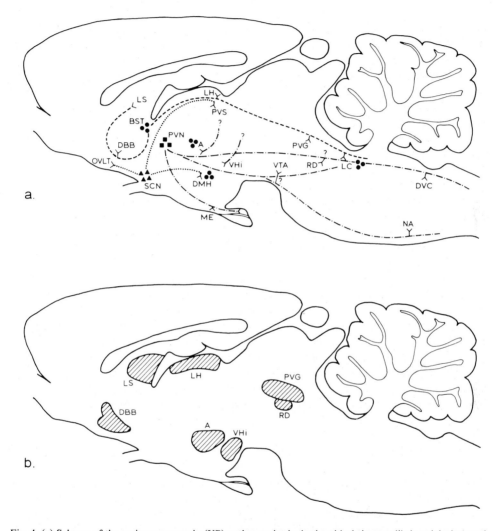

Fig. 4. (a) Scheme of the major vasopressin (VP) pathways in the brain with their most likely origin (see text). — · — · —, pathways from the paraventricular nucleus (PVN); ··········, pathways from the suprachiasmatic nucleus (SCN); -----------, pathways from the bed nucleus of the stria terminalis (BST). Squares, triangles, and dots indicate, respectively, VP cell groups in the PVN, SCN, and cell groups which were found only after colchi-cine treatment, e.g., in the BST. A question mark indicates that the source of the VP innervation in that particular area is still uncertain. (b) Scheme indicating the major (hatched) areas where VP fibers were seen to disappear after gonadectomy. Note that the fibers disappear from all areas to which the BST presumably projects and from the areas where the origin of the fibers is unknown. A, amygdala; DBB, diagonal band of Broca; DMH, dorsome-dial nucleus of the hypothalamus; DVC, dorsal vagal complex; LC, locus coeruleus; LH, lateral habenula; LS, lateral septum; ME, median eminence; NA, nucleus ambiguus; OVLT, organum vasculosum lamina terminalis; PVG, periventricular grey; PVS, periventricular nucleus; RD, dorsal raphe nucleus; VHi, ventral hippocampus; VTA, ventral tegmental area. (Fig. 4a from Buijs et al., 1983.)

results of the previously mentioned castration and ovariectomy experiments provide an additional argument in favor of the BST: all areas to which the VP neurons of the BST presumably project, displayed a very strong regression in the VP fiber density following gonadectomy of adult male and female rats. After testosterone replacement therapy in the castrated males, VP fibers reappeared in these areas (Fig. 3) (De Vries et al., 1984). The stainability of VP neurons in the BST followed the same pattern, i.e., no cells were found in the long-term castrated rats, but they reappeared after testosterone replacement therapy (Van Leeuwen et al., in preparation). Interestingly, similar changes in the VP innervation were found in the medial amygdaloid nucleus, the ventral hippocampus and the ventral tegmental area. The origin of these VP fibers is unknown, although they might be derived from the most ventral part of the BST which was not affected in the previously mentioned lesion studies. An additional possibility is that VP cells in the medial amygdaloid nucleus form the source (Caffe and Van Leeuwen, 1983) since these cells showed similar changes as the BST cells following hormonal manipulations (De Vries, in preparation). No changes following the hormonal manipulations were found in the VP projections from the SCN and PVN (for a schematic representation of the changes observed after gonadectomy, see Fig. 4). Taken together, these results demonstrate not only that the VP innervation of the brain can be subdivided as to origin, but also that these subdivisions respond differently to hormonal stimuli and, presumably participate in different ways in neurally regulated functions.

Questions on the action of gonadal hormones on the VP fiber density

The site where gonadal hormones act so as to influence the VP projections of the BST is unknown. Gonadal steroid implantation studies (cf. Christensen and Gorski, 1978) might be used in order to shed light on this problem. It might be that they act directly upon the BST, because many neurons in this area have been shown to concentrate gonadal steroids (Pfaff and Keiner, 1973; Stumpf and Sar, 1976). Such an action could be directed either to the VP neurons in this area, or at other neurons which in turn would influence the VP neurons. The latter situation might apply to those preoptic neurons which contain "luteinizing hormone-releasing hormone" (LHRH): although the fiber projections of these cells are affected by gonadectomy (Shivers et al., 1983a), a combination of autoradiography and immunocyto-chemistry has made it clear that almost no LHRH cells concentrate estradiol (Shivers et al., 1983b).

Besides the question of where gonadal hormones act so as to change VP projections, it is not clear in what way such changes should be explained. Should one see the disappearance and reappearance of fiber staining as an actual outgrowth and retraction of VP fibers or merely as changes in the state of filling of otherwise intact fibers following hormonal manipulations? The aforementioned effects of androgens on the developing VP innervation might be reasonably interpreted as a stimulation of nerve fiber outgrowth. Such a mechanism would then be in line with the observations of Toran-Allerand (1976, 1984) who has demonstrated that steroids promote neurite outgrowth in cultures of newborn mouse hypothalamus and in explants derived from the BST. That a similar process also takes place in adulthood, viz., a complete retraction of the VP fibers after gonadectomy and again an outgrowth after steroid replacement therapy, seems unprobable. However, stimulation of dendritic growth under the influence of gonadal steroids has been demonstrated in the adult avian brain (DeVoogd and Nottebohm, 1981) while electron microscopic analysis has demonstrated that the mammalian brain too displays structural plasticity in adulthood, at least with respect to the number and nature of synaptic contacts (Dyer, 1984). As for the VP pathways, it could well be that the changes in fiber staining represent a combination of both possibilities, i.e., the axonal length and branching change in parallel with alterations in the state of filling of the fibers.

Another problem concerns the nature of the sex difference in the lateral septum. In the first place, also in this case one cannot say whether females really contain fewer VP fibers than do males, or simply that the VP content in many of the fibers is below the level of detection. Secondly, it is still not clear whether the sex difference is maintained in adulthood exclusively by differences in the hormonal milieu, or whether it reflects a sex difference in the brain that was established during development. An indication that the differences are not due solely to hormonal conditions in adulthood is given by the fact that, whereas testosterone replacement therapy in adult castrated male rats restores the VP fiber density in the lateral septum to the original density, the same treatment can bring the fiber density in adult ovariectomized female rats only at the level characteristic for normal females (observations of Wouter Duetz, in our laboratory). If the sexual dimorphism is indeed inherent to a differentiated VP system, it might for instance be the consequence of sex differences in the ramifications of VP fibers or the number of VP cells in the BST. Interesting in this respect is, that about twice as many VP cells are found in male than in female rats after colchicine treatment (Fig. 4) (Van Leeuwen et al., in preparation). Again, the actual number of VP cells might be higher than that observed in the immunocytochemically stained sections, which possibility seems to be corroborated by the aforementioned disappearance of the cells after gonadectomy and reappearance after testosterone replacement therapy. It is noteworthy, however, that a sex difference has been found in the BST of the guinea pig, comparable to that in the SDN-POA of the rat (Hines et al., 1983). This finding suggests that the BST of the rat might contain structural sex differences which could include VP cells as well.

Possible functions of the VP innervation of the brain

The earlier mentioned classification one can make as to the origin of the VP innervation may give a lead as to what functions the various subdivisions might be involved in. The VP projections of the SCN follow closely all the projections of the SCN as established by antero-grade tracing techniques (Berk and Finkelstein, 1981; Hoorneman and Buijs, 1982). Since the SCN plays a keyrole in the generation of circadian rhythms (Moore, 1978) and the estrous cycle (Brown-Grant and Raisman, 1977) the VP projections of this nucleus might be involved in these rhythms as well.

VP projections of the PVN run predominantly to the medulla and the spinal cord where they innervate areas such as the nucleus of the solitary tract, which are involved in the regula-tion of autonomic functions (see e.g., Palkovits and Zaborsky, 1977). These VP projections indeed may play a role in such functions, since central administration of VP influences blood pressure and heart rate, especially when injected into the hind brain (Bohus, 1980; Matsu-guchi et al., 1982; Pittman et al., 1982). Since those areas project in turn to the PVN and SON, it is possible that the VP projections of the PVN influence, via a feedback loop the release of VP into the blood stream (see Buijs et al., 1983; Swanson and Sawchenko, 1980).

The observed sex differences and the changes under influence of hormonal manipulations in the remaining part of the VP fiber pathways (which for matters of convenience will be referred to as "the sexually dimorphic VP projections") suggest that these VP pathways are probably involved in functions which are strongly influenced by gonadal steroids. Such functions would, however, not necessarily have to play a part in reproductive processes like gonadotropin secretion or sexual behavior. A variety of neurally regulated functions such as feeding, learning, and aggressive behavior are sexually dimorphic or strongly influenced by gonadal steroids in adulthood (for reviews see Van de Poll et al., 1978; Goy and McEwen, 1980; Beatty, 1984). The sexually dimorphic VP projections could be involved in such an apparently non-reproductive but still sexually dimorphic function.

A good candidate for such a function is the regulation of VP release into the blood by the neurohypophysis: whereas VP secretion is rather constant in male rats, in females it follows a cyclic pattern, which is synchronized with the estrous cycle (Swaab and Jongkind, 1970; Skowsky et al., 1979). Furthermore, the administration of estrogen to gonadectomized rats stimulated VP release, while androgens inhibited it (Skowsky et al., 1979). There are indications that the sexually dimorphic VP projections to areas such as the septum and the amygdala are indirectly involved in the control of VP secretion by the neurohypophysis. Thus, both the septum and the amygdala send projections to the PVN and SON (Garris, 1979; Silverman et al., 1981; Tribollet and Dreifuss, 1981; Oldfield et al., 1983), and electrical stimulation of the former areas indeed results in a change in spike frequency of the neurosecretory cells of the PVN and SON (Negoro et al., 1973; Poulain et al., 1980).

The changes in peripheral VP levels which are induced by gonadal hormones might be caused by a direct action of steroids upon hypothalamic neurosecretory neurons. The VP-containing neurosecretory neurons of the PVN and SON of the mouse concentrate estrogens (Sar and Stumpf, 1980). In the rat, however, no estradiol-concentrating cells have been found in the SON, while in the PVN such cells were found only in regions containing predominantly oxytocin cells (Rhodes et al., 1981). The same regions contain only very few vasopressin cells most of which project to the medulla and spinal cord rather than to the neurohypophysis. This led the authors to conclude that in the rat gonadal steroids exert no direct action upon the neurosecretory neurons and therefore influence VP release via an indirect mechanism (Rhodes et al., 1981). If the sexually dimorphic VP projections indeed turn out to be implicated in the regulation of VP release, it will be of great interest to investigate whether or not the influence of gonadal steroids on VP release is mediated via this system.

Vasopressin and reproductive functions

A clue to the function of the sexually dimorphic VP projections might be found in the dynamics of the observed changes in fiber density after gonadectomy (viz., a decrease over 15 weeks versus a restoration of the original fiber density within 4 weeks; results of Wouter Duetz in our laboratory). These changes are rather slow when compared with the changes in LHRH innervation in the midbrain central grey, which decreases drastically within a week following gonadectomy of male rats or after estrogen replacement in gonadectomized females (Shivers et al., 1983a). The time course of these last changes is consistent with the postulated involvement of LHRH fibers within the midbrain central grey in lordosis behavior (Riskind and Moss, 1979; Sakuma and Pfaff, 1980), since this behavior too disappears shortly after ovariectomy and reappears within a few days following estrogen administration (Harlan et al., 1984). By contrast, male sexual behavior decreases with a time course comparable to the changes in the density of the sexually dimorphic VP projections after castration (Davidson, 1966). Noteworthy in this respect is the fact that Bohus (1977) has demonstrated, using pharmacological methods, that VP might be involved in the maintenance of post-castration male copulatory behavior.

Another indication that centrally acting VP is involved in reproductive processes is given by its inhibitory effect on female sexual behavior after intracerebroventricular administration of VP (Södersten et al., 1983; Södersten, 1984). Although it is not known via what mechanism VP exerts this action, the substrate could be constituted by the sexually dimorphic innervation of the lateral septum, especially since various studies have demonstrated that the septal nuclei are implicated in the (predominantly) inhibitory control of feminine sexual receptivity (Nance et al., 1974; Zasorin et al., 1975; McGinnis and Gorski, 1976; Gorzalka and Gray, 1981; Nance, 1982). The question of whether or not VP is indeed implicated in the central regulation of male and female sexual behavior and, if so, by which part of the VP innervation, might be studied e.g. by means of local administration of VP agonists and antagonists in specific brain regions.

Besides the data obtained from the aforementioned pharmacological studies also comparative studies are in support of a role for VP in reproductive functions. Non-mammalian vertebrates do not synthesize the neurohypophyseal hormone VP, the homologue hormone in these classes being vasotocin (Pickering, 1978). Several studies have demonstrated that in many species vasotocin is implicated in reproductive processes (for review see Moore and Miller, 1983). The effects of central injection of vasotocin and antagonists or vasotocin antisera in the newt indicate that vasotocin stimulates male sexual behavior at the level of the brain (Moore and Miller, 1983). That vasotocin and vasopressin may be involved in similar central processes is suggested by a recent finding of Stoll and Voorn (1983) who reported that the vasotocin innervation of the lateral septum of *Gecko gekko* — a lizard species — displays similar sex differences as does the VP innervation in the rat.

CONCLUDING REMARKS

Studies of the vasopressinergic innervation of the brain have demonstrated that immunocytochemistry in conjunction with tracing and lesion studies forms a powerful tool to study the anatomical background of a particular sex difference. Furthermore, it shows that it might be used to study the influences of gonadal hormones, either in development or in adulthood, upon a specific neurotransmitter system. However, immunocytochemical methods have certain inherent drawbacks. One major problem is that it is difficult to raise an antiserum which is directed specifically against a single antigen, which makes it necessary to extensively test all sera and, if necessary, to purify them (Pool et al., 1983). Furthermore, once a section has been stained immunocytochemically, the absence of staining does not exclude the presence of the antigen against which the serum was raised, as has been discussed above. An advantage of the application of immunocytochemistry is that it can readily be combined with other techniques, e.g., with steroid receptor labeling as mentioned previously (Sar and Stumpf, 1980; see also Harlan et al., 1984), with retrograde tracing techniques (Sofroniew and Schrell, 1981; Sawchenko and Swanson, 1982), and even with electrophysiology for identifying the cells recorded from (Skirbol et al., 1981). This approach enables the simultaneous study of several features of one and the same cell. To conclude the study of the neurotransmitter content of the various components of a given sexually dimorphic system (in addition to, e.g., electrophysiological studies, steroid implantation studies, lesion studies (reviewed by Gorski, 1984; Dyer, 1984; Harlan et al., 1984)) can also help to elucidate its functional significance, if only because the knowledge about the neurotransmitters involved makes it possible to use pharmacological tools such as local administration of specific agonists or antagonists.

REFERENCES

Alderson, L.M. and Baum, M.J. (1981) Differential effects of gonadal steroids on dopamine metabolism in mesolimbic and nigro-striatal pathways of male rat brain. *Brain Res.*, 218: 189–206.

Arendash, G.W. and Gorski, R.A. (1983) Effects of discrete lesions of the sexually dimorphic nucleus of the preoptic area or other medial preoptic regions on the sexual behavior of male rats. *Brain Res. Bull.*, 10: 147–154.

Arimatsu, Y. (1983) Short- and long-term influences of neonatal sex steroids on a-bungarotoxin binding capacity in the mouse amygdala. *Neuroscience*, 9: 873–877.

Arimatsu, Y., Seto, A. and Amano, T. (1981) Sexual dimorphism in a-bungarotoxin binding capacity in the mouse amygdala. *Brain Res.*, 213: 432–437.

Avissar, S., Egozi, Y. and Sokolovsky, M. (1981) Studies of muscarinic receptors in mouse and rat hypothalamus: a comparison of sex and cyclical differences. *Neuroendocrinology*, 32: 295–302.

Barchas, J.D., Akil, H., Elliott, G.R., Holman, R.B. and Watson, S.J. (1978) Behavioral neurochemistry: neuroregulators and behavioral states. *Science*, 200: 964–973.

Bargman, W. and Scharrer, E. (1951) The site of origin of the hormones of the posterior pituitary. *Am. Scient.*, 39: 255–259.

Baskin, D.G., Petracca, F. and Dorsa, D.M. (1983) Autoradiographic localization of specific binding sites for [H][Arg]vasopressin in the septum of the rat brain with tritium-sensitive film. *Eur. J. Pharmacol.*, 90: 155–157.

Baum, M.J. and Starr, M.S. (1979) Inhibition of sexual behavior by dopamine antagonists or serotonin agonist drugs in castrated male rats given estradiol or dihydrotestosterone. *Pharmacol. Biochem. Behav.*, 13: 57–67.

Beatty, W.W. (1984) Hormonal organization of sex differences in play fighting and spatial behavior. In: G.J. De Vries, J.P.C. De Bruin, H.B.M. Uylings and M.A. Corner (Eds.), *Sex Differences in the Brain. The Relation between Structure and Function. Progress in Brain Research*, this volume, Ch. 19.

Berk, M.L. and Finkelstein, J.A. (1981) An autoradiographic determination of the efferent projections of the suprachiasmatic nucleus of the hypothalamus. *Brain Res.*, 226: 1–13.

Boer, G.J., Buijs, R.M., Swaab, D.F. and De Vries, G.J. (1980) Vasopressin and the developing rat brain. *Peptides*, 1, Suppl. 1: 203–209.

Bohus, B. (1977) The influence of pituitary neuropeptides on sexual behavior. In: H.P. Klotz (Ed.), *Hormones et Sexualité. Problèmes Actuels d'Endocrinologie et de Nutrition. II*, Expansion Scientifique, Paris, pp. 235–246.

Bohus, B. (1980) Effects of neuropeptides on adaptive autonomic processes. In: D. De Wied and P.A. Van Keep (Eds.), *Hormones and the Brain*, MTP Press, Lancaster.

Breedlove, S.M. (1984) Steroid influences on the development and function of a neuromuscular system. In: G.J. De Vries, J.P.C. De Bruin, H.B.M. Uylings and M.A. Corner (Eds.), *Sex Differences in the Brain. The Relation between Structure and Function. Progress in Brain Research*, this volume, Ch. 8.

Breedlove, S.M. and Arnold, A.P. (1980) Hormone accumulation in a sexually dimorphic nucleus in the rat spinal cord. *Science*, 210: 564–566.

Brown-Grant, K. and Raisman, G. (1977) Abnormalities in reproductive function associated with the destruction of the suprachiasmatic nuclei in female rats. *Proc. Roy. Soc. Lond. B*, 198: 279–296.

Buijs, R.M. (1978) Intra- and extrahypothalamic vasopressin and oxytocin pathways in the rat: pathways to the limbic system, medulla oblongata and spinal cord. *Cell Tissue Res.*, 192: 423–435.

Buijs, R.M. and Swaab, D.F. (1979) Immuno-electron microscopical demonstration of vasopressin and oxytocin synapses in the limbic system of the rat. *Cell Tissue Res.*, 204: 355–365.

Buijs, R.M. and Van Heerikhuijze, J.J. (1982) Vasopressin and oxytocin release in the brain: a synaptic event. *Brain Res.*, 252: 71–76.

Buijs, R.M., Velis, D.N. and Swaab, D.F. (1980) Ontogeny of vasopressin and oxytocin in the fetal rat: early vasopressinergic innervation of the fetal brain. *Peptides*, 1: 315–324.

Buijs, R.M., De Vries, G.J., Van Leeuwen, F.W. and Swaab, D.F. (1983) Vasopressin and oxytocin distribution and putative functions in the brain. In: B.A. Cross and G. Leng (Eds.), *The Neurohypophysis: Structure, Function and Control, Progress in Brain Research, Vol. 60*, Elsevier, Amsterdam, pp. 115–122.

Burbach, J.P.H., Kovacs, G.L., De Wied, D., Van Nispen, J.W. and Greven, H.M. (1983) A major metabolite of arginine vasopressin in the brain is a highly potent neuropeptide. *Science*, 221: 1310–1312.

Caffe, A.R. and Van Leeuwen, F.W. (1983) Vasopressin-immunoreactive cells in the dorsomedial hypothalamic region, medial amygdaloid nucleus and locus coeruleus of the rat. *Cell Tissue Res.*, 233: 23–33.

Caggiula, A.R., Shaw, D.H., Antelman, S.M. and Edwards, D.J. (1976) Interactive effects of brain catecholamine and variations in sexual and non-sexual arousal on copulatory behavior of male rats. *Brain Res.*, 111: 321–336.

Christensen, L.W. and Gorski, R.A. (1978) Independent masculinization of endocrine systems by intracerebral implants of testosterone or estradiol on the neonatal female rat. *Brain Res.*, 146: 325–340.

Clemens, L.G., Dohanich, G.P. and Witcher, J.A. (1981) Cholinergic influences on estrogen-dependent sexual behaviour in female rats. *J. Comp. Physiol. Psychol.*, 95: 763–770.

Conrad, L.C.A. and Pfaff, D.W. (1976) Efferents from medial basal forebrain and hypothalamus in the rat. II. An autoradiographic study of the anterior hypothalamus. *J. Comp. Neurol.*, 169: 221–262.

Cooper, K.E., Kasting, N.W., Lederis, K. and Veale, W.L. (1979) Evidence supporting a role for endogenous vasopressin in natural suppression of fever in the sheep. *J. Physiol. (London)*, 295: 33–45.

Davidson, J.M. (1966) Characteristics of sex behaviour in male rats following castration. *Animal Behav.*, 14: 266–272.

DeVoogd, T. (1984) The avian song system: relating sex differences in behavior to dimorphism in the central nervous system. In: G.J. De Vries, J.P.C. De Bruin, H.B.M. Uylings and M.A. Corner (Eds.), *Sex Differences in the Brain. The Relation between Structure and Function. Progress in Brain Research*, this volume, Ch. 9.

DeVoogd, T.J. and Nottebohm, F. (1981) Gonadal hormones induce growth in the adult avian brain. *Science*, 214: 202–204.

De Vries, G.J. and Buijs, R.M. (1983) The origin of the vasopressinergic and oxytocinergic innervation of the rat brain; with special reference to the lateral septum. *Brain Res.*, 273: 307–317.

De Vries, G.J., Buijs, R.M. and Swaab, D.F. (1981) Ontogeny of the vasopressinergic neurons of the suprachiasmatic nucleus and their extrahypothalamic projections in the rat brain — presence of a sex difference in the lateral septum. *Brain Res.*, 218: 67–78.

De Vries, G.J., Best, W. and Sluiter, A.A. (1983) The influence of gonadal steroids on a sex difference in the vasopressinergic innervation of the brain. *Develop. Brain Res.*, 8: 377–380.

De Vries, G.J., Buijs, R.M. and Sluiter, A.A. (1984) Gonadal hormone actions on the morphology of the vasopressinergic innervation of the adult rat brain. *Brain Res.*, in press.

Dyer, R.G. (1984) Sexual differentiation of the forebrain — relationship to gonadotrophin secretion. In: G.J. De Vries, J.P.C. De Bruin, H.B.M. Uylings and M.A. Corner (Eds.), *Sex Differences in the Brain. The Relation between Structure and Function. Progress in Brain Research*, this volume, Ch. 13.

Everitt, B.J., Fuxe, K., Hokfelt, T. and Jonsson, G. (1975) Role of monoamines in the control by hormones of sexual receptivity in the female rat. *J. Comp. Physiol. Psychol.*, 89: 556–572.

Fischette, C.T., Biegon, A. and McEwen, B.S. (1983) Sex differences in serotonin 1 receptor binding in rat brain. *Science*, 222: 333–335.

Garris, D.R. (1979) Direct septo-hypothalamic projections in the rat. *Neurosci. Lett.*, 13: 83–90.

Giulian, D., Pohorecky, L.A. and McEwen, B.S. (1973) Effects of gonadal steroids upon brain 5-hydroxytryptamine levels of the neonatal rat. *Endocrinology*, 93: 1329–1335.

Gordon, J.H. and Shellenberger, M.K. (1974) Regional catecholamine content in the rat brain: sex difference and correlation with motor activity. *Neuropharmacology*, 13: 129–137.

Gorski, R.A. (1984) Critical role for the medial preoptic area in the sexual differentiation of the brain. In: G.J. De Vries, J.P.C. De Bruin, H.B.M. Uylings and M.A. Corner (Eds.), *Sex Differences in the Brain. The Relation between Structure and Function. Progress in Brain Research*, this volume, Ch. 7.

Gorski, R.A., Gordon, J.H., Shryne, J.E. and Southam, A.M. (1978) Evidence for a morphological sex difference within the medial preoptic area of the rat brain. *Brain Res.*, 148: 333–346.

Gorzalka, B.B. and Gray, D.S. (1981) Receptivity, rejection and reactivity in female rats following kainic acid and electrolytic septal lesions. *Physiol. Behav.*, 26: 39–44.

Goy, R.W. and McEwen, B.S. (1980) *Sexual Differentiation of the Brain*. MIT Press, Boston, MA, 223 pp.

Harlan, R.E., Shivers, B.D. and Pfaff, D.W. (1984) Lordosis as a sexually dimorphic neural function. In: G.J. De Vries, J.P.C. De Bruin, H.B.M. Uylings and M.A. Corner (Eds.), *Sex Differences in the Brain. The Relation between Structure and Function. Progress in Brain Research*, this volume, Ch. 14.

Hery, M., Laplante, E. and Kordon, C. (1976) Participation of serotonin in the phasic release of LH. I. Evidence from pharmacological experiments. *Endocrinology*, 98: 743–747.

Hines, M., Coquelin, A., Davis, F.C., Goy, R.W. and Gorski, R.A. (1983) Sex differences in the preoptic area and the bed nucleus of the stria terminalis in the guinea pig are not a function of the adult hormonal environment. *Soc. Neurosci. Abstr.*, 9: 1094.

Hoorneman, E.M.D. and Buijs, R.M. (1982) Vasopressin fiber pathways in the rat brain following suprachiasmatic nucleus lesioning. *Brain Res.*, 243: 235–241.

Hywiler, T. and Felix, D. (1980) Angiotensin II-sensitive neurons in septal areas of the rat. *Brain Res.*, 195: 187–195.

Jarzab, B. and Döhler, K.D. (1984) Serotoninergic influences on sexual differentiation of the rat brain. In: G.J. De Vries, J.P.C. De Bruin, H.B.M. Uylings and M.A. Corner (Eds.), *Sex Differences in the Brain. The Relation between Structure and Function. Progress in Brain Research*, this volume, Ch. 6.

Joëls, M. and Urban, I.J.A. (1982) The effect of microiontophoretically applied vasopressin and oxytocin on single neurones in the septum. *Neurosci. Lett.*, 33: 79–84.

Kato, R. (1960) Serotonin content of rat brain in relation to sex and age. *J. Neurochem.*, 5: 202.

Kelly, J. and Swanson, L.W. (1980) Additional forebrain regions projecting to the posterior pituitary: preoptic region, bed nucleus of the stria terminalis, and zona incerta, *Brain Res.*, 197: 1–9.

Ladosky, W. and Gaziri, L.C.J. (1970) Brain serotonin and sexual differentiation of the nervous system. *Neuroendocrinology*, 36: 168–174.

Lewis, J.W., Ryan, S.M., Butcher, L.L. and Arnold, A.P. (1981) Evidence for a catecholaminergic projection to area X in the zebra finch. *J. Comp. Neurol.*, 196: 347–354.

Libertun, C., Timiras, P.S. and Kragt, C.L. (1973) Sexual differences in the hypothalamic cholinergic system before and after puberty. Inductory effect of testosterone. *Neuroendocrinology*, 12: 73–85.

Livett, B.G. (1978) Immunohistochemical localization of nervous system specific proteins and peptides. *Int. Rev. Cytol.*, Suppl. 7: 53–237.

Luine, V.N. and McEwen, B.S. (1983) Sex differences in cholinergic enzymes of diagonal band nuclei in the rat preoptic area. *Neuroendocrinology*, 36: 475–482.

Luine, V.N. and Rhodes, J.C. (1983) Gonadal hormone regulation of MAO and other enzymes in hypothalamic areas. *Neuroendocrinology*, 36: 235–241.

Malmnas, C.O. (1977) Dopaminergic reversal of decline after castration of rat copulatory behavior. *J. Endocrinol.*, 73: 187–188

Matsuguchi, H., Sharabi, F.M., Gordon, F.J., Johnson, A.K. and Schmid, P.G. (1982) Blood pressure and heart response to microinjection of vasopressin in the nucleus of the solitarius region in the rat. *Neuropharmacology*, 21: 687–693.

McGinnis, M.Y. and Gorski, R.A. (1976) Sexual behavior of male and female rats. *Physiol. Behav.*, 24: 569–573.

Meyerson, B.J. (1984) Hormone-dependent socio-sexual behaviors and neurotransmitters. In: G.J. De Vries, J.P.C. De Bruin, H.B.M. Uylings and M.A. Corner (Eds.), *Sex Differences in the Brain. The Relation between Structure and Function. Progress in Brain Research*, this volume, Ch. 16.

Moore, R.Y. (1978) Central neural control of circadian rhythms. *Front. Neuroendocrinol.*, 5: 185–206.

Moore, F.L. and Miller, L.J. (1983) Arginine vasotocin induces sexual behavior of newts by acting on cells in the brain. *Peptides*, 4: 97–102.

Mühlethaler, M., Dreifuss, J.J. and Gähwiler, B.H. (1982) Vasopressin excites hippocampal neurones. *Nature (London)*, 296: 749–751.

Muth, E.A., Crowley, W.R. and Jacobowitz, D.M. (1980) Effect of gonadal hormones on luteinizing hormone in plasma and on choline acetyltransferase activity and acetylcholine levels in discrete nuclei of the rat brain. *Neuroendocrinology*, 30: 329–336.

Nance, D.M. (1982) Psychoneuroendocrine effects of neurotoxic lesions in the septum and striatum of rats. *Pharmacol. Biochem. Behav.*, 18: 605–609.

Nance, D.M., Shryne, J. and Gorski, R.A. (1974) Septal lesions: Effect on lordosis behavior and pattern of gonadotropin release. *Hormone Behav.*, 5: 73–81.

Negoro, H., Visessuwan, S. and Holland, R.C. (1973) Inhibition and excitation of units in paraventricular nucleus after stimulation of septum, amygdala and neurohypophysis. *Brain Res.*, 57: 479–483.

Nottebohm, F. and Arnold, A.P. (1976) Sexual dimorphism in vocal control areas of the songbird brain. *Science*, 194: 211–213.

Nottebohm, F., Stokes, T.M. and Leonard, C.M. (1976) Central control of song in the canary, *Serinus canarius*. *J. Comp. Neurol.*, 165: 457–486.

Oldfield, B.J., Hou-yu, A. and Silverman, A.J. (1983) Technique for the simultaneous ultrastructural demonstration of anterogradely transported horseradish peroxidase and an immunocytochemically identified neuropeptide. *J. Histochem. Cytochem.*, 31: 1145–1150.

Orensanz, L.M., Guillamon, A., Ambrosio, E., Segovia, S. and Azuara, M.C. (1982) Sex differences in alpha-adrenergic receptors in the rat brain. *Neurosci. Lett.*, 30: 275–278.

Palay, S.L. and Chan-Palay, V. (1982) *Cytochemical Methods in Neuroanatomy*, Alan R. Liss, New York, 568 pp.

Palkovits, H. and Zaborsky, L. (1977) Neuroanatomy of central cardiovascular control. Nucleus tractus solitarius: afferent and efferent neuronal connections in relation to the baroreceptor reflex arc. In: W. De Jong,

A.P. Provoost and A.P. Shapiro (Eds.), *Hypertension and Brain Mechanisms. Progress in Brain Research*, *Vol. 47*, Elsevier/North-Holland, Amsterdam, pp. 9–34.

Pfaff, D.W. and Keiner, M. (1973) Atlas of estradiol-concentrating cells in the central nervous system of the female rat. *J. Comp. Neurol.*, 151: 121–158.

Pickering (1978) Posterior-lobe hormones — Comparative aspects. In: *Hypothalamic Hormones*, Academic Press, New York.

Pittman, Q.J., Lawrence, D. and McLean, L. (1982) Central effects of vasopressin on blood pressure in rats. *Endocrinology*, 110: 1058.

Pool, C.W., Buijs, R.M., Swaab, D.F., Boer, G.J. and Van Leeuwen, F.W. (1983) On the way to a specific immunocytochemical localization. In: A.C. Cuello (Ed.), *Immunohistochemistry, IBRO Handbook Series: Methods in the Neurosciences, Vol. 3*, John Wiley, Chichester, pp. 1–45.

Poulain, D.A., Ellendorf, F. and Vincent, J.D. (1980) Septal connections with identified oxytocin and vasopressin neurones in the supraoptic nucleus of the rat. An electrophysiological investigation. *Neuroscience*, 5: 379–387.

Raisman, G. and Field, P.M. (1971) Sexual dimorphism in the preoptic area of the rat. *Science*, 173: 731–733.

Reznikov, A.G. (1978) Neurotransmitters and brain sexual differentiation. In: G. Dorner and M. Kawakami (Eds.), *Hormones and Brain Development*, Elsevier/North-Holland, Amsterdam, pp. 175–179.

Rhodes, C.H., Morell, J.I. and Pfaff, D.W. (1981) Distribution of estrogen-concentrating, neurophysin-containing magnocellular neurons in the rat hypothalamus as demonstrated by a technique combining steroid autoradiography and immunohistology in the same tissue. *Neuroendocrinology*, 33: 18–23.

Riskind, P. and Moss, R.L. (1979) Midbrain central grey: LHRH infusion enhances lordotic behaviour in estrogen-primed ovariectomized rats. *Brain Res. Bull.*, 4: 203–205.

Ryan, S.M. and Arnold, A.P. (1981) Evidence for cholinergic participation in the control of bird song: acetylcholinesterase distribution and muscarinic receptor autoradiography in the zebra finch brain. *J. Comp. Neurol.*, 202: 211–219.

Ryan, S.M., Arnold, A.P. and Elde, R.P. (1981) Enkephalin-like immunoreactivity in vocal control regions of the zebra finch brain. *Brain Res.*, 229: 236–240.

Sakuma, Y. and Pfaff, D.W. (1980) LH-RH in the mesencephalic central grey can potentiate lordosis reflex of female rats. *Nature (London)*, 283: 566–567.

Sar, M. and Stumpf, W.E. (1980) Simultaneous localization of [^{3}H]-oestradiol and neurophysin I or arginine vasopressin in hypothalamic neurons demonstrated by a combined technique of dry-mount autoradiography and immunohistochemistry. *Neurosci. Lett.*, 17: 179–184.

Sawchenko, P.E. and Swanson, L.W. (1982) Immunohistochemical identification of neurons in the paraventricular nucleus of the hypothalamus that project to the medulla or to the spinal cord in the rat. *J. Comp. Neurol.*, 205: 260–272.

Shivers, B.D., Harlan, R.E., Morell, J.I. and Pfaff, D.W. (1983a) Immunocytochemical localization of luteinizing hormone-releasing hormone in male and female rat brains. Quantitative studies on the effect of gonadal steroids. *Neuroendocrinology*, 36: 1–12.

Shivers, B.D., Harlan, R.E., Morell, J.I. and Pfaff, D.W. (1983b) Absence of oestradiol concentration in cell nuclei of LHRH-immunoreactive neurones. *Nature (London)*, 304: 345–347.

Silverman, A.J., Hoffman, D.L. and Zimmerman, E.A. (1981) The descending afferent connections of the paraventricular nucleus of the hypothalamus (PVN). *Brain Res. Bull.*, 6: 47–61.

Simerly, R.B., Swanson, L.W. and Gorski, R.A. (1983) Demonstration of a sexual dimorphism in the distribution of serotonin immunoreactive fibers in the medial preoptic nucleus of the rat. *Anat. Rec.*, 205: 185A.

Skirbol, L.R., Grace, A.A., Hommer, D.W., Rehfield, J., Goldstein, M., Hökfelt, T. and Bunney, B.S. (1981) Peptide-monoamine coexistence: studies of the actions of cholecystokinin-like peptide on the electrical activity of midbrain dopamine neurons. *Neuroscience*, 6: 2111–2123.

Skowsky, W.R., Swan, L. and Smith, P. (1979) Effects of sex steroid hormones on arginine vasopressin in intact and castrated male and female rats. *Endocrinology*, 104: 105–108.

Sladek, J.R., Fields, J.A. and Jacobson, C.D. (1983) The sexually dimorphic nucleus of the preoptic area: catecholamine innervation. *Anat. Rec.*, 205: 187A.

Södersten, P. (1984) Sexual differentiation: do males differ from females in behavioral sensitivity to gonadal hormones? In: G.J. De Vries, J.P.C. De Bruin, H.B.M. Uylings and M.A. Corner (Eds.), *Sex Differences in the Brain. The Relation between Structure and Function. Progress in Brain Research*, this volume, Ch. 15.

Södersten, P., Henning, M., Melin, P. and Lundin, S. (1983) Vasopressin alters female sexual behaviour by acting on the brain independently of alterations in blood pressure. *Nature (London)*, 301: 608–610.

Sofroniew, M.V. and Schrell, U. (1981) Evidence for a direct projection from oxytocin and vasopressin neurons in the hypothalamic paraventricular nucleus to the medulla oblongata: immunohistochemical visualization of both the horseradish peroxidase transported and the peptide produced by the same neurons. *Neurosci. Lett.*, 22: 221–227.

Sofroniew, M.V. and Weindl, A. (1978) Projections from the parvocellular vasopressin and neurophysin-containing neurons of the suprachiasmatic nucleus. *Am. J. Anat.*, 153: 391–430.

Stoll, C.J. and Voorn, P. (1983) Sex differences in the vasotocin innervation of the brain of the lizard (*Gecko gekko*). *Proc. Int. Summer Sch. Brain Res.*, 13: 114.

Stumpf, W.E. and Sar, M. (1976) Steroid hormone target sites in the brain: the differential distribution of estrogen, progestin, androgen and glucocorticosteroid. *J. Steroid Biochem.*, 7: 1163–1170.

Swaab, D.F. and Jongkind, J.F. (1970) The hypothalamic neurosecretory activity during the oestrus cycle, pregnancy, parturition, lactation and persistent oestrus, and after gonadectomy, in the rat. *Neuroendocrinology*, 6: 133–145.

Swaab, D.F. and Pool, C.W. (1975) Specificity of oxytocin and vasopressin immunofluorescence. *J. Endocrinol.*, 66: 263–373.

Swanson, L.W. and Sawchenko, P.E. (1980) Paraventricular nucleus: a site for integration of neuroendocrine and autonomic mechanisms. *Neuroendocrinology*, 31: 410–417.

Swanson, L.W. and Sawchenko, P.E. (1983) Hypothalamic integration: organization of the paraventricular and supraoptic nuclei. *Annu. Rev. Neurosci.*, 6: 269–324.

Torand-Allerand, C.D. (1976) Sex steroids and the development of the newborn mouse hypothalamus and preoptic area in vitro: implications for sexual differentiation. *Brain Res.*, 106: 407–412.

Toran-Allerand, C.D. (1984) On the genesis of sexual differentiation of the central nervous system: morphogenetic consequences of steroidal exposure and possible role of α-fetoprotein. In: G.J. De Vries, J.P.C. De Bruin, H.B.M. Uylings and M.A. Corner (Eds.), *Sex Differences in the Brain. The Relation between Structure and Function. Progress in Brain Research*, this volume, Ch. 4.

Tribollet, E. and Dreifuss, J.J. (1981) Localization of neurons projecting to the hypothalamic paraventricular nucleus area of the rat: a horseradish peroxidase study. *Neuroscience*, 6: 1315–1328.

Troiano, R. and Siegel, A. (1975) The ascending and descending connections of the hypothalamus in the cat. *Exp. Neurol.*, 49: 161–173.

Vaccari, A. (1980) Sexual differentiation of monoamine neurotransmitters. In: H. Parvez and S. Parvez (Eds.), *Biogenic Amines in Development*, Elsevier/North-Holland, Amsterdam, pp. 327–352.

Van de Poll, N.E., De Bruin, J.P.C., Van Dis, M. and Van Oyen, H.G. (1978) Gonadal hormones and the differentiation of sexual and aggressive behavior and learning in the rat. In: M.A. Corner, R.E. Baker, N.E. Van de Poll, D.F. Swaab and H.B.M. Uylings (Eds.), *Maturation of the Nervous System. Progress in Brain Research, Vol. 48*, Elsevier, Amsterdam, pp. 309–325.

Vandesande, F., Dierickx, K. and De Mey, J. (1975) Identification of the vasopressin-neurophysin producing neurons of the rat suprachiasmatic nuclei. *Cell Tissue Res.*, 156: 377–380.

Van Leeuwen, F.W. and Caffe, R. (1983) Vasopressin-immunoreactive cell bodies in the bed nucleus of the stria terminalis of the rat. *Cell Tissue Res.*, 228: 525–534.

Van Leeuwen, F.W. and Wolters, P. (1983) Light microscopic autoradiographic localization of [³H]arginine-vasopressin binding sites in the rat brain and kidney. *Neurosci. Lett.*, 41: 61–66.

Voorn, P. and Buijs, R.M. (1983) An immuno-electronmicroscopical study comparing vasopressin, oxytocin, substance P and enkephalin containing nerve terminals in the nucleus of the solitary tract of the rat. *Brain Res.*, 270: 169–173.

Watson, R.E. and Hoffman, G.E. (1983) The sexually dimorphic nucleus of the preoptic area: peptidergic components. *Anat. Rec.*, 205: 210A.

Zasorin, N.L., Malsbury, C.W. and Pfaff, D.W. (1975) Suppression of lordosis in the hormone-primed female hamster by electrical stimulation of the septal area. *Physiol. Behav.*, 14: 595–600.

DISCUSSION

K.D. DÖHLER: Concerning a possible function for the sexual dimorphism of the vasopressinergic innervation of the lateral septum; may it be more than just a coincidence that Nance et al. (1975) induced lordosis behavior in male rats after lesioning the lateral septum, whereas Södersten et al. (1983) inhibited lordosis behavior in female rats after treatment with vasopressin? May this not indicate that the lateral septum and/or vasopressin in this area are inhibitory for lordosis behavior?

G.J. DE VRIES: Lesioning of the lateral septum increased indeed estrogen-induced feminine sexual behavior in the female. In male rats, however, an increase was found only after chronic estrogen treatment following surgery with estrogen (Nance et al., 1975). Another confusing fact in this respect is, that while the lateral habenular nucleus shows a similar sex difference in the VP innervation, lesions of this structure reduce female sexual behavior (Modianus et al., 1974).

P. SÖDERSTEN: Lesions in the lateral septum have been shown to facilitate female sexual behavior in female rats. Can the VP innervation of the lateral septum be important in this? Probably not, since the VP innervation in the lateral septum disappears after castration of male rats and this does not facilitate female sexual behavior in the male.

G.J. DE VRIES: Together with VP many other neurotransmitter systems show changes after gonadectomy (see this chapter). This obviously makes it very difficult to relate changes or the absence of changes in behavior after gonadectomy to the effects observed in one single neurotransmitter system. It therefore seems preliminary to exclude that the VP innervation of the lateral septum exerts an inhibitory influence on female sexual behavior.

C.D. TORAN-ALLERAND: Do you have any evidence as to whether or not the loss of immunoreactivity in the castrated adult male is due to loss of fibers or to loss of product?

G.J. DE VRIES: No we have not. Taking into account, however, that DeVoogd and Nottebohm (1981) have shown that steroids can induce neurite outgrowth in the adult bird brain one should not exclude that changes in neuritic length under influence of steroid hormones could also occur in the adult mammalian brain which might include VP fibers as well.

R. DYER: Following the line of reasoning of the last question I would like to know whether there are any circumstances where physiological stimuli can be used to change the density of immunohistochemically stained VP fibers. What happens for example to the density of staining when rats are salt-loaded? This stimulus will activate the VP release system.

R. RAVID: Water deprivation causes significant changes in the VP content and distribution in the rat brain (Epstein et al., 1983). Radioimmunoassay shows that VP decreases in the hypothalamus, thalamus, septum, striatum, and amygdala. Pituitary VP decreases too, while plasma VP rises. Immunocytochemical staining demonstrates a decrease in VP immunoreactivity in perikarya of the PVN and SCN, while magnocellular fibers are more pronounced due to the presence of large Herring bodies. In the thalamus and septum VP immunoreactivity is very much reduced. This reduction appeared as a loss of immunoreactivity per individual fiber. A clear change in fiber density was, however, not noted.

REFERENCES

DeVoogd, T.J. and Nottebohm, F. (1981) Gonadal hormones induce growth in the adult avian brain. *Science*, 214: 202–204.

Epstein, Y., Castel, M., Glick, S.M., Sivan, N. and Ravid, R. (1983) Changes in hypothalamic and extra-hypothalamic vasopressin content in water-deprived rats. *Cell Tissue Res.*, 233: 99–111.

Modianus, D.T., Hitt, J.C. and Flexman, J. (1974) Habenular lesions produce decrements in feminine, but not masculine, sexual behavior in rats. *Behav. Biol.*, 10: 75–87.

Nance, D.W., Shryne, J.E. and Gorski, R.A. (1975) Facilitation of female sexual behavior in male rats by septal lesions: An interaction with estrogen. *Hormone Behav.*, 6: 289–299.

Södersten, P., Henning, M., Melin, P. and Lundin, S. (1983) Vasopressin alters female sexual behaviour by acting on the brain independently of alterations in blood pressure. *Nature (London)*, 301: 608–610.

G.J. De Vries et al. (Eds.),
Progress in Brain Research, Vol. 61
© 1984   Elsevier Science Publishers B.V., Amsterdam

Sex Differences in Developmental Plasticity in the Visual Cortex and Hippocampal Dentate Gyrus

JANICE M. JURASKA

Department of Psychology, Indiana University, Bloomington, IN 47405 (U.S.A.)

INTRODUCTION

Sex differences in the morphology of brain areas important in reproduction have been described at several levels in the rodent (e.g., Raisman and Field, 1971; Greenough et al., 1977; Gorski et al., 1978). Less attention has been paid to other brain areas, such as the cortex and hippocampus, even though sex differences in non-reproductive behavior have been well documented (Beatty, 1979). There is evidence of gross size differences between the sexes in many brain regions. For example, Pfaff (1966) found that male rats had larger neocortical and hippocampal cross-sectional areas than females. Using nucleolar size as an index of cell size, Pfaff showed that male dentate and cortical pyramidal neurons were larger while neuron number was the same in both sexes. Yanai (1979a) reported no sex differences in the sagittal area of the rat cortex, hippocampus and dentate gyrus. Yet Yanai (1979b) documented a larger sagittal area for the male rat cortex than for the female with an increased cell density in the females that resulted in equal cell numbers for both sexes. Thus there appear to be sex differences in the size of the cortex and hippocampus that are small and sometimes not readily replicable. The nature of these size differences in terms of anatomical fine structure, such as the amount and distribution of dendritic material or number of synapses, is not known.

The size of the cortex and hippocampus are themselves not constant within a sex, but vary with the nature of the environment, especially the rearing environment. The cortex, notably the visual cortex, is thicker in rats that have been raised in a complex environment (EC) with various objects and other rats in comparison to rats raised in isolation (IC) from weaning (Rosenzweig et al., 1972). Most of these studies have used only male rats. Rosenzweig and Bennett (1977) measured cortical weight and the cortical/subcortical ratio in male and female rats, differentially reared from weaning, with equivocal results. They also compared environmental effects in each sex separately without direct statistical comparisons between the sexes. The few studies of cortical thickness that used female rats have started the differential environments in young adulthood and also not made statistical comparisons to male rat cortical changes (Diamond et al., 1971; Hamilton et al., 1977). The results of this work indicate that the female visual cortex changes with the rearing environment but that the difference may not be as much as in the male. It is also known that following differential rearing there are changes in dendrites and synaptic structure in the male visual cortex (Volkmar and Greenough, 1972; Globus et al., 1973; Greenough et al., 1978). Whether such fine structural changes occur to the same degree in female rats is unknown.

Gross size differences have been documented in the hippocampus following differential rearing in males (Walsh et al., 1969), although such changes have not always been replicable (Diamond et al., 1976; Jones and Smith, 1980). Dendritic differences between male EC and IC rats have been reported in dentate granule neurons (Fiala et al., 1978). Once again, the possibility of such plasticity in the female dentate gyrus has not been explored.

A growing body of evidence suggests that in some cases females may be less susceptible to changes in their early environment than males. Early malnutrition affects the growth of body and brain (Crutchfield and Dratman, 1980; McConnell et al., 1981; Jones and Friedman, 1982) and behavior (Galler and Manes, 1980) in male rats to a greater degree than in female rats. Some of the behavioral and physiological changes that accompany early handling are more evident in male than female rats (Levine, 1974; Weinberg and Levine, 1977). Sackett (1974) has reported that the primate isolation syndrome is more pronounced in males. We have found that male IC rats are much more variable in their response to sodium pentobarbital than EC males or females from either environmental condition (Juraska et al., 1983). Thus males appear to be more vulnerable to their early environment experiences while females are more buffered.

Because of evidence of sex differences in environmental susceptibility, I have hypothesized that there may be both quantitative and qualitative differences in dendritic responsiveness between the sexes following differential rearing. As a test of this, we have been examining dendritic parameters in the visual cortex and hippocampal dentate gyrus in both male and female hooded rats raised in either EC or IC. These studies examine whether there are sex differences in the dendritic structure of these areas, as well as possible sex differences in susceptibility to the differential environments.

At weaning, littermate sets of rats were placed in EC or IC. EC consisted of 12 same sex rats housed in a large wire mesh cage with a large set of objects changed daily. In addition, EC rats interacted with another set of objects (also changed daily) in a playbox. IC rats were housed alone in standard laboratory cages in the same room as the EC rats. IC rats of each sex weighed more than EC rats of each sex after 1 month of differential rearing as in previous work (Juraska et al., 1983). After 1 month of the differential environments, the brains were Golgi–Cox stained according to Van der Loos (1956). Neurons were traced with the aid of a camera lucida and neuron drawings were scored for number and length of branches. Three-way analyses of variance were performed on each measure with environment, sex and litter as factors. The individual animal was the unit of analysis with neurons nested in animal. Details of the rearing and histological procedures appear elsewhere (Juraska, 1984).

VISUAL CORTEX

We sampled 3 cell populations from 100 μm coronal sections in the visual cortex (area 17) — layer III pyramidal neurons, layer IV stellate neurons, and layer V pyramidal neurons. 19 neurons were drawn per animal from 5 littermate sets (380 neurons total) for layer III and 15 neurons per animal from 7 sets (420 neurons per cell type) for layers IV and V. Fig. 1 illustrates total dendritic length, the result of adding together the length of all dendritic branches per neuron (basilar and apical dendritic trees were separated). Every cell population showed a different pattern of changes. The largest total dendritic length differences were in the layer III basilar dendrites (Fig. 1a). There was a significant effect ($P < 0.00001$) of the environment in favor of the EC rats of both sexes. In addition, a sex-by-environment interaction was significant such that total dendritic length was greater in male EC rats ($P < 0.01$)

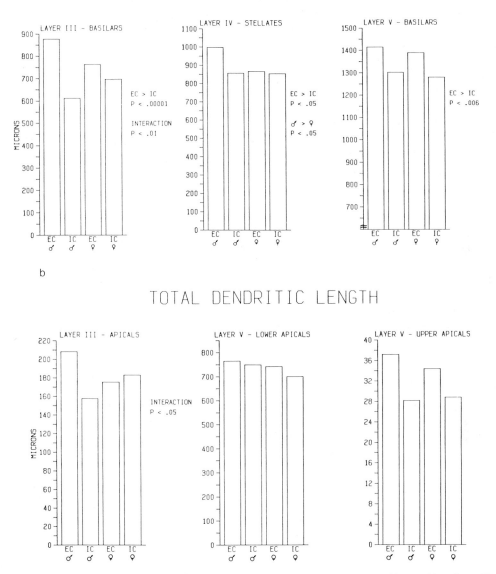

Fig. 1. The average total dendritic length per neuron (a) for layer III basilar pyramidal dendrites, layer IV stellate dendrites and layer V basilar pyramidal dendrites and (b) for layer III apical oblique dendrites and upper (> 250 μm from the soma) and lower (< 250 μm from the soma) layer V apical oblique dendrites. (From Juraska, 1984.)

than in any other group. This interaction pattern, which will appear again, indicates that males are showing more differences in response to the environment than females, and that sex differences appear in EC, but not in IC, rats. A similar pattern of a sex-by-environment interaction was evident in the layer III apical oblique total dendritic length ($P < 0.05$) (Fig. 1b). Once again, the male EC group had more dendritic material than any other group.

In the layer IV stellates, there was an environmental effect ($P < 0.05$; EC > IC) and a sex effect ($P < 0.05$; male > female). From Fig. 1a, it would appear that there should again be a sex-by-environment interaction. The interaction just missed significance ($P = 0.059$). Closer examination revealed that the large variance of the female groups probably obscured the interaction.

In contrast to layers III and IV, layer V basilar dendrites showed an environment effect ($P < 0.006$; EC > IC) but no interaction or trend toward an interaction (Fig. 1a). There were no sex differences in this cell population, and both sexes showed equal amounts of plasticity. There were no differences in either upper (> 250 μm from the cell body) or lower (< 250 μm from the cell body) apical oblique total length (Fig. 1b).

Lengths of individual branches were classified as bifurcating, terminal or cut off/obscured. This classification scheme has proved useful in previous studies (Uylings et al., 1978; Juraska et al., 1980). Analyzed alone, bifurcating branches did not change in any cell population. On the other hand, terminal branches, the growing tips of the dendritic tree, were significantly longer in EC rats in all cell populations ($P < 0.05$) except layer V upper apical oblique dendrites, regardless of sex. Males had longer terminal branches in layer IV stellates ($P < 0.01$) and layer V lower apical oblique branches ($P < 0.0006$). The only interaction ($P < 0.05$) occurred in layer III apical dendrites where male EC rats had longer terminals than all other groups.

The number of dendritic branches at each centrifugal order from the cell body or apical shaft were analyzed with branches originating at the cell body as first order (1), after one bifurcation, second order (2), etc. The most dramatic effects occurred in the layer III basilar dendritic tree (Fig. 2). At orders 2 and 4 there was an environment effect ($P < 0.01$ and $P < 0.002$) while at orders 3 and 5 there was an interaction ($P < 0.01$ and $P < 0.05$) with the

Layer III Pyramidal

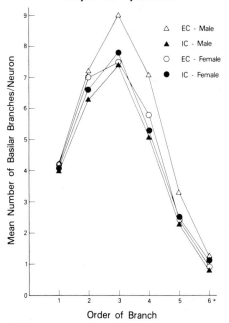

Fig. 2. The average number of basilar branches per layer III pyramidal neuron at each order from the cell body. Orders 2 and 4 show a significant environment effect (EC > IC) and orders 3 and 5 a significant interaction between sex and the environment. (From Juraska, 1984.)

male EC group having more branches than any other group. In layer IV stellates there was an environment effect ($P < 0.02$) in first-order branches in favor of the EC rats of both sexes. There also were no sex differences in layer V pyramidal neurons. However, significant environment effects (EC > IC) were seen for order 4 ($P < 0.05$) and total higher-order (3 and above) basilar branches ($P < 0.02$) and the total number of upper apical oblique branches ($P < 0.02$). A similar change in the upper apical oblique branches has been reported following extensive maze training (Greenough et al., 1979).

Significant litter differences were found in nearly all measures that also showed other significant effects (environment, sex or environment-by-sex interactions). Conversely, very few significant litter differences appeared in measures that were not significant for the other major variables.

Taken as a whole, it is evident that while female rats show changes in several dendritic measures in the visual cortex in response to differential environments, they are not as responsive or as vulnerable to the environments as males. This is consistent with the existing literature in which females have been described as the more buffered sex. This buffering is not absolute — in layer V pyramidal neurons female differences were the same as the males. In layer IV stellates there was a tendency for males to show larger effects, while in layer III pyramidal neurons male rats showed far more pronounced differences than female rats in several measures. Thus there are several different patterns of sex differences in plasticity exhibited within the visual cortex.

These data also show that sex differences are often relative to the rearing environment. If only IC males and females had been examined for sex differences, none would have been found. However, sex differences are evident in EC males and females in layer III pyramidal and layer IV stellate neurons with males having more dendritic material. These results make the question "Are there sex differences in the rat cortex?" too simplistic. A more appropriate formulation would be: "Under what conditions are there sex differences in the rat cortex?".

DENTATE GYRUS

We raised male and female rats in EC and IC in two separate replications. In each replication dentate granule neurons were sampled from 7 littermate sets, 20 neurons per animal (560 neurons per replication) in 150-μm coronal sections. We noted in which third of the granule cell layer each neuron was located (total granule layer thickness was approximately 135 μm) since early-forming granule cells are located in the top of the layer while later-forming neurons are progressively added to the bottom of the layer. Cell proliferation continues in the dentate past weaning age to at least 1 year of age (Bayer et al., 1982). We sampled from both the dorsal and ventral blades of the dentate gyrus avoiding the bend where the blades meet. Sampling was restricted to the septal region of the dentate gyrus.

We analyzed each neuron by counting the number of intersections between the dendrites and a series of concentric rings, 20 μm apart, centered on the cell body (Sholl, 1956). The concentric ring analysis indicates both amount and location of dendritic material relative to the cell body. This is especially useful information for granule cells since the input to the dentate is segregated in a laminar fashion. Fig. 3 shows the results of this analysis for replication 1 and Fig. 4 for replication 2. The pattern of results is completely different than any cell population examined in the cortex. Many rings show a sex-by-environment interaction, which mainly consists of females showing more plasticity than males. In fact, the male means are often reversed. In replication 1, the reversed male trend (IC > EC) only was significant

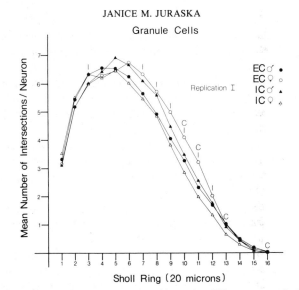

Fig. 3. The number of dendritic intersections per neuron with a series of 20-μm concentric rings for granule cells in replication 1. C indicates a significant environmental condition effect and I a significant sex-by-environment interaction.

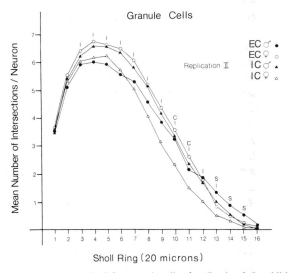

Fig. 4. The concentric ring analyses as in Fig. 3 for granule cells of replication 2. In addition, S indicates a significant sex effect.

($P < 0.05$) in ring 8. However, in replication 2, this reversal occurred in rings 4, 5, 6 and 8 ($P < 0.05$) in males. Females, on the other hand, showed a significant effect (EC > IC) in rings 9, 10, 11, 12 and 13 ($P < 0.02$) and a marginal effect ($P < 0.10$) in rings 3, 7, 8, 16 in replication 1 and a significant effect in rings 4 and 6–12 ($P < 0.05$) with a marginal effect in ring 3 in replication 2. Females are reversed (IC > EC) in ring 1 ($P < 0.05$) of replication 1. It is obvious that in the dentate female rats show a strong response to the environment while males show very little plasticity and often in an unexpected direction.

We also examined the data for sex differences within an environment. For IC rats, males had more dendritic material than females in rings 6–11 ($P < 0.02$) in replication 1 and 6–14 ($P < 0.05$) in replication 2. There was one reversal of this pattern in ring 1 of replication 1 (female > male) ($P < 0.03$). When the EC rats were examined for sex differences, females had more dendritic material than males in rings 10 and 11 ($P < 0.05$) of replication 1 and rings 2–7 ($P < 0.05$) of replication 2. Thus the pattern of sex differences was completely dependent on the rearing environment and bore no resemblance to the results found in the cortex.

As in the visual cortex, significant litter differences were found in most of the rings that exhibited significant environment differences or sex-by-environment interactions.

We also broke down the concentric ring analysis into upper one-third granule cells (older) and lower two-thirds granule cells (newer). We combined the bottom two-thirds because very few of the lowest one-third neurons stained in our Golgi–Cox preparation. This may reflect a staining bias against the very newest cells since the lowest cells in the granule cell layer are formed the latest. In replication 1, 43% of the sampled cells were from the upper one-third of the granule cell layer and 57% were from the lower two-thirds of the layer. In replication 2, equal numbers of cells were sampled from the upper and lower portions of the layer. The pattern of results seen in each replication across layer areas was also seen in the separate analyses of upper and lower granule layer cells. The effects were statistically strong in the upper granule layer and less so in the lower layer cells, especially in replication 1. This indicates that earlier-forming neurons are somewhat more plastic than later-forming neurons in this brain area of females.

Breaking the granule cells into upper and lower according to cell layer position did not shed light on the surprising lack of male differences or on the prominent female plasticity in this area. However, examination of characteristics of cells in each of these categories may help to explain why we did not replicate the findings of Fiala et al. (1978) who found significant differences between male EC and IC rats in the inner rings (near the cell body) of granule cells. We found differences in ring intersections between upper and lower granule cells that ranged from being equal to 3.5 times the differences found between the groups in the Fiala et al. study. While we cannot prove that we can account for the Fiala findings, it is possible that differences between groups in the number of upper and lower granule cells sampled in the Fiala study may have resulted in artificial differences in the lower rings. It is interesting to note that we have found the largest differences between the upper and lower granule cells in the inner rings.

There is one piece of support for the greater plasticity shown by the females in the hippocampal dentate gyrus in this study. Loy and Milner (1980) found that following fimbrial lesions (cutting the septohippocampal pathway), female rats exhibit greater sprouting of sympathetic, norepinephrine-containing axons in the dentate gyrus than male rats. Davis and Martin (1982), who failed to find this sex difference with medial septal lesions, suggested that sex differences may exist in the location of neurons contributing to the septohippocampal pathway. Additional evidence comes from the work of Drewett et al. (1977) who reported a sex difference in the characteristics of the septal driving of the hippocampal theta rhythm. Thus there may be sex differences in the connections of the hippocampal formation. Such differences in the pattern of connections could also contribute to the dimorphic response to the environment seen in the dentate gyrus. Most of the female environmental differences occur in the middle to upper dendritic tree, and one of the principle inputs to this dendritic area is the perforant pathway from the entorhinal area (Storm-Mathisen, 1977). One could speculate that this pathway may be sensitive to environmental events in females, or females could receive some other input in this part of the dendritic tree that males do not, which might be environmentally sensitive. Another possibility is that the entorhinal input is rerouted (sprouts in non-dentate gyrus areas) in male EC rats that could explain not only the lack of environmental differences but also the reversals (IC > EC) in this part of the dendritic tree.

GENERAL DISCUSSION

It is clear from the results in both the visual cortex and dentate gyrus that the female rat brain is not merely a miniaturized version of the male brain. Patterns of sex differences in dendritic structure vary with the area of the brain, cell population and rearing environment. Males exhibit greater differences in response to the environment in the visual cortex but not in every cell population. On the other hand, females show greater plasticity following differential rearing environments in the hippocampal dentate gyrus. This result in the dentate gyrus at first seems surprising in light of the literature on females as the more buffered sex and the cortical results presented here. The dentate gyrus results indicate that no generalization can be made concerning sex differences in plasticity. The pattern of changes is less puzzling if viewed as a piece of a larger set of rearrangements of connections that may be environmentally influenced or directed in many areas of the brain. For example, the possible increase in entorhinal input for female EC rats could be occurring in another part of the brain for male EC rats. These sexually dimorphic responses to the environment obviously imply sex differences in behavioral responses to the environment. However, the pattern of changes are, at present, too fragmented to predict how the sexes will differ.

The possible hormonal basis for any of the dendritic differences described here is not known. Both perinatal and post-puberal hormones could be responsible. Estrogen receptors appear in both the rat cortex and, to a lesser extent, hippocampus perinatally (Sheridan, 1979). Progesterone receptors also are found in the perinatal cortex (Kato and Onouchi, 1981). In adulthood, the cortex has low levels of estrogen and progesterone receptors (MacLusky and McEwen, 1978; MacLusky et al., 1979), while the hippocampus has estrogen and androgen receptors (Pfaff and Keiner, 1973; Stumpf and Sar, 1978). In addition, the hippocampus has high levels of corticosterone receptors (Stumpf and Sar, 1978), so that interactions between the gonadal steroids and the corticosteroids could influence the hippocampus. The dendritic sexual dimorphism in the cortex and hippocampus may also be influenced by input from other brain areas that have gonadal hormone receptors. More work needs to be done to understand not only the possible hormonal basis for sexual dimorphism in the cortex and hippocampus, but also how the environment may interact with hormones that result in sex differences in response to the environment.

CONCLUSIONS

Male rats showed larger dendritic differences in response to stimulating and isolated environments than females in some, but not all, visual cortex neuronal populations. This pattern was reversed in the granule cells of the hippocampal dentate gyrus, where female rats exhibited more environmental differences than male rats. Sex differences in these two brain areas were not absolute but varied with the rearing environment. In the visual cortex, males had more dendritic material than females in some neuronal populations when both were raised in a stimulating environment while there were no sex differences in rats from the isolated environment. Once again, this pattern was reversed in the dentate gyrus where isolated males had more dendritic material than isolated females while females had more dendrites after a stimulating environment than males. Therefore, sex differences exist in areas of the rat brain that are not directly involved with reproduction but no simple generalizations can be made concerning their direction.

ACKNOWLEDGEMENTS

I would like to thank Jonathan Fitch, Constance Henderson and Natalie Rivers for their assistance. This work was supported by NIH (HD 14949) and the John D. and Catherine T. MacArthur Foundation.

REFERENCES

Bayer, S.A., Yackel, J.W. and Puri, P.S. (1982) Neurons in the rat dentate gyrus granular layer substantially increase during juvenile and adult life. *Science*, 216: 890–892.

Beatty, W.W. (1979) Gonadal hormones and sex differences in nonreproductive behaviors in rodents: organizational and activational influences. *Hormone Behav.*, 12: 112–163.

Crutchfield, F.L. and Dratman, M.B. (1980) Growth and development of the neonatal rat: particular vulnerability of males to disadvantageous conditions during rearing. *Biol. Neonate*, 38: 203–209.

Davis, J.N. and Martin, B. (1982) Sympathetic ingrowth in the hippocampus: evidence for regulation by mossy fibers in thyroxin-treated rats. *Brain Res.*, 247: 145–148.

Diamond, M.C., Johnson, R.E. and Ingham, C. (1971) Brain plasticity induced by environment and pregnancy. *Int. J. Neurosci.*, 2: 171–178.

Diamond, M.C., Ingham, C.A., Johnson, R.E., Bennett, E.L. and Rosenzweig, M.R. (1976) Effects of environments on morphology of rat cerebral cortex and hippocampus. *J. Neurobiol.*, 7: 75–85.

Drewett, R.F., Gray, J.A., James, D.T.D., McNaughton, M., Valero, I. and Dudderidge, H.J. (1977) Sex and strain differences in septal driving of the hippocampal theta rhythm as a function of frequency: effects of gonadectomy and gonadal hormones. *Neuroscience*, 2: 1033–1041.

Fiala, B.A., Joyce, J.N. and Greenough, W.T. (1978) Environmental complexity modulates growth of granule cell dendrites in developing but not adult hippocampus of rats. *Exp. Neurol.*, 59: 372–383.

Galler, J.R. and Manes, M. (1980) Gender differences in visual discrimination by rats in response to malnutrition of varying durations. *Develop. Psychobiol.*, 13: 409–416.

Globus, A., Rosenzweig, M.R., Bennett, E.L. and Diamond, M.C. (1973) Effects of differential experience on dendritic spine counts in rat cerebral cortex. *J. Comp. Physiol. Psychol.*, 82: 175–181.

Gorski, R.A., Gordon, J.H., Shryne, J.E. and Southam, A.M. (1978) Evidence for a morphological sex difference within the medial preoptic area of the rat brain. *Brain Res.*, 148: 333–346.

Greenough, W.T., Carter, C.S., Steerman, C. and DeVoogd, T.J. (1977) Sex differences in dendritic patterns in hamster preoptic area. *Brain Res.*, 126: 63–72.

Greenough, W.T., West, R.W. and DeVoogd, T.J. (1978) Subsynaptic plate perforations: changes with age and experience in the rat. *Science*, 202: 1096–1098.

Greenough, W.T., Juraska, J.M. and Volkmar, F.R. (1979) Maze training effects on dendritic branching in occipital cortex of adult rats. *Behav. Neurol. Biol.*, 26: 287–297.

Hamilton, W.L., Diamond, M.C., Johnson, R.E. and Ingham, C.A. (1977) Effects of pregnancy and differential environments on rat cerebral cortical depth. *Behav. Biol.*, 19: 333–340.

Jones, A.P. and Friedman, M.I. (1982) Obesity and adipocyte abnormalities in offspring of rats undernourished during pregnancy. *Science*, 215: 1518–1519.

Jones, D.G. and Smith, B.J. (1980) Morphological analysis of the hippocampus following differential rearing in environments of varying social and physical complexity. *Behav. Neurol. Biol.*, 30: 135–147.

Juraska, J.M. (1984) Sex differences in dendritic response to differential experience in the rat visual cortex. *Brain Res.*, 295: 27–34.

Juraska, J.M., Greenough, W.T., Elliott, C., Mack, K.J. and Berkowitz, R. (1980) Plasticity in adult rat visual cortex: an examination of several cell populations after differential rearing. *Behav. Neurol. Biol.*, 29: 157–167.

Juraska, J.M., Greenough, W.T. and Conlee, J.W. (1983) Differential rearing affects responsiveness of rats to depressant and convulsant drugs. *Physiol. Behav.*, 31: 711–715.

Kato, J. and Onouchi, T. (1981) Progesterone receptors in the cerebral cortex of neonatal female rats. *Develop. Neurosci.*, 4: 427–432.

Levine, S. (1974) Differential response to early experience as a function of sex difference. In: R.C. Friedman, R.M. Richart and R.L. Vande Wiele (Eds.), *Sex Differences in Behavior*, John Wiley, New York, pp. 87–98.

Loy, R. and Milner, T.A. (1980) Sexual dimorphism in extent of axonal sprouting in rat hippocampus. *Science*, 208: 1282–1284.

MacLusky, N.J. and McEwen, B.S. (1978) Oestrogen modulates progestin receptor concentrations in some rat brain regions but not in others. *Nature (London)*, 274: 276–278.

MacLusky, N.J., Chaptal, C. and McEwen, B.S. (1979) The development of estrogen receptor systems in the rat brain and pituitary: postnatal development. *Brain Res.*, 178: 143–160.

McConnell, P., Uylings, H.B.M., Swanson, H.H. and Verwer, R.W.H. (1981) Sex differences in effects of environmental stimulation on brain weight of previously undernourished rats. *Behav. Brain Res.*, 3: 411–415.

Pfaff, D.W. (1966) Morphological changes in the brains of adult male rats after neonatal castration. *J. Endocrinol.*, 36: 415–416.

Pfaff, D. and Keiner, M. (1973) Atlas of estradiol-concentrating cells in the central nervous system of the female rat. *J. Comp. Neurol.*, 151: 121–158.

Raisman, G. and Field, P.M. (1971) Sexual dimorphism in the preoptic area of the rat. *Science*, 173: 731–733.

Rosenzweig, M.R. and Bennett, E.L. (1977) Effects of environmental enrichment or impoverishment on learning and on brain values in rodents. In: A. Oliverio (Ed.), *Genetics, Environment and Intelligence*, Elsevier, Amsterdam, pp. 163–196.

Rosenzweig, M.R., Bennett, E.L. and Diamond, M.C. (1972) Chemical and anatomical plasticity of brain: replications and extensions. In: J. Gaito (Ed.), *Macromolecules and Behavior*, Appleton Century Crofts, New York, pp. 205–277.

Sackett, G.P. (1974) Sex differences in rhesus monkeys following varied rearing experience. In: R.C. Friedman, R.M. Richart and R.L. Vande Wiele (Eds.), *Sex Differences in Behavior*, J. Wiley, New York, pp. 99–122.

Sheridan, P.J. (1979) Estrogen binding in the neonatal neocortex. *Brain Res.*, 178:201–206.

Sholl, D.A. (1956) *The Organization of the Cerebral Cortex*, Methuen, London.

Storm-Mathisen, J. (1977) Localization of transmitter candidates in the brain: the hippocampal formation as a model. *Progr. Neurobiol.*, 8: 119–181.

Stumpf, W.E. and Sar, M. (1978) Anatomical distribution of estrogen, androgen, progestin, corticosteroid and thyroid hormone target sites in the brain of mammals: phylogeny and ontogeny. *Am. Zool.*, 18: 435–445.

Uylings, H.B.M., Kuypers, K., Diamond, M.C. and Veltman, W.A.M. (1978) Effects of differential environments on plasticity of dendrites of cortical pyramidal neurons in adult rats. *Exp. Neurol.*, 62: 658–677.

Van der Loos, H. (1956) Une combinaison de deux vieilles méthodes histologiques pour le système nerveux central. *Mschr. Psychiat. Neurol.*, 132: 331–334.

Volkmar, F.R. and Greenough, W.T. (1972) Rearing complexity affects branching of dendrites in the visual cortex of the rat. *Science*, 176: 1445–1447.

Walsh, R.N., Budtz-Olsen, O.E., Penny, J.E. and Cummins, R.A. (1969) The effects of environmental complexity on the histology of the rat hippocampus. *J. Comp. Neurol.*, 137: 361–366.

Weinberg, J. and Levine, S. (1977) Early handling influences on behavioral and physiological responses during active avoidance. *Develop. Psychobiol.*, 10: 161–169.

Yanai, J. (1979a) Strain and sex differences in the rat brain. *Acta Anat.*, 103: 150–158.

Yanai, J. (1979b) Delayed maturation of the male cerebral cortex in rats. *Acta Anat.*, 104: 335–339.

DISCUSSION

W.W. BEATTY: Have you looked for evidence of differences in the environmental and sex effects between the left and right hemisphere?

J.M. JURASKA: I did not keep track of left and right sides in the visual cortex. In the dentate gyrus studies, I looked for left/right differences and did not find any.

G.J. De Vries et al. (Eds.),
Progress in Brain Research, Vol. 61
© 1984 Elsevier Science Publishers B.V., Amsterdam

Morphometric Methods
in Sexual Dimorphism Research
on the Central Nervous System

H.B.M. UYLINGS, C.G. VAN EDEN and R.W.H. VERWER

Netherlands Institute for Brain Research, Meibergdreef 33, 1105 AZ Amsterdam (The Netherlands)

INTRODUCTION

It was not until the last few decades that structural sex differences were demonstrated in the brain of mammals and birds. Especially the paper of Raisman and Field (1973), but also those of Pfaff (1965) and of Nottebohm and Arnold (1976), formed the impetus for the study of structural correlates of sex differences in the brain, using morphometric methods. Interesting results have been reported regarding the presence of (a) a 5 times larger sexual dimorphic nucleus of the preoptic area (SON-POA) in male rats as compared with female rats (Gorski et al., 1980; Gorski, 1984); 3 strikingly larger vocal control *brain areas* in male songbirds (Nottebohm and Arnold, 1976); (b) sex differences in the size of *neuronal somata* and in *neuronal density* (e.g. Gorski et al., 1980); (c) sex differences in *dendritic size* in the primate and rodent preoptic area (Greenough et al., 1977; Ayoub et al., 1983) and in a vocal brain area in the canary (e.g., DeVoogd, 1984); (d) sex differences in the *synaptology* in the dorsomedial preoptic area (Raisman and Field, 1973), in the hypothalamic arcuate nucleus and the medial amygdaloid nucleus (e.g. Arai, 1981). In addition, sex differences have been shown by Juraska (1984) in the response of dendritic patterns in the rodent occipital cortex and hippocampus to enriched environment. Furthermore, Diamond and collaborators (1981, 1982, 1983) showed that cerebral cortical and hippocampal *thicknesses* are differentially lateralized. In adult male rats some of the locations measured in the right cerebral cortex and hippocampus were significantly thicker than those in the left, whereas in adult female rats the laterality in thickness was not well defined. Van Eden et al. (1984) found a significant effect of sex on the degree of volumetric asymmetry in the rat orbital prefrontal cortex (viz. the dorsal agranular insular cortex). Throughout the period investigated (6–90 days post partum) this area was more strongly asymmetric in male than in female rats, with significant right-over-left asymmetries on days 14, 30 and 90. In the medial prefrontal cortex, on the other hand, the observed significant left-over-right volume asymmetry was equally pronounced in female and male rats.

All these results have been obtained by morphometric analysis. In this kind of research, however, the application of accurate analytical methods is crucial, since it may well be decisive for the final outcome of the results. Reviewing the morphometric studies performed in the field of sex dimorphism research we felt that it would be useful to briefly describe several currently employed morphometric methods. This may reduce the measuring error and, therefore, more readily reveal the existence of differences between the sexes in the — partly overlapping — distributions of a given parameter. In this paper, we will restrict ourselves to (i) the analysis of thickness of cortical structures, (ii) the volume of different brain regions and (iii) cell and synapse counting within a given brain area. For a review on metric analysis of dendritic patterns, we refer to Uylings et al. (1981); for topological analysis of dendritic structures we refer to Van Pelt and Verwer (1983), Verwer and Van Pelt (1983), and Sadler and Berry (1983).

CORTICAL THICKNESS ANALYSIS

The analysis of thickness of a given brain region is important in cases where we are dealing with a large structure such as the cerebral cortex, where an initial screening for detecting differences between two or more groups is desirable before proceeding to a more detailed analysis. If, however, the shape of the brain region itself is too complex (e.g., rather curved and/or twisted), the linear parameter "thickness" may easily become too insensitive to detect any but the largest differences between the groups. The hippocampus, for instance, is a highly curved structure composed of different regions, such as fascia dentata, CA1, CA3 and subiculum, which are twisted in a complex fashion in the three-dimensional space. As an illustration of this difficulty, thickness measurements in the dorsal hippocampus did not reveal any clear-cut effects of undernutrition (e.g., Noback and Eisenman, 1981), whereas a volumetric analysis of the different hippocampal regions shows deficits as large as 25% (Uylings et al., in preparation).

When a cortical thickness analysis is performed involving groups with a chance that not all cortical areas will be equally affected, identical cortical regions obviously must be compared. If no cytoarchitectonic criteria but subcortical landmarks (e.g., Diamond et al., 1981) or a position in the cerebral cortex proportional to the rostrocaudal length of the corpus callosum (e.g., Uylings et al., 1983) are applied for selecting the region to be used for the thickness measurements, it is essential to control for the plane of cutting and its variation between the different brains proposed to be examined. In brains which are cut in planes that deviate too much from each other, the thickness measurements will in fact be obtained from different cortical areas. As far as we know the literature, no methods have been described for determining limits and no rodent study (with the exception of Finlay and Slattery, 1983) mentioned the use of limits for selection of brains which are coronally sectioned. Finlay and Slattery (1983) arbitrarily chose a 1% deviation from the coronal plane as the maximum to be allowed.

In Fig. 1 we indicate the two kinds of deviation from a coronal plane caused by, respectively, *asymmetrical* cutting (i.e., cutting in a plane not perpendicular to the midsagittal sulcus: Fig. 1a,b), and *oblique* cutting (i.e., plane of section not perpendicular to the dorsal pial surface: Fig. 1c,d). A combination of these two types of deviation usually occurs. The procedure which we use in the rat for determining the degree of both types of deviation is shrinkage-independent, under the assumption only that the shrinkage is similar in the length and width dimension of the cerebrum. The degree of *asymmetric cutting* can be determined on the basis of characteristic fusion of the strata pyramidale of the dorsal and ventral hippocampus (see Fig. 1b). If the sections are perfectly coronal, the fusion of these strata pyramidale in the left and right hemispheres should occur in the same section. No objective criteria, however, have yet been established for limiting the permissible range of the angle of asymmetric cutting, a. Subjectively, we chose an a value of 3.5° as the maximal permissible deviation angle on the basis of the number of different cytoarchitectonic cortical regions which will be compared as estimated by the broken line in Fig. 1a relative to the unbroken straight line in Fig. 1a, showing the ideal coronal plane.

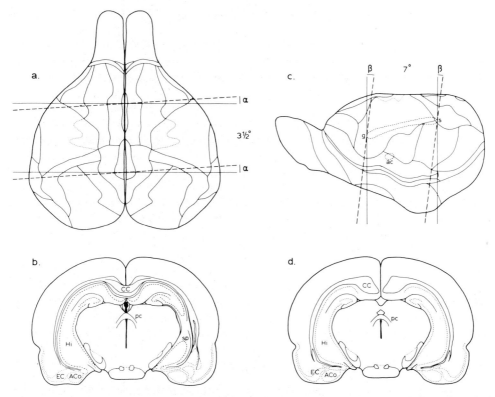

Fig. 1. The effect of the maximum angle of deviation from the coronal plane on the cytoarchitectonic cortical regions for, respectively, "asymmetric" cutting (angle a) and "oblique cutting" angle (angle β). The rat cytoarchitectonic areas displayed in a and c are based on Zilles et al. (1980). The cross-sectional sections in b and d show the effects of the maximum angle a and β, respectively. The composite drawings b and d are based on König and Klippel (1963). CC, corpus callosum; pc, posterior commissure; Hi, hippocampus; sp, stratum pyramidale; EC, entorhinal cortex; ACo, cortical amygdaloid nucleus.

The size of "*oblique cutting*" can be determined by two, respectively, dorsal and ventral landmarks in the cerebrum. For these characteristic landmarks, we selected the splenium (i.e., the caudal midsagittal extremity of the corpus callosum) and the caudal border of the cortical amygdaloid nucleus (ACo). If the planes of sections are according to the stereotactic atlas of König and Klippel (1963), then the splenium will occur in about the same plane as the caudal border of the ACo. In view of the number of different cytoarchitectonic cortical areas sectioned as compared with those in the ideal coronal plane (continuous line in Fig. 1c), we chose the β value of $-7°$ and $+7°$ as the maximum allowed angle of deviation. For β is $\pm 7°$, the cortical thickness itself changes only by about 0.7%.

An example of the effects of the a and β angle limits is the following. In the course of an experimental study at our institute, 78 rat brains embedded in celloidin were cut coronally after orienting the tissue blocks at the sliding microtome by workers recently involved in this type of study. Following the a criterion, 17%, i.e., 13 animals and, following the β criterion, 32%, i.e., 25 animals, had to be excluded. Combination of the a and β angle limits led to the exclusion of a total of 27 animals from further analysis.

VOLUMETRIC ANALYSIS

The weight analysis of dissected brain regions (e.g. 8 regions in rat brain) can be regarded as a rough but rapid volumetric screening procedure for detecting large differences (e.g., Mirmiran and Uylings, 1983). In histological preparations volumetric analysis will be preferred to thickness analysis in cases where the boundaries of the relevant regions can be defined and the region has a rather curved or complex structure (see above). Various approaches are available for the calculation of the volume. The cutting plane is usually irrelevant for the volumetric analysis. When a large number of structures (animals and/or brain regions) has to be analyzed and compared with other groups, the use of a computer for volume calculations and statistical analysis is practical for the processing of on-line data of cross-sectional area measurements. In our analysis, we use the "arithmetic mean" approximation for volume calculation (e.g., Wingert, 1969; West et al., 1978; Van Eden et al., 1984), assuming that any change in cross-sectional area between the slides measured is linear:

$$V = \frac{1}{M^2} \sum_{i=1}^{n-1} \frac{A_i + A_{i+1}}{2} \, d_i \qquad (1)$$

in which A_i = surface area in ith section, n = number of sections measured, d_i = distance between surface area A_i and A_{i+1}, and M is the linear magnification. Another approximation which is frequently used is the "cylindrical" approximation (e.g., Wingert, 1969; Konigsmark, 1970, his Eqn. 9; Jacobson et al., 1981), given by

$$V = \frac{1}{M^2} \sum_{i=1}^{n} A_i d_i \qquad (2)$$

Eqn. 2 can easily lead to an overestimation if d_i is constant and the effect at both poles of the region to be studied cannot be neglected.

For an accurate volumetric analysis, based upon transectional area measurements, not all of the sections need to be measured. Usually, a certain prefixed distance has been taken between the sections to be analyzed. In practice, however, the cross-sectional area of the pertinent brain region may vary in size and shape in a rather irregular fashion. This would require a very fine grading of the prefixed distance, if Eqn. 2 is used. Sometimes visual inspection of a series of sections of a particular brain region shows large changes in the cross-sectional surface area over relatively few consecutive sections, whereas in other parts the surface area remains about the same over a large number of consecutive sections. For an accurate estimation the distance between measured sections has to be small in the rapidly changing parts, but may be larger in the more "stable" parts. In such a situation, Eqn. 1 is applied (e.g., Van Eden et al., 1984). In addition, in order to increase the accuracy of the volumetric analysis, a plane of section would be preferred that is perpendicular to the longitudinal axis of the brain region (e.g., the horizontal planes in the case of the hippocampus (West et al., 1978)).

Volumetric and cortical thickness analyses can be affected by *shrinkage* of the tissue (during fixation, embedding and staining) if groups are compared which are differentially shrunken by these procedures. As far as we know, this has not been reported for male vs. female brains (Leibnitz, 1971). The shrinkage of tissue from young animals, however, is systematically larger than from older animals (e.g., Zilles, 1978), since the brains of immature animals have a higher water content and more extracellular space. In developmental studies, therefore, the application either of relative parameters (i.e., insensitive for shrinkage) or the correction of the volumetric data by the estimated degree of shrinkage is necessary. The following shrinkage-insensitive, relative parameter for estimating the degree of interhemispheric asymmetry, i.e., the *lateralization ratio*, *LR*, has been defined in the analysis of the volumetric development of the left and right prefrontal cortex (Van Eden et al., 1984)

$$LR = 2 \ (V_1 - V_r) \ / \ (V_1 + V_r) \tag{3}$$

where V_1 and V_r indicate the volume of the region in the left and right hemispheres, respectively. In addition, these parameters allow for comparisons between brains of different sizes. Use of this parameter revealed the above-mentioned sex difference in the extent of lateralization of male and female rats during the development of the agranular dorsal insular region of the orbital prefrontal cortex (see Fig. 2) (Van Eden et al., 1984). Furthermore, both in male and female rats, the medial prefrontal cortex showed a left-over-right asymmetry in adulthood, which was also clearly evident from day 10 until day 18. In addition, it is noteworthy that our measurements of the absolute cortical depth in this curved area did not show any significant difference between the hemispheres on day 18.

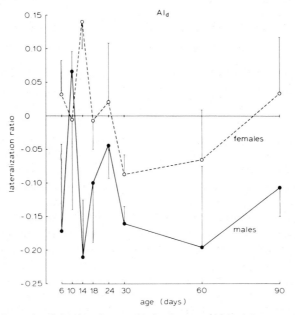

Fig. 2. The lateralization ratio of the dorsal agranular insular area (AI_d) of the rat prefrontal cortex during postnatal development. The bars indicate the S.E.M. values.

COUNTING OF CELLS AND SYNAPSES

Given the volume of a specific region as determined by the above-mentioned equations, the total cell or neuron number can be derived once the number per unit volume has been determined. Quite frequently, however, published counts of cells, spines and synapses are limited to the number of profiles per unit section area which is subsequently used for comparing different groups (e.g., males and females). This parameter, however, is *non-informative*: a quite different number of cell or synapse profiles per unit section area may be obtained for groups even though the total number per unit volume is equal, and vice versa.

This can occur when the counted particles have (i) a differential *orientation* from one group to another, (ii) a differential *size distribution* and/or (iii) a differential variation in *shape*. Therefore, it is necessary to determine the number of particles (e.g., cells and synapses) per unit tissue volume. Several approaches are reported in the literature, which can be divided into those with and those without assumptions concerning shape. In view of the limited scope of this article we will refer only to Weibel (1979, 1980), Cruz-Orive (1983) and Taylor (1983) for reviews of methods with shape assumptions, especially the so-called unfolding methods. The unfolding method is the most practical one in situations where section thickness is not negligible and/or many profiles, which were not detectable in the preparation due to the smallness and/or their too low contrast, are missed. When the section thickness cannot be neglected, a simple estimate of the mean cell or nucleus diameter, $\bar{D}$, from the observed mean profile diameter, $\bar{d}$, given by the relation $\bar{D} = (4/\pi)\,\bar{d}$ will lead to overestimation up to 27%). This $\bar{D}$ estimate will therefore lead to underestimation of the numerical density per unit volume, if the Abercrombie formula (see e.g., Konigsmark, 1970; Haug, 1972; Weibel, 1979, p. 158) is used. Furthermore, missed profiles will give rise to an underestimation of the numerical profile density per unit section area and, therefore, an underestimation of the numerical density per unit volume, calculated with the Abercrombie formula. However, all of the methods that embody shape assumptions can be applied in structural sexual dimorphism research only, if the shapes of the counted structures are similar in male and female brains. In addition, they should be randomly (isotropically) oriented and randomly distributed within the region selected for counting. If these conditions are not satisfied, methods without shape assumptions are to be preferred (see Cruz-Orive, 1980; Verwer and De Groot, 1982; Sterio, 1984).

The method of *sampling* in order to obtain the data is of crucial importance. A wrong sampling design may easily lead to a serious biasing of the final results (e.g., Shay, 1975; Cochran, 1977). The analysis of sampling design examines the variation contribution of each of the different hierarchical levels present in (neuro)morphometric studies. The levels generally distinguished are: treatment — sex — individual animal — brain region — section — micrograph or microscopical field — test frame. On the basis of pilot studies and the analysis of sampling variances, an efficient design for sampling at the different hierarchical levels can be composed. Sometimes it will turn out that a real study (as opposed to a pilot study) is extremely difficult to perform in a satisfactory way. For definitely establishing, for instance, the indications for the existence of a sex difference in the lateralization (ratio) of the prelimbic cortex found in our study, the use of groups with very large numbers of animals appears to be necessary given the large variance of the lateralization ratio and the magnitude of sex difference (Van Eden et al., 1984).

In conclusion, in this paper we have briefly reviewed methods for the determination of cortical thickness and of the volume of brain regions. Relative (shrinkage-insensitive) parameters appeared to be profitable in demonstrating a sex dimorphism in the lateralization of the orbital prefrontal cortex both during development and in adulthood. For counting synapses and neurons, the numerical density per unit section area is non-informative. A better parameter is either the numerical density per unit volume or the total number in a particular brain region.

ACKNOWLEDGMENT

We acknowledge Mr. H. Stoffels for his art-work.

REFERENCES

Arai, Y. (1981) Synaptic correlates of sexual differentiation. *Trends Neurosci.*, 4: 291–293.

Ayoub, D.M., Greenough, W.T. and Juraska, J.M. (1983) Sex differences in dendritic structure in the preoptic area of the juvenile macaque monkey brain. *Science*, 219: 197–198.

Cochran, W.C. (1977) *Sampling Techniques*, 3rd Edn., Wiley, New York.

Cruz-Orive, L.M. (1980) On the estimation of particle number. *J. Microsc.*, 120: 15–27.

Cruz-Orive, L.M. (1983) Estimation sphere size distribution from slabs. *J. Microsc.*, 131: 265–290.

DeVoogd, T. (1984) The avian song system: relating sex differences in behavior to dimorphism in the central nervous system. In: G.J. De Vries, J.P.C. De Bruin, H.B.M. Uylings and M.A. Corner (Eds.), *Sex Differences in the Brain. The Relation between Structure and Function. Progress in Brain Research*, this volume, Ch. 9.

Diamond, M.C., Dowling, G.A. and Johnson, R.E. (1981) Morphologic cerebral cortical asymmetry in male and female rats. *Exp. Neurol.*, 71: 261–268.

Diamond, M.C., Murphy Jr., G.M., Akiyama, K. and Johnson, R.E. (1982) Morphologic hippocampal asymmetry in male and female rats. *Exp. Neurol.*, 76: 553–556.

Diamond, M.C., Johnson, R.E., Young, D. and Singh, S.S. (1983) Age-related morphologic differences in the rat cerebral cortex and hippocampus: male–female; right–left. *Exp. Neurol.*, 81: 1–13.

Finlay, B.L. and Slattery, M. (1983) Local differences in the amount of early cell death in neocortex predict adult local specializations. *Science*, 219: 1349–1351.

Gorski, R.A. (1984) Critical role for the medial preoptic area in the sexual differentiation of the brain. In: G.J. De Vries, J.P.C. De Bruin, H.B.M. Uylings and M.A. Corner (Eds.), *Sex Differences in the Brain. The Relation between Structure and Function. Progress in Brain Research*, this volume, Ch. 7.

Gorski, R.A., Harlan, R.E., Jacobson, C.D., Shryne, J.E. and Southam, A.M. (1980) Evidence for the existence of a sexually dimorphic nucleus in the preoptic area of the rat. *J. Comp. Neurol.*, 193: 529–539.

Greenough, W.T., Carter, C.S., Steerman, C. and DeVoogd, T.J. (1977) Sex differences in dendritic patterns in hamster preoptic area. *Brain Res.*, 126: 63–72.

Haug, H. (1972) Stereological methods in the analysis of neuronal parameters in the central nervous system. J. Microsc., 95: 165–180.

Jacobson, C.D., Csernus, V.J., Shryne, J.E. and Gorski, R.A. (1981) The influence of gonadectomy, androgen exposure or a gonadal graft in the neonatal rat on the volume of the sexually dimorphic nucleus of the preoptic area. *J. Neurosci.*, 1: 1142–1147.

Juraska, J.M. (1984) Sex differences in developmental plasticity in the visual cortex and hippocampal dentate gyrus. In: G.J. De Vries, J.P.C. De Bruin, H.B.M. Uylings and M.A. Corner (Eds.), *Sex Differences in the Brain. The Relation between Structure and Function. Progress in Brain Research*, this volume, Ch. 11.

König, J.F.R. and Klippel, R.A. (1963) *The Rat Brain. A Stereotaxic Atlas*. Williams and Wilkins, Baltimore, MD.

Konigsmark, B.W. (1970) Methods for the counting of neurons. In: W.J.H. Nauta and S.O.E. Ebbeson (Eds.), *Contemporary Research Methods in Neuroanatomy*, Springer, Berlin, pp. 315–340.

Leibnitz, L. (1971) Untersuchungen zur Optimierung der Gewichts- und Volumenänderungen von Hirnen während der Fixierung, Dehydrierung und Aufhellung sowie über Rückschüsse vom Gewicht des Behandelten auf das Volumen des frischen Gehirns. *J. Hirnforsch.*, 13: 321–329.

Mirmiran, M. and Uylings, H.B.M. (1983) The environmental enrichment effect upon cortical growth is neutralized by concomitant pharmacological suppression of active sleep in female rats. *Brain Res.*, 261: 331–334.

Noback, C.R. and Eisenman, L.M. (1981) Some effects of protein-calorie undernutrition on the developing central nervous system of the rat. *Anat. Rec.*, 201: 67–73.

Nottebohm, F. and Arnold, A.P. (1976) Sexual dimorphism in vocal control areas of the songbird brain. *Science*, 194: 211–213.

Pfaff, D.W. (1966) Morphological changes in the brains of adult male rats after neonatal castration. *J. Endocrinol.*, 36: 415–416.

Raisman, G. and Field, P.M. (1973) Sexual dimorphism in the neuropil of the preoptic area of the rat and its dependence on neonatal androgen. *Brain Res.*, 54: 1–29.

Sadler, M. and Berry, M. (1983) Morphometric study of the development of Purkinje cell dendritic trees in the mouse using vertex analysis. *J. Microsc.*, 131: 341–354.

Shay, J. (1975) Economy of effort in electron microscope morphometry. *Am. J. Pathol.*, 81: 503–512.

Sterio, D.C. (1984) The unbiased estimation of number and sizes of arbitrary particles using the disector. *J. Microsc.*, 134:127–136.

Uylings, H.B.M., Parnavelas, J.G. and Walg, H.L. (1981) Morphometry of cortical dendrites. In: E.A. Vidrio and M.A. Galina (Eds.), *Advances in the Morphology of Cells and Tissues, Progr. Clin. Biol. Res., Vol. 59*, Alan Liss, New York, pp. 185–192.

Uylings, H.B.M., McConnell, P., Ruiz-Marcos, A., Van Pelt, J. and Verwer, R.W.H. (1983) Differential changes in dendritic patterns of pyramidal and non-pyramidal neurons after undernutrition and its subsequent rehabilitation. In: *The Cell Biology of Neuronal Plasticity*, Abstractbook No. 1, Fidia Res. Ser. Frontiers Neurosci., pp. 295–297.

Van Eden, C.G., Uylings, H.B.M. and Van Pelt, J. (1984) Sex difference and left–right asymmetries in the prefrontal cortex during postnatal development in the rat. *Develop. Brain Res.*, 12: 146–153.

Van Pelt, J. and Verwer, R.W.H. (1983) Exact probabilities of branching patterns under terminal and segmental growth hypotheses. *Bull. Math. Biol.*, 45: 269–285.

Verwer, R.W.H. and De Groot, D.M.G. (1982) The effect of shape assumptions on the estimation of the numerical density of synapses from thin sections. In: R.M. Buijs, P. Pévet and D.F. Swaab (Eds.), *Chemical Transmission in the Brain, Progress in Brain Research, Vol. 55*, Elsevier, Amsterdam, pp. 195–203.

Verwer, R.W.H. and Van Pelt, J. (1983) A new method for the topological analysis of neuronal tree structures. *J. Neurosci. Meth.*, 8: 335–351.

Weibel, E.R. (1979) *Stereological Methods, Vol. 1, Practical Methods for Biological Morphometry*, Academic Press, London.

Weibel, E.R. (1980) *Stereological Methods, Vol. 2, Theoretical Foundations*, Academic Press, London.

West, M.J., Danscher, G. and Gydesen, H. (1978) A determination of the volumes of the layers of the rat hippocampal region. *Cell Tissue Res.*, 188: 345–359.

Wingert, F. (1969) Biometrische Analyse der Wachstumsfunktionen von Hirnteilen und Körpergewicht der Albinomaus. *J. Hirnforsch.*, 11: 133–197.

Zilles, K.J. (1978) Ontogenesis of the visual system. *Adv. Anat. Embryol. Cell Biol.*, 53: (3) 1–138.

Zilles, K.J., Zilles, B. and Schleicher, A. (1980) A quantitative approach to cytoarchitectonics. VI. The areal pattern of the cortex of the albino rat. *Anat. Embryol.*, 159: 335–360.

G.J. De Vries et al. (Eds.),
Progress in Brain Research, Vol. 61
© 1984 Elsevier Science Publishers B.V., Amsterdam

Sexual Differentiation of the Forebrain — Relationship to Gonadotrophin Secretion

R.G. DYER

ARC Institute of Animal Physiology, Babraham, Cambridge CB2 4AT (Great Britain)

INTRODUCTION

The concept of sexual differentiation of the brain is not new. For example, a little over 100 years ago Crichton-Browne (1880) reported a sex difference in the left–right asymmetry of the human cerebral cortex. This was not the first such observation, for 2 years earlier Heschl (1878) had described briefly a sex difference in the structure of the human temporal lobe. The analyses which led to these and later similar conclusions were based on the classical anatomical procedures of weighing and/or measuring the tissue under investigation. Such analytical procedures, albeit utilising more sophisticated statistical evaluations, continue to be used for the assessment of differences in the structure of the cerebral cortex in males and females (e.g. Diamond et al., 1981). In all these experiments attempts have been made to relate the sexually differentiated structures to differences in male–female physiology. Thus when gonadotrophin secretion was found to be a sexually differentiated process in a number of mammalian species (e.g. Everett et al., 1949; Harris, 1964; Neumann and Kramer, 1967) the search commenced to find the anatomical basis for this important sex difference (e.g. Barraclough and Gorski, 1961; Gorski, 1971). The pituitary gland itself was excluded as a possible site (Harris and Jacobsohn, 1952; Davidson, 1966) and attention was focussed upon the hypothalamus and limbic structures implicated in the control of gonadotrophin secretion (Velasco and Taleisnik, 1969; Everett, 1969; Gorski, 1971). This chapter presents an overview of the known sexually differentiated sites in the hypothalamus, explains why there is now an impasse in understanding the precise role of the sexually dimorphic structures and outlines a strategy for overcoming this problem.

SEXUAL DIFFERENTIATION OF THE PREOPTIC AREA

Although most aspects of luteinising hormone (LH) secretion in male and female rats appear similar there is one striking difference between the sexes. Adult male rats cannot generate an LH surge of preovulatory proportions in response to injections of oestrogen. LH secretion in adult female rats also cannot be stimulated by oestrogen if the animals have been exposed to testosterone in the immediate postnatal period (see Neill, 1972; Brown-Grant, 1972). For this chapter both normal males and testosterone-treated females will frequently be grouped together as "endocrine males". However, the reader should be aware that there are important differences between the two types of "endocrine male". In particular, female rats given testosterone propionate at birth often show a few ovulatory cycles immediately after puberty before the anovulatory syndrome is established (Swanson and Van der Werff ten Bosch, 1964; Brown-Grant, 1974). Likewise, because castration immediately after birth allows LH secretion to be stimulated by oestrogen in otherwise normal genetic males these rats and normal females will be referred to as "endocrine females" (see Neill, 1972; Gorski, 1971, 1973, for reviews).

Thus the sexually differentiated aspect of LH secretion concerns the ability to trigger an LH surge in response to oestrogen. Because this function is controlled by the medial preoptic area (MPOA; Everett, 1964) this part of the brain was examined by Raisman and Field (1971, 1973a) to try to find a difference between "endocrine males" and "endocrine females". They studied the ultrastructure of the dendrites, in a small part of the dorsal MPOA, to calculate the density of different types of axo-dendritic synapse in the two groups of rats. In particular, they distinguished synapses ending on dendritic spines from those ending on the shaft of the dendrite, and synapses originating from axons passing in the stria terminalis from all the others (see Fig. 1). The most striking discovery made was that "endocrine females" had significantly more spine synapses of non-strial origin than the "endocrine males". Numbers of spine synapses of strial origin, which are the endings of neurones located in the corticomedial amygdala, were not sexually differentiated, nor was any sex difference reported for synapses located upon dendritic shafts. Since there are 12 times more shaft synapses than spine synapses in the MPOA, and because one-third of the spine synapses are of strial origin (Raisman and Field, 1973a), it may be calculated that the sexually differentiated synapses account for only about 5% of all dendritic synapses in this region. Similar sexual differentiation of synaptic inputs was not observed in the ventromedial nucleus (Raisman and Field, 1973a), or in the projections of the fimbria to the septal nucleus (Raisman and Field, 1973b).

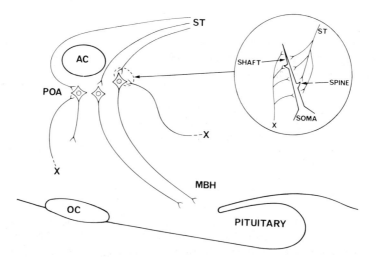

Fig. 1. Diagram of a parasagittal section through the hypothalamus to depict the experimental protocol used in the experiments of Raisman and Field (1973a; see text). Only synapses on preoptic (POA) neurones immediately under the anterior commissure (AC) were studied. The work involved separate analysis of synapses terminating on dendritic spines and shafts and inputs from the amygdala via the stria terminalis (ST) were distinguished from those originating from other unknown (X) structures (inset). Note that only the spine synapses of the non-strial input were sexually differentiated. Other abbreviations: OC, optic chiasm; MBH, mediobasal hypothalamus.

We (Dyer et al., 1976) have used electrophysiological techniques to investigate possible sexual differentiation of preoptic synapses. The experiments involved first identifying individual preoptic neurones on the basis of their connections with the mediobasal hypothalamus (Dyer, 1973) and then quantifying the response of these neurones to electrical stimulation of the corticomedial amygdala. Two noteworthy results were obtained. First, the cells having no direct connection (either afferent or efferent and therefore putative preoptic interneurones) with the mediobasal hypothalamus, showed significantly more spontaneous electrical activity when recorded in "endocrine females" than when recorded in "endocrine males" (Fig. 2). However there was no sexual differentiation of their amygdaloid input. By contrast, second, in "endocrine females" significantly fewer of the neurones, identified as projecting directly to the mediobasal hypothalamus, responded to stimulation of the amygdala than was observed in normal males. The other group of "endocrine males" (the females given testosterone within a few days of birth) had responses intermediate between those of normal males and normal females (Fig. 2).

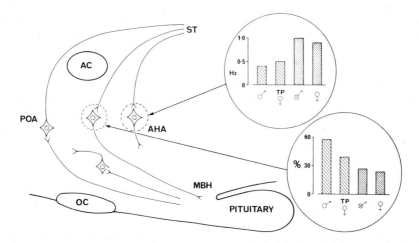

Fig. 2. Diagram of a parasagittal section through the rat hypothalamus to outline the experiments of Dyer et al. (1976; see text). Action potentials were recorded from neurones throughout the preoptic area (POA) and into the anterior hypothalamic area (AHA). Each cell was identified on the basis of its connections with the mediobasal hypothalamus (MBH) and corticomedial amygdala (via the stria terminalis — ST). Note (i) that the neurones having no direct afferent or efferent connection with the mediobasal hypothalamus were more active in the "endocrine females" than in the "endocrine males" (top inset; Hz, mean firing rate of the cells; TP, females given testosterone propionate on the first day of life) and (ii), that in "endocrine females" the cells identified as projecting directly to the MBH received fewer inputs via the ST than observed in normal males (lower inset; %, percentage of recorded cells responding to stimulation of the corticomedial amygdala).

Because Raisman and Field (1971, 1973a) found no sexual differentiation of the afferents from the amygdala to the MPOA, whereas we did (Dyer et al., 1976), the two sets of data are not easily reconcileable. There was, however, at least one important difference between the two series of experiments. Raisman and Field analysed only a part of the dorsal MPOA, whereas our electrophysiological experiments involved the full dorsal-ventral extent of the MPOA and extended into the anterior hypothalamic region. Nonetheless, if spine synapses are excitatory (Diamond et al., 1970), cells found to be more active in "endocrine females" than "endocrine males" may reflect the greater number of spine synapses in the former group (Raisman and Field, 1973a). However the region we studied with microelec-trodes overlapped more substantially with the sexually dimorphic zone of the MPOA described by Gorski et al. (1978) (where the density of neurones is greater in male rats than in females; see also Gorski, 1984; Gorski et al., 1980), than with the region analysed by Raisman and Field (1971, 1973a) and therefore it may not be important that different inter-pretations were made from the two sets of data.

SEXUAL DIFFERENTIATION OF THE ARCUATE NUCLEUS

More than 90% of the synapses in the rat arcuate nucleus develop after birth (Matsumoto and Arai, 1976; Arai and Matsumoto, 1978). However, the undeveloped neurones in this area already contain receptors for sex steroids (Sheridan et al., 1974). Therefore following the discoveries about sexually differentiated synapses in the preoptic area, it was logical to seek an organisational effect of testosterone upon synapse formation in the arcuate nucleus. In an exhaustive series of experiments Arai and associates (see Arai, 1981) have demon-strated that this nucleus is also sexually differentiated. In particular "endocrine females" had significantly more axo-dendritic spine synapses than "endocrine males". No sexual dimor-phism was shown for axo-dendritic shaft synapses (Matsumoto and Arai, 1980). These results are essentially analogous to those reported by Raisman and Field (1973a) for the dorsal MPOA. However Matsumoto and Arai (1980) were also able to describe a sex differ-ence in the synaptic input to the cell bodies. This difference was the inverse of that detected on the spine synapses. Thus "endocrine males" had significantly more axosomatic synapses than the "endocrine females".

DO SYNAPSES ONTO DENDRITIC SPINES
HAVE A PARTICULAR FUNCTION?

The two morphological experiments outlined above established that axo-dendritic spine synapses in the preoptic area and arcuate nucleus are sexually differentiated. The signifi-cance of this sexual dimorphism might be more readily appreciated if the function of spine synapses were understood. Unfortunately it is not.

There are two current hypotheses about the function of dendritic spines. The first, and oldest, suggests that they serve only to increase the area of dendrite available for presynaptic contacts (for recent statement of the relevant arguments see Swindale, 1981). If this is correct, some refinement of the hypothesis is needed to explain why particular inputs go to the dendritic spines. The sexually differentiated inputs under consideration provide an example of where such an explanation is necessary.

The second hypothesis gives the dendritic spines an important role in neuronal plasticity (Rall, 1974). Each spine often connects with the dendrite via a narrow neck. At the distal end the neck dilates and it is on this dilation that the synapses are to be found. Postsynaptic potentials must pass along the relatively narrow neck region of the spine before they reach the parent dendrite. Therefore if the diameter of the neck region changed, the efficacy of transmission from the synapse to the shaft of the dendrite might change also. The shape of the neck region of dendritic spines in the hippocampus is known to change after stimulation of the perforant path (Van Harreveld and Fifkova, 1975; Fifkova and Van Harreveld, 1977; Fifkova and Anderson, 1981), and recent computer modelling has provided evidence that a reduction in the length of the neck could increase the size of the postsynaptic potential arriving on the shaft of the dendrite (Koch and Poggio, 1983). If this second hypothesis is correct, a reduced input onto dendritic spines implies that the brain has reduced capacity to modify the strength of the input at the level of the synapse. Such considerations would apply to the sexually differentiated synapses found on dendritic spines. For example, suppose that at puberty oestrogen influenced the neck of dendritic spines in the MPOA to facilitate activation of the LH release system and this facilitation was essential for regular oestrous cycles to continue. If this were to happen, then females given testosterone propionate at birth might rapidly become acyclic after puberty because they have fewer spine synapses than normal females.

IS THE ORGANISATION OF THE SEXUALLY DIFFERENTIATED SYNAPSES IMMUTABLE IN ADULT RATS?

In all these experiments on the sexually differentiated organisation of synapses there is an important underlying assumption. That is, the synaptic structure is permanently altered by a single neonatal exposure to testosterone. This implicit assumption may be correct, and was certainly reasonable several years ago when the structure of the developed brain was considered a relatively fixed entity. However brain structure is more plastic than once thought. For example, in the supraoptic nucleus of the hypothalamus there is a dramatic increase in double synapses (i.e., synapses making contact with two neurones) during lactation in the rat. Double synapses are practically non-existent in virgin females, increase in number during pregnancy to peak during lactation and thereafter decline back to the non-pregnant density when lactation ceases (Hatton and Tweedle, 1982; Theodosis and Poulain, 1983). These changes are associated with an increase in soma-somatic contact during lactation caused by retraction of glial processes (for review see Hatton et al., 1984). Recent work in our laboratory (Bicknell et al., 1983) has demonstrated that, in culture, the specialised glial cells of the neurohypophysis (pituicytes) exhibit rapid and dramatic changes in morphology in response to some neurotransmitters.

These recent experiments indicate that the structure of the hypothalamus can change rapidly in response to physiological stimuli. Is it possible that the sexually differentiated structures are not so immutable as we now believe? There is just a hint that this could be the case. Thus although Raisman and Field (1973a) and Matsumoto and Arai (1980) showed that the sexually dimorphic synapses in female rats, treated neonatally with testosterone propionate, are quantitatively identical with those found in normal males, we know that immediately after puberty these females are likely to show a few ovulatory cycles. If the rats ovulate once or twice might it be possible to reinitiate cycles in the young adults? Finally, if sexually differentiated synapses are involved in control of the preovulatory LH surge, are they of the "endocrine male" or "endocrine female" type in testosterone-treated females at puberty?

THE ROLE OF SEXUALLY DIMORPHIC NEURONES IN CONTROL OF LH SECRETION

What effect, if any, do these morphological sex differences have on the functioning of the hypothalamus? At the present time the precise role of the sexually differentiated neural structures is not known. This has not prevented speculation about the possible involvement of these structures in the control of gonadotrophin secretion. However the most appropriate way to relate structure with function is to first define how the function is controlled and then ascertain how changes in structure alter the function. This, of course, is considered to be a standard and obvious experimental approach but it is frequently unsatisfactory because the structure and function are not analysed at the same level of complexity. For example, when sexual differentiation is investigated at a synaptic level it is difficult to relate the data to control of gonadotrophin secretion because we have little knowledge of how individual neurones or synapses regulate the release of these hormones. We have attempted to overcome this problem, by defining the synaptic connections between neurones which are able to regulate LH release, in the belief that this knowledge will allow us to generate testable hypotheses about possible roles for the sexually differentiated structures in the hypothalamus. The remainder of this chapter outlines our current view of the role of preoptic and arcuate/tuberoinfundibular neurones in controlling LH secretion and concludes by suggesting how the sexually differentiated structures might interact with this control process.

OESTROGEN, PREOPTIC NEURONES AND THE LH SURGE

In the rat the MPOA triggers ovulation by responding to the rising titre of systemic oestradiol in such a way as to initiate an LH surge. This response probably involves either an increase in the amount of gonadotrophin-releasing hormone (GnRH) secreted into the hypophysial portal vessels and/or a change in the pattern of its release to optimise its action upon the gonadotrophs of the anterior pituitary gland (Levine and Ramirez, 1982; Ching, 1982). The oestradiol also acts to increase the responsiveness of the pituitary gland to GnRH (Fink et al., 1976; Savoy-Moore et al., 1980) and although advances have been made in understanding this action of the steroid, progress in understanding its action upon the brain has not been so good. One reason for this is that the oestrogen-stimulated LH surge is blocked by the anaesthetics often required for in vivo investigation of brain function (Everett and Sawyer, 1950; Everett, 1964; Dyer and Mansfield, 1980). We have overcome this difficulty by utilising a slightly modified version of the Cross and Kitay (1967) technique for making hypothalamic islands. In this preparation a cylindrical cutting device is lowered through the brain of an anaesthetised rat to enclose the diencephalon and permit removal of all adjacent forebrain structures. The non-sentient preparation is then allowed to recover from the anaesthesia and may be used for manipulative experiments, including electrophysiology, upon hypothalamic neurones.

In earlier experiments ovulation induced by steroid-stimulated LH surges did not occur in island bearing rats (Cross and Dyer, 1972). However more recently Weick and Dyer (1982) found that by increasing the diameter of the island by 1.0 mm, small but reproducible LH surges occurred 6 h after ovariectomised female rats had been given the second of two steroid injections; each separated by 72 h, the first of oestradiol benzoate (OB) and the second of progesterone (P); for a discussion on this and other models for stimulating the preovulatory LH surge see Brown-Grant (1976). These procedures allowed us to record the electrical activity of hypothalamic neurones during the period that the preoptic area responds to circulating ovarian steroid and initiates the LH surge.

Data were obtained from 192 neurones recorded from 13 rats given oestrogen followed by progesterone and 161 neurones from the 9 oil-treated control rats. Subsequent histology demonstrated that a total of 153 of these cells were recorded from the MPOA and a further

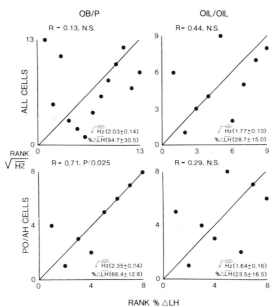

Fig. 3. Graphs showing the correlation between the firing rate (Hz) of recorded neurones and the increase in plasma LH concentrations (ΔLH) during the recording period, after injection of oestradiol benzoate (OB) and progesterone (P) to ovariectomised female rats. Control animals were given 2 injections of oil and hypothalamic islands were made in all rats immediately prior to the electrophysiological experiments. Note that no correlation between Hz and ΔLH could be established when all the cells were analysed together but that when preoptic and anterior hypothalamic (PO/AH) neurones recorded in OB/P-treated rats were analysed separately a significant correlation was obtained (solid line through some points represents complete correlation between rank values). (From Weick and Dyer, 1982.)

25 from the anterior hypothalamic area (AHA). Considered together the MPOA/AHA neurones recorded from the OB/P-treated rats showed a significant increase in their spontaneous activity; this being approximately twice that recorded from the control rats. A similar difference was not demonstrated for other groups of cells. The steroid treatment also significantly increased plasma concentrations of luteinising hormone and we were able to establish that the two phenomena were related. This was achieved by ranking the increases in plasma LH obtained for each rat and plotting them against a ranked quantification of the electrical activity recorded in the same animal (see Weick and Dyer, 1982). The results are summarised in the 4 graphs shown in Fig. 3. There was no correlation between the percentage increase in LH and the firing rate (Hz) when all cells were pooled together, either in steroid-treated (OB/P) or in control (oil/oil) rats. By contrast, when the MPOA/AHA neurones were analysed separately the OB/P rats, but not the controls, showed a significant correlation between their electrical activity and the increase in plasma LH. The data indicate that increased firing of MPOA/AHA neurones is associated with increased secretion of LH. If the correlation had reflected a feedback action of LH upon MPOA/AHA neurones, then it should have been observed also in the control rats. Because these had not received any oestrogen their plasma LH concentrations were relatively high, but they did not significantly increase LH secretion during the recording period.

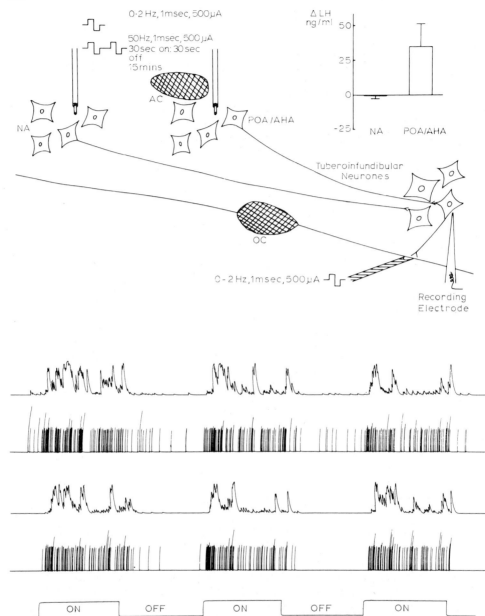

Fig. 4. Above: Diagram of a parasagittal section through the hypothalamus to show the arrangement for electro-physiological investigation of transmission from the preoptic and anterior hypothalamic areas (POA/AHA) to the tuberoinfundibular neurones in the mediobasal hypothalamus. These neurones were recorded during stimulation of POA/AHA with trains of stimuli sufficient to cause a significant increase in plasma LH concentrations. Inset: Graph representing the rise in plasma LH after stimulation of the POA/AHA or the nucleus accumbens (NA); note that when the NA was stimulated, as a consequence of inaccurate stereotaxic procedures, plasma LH was not affected. Below: Polygraph recording of action potentials generated by a tuberoinfundibular neurone during stimulation of POA/AHA to release LH. Note the bursting activity resulting from steady 50-Hz stimulation during the ON periods (top trace in each pair is a record of integrated activity and the bottom trace shows a pen deflection for each action potential). (From Saphier and Dyer, 1980.)

EXCITATION OF THE PREOPTIC AREA AND THE RESPONSE
OF TUBEROINFUNDIBULAR NEURONES

How do the tuberoinfundibular neurones, which project to the median eminence and secrete releasing and inhibiting hormones into the hypophysial portal vessels, respond to the increased firing of preoptic neurones? This question has been answered by recording from tuberoinfundibular neurones during stimulation of the preoptic area at a sufficient intensity to cause a significant increase in plasma LH concentrations. The arrangement for these experiments, which were performed on anaesthetised pro-oestrous rats, is shown in Fig. 4 (above). The stimulating electrode on the median eminence allowed identification of the tuberoinfundibular neurones following antidromic activation. Electrical stimulation in MPOA/AHA for 15 min (30 sec on, 30 sec off; 50 Hz at 500 μA) evoked a significant ($P < 0.02$; Mann–Whitney U test) rise in plasma LH. Such a rise was not observed when the stimulating electrode was placed in too rostral a position (in this case in the nucleus accumbens), even though the stimulation changed the firing rate of some tuberoinfundibular cells (see inset graph in Fig. 4; Dyer and Saphier, unpublished observations).

When the tuberoinfundibular neurones were recorded through the periods of MPOA/AHA stimulation, we observed (Saphier and Dyer, 1980) first that they did not follow the applied stimuli on a 1 : 1 basis. Indeed an average of 18 pulses in MPOA/AHA

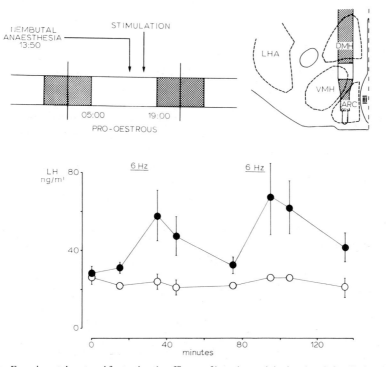

Fig. 5. Above: Experimental protocol for testing the efficacy of bursting activity in tuberoinfundibular neurones in causing LH secretion. Abbreviations: ARC, arcuate nucleus; DMH, dorsomedial nucleus; LHA, lateral hypothalamic area; VMH ventromedial nucleus. Below: Plasma LH concentrations before and after 2 periods of stimulation at 6 Hz in the mediobasal hypothalamus of pentobarbitone-anaesthetised pro-oestrous rats. The group of rats shown as open circles were stimulated at a constant 6 Hz whereas the group shown as filled circles had an average of 6 Hz stimulation but delivered in a bursting pattern.

was required to cause one extra action potential in the excited tuberoinfundibular neurones. The second point we observed was that when the tuberoinfundibular neurones were excited by the MPOA/AHA stimulation the excitation was in the form of brief bursts of activity in nearly 40% of the tested cells. An example of this bursting activity is shown in Fig. 4 below.

Does this bursting activity optimise release of hypothalamic hormones? We know that phasic firing in vasopressin-secreting neurones enhances the effectiveness of each action potential in causing hormone release (Dutton and Dyball, 1979). Indeed bursting activity may be a characteristic firing pattern for most peptide-secreting neurones during periods of activation. Recently we have investigated the effectiveness of the bursting activity, recorded from tuberoinfundibular neurones, in stimulating LH secretion. A stimulating electrode was inserted into the hypothalamus of anaesthetised pro-oestrous rats to allow electrical stimulation of the arcuate nucleus/median eminence (see top of Fig. 5). The stimulator was triggered by a recording of bursting activity in a tuberoinfundibular neurone, to mimic faithfully the pattern of electrical activity known to occur in this region during periods of MPOA/AHA activation. Two 5-min periods of stimulation were applied to each rat. The control animals receiving a regular train of pulses at almost exactly 6 Hz, by which the total number of pulses equals that of the brief bursts applied to the experimental group. The results of this experiment, which are shown in the lower part of Fig. 5, demonstrate that whereas the bursting pattern of stimulation caused a significant rise in plasma LH concentrations steady stimulation at the same overall frequency was without effect.

CONCLUSIONS

The various experiments outlined in the previous two sections provide sufficient data to construct a useful model to describe how the brain controls the preovulatory LH surge in the rat. Thus the oestrogen secreted by the developing ovarian follicle causes an increase in the electrical activity of MPOA/AHA neurones, which results in the generation of a characteristic bursting pattern of impulse generation in tuberoinfundibular neurones. This in turn facilitates GnRH secretion, thereby potentiating release of LH from the adenohypophysis. Communication between neurones in these two distinct parts of the hypothalamus is dependent upon the synaptic organisation of the constituent cells. Any change in the synaptic arrangements is likely to change also the nature of the communication. Thus, since some aspects of the synaptic arrangements in both MPOA/AHA and the arcuate nucleus are sexually differentiated, transmission between these two areas may also be sexually differentiated. If this sexual differentiation is related to control of gonadotrophin secretion, and especially the preovulatory LH surge, then some effect of endocrine sex upon the control mechanism proposed for the regulation of LH secretion should be detectable. It is also possible that oestrogen does not excite MPOA/AHA neurones in "endocrine males" to the same extent as in "endocrine females". This would be consistent with our finding that presumptive MPOA/AHA interneurones show more spontaneous electrical activity in "endocrine females" than in "endocrine males" (Dyer et al., 1976). Therefore, because rats with "male" brains have relatively less active MPOA/AHA neurones they may be unable to drive the important bursting activity in tuberoinfundibular neurones now described in normal female brains. These and related hypotheses will be tested in future experiments. It seems clear that the physiological consequence of hormonally induced changes in the ultrastructure of particular hypothalamic neurones will remain uncertain until the function of the neurone involved is better understood.

ACKNOWLEDGEMENTS

I thank Drs. G.I. Hatton, G. Leng and W.T. Mason for their helpful and constructive comments on the text. I am also grateful to R. Bunting, M. Marsh and A. Setchell for rapidly making the figures and to Mrs. J. Cummings and Mrs. S. Mansfield for help in the preparation of the manuscript.

REFERENCES

Arai, Y. (1981) Synaptic correlates of sexual differentiation. *Trends Neurosci.*, 4: 91–293.

Arai, Y. and Matsumoto, A. (1978) Synapse formation of the hypothalamic arcuate nucleus during post-natal development in the female rat and its modification by neonatal estrogen treatment. *Psychoneuroendocrinology*, 3: 31–45.

Barraclough, C.A. and Gorski, R.A. (1961) Evidence that the hypothalamus is responsible for androgen-induced sterility in the female rat. *Endocrinology*, 68: 68–79.

Bicknell, R.J., Leendertz, J. and Worley, R.T.S. (1983) Time lapse video recording of rapid morphological changes of rat pituicytes in culture. *J. Physiol. (London)*, in press.

Brown-Grant, K. (1972) Recent studies on the sexual differentiation of the brain. In: R.S. Comline, G.S. Dawes, P.W. Nathanielsz and K.W. Cross (Eds.), *Foetal and Neonatal Physiology*, Cambridge University Press, Cambridge, pp. 527–545.

Brown-Grant, K. (1974) On "critical periods" during the postnatal development of the rat. In: M.G. Forest and J. Bertrand (Eds.), *Endocrinologie Sexuelle de la Période Périnatale*, INSERM, Paris, pp. 357–376.

Brown-Grant, K. (1976) Control of gonadotrophin secretion. In: F. Naftolin, K.J. Ryan and J. Davies (Eds.), *Subcellular Mechanisms in Reproductive Neuroendocrinology*, Elsevier, Amsterdam, pp. 485–501.

Crichton-Browne, J. (1880) On the weight of the brain and its component parts in the insane. *Brain*, 2: 42–67.

Cross, B.A. and Dyer, R.G. (1972) Cyclic changes in neurons of the anterior hypothalamus during the rat estrous cycle and the effect of anaesthesia. In: C.H. Sawyer and R. Gorski (Eds.), *Steroid Hormones and Brain Function*, University of California Press, Los Angeles, CA, pp. 95–102.

Cross, B.A. and Kitay, J. (1967) Unit activity in rat diencephalic islands. *Exp. Neurol.*, 19: 316–330.

Davidson, J.M. (1966) Control of gonadotropin secretion in the male. In: L. Martini and W.F. Ganong (Eds.), *Neuroendocrinology, Vol. 2*, Academic Press, New York, pp. 565–611.

Diamond, J., Gray, E.G. and Yasargil, G.M. (1970) The function of the dendritic spine: an hypothesis. In: J. Jannsen and P. Andersen (Eds.), *Excitatory Synaptic Mechanisms*, Scandinavian University Books, Oslo, pp. 213–222.

Diamond, M.C., Dowling, G.A. and Johnson, R.E. (1981) Morphological cerebral cortical asymmetry in male and female rats. *Exp. Neurol.*, 71: 261–268.

Dutton, A. and Dyball, R.E.J. (1979) Phasic firing enhances vasopressin release from the rat neurohypophysis. *J. Physiol. (London)*, 290: 433–440.

Dyer, R.G. (1973) An electrophysiological dissection of the hypothalamic regions which regulate the pre-ovulatory secretion of luteinising hormone in the rat. *J. Physiol. (London)*, 234: 421–442.

Dyer, R.G. and Mansfield, S. (1980) Relationship between duration of urethane or pentobarbitone anaesthesia in male and female rats and adenohypophysial response to luteinising hormone-releasing hormone. *Br. J. Pharmacol.*, 69: 139–143.

Dyer, R.G. and Weick, R.F. (1981) A preparation suitable for recording the activity of single neurones during the LH surge in the rat. *J. Physiol. (London)*, 319: 14–15P.

Dyer, R.G., MacLeod, N.K. and Ellendorff, F. (1976) Electrophysiological evidence for sexual dimorphism and synaptic convergence in the preoptic and anterior hypothalamic areas of the rat. *Proc. R. Soc. Lond. B*, 193: 421–440.

Everett, J.W. (1964) Central neural control of reproductive functions of the adenohypophysis. *Physiol. Behav.*, 44: 373–431.

Everett, J.W. (1969) Neuroendocrine aspects of mammalian reproduction. *Annu. Rev. Physiol.*, 31: 383–416.

Everett, J.W. and Sawyer, C.H. (1950) A 24-hours periodicity in the "LH-release apparatus" of female rats, disclosed by barbiturate sedation. *Endocrinology*, 47: 198–218.

Everett, J.W., Sawyer, C.H. and Markee, J.E. (1949) A neurogenic timing factor in control of the ovulatory discharge of luteinising hormone in the cyclic rat. *Endocrinology*, 44: 234–250.

Fifkova, E. and Anderson, C.L. (1981) Stimulation-induced changes in dimensions of stalks of dendritic spines in the dentate molecular layer. *Exp. Neurol.*, 74: 621–627.

Fifkova, E. and Van Harreveld, A. (1977) Long-lasting morphological changes in dendritic spines of dentate granular cells following stimulation of the entorhinal area. *J. Neurocytol.*, 6: 211–230.

Fink, G., Chiappa, S.A. and Aiyer, M.S. (1976) Priming effect of luteinising hormone releasing factor elicited by preoptic stimulation and by intravenous infusion and multiple injections of the synthetic decapeptide. *J. Endocrinol.*, 69: 359–372.

Gorski, R.A. (1971) Gonadal hormones and the perinatal development of neuroendocrine function. In: L. Martini and W.F. Ganong (Eds.), *Frontiers in Neuroendocrinology*, Oxford University Press, New York, pp. 237–290.

Gorski, R.A. (1973) Perinatal effects of sex steroids on brain development and function. *Progr. Brain Res.*, 39: 149–162.

Gorski, R.A. (1984) Critical role for the medial preoptic area in the sexual differentiation of the brain. In: G.J. De Vries, J.P.C. De Bruin, H.B.M. Uylings and M.A. Corner (Eds.), *Sex Differences in the Brain. The Relation between Structure and Function. Progress in Brain Research*, this volume, Ch. 7.

Gorski, R.A., Gordon, J.H., Shryne, J.E. and Southam, A.M. (1978) Evidence for a morphological sex difference within the medial preoptic areas of the rat brain. *Brain Res.*, 148: 333–346.

Gorski, R.A., Harlan, R.E., Jacobson, C.D., Shryne, J.E. and Southam, A.M. (1980) Evidence for the existence of a sexually dimorphic nucleus in the preoptic area of the rat. *J. Comp. Neurol.*, 193: 529–539.

Harris, G.W. (1964) Sex hormones, brain development and brain function. *Endocrinology*, 75: 627–648.

Harris, G.W. and Jacobsohn, D. (1952) Functional grafts of the anterior pituitary gland. *Proc. Soc. Lond. B*, 139: 263–276.

Hatton, G.I. and Tweedle, C.D. (1982) Magnocellular neuropeptidergic neurons in hypothalamus: increase in membrane apposition and number of specialised synapses from pregnancy to lactation. *Brain Res. Bull.*, 8: 197–204.

Hatton, G.I., Perlmutter, L.S., Salm, A.K. and Tweedle, D. (1984) Dynamic neuronal-glial interactions in hypothalamus and pituitary: implications for control of hormone synthesis and release. *Peptides*, in Press.

Heschl, R. (1878) Abstract translated by D. Kimura and referred to by J. McClone (1980) *Behav. Brain Sci.*, 3: 215–263.

Koch, C. and Poggio, T. (1983) A theoretical analysis of electrical properties of spines. *Proc. R. Soc. Lond. B*, 218: 455–477.

Levine, J.E. and Ramirez, V.D. (1982) Luteinising hormone-releasing hormone release during the rat estrous cycle and after ovariectomy, as estimated with push-pull cannulae. *Endocrinology*, 111: 1439–1448.

Matsumoto, A. and Arai, Y. (1976) Developmental changes in synaptic formation in the hypothalamic arcuate nucleus of female rats. *Cell Tissue Res.*, 169: 143–156.

Matsumoto, A. and Arai, Y. (1980) Sexual dimorphism in 'wiring pattern' in the hypothalamic arcuate nucleus and its modification by neonatal hormonal environment. *Brain Res.*, 190: 238–242.

Neill, J.D. (1972) Sexual difference in the hypothalamic regulation of prolactin secretion. *Endocrinology*, 90: 1154–1159.

Neumann, F. and Kramer, M. (1967) Female brain differentiation of male rats as a result of early treatment with an androgen antagonist. In: L. Martini, F. Fraschini and M. Motta (Eds.), *Hormonal Steroids*, Excerpta Medica, Amsterdam, pp. 932–941.

Raisman, G. and Field, P.M. (1971) Sexual dimorphism in the preoptic area of the rat. *Science*, 173: 731–733.

Raisman, G. and Field, P.M. (1973a) Sexual dimorphism in the neuropil of the preoptic area of the rat and its dependence on neonatal androgen. *Brain Res.*, 54: 1–29.

Raisman, G. and Field, P.M. (1973b) A quantitative investigation of the development of collateral reinnervation after partial deafferentation of the septal nuclei. *Brain Res.*, 50: 241–264.

Rall, W. (1974) Dendritic spines, synaptic potency and neuronal plasticity. *Brain Inf. Serv. Res. Rep.*, 3: 13–21.

Saphier, D.J. and Dyer, R.G. (1980) Bursting activity in tuberoinfundibular neurones during electrical stimulation of the rostral hypothalamus. *Exp. Brain Res.*, 39: 113–116.

Savoy-Moore, R.T., Schwartz, N.B., Duncan, J.A. and Marshall, J.C. (1980) Pituitary gonadotrophin-releasing hormone receptors during the rat estrous cycle. *Science*, 209: 942–944

Sheridan, P.J., Sar, M. and Stumpf, W.E. (1974) Autoradiographic localisation of ^{3}H-estradiol or its metabolites in the central nervous system of the developing rat. *Endocrinology*, 94: 1386–1390.

Swanson, H.E. and Van der Werff ten Bosch, J.J. (1964) The "early androgen" syndrome; differences in response to pre-natal and post-natal administration of various doses of testosterone propionate in female and male rats. *Acta Endocrinol.*, 47: 37–50.

Swindale, N.V. (1981) Dendritic spines only connect. *Trends Neurosci.*, 4: 240–241.

Theodosis, D.T. and Poulain, D.A. (1983) Evidence for structural plasticity in the supraoptic nucleus of the rat hypothalamus in relation to gestation and lactation. *Neuroscience*, in press.

Van Harreveld, A. and Fifkova, E. (1975) Swelling of dendritic spines in the fascia dentata after stimulation of the perforant fibres as a mechanism of post-tetanic potentiation. *Exp Neurol.*, 49: 736–749.

Velasco, M.E. and Taleisnik, S. (1969) Release of gonadotropins induced by amygdaloid stimulation in the rat. *Endocrinology*, 84: 132–139.

Weick, R.F. and Dyer, R.G. (1982) Stimulation of single unit activity in the preoptic area and anterior hypothalamus, and secretion of luteinising hormone, by ovarian steroids in ovariectomised rats with diencephalic islands. *Proc. R. Soc. Lond. B*, 216: 461–473.

DISCUSSION

J.C. KING: The area of stimulation in the preoptic area in the rat is one in which there is a large accumulation of LHRH neurones. These cells may not only send their fibres to the median eminence but also their collaterals to the arcuate nucleus. You may be stimulating these neurones directly.

R.G. DYER: Of course electrical stimulation in the preoptic area should activate the LHRH-containing neurones that you and others have shown to be present in the rostral hypothalamus. I did not say, or mean to imply, that I thought the bursting activity we recorded in tuberoinfundibular neurones was obtained from LHRH-secreting cells. We did the experiments to assess that these neurosecretory cells might fire when a pathway projecting to them is excited. Most of the tuberoinfundibular neurones that generated bursting activity were recorded outside the arcuate nucleus. Cells in the arcuate nucleus were often inhibited during MPOA/AHA stimulation and these are good candidates to be the dopamine (prolactin-inhibitory factor-secreting neurones. Therefore the other tuberoinfundibular neurones are likely to be peptide secreting. It is noteworthy that bursting activity may be a characteristic of all peptide-secreting cells when they are stimulated to release their hormone.

The fact remains, however, that LHRH-containing cells have been shown to exist in the mediobasal hypothalamus of the rat and there is substantial physiological evidence to support the view that they must have an important role. Questions to be answered now are first, do the different populations of LHRH-containing neurones have different functions? Second, are all LHRH-containing neurones equal in their capacity to release hormone? Third, is there a population of LHRH-secreting neurones that is so active that they have minimal stores and are thus not detected by immunohistochemical techniques?

J.C. KING: The data regarding the amount of peptide released may be very important in ascertaining the role of LHRH neurones which are present in the mediobasal hypothalamus. We have previously shown (King et al., 1980) that about 30% of LHRH population is present there. These data will allow us to examine the role of subpopulations of this diffuse LHRH population in various endocrine states.

D.W. PFAFF: If from endocrine physiological points you suspect there are LHRH-producing cells in MBH, what acounts for the relative difficulty of immunocytochemistry in showing these cells?

R.G. DYER: Yes, I do think that there is substantial physiological evidence to support the view that all of the LHRH neurones in the rat are unlikely to be in the medial preoptic area. First, complete destruction of the medial preoptic area abolishes only the preovulatory LH surge. Basal secretion continues normally, thus ovariectomy in rats with a lesioned preoptic area results in elevated LH secretion. Second, cuts between the preoptic area and mediobasal hypothalamus, which would be expected to sever the axons of the LHRH neurones projecting down to the median eminence, block only the preovulatory LH surge. Pulsatile LH secretion is normal. My position is that it is unreasonable to jettison the conclusions that may be drawn from these experiments on the basis of the inability to demonstrate LHRH-containing pericarya in the mediobasal hypothalamus.

As to accounting for the "relative difficulty" in staining LHRH neurones, the problems have been discussed many times before. However, I think one should be uneasy about any answers that depend so substantially upon the antisera used. We know that in the rat the same laboratory will find a very different distribution of stained LHRH-containing cell bodies when they use a variety of apparently good antisera to the decapeptide. In any case, what does the immunofluorescence actually mean? If cells are active, and therefore discharge their contents rapidly without allowing stores to build up, they may not be stained. Perhaps the only detectable LHRH neurones are those which are not very active. Hopefully future work in this field will follow in the direction that you have embarked upon and try to relate intensity of fluorescence with physiological states. In the meantime I suggest that every immunohistochemist writes the motto "Lack of evidence is not necessarily evidence of lack" on the wall above his or her desk!

D.W. PFAFF: For the reduction in numbers of electrical pulses from MPOA to tuberoinfundibular cells, were you calculating for the individual cells your electrode sampled, or for the total arcuate nucleus?

R.G. DYER: It was not a calculation for the arcuate nucleus as a whole. We do not have the data to make such a calculation. In fact many of the tuberoinfundibular neurones were recorded outside of the arcuate nucleus. This applies especially to those that were excited by MPOA/AHA stimulation. It is of considerable interest to us that this stimulation usually inhibited neurones recorded within the arcuate nucleus, and since MPOA/AHA stimulation releases prolactin we think that the inhibited neurones are good candidates to be the prolactin-inhibiting factor-releasing cells.

The evidence for the transmission loss between MPOA/AHA and tuberoinfundibular neurones was derived from noting the total number of stimulus pulses applied to MPOA/AHA and finding that the tuberoinfundibular neurone was excited to this extent. In fact during the 50-Hz stimulation in MPOA/AHA, which continued for 30 sec, no recorded cell ever fired at this frequency for even 1 sec.

D.F. SWAAB: Are you able to synthesise your data in such a way that it might give us an idea about the amount of information concealed in the frequency of the firing rate and in the pattern of firing? (Cf. the increased efficiency of AVP release using the natural firing pattern.)

R.G. DYER: This might be a dangerous calculation to make at the present time. I say this because the example I have given showed that LH secretion could not be increased at all when the median eminence was stimulated at a constant 6 Hz. Increased secretion only occurred when an average of 6 Hz was applied in the form of bursts of activity. Thus one could calculate that the pattern was all important. Such a conclusion would of course be wrong since we know that, at higher frequencies, steady stimulation can increase LH secretion. At the present time I can state only that the patterning is likely to be of considerable importance.

C.D. TORAN-ALLERAND: Matsumoto and Arai (1981) showed that in ovariectomised deafferented females oestrogen elicits an increase in synaptogenesis in the arcuate nucleus. In your deafferented model, do you think that such a phenomenon may be playing a role in your responses?

R.G. DYER: I have no data to provide an answer to this question. The steroid-primed hypothalamic island model we used certainly allowed us to investigate the electrical activation of MPOA/AHA neurones during steroid-stimulated LH secretion. However, the amounts of LH released were substantially less than we normally obtain in our rats, after ovariectomy and subsequent priming with oestrogen and progesterone. This may be because of damage resulting from the surgery or removal of structures normally involved in stimulating the LH surge or possibly even inappropriate synaptogenesis in the arcuate nucleus.

REFERENCES

King, J.C., Tobet, S.A., Snavely, F.L. and Arimura, A.A. (1980) The LHRH system in normal and neonatally androgenized female rats. *Peptides*, 1, Suppl. 1: 85–100.
Matsumoto, A. and Arai, Y. (1981) Neuronal plasticity in the deafferented hypothalamic arcuate nucleus of adult female rats and its enhancement by treatment with estrogen. *J. Comp. Neurol.*, 197: 197–205.

SECTION 3

FUNCTIONAL SEX DIFFERENCES IN THE BRAIN

G.J. De Vries et al. (Eds.),
Progress in Brain Research, Vol. 61
© 1984 Elsevier Science Publishers B.V., Amsterdam

Lordosis as a Sexually Dimorphic Neural Function

RICHARD E. HARLAN, BRENDA D. SHIVERS and DONALD W. PFAFF

The Rockefeller University, 1230 York Avenue, New York, NY 10021 (U.S.A.)

INTRODUCTION

The study of sex differences in brain structure or function aids our understanding of the nervous system in at least two ways. First, detailed examination of sex differences in a neural circuit of known behavioral or physiological function may provide insight regarding those aspects of the neural circuit that are critically involved in the display of the function under question. Secondly, sexual differentiation is a process fundamental to development, so that understanding it better may lead to a deeper insight into the general processes involved in differentiation and specialization of nerve cells and their patterns of connectivity.

There are two general approaches to the study of sex differences within the nervous system. In one approach, researchers examine the nervous system for sex differences in any parameter which can be measured with available techniques. Once a sex difference has been found, attempts are made to relate it to known sexually dimorphic functions. Many parameters in mammalian brains are indeed sexually dimorphic, and the list is growing rapidly. Since many of these sexually dimorphic parameters are discussed in detail in other chapters of this volume, no attempt will be made here to review this literature.

The second overall approach to the study of sex differences in the nervous system begins with documentation of a sexually dimorphic neural function, especially one which is extreme in its dimorphism. One can then study in detail the neural circuitry underlying this function, especially in the sex in which it is best displayed. Given a detailed description of the physiology, anatomy and biochemistry of this circuit, one can then try to determine where, within it, the sex difference(s) reside. This is the approach that we have adopted, and the sexually dimorphic function that we study is the lordosis response, displayed by sexually receptive female rats.

LORDOSIS AS A SEXUALLY DIMORPHIC FUNCTION

In rats, lordosis is a stereotyped reflex consisting of dorsiflexion (extension) of the vertebral column, which produces an elevation of the head and the hind quarters region (Pfaff and Lewis, 1974; Pfaff et al., 1978). Accompanying this vertebral dorsiflexion is a slight extension of the hind limbs. This posture facilitates intromission by male rats. It can be quantified easily either by tests with male rats (resulting in a lordosis quotient: percentage of male mounts that result in lordosis) or by a manual stimulation technique (resulting in a lordosis reflex score: degree of dorsiflexion; Pfaff et al., 1977; Harlan et al., 1982a). We have utilized the manual stimulation technique extensively, and have found that the technique produces reliable and reproducible results (Harlan et al., 1983a,b).

That lordotic responsiveness in rats is highly sexually dimorphic has been known for many years (Barraclough and Gorski, 1962; Harris and Levine, 1965). In the strain of rats that we commonly use (derived from Sprague–Dawley), female rats readily display maximal lordosis when given appropriate steroid hormones, whereas male rats, given the same steroid treatment, display little or no lordosis. The availability of gonadal steroids during a perinatal "critical period" is crucial for the development of this sex difference (Gorski, 1971; Harlan et al., 1979). Thus, a careful examination of the mechanisms underlying this sex difference in lordotic responsiveness in adult rats should provide insight into the process of sexual differentiation of the brain.

In addition to the extreme sexual dimorphism in lordotic responsiveness, there are several advantages to studying lordosis. First of all, the behavior is of vital importance to reproduction, and thus plays a central role in the behavioral repertoire of this species. Secondly, lordosis is a reflex, i.e. a motor response which occurs at a more or less constant interval following application of appropriate sensory stimuli (Pfaff et al., 1977). The sensory stimuli needed to elicit lordosis are well defined, consisting of pressure on the flanks and perineal region (Pfaff et al., 1977; Kow et al., 1979). It can therefore be elicited "on demand". Moreover, the neural circuitry controlling this reflex can be reduced to an input–output relationship, thus greatly facilitating a systematic analysis of the neural circuitry. An additional advantage is that in the strain of rats which we use, lordotic responsiveness does not vary as a function of time of day (Harlan et al., 1980). Finally, lordosis is entirely dependent on prior exposure of the brain to gonadal steroids. During the estrous cycle, lordotic responsiveness is induced by an interaction between estrogen and progesterone, but full lordotic responsiveness can be induced in ovariectomized rats by the administration of estradiol alone (Davidson et al., 1968; Pfaff, 1980). Elimination of the interaction between the two steroids greatly facilitates the investigation into the mechanism of estrogenic action on the brain. Moreover, research into the effects of estrogen upon brain function may provide new insights into one of the most basic biological processes, viz. the interactions between endocrine and nervous systems.

RELATIONSHIP BETWEEN THE ENDOCRINE AND NERVOUS SYSTEMS

Two regulatory systems have evolved in vertebrates in order to facilitate such functions as homeostasis and transmission of genetic information to offspring, i.e. the endocrine and nervous systems. These two systems interact in a variety of ways, and a study of this interaction should yield new insights into information-processing capabilities in the nervous system. Both the nervous and endocrine systems handle information, but the forms of information as well as the response properties of the cells involved differ markedly. The nervous system responds rapidly (in a millisecond time frame), habituates rapidly and is responsive to discrete signals; it transmits information to a limited number of cells at highly localized points, the synapses. The endocrine system responds much more slowly (in a time frame of minutes to hours to days), habituates slowly and is responsive to continuous signals (usually in the form of circulating hormones); it transmits information (or potential information) to all cells of the body, via the systemic circulation.

Since the two systems handle different forms of information, there is a requirement for cells at the interface that transduces the information handled by one system into a form recognizable by cells in the other system. Moreover, since information is transduced from the nervous to the endocrine system, and vice versa, such transducer cells must be of at least two functional types. One of these cell types has been defined previously by Wurtman (1973) as the *neuroendocrine transducer*, i.e. a cell which transduces neural signals into an endocrine output (Fig. 1). Two examples of neuroendocrine transducers are cells in the adrenal medulla (which transduce preganglionic sympathetic nerve impulses into catecholamine release into the systemic circulation), and the magnocellular neurosecretory cells of the supraoptic and paraventricular nuclei (which transduce a variety of neural signals into secretion of oxytocin and vasopressin from the posterior pituitary). Certain nerve cells, in turn, respond to circulating hormones, transducing endocrine signals into a form recognizable by nerve cells. These hormone-responsive cells can be called *endocrineural transducers* (Fig. 1).

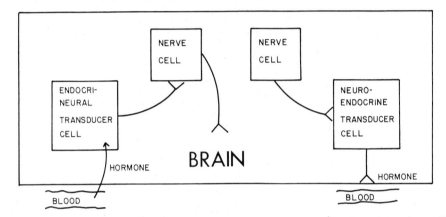

Fig. 1. Schematic of interfaces between the nervous and endocrine systems. Endocrineural transducer cells are sensitive to hormones in the circulation and transduce this information into a form recognizable by other nerve cells. Neuroendocrine transducer cells receive input from nerve cells and transduce this information into endocrine signals released into the blood stream.

Particular advantages and disadvantages are found for the study of neuroendocrine and endocrineural transducers. For neuroendocrine transducers, the nature of the output information is easily determined since the output can be readily measured in the blood, but since the cells may be embedded in a matrix of hundreds of thousands of synaptic inputs, the inputs to these cells are generally difficult to study. For endocrineural transducers, the reverse is the case; the cells usually can be characterized on the basis of their output (e.g., accumulation of radiolabeled hormones from the circulation) but the nature of the neural signals generated by endocrineural transducer cells is not so easily characterized. From an understanding of some of the response characteristics of the nervous and endocrine systems, as sketched above, some predictions can be made about the response properties of endocrineural transducers. For instance, one would predict that endocrineural transducer cells respond to slowly changing (or even static) signals, but that the output information is transmitted locally at synapses. Moreover, the secretory products released at such synapses might retain the characteristics of a prolonged duration of action, thus transmitting information about slowly changing or static input. As will be described in detail, the hypothalamic cells which respond to estrogen and are necessary for lordosis appear to display several of these predicted properties of endocrineural transducer cells.

THE NEURAL CIRCUITRY CONTROLLING LORDOSIS

Given that lordosis is a hormonally induced reflex, the simplest possible model for lordosis-relevant neural circuitry consists of an "integrator" which (a) responds to appropriate somatosensory input, (b) triggers a motor output (lordosis) and (c) is responsive to circulating hormones. Within this "integrator", however, must be some fairly complicated neural circuitry. Much detail has been added in recent years to our understanding of this neural circuitry, and although a detailed summary of the experiments which have led to this model is beyond the scope of this chapter, its basic elements can be described (Fig. 2). Somatosensory input is illustrated as stimuli applied to the flanks, rump, tailbase and perineum. Motor output is represented by spinal motoneurons innervating the lateral longissimus and the transversospinalis muscle systems. Hormonal input is shown as estradiol action on cells in the medial preoptic, medial anterior hypothalamic and ventromedial hypothalamic areas. These cells project to the midbrain and central grey, stimulation of which elicits lordosis-like movements (Pfaff et al., 1973). In addition, inhibition of electrical activity by microinfusion of anesthetics or tetrodotoxin (TTX) locally into the dorsal

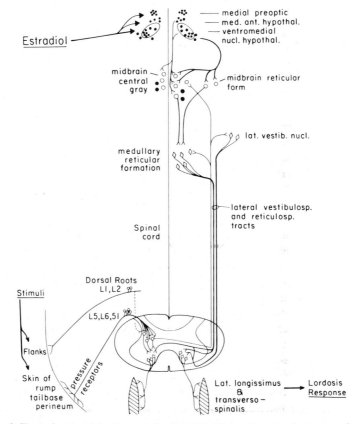

Fig. 2. Schematic illustrating the minimal neural circuitry for lordosis. Although stimuli, responses, circuitry and hormone effects are all bilateral, they are shown on one side only, for convenience. From Pfaff (1980), reprinted by permission.

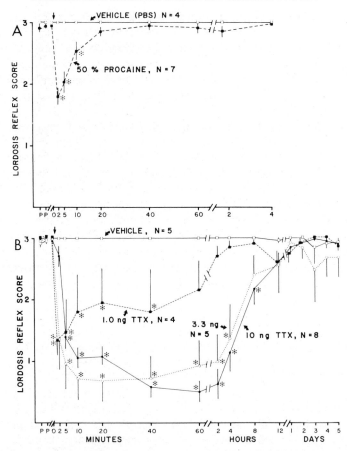

Fig. 3. Effect on lordotic responsiveness of microinfusion of vehicle, 50% procaine (A) or different doses of tetrodotoxin (B). Vertical lines are standard errors of the means. Asterisks indicate significant differences ($P < 0.05$ or less, Mann-Whitney U tests) from vehicle-infused rats. Procedures were as described in Harlan et al. (1983a,b). P, pretests conducted 10–45 min prior to microinfusion (arrows); TTX, tetrodotoxin.

midbrain resulted in an immediate decrease in lordotic responsiveness, with recovery to preinfusion levels by 20 min after infusion when 50% procaine was used, or by 1–12 h depending on the dose when TTX was used (Fig. 3).

Within the neural circuit controlling lordosis as it is now understood, we can make some speculations about possible sites of sexual differentiation. Since many sexually dimorphic functions are also hormonally responsive (Harlan et al., 1979), a good place to begin an analysis of possible sex differences would be those cells in the preoptic area and medial hypothalamus that respond to estrogen in such a manner as to result in facilitation of lordosis. Moreover, analysis of properties of these estrogen-responsive cells should provide greater insight into the properties of endocrineural transducers. For these reasons, discussion of the neural circuitry underlying lordosis will be limited to those neurons that respond to estrogen and produce signals which are transmitted to other parts of the brain, especially the midbrain.

Cells that can respond genomically to estrogen can be identified autoradiographically following systemic administration of tritiated estradiol (Pfaff, 1968; Pfaff and Keiner, 1973).

A specific subset of these estrogen-concentrating cells is critical for lordosis, as determined by lesions, knife cuts and localized hormone implants (Pfaff, 1980). The primary site in the brain at which estrogen acts (to increase lordotic responsiveness) consists of cells in the mediobasal hypothalamus, especially in the ventrolateral portion of the ventromedial nuclei, and the surrounding cells. The pathways by which "lordosis-relevant" hypothalamic cells transmit information to other brain cells have been determined anatomically, by retrograde and orthograde filling of neurons (Saper et al., 1976; Kreiger et al., 1979; Morrell et al., 1981) and behaviorally, by strategic placement of knife cuts (Malsbury and Daood, 1978; Phelps and Nance, 1979; Manogue et al., 1980; Edwards and Pfeifle, 1981). Hypothalamic projections to the dorsal midbrain, in and around the central grey, are of critical importance to lordosis. Moreover, a substantial portion of the estrogen-concentrating cells in the ventromedial nucleus project directly to the dorsal midbrain (Morrell and Pfaff, 1982). Mediobasal hypothalamic outputs to the midbrain central grey follow two major pathways (Saper et al., 1976; Kreiger et al., 1979); (a) laterally across the supraoptic commissures, around the dorsolateral aspect of the thalamus, and then medially to the central grey; (b) medially, following the trajectory of the caudal portion of the third ventricles as it moves dorsally to form the cerebral aqueduct. Although both pathways appear to be involved in lordosis, the lateral projection is quantitatively more critical (Manogue et al., 1980).

HOW DO HYPOTHALAMIC NERVE CELLS RESPOND TO ESTROGEN SO AS TO FACILITATE LORDOSIS?

Concentrating on the hypothalamic projections to midbrain, we have begun to question the cellular responses to estrogen that are necessary for lordosis. Although it is difficult to test the hypothesis directly, all available evidence suggests that concentration of estradiol by the nuclei of hypothalamic cells is a necessary step in the production of lordosis (Pfaff, 1980). Current models of estrogenic action indicate that nuclear concentration of estradiol promotes transcription of RNA, leading to new protein synthesis (O'Malley and Means, 1974; McEwen et al., 1979). Consistent with the hypothesis that estrogenic action on nerve cells involves RNA synthesis is the finding that intrahypothalamic infusion of actinomycin D, which blocks DNA-dependent RNA synthesis (Samuels, 1964), attenuates the effect of estrogen on lordosis (Quadagno et al., 1971; Terkel et al., 1973; Shivers et al., 1980). Moreover, recent ultrastructural evidence indicates that estrogen modifies the morphology of the nucleoli of certain mediobasal hypothalamic cells, suggesting that increased ribosomal RNA synthesis occurs following treatment with estradiol (Cohen and Pfaff, 1982).

That protein synthesis is necessary for the estrogenic induction of lordosis is indicated by the inhibitory effects of intrahypothalamic administration of protein synthesis inhibitors (Quadagno and Ho, 1975; Rainbow et al., 1980). Ultrastructural studies demonstrating an extension of the rough endoplasmic reticulum and Golgi apparatus further suggest a stimulatory action of estrogen on protein synthesis of many cells in the mediobasal hypothalamus (Cohen and Pfaff, 1981; Carrer and Aoki, 1982). The full range of proteins synthesized in hypothalamic cells in response to estrogen has not been determined. Two examples of proteins whose synthesis rates are altered in brain cells by estrogen are (i) enzymes involved in neurotransmitter synthesis (Luine et al., 1974, 1975; Luine and Rhodes, 1983) and (ii) receptor molecules for progesterone (Blaustein and Feder, 1979; MacLusky and McEwen, 1980).

Since hypothalamic cells involved in lordosis send projections to the dorsal midbrain, we addressed the question as to whether axoplasmic transport of substances out of the hypothalamus is necessary for estrogenic action on lordosis (Harlan et al., 1982a). We microinfused colchicine, which blocks fast axoplasmic transport (Schwartz, 1980), into the mediobasal hypothalamus 24 h before administration of estrogen to ovariectomized rats. This treatment indeed resulted in a 2-day delay in the induction of lordotic responsiveness, in comparison

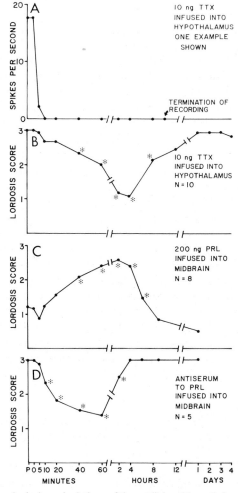

Fig. 4. Summary of pharmacological manipulations of the mediobasal hypothalamus (A, B) or dorsal midbrain (C, D). (A) Effect on hypothalamic multiunit activity of hypothalamic microinfusion of tetrodotoxin (TTX). Data from 1 Expt. are illustrated schematically, and are representative of the result obtained in 5 out of 6 Expts. involving this dose of TTX. Data from Harlan et al. (1983b). (B) Effect on lordotic responsiveness of hypothalamic microinfusion of TTX. Data from Harlan et al. (1983b). (C) Effect on lordotic responsiveness of microinfusion of prolactin into the dorsal midbrain in estrogen-treated rats displaying low-to-moderate lordosis. Data from Harlan et al. (1983a). (D) Effect on lordotic responsiveness of microinfusion of antiserum to prolactin into the dorsal midbrain of estrogen-treated rats displaying maximal lordosis. Data from Harlan et al. (1983a). The error bars have been eliminated, for convenience. Abbreviations: P, pretest conducted 10–30 min prior to microinfusion; PRL, prolactin; TTX, tetrodotoxin. Asterisks indicate significant differences ($P < 0.05$ or less; Mann–Whitney U tests) from vehicle-infused rats (not shown).

with rats infused with vehicle only. Similar intrahypothalamic microinfusion of colchicine into rats displaying maximal lordotic responsiveness due to prolonged administration of estrogen, resulted in a disruption of lordotic responsiveness lasting for several days. In neither estrogen treatment group did microinfusion of colchicine into the dorsal thalamus affect lordosis, indicating that the lordosis-disrupting effect of intrahypothalamic colchicine infusion was not due to widespread neuronal damage. The simplest interpretation of these data is that fast axoplasmic transport of substances in hypothalamic cells is a necessary factor in estrogenic action on lordosis.

In the extensively studied optic nerve and peripheral nervous system, substances carried by fast axoplasmic transport are contained within vesicles and are usually either involved in neurosecretion or are the secreted products themselves (Lorenz and Willard, 1978; Tytell et al., 1981). Given a rich body of literature on stimulus secretion coupling, it is reasonable to predict that lordosis-relevant hypothalamic substances might be released within the dorsal midbrain in response to action potentials. We have therefore addressed the requirement for hypothalamic action potentials in mediating estrogenic actions upon lordosis (Harlan et al., 1983b). We were able to decrease multiunit electrical activity (MUA) in the mediobasal hypothalamus by microinfusion of local anesthetics, which produced MUA decreases for periods ranging from about 5 min to an hour, but had no effect whatsoever on lordosis. In contrast, microinfusion of TTX into the hypothalamus eliminated MUA within a few minutes, lasting several hours (Fig. 4A), with a concomitant disruption of lordotic responsiveness (Fig. 4B). It is noteworthy that, despite the rapid suppression of hypothalamic MUA, a significant decrease in lordotic responsiveness occurred only 40 min after the intrahypothalamic microinfusion. Lordosis reflex scores then continued to drop, reaching a minimum 2–4 h after infusion of TTX, and recovery of lordotic responsiveness to preinfusion levels was complete by 12–24 h after infusion. Microinfusion of TTX into the dorsal thalamus had no effect on lordosis, which is consistent with the notion that hypothalamic action potentials are necessary for estrogenic action on lordosis. Presumably release of neurosecretory products from midbrain terminals of hypothalamic cells occurs in response to action potentials, and this release in turn facilitates the lordosis mechanisms. Since midbrain microinfusion of procaine or TTX resulted in an immediate inhibition of lordosis (Fig. 3), it is likely that neurosecretory products of hypothalamic origin released in the midbrain have a prolonged duration of action.

PEPTIDES INVOLVED IN THE SUPPORT
OF HYPOTHALAMIC CONTROL OF LORDOSIS

The data described above are consistent with the hypothesis that at least part of the action of estrogen on lordosis-relevant hypothalamic cells is mediated through synthesis of substances, some of which are transported to terminals within the midbrain where one or more are released in response to the arrival of action potentials. Once released, these neurosecretory products have a prolonged duration of action on midbrain cells. A question of major importance becomes: What are these lordosis-facilitating neurosecretory products released by hypothalamic projections to the midbrain? We have investigated several neural peptides as candidates for these lordosis-relevant neurosecretory products.

About a decade ago, evidence was presented that the peptide luteinizing hormone-releasing hormone (LHRH) could facilitate lordotic responsiveness when given systemically (Moss and McCann, 1973; Pfaff, 1973). More recent studies have indicated that the midbrain central grey is a primary neural site at which LHRH facilitates lordosis (Riskind and Moss, 1979; Sakuma and Pfaff, 1980, 1983). Release of endogenous LHRH appears in fact to be necessary for lordosis, since infusion of antibodies to LHRH into the midbrain central grey decreases lordotic responsiveness (Sakuma and Pfaff, 1980, 1983). LHRH-containing fibers have been demonstrated within the midbrain central grey (Liposits and Sétáló, 1980; Witkin et al., 1982; Shivers et al., 1983a), which is further support for a role of this peptide in lordosis. However, extensive immunocytochemical screening of brains for LHRH-containing cell bodies within the mediobasal hypothalamus has been largely negative (Witkin et al., 1982; Shivers et al., 1983a,d). The great majority of LHRH cell bodies is found in the diagonal band of Broca, the medial preoptic area and the anterior hypothalamic area, especially immediately dorsal to the supraoptic nuclei. The population of LHRH neurons in the mediobasal hypothalamus seems to be insufficient to account fully for the lordosis-facilitating effect of estrogen on this part of the brain.

A much larger population of mediobasal hypothalamic neurons produces pro-opiomelanocortin (POMC) and its biologically active fragments (Watson et al., 1977; Bloom et al., 1978; Nilaver et al., 1979) and these cells provide a substantial projection to the midbrain central grey (Bloom et al., 1978; Finley et al., 1981). Both α-MSH (Thody et al., 1979) and ACTH, as well as fragments (Wilson et al., 1979), have been reported to affect lordotic responsiveness when given systemically, but, in our studies, microinfusion of $ACTH_{1-24}$ into the dorsal midbrain had no effect on lordosis (Harlan et al., 1983a). Microinfusion of β-endorphin into the midbrain central grey has been reported to decrease lordotic responsiveness, perhaps by decreasing endogenous release of LHRH from terminals (Sirinathsinghji et al., 1983). Suppression of lordotic responsiveness following infusion of β-endorphin into the third ventricle has also been reported (Weisner and Moss, 1982). Although additional POMC-derived peptides have not been tested for effects on lordosis, the peptides that have been tested to date do not appear to meet the criteria for concluding that they are produced within hypothalamic cell bodies, transported to the midbrain and released there at the appropriate target sites.

Stimulated by a report of a prolactin-like substance in cell bodies in the mediobasal hypothalamus and in fibers in the midbrain central grey (Toubeau et al., 1979), we have investigated the candidacy of prolactin as a lordosis-facilitating peptide (Harlan et al., 1983a). Microinfusion of prolactin into the dorsal midbrain of estrogen-treated rats displaying low-to-moderate levels of lordosis greatly facilitated lordotic responsiveness, with a latency of about 40 min (Fig. 4C). Maximal lordotic responsiveness was reached about 90 min after microinfusion, and returned to the level of vehicle-infused rats by about 6 h after infusion. Microinfusion of growth hormone, oxytocin, vasopressin or $ACTH_{1-24}$ into the dorsal midbrain had no effect on lordosis, nor did microinfusion of prolactin into the cerebral cortex overlying the midbrain. To address the question as to whether or not endogenous release of a prolactin-like substance is necessary for lordosis, we microinfused anti-prolactin immune serum into the dorsal midbrain of estrogen-treated rats which displayed a maximal lordosis response. This infusion decreased lordotic responsiveness, beginning about 10 min after infusion and lasting for more than 2 h (Fig. 4D). Infusion of normal rabbit serum had no effect.

We have also confirmed and greatly extended the immunocytochemical localization of immunoreactive (ir) prolactin in the rat brain (Harlan et al., 1983a; Shivers et al., 1983c). Cell bodies containing ir prolactin (Fig. 5) have been located exclusively in the mediobasal hypothalamus, viz. in the arcuate nuclei and in a band extending ventral and lateral to the ventromedial nuclei. Immunopositive cell bodies have been found in all tissue sections from

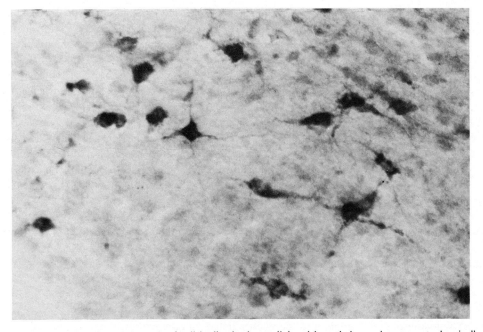

Fig. 5. Bright-field photomicrograph of cell bodies in the mediobasal hypothalamus immunocytochemically stained with antiserum to prolactin obtained from the National Hormone and Pituitary Program, and diluted 1 : 1000. The antigen was visualized by the avidin-biotin system and diaminobenzidine.

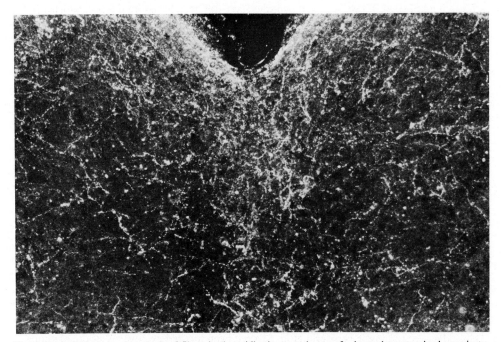

Fig. 6. Dark-field photomicrograph of fibers in the midbrain central grey of a hypophysectomized, ovariectomized rat, immunocytochemically stained with antiserum to prolactin, as indicated in legend to Fig. 5. The ventral edge of the cerebral aqueduct can be seen in the top center of the photograph.

the retrochiasmatic area up to the caudal extent of the mammillary recess, and we have estimated that 2000–3000 ir prolactin cell bodies exist in the hypothalamus. Fibers containing ir prolactin have been found throughout the brain, from olfactory regions of the forebrain to the sacral spinal cord. The midbrain central grey is particularly rich in immunocytochemically stained fibers (Fig. 6), many of which branch extensively to form what appears at the light microscopical level to be terminals surrounding midbrain cells. Ir prolactin fibers take both medial and lateral pathways from the hypothalamus to the midbrain central grey, a finding which fits very well with previous anatomical studies (Saper et al., 1976; Kreiger et al., 1979) and which is consistent with a role of ir prolactin in the neural mechanisms controlling lordosis.

These data support the candidacy of a prolactin-like substance as a product produced by hypothalamic cell bodies, transported to the midbrain central grey, and there released in such a way as to facilitate lordosis. Is this prolactin-like substance really prolactin? We have approached this question with two methods. In one approach, we have immunoprecipitated ir prolactin from the hypothalamus and electrophoresed the immunoprecipitate on an SDS/polyacrylamide gel in order to determine the apparent molecular weight. In preliminary studies, the molecular weight of the brain ir prolactin appears to be indistinguishable from that of pituitary prolactin. Given the presence of the latter in the circulation perfusing the brain, it will be necessary to repeat our findings in hypophysectomized animals. It should be noted, however, that immunocytochemically visualized ir prolactin remains in the brain for at least several months following hypophysectomy (unpublished observations; Fuxe et al., 1977; Toubeau et al., 1979).

In a second approach addressed to the question of whether ir prolactin in the brain is identical to pituitary prolactin, we have used recombinant DNA techniques to see if prolactin mRNA is present in the brain. We have obtained strong evidence that an mRNA species in the brain hybridizes to DNA which is known to be complementary to prolactin mRNA (Schachter, Durgerian, Harlan, Pfaff and Shivers, in preparation); the hybridizable brain mRNA (which is found in the hypothalamus and in the amygdala) is indistinguishable from mature pituitary prolactin mRNA, as determined by sizing on agarose gels. We have also performed in situ hybridization experiments, and have found a population of cell bodies in the mediobasal hypothalamus which contains RNA that hybridizes to the prolactin cDNA probe. The distribution of these cell bodies is "remarkably similar" to the distribution of cells containing ir prolactin (Schachter et al., 1983). These data thus strengthen the candidacy of prolactin (or a prolactin-like substance) as a gene product produced by hypothalamic cells, transported to the target cells within the midbrain central grey, and released so as to activate the mechanism underlying lordosis.

To establish a given peptide as an estrogen-induced substance, a first step is to demonstrate effects of estrogen on the production of the substance in question. For instance, quantitative immunocytochemical studies have revealed effects of gonadal steroid manipulations on the content of LHRH in nerve cell bodies and fibers in two of the three terminal fields so far examined (Shivers et al., 1983a). In addition to effects on peptide production, it is also possible to determine autoradiographically whether individual cell bodies which produce a particular substance concentrate tritiated estradiol when this ligand is given systemically. We have performed such experiments in the rat, in order to determine whether or not estrogen has a direct, genomic action on LHRH-containing brain cells; out of more than 400 LHRH-positive cell bodies, only one showed nuclear concentration of tritiated estradiol (Shivers et al., 1983b). In many cases, however, LHRH neurons were located only a few micrometers away from estradiol-concentrating cells. These data indicate that different cells mediate genomic actions of estradiol on, respectively, LHRH synthesis and release (Jackson, 1973, 1975). Additional work from this laboratory has indicated that a small proportion of POMC cells in the mediobasal hypothalamus concentrate estradiol (Morrell et al., 1983) and we are currently determining whether cells containing ir prolactin also do so.

A MODEL FOR THE ACTIONS OF ESTROGEN ON LORDOSIS-RELEVANT HYPOTHALAMIC CELLS

The data reviewed above are consistent with the following working model for estrogen on lordosis. Estrogen acts on mediobasal hypothalamic neurons that project to the midbrain central grey, to increase synthesis of proteins and/or peptides. One or more of these substances are carried via fast axonal transport to terminals in the midbrain, where the substance(s) may be stored until released. Arrival of action potentials at the nerve terminals triggers the release of one or more of these substances onto postsynaptic receptors. The released substance(s) presumably alter the firing rate and/or synthetic activity of midbrain cells over a prolonged period (measured in minutes). One of the substances released appears to be very similar, and may even be identical to, prolactin.

How does this model compare to the predicted properties of endocrineural transducers, which should be responsive to slowly changing, or even static, continuous, inputs. Estrogen-concentrating cells in the mediobasal hypothalamus, some of which may contain prolactin, appear to meet this criterion. Endocrineural transducer cells would be expected to transmit information to other brain cells at highly localized transmission points, synapses for instance. Although the existence of ir prolactin in nerve terminals in the midbrain central grey has not been definitively established, our immunocytochemical evidence at the light microscopic level is certainly suggestive of this. Finally, it is predicted that neurosecretory products released from the terminals of endocrineural transducer cells would retain the characteristic of a long duration of action, thus transmitting information about slowly changing input. Our results of microinfusion of TTX into the hypothalamus support the hypothesis that lordosis-relevant neurotransmitters released from terminals of hypothalamic cells indeed have a prolonged duration of action. If one of the main functions of estrogen-sensitive hypothalamic neurons is to inform specific midbrain neurons about the levels of circulating estrogen, the hypothalamic cells would not need to inform the midbrain cells on a millisecond-by-millisecond basis, but rather in a time frame of minutes. Moreover, the effects of infusion of prolactin and anti-prolactin immune serum into the dorsal midbrain suggest that prolactin might be one of the neurotransmitters in question.

POSSIBLE SEX DIFFERENCES IN THE NEURAL CIRCUITRY CONTROLLING LORDOSIS

The lack of definitive evidence concerning the location(s) of sex differences in the neural circuitry controlling lordosis requires us to speculate about different possibilities. Given the emphasis in this chapter on lordosis-relevant, estrogen-sensitive hypothalamic cells with projections to the dorsal midbrain, we will limit our speculations to possible sex differences in the anatomy, physiology or biochemistry of these particular cells.

One possibility is that the sex difference in lordotic responsiveness relates to differences in nuclear uptake of steroids. Although several studies have failed to reveal any sex difference in the number of estrogen receptors in different brain regions (Maurer and Woolley, 1975; Lieberburg et al., 1980), more recent work (using brain tissue finely dissected by a "punch" technique) has indicated that female rats have more cytoplasmic estrogen receptors per mg protein than male rats (Rainbow et al., 1982). There is no way of determining from these data whether this difference is limited to, or even involves, cells that are related to lordosis behavior.

Another possible sex difference in lordosis-relevant hypothalamic cells might reside in their biochemical responses to steroids. Sex differences have been reported lately in the effects of estradiol on cholinergic enzyme activities within the preoptic area and diagonal bands of Broca (Luine and McEwen, 1983). Sex differences in estrogen-induced progestin receptors have also been found in the mediobasal hypothalamus (Rainbow et al., 1982). The specific roles of either cholinergic enzymes or estrogen-inducible progestin receptors in the control of lordosis are not known. Cholinergic agonists have been reported to facilitate lordotic responsiveness (Dohanich and Clemens, 1981), but a neural site of action for this effect has not been identified. Under many circumstances, the induction of hypothalamic progestin receptors correlates with the ability of progesterone to facilitate lordosis in estrogen-treated rats (Parsons et al., 1982), but a causal relationship has not been established, although a variety of circumstantial evidence points to this conclusion. At the very best, however, estrogen-inducible progestin receptors are a convenient marker for estrogen-stimulated biochemical events. There is always the possibility that the sex difference in estrogen-inducible hypothalamic progestin receptors represents only the tip of the iceberg as far as sex differences in biochemical responses to gonadal steroids are concerned.

Sex differences could also exist in the *physiology* of lordosis-relevant hypothalamic neurons projecting to the midbrain. In fact, Sakuma and Pfaff (1981) have provided evidence for a sex difference in antidromic latencies of mediobasal hypothalamic neurons with projections to the dorsal midbrain, but it is not known whether this difference relates to differences in axon thickness, axon trajectories or other factors.

Sex differences in the *anatomical* organization of such lordosis-relevant cells might also exist. Sex differences in the anatomy of the medial preoptic/anterior hypothalamic area have in fact been demonstrated in several rodent species (Greenough et al., 1977; Gorski et al., 1978, 1980; Bleier et al., 1982), and we are currently investigating whether there is a sex difference in the organization of cells and fibers containing ir prolactin.

It is evident that our cellular analysis of estrogenic action on neural circuitries producing lordosis is far from complete. However, the model that we have proposed may allow us to carry out a study of the putative sex differences in this system.

REFERENCES

Barraclough, C.A. and Gorski, R.A. (1962) Studies on mating behavior in the androgen-sterilized rat and their relation to the hypothalamic regulation of sexual behavior in the female rat. *J. Endocrinol.*, 25: 175–182.

Blaustein, J.D. and Feder, H.H. (1979) Cytoplasmic progestin receptors in guinea pig: Characteristics and relationship to the induction of sexual behavior. *Brain Res.*, 169: 481–497.

Bleier, R., Byne, W. and Siggelkow, I. (1982) Cytoarchitectonic sexual dimorphisms of the medial preoptic and anterior hypothalamic areas in guinea pig, rat, hamster, and mouse. *J. Comp. Neurol.*, 212: 118–130.

Bloom, F., Battenberg, E., Rossier, J., Ling, N. and Guillemin, R. (1978) Neurons containing β-endorphin in rat brain exist separately from those containing enkephalin: Immunocytochemical studies. *Proc. Natl. Acad. Sci. (U.S.A.)*, 75: 1591–1595.

Carrer, H.F. and Aoki, A. (1982) Ultrastructural changes in the hypothalamic ventromedial nucleus of ovariectomized rats after estrogen treatment. *Brain Res.*, 240: 221–233.

Cohen, R.S. and Pfaff, D.W. (1981) Ultrastructure of neurons in the ventromedial nucleus of the hypothalamus in ovariectomized rats with or without estrogen treatment. *Cell Tissue Res.*, 217: 451–470.

Cohen, R.S. and Pfaff, D.W. (1982) Estrogen alters nerve cell nucleoli in rat hypothalamus. *Abstr. Soc. Neurosci.*, 8: 531.

Davidson, J.M., Smith, E.R., Rodgers, C.H. and Bloch, G.J. (1968) Relative thresholds of behavioral and somatic responses to estrogen. *Physiol. Behav.*, 3: 227–229.

Dohanich, G.P. and Clemens, L.G. (1981) Brain areas implicated in cholinergic regulation of sexual behavior. *Hormone Behav.*, 15: 157–167.

Edwards, D.A. and Pfeifle, J.K. (1981) Hypothalamic and midbrain control of sexual receptivity in the female rat. *Physiol. Behav.*, 26: 1061–1067.

Finley, J.C.W., Lindstrom, P. and Petrusz, P. (1981) Immunocytochemical localization of β-endorphin-containing neurons in the rat brain. *Neuroendocrinology*, 33: 28–42.

Fuxe, K., Hokfelt, T., Eneroth, P., Gustafsson, J.-A. and Skett, P. (1977) Prolactin-like immunoreactivity: Localization in nerve terminals of rat hypothalamus. *Science*, 196: 899–900.

Gorski, R.A. (1971) Gonadal hormones and the perinatal development of neuroendocrine function. In: L. Martini and W.F. Ganong (Eds.), *Frontiers in Neuroendocrinology 1971*, Oxford University Press, New York, pp. 237–290.

Gorski, R.A., Gordon, J.H., Shryne, J.E. and Southam, A.M. (1978) Evidence for a morphological sex difference within the medial preoptic area of the rat brain. *Brain Res.*, 148: 333–346.

Gorski, R.A., Harlan, R.E., Jacobson, C.D., Shryne, J.E. and Southam, A.M. (1980) Evidence for the existence of a sexually dimorphic nucleus in the preoptic area of the rat. *J. Comp. Neurol.*, 193: 529–539.

Greenough, W.T., Carter, C.S., Steerman, C. and DeVoogd, T.J. (1977) Sex differences in dendritic patterns in hamster preoptic area. *Brain Res.*, 126: 63–72.

Harlan, R.E., Gordon, J.H. and Gorski, R.A. (1979) Sexual differentiation of the brain: Implications for neuroscience. In: D. Schneider (Ed.), *Reviews of Neuroscience*, Raven, New York, pp. 31–71.

Harlan, R.E., Shivers, B.D., Moss, R.L., Shryne, J.E. and Gorski, R.A. (1980) Sexual performance as a function of time of day in male and female rats. *Biol. Reprod.*, 23: 64–71.

Harlan, R.E., Shivers, B.D., Kow, L.-M. and Pfaff, D.W. (1982a) Intrahypothalamic colchicine infusions disrupt lordotic responsiveness in estrogen-treated female rats. *Brain Res.*, 238: 153–167.

Harlan, R.E., Shivers, B.D. and Pfaff, D.W. (1982b) Dorsal midbrain sodium currents are required for the lordosis reflex in female rats. *Abstr. Soc. Neurosci.*, 8: 930.

Harlan, R.E., Shivers, B.D. and Pfaff, D.W. (1983a) Midbrain microinfusions of prolactin increase the estrogen-dependent behavior, lordosis. *Science*, 219: 1451–1453.

Harlan, R.E., Shivers, B.D., Kow, L.-M. and Pfaff, D.W. (1983b) Estrogenic maintenance of lordotic responsiveness: Requirement for hypothalamic action potentials. *Brain Res.*, 268: 67–78.

Harris, G.W. and Levine, S. (1965) Sexual differentiation of the brain and its experimental control. *J. Physiol. (London)*, 181: 379–400.

Jackson, G.L. (1973) Time interval between injection of estradiol benzoate and LH release in the rat and effect of actinomycin D or cycloheximide. *Endocrinology*, 93: 887–892.

Jackson, G.L. (1975) Blockage of progesterone-induced release of LH by intrabrain implants of actinomycin D. *Neuroendocrinology*, 17: 236–244.

Kow, L.-M., Montgomery, M.O. and Pfaff, D.W. (1979) Triggering of lordosis reflex in female rats with somatosensory stimulation: Quantitative determination of stimulus parameters. *J. Neurophysiol.*, 42: 195–202.

Kreiger, M.S., Conrad, L.C.A. and Pfaff, D.W. (1979) An autoradiographic study of the efferent connections of the ventromedial nucleus of the hypothalamus. *J. Comp. Neurol.*, 183: 785–816.

Lieberburg, I., MacLusky, N. and McEwen, B.S. (1980) Cytoplasmic and nuclear estradiol 17-β binding in male and female rat brain: Regional distribution, temporal aspects and metabolism. *Brain Res.*, 193: 487–503.

Liposits, Z. and Sétáló, G. (1980) Descending luteinizing hormone-releasing hormone (LHRH) nerve fibers to the midbrain of the rat. *Neurosci. Lett.*, 20: 1–4.

Lorenz, T. and Willard, M. (1978) Subcellular fractionation of intra-axonally transported polypeptides in the rabbit visual system. *Proc. Natl. Acad. Sci. (U.S.A.)*, 75: 505–509.

Luine, V.N. and McEwen, B.S. (1983) Sex differences in cholinergic enzymes of diagonal band nuclei in the rat preoptic area. *Neuroendocrinology*, 36: 475–482.

Luine, V.N. and Rhodes, J.C. (1983) Gonadal hormone regulation of MAO and other enzymes in hypothalamic areas. *Neuroendocrinology*, 36: 235–241.

Luine, V.N., Khylchevskaya, R.I. and McEwen, B.S. (1974) Oestrogen effects on brain and pituitary enzyme activities. *J. Neurochem.*, 23: 925–934.

Luine, V.N., Khylchevskaya, R.I. and McEwen, B.S. (1975) Effects of gonadal hormones on enzyme activities in brain and pituitary of male and female rats. *Brain Res.*, 86: 283–292.

MacLusky, N.J. and McEwen, B.S. (1980) Progestin receptors in rat brain: Distribution and properties of cytoplasmic progestin binding sites. *Endocrinology*, 106: 192–202.

Malsbury, C.W. and Daood, J.T. (1978) Sexual receptivity: Critical importance of supraoptic connections of the ventromedial hypothalamus. *Brain Res.*, 159: 451–457.

Manogue, K.R., Kow, L.-M. and Pfaff, D.W. (1980) Selective brain stem transections affecting reproductive behavior of female rats: The role of hypothalamic output to the midbrain. *Hormone Behav.*, 14: 277–302.

Maurer, R.A. and Woolley, D.E. (1975) ³H-Estradiol distribution in female, androgenized female, and male rats at 100 and 200 days of age. *Endocrinology*, 96: 755–765.

McEwen, B.S., Davis, P.G., Parsons, B. and Pfaff, D.W. (1979) The brain as a target for steroid hormone action. *Annu. Rev. Neurosci.*, 2: 65–112.

Morrell, J.I. and Pfaff, D.W. (1982) Characterization of estrogen-concentrating hypothalamic neurons by their axonal projections. *Science*, 217: 1273–1275.

Morrell, J.I., Greenberger, L.M. and Pfaff, D.W. (1981) Hypothalamic, other diencephalic, and telencephalic neurons that project to the dorsal midbrain. *J. Comp. Neurol.*, 201: 589–620.

Morrell, J.I., McGinty, J. and Pfaff, D.W. (1983) Some steroid hormone concentrating cells in the medial basal hypothalamus (MBH) and anterior pituitary contain β-endorphin or dynorphin. *Abstr. Soc. Neurosci.*, 9.

Moss, R.L. and McCann, S.M. (1973) Induction of mating behavior in rats by luteinizing hormone-releasing factor. *Science*, 181: 177–179.

Nilaver, G., Zimmerman, E.A., Defendini, R., Liotta, A.S., Krieger, D.T. and Brownstein, M.J. (1979) Adreno-corticotropin and β-lipotropin in the hypothalamus. Localization in the same arcuate neurons by sequential immunocytochemical procedures. *J. Cell Biol.*, 81: 50–58.

O'Malley, B.W. and Means, A.R. (1974) Female steroid hormones and target cell nuclei. *Science*, 183: 610–620.

Parsons, B., McEwen, B.S. and Pfaff, D.W. (1982) A discontinuous schedule of estradiol treatment is sufficient to activate progesterone-facilitated feminine sexual behavior and to increase cytosol receptors for progestins in the hypothalamus of the rat. *Endocrinology*, 110: 613–619.

Pfaff, D.W. (1968) Autoradiographic localization of radioactivity in the rat brain after injection of tritiated sex hormones. *Science*, 161: 1355–1356.

Pfaff, D.W. (1973) Luteinizing hormone-releasing factor potentiates lordosis behavior in hypophysectomized ovariectomized female rats. *Science*, 182: 1148–1149.

Pfaff, D.W. (1980) *Estrogens and Brain Function*, Springer, New York.

Pfaff, D.W. and Keiner, M. (1973) Atlas of estradiol-concentrating cells in the central nervous system of the female rat. *J. Comp. Neurol.*, 151: 121–158.

Pfaff, D.W. and Lewis, C. (1974) Film analyses of lordosis in female rats. *Hormone Behav.*, 5: 317–335.

Pfaff, D.W., Lewis, C., Diakow, C. and Keiner, M. (1973) Neurophysiological analysis of mating behavior responses as hormone sensitive reflexes. *Progr. Physiol. Psychol.*, 5: 253–297.

Pfaff, D.W., Montgomery, M. and Lewis, C. (1977) Somatosensory determinants of lordosis in female rats: Behavioral definition of the estrogen effect. *J. Comp. Physiol. Psychol.*, 91: 134–145.

Pfaff, D.W., Diakow, C., Montgomery, M. and Jenkins, F.A. (1978) X-ray cinematographic analysis of lordosis in female rats. *J. Comp. Physiol. Psychol.*, 92: 937–941.

Phelps, C.P. and Nance, D.M. (1979) Sexual behavior and neural degeneration following hypothalamic knife cuts. *Brain. Res. Bull.*, 4: 423–429.

Quadagno, D.M. and Ho, G.K.W. (1975) The reversible inhibition of steroid-induced sexual behavior by intra-cranial cycloheximide. *Hormone Behav.*, 6: 19–26.

Quadagno, D.M., Shryne, J. and Gorski, R.A. (1971) The inhibition of steroid-induced sexual behavior by intra-hypothalamic actinomycin D. *Hormone Behav.*, 2: 1–10.

Rainbow, T.C., Davis, P.G. and McEwen, B.S. (1980) Anisomycin inhibits the activation of sexual behavior by estradiol and progesterone. *Brain Res.*, 194: 548–555.

Rainbow, T.C., Parsons, B. and McEwen, B.S. (1982) Sex differences in rat brain oestrogen and progestin receptors. *Nature (London)*, 300: 648–650.

Riskind, P. and Moss, R.L. (1979) Midbrain central gray: LHRH infusion enhances lordotic behavior in estrogen-primed ovariectomized rats. *Brain Res. Bull.*, 4: 203–205.

Sakuma, Y. and Pfaff, D.W. (1980) LH-RH in the mesencephalic central grey can potentiate lordosis reflex of female rats. *Nature (London)*, 283: 566–567.

Sakuma, Y. and Pfaff, D.W. (1981) Electrophysiological determination of projections from ventromedial hypothalamus to midbrain central gray: differences between female and male rats. *Brain Res.*, 225: 184–188.

Sakuma, Y. and Pfaff, D.W. (1983) Modulation of the lordosis reflex of female rats by LHRH, its antiserum and analogs in the mesencephalic central gray. *Neuroendocrinology*, 36: 218–224.

Samuels, L.D. (1964) Actinomycin and its effects. Influence of an effector for hormonal control. *New Engl. J. Med.*, 271: 1252–1258.

Saper, C.B., Swanson, L.W. and Cowan, W.M. (1976) The efferent connections of the ventromedial nucleus of the hypothalamus of the rat. *J. Comp. Neurol.*, 169: 409–442.

Schachter, B., Shivers, B., Harlan, R. and Pfaff, D. (1983) Evidence for prolactin messenger RNA in the rat brain. *Abstr. Endocr. Soc.*

Schwartz, J.H. (1980) The transport of substances in nerve cells. *Sci. Am.*, 242: (4) 152–171.

Shivers, B.D., Harlan, R.E., Parker Jr., C.R. and Moss, R.L. (1980) Sequential inhibitory effect of progesterone on lordotic responsiveness in rats: Time course, estrogenic nullification and actinomycin-D insensitivity. *Biol. Reprod.*, 23: 963–973.

Shivers, B.D., Harlan, R.E., Morell, J.I. and Pfaff, D.W. (1983a) Immunocytochemical localization of luteinizing hormone-releasing hormone in male and female rat brain: Quantitative studies on the effect of gonadal steroids. *Neuroendocrinology*, 36: 1–12.

Shivers, B.D., Harlan, R.E., Morrell, J.I. and Pfaff, D.W. (1983b) Absence of oestradiol concentration in cell nuclei of LHRH-immunoreactive neurones. *Nature (London)*, 304: 345–347.

Shivers, B.D., Harlan, R.E. and Pfaff, D.W. (1983c) Immunocytochemical mapping of immunoreactive prolactin in female rat brain. *Abstr. Soc. Neurosci.*, 9: 1018.

Shivers, B.D., Harlan, R.E. and Pfaff, D.W. (1983d) Reproduction: The central nervous system role of luteinizing hormone releasing hormone. In: D. Krieger, J. Martin and M. Brownstein (Eds.), *Brain Peptides*, Wiley, New York, pp. 389–412.

Sirinathsinghji, D.J.S., Whittington, P.E., Audsley, A. and Fraser, H.M. (1983) β-Endorphin regulates lordosis in female rats by modulating LH-RH release. *Nature (London)*, 301: 62–64.

Terkel, A.S., Shryne, J. and Gorski, R.A. (1973) Inhibition of estrogen-facilitation of sexual behavior by the intracranial infusion of actinomycin-D. *Hormone Behav.*, 4: 377–386.

Thody, A.J., Wilson, C.A. and Everard, D. (1979) Facilitation and inhibition of sexual receptivity in the female rat by a-MSH. *Physiol. Behav.*, 22: 447–450.

Toubeau, G., Desclin, J., Parmentier, M. and Pasteels, J.L. (1979) Cellular localization of a prolactin-like antigen in the rat brain. *J. Endocrinol.*, 83: 261–266.

Tytell, M., Black, M.M., Garner, J.A. and Lasek, R.J. (1981) Axonal transport: Each major rate component reflects the movement of distinct macromolecular complexes. *Science*, 214: 179–181.

Watson, S.J., Barchas, J.D. and Li, C.H. (1977) β-Lipotropin: Localization of cells and axons in rat brain by immunocytochemistry. *Proc. Natl. Acad. Sci. (U.S.A.)*, 74: 5155–5158.

Weisner, J.B. and Moss, R.L. (1982) β-Endorphin suppression of mating behavior and plasma luteinizing hormone in the female rat. *Abstr. Soc. Neurosci.*, 8: 930.

Wilson, C.A., Thody, A.J. and Everard, D. (1979) Effect of various ACTH analogs on lordosis behavior in the female rat. *Hormone Behav.*, 13: 293–300.

Witkin, J.W., Paden, C.M. and Silverman, A.-J. (1982) The luteinizing hormone-releasing hormone (LHRH) systems in the rat brain. *Neuroendocrinology*, 35: 429–438.

Wurtman, R.J. (1973) Neuroendocrine transducers and monoamines. *Fed. Proc.*, 32: 1769–1771.

DISCUSSION

D.F. SWAAB: The prolactin immunocytochemistry (ICC) and gene localization seem to match beautifully. However, I wonder whether both methods are yet not subject to specificity problems. Concerning the ICC data we have to consider e.g. the biological source of the antigen, which might give rise to all kinds of unexpected crossreactions. With regard to the new gene localization technique, I can think of no specificity problems of this procedure, but only due to lack of knowledge. Could you please elaborate on such problems?

D.W. PFAFF: We have carried out a number of immunocytochemical controls to show that the specifically recognized cells in the hypothalamus are really due to prolactin. Possible contaminants of prolactin preparations used for generating antisera did not, in preabsorption controls, abolish these ICC results (Shivers et al., 1983). Successful ICC-stained cells in hypophysectomized rats and positive cDNA hybridization in medial basal hypothalamus further support the initial ICC results, and suggest that these hypothalamic neurons are actually producing prolactin (Schachter et al., 1983).

M.A. CORNER: Does the electrical induction of lordosis behavior require estrogen priming, and what is the *latency* before lordosis results?

D.W. PFAFF: For electrical stimulation of ventromedial hypothalamus to lead to lordosis behavior, a background of low-dose estrogen priming is required, and the behavioral increases have latencies longer than 25 min (Pfaff and Sakuma, 1979).

J. RODRIGUEZ-SIERRA: In your protocols you always use estrogen-primed animals. If estrogen is to be the factor that stimulates sexual behavior, then the effects of prolactin, progesterone, LHRH, etc. are not responsible for the behavior, but instead the early effects of estrogen are the important key to the causal mechanism of female sexual receptivity.

D.W. PFAFF: The behavior, highly integrated with endocrine and environmental states, is not singly determined. While the agents you mentioned are important, we are especially excited about preliminary findings in which we are studying hypothalamic proteins whose synthesis is increased soon after the beginning of estrogen treatment.

J.B. HUTCHISON: Can estrogen-sensitive brain cells associated with female sexual behavior be identified and, if so, do they have characteristics which distinguish them from estrogen-sensitive cells of the neuroendocrine system?

D.W. PFAFF: We can narrow to small groups of estrogen-sensitive neurons and study properties of individual cells in those groups (e.g. Morrell and Pfaff, 1982), but have not been able to directly relate activity in individual cells to a particular reproductive behavior.

E.B. KEVERNE: Since the distribution of steroid-binding receptors in the brain is remarkably similar phylogenetically and a primary consequence of estrogen binding is the synthesis of progesterone receptors, how do you account for the remarkably different behavioral effects of progesterone? For example, progesterone priming is necessary prior to estrogen to promote sexual activity in the ewe, progesterone enhances sexual proceptivity/ receptivity in the rat, but is inhibitory in the guinea pig, while in the monkey there are no physiological effects of progesterone on proceptivity/receptivity.

D.W. PFAFF: For comparative neuroanatomical approaches to steroid hormone-binding cells, estrogens and androgens have been used much more extensively than progestins (Morrell and Pfaff, 1978). This was partly because progesterone was a poor subject for steroid autoradiography, due to extensive metabolism of the labeled hormone. In the future, $[^3H]R5020$ will be useful for comparative steroidal autoradiography. Where two species have similar neuroanatomical binding patterns but different relations to behavior, the cellular consequences of progestin binding must be different.

C. FABRE-NYS: What would you say about DHT found autoradiographically in places important for behavior, even in places where it does not play a behavioral role?

D.W. PFAFF: We would predict that where a steroid hormone normally circulating in the animal studied is bound to a nerve cell group, that a behavioral or endocrine function modulated by the hormone through that nerve cell group will be found. So we hope the steroid autoradiography will be used as a clue, in that regard.

REFERENCES

Morrell, J.I. and Pfaff, D.W. (1978) A neuroendocrine approach to brain function. Localization of sex steroid concentrating cells in vertebrate brains. *Am. Zool.*, 18: 447–460.

Morrell, J.I. and Pfaff, D.W. (1982) Characterization of estrogen-concentrating hypothalamic neurons by their axonal projections. *Science*, 217: 1273–1276.

Pfaff, D.W. and Sakuma, Y. (1979) Facilitation of the lordosis reflex of female rats from the ventromedial nucleus of the hypothalamus. *J. Physiol. (London)*, 288: 189–202.

Schachter, B., Shivers, B., Harlan, R.E. and Pfaff, D.W. (1983) Evidence for prolactin messenger RNA in the rat brain. *Abstr. Endocr. Soc.*

Shivers, B.D., Harlan, R.E. and Pfaff, D.W. (1983) Immunocytochemical mapping of immunoreactive prolactin in female rat brain. *Abstr. Soc. Neurosci.*, 9: 1018.

G.J. De Vries et al. (Eds.),
Progress in Brain Research, Vol. 61
© 1984   Elsevier Science Publishers B.V., Amsterdam

Sexual Differentiation:
Do Males Differ from Females
in Behavioral Sensitivity to Gonadal Hormones?

P. SÖDERSTEN

Department of Psychiatry, Karolinska Institute, S-141 86 Huddinge (Sweden)

INTRODUCTION

The principles of gonadal steroid hormone action on sexual behavior were outlined by W.C. Young, beginning in the mid 1930s (reviewed by Young, 1961, 1969). *Activational* effects of sex hormones were defined as reversible effects by which the gonadal hormones temporarily activated the behaviors in adult animals. Individual differences in the activational effects of, e.g. testosterone (T) on sexual behavior of male guinea pigs were found to be pronounced (Grunt and Young, 1952), and were regarded as due to individual differences in the *sensitivities of the tissues*, neural and genital, upon which T acted to induce the behavior. Individual differences in tissue sensitivity were, in turn, shown to be the consequence of the *organizational* effects of T on these tissues in early life. Exposure to T during a "critical" period in perinatal life decreased tissue sensitivity to ovarian hormones (Phoenix et al., 1959) and increased tissue sensitivity to T (Grady et al., 1965) in adulthood. These organizational effects of early T treatment on adult behavior were believed to be irreversible. The concepts of *activational* and *organizational* effects of gonadal hormones as well as that of *tissue sensitivity* have been useful theoretical concepts and have, therefore, permeated research on the endocrinology of sexual differentiation. However, the usefulness of concepts such as "neural tissues mediating mating behavior", and "organizational" effects of sex hormones was questioned by Beach (1971), who argued that sex hormones should not be regarded as "...organizing agents but as chemical sensitizers, which alter the stimulability of critical mechanisms within the central nervous system" (Beach, 1945) and questioned the notion that sex hormones, in fact, can organize neural tissues. However, numerous examples that this can occur are now available (see this volume). Yet, the relationships between hormone-induced alterations in neural structure and sex differences in the display of sexual and other behaviors by adult rodents are not always clear. One reason for this may simply be that the necessary methodology has not yet been achieved. Another reason why brain dimorphism cannot readily be related to sex differences in behavior could be that sex differences in behavior have been overestimated, i.e. that the similarities in the behavioral capacity of males and females are more striking than the differences. Beach (1975) suggested that perinatal T stimulation defeminizes and, at the same time (although perhaps by a different mechanism) masculinizes the animal. However, there is some evidence that at least one human male, undoubtedly exposed to physiological amounts of T, is in no way defeminized but perfectly capable of showing the full repertoire of what has traditionally been considered "feminine" and "masculine" behaviors (Fig. 1). The appearance of the individual shown in Fig. 1 in

Fig. 1. Actor Dustin Hoffman displays feminine behavior in the recent movie "Tootsie". (Reproduced with permission of Columbia Picture Industries, Inc.)

1982 caused some confusion about what we should consider feminine and masculine behavior, and opened the possibility that the potential for display of "male" and "female" behavior patterns can co-exist in an individual independently of whatever organizing effect perinatal T might have had on neural and genital anatomy. We will present additional data in support for this possibility using the sexual behavior of a Danish strain of Wistar rats as the model.

LORDOSIS BEHAVIOR: DECREASED BEHAVIORAL ESTROGEN SENSITIVITY AFTER NEONATAL TESTOSTERONE TREATMENT?

Defeminization occurs physiologically in male rats and is traditionally measured by the display of female sexual behavior (lordosis behavior, measured by the lordosis quotient, LQ = lordosis to mount ratio; Södersten, 1976) after castration in adulthood followed by exogenous treatment with estradiol benzoate (EB) and progesterone (P). Characteristically, gonadectomized males are less sensitive to EB and insensitive to P in this paradigm (McEwen, 1981; Rainbow et al., 1982). In a series of experiments behavioral responses of male rats to EB and P were compared with those of females treated with oil (females) or 1 mg testosterone propionate (TP) between 96 and 120 h after birth (androgenized females) (Södersten, 1976). The males were castrated at 30 days of age and the females ovariectomized between 71 and 90 days of age. Fig. 2 shows that the males showed lower LQs than both groups of females in response to 7 daily injections of various doses of EB. The androgenized females, however, did not differ from the females with respect to EB sensitivity. Treatment of adult gonadectomized male, female and androgenized female rats with 10 μg EB/kg plus, 42 h later, various doses of P, was followed 6 h later by a dose-dependent increase of LQs in all three groups, but females showed higher LQs than the other two groups. These results indicated that, although males can show female behavior pattern in response to EB or EB and P treatment, the frequency of such behavior is lower than in

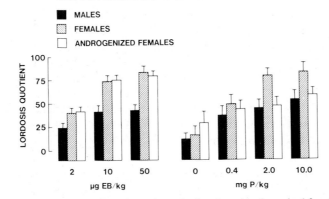

Fig. 2. Mean (± S.E.M.) lordosis quotients shown by male, female and androgenized female (given 1 mg testosterone propionate between 96 and 120 h after birth) rats in response to 7 daily injections of various doses of
estradiol benzoate (EB, left) or after treatment with 10 μg EB/kg in combination with various doses of progesterone (P). Males were castrated at 30 days of age, females were ovariectomized between 71 and 90 days of age.

females. This can, however, not be due only to perinatal androgen secretions in the males,
since androgenized females showed similar LQ scores as did normal females.

Behavioral P sensitivity was suppressed in males and androgenized females. In the male
this may have been due to deficient EB pretreatment rather than a deficient ability to respond
to P. Thus, when a high dose of EB (100 μg) was given to castrated males followed by a high
dose of P (2 mg) on 5 consecutive weeks and the animals were tested weekly 6 h after the P
treatment, P clearly facilitated the display of lordosis in the males (Table I). In addition, the
animals showed ear wiggling and hopping behavior, i.e. higher levels of female sexuality
termed proceptive behavior by Beach (1976).

The retained estrogen sensitivity of the androgenized females was surprising since an
overwhelming literature had indicated that neonatal TP treatment reduces adult behavioral
estrogen sensitivity (e.g. Beach, 1971). The high estrogen sensitivity of these rats was found
to be due to the presence of the ovaries until adulthood. Thus, if the animals were ovariectomized at the time of neonatal TP treatment, they were less sensitive to EB than neonatally
ovariectomized and oil-treated females. This effect was, however, completely eliminated by

TABLE I

LORDOSIS QUOTIENTS (LQ) AND PROCEPTIVE BEHAVIOR (EAR WIGGLING)
IN CASTRATED MALE RATS TREATED WITH 100 μg ESTRADIOL BENZOATE (EB)
IN COMBINATION WITH ARACHIDIS OIL (O) ($n = 10$) or 2 mg PROGESTERONE (P) ($n = 11$)

Test	LQ (mean ± S.E.M.)			Number of rats showing ear wiggling (%)		
	EB + O	EB + P	P*	EB + O	EB + P	P**
1	39.9 ± 10.1	38.0 ± 10.1	N.S.	0	27.3	N.S.
2	46.0 ± 13.3	74.5 ± 8.9	N.S.	10	45.5	N.S.
3	48.0 ± 11.6	89.0 ± 6.6	< 0.02	10	81.8	< 0.01
4	43.0 ± 12.7	82.7 ± 6.0	< 0.05	10	54.6	< 0.05
5	37.0 ± 11.0	89.1 ± 3.0	< 0.02	0	45.5	< 0.05

* Mann–Whitney U test (two-tailed).
** Fisher exact probability test (two-tailed).

the presence of the ovaries during development, i.e. if the ovariectomy was postponed until adulthood (Fig. 3). Interestingly, female rats given oil and ovariectomized neonatally did not show higher LQs in adulthood than day-30-castrated male rats (Södersten, 1976).

These results showed that normal male rats are sensitive to the behavioral effects of both EB and P and have the capacity to show all aspects of female behavior, including proceptive behaviors. Additionally, the results showed that exposure to ovarian hormones during development can mask the effect of TP treatment during the "critical" neonatal period of sexual differentiation. The theory that the "organizational" effect of perinatal T treatment is irreversible is, therefore, questionable.

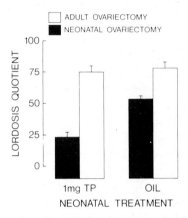

Fig. 3. Mean (± S.E.M.) lordosis quotients shown by female rats treated with 1 mg testosterone propionate (TP) or oil between 96 and 120 h after birth and ovariectomized neonatally or in adulthood. The animals received 7 daily injections of 10 μg estradiol benzoate/kg as adults.

MOUNTING BEHAVIOR: INCREASED BEHAVIORAL ESTROGEN SENSITIVITY AFTER NEONATAL TESTOSTERONE TREATMENT

Another problem with the notion of reduced behavioral estrogen sensitivity in males and androgenized females is that if estrogen sensitivity is measured, not by female sexual behavior, but by another estrogen-dependent behavior, male and androgenized female rats turn out to be *more* sensitive than females. One such behavior is male sexual behavior. An extensive literature indicates that estradiol is the physiological stimulator of masculine sexual behavior (Södersten, 1979). Thus, it is now well known that (1) T is metabolized to estradiol in the male rat brain (McEwen, 1981); (2) there are estradiol receptors in the male rat brain (Vreeburg et al., 1975); and (3) systemic injections or intrahypothalamic implantation of estradiol readily activate male sexual behavior in castrated male rats (Christensen and Clemens, 1974; Södersten, 1973a). Neonatally ovariectomized female rats, given a single injection of 1 mg TP 4 days after birth and tested for lordosis after daily EB treatment in adulthood (10 μg EB/kg) show lower LQs than neonatally oil-treated controls, but higher rates of male-like mounting behavior if tested with sexually receptive stimulus females (Fig. 4) (Södersten, 1973b). Clearly, an evaluation of the effect of perinatal androgen stimulation on estrogen sensitivity in adulthood depends upon the behavioral index used.

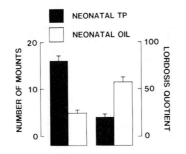

Fig. 4. Mean ($\pm$ S.E.M.) number of mounts and mean ($\pm$ S.E.M.) lordosis quotients shown by female rats treated with 1 mg testosterone propionate (TP) or oil between 96 and 120 h after birth. The animals received daily injections of 10 μg estradiol benzoate/kg as adults.

A recent trend in the search for sex differences in the brain is to look for regional differences in gonadal steroid hormone receptor concentrations (McEwen, 1981; Hutchison and Steimer, 1984) and attempt to relate these to differences in behavior and/or pituitary luteinizing hormone (LH) secretion, the assumption being that high concentrations of neural receptors should be positively correlated with high levels of behavioral responses or with alterations in the capacity for a secretory surge of LH. It has been shown that there is a marked sex difference in medial preoptic area estrogen receptor concentrations, with males having much lower receptor levels than females. This finding was proposed as an explanation of the failure of male rats to show surge secretion of LH in response to estrogen treatment (Rainbow et al., 1982), but it is not readily reconciled with the fact that the medial preoptic area is also the neural site where estrogens are believed to act in the control of male sexual behavior (Christensen and Clemens, 1974). As we have seen above males (and androgenized females) are actually more sensitive to estrogen than females if display of masculine behavior (rather than female behavior or pituitary LH release), is used as the criterion.

ABOLITION OF THE SEX DIFFERENCE IN LORDOSIS
BY PULSE ADMINISTRATION OF ESTRADIOL

If ovarian secretions during development can mask the behavioral effects of perinatal T treatment (see above) it becomes of interest to determine the exact nature of these secretions. The cycling female rat, of course, displays a succession of estrous cycles in which she is repeatedly exposed to ovarian estradiol and P secretion. In a series of experiments we have determined the precise characteristics of the estradiol stimulus sufficient for induction of behavioral estrus in ovariectomized rats (Södersten et al., 1981a). If treatment with estradiol is initiated 32 h before behavioral testing, with P given 6 h before testing, rats show almost maximal LQ scores (Fig. 5). The estrogen stimulus in these experiments was an estradiol-filled constant-release implant, which can be subcutaneously inserted and subsequently removed without anesthesia and with a minimum of stress for the animal (Södersten et al., 1981a). Fig. 5 also shows that the estrogen stimulus could be interrupted 20 h after its initiation and, most interestingly, a 20-h period could be replaced by two 4-h pulses, one at the beginning and one at the end of the 20-h period. If, however, the internal relationship between the two estrogen pulses was distorted, i.e., the first pulse was advanced or the second pulse delayed, the behavioral effect was greatly reduced (Fig. 5).

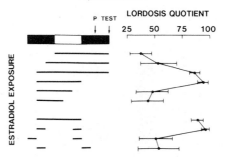

Fig. 5. Mean (± S.E.M.) lordosis quotients shown by ovariectomized rats exposed to estradiol (horizontal black lines) during various time intervals and given 0.5 mg progesterone (P) 6 h before testing (arrow). The black and white horizontal bars indicate the light : darkness cycle.

Since serum levels of estradiol fluctuate markedly in blood samples obtained from groups of rats decapitated during various phases of the estrous cycle (Södersten and Eneroth, 1981), and since behavioral responses could be effectively induced by a pulsatile schedule of estradiol administration we considered the possibility that the ovaries of proestrous rats might secrete estradiol in a pulsatile manner. This was shown to be the case (Södersten et al., 1983a). Fig. 6A shows that serum levels of estradiol fluctuate markedly in sequential blood

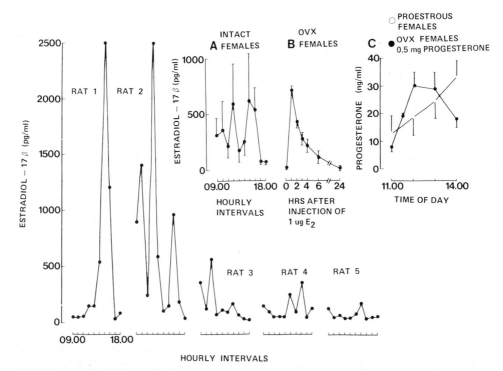

Fig. 6. Serum levels of 17β-estradiol (E$_2$) in 5 individual intact female rats bled at hourly intervals between 09.00 and 18.00 h of the day before behavioral estrus (left and lower part of figure). Mean (± S.E.M.) E$_2$ levels of all 5 individuals are shown in A. B shows E$_2$ levels in ovariectomized (OVX) rats injected with 1 μg E$_2$, while C shows serum progesterone levels in OVX rats injected with 0.5 mg progesterone and in intact proestrous rats. (Reproduced with permission from *Endocrinology*, 112: 1883–1885.)

samples obtained at hourly intervals from freely moving proestrous rats and the lower part of Fig. 6 shows that ovarian estradiol secretion was episodic in all of 5 rats studied. Episodic secretion of estradiol is commonly seen in several mammalian species (Bäckström et al., 1983; Baird, 1978) and is the result of a pulsatile pattern of pituitary gonadotropin secretion, driven in turn by the episodic secretion of gonadotropin-releasing hormone by the brain (Knobil et al., 1980; Levine et al., 1982). Interestingly, the pulsatile pattern of gonadotropin secretion in long-term gonadectomized rats, a reflection of the pulsatile secretion of hypothalamic gonadotropin-releasing hormone, is not sexually dimorphic in the rat (Gay and Sheth, 1972) and is not influenced by perinatal T treatment (Södersten and Eneroth, 1983).

Fig. 6B shows that injections of 1 μg estradiol produced serum estradiol levels which varied within the physiological range. Injection of 0.5 mg P produced serum P levels which also were within the physiological range of variation. Two injections of 1 μg estradiol (and lower doses) followed by 0.5 mg P according to the schedule of administration outlined in Fig. 5 were then given to adult gonadectomized male and female rats at 4-day intervals to simulate the pattern of hormone secretion occurring during the estrous cycle. It was expected that these artificial estrous cycles might eliminate the sex difference in lordosis responding, since ovarian secretions during development had been found to do so (see above). This was shown to be the case (Södersten et al., 1983a). Fig. 7A shows that no sex differences were

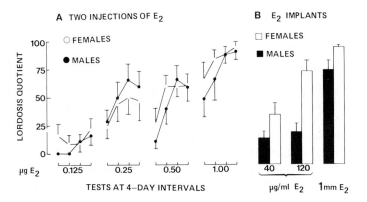

Fig. 7. Mean ($\pm$ S.E.M.) lordosis quotients shown by gonadectomized female and male rats treated with two injections of various doses of estradiol (E_2) in combination with 0.5 mg progesterone (A) or with constant-release implants filled with E_2 (B). (Reproduced with permission from *Endocrinology*, 112: 1883–1885.)

found in the response to a wide range of low doses of estradiol, administered in two pulses and followed by P. In contrast, if the rats were given constant-release implants filled with oil solutions of estradiol or crystalline estradiol clear-cut sex differences in lordosis behavior were found (Fig. 7B). Obviously, male rats exposed to perinatal T through testicular secretions in early life, are capable of showing the same behavioral responses to physiological doses of estradiol and P in adulthood as females. The notion that perinatal T stimulation causes irreversible alterations in adult behavioral sensitivity to ovarian hormones is, therefore, further challenged.

SEXUAL DIFFERENTIATION OF REPRODUCTIVE
NEUROENDOCRINE RHYTHMS

Lordosis behavior

The observation that a sex difference in the lordosis response could be demonstrated under conditions of constant stimulation with estradiol (Fig. 7B) but not when estradiol was given in a pulsatile manner (Fig. 7A), raises the question of how the observed sex difference should be interpreted. In an experiment on the role of ovarian hormones in the termination of sexual receptivity in ovariectomized rats, it was found that the behavior of receptive rats declined despite the continued presence of a constant amount of estradiol (Hansen and Södersten, 1978). This suggested that the behavior of ovariectomized rats, treated with a constant-release implant filled with estradiol, should vary rhythmically with the phase of the light: darkness (LD) cycle. Lordosis was indeed displayed rhythmically, by estradiol-treated ovariectomized rats (Hansen et al., 1979), with maximum levels during the D phase and minimum levels during the L phase (Fig. 8). This is similar to surge secretion of LH by the pituitary gland, which is controlled by a neural mechanism with a 24-h periodicity (Everett and Sawyer, 1950) that, in ovariectomized estradiol-treated rats, comes to expression every 24 h (Legan et al., 1975).

Male rats lack the capacity for a daily LH surge in response to estradiol treatment (Henderson et al., 1977) and do not show an LD-dependent rhythm in estradiol-activated lordosis behavior (Fig. 8). The data in Fig. 8 thus show that behavioral estrogen sensitivity depends not only upon the behavioral criterion used, but also upon the time of testing. Any outcome, i.e. less, equal and more sensitive to estradiol, of such a comparison seems possible. Clearly, there are enough drawbacks with the notion that perinatal T treatment causes a decrement in adult behavioral estrogen sensitivity to warrant an alternative definition of the alteration in adult behavior caused by early T stimulation. One such alternative definition is that behavioral estrogen sensitivity is in fact retained in male rats but that the temporal organization of behavioral responses has been changed.

Rhythms in behavior with a 24-h periodicity are controlled by the suprachiasmatic nuclei (SCN) of the hypothalamus (Rusak and Zucker, 1979) and SCN lesions disrupted the LD-dependent rhythm in lordosis behavior seen in estradiol-treated female rats (Fig. 9). Neonatal T treatment also disrupted adult rhythmicity in lordosis behavior and it was there-

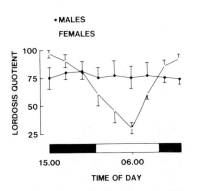

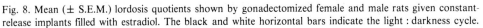

Fig. 8. Mean (± S.E.M.) lordosis quotients shown by gonadectomized female and male rats given constant-release implants filled with estradiol. The black and white horizontal bars indicate the light : darkness cycle.

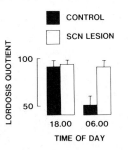

Fig. 9. Mean (± S.E.M.) lordosis quotients shown by ovariectomized rats given constant-release implants filled with estradiol in combination with lesions in the suprachiasmatic nuclei of the hypothalamus (SCN) or control lesions. The rats were tested during the dark (18.00) and light (06.00) phase of the light : darkness cycle.

fore suggested that perinatal T stimulation causes uncoupling of the SCN generator of circadian rhythms from brain mechanisms of sexual behavior in adult animals (Hansen et al., 1979).

The way in which the SCN control behavioral rhythms is unknown. It can be observed in Figs. 8 and 9, however, that, whereas the LQs of neurologically intact female rats were low during the L phase of the LD cycle and high during the D phase they were uniformly high throughout the LD cycle in rats with SCN lesions. The SCN, therefore, appear to inhibit the display of lordosis during the L phase of the LD cycle. Interestingly, the metabolic (Schwartz et al., 1980) and neurophysiological (Inouye and Kawamura, 1979) activities of the SCN are maximal during the L phase of the LD cycle. Of all the potential neurotransmitters produced by the SCN (Card et al., 1981) vasopressin (AVP) (De Vries et al., 1984) is particularly interesting in this context since cerebrospinal fluid (but not peripheral blood) levels of AVP vary rhythmically with the LD cycle (Reppert et al., 1981), with maximal daily concentrations coinciding with the time of maximal activity of the SCN neurons and maximal inhibition of lordosis behavior. In a recent study (Södersten et al., 1983b), it was found that intracerebroventricular (1 ng), but not peripheral (1000 ng) injections of AVP inhibited the behavior of sexually receptive rats. AVP might, therefore, be the secretory product from the SCN which rhythmically inhibits the display of lordosis in female rats. In this context it is of interest that AVP projections of the bed nucleus of the stria terminalis, which form a considerable part of the AVP innervation of the brain, are clearly sexually dimorphic, and are strongly influenced by gonadal hormones, both during development and in adulthood (De Vries et al., 1984). However, such a dimorphism was not found in the AVP projections of the SCN. It remains therefore questionable whether the aforementioned behavioral effects of AVP reflect the normally occurring physiological actions of the SCN, or are caused by e.g. interference with the AVP projections of the stria terminalis.

Male sexual behavior

Male rats show a rhythm in male sexual behavior, which is reflected in a progressive decrease in the latency to ejaculation as the D phase of the LD cycle progresses (Södersten and Eneroth, 1980). On the assumption (see above) that perinatal T stimulation causes uncoupling of the SCN rhythm generator from the neural substrates of sexual behavior in the adult female rat it was predicted that reduced perinatal T stimulation of the brain should enhance the rhythmicity in adult sexual behavior in male rats (Södersten and Eneroth, 1980).

Estradiol is the mediator of the effects of T in the brain, not only in the adult but also in the newborn rat (Södersten, 1979). It is possible, therefore, to antagonize the effects of perinatal T exposure by perinatal anti-estrogen treatment, without disturbing the development of the peripheral masculine anatomy (which is dependent upon androgenic rather than estrogenic stimulation) (Södersten, 1978; Breedlove, 1984). Neonatally anti-estrogen-treated male rats, with their testes intact throughout development, grow up with normal serum T concentrations and show both male and female sexual behavior in the absence of exogenous hormone treatment in adulthood (Fig. 10) (Södersten, 1978). There is a statistically significant, but slight, reduction in the number of ejaculations (Fig. 10), but the important point in this context is that neonatally anti-estrogen-treated rats readily show both male and female behavior. When tested during various phases of the LD cycle these anti-estrogen-treated animals had great difficulty in ejaculating at the time of lights off (11.00 h in Fig. 11), some

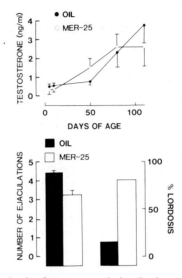

Fig. 10. Mean (± S.E.M.) serum levels of testosterone during development and number of ejaculations and percentage showing lordosis of male rats treated neonatally with anti-estrogen (10 daily injections of 100 μg MER-25) or oil.

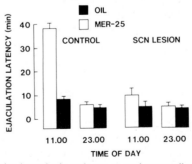

Fig. 11. Mean (± S.E.M.) ejaculation latencies in male rats treated neonatally with anti-estrogen (10 daily injections of 100 μg MER-25) or oil during the first 10 days of postnatal life. The rats received control lesions or lesions in the suprachiasmatic nuclei of the hypothalamus (SCN) as adults and were tested during the late light (11.00) and the late dark (23.00) phase of the light : darkness cycle.

rats requiring 1 h to ejaculate, although they initiated sexual activity with the females as quickly as the controls. In a test 12 h later, however, the anti-estrogen-treated rats ejaculated as quickly as the controls (23.00 h in Fig. 11). Clearly, the diurnal rhythmicity in the behavior of these animals had been enhanced. Additionally, these males developed a rhythm in the display of lordosis behavior (Södersten and Eneroth, 1980). A subsequent SCN lesion markedly reduced the ejaculation latency in the 11.00-h test and eliminated the rhythmicity in the behavior as well as the difference between the neonatally anti-estrogen- and oil-treated rats (Fig. 11). The lesions also eliminated the rhythmic display of lordosis by the anti-estrogen-treated rats (Södersten et al., 1981b). Neonatally anti-estrogen-treated males which were subjected to SCN lesions as adults showed intense male and intense female behavior at all times of the LD cycle even without exogenous hormone treatment (Södersten et al., 1981b). These results show, in 25-year-old terminology, that "the neural tissues mediating both male and female mating behavior" can develop side by side in male rats in which the "organizational action" of neonatal T has been antagonized. The results, in addition, support the hypothesis that perinatal T stimulation uncouples the SCN rhythm generator from these "neural tissues" in adulthood (Rusak and Zucker, 1975).

This hypothesis of the "organizational" action of perinatal T stimulation on adult neuroendocrine function is applicable, not only to female sexual behavior (Hansen et al., 1979), male sexual behavior (Södersten and Eneroth, 1980; Södersten et al., 1981b) and surge secretion of LH (Södersten and Eneroth, 1983) but also to the circadian components of the neuroendocrine regulation of prolactin secretion (Gunnett and Freeman, 1983).

SUMMARY AND CONCLUSIONS

Sex differences in behavioral estrogen sensitivity, measured by the display of female sexual behavior, can be demonstrated in gonadectomized adult animals after treatment either with long-acting forms of estradiol or with constant-release implants filled with estradiol. However, no such differences in behavior are observed if estradiol is administered in a manner which mimics the pulsatile secretion of ovarian estradiol observed in proestrous rats. Thus, the capacity to respond behaviorally to physiological doses of estradiol by display of all aspects of feminine behavior is retained in normal male rats.

Ovariectomized estradiol-treated female rats show a diurnal rhythm in lordosis behavior which is eliminated by suprachiasmatic lesions or by neonatal testosterone treatment, and it is suggested that vasopressinergic neurons in the suprachiasmatic nuclei of the hypothalamus are responsible for the rhythmical inhibition of this behavior in neurologically intact rats.

Male rats in which the developmental effect of neonatal testosterone stimulation has been antagonized by an anti-estrogen, show an enhanced rhythmicity in both adult male and female sexual behavior, which is eliminated by suprachiasmatic lesions.

Rusak and Zucker's (1975) hypothesis that perinatal androgen stimulation causes uncoupling of the central nervous generator of circadian rhythms from the mechanisms of reproductive neuroendocrine functions is a plausible alternative to the traditional view that perinatal androgen treatment "defeminizes" and/or "masculinizes" the brain mechanisms for these patterns of behavior.

ACKNOWLEDGEMENTS

This work has been supported by the Swedish Council for Research in the Humanities and Social Sciences.

We thank the Journal of Endocrinology, Ltd. and the Williams and Wilkins Company for permission to use previously published material and Ms. Christina Andersson of Columbia Picture Industries Inc. for permission to publish Fig. 1.

REFERENCES

Bäckström, C.T., McNeilly, A.S., Leask, R.M. and Baird, D.T. (1983) Pulsatile secretion of LH, FSH, prolactin, oestradiol and progesterone during the human menstrual cycle. *Clin. Endocrinol.*, 17: 29–35.

Baird, D.T. (1978) Pulsatile secretion of LH and ovarian estradiol during the follicular phase of the sheep estrous cycle. *Biol. Reprod.*, 18: 359–364.

Beach, F.A. (1945) Bisexual mating behavior in the male rat: Effects of castration and hormone administration. *Physiol. Zool.*, 18: 390–402.

Beach, F.A. (1971) Hormonal factors controlling the differentiation, development, and display of copulatory behavior in the ramstergig and related species. In: E. Tobach, L.R. Aronson and E. Shaw (Eds.), *The Biopsychology of Development*, Academic Press, New York, pp. 249–296.

Beach, F.A. (1975) Hormonal modification of sexually dimorphic behavior. *Psychoneuroendocrinology*, 1: 3–23.

Beach, F.A. (1976) Sexual attractivity, proceptivity, and receptivity in female mammals. *Hormone Behav.*, 7: 105–138.

Breedlove, S.M. (1984) Steroid influences on the development and function of a neuromuscular system. In: G.F. De Vries, J.P.C. De Bruin, H.B.M. Uylings and M.A. Corner (Eds.), *Sex Differences in the Brain. The Relation between Structure and Function. Progress in Brain Research*, this volume, Ch. 8.

Card, J.P., Brecha, N., Karten, H.J. and Moore, R.Y. (1981) Immunocytochemical localization of vasoactive intestinal polypeptide-containing cells and processes in the suprachiasmatic nucleus of the rat: light and electron microscopic analysis. *J. Neurosci.*, 1: 1289–1303.

Christensen, L.W. and Clemens, L.G. (1974) Intrahypothalamic implants of testosterone or estradiol and resumption of masculine sexual behavior in long-term castrated male rats. *Endocrinology*, 95: 984–990.

De Vries, G.J., Buijs, R.M. and Van Leeuwen, F.W. (1984) Sex differences in vasopressin and other neurotransmitter systems in the brain. In: G.J. De Vries, J.P.C. De Bruin, H.B.M. Uylings and M.A. Corner (Eds.), *Sex Differences in the Brain. The Relation between Structure and Function. Progress in Brain Research*, this volume, Ch. 10.

Everett, J.W. and Sawyer, C.H. (1950) A 24-hour periodicity in the 'LH-release apparatus' disclosed by barbiturate sedation. *Endocrinology*, 47: 198–218.

Gay, V.L. and Sheth, N.A. (1972) Evidence for a periodic release of LH in castrated male and female rats. *Endocrinology*, 90: 158–162.

Grady, K.L., Phoenix, C.H. and Young, W.C. (1965) Role of the developing rat testis in the differentiation of the neural tissues mediating mating behavior. *J. Comp. Physiol. Psychol.*, 59: 176–182.

Grunt, J.A. and Young, W.C. (1952) Differential reactivity of individuals and the response of male guinea pigs to testosterone propionate. *Endocrinology*, 51: 237–248.

Gunnett, J.W. and Freeman, M.C. (1983) The mating-induced release of prolactin: a unique neuroendocrine response. *Endocr. Rev.*, 4: 44–61.

Hansen, S. and Södersten, P. (1978) Effects of subcutaneous implants of progesterone on the induction and duration of sexual receptivity in ovariectomized rats. *J. Endocrinol.*, 77: 373–379.

Hansen, S., Södersten, P., Eneroth, P., Srebro, B. and Hole, K. (1979) A sexually dimorphic rhythm in oestradiol-activated lordosis behaviour in the rat. *J. Endocrinol.*, 83: 267–274.

Henderson, S.R., Baker, C. and Fink, G. (1977) Effect of oestradiol-17β exposure on the spontaneous secretion of gonadotrophins in chronically gonadectomized rats. *J. Endocrinol.*, 73: 455–462.

Hutchison, J.B. and Steimer, T. (1984) Androgen metabolism in the brain: behavioural correlates. In: G.J. De Vries, J.P.C. De Bruin, H.B.M. Uylings and M.A. Corner (Eds.), *Sex Differences in the Brain. The Relation between Structure and Function. Progress in Brain Research*, this volume, Ch. 2.

Inouye, S.-I. and Kawamura, H. (1979) Persistence of circadian rhythmicity in a mammalian hypothalamic island containing the suprachiasmatic nucleus. *Proc. Natl. Acad. Sci. (U.S.A.)*, 76: 5962–5966.

Knobil, E., Plant, T.M., Wildt, L., Belchetz, P.E. and Marshall, G. (1980) Control of rhesus monkey menstrual cycle: permissive role of hypothalamic gonadotropin-releasing hormone. *Science*, 207: 1371–1373.

Legan, S.J., Coon, G.A. and Karsch, F.J. (1975) Role of estrogen as initiator of the daily LH surges in the ovariectomized rat. *Endocrinology*, 96: 50–56.

Levine, J.E., Pau, K.F., Ramirez, V.D. and Jackson, G.L. (1982) Simultaneous measurement of luteinizing hormone-releasing hormone and luteinizing hormone release in unanesthetized ovariectomized sheep. *Endocrinology*, 111: 1449–1455.

McEwen, B.S. (1981) Neural gonadal steroid actions. *Science*, 211: 1303–1311.

Phoenix, C.H., Gerall, A.A., Goy, R.W. and Young, W.C. (1959) Organizational action of prenatally administered testosterone propionate on the tissues mediating mating behavior in the female guinea pig. *Endocrinology*, 65: 369–382.

Rainbow, T.C., Parsons, B. and McEwen, B.S. (1982) Sex differences in rat brain oestrogen and progestin receptors. *Nature (London)*, 300: 648–649.

Reppert, S.M., Artman, H.G., Swaminathan, S. and Fisher, D.A. (1981) Vasopressin exhibits a rhythmic pattern in cerebrospinal fluid but not in blood. *Science*, 213: 1256–1257.

Rusak, B. and Zucker, I. (1975) Biological rhythms and animal behavior. *Annu. Rev. Psychol.*, 26: 137–171.

Rusak, B. and Zucker, I. (1979) Neural regulation of circadian rhythms. *Physiol. Rev.*, 59: 449–526.

Schwartz, W.J., Davidsen, C.C. and Smith, C.B. (1980) In vivo metabolic activity of a putative circadian oscillator, the rat suprachiasmatic nucleus. *J. Comp. Neurol.*, 189: 157–167.

Södersten, P. (1973a) Estrogen-activated sexual behavior in male rats. *Hormone Behav.*, 4: 247–256.

Södersten, P. (1973b) Increased mounting behavior in the female rat following a single neonatal injection of testosterone propionate. *Hormone Behav.*, 4: 1–17.

Södersten, P. (1976) Lordosis behaviour in male, female and androgenized female rats. *J. Endocrinol.*, 70: 409–420.

Södersten, P. (1978) Effects of anti-oestrogen treatment of neonatal male rats on lordosis behaviour and mounting behaviour in the adult. *J. Endocrinol.*, 76: 241–249.

Södersten, P. (1979) Role of estrogen in the display and development of sexual behaviour in male rats. In: C. Beyer (Ed.), *Endocrine Control of Sexual Behavior*, Raven, New York, pp. 305–315.

Södersten, P. and Eneroth, P. (1980) Neonatal treatment with anti-oestrogen increases the diurnal rhythmicity in the sexual behavior of adult male rats. *J. Endocrinol.*, 85: 331–339.

Södersten, P. and Eneroth, P. (1981) Serum levels of oestradiol-17β and progesterone in relation to sexual behaviour in intact and ovarectomized rats. *J. Endocrinol.*, 89: 45–54;

Södersten, P. and Eneroth, P. (1983) Reproductive neuroendocrine rhythms. In: J. Balthazart, E. Pröve and R. Gilles (Eds.), *Hormones and Behavior in Higher Vertebrates*, Springer, Berlin, in press.

Södersten, P., Eneroth, P. and Hansen, S. (1981a) Induction of sexual receptivity in ovariectomized rats by pulse administration of oestradiol-17β. *J. Endocrinol.*, 89: 55–62.

Södersten, P., Hansen, S. and Srebro, B. (1981b) Suprachiasmatic lesions disrupt the daily rhythmicity in the sexual behaviour of normal male rats and of male rats treated neonatally with antioestrogen. *J. Endocrinol.*, 88: 125–130.

Södersten, P., Pettersson, A. and Eneroth, P. (1983a) Pulse administration of estradiol-17β cancels sex difference in behavioral estrogen sensitivity. *Endocrinology*, 112: 1883–1885.

Södersten, P., Henning, M., Melin, P. and Lundin, S. (1983b) Vasopressin alters female sexual behaviour by acting on the brain independently of alterations in blood pressure. *Nature (London)*, 301: 608–610.

Vreeburg, J.T.M., Schretlen, P.J.M. and Baum, M.J. (1975) Specific, high-affinity binding of 17β-estradiol in cytosols from several brain regions and pituitary of intact and castrated adult male rats. *Endocrinology*, 97: 969–977.

Young, W.C. (1961) The hormones and mating behavior. In: W.C. Young (Ed.), *Sex and Internal Secretions, Vol. 2*, Williams and Wilkins, Baltimore, MD, pp. 1173–1239.

Young, W.C. (1969) Psychobiology of sexual behavior in the guinea pig. In: D.S. Lehrman, R.A. Hinde and E. Shaw (Eds.), *Advances in the Study of Behavior, Vol. 2*, Academic Press, New York, pp. 1–110.

DISCUSSION

S.M. BREEDLOVE: Do you know whether the neonatal treatment of intact males with the anti-estrogen MER-25 had any effect on testosterone secretion from the testes? For example, did you measure testis weight at the end of the experiment?

P. SÖDERSTEN: We measured serum testosterone levels at various developmental ages, and these were unaffected by the neonatal anti-estrogen treatment. In other groups of neonatally anti-estrogen-treated rats we investigated the responses of the accessory sexual glands and penis to testosterone after castration and these were also comparable to those of oil-injected controls.

C.D. TORAN-ALLERAND: You have an unusually interesting strain with respect to its high incidence of lordosis. Have you ever looked at this phenomenon in another strain?

P. SÖDERSTEN: The only other reports on feminine behavior in intact rats I know of are the old studies by Stone and Beach performed before 1945, in which individual rats, given no hormone treatment, were found to display lordosis behavior spontaneously.

J.F. RODRIQUEZ-SIERRA: Have you tested your strain of males for inhibitory effect of progesterone on lordosis or for inhibitory effects of progesterone on LH release?

P. SÖDERSTEN: No, we have not tested for inhibitory effects of progesterone, since we have shown that such effects probably have no physiological significance in female rats. We did not test the possible effects of progesterone on LH feedback.

J.M. REINISCH: Our data regarding reduced rhythmicity in human males exposed prenatally to 19 NET when compared to unexposed brother(s), have not yet been demonstrated to also reflect a sex difference. That is, we have not shown as yet that males are less rhythmic in temperament than females. This awaits the testing of enough male and female subjects with the New York Longitudinal Temperament Questionnaire-adult form (Thomas, Chess and Birch) to develop norms.

P. SÖDERSTEN: Even though your data on rhythmicity in human behavior may be preliminary, they suggest that prenatal androgens may suppress a rhythmiticy in adult behavior.

J.M. REINISCH: Your rats remind me of Richard Whalen's animals who were treated with androstenedione instead of T during early life. These subjects exhibited high levels of both lordosis and mounting, e.g. they would be categorized on the orthogonal or oblique model of masculinity and femininity as androgenous.

P. SÖDERSTEN: Yes, the rat strain we use may be categorized as androgenous.

G.J. De Vries et al. (Eds.),
Progress in Brain Research, Vol. 61
© 1984   Elsevier Science Publishers B.V., Amsterdam

Hormone-Dependent Socio-Sexual Behaviors and Neurotransmitters

BENGT J. MEYERSON

Department of Medical Pharmacology, Box 573, Biomedicum, S-75123 Uppsala (Sweden)

INTRODUCTION

The role of neurotransmitter mechanisms in the activation and modulation of behavior has become increasingly interesting in the light of the evidence of coexistence and presumable cofunction of traditional neurotransmitters, steroid hormones and neuropeptides in the mammalian brain. The general topic to be dealt with here is the relationship between hormone-dependent dimorphic socio-sexual behaviors and certain forms of neurotransmission. The specific question to be raised is which transmitter systems are involved in copulatory behavior (mounting and lordosis response) and sexual motivation in male and female rats.

Psychotrophic drugs have been utilized to investigate the biochemical basis of socio-sexual behaviors. The availability of substances which selectively influence the activity of certain types of neurons opens the possibility of determining whether a given class of neurons (e.g. utilizing a common transmitter) is implicated in the activation and maintenance of specific elements of sexually dimorphic behaviors. Monoaminergic mechanisms have been demonstrated in different elements of sexual behaviors, such as sexual approach behavior and female and male copulatory behavior. Certain agents also change the incentive quality, c.q. attractiveness of the individual (for reviews see Meyerson and Malmnäs, 1978; Meyerson, 1978; Everitt, 1978; Crowley and Zemlan, 1981).

In the following presentation some general aspects of behavioral pharmacology will be discussed first. This will be followed by a brief summary of earlier results in the field concerning the role of serotonin and dopamine. Finally some recent results will be presented, which may hopefully serve as a trigger for future lines of research.

BEHAVIORAL PHARMACOLOGY: METHODOLOGICAL ASPECTS

For a fuller understanding of the potentialities and limitations of the techniques employed in behavioral pharmacology, certain concepts need to be discussed first.

The steroid hormone/neurotransmitter relationship

Our knowledge in this field is mainly based on neuropharmacological studies of hormone-dependent behaviors. Psychotrophic drugs with known effects on transmitter mechanisms have been used. Although gonadal hormones control certain behaviors by acting locally in the brain (Harlan et al., 1984), neuropharmacological experiments suggest that concomitant activation of specific transmitter mechanisms is also important. However, the fact that a hormone-dependent behavior covaries with a certain transmitter activity does not necessarily mean that there is a direct causal relationship between the hormonal action and the transmitter mechanisms in question. For some hormone-influenced behaviors, e.g. the progesterone-induced lordosis response (see below) evidence for the involvement of serotoninergic mechanisms has been obtained (see Sietnieks and Meyerson, 1980, 1982, 1983; Franck and Ward, 1981), but for many others no such relationship has been convincingly demonstrated.

Behavior/neurotransmitter relationships

Behavior usually consists of a sequence of motor patterns, each of which can be measured in terms of (1) *latency*, i.e. the time between the presentation of the stimulus and the onset of the behavioral response; (2) *frequency*, i.e. the number of times a given pattern is exhibited within a specified time; (3) *duration* and (4) *incidence*, i.e. the proportion of subjects displaying the response.

Drugs may influence each of these measures differently. For instance, in spite of a prolonged mount latency, indicating inhibition of this behavior, the mount frequency may be abnormally high once the behavior is initiated. However, it is also possible that all measures of a certain behavior (for instance mounting behavior) are facilitated by a given treatment. We may also ask whether or not functionally related behaviors are influenced in the same way. Thus, sexual behavior consists of appetitive components, such as seeking, orientation, making contact, and, finally, the consummatory act of copulation itself. Certain neuronal pathways may facilitate or inhibit the entire functional sequence of such behavioral elements.

There is a third factor to be considered. In order for behavior to occur in a biologically meaningful way, certain fundamental processes such as perception and the ability to recognize and store incoming information are necessarily involved. Socio-sexual behaviors can therefore be influenced by changes in the transmitter activity of such systems, which will have to be borne in mind when selective neuropharmacological influences on sexual behavior are investigated.

The drug selectivity problem

Progress in behavioral pharmacology is closely linked to the problem of achieving a selective effect on a defined behavioral response. To this end, this type of research has focused for a long time on agents acting upon neurotransmitter mechanisms, especially receptor binding (agonists, antagonists). The increasing amount of data regarding different subpopulations of pre- and postsynaptic receptors continuously opens new possibilities of developing selectively active compounds. The most recently developed agents in this area have not been fully utilized with respect to sexually dimorphic behaviors. Further progress and perhaps new concepts may therefore be expected in this field.

The loci for hormone/neurotransmitter interaction

There are several lines of evidence suggesting that gonadal hormones activate behavior in part by acting upon the neuronal genome. This evidence has been obtained by, among other methods, the use of protein synthesis inhibitors (Meyerson, 1973; Terkel et al., 1973; Quadagno and Ho, 1975; Rainbow et al., 1980). Furthermore, cyclic AMP mechanisms may be directly or indirectly related to the steroid hormone effect (Beyer et al., 1981). How these mechanisms influence the neuronal activity relevant to behavior is not understood, however. It seems that estrogen activation of female lordotic behavior and wheel-running activity involves a factor requiring axonal transport (Meyerson, 1973, 1982). Whether or not this holds true for other hormones such as testosterone and progesterone, has not yet been established.

COPULATORY BEHAVIOR

In the male rat copulatory behavior is characterized by repetitive mounting of the female partner, with or without penile intromission into the female's vagina, until terminated by ejaculation. If intromission is achieved, a vigorous backward lunge is displayed by the male during the mount. After several mounts with intromission, the ejaculatory reflex is triggered, characterized by a prolonged intromission with intense clasping of the female, followed by a slow dismount and subsequent genital licking. The dependence of these components of the sexual performance upon testosterone and testosterone metabolites is abundantly documented (see Feder, 1978). In castrated male laboratory rats given exogenous testosterone replacement, Malmnäs (1973) worked out an appropriate model for analyzing drug-induced effects on elements of male copulatory behavior (see below).

In female laboratory rats both mounting and patterns suggestive of intromission and ejaculation have been described (Beach, 1942a; Levine and Mullins, 1964; Ward, 1969). Male-like mounting behavior can be induced by testosterone (Beach, 1942a; Södersten, 1972; Feder, 1978) and masculine copulatory behaviors can be activated in "normal" female rats under appropriate hormonal and environmental stimulus conditions. "Normal" here refers to females that have not been experimentally manipulated during the perinatal period.

The most characteristic element in the copulatory behavior of the female rat is the lordosis response, i.e. the posture taken up by the female upon being mounted by a male. Both its dependence upon estrogen and the facilitatory effects of progesterone have long been well known (see Feder, 1978; Södersten, 1984). Lordotic behavior can be induced in "normal" male rats by administration of estrogen (Beach, 1942b; Feder and Wahlen, 1965). However, progesterone does not seem to exert a facilitatory effect when injected after estrogen (Meyerson, 1968; Davidson and Levine, 1969).

Monoamines and, respectively, homotypic and heterotypic copulatory behavior

Let us now consider the question raised in the introduction, viz.: Are the same pathways involved in female and male copulatory behavior in both sexes? To discuss this we shall first have to summarize what is known about pathways involved in homotypic copulatory behavior in the male and female rat. We shall restrict the discussion to mounting behavior, lordotic behavior and monoaminergic pathways. Extensive reviews are available and are beyond the scope of this presentation (for references see Introduction). The data referred to below were selected with respect to the question put above.

Behavioral pharmacological studies have employed various experimental models in studying male mounting behavior. Some authors have studied intact male rats, while others have used castrated males with testosterone replacement therapy. The most frequently employed stimulus object is an ovariectomized female brought into artificial estrus by estradiol and progesterone. However, another male has also been used as the stimulus object, in male-to-male sexual encounters. Regardless of the experimental model, it is a consistent finding that an increase in serotoninergic postsynaptic receptor activity has an inhibitory effect on male copulatory behavior, i.e. it results in decreased mount and intromission percentages, in prolonged mount and intromission latencies and in a decreased mount frequency (for definition of measures, see Malmnäs, 1973). Decreased biosynthesis of serotonin caused by *para*-chlorophenyl alanine (PCPA) treatment facilitates several components of male copulatory behavior.

In contrast to the inhibitory influence of serotonin, an increase in dopaminergic activity (induced by treatment with agonists or a precursor (DOPA)) facilitates all elements of male mating behavior. These effects are blocked by dopamine antagonists. In analogous experiments, drugs acting selectively on the norepinephrine system failed to facilitate this behavior; certain elements were in fact inhibited (prolonged mount latency, decrease in mounts per minute). It is worth noting that the facilitatory effect of DOPA is dose-related, with very high doses causing an inhibition. The question of high doses was thoroughly analyzed by Malmnäs (1976) in a study using DOPA in combination with a monoamine oxidase inhibitor (pargyline) plus a peripherally acting inhibitor of decarboxylase (MK486). Malmnäs also used the dopamine antagonist pimozide in order to test the hypothesis that the stimulatory effect is likely to be postsynaptic, while the inhibitory effect may be due to mere disturbances in the locomotor system, to a displacement of serotonin, or to other non-specific influences. Thus, on the basis of data available we can conclude that within a certain dose range psychotrophic agents which increase dopaminergic activity will facilitate copulatory behavior, whereas serotonin seems to have an inhibitory effect.

TABLE I

Treatment (mg/kg i.p.)		EB, 25 µg/kg Lordosis		TP 1.0 mg/kg Mount		TP 1.0 mg/kg + prog. 1.0 mg Lordosis	
		%	N	%	N	%	N
Apomorphine	0.10[1] 0.15[2]	29[2]	24	75 *,[1]	30	40[1]	24
	0.30	17 **	24	33	12	15 *	25
Saline	0.2 ml	47	24	33	30	67	24
Reserpine	1.0	83 ***	36				
PCPA	4 × 100	72 ***	36				
αMtyr	150	64 **	36				
Saline	0.2 ml	25	36				

Hormone treatment: estradiol benzoate (EB) was given 56 h before tests and testosterone propionate (TP) 56 h before test of mounting and 76 h before test of lordosis. Progesterone (prog.) was given 4 h before test. Drug treatment: apomorphine was given 15 min, reserpine 24 h, *p*-chlorophenylalanine (PCPA) 78, 54, 30 and 6 h and α-methyltyrosine (αMtyr) 6 h before test.
Comparisons between saline and drug treatment (χ^2 test): * $P < 0.05$, ** $P < 0.01$, *** $P < 0.001$. (Data taken from Meyerson and Malmnäs, 1978.)

What then, regulates the mounting behavior displayed by females? Unfortunately, very little research has been done in this field. We have tested ovariectomized females treated with testosterone propionate with stimulus females treated with estradiol + progesterone. The dopamine agonist apomorphine when given intraperitoneally (100 μg/kg) significantly increased the proportion of females which exhibited mounting during the 3-min testing period (Table I). In females implanted with estrogen, Emery and Sachs (1975) found that PCPA treatment facilitated ejaculatory behavior patterns. These results are in agreement with the data available for the male rat, indicating that increased dopaminergic activity enhances mounting behavior in both males and females, while decreased serotoninergic activity facilitates copulatory behavior in the male as well as "masculine" ejaculatory patterns in the female rat.

Evidence is building up that endogenous opioid peptides participate in the regulation of male sexual behavior (Meyerson and Terenius, 1977; Hetta, 1977; Myers and Baum, 1979, 1980; Pelegrini-Quarantotti et al., 1978). β-Endorphin inhibits elements of male copulatory behavior in intact and in castrated, testosterone-treated male rats. The exploration of the relationship between β-endorphin effects and monoaminergic mechanisms is in an early phase. Sexual behavior deficits induced by β-endorphin have been reported to be correlated with a significant increase in hypothalamic norepinephrine levels (McIntosh et al., 1980). Administration of PCPA (which facilitates mounting behavior) was found, paradoxically, to enhance the β-endorphin inhibition (Meyerson, 1983).

There is abundant documentation on the effects of psychotrophic compounds on copulatory behavior in female rats (for references see Introduction). In general, an increase in postsynaptic serotoninergic receptor activity has inhibitory effects upon such behaviors. This holds true also for dopamine. However, evidence for a facilitatory effect of increased presynaptic serotoninergic or dopaminergic activity on lordotic behavior stems from experiments in which very low doses of agonists were given (Everitt et al., 1975; Everitt and Fuxe, 1977a,b; Sietnieks and Meyerson, 1983). Such low dose levels presumably gave rise to presynaptic receptor activation as a result of which, according to current transmitter mechanism theories, postsynaptic activity would decrease.

Recent findings suggest that opioid receptors are also involved in the regulation of lordotic behavior in the female rat. It has been proposed that this effect may be exerted indirectly via luteinizing hormone-releasing hormone (LHRH) mechanisms (Sirinathsinghji et al., 1983). The relationship between endorphins and monoaminergic mechanisms has not yet been investigated, however.

In our studies, using male rats castrated in adulthood, lordotic behavior was activated by estradiol benzoate, given subcutaneously (25 μg/kg) (see Table I). Note that no progesterone was given. This is mentioned in view of the fact that we recently reported that, in female rats, progesterone acts synergistically both with serotoninergic agonists and with the serotonin precursor 5-hydroxytryptamine (5-HT) (Sietniek and Meyerson, 1980, 1982, 1983). Apomorphine clearly increased the percentage of males which, after treatment with estradiol alone, displayed lordotic behavior when mounted by a vigorous stimulus male (Table I). Monoamine depression, either as a general effect induced by reserpine, or as a more selective one caused by PCPA or α-methyltyrosine, significantly facilitated the lordotic response in the estradiol-treated males.

In summary, the above findings justify the working hypothesis that heterotypic mating behavior in one sex and homotypic mating behavior in the opposite sex are influenced analogously by monoaminergic mechanisms.

SEXUAL MOTIVATION

Most investigations into the relationships between hormones, neurotransmitters and sexual behavior were concerned with copulatory behavior, which represents an easily recognizable and hormone-dependent sequence of motor patterns. It is likely that the behavioral acts which precede copulation itself are maintained by a physiological state which causes the animal to actively seek sexual contact with a conspecific. The concept of sexual "motivation" can in fact only be given an operational definition at the present moment. It might be wiser to use a more descriptive term. In the following discussion, therefore, two concepts will be used: (a) *sex-specific approach behavior*, i.e. the extent to which the animal preferentially locates itself in the environment of the opposite sex; and (b) *sexual approach behavior*, i.e. the approach of the rat to a stimulus object if "related to" sexual activity (Fig. 1). Approach behavior and orientation will be used synonymously, and the term "socio-sexual" will cover both concepts a and b.

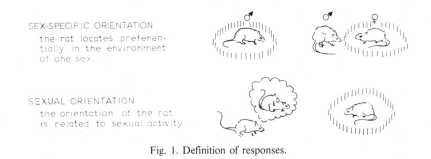

Fig. 1. Definition of responses.

In order to study the influence of gonadal hormones on socio-sexual approach behaviors, we have employed several techniques. Each technique included measures of how the experimental animal sought contact with incentive animals possessing various characteristics, such as gender and endocrine state.

Hormone-dependent socio-sexual approach behavior has been demonstrated both in adult female (Meyerson and Lindström, 1973; Meyerson et al., 1979; McDonald and Meyerson, 1973; Eliasson and Meyerson, 1975) and in adult male rats (Hetta and Meyerson, 1978). Female rats spent more time in the vicinity of males during estrus–proestrus than during diestrus. In the ovariectomized animals, this orientation was activated by exogenous administration of estrogen in a dose-dependent fashion. Experiments in which different stimulus situations and incentive animals were used, suggested that the predominant stimulus for seeking contact with a male was sexual rather than social. In analogous studies it was demonstrated that male rats spend more time in the vicinity of an estrous than of an anestrous female. Female-directed orientation was also related to the dose of estrogen given to an ovariectomized female. It was also shown that the female-directed orientation declines after castration of the male but could be restored by testosterone treatment. Thus, male and female rats have a hormone-dependent tendency to seek contact with the opposite sex. Available information suggests that this approach primarily has a sexual function.

We have also studied the development of the adult pattern of socio-sexual orientation (Eliasson and Meyerson, 1981; Meyerson et al., 1979). This pattern gradually appears in the female from the time of vaginal opening and is fully established by the time of regular estrous cycles. In the male the adult pattern is more obviously related to the time of puberty.

The neuropharmacology of socio-sexual approach behavior has not been greatly explored as yet. In our own laboratory there have only been a few preliminary studies comparing the effects of increasing and decreasing serotoninergic activity in estrogen-treated ovariectomized female rats (Meyerson, 1975). Sex-specific approach behavior, as defined above, was used as the study parameter. It was found that decreased serotonin biosynthesis led to a reduction in male-directed orientation. An increase in brain serotonin levels led to an increased preference for the incentive male rat. The latter effect was also accomplished by pretreatment with a monoamine oxidase inhibitor alone, along with a peripheral decarboxylase inhibitor. Lately this approach has been re-adopted for more detailed studies. We have chosen to work with the "open-field choice technique", which has now been redesigned to include a television-video-computer system for recording and computing the data (Höglund et al., 1983). In addition to the duration of stay in the vicinity of the incentive animal, we can now also record the number of visits to the incentive area, the latency to the first visit and a general locomotor activity score.

The purpose of the experiments described below was to investigate the possible involvement of dopaminergic mechanisms in socio-sexual approach behavior. In the first series of experiments we studied the effect of apomorphine on sex-specific and sexual orientation behavior in sexually experienced female rats. The females were ovariectomized as adults and were allowed to adapt to the experimental apparatus during three 30-min trials (no incentive animals in goal boxes). Estradiol benzoate, 10 μg/kg s.c., was given 52 h before the experimental test session. Apomorphine, in a dose of either 50 or 500 μg/kg s.c., was given just before the start of the test. The following two measures will be discussed below: the duration and the frequency of visits.

Duration is defined as the percentage amount of test time spent by the animals in different areas. Two areas are of principal interest in the present context: area 1, the area just in front of the goal cage and area 2, the zone outside area 1 (see Figs. 2 and 3). In saline-treated control females, as was expected from earlier data, more time was spent with, and more visits were paid to, the incentive male. This preference for male company was seen no longer after treatment with apomorphine. The most marked effect was the decrease in amount of time spent in the area adjacent to the goal cage. In area 2, by contrast, there was a slight increase in duration. The time spent by the female close the incentive female was slightly reduced by the high dose of apomorphine. The large number of visits to the different areas indicates that the locomotor ability was not influenced by drug treatment, which precludes the possibility that the effects seen in the duration are simply non-specific, due to some motor disturbance. In an analogous experiment, but with a castrated male and an intact male as stimulus objects, a similar effect was observed. Again, the baseline response was characterized by a clear-cut preference for the intact male, which was neutralized by apomorphine. It is concluded that apomorphine influences socio-sexual approach behavior by inhibiting the sexual orientation.

In the second series of experiments, sexually experienced male rats, castrated in adulthood and maintained on a substitution treatment with testosterone propionate (0.5 mg/kg/week), were tested for sexual orientation. In this experiment, the drug treatment was as follows: The catecholamine precursor DOPA was given after pretreatment with the monoamine oxidase inhibitor pargyline and a peripheral decarboxylase inhibitor, RO 4602. Controls (saline only) spent more time in the area of the estrous female. After administration of pargyline + RO 4602 + DOPA, the duration in the area of the estrous female (area 1) decreased. The time spent in the outer zone (area 2) was not affected and the number of visits was only slightly — and not significantly — decreased. DOPA had no marked effect on the male performance with regard to the anestrous female. There was a slight decrease in length of

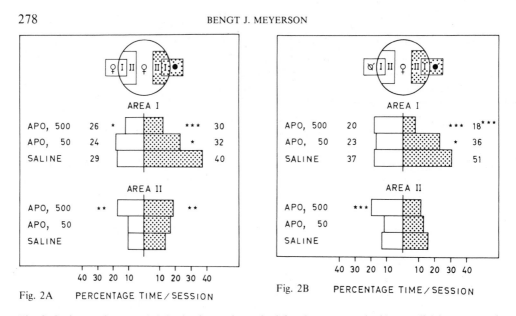

Fig. 2A   PERCENTAGE TIME / SESSION

Fig. 2B   PERCENTAGE TIME / SESSION

Fig. 2. Socio-sexual approach behavior in ovariectomized female rats treated with estradiol benzoate and apomorphine (APO). Estradiol benzoate 10 μg/kg s.c. was given 52 h before the experimental test session. APO 50 or 500 μg/kg s.c. was given just before the start of the test. Test session = 30 min. Data are given from time 15–30 of the test session. Number of animals tested in each category = 12. Columns = duration; figures = number of visits. * $P < 0.05$; ** $P < 0.01$; *** $P < 0.001$ (comparison to saline group).

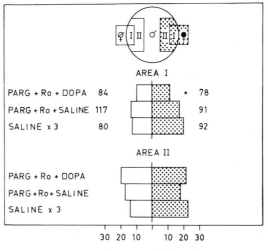

PERCENTAGE TIME / SESSION

Fig. 3. Socio-sexual approach behavior in castrated male rats treated with testosterone proprionate and pargyline + RO 4602 + DOPA. Testosterone was given 52 h before the experimental test session. Pargyline 20 mg/kg, RO 4602 25 mg/kg and L-DOPA 2.5 mg/kg was given 90, 60 and 30 min respectively before the test session. Test session = 30 min. Data represent the whole test session. Number of animals tested in each category = 6. Columns = duration; figures = number of visits. * $P < 0.05$ (comparison to saline group).

time for which the male sat close to the female, but a corresponding increase in the time spent in area 2. The data indicate that an increase in dopamine and/or norepinephrine inhibits heterosexual approach behavior in both sexes.

SUMMARY AND CONCLUSIONS

With regard to the question posed in the Introduction, the data available so far allow us to draw the following tentative conclusions. An increase in dopaminergic activity stimulates most elements of the testosterone-dependent male copulatory behavior pattern, as was demonstrated in genetic male rats. The initiation of mounting also seems to be facilitated by a dopamine agonist in testosterone-treated spayed females. Lordotic behavior is inhibited by dopamine in both females and males. The sexual approach displayed by males towards a sexually active female seems to be inhibited by dopamine and/or norepinephrine. Hetero-sexual approach in the female was clearly suppressed by apomorphine, thus implicating dopaminergic inhibitory mechanisms in this behavior.

More experiments are certainly required before any definite conclusions can be drawn. A variety of psychotrophic drugs with selective effects need to be tested together with different hormonal combinations. It is also possible that differential effects could be obtained by various neuropeptides. However, it would seem that heterotypic copulatory behavior in a given sex and homotypic copulatory behavior in the opposite sex are influenced in an analogous fashion by monoaminergic systems.

ACKNOWLEDGMENT

Research was supported by Grant B83-04X-00064-19C from the Swedish Medical Research Council.

REFERENCES

Beach, F.A. (1942a) Male and female mating behavior in prepuberally castrated female rats treated with andro-gens. *Endocrinology*, 31: 373–378.

Beach, F.A. (1942b) Copulatory behavior in prepuberally castrated male rats and its modification by estrogen administration. *Endocrinology*, 31: 679–683.

Beyer, C., Canchola, E. and Larsson, K. (1981) Facilitation of lordosis behavior in the ovariectomized estrogen primed rat by dibutyryl cAMP. *Physiol. Behav.*, 26: 249–251.

Crowley, W. and Zemlan, F.P. (1981) The neurochemical control of mating behavior. In: N.T. Adler (Ed.), *Neuroendocrinology of Reproduction*, Plenum, New York, pp. 451–484.

Davidson, J.M. and Levine, S. (1969) Progesterone and heterotypical sexual behavior in the male rat. *J. Endocrinol.*, 44: 129–130.

Eliasson, M. and Meyerson, B.J. (1975) Sexual preference in female rats during estrous cycle, pregnancy and lactation. *Physiol. Behav.*, 14: 705–710.

Eliasson, M. and Meyerson, B.J. (1981) Development of socio-sexual approach behavior in male laboratory rats. *J. Comp. Physiol. Psychol.*, 95: 160–165.

Emery, D.E. and Sachs, B.D. (1975) Ejaculatory pattern in female rats without androgen treatment. *Science*, 190: 484–485.

Everitt, B.J. (1978) A neuroanatomical approach to the study of monoamines and sexual behavior. In: J.B. Hutchison (Ed.), *Biological Determinants of Sexual Behaviour*, Wiley, Chicester, pp. 555–574.

Everitt, B.J. and Fuxe, K. (1977a) Dopamine and sexual behavior of female rats. Effects of dopamine receptor agonists and sulpiride. *Neurosci. Lett.*, 4: 209–213.

Everitt, B.J. and Fuxe, K. (1977b) Serotonin and sexual behavior of female rats. Effects of hallucinogenic indolealkylamines and phenylethylamines. *Neurosci. Lett.*, 4: 213–220.

Everitt, B.J., Fuxe, K., Hökfelt, T. and Jonsson, G. (1975) Role of monoamines in the control by hormones of sexual receptivity in the female rat. *J. Comp. Physiol. Psychol.*, 89: 556–572.

Feder, H.H. (1978) Specificity of steroid hormone activation of sexual behaviour in rodents. In: J.B. Hutchison (Ed.), *Biological Determinants of Sexual Behaviour*, Wiley, Chicester, pp. 395–424.

Feder, H.H. and Wahlen, R.E. (1965) Feminine behavior in neonatally castrated and estrogen treated male rats. *Science*, 147: 306–307.

Franck, J.A. and Ward, I.L. (1981) Intralimbic progesterone and methysergide facilitate lordotic behavior in estrogen-primed female rats. *Neuroendocrinology*, 32: 50–56.

Harlan, R.E., Shrivers, B.D. and Pfaff, D.W. (1984) Lordosis as a sexually dimorphic neural function. In: G.J. De Vries, J.P.C. De Bruin, H.B.M. Uylings and M.A. Corner (Eds.), *Sex Differences in the Brain. The Relation between Structure and Function. Progress in Brain Research*, this volume, Ch. 14.

Hetta, J. (1977) Effects of morphine and naltrexone on sexual behavior of the male rat. *Acta Pharmacol. Toxicol.*, 41, Suppl. 4: 53.

Hetta, J. and Meyerson, B.J. (1978) Sexual motivation in the male rat. A methodological study of sex-specific orientation, and the effects of gonadal hormones. *Acta Physiol. Scand.*, Suppl. 453: 1–68.

Höglund, A.U., Hägglund, J.-E. and Meyerson, B.J. (1983) A video interface for behavioural recordings with applications. *Physiol. Behav.*, 30: 489–492.

Levine, S. and Mullins Jr., R.F. (1964) Estrogen administered neonatally affects adult sexual behavior in male and female rats. *Science*, 144: 185–187.

Malmnäs, C.O. (1973) Monoaminergic influence of testosterone-activated copulatory behavior in the castrated male rat. *Acta Physiol. Scand.*, Suppl. 395: 1–128.

Malmnäs, C.O. (1976) The significance of dopamine, versus other catecholamines for L-DOPA induced facilitation of sexual behavior in the castrated male rats. *Pharmacol. Biochem. Behav.*, 4: 521–526.

McDonald, P. and Meyerson, B.J. (1973) The effect of oestradiol, testosterone on sexual motivation in ovariectomized female rats. *Physiol. Behav.*, 11: 515–520.

McIntosh, T.K., Vallano, M.L. and Barfield, R.J. (1980) Effects of morphine, β-endorphin and naloxone on catecholamine levels and sexual behavior in the male rat. *Pharmacol. Biochem. Behav.*, 13: 435–441.

Meyerson, B.J. (1968) Female copulatory behaviour in male and androgenized female rats after oestrogen/amine depletor treatment. *Nature (London)*, 217: 683–684.

Meyerson, B.J. (1973) Mechanisms of action of sex steroids on behavior; inhibition of estrogen-activated behavior by ethamoxy-triphetol (MER-25), colchicine and cycloheximide. In: E. Zimmermann, W.H. Gispen, B.H. Marks and D. de Wied (Eds.), *Progress in Brain Research, Vol. 39*, Elsevier, Amsterdam, pp. 135–146.

Meyerson, B.J. (1975) Drugs and sexual motivation in the female rat. In: M. Sandler and G.L. Gessa (Eds.), *Sexual Behavior, Pharmacology and Biochemistry*, Raven, New York, pp. 21–31.

Meyerson, B.J. (1978) Psychotropic drugs and sexual behavior. In: P. Deniker, C. Radovco-Thomas and A. Villeneove (Eds.), *Neuro-Psychopharmacology*, Pergamon, New York, pp. 971–980.

Meyerson, B.J. (1982) Colchicine delays the estrogen-induced copulatory response in the ovariectomized female rat. *Brain Res.*, 253: 281–286.

Meyerson, B.J. (1983) Endorphin–monoamine interaction and steroid-dependent behavior. In: J. Balthazart, R. Pröve and R. Gilles (Eds.), *Hormones and Behaviour in Higher Vertebrates*, Springer, Berlin, pp. 111–117.

Meyerson, B.J. and Lindström, L.H. (1973) Sexual motivation in the female rat. A methodological study applied to the investigation of the effect of estradiol benzoate. *Acta Physiol. Scand.*, Suppl. 389: 1–80.

Meyerson, B.J. and Malmnäs, C.O. (1978) Brain monoamines and sexual behaviour. In: J.B. Hutchison (Ed.), *Biological Determinants of Sexual Behaviour*, Wiley, Chicester, pp. 521–554.

Meyerson, B.J. and Terenius, L. (1977) β-Endorphin and male sexual behavior. *Eur. J. Pharmacol*, 42: 191–192.

Meyerson, B.J., Eliasson, M. and Hetta, J. (1979) Sex specific orientation in female and male rats. Development and effects of early endocrine manipulation. In: A.M. Kaye and M. Kaye (Eds.), *Advances in Bioscience, Vol. 25*, Pergamon, New York, pp. 451–460.

Myers, B.M. and Baum, M.J. (1979) Facilitation by opiate antagonists of sexual performance in the male rat. *Pharmacol. Biochem. Behav.*, 10: 615–618.

Myers, B.M. and Baum, M.J. (1980) Facilitation of copulatory performance by naloxone: Effects of hypophysectomy, 17a-estradiol, and luteinizing releasing hormone. *Pharmacol. Biochem. Behav.*, 12: 365–371.

Pellegrini-Quarantotti, B., Corda, M.G., Paglietti, E., Biggio, G. and Gessa, G.L. (1978) Inhibition of copulatory behavior in male rats by D-ACA^2-metenkephalinamide. *Life Sci.*, 23: 673–678.

Quadagno, D.M. and Ho, G.K.W. (1975) The reversible inhibition of steroid-induced sexual behavior by intra-cranial cycloheximide. *Hormone Behav.*, 6: 19–26.

Rainbow, T.C., Davis, P.G. and McEwen, B.S. (1980) Anisomycin inhibits the activation of sexual behavior by estradiol and progesterone. *Brain Res.*, 194: 548–555.

Sietnieks, A. and Meyerson, B.J. (1980) Enhancement by progesterone of lysergic acid diethylamide inhibition of copulatory response in the female rat. *Eur. J. Pharmacol.*, 63: 57–64.

Sietnieks, A. and Meyerson, B.J. (1982) Enhancement by progesterone of 5-hydroxytryptophan inhibition of the copulatory response in the female rat. *Neuroendocrinology*, 35: 321–326.

Sietnieks, A. and Meyerson, B.J. (1983) Progesterone enhancement of lysergic acid diethylamide (LSD) and *levo*-5-hydroxytryptophan stimulation of the copulatory response in the female rat. *Neuroendocrinology*, 36: 462–467.

Sirinathsinghji, D.J., Whittington, P.E., Andsley, A. and Fraser, H.M. (1983) β-Endorphin regulates lordosis in female rats by modulating LH-RH release. *Nature (London)*, 301: 62–64.

Södersten, P. (1972) Mounting behavior in the female rat during the estrous cycle, after ovariectomy and after estrogen or testosterone administration. *Hormone Behav.*, 3: 307–320.

Södersten, P. (1984) Sexual differentiation: do males differ from females in behavioral sensitivity to gonadal hormones? In: G.J. De Vries, J.P.C. De Bruin, H.B.M. Uylings and M.A. Corner (Eds.), *Sex Differences in the Brain. The Relation between Structure and Function. Progress in Brain Research*, this volume, Ch. 5.

Terkel, A.S., Shregne, J. and Gorski, R.A. (1973) Inhibition of estrogen facilitation of sexual behavior by the intracerebral infusion of actinomycin-D. *Hormone Behav.*, 4: 377–386.

Ward, I. (1969) Differential effect of pre- and postnatal androgen on the sexual behavior of intact and spayed female rats. *Hormone Behav.*, 1: 25–36.

DISCUSSION

E. ERIKSSON: Are there any data from biochemical studies or radioligand binding experiments supporting your postulated influence of progesterone on 5-HT neurotransmission?

B. MEYERSON: There are a couple of studies indicating a relationship between estrogen/progesterone effects on 5-HT binding and turnover (Fichette et al., 1983). However, it is not possible to relate these effects to functional significance for the behavior.

K.-D. DÖHLER: You have shown that a test animal will prefer to approach a sexually active animal of the other sex, rather than a sexually non-active animal of the other sex. Will a test animal prefer to approach sexually active animals in general, including sexually active members of the same sex as compared to sexually non-active members of the same sex?

B. MEYERSON: No, e.g. a male has a clear preference for a castrate male vs. an intact male.

REFERENCE

Fichette, C.T., Biegon, A. and McEwen, B.S. (1983) Sex differences in serotonin-1 receptor binding in rat brain. *Science*, 222: 333–335.

G.J. De Vries et al. (Eds.),
Progress in Brain Research, Vol. 61
© 1984 Elsevier Science Publishers B.V., Amsterdam

Relationships between Sexual and Aggressive Behavior in Male and Female Rats: Effects of Gonadal Hormones

F.H. DE JONGE and N.E. VAN DE POLL

Netherlands Institute for Brain Research, Amsterdam (The Netherlands)

INTRODUCTION

Ideas concerning a general link between sexuality and aggression have been advanced both from psychological theories and from biological studies in animals. Elements of aggressive behavior observed in human heterosexual relations not only stimulated Freud (1933) to formulate a link between these two classes of motives but also founded the impetus for empirical studies which demonstrated that sexual arousal could indeed influence aggression. In one such study based upon these considerations, Jaffe et al. (1974) investigated the effects of sexual arousal upon experimentally operationalized aggression in male and female students. Sexually aroused subjects delivered more intense shocks than did control subjects to a confederate of the experimenter who was operating the so-called "Buss aggression machine" (Buss, 1961). Although males delivered stronger shocks than did females, neither the gender of the experimental subject nor that of the feigned recipient of the shock (which were varied as factors in the experimental design), interacted with the induced increase in aggression.

Several biological factors, the relevance of which was established in animal studies on sexual and aggressive behavior, may underly the link between these two classes of motives. Endocrinological experiments have indicated that testosterone activates masculine sexual behavior (reviewed by Young, 1961) along with aggressive tendencies (reviewed by Moyer, 1976) in the male and female rat, but also feminine sexual behavior (i.e., the assumption of a lordosis posture) specifically in the female (reviewed by Feder, 1978). Estrogen in contrast elicits masculine and feminine sexual responses in both sexes (Davidson, 1969; Aren-Engelbrektsson et al., 1970; Södersten, 1972, 1973; van de Poll and van Dis, 1977), but aggressive behavior only in the male (Edwards and Burge, 1971; van de Poll et al., 1981a).

The now rapidly growing knowledge on local hormonal effects on the brain — studies using brain implants of crystalline hormones — strongly suggests that neural systems involving receptors for these hormones, which influence these behaviors, either overlap or are intimately linked (for a review see Barfield, 1983). The importance of the medial preoptic anterior hypothalamic continuum (APOA/AHA) for the female's pattern of sexual behavior was established by means of intracerebral implants of estradiol (Lisk, 1962; Barfield and Chen, 1977) while preoptic lesions facilitated sexual receptivity (Powers and Valenstein, 1972). With respect to masculine sexual behavior in male animals, here too the medial preoptic area was found to be a site of action of gonadal hormones, on the basis of implantation (Davidson, 1966) and lesion studies (Heimer and Larsson, 1966/67; van de Poll and van

Dis, 1979). The relationship between electrical self-stimulation and sexual behavior suggested that motivational aspects of masculine sexual behavior are involved (van de Poll and van Dis, 1971).

The few studies aimed at localizing the site of action of steroid hormones in aggressive behavior revealed that testosterone implanted in the septal and medial preoptic areas, raised the response levels in castrated male mice and rats, although the effects were not very striking (Christie and Barfield, 1973; Owen et al., 1974; Bean and Conner, 1978). In reviewing this work and some studies of his own lab, Barfield (1983) came to the conclusion that "no single area appears to be responsible for androgen effects in the enhancement of aggressiveness of males as seems the case of sexual behavior". However, the apparent simple "one hormone–one target site–one behavior" relationship is in fact also intenable in the case of sexual behavior (Barfield, 1983). Recent experiments indicate that, in the activation of masculine and feminine sexual behavior, androgens not only derive their effects from estrogenic metabolites acting upon the hypothalamus and preoptic area but that 5α-reduced androgens act within the brain so as to influence behavior (Dohanich and Ward, 1980; Baum et al., 1982; Tobet and Baum, 1982). Thus, the lateral septum and the medial amygdala were implicated both in the facilitation of masculine sexual behavior and in the inhibition of feminine responses.

There is evidence, apparently, that biological mechanisms mediating the display of sexual and aggressive behaviors overlap. Typically, however, experiments (and especially studies on sex differences), have been studying these behaviors as separate entities under stimulus conditions which are optimal for only one type of behavior to occur thus obscuring possible relations. In the present paper it will be argued that the study of masculine and feminine sexual behavior and aggression as separate behavioral entities limits the possibilities to define the relevance of differences between males and females thus observed. In the first place it will be argued that sex differences in behavior as a function of hormone treatment can only be interpreted if the relative importance of experiential factors and/or stimulus conditions in modifying sex differences have been established. This is of special importance for the development of an animal model for the study of biological factors underlying sex differences in man, as typically previous experience is assumed to contribute as a major factor to the development of human behavior. Furthermore it will be shown that the facilitation or inhibition of one type of behavior — when going together with a facilitation of another type of behavior — can only be interpreted when the animal is placed in a test environment, appropriate for the display of both behaviors or revealing the choice between one or the other stimulus situation. In a last section, data will be presented which point to the role of aromatization of testosterone and the relative contributions of its metabolites in eliciting sexual and aggressive responses.

SEX DIFFERENCES IN THE SEQUELAE TO AGGRESSIVE EXPERIENCES

Most research on activating effects of testosterone on aggressive behavior has focused upon the so-called "inter-male" or social aggression as a form that is particularly relevant in reproductive behavior of both sexes. Sex differences which could be attributed to an organizational effect of perinatal gonadal steroid hormones in mice have been reported in several experiments (Von Saal et al., 1976; Barkley and Goldman, 1977), although the magnitude of the effects is a matter of debate. A possible source of variation between results of different experimenters might lie in factors other than hormonal treatment, which affect aggression to a large extent. Therefore, in a series of experiments, sex differences in testosterone propionate (TP)-induced agonistic behavior were evaluated as a function of two such factors: (1) the hormonal condition of the opponent and (2) the subject's previous experiences with aggressive encounters.

It was previously shown that TP-treated mice, male as well as female, elicited far more attacks from male fighter mice than did oil-treated animals (Mugford and Nowell, 1971; Mugford, 1974). In our tests (van de Poll et al., 1981b) in which an agonistic interaction of animals of the same sex was studied, it was shown that TP (500 μg/rat) activated aggressive behavior in male and female rats equally and, moreover, that the gonadal condition of the opponent was as relevant a factor for males as for females: TP treatment of the opponent increased aggression both in oil-treated and TP-treated males and females (see Fig. 1). The possibility that a lower dose of TP would reveal a sex difference was eliminated by a subsequent replication of this experiment with varying doses of TP (250 resp. 100 μg) (Van de Poll et al., 1981a, 1983). Since the actual patterns of agonistic responses did not differ between the sexes, and since females and males reacted equally aggressively to the hormonal condition of the opponent, regardless of the dose, it was concluded that neither the quantity nor the quality of this kind of aggressive behavior differed between male and female rats.

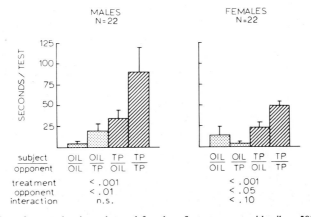

Fig. 1. Mean duration of aggression in males and females after treatment with oil or 500 μg TP (treatment subject). Individuals of all groups were tested either against oil-treated opponents or against TP-treated opponents (treatment opponent) of the same sex. Analysis of variance indicated that TP activated aggression in males and females equally (treatment: $P < 0.001$) and that hormonal treatment of the opponent was a relevant factor both in males and in females (opponent: $P < 0.05$).

In all experiments mentioned thus far, a procedure was used which minimized the role of experiential factors in agonistic responding. The relevance of such a factor could be clearly seen however, during the tests which endured 15 min: Equally treated animals readily developed a dominance–submission relationship which affected the subsequent levels of aggression. Indeed, although no sex differences were found in an initial aggressive encounter, subsequent testing revealed that the sexes in fact differed in their long-term reaction to the experience of winning or losing, and that this difference was clearly hormone dependent. Male and female rats were exposed to winning and losing experiences by confronting them to conspecifics from more or less aggressive strains (for details of the procedure, see van de Poll et al., 1982a,b). After three such confrontations the aggression of the loser rats was clearly inhibited as compared to winners, both in testosterone- and in oil-treated subjects. Typically,

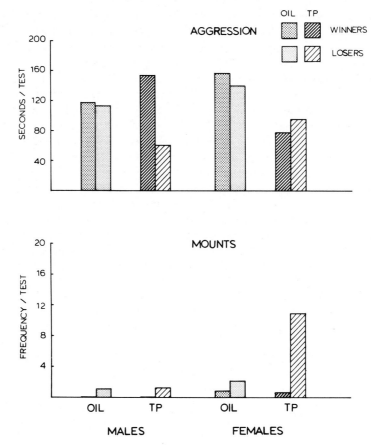

Fig. 2. After 3 days of victory (WINNERS) or defeat (LOSERS), winners and losers were confronted with each other. Effects of victory or defeat were observed with respect to aggressive behavior in males (but not in females) and with respect to mounting behavior in females (but not in males). These effects only occurred in TP-treated animals (250 μg/14 days/rat). (Taken from van de Poll et al., 1982b.)

an inhibition of social initiative and activity was observed in the losers, which in addition showed a loss in body weight. After this "induction", winners were confronted with losers of the same sex and prior treatment (see Fig. 2). In these tests, clear-cut sex differences emerged which were still present 14 days later: whereas TP-treated male winners exhibited high levels of aggression, the TP-treated male losers' aggression was severely inhibited. TP-treated females, in contrast, reacted with the same amount of aggression, whether they had previously experienced victory or defeat. Oil-treated animals of both sexes reacted with equal levels of aggression, irrespective of their previous experience. In conclusion, activating effects of testosterone on aggression clearly interact with agonistic experience in a sex-specific manner: in response to earlier victory or defeat, lasting changes in aggressive behavior emerged, but only in males.

The relevance of behavioral changes as a result of winning or losing a conspecific encounter, has been previously described in terms of hormonal feedback mechanisms (Leshner, 1980). However, such behavioral changes have been scarcely studied (Kahn, 1951; Scott and Marston, 1953; Bevan et al., 1960; Frischknecht et al., 1982), with only a few studies in rats and monkeys (see Keverne et al., 1984), indicating the existence of sex differences in this aspect of agonistic behavior. Seward (1945, 1946) reported that in male encounters the first fight was usually decisive in establishing dominance. After being defeated the loser assumed a submissive status even with different opponents. Fights among females, although occurring frequently in his experiments, were characteristically less violent and failed to have a decisive outcome. After fighting and "defeat" contact was re-established and losing females did not assume a subordinate position. Our results, however, do not support Seward's hypothesis that sex differences are due to more intense fighting and forthcoming pain in males than in females. On the contrary, our females in many cases fought even more fiercely than did the males, probably due to the absence of "behavioral inhibition".

MOUNTING BEHAVIOR: ITS RELATION TO AGGRESSION

When activational effects of gonadal hormones upon sexual and aggressive behavior are investigated, involuntarily estrogenic induction of lordosis stands as a model for the effects, in which case a period of hormonal exposure precedes the behavioral response that is highly stereotyped. Aggressive behavior is different in this respect, since this behavior is not dependent on the presence of gonadal hormones. If present, however, gonadal hormones certainly affect levels of aggressive responding, but, as is illustrated in the first section, their influence comprises interactions with both environmental factors and former social experience (van de Poll et al., 1982a,b). From the literature it is known that, at least in males, this is also the case with masculine sexual behavior (Larsson, 1978). This is of special interest when possible relations between sexual an aggressive behavior are considered.

Sexual behaviors frequently occur during aggressive encounters and examples can be found in the literature of a relationship between social status or dominance and sexual activity in male rodents and primates (Goldfoot, 1971; Dewsbury, 1981). Male Wistar rats living in an established colony, for instance, do not fight very often but a male intruder is fiercely attacked by the dominant male (Adams and Boice, 1983). Females attack female intruders in a similar fashion, but exposure of a female to testosterone leads her to attack male intruders as well (Brain et al., 1983; De Bold and Miczek, 1981).

Illustrations of an influence of social status on sexual activity can be given by observations from our lab: The majority of male rats living peacefully in an enriched environment in which they had been reared, totally ignored a female in heat that was introduced into the cage (Swanson and van de Poll, 1983). Only one or two males mated with such females even when each male was tested individually. On the other hand, it has been reported that prior sexual experience may influence consequent aggressive behavior: Cohabitation with intact females — but not with ovariectomized females or intact males (Goyens and Noirot, 1974; Flannelly and Lore, 1977) — or prior experience with copulation (Flannelly et al., 1982) increased aggressiveness on the part of resident males towards unfamiliar male intruders. When exposed to inaccessible estrous females, both dominant and submissive male rats reacted with increased approach and aggressive behavior towards aggressive target males (Taylor, 1975, 1976).

Although sexual behaviors frequently occur during aggressive encounters, only a few studies have reported and interpreted interactions at this level. Grant and McIntosh (1963), in a study on rank orders in caged male rats, found a positive correlation between mounting responses and dominance in males. And Lagerspetz and Hautojärvi (1967), studying the

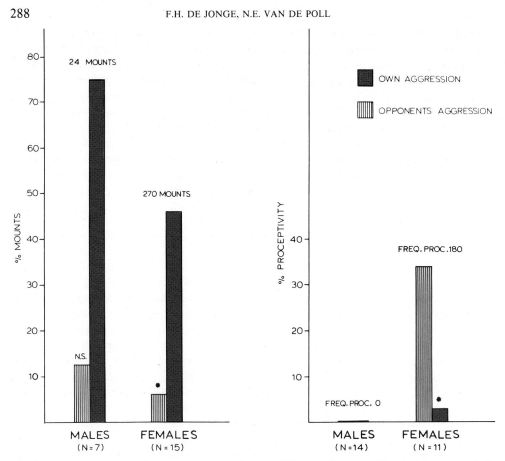

Fig. 3. Sequences of sexual and aggressive responses in pairs of TP-treated males and females: percentage of all mounts (left) or proceptive behaviors (right) followed (within 7 sec) by aggression of the animal or followed by aggression of the opponent. These sequences were calculated on the basis of the total number of mounts or proceptive behaviors (presented on top of the bars). Mounting females elicited aggression from the opponent, whereas proceptive behaviors were frequently followed by aggression in the proceptive animal. Results in males, apparently, were equal to those of females but the low frequencies of mounting prohibited significance. * $P < 0.05$; N.S., not significant.

aggressive behavior of naive male mice versus sexually experienced males, found that (in contrast to the earlier mentioned papers) aggressive behavior was inhibited in sexually experienced males, while mounting behavior was increased during the aggressive encounter. This was interpreted as "that the kind of arousal which has been learned tends to be reactivated and may cause inappropriate behavior, i.e. homosexuality...".

In our experiments, described in the first section, mounting behavior was commonly observed in males and even more so, in females (van de Poll et al., 1982b). The consistency with which this behavior was observed indicated that mounting behavior is, rather than "inappropriate", an integrative part of the male's and female's aggressive repertoire and that it possibly serves a specific function. After repeated exposure, TP-treated female losers mounted 3 times more than did winners, while males did not react to victory or defeat with differential mount frequencies (see Fig. 2). Apparently, experience of victory or defeat changes the male's aggressive behavior and aggressive initiative, leaving mounting responses unaffected, while TP-treated females, as a contrast, react with equal levels of aggressive behaviors and with differential levels of masculine sexual behavior. Based on these observations, it should be considered if the concept of dominance, traditionally described in terms of overt aggressive behavior as a result of previous aggressive interactions (in males!), should be re-evaluated and extended to the analysis of masculine sexual behaviors, if a proper comparison between the sexes is to be made.

Interactions between sexual and aggressive behaviors can be further illustrated by observations on the relationship between masculine and feminine sexual behavior patterns in female rats during aggressive encounters. Of special interest in this respect are dyads of TP-treated naive female rats (see Fig. 3), showing all of the known components of sexual behavior together with fierce fighting. High levels of proceptive behavior, which elicit masculine sexual behavior from the partner, are followed by attacks from this proceptive female as soon as mounting occurs. In accordance with the results from the winner/loser experiment, females losing a fight react with high levels of mounting behavior (de Jonge et al., 1983b).

MOUNTING BEHAVIOR: ITS RELATION TO SEXUAL MOTIVATION

Female rats show (1) feminine sexual responses when exposed to a male and (2) masculine sexual responses when exposed to another female in heat. Typically, feminine sexual responses only occur after proper hormonal stimulation, whereas mounting occurs in the ovariectomized non-treated female rat as well. Feminine sexual responses (i.e. lordosis behavior) in the female have implicitly been taken as a sign for feminine sexual motivation (i.e. a preference to approach or copulate with a male). However, tests for homotypical or heterotypical sexual behavior either in male or in female rats, generally do not include parameters for sexual motivation. Partner preference tests and tests measuring the motivation to copulate with a male provided arguments that indeed both lordosis behavior and the motivation to approach or copulate with a male are stimulated by estrogen treatment (Meyerson and Lindström, 1973; Pfaff, 1982). Others (de Jonge and van de Poll, 1982) have stressed the relationship between the motivation to copulate with a male and proceptive behaviors (presenting hopping, darting and ear wiggling), which are assumed to elicit copulatory activity from the male (Madlafousek and Hlinak, 1977). Possible relations between mounting behavior of the female and sexual motivation are not investigated yet. Although mounting would be expected to correlate with motivation to approach or copulate with a receptive female (i.e. masculine sexual motivation), some authors tentatively suggested that in females mounting is rather related to motivation to copulate with a male (i.e. feminine sexual motivation) (discussed by Beach, 1968).

In male rats, Hetta and Meyerson (1978a) extensively studied the relation between copulatory performance and their approach behavior towards estrous females — as a measure of sexual motivation — as a function of hormone treatment. In studies in which males were castrated and then allowed the choice to approach either a sexually active male or an estrous female, the preference for the estrous female gradually disappeared after castration. This went together with a decrement in sexual performance (ejaculations, intromissions and eventually, mounting) (Hetta and Meyerson, 1978b).

The study of motivation underlying sexual behavior is of special relevance for an appreciation of the organizing effects of androgens on the development of sexual behavior. Neonatal androgenization of female rats, for instance, is generally thought to masculinize the brain as a result of which feminine sexual responses are inhibited, whereas masculine sexual responses are facilitated in these animals. The question arises, however, if the observed changes in sexual behavior reflect an increased motivation to copulate with a female as well. This question is especially difficult to answer, since the relationship between masculine sexual behavior and sexual motivation in normally developed female rats has never been investigated.

In order to evaluate the significance of mounting in females, and its possible relationship to sexually motivated behavior, two experiments were carried out in our lab. In the first experiment, effects of TP — chosen as a hormone which particularly stimulates mounting in the female — on measures of masculine and feminine sexual behavior and partner preference were studied (Scholtens et al., 1980). In a second experiment, an attempt was made to correlate mounting with sexual motivation both in ovariectomized, non-treated female rats and in other animals in which mounting behavior had been facilitated by TP treatment.

In the first experiment, ovariectomized TP-treated female rats (100 μg, 14 days) were tested for mounting behavior towards highly receptive females and for lordosis in reaction to vigorous mounts by a stimulus male. As can be seen from the results presented in Fig. 4, mounting is significantly (U-test; $p < 0.01$) facilitated in TP-treated animals, while receptive behavior is not significant increased as compared to controls. Then, naive, TP-or oil-treated

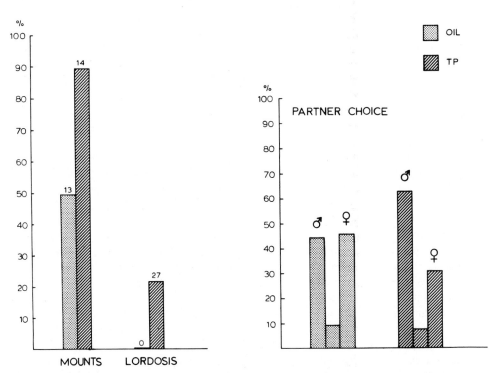

Fig. 4. The percentage of females responding with masculine sexual behavior (mounting) or feminine sexual behavior (lordosis) after treatment with TP. Mean mount frequencies per 20 min and lordosis quotients, based on 10 mounts, are presented on top of the bars. Partner choice was tested in a runway–choice apparatus and is presented at the right side, as the percentage of trials in which a female chose to approach either a sexually active male or a receptive female or neither of them (middle column). Apparently, treatment with 100 μg TP/14 days facilitated both masculine and feminine sexual behavior, although levels of receptive behavior were very low. Interestingly, this treatment resulted in a choice for sexually active males.

females were tested in a Y maze, allowing them to gain access to either a sexually active male or an estrous female. The results show that, in contrast to oil-treated controls, TP-treated females preferred active males over sexually active females (U-test; $p < 0.01$; Fig. 4). Thus, on the basis of these results, mounting behavior by TP-treated females directed towards estrous females could be taken as indicative of a high degree of motivation to approach sexual active males (i.e. feminine sexual motivation), which, interestingly enough, was activated by doses of testosterone that were insufficient to stimulate lordosis to a significant extent. Support for the notion that testosterone affects feminine sexual motivation stems from some literature in monkeys (Herbert and Trimble, 1967; Everitt and Herbert, 1972) and humans (Waxenburg et al., 1959; Gorzynski and Katz, 1977) where this hormone affects the proceptive part of the feminine sexual behavioral repertoire, while leaving the receptive and attractive components relatively unaffected. In accordance with this hypothesis, masculine responses, facilitated in TP-treated female rats, could indeed be taken as an indication for the females' increased level of feminine sexual motivation.

Since mounting in the female is a rather variable behavior, it was the aim of the second experiment to establish individual levels of mount frequencies after introduction of a receptive female and to correlate these mount frequencies with approach behavior towards sexually active male or female "incentive" animals. For this purpose, ovariectomized female rats were repeatedly exposed to estrous females in order to acquire repeated measurements of mount frequencies, before tests for sociosexual approach behavior started. These females were tested every third day and mount frequencies increased while testing proceeded. In addition, individual frequencies were highly correlated between tests: Those females which mounted most frequently on the first test did so on subsequent tests as well. After 8 tests, effects of a single injection of testosterone propionate (TP: 500 μg) upon masculine sexual behavior were established. TP given 48 h prior to testing facilitated mounting in these "experienced" females (Wilcoxon, $p < 0.01$). In contrast, a control group of females, tested only once before and once after TP treatment, did not show this facilitation, although they started with only a few mounts per test. It can be said that mount experience sensitized the females for the activating effects of TP treatment (see Fig. 5).

Subsequently, sociosexual approach behavior (towards sexually active males or estrous females) of the "experienced" group of females was registrated first under oil conditions and then 48 h after TP treatment. A control group of "naive" ovariectomized females (which had never been introduced to receptive females) was tested for sociosexual approach behavior as well, the mount frequencies being registered after this test (see Fig. 5). In accordance with earlier reports (McDonald and Meyerson, 1973; Meyerson et al., 1973) naive females did not show any preference for one or the other incentive, while minimal doses of TP induced a preference for active males, despite the fact that neither masculine nor feminine sexual behavior as such was facilitated after this treatment. In contrast, females which had previously been exposed to estrous females, and consequently attained relatively high levels of mounting behavior, consistently preferred the estrous females both before and after the hormone treatment (U-test; $p < 0.01$). Remarkably, however, mount frequencies (which had gradually increased during the test period in the experienced females) were in no way correlated either with the degree of preference for the estrous females or with the time spent with the active male.

The results show that effects of TP on both mounting behavior and partner preference depend on previous sexual experience. Whereas chronically applied TP is capable of activating mounting in naive females, a single injection only facilitates mounting in females repeatedly exposed to estrous females previously. Both with and in the absence of hormonal treat-

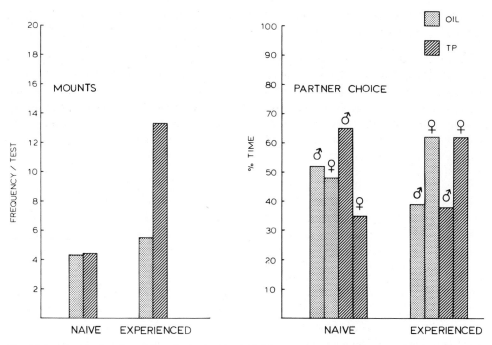

Fig. 5. Mean frequencies of mounting of naive females (which have not been introduced to other receptive females before) and of experienced females (which have been introduced to receptive females repeatedly). Partner choice is presented as the percentage of the total time that naive or experienced females spend near sexually active males or receptive females. Apparently, effects of hormonal treatment and former sexual experience interact with each other.

ment, the preference for sexually active males or alternatively, estrous females appears to be highly dependent upon previous experience as well. Moreover, facilitation of mounting behavior in females in no way predicts the preference for either a male or a female incentive, although sexual experience and/or TP treatment affects both mounting behavior and approach behavior. Apparently, a facilitation or inhibition of masculine sexual behavior, generally observed in test situations which maximize the chance of occurrence of that behavior, has little predictive value for an estimation of the motivation underlying that behavior: the mechanism which regulates preference for one rather than the other incentive is different from that regulating the display of masculine or feminine sexual behaviors occurring when exposed to these incentives.

THE ROLE OF METABOLITES OF TESTOSTERONE IN THE ACTIVATION OF SEXUAL AND AGGRESSIVE BEHAVIOR

Androgenic stimulation in an adult animal may lead to masculine as well as feminine sexual responses. Commonly this is interpreted in terms of the so-called aromatization hypothesis, which states that androgens are aromatized to estrogenic metabolites before they can exert motivational effects upon the brain (Naftolin et al., 1975). There is evidence that this theory is also relevant for other androgen-mediated behaviors, including aggression, and in a variety of species (see review by Brain, 1977; Bowden, 1979). Estrogenic arousal of aggression in male rats and mice has been reported previously (Edwards and Burge, 1971; Brain and Poole, 1976; Christie and Barfield, 1979). In our experiments (van de Poll et al., 1983), males and females were injected with estradiol benzoate (10 μg/14 days) and tested for aggression against TP-treated opponents of the same sex. Although a huge sex difference was established in these animals, the males showing levels of aggression which equaled those of testosterone-treated males (100 μg/14 days) while the females predominantly showed proceptive and receptive responses, it was evident that even estrogen-treated females could occasionally pass into aggressiveness (see van de Poll et al., 1981b). The interpretation of results of androgen-mediated behaviors in terms of the aromatization hypothesis is of

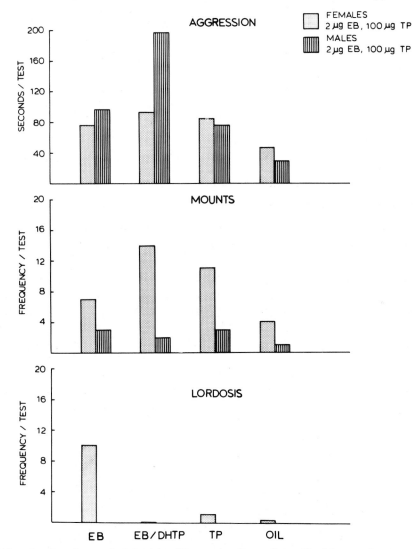

Fig. 6. Mean duration of aggressive behavior and frequencies of masculine and feminine sexual responses in males and females treated with different gonadal hormones. This low dose of EB did not differentially affect the male's and female's aggression. Males were more aggressive than females only after combined EB/DHTP treatment (U-test, $p < 0.05$). During these aggressive encounters, females, in general, showed more masculine sexual behavior than males. For further details see text.

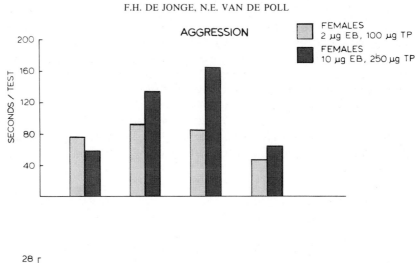

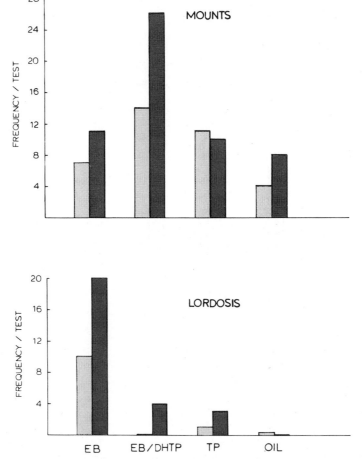

Fig. 7. Mean duration of aggressive behavior and frequencies of masculine and feminine sexual responses of females treated with different gonadal hormones. In the group treated with a higher dose of EB sexual behavior was increased (U-test, $p < 0.05$) and aggression tended to be lower (n.s.). When DHTP was added to EB aggression was increased to levels equal to those of TP-treated females. For further details see text.

special relevance for the appreciation of sex differences in sexual and aggressive behavior since both behaviors have been implicated in the "organizing" effects of gonadal hormones during development, and various metabolites of testosterone could be differentially involved according to the gender of the animal. Indeed, it was found that adult ovariectomized female mice, when treated with estrogen, would only fight if they had been androgenized neonatally (Simon and Gandelman, 1978).

Evidence is now emerging that not only estrogenic metabolites but also $5a$-reduced androgens, derived from testosterone, act together with estrogen both to augment masculine sexual behavior (Lodder and Baum, 1977; Baum and Vreeburg, 1973), and to inhibit feminine sexual responses (Baum and Vreeburg, 1976). Implantation of dihydrotestosterone into the lateral septum facilitated copulation in castrated male rats given estradiol and inhibited feminine sexual responses in estrogen-pretreated ovariectomized female rats (Baum et al., 1982; Tobet and Baum, 1982). Both the preoptic area and the lateral septal area have been shown to contain androgen receptors (Heritage et al., 1981).

For the comparison of effects of testosterone and its major metabolites on aggression, separate groups of males and females were treated with estradiol benzoate (EB: $2 \mu g/14$ days/animal), dihydrotestosterone (DHTP: $1000 \mu g/14$ days/animal) and the combinations of EB and DHTP. An additional group received testosterone propionate (TP: $100 \mu g/14$ days/animal) (Fig. 6). In a subsequent experiment, in which the same hormones were injected in females only, the doses of EB and TP were increased to 10 and $250 \mu g$ respectively. Oil-treated animals were run as controls and all groups were tested against TP-treated opponents of the same sex ($100 \mu g$: Expt. 1, $250 \mu g$: Expt. 2). All females were ovariectomized for at least 6 weeks, and the methodology and procedure were the same as in our earlier experiments (van de Poll et al., 1981a). Not only aggressive responses were scored, but also masculine and feminine sexual responses, frequently occurring in some of these tests (Fig. 7).

Females, treated with TP, showed significant and consistent levels of masculine sexual responses in the aggression tests. In fact, the frequencies of mounting were significantly higher than those observed in the males (Fig. 6). As was already reported in literature on masculine sexual behavior, adding DHTP to EB injections enhanced masculine sexual behavior (Baum and Vreeburg, 1976), which, in the present experiment, led to remarkably frequent mounting when the high dose of estrogen was combined with DHTP. EB and DHTP on their own did not raise mounting levels above those of oil-treated females, but it is noteworthy that mounting was occasionally seen in all these groups.

Feminine sexual responses — the proceptive behaviors hopping and darting, as well as receptive behavior (lordosis) — were most frequently observed in the EB-treated females, especially when the higher dose was administered. These data are consistent with earlier results from our lab which show that estradiol treatment, even in the absence of progesterone, activates complete feminine sexual behavior (de Jonge et al., 1983a). As was expected from earlier results (van de Poll et al., 1981b, 1982c), TP treatment of the females resulted in low but consistent levels of feminine sexual responding. DHTP, when added to EB, drastically inhibited feminine sexual responding: in the low EB dose this behavior was virtually absent, in the higher EB dose females occasionally reacted with lordosis and proceptive behavior. These findings on masculine and feminine sexual responses indicate that DHTP may act directly upon the brain both by stimulating masculine behavior and inhibiting feminine behavior.

If androgenic stimulation leads to feminine sexual behavior by the aromatization of a proportion of the androgen to estrogen (Naftolin et al., 1972), and androgenic metabolites act to inhibit feminine sexual responses, the ultimate levels would depend upon the relative contribution of estrogen activation and (5α-reduced) androgen inhibition of this behavior thus "tuning" masculine and feminine sexual tendencies. What, then, are the implications of this for the sex differences in these behaviors and for the activation of aggression in both sexes? With respect to the latter, our results clearly showed higher levels of aggression in EB/DHTP- and TP-treated females — compared to EB only — when these were treated with the higher dose of EB and TP. This increased aggression went together with an increase in masculine sexual, and a decrease in feminine sexual responding, although this latter was not completely absent in all of the females. Sequence analysis of sexual and aggressive responses indicated that in some females and especially in TP- and EB/DHTP-treated females, being mounted acted to strongly stimulate aggression, whereas mounting tendencies themselves were also strongly increased. Mounting, however, could occur in the most aggressive as well as in the least aggressive females, as was noted earlier (van de Poll et al., 1983).

It will be clear that, given these results, it cannot be stated with certainty whether the hormonal stimulation activated aggression directly and to which extent influences upon sexual behavior contribute to the effects. Two aspects of the increase of aggression may plead for a direct stimulatory effect. Correlation coefficients calculated for the sexual and aggressive responses — either within an animal or between animals — were low and non-significant, despite the fact that sequence analysis led us to conclude that sexual behavior in particular serves as a stimulus for consequent aggressive interactions. Levels of aggression and sexual behavior, moreover, were extremely variable between pairs of animals. As a second argument, aggression and sexual tendencies changed rapidly in the course of the interaction (15 min) and often stabilized in the form of certain roles, which also might indicate that independent tendencies existed at the start of the interaction. The results on the males in these and earlier experiments (van de Poll et al., 1982a,b) can be interpreted as an additional argument for the relative independence of these behaviors, as mounting and especially feminine responses were virtually absent and still aggression was high in TP- and EB/DHTP-treated males.

With respect to sex differences in the hormonal mediation of sexual and aggressive behavior, only tentative conclusions can be drawn as yet. Testosterone and EB/DHTP activated aggression in male and female rats (these experiments and van de Poll et al., 1983). In contrast estradiol consistently increased aggression above the levels seen in oil-treated animals only, when given to male rats (Christie and Barfield, 1979; van de Poll et al., 1981b) and mice (Edwards and Burge, 1971; Brain and Poole, 1976; Bowden, 1979) or androgenized female mice (Simon and Gandelman, 1978). It could be questioned whether sex differences in feminine sexual responding (which have been most consistently found to be influenced by organizing activity of gonadal hormones during the perinatal period) are differently organized into the sexual and aggressive behaviors of males and females. In this respect it remains to be established whether it is the occurrence of feminine sexual responses (in the female) in itself which inhibits aggression in the female, or whether the females' aggression is not activated by estrogen at all. If the absence of sex differences in testosterone-activated aggression would result from specific androgenic activation together with additional reactive aggression which is elicited by being mounted, this latter component would greatly contribute to the overall levels of aggression in the females as the result of excessive frequencies of mounting seen in them. Whether the actual activation and execution of feminine responses directly contributes to an inhibition of aggression in the female is difficult to establish. In that respect a possible role of progesterone is of importance which greatly enhances feminine sexual responding in the female and far less so in the male (reviewed by

Feder, 1978). Preliminary results indeed seem to indicate that progesterone further increases sexual behavior and inhibits the outbursts of aggression which occasionally occurred in individual females (de Jonge et al., 1983b).

IMPLICATIONS FOR A BIOLOGICAl MODEL UNDERLYING SEX DIFFERENCES IN THE HUMAN

Animal studies on the biological factors underlying sex differences in behavior have thus far been considered to be of limited value as a model for the ontogeny of behavioral sex differences in man. As stated in the introduction, two factors limit the extrapolation of animal results to the human. First of all, previous experience of animals influencing adult hormone-activated behavior has been looked upon as being a hazardous introduction of variance into experiments. In animals as in men, however, previous agonistic or sexual experiences have been shown to affect adult behavior, and it seems probable that this effect will be different in males and females. In that respect, in animal as well as in human research, individual differences deserve more attention with respect to the possibility that hormonally induced behavioral changes interact with experiential factors, and possibly can be described in terms of hormonal feedback mechanisms, as noted earlier in rats (Leshner, 1980). Some incidental observations implicated such mechanisms in man as well: studies by Elias (1981) and one by Mazur and Lamb (1980) reported a correlation between individual changes in plasma testosterone levels and previous experience of either winning or losing a boxing match or a tennis competition. The outcome revealed that plasma testosterone levels, as in rats, increased as a result of winning, while decreasing as a result of losing. Data presented in this paper illustrated that sex differences, that are related to the presence of testosterone, can be modified as a function of previous experience: sex differences in agonistic behavior emerged as a consequence of previous victory and defeat. Sexually dimorphic, TP-induced partner preferences were completely changed when females were repeatedly exposed to estrous females (and thus obtained mounting experience). Even the sex difference in estrogen-activated aggression in rats was abolished when pairs of animals were tested in subsequent tests (van de Poll et al., 1983).

A second point stressed in this article concerns the relevance of the interaction of the behavior-eliciting stimuli with the activating hormone. It can be assumed that, in the human, stimuli which elicit aggressive or sexual responses can — at least partially — be selected on the basis of cognitive and motivational factors. Especially when sexual and aggressive behaviors are concerned, all being facilitated by testosterone or its metabolites, it is of major interest to know if all behaviors are indeed stimulated under all possible test situations rather than being facilitated in one situation while being inhibited in the other. Concerning this point, our data give evidence for both possibilities and it must be concluded that data are insufficient to elucidate this point yet. Evidence was presented that the facilitation of either masculine or feminine sexual behavior in the female rat is in no way predictive for the motivation to choose an appropriate incentive to elicit this behavior.

Naturally, studies on sex differences in the human with respect to sexual and aggressive responses were greatly stimulated by the establishment of organizing effects of gonadal hormones in rodents. Thus far, many investigations have concerned possible influences of naturally occurring endocrine syndromes such as CAH and partial androgen insensitivity, and more recently reports of consequences of prenatal exposure to exogenous hormones which were prescribed to the mother (see contribution of Meyer-Bahlburg, 1984; Reinish, 1981). Self-evidently such research exerted great strength in finding positive evidence of sexual dimorphic aspects of behavior which could be shown to be affected by such a factor. Changes in sexual orientation which could be unequivocally related to endocrine factors during development or in adulthood have not been established so far, and the relationship between animal studies involving sexual behavior, on the one hand, and preferential and motivational or attitudinal measures in men, on the other hand, is difficult to assess. Meyer-Bahlburg (1977, 1982), commenting on these typical problems of interspecies comparison, rightly stressed the necessity of studying preferential aspects of sexuality in animals and the misleading notion of stereotypic uniformity in animal sexual behavior, and puts great emphasis upon learning and experiential aspects which in themselves could interact with hormonal factors during puberty and early adulthood, as an alternatively learning-theory-based etiology of human homosexual orientation. Some of the results of this article could be interpreted as an encouragement for investigating the significance of such factors for the development of animal behavior.

In the majority of studies concerning sexual differentiation little attention has been paid to experiential factors, and only a limited number of studies have reported on the differentiation and development of motivational factors underlying sexuality (Meyerson et al., 1979; Eliasson and Meyerson, 1981; de Jonge and Meyerson, 1982). For instance, differential sexual or aggressive experiences during development with littermates or during puberty as a result of early endocrine manipulations have been largely ignored. Although neonatally androgenized female rats have been shown to display more masculine sexual behavior, together with an increased motivation to approach female incentives (Meyerson et al., 1979), the possibility that the increase in female-directed motivation in androgenized females is merely the result of the fact that these animals display more mounting behavior towards cage mates during development (due to elevated estrogen secretion from the ovaries) has not yet been investigated. Moreover, studies in which partner preferences are studied in neonatally demasculinized male rats suggest that, indeed, increased frequencies of lordosis do not necessarily go together with a reversed partner preference (Hetta, 1978a,b; Davis et al., 1979). ATD-treated male rats, as for instance shown in the study by Davis et al. (1979), showed increased levels of feminine sexual responses, but preferred access to an estrous female. Differences with respect to control males were only expressed by the fact that ATD males copulated on all visits, with both males and females, while control males copulated only when visiting an estrous female.

With respect to aggression, as a putative sexually dimorphic aspect of behavior, recent evidence suggests that human prenatal exposure to exogenous sex hormones might affect measures of aggression. However these studies are highly heterogenous in methodology and experimental variables, which led Meyer-Bahlburg (1982) to conclude that "neither the replicability of the aggression results nor the validity of the hormonal interpretation is yet established". Even more so than in the case of sexual behavior, aggressive responses are modulated by experiential factors, not only during development but also in adulthood; even in rats (!) experiential factors can be shown to overrule the activating effects of gonadal hormones. It is therefore not surprising that, despite some positive findings, most studies on the possible relationship between hormones and aggression suggest that androgens influence human aggression only slightly, and possibly only during some psychologically "critical" periods in development. Most authors, comparing animal and human research, stress the importance of social and cultural influences on human behavior, which would make it difficult to distinguish social from biological mechanisms (Benton, 1981). There is no reason to deny the significance of such factors in man but it seems urgent to incorporate learning principles in hormonally mediated behaviors in animals.

ACKNOWLEDGEMENTS

Part of this research was conducted while the first author was being supported by a grant from the Netherlands Psychonomics Foundation (Z.W.O. No. 15-25-09) awarded to dr. N.E. van de Poll. Research on the hormonal effects on aggression was greatly stimulated by a Twinning Grant obtained from the European Training Program together with Dr. D.F. Brain, University of Swansea.

Excellent drawings were prepared by Ellen Verbraak.

REFERENCES

Adams, N. and Boice, R. (1983) A longitudinal study of dominance in an outdoor colony of domestic rats. *J. Comp. Psychol.*, 97: 24–33.

Aren-Engelbrektsson, B., Larsson, K., Södersten, P. and Wilhelmson, M. (1970) The female lordosis pattern induced in male rats by estrogen. *Hormone Behav.*, 1: 181–188.

Barfield, R.J. (1983) Reproductive hormones and aggressive behavior. In: D.C. Blanchard, K.J. Flannely and R.J. Blanchard (Eds.), *Biological Perspectives on Aggression*, Alan R. Liss, New York, in press.

Barkley, M.S. and Goldman, B.D. (1977) Testosterone-induced aggression in adult female mice. *Hormone Behav.*, 9: 76–84.

Baum, M.J. and Vreeburg, J.I.H. (1973) Copulation in castrated male rats following combined treatment with estradiol and dihydrotestosterone. *Science*, 182: 283–285.

Baum, M.J. and Vreeburg, J.I.H. (1976) Differential effects of the anti-estrogen MER-25 and of three 5a-reduced androgens on mounting and lordosis behavior in the rat. *Hormone Behav.*, 7: 87–104.

Baum, M.J., Tobet, S.A., Starr, M.S. and Bradshaw, W.G. (1982) Implantation of dihydrotestosterone propionate into the lateral septum or medial amygdala facilitates copulation in castrated male rats given estradiol systemically. *Hormone Behav.*, 16: 208–223.

Beach, F.A. (1968) Factors involved in the control of mounting behavior by female mammals. In: M. Diamond (Ed.), *Perspective in Reproduction and Sexual Behavior*, Indiana University Press, Bloomington, IN, pp. 83–131.

Bean, N.J. and Conner, R. (1978) Central hormonal replacement and home-cage dominance in castrated rats. *Hormone Behav.*, 11: 100–109.

Benton, D. (1981) The extrapolation from animal to man: the example of testosterone and aggression. In: P.F. Brain and D. Benton (Eds.), *Multidisciplinary Approaches to Aggression Research*, Elsevier/North-Holland Biomedical Press, Amsterdam.

Bevan, W., Daves, W.F. and Levy, G.W. (1960) The relation of castration, androgen therapy and pre-test fighting experience to competitive aggression in male C57B1/10 mice. *Anim. Behav.*, 8: 6–12.

Bowden, N.J. (1979) *Studies on the Manner in which Steroids Influence Aggressiveness in Mus Musculus*, Ph.D. Thesis, University of Wales.

Brain, P.F. (1977) Hormones and aggression. *Annu. Res. Rev.*, 1.

Brain, P.F. and Poole, A.E. (1976) The role of endocrines in isolation-induced intermale fighting in albino laboratory mice. II. Sex-steroid influences in aggressive mice. *Aggress. Behav.*, 2: 55–76.

Brain, P.F., Benton, D., Howell, P.A. and Jones, S.E. (1983) Residents rats' aggression toward intruders. *Anim. Learn. Behav.*, 8: 331–335.

Buss, A. (1961) *The Psychology of Aggression*, Wiley, New York.

Christie, M.H. and Barfield, R.J. (1973) Restoration of social aggression by androgen implanted into the brain of castrated male rats. *Am. Zool.*, 13: 1267 (abstr.).

Christie, M.H. and Barfield, R.J. (1979) Effects of aromatizable androgens on aggressive behavior among rats (*Rattus norvegicus*). *J. Endocrinol.*, 83: 17–26.

Davidson, J.M. (1966) Activation of male rat's sexual behavior by intracerebral implantation of androgen. *Endocrinology*, 79: 783–794.

Davidson, J.M. (1969) Effects of estrogen on the sexual behavior of male rats. *Endocrinology*, 84: 1365–1372.

Davis, P.G., Chaptal, C.V. and McEwen, B.S. (1979) Independence of the differentiation of masculine and feminine sexual behavior in rats. *Hormone Behav.*, 12: 12–19.

De Bold, J.F. and Miczek, K.A. (1981) Sexual dimorphism in the hormonal control of aggressive behavior of rats. *Pharmacol. Biochem. Behav.*, 14, Suppl.: 89–94.

de Jonge, F.H. and Meyerson, B.J. (1982) Attractivity of male and female rats after early endocrine manipulation. *Hormone Behav.*, 16: 1–12.

de Jonge, F.H. and van de Poll, N.E. (1982) Sexual motivation and proceptive behavior in the rat. In: *Abstracts, 4th ESCAB Conference, Bielefeld, September 1982*, pp. 254–255.

de Jonge, F.H., Burger, J. and van de Poll, N.E. (1983a) Lordosis and mounting behavior in the female rat. In: *Abstracts, First European Meeting on the Experimental Analysis of Behaviour, Behaviour Analysis and Contemporary Psychology*, in press.

de Jonge, F.H., Eerland, E.M.J. and van de Poll, N.E. (1983b) Functional relationships between sexual and aggressive behavior. In: *Abstracts, Second European ISRA Conference, September 26–30, Zeist*, in press.

Dewsbury, D.A. (1981) Social dominance, copulatory behavior, and differential reproduction in deer mice (*Peromyscus maniculatus*). *J. Comp. Physiol. Psychol.*, 95: 880–895.

Dohanich, G.P. and Ward, I.W. (1980) Sexual behavior in male rats following intracerebral estrogen application. *J. Comp. Physiol. Psychol.*, 94: 634–640.

Edwards, D.A. and Burge, K.G. (1971) Estrogenic arousal of aggressive behavior and masculine sexual behavior in male and female mice. *Hormone Behav.*, 2: 239–245.

Elias, M. (1981) Serum cortisol, testosterone, and testosterone-binding globulin responses to competitive fighting in human males. *Aggress. Behav.*, 7: 215–224.

Eliasson, M. and Meyerson, B.J. (1981) Development of sociosexual approach behavior in male laboratory rats. *J. Comp. Physiol. Psychol.*, 95: 160–165.

Everitt, B.J. and Herbert, J. (1972) Hormonal correlates of sexual behaviour in subhuman primates. *Dan. Med. Bull.*, 19: 246–258.

Feder, H.H. (1978) Specificity of steroid hormone activation of sexual behaviour in rodents. In: J.B. Hutchinson (Ed.), *Biological Determinants of Sexual Behavior*, John Wiley, New York.

Flannelly, K. and Lore, R. (1977) The influence of females upon aggression in domesticated male rats (*Rattus norvegicus*). *Anim. Behav.*, 25: 654–659.

Flannelly, K.J., Blanchard, R.J., Muraoka, M.Y. and Flannelly, L. (1982) Copulation increases offensive attack in male rats. *Physiol. Behav.*, 29: 381–385.

Freud, S. (1933) *New Introductory Lectures on Psychoanalysis*, Norton, New York.

Frishknecht, H., Siegfried, B. and Waser, P.G. (1982) Learning of submissive behavior in mice: A new model. *Behav. Proc.*, 7: 235–245.

Goldfoot, D.A. (1971) Hormonal and social determinants of sexual behavior in the pigtail monkey (M. nemestrina). In: G.B. Stoelinge and J.J. van der Werff ten Bosch (Eds.), *Normal and Abnormal Development of Brain and Behaviour*, Leiden, pp. 325–342.

Gorzynski, G. and Katz, J.L. (1977) The polycystic ovary syndrome: psychosexual correlates. *Arch. Sex. Behav.*, 6: 215.

Goyens, J. and Noirot, E. (1974) Effects of cohabitation with females on aggressive behavior between male mice. *Develop. Psychobiol.*, 8: 79–84.

Grant, E.C. and McIntosh, J.H. (1963) A comparison of the social postures of some common laboratory rodents. *Behaviour*, 21: 246–259.

Heimer, L. and Larsson, K. (1966/67) Impairment of mating behavior in male rats following lesions in the preoptic-anterior hypothalamic continuum. *Brain Res.*, 3: 248–263.

Herbert, J. and Trimble, M.R. (1967) Effect of oestradiol and testosterone on the sexual receptivity and attractiveness of the female rhesus monkey. *Nature (London)*, 216: 165–166.

Heritage, A.S., Stumpf, W.E., Sarr, M. and Grant, C.D. (1981) ³H-Dihydrotestosterone in catecholamine neurons of rat brain stem: combined localisation by autoradiography and formaldehyde-induced fluorescence. *J. Comp. Neurol.*, 200: 289–307.

Hetta, J. (1978a) *The Effects of Neonatal Castration on Sex-Specific Orientation in the Male Rat*, Doctoral dissertation, Uppsala University.

Hetta, J. (1978b) *Opposite Effects of Testosterone and Estrogen on Sex-Specific Orientation in the Neonatally Castrated Male Rat*, Doctoral dissertation, Uppsala University.

Hetta, J. and Meyerson, B.J. (1978a) Sexual motivation in the male rat. A methodological study of sex-specific orientation and the effects of gonadal hormones. *Acta. Physiol. Scand.*, Suppl. 453.

Hetta, J. and Meyerson, B.J. (1978b) Effects of castration and testosterone treatment on sex-specific orientation in the male rat. *Acta Physiol. Scand.*, Suppl. 453: 47–62.

Jaffe, Y., Malamuth, N., Feingold, J. and Feshback, S. (1974) Sexual arousal and behavioral aggression. *J. Pers. Soc. Psychol.*, 30: 759–764.

Kahn, M.W. (1951) The effect of severe defeat at various age levels on the aggressive behavior of mice. *J. Genet. Psychol.*, 79: 117–130.

Keverne, E.B., Eberhart, J.A., Yodyingyuad, U. and Abbott, D.H. (1984) Social influences on sex differences in the behaviour and endocrine state of talapoin monkeys. In: G.J. De Vries, J.P.C. De Bruin, H.B.M. Uylings and M.A Corner (Eds.), *Sex Differences in the Brain. The Relation between Structure and Function. Progress in Brain Research*, this volume, Ch. 20.

Lagerspetz, K. and Hautojärvi, S. (1967) The effect of prior aggressive or sexual arousal on subsequent aggressive or sexual reactions in male mice. *Scand. J. Psychol.*, 8: 1–6.

Larsson, K. (1978) Experiential factors in the development of sexual behaviour. In: J.B. Hutchinson (Ed.), *Biological Determinants of Sexual Behavior*, John Wiley, New York.

Leshner, A.I. (1980) The interaction of experience and neuroendocrine factors in determining behavioral adaptations to aggression. In: P.S. McConnell, G.J. Boer, H.J. Romijn, N.E. van de Poll and M.A. Corner (Eds.), *Adaptive Capabilities of the Nervous System, Progress in Brain Research, Vol. 53*, Elsevier/North-Holland, Amsterdam, pp. 427–438.

Lisk, R.D. (1962) Diencephalic placement of estradiol and sexual receptivity in the female rat. *Am. J. Physiol.*, 203: 493–496.

Lodder, J. and Baum, M.J. (1977) Facilitation of mounting behavior by dihydrotestosteronepropionate in castrated estradiolbenzoate-treated male rats following pudendectomy. *Behav. Biol.*, 20: 141–148.

Madlafousek, J. and Hlinak, Z. (1977) Sexual behaviour of female laboratory rat. Inventory, patterning, and measurement. *Behaviour*, 63: 129–174.

Mainwaring, W.I.P. (1977) *The Mechanism of Action of Androgens*, Springer, New York.

Mazur, A. and Lamb, T.A. (1980) Testosterone, status, and mood in human males. *Hormone Behav.*, 14: 236–246.

McDonald, P.G. and Meyerson, B.J. (1973) The effect of oestradiol, testosterone and dihydrotestosterone on sexual motivation in the ovariectomized female rat. *Physiol. Behav.*, 11: 515–520.

Meyer-Bahlburg, H.F.L. (1977) Sex hormones and male homosexuality in comparative perspective. *Arch. Sex. Behav.*, 6: 297–325.

Meyer-Bahlburg, H.F.L. (1982) Prenatal sex hormones and human aggression: A review, and new data on progestagen effects. *Aggress. Behav.*, 8: 39–62.

Meyer-Bahlburg, H.F.L. (1984) Psychoendocrine research on sexual orientation. Current status and future options. In: G.J. De Vries, J.P.C. De Bruin, H.B.M. Uylings and M.A. Corner (Eds.), *Sex Differences in the Brain. The Relation between Structure and Function. Progress in Brain Research*, this volume, Ch. 23.

Meyerson, B.J. and Lindström, L. (1973) Sexual motivation in the female rat. A methodological study applied to the investigation of the effect of estradiol benzoate. *Acta Physiol. Scand.*, Suppl. 389.

Meyerson, B.J., Lindström, L., Nordström, E.-B., Ågmo, A. (1973) Sexual motivation in the female rat after testosterone treatment. *Physiol. Behav.*, 11: 421–428.

Meyerson, B.J., Eliasson, M. and Hetta, J. (1979) Sex-specific orientation in female and male rats: Development and effects of early endocrine manipulation. In: A.M. Kaye and M. Kaye (Eds.), *Development of Responsiveness to Steroid Hormones, Advances in the Biosciences, Vol. 25*, Pergamon, Oxford, pp. 451–460.

Moyer, K.E. (1976) Kinds of aggression and their physiological basis. In: K.E. Moyer (Ed.), *Physiology of Aggression and Implications for Control: An Anthology of Readings*, Raven, New York.

Mugford, R.A. (1974) Androgenic stimulation of aggression eliciting cues in adult opponent mice castrated at birth, weaning or maturity. *Hormone Behav.*, 5: 93–102.

Mugford, R.A. and Nowell, N.W. (1971) Endocrine control over production and activity of the anti-aggressive pheromone from female mice. *J. Endocrinol.*, 49: 225–232.

Naftolin, F., Ryan, K.J. and Petro, Z. (1972) Aromatization of androstenedione by the anterior hypothalamus of adult male and female rats. *Endocrinology*, 90: 295–298.

Naftolin, F., Ryan, K.J., Davies, I.J., Reddy, V.V., Flores, F., Petro, Z., Kuhn, M., White, R.J., Takaoka, Y. and Wolin, L. (1975) The formation of estrogens by central neuroendocrine tissues. *Recent Progr. Hormone Res.*, 31: 295–319.

Owen, K., Peters, P.J. and Bronson, F.H. (1974) Effects of intracranial implants of testosterone propionate on intermale aggression in the castrated male mouse. *Hormone Behav.*, 5: 83–92.

Pfaff, D.W. (1982) Neurobiological mechanisms of sexual motivation. In: D.W. Pfaff (Ed.), *The Physiological Mechanisms of Motivation*, Springer, New York.

302   F.H. DE JONGE, N.E. VAN DE POLL

Powers, B. and Valenstein, E.S. (1972) Sexual receptivity: Facilitation by medial preoptic lesions in female rats. *Science*, 175: 1003–1005.

Reinish, J. (1981) Prenatal exposure to synthetic progestins increases potential for aggression in humans. *Science*, 211: 1171–1173.

Scholtens, J., van de Poll, N.E. and van Oyen, H.G. (1980) Gonadal hormones and sexual motivation in the female rat. In: *Proc. of the 21st Dutch Federation Meeting, Nijmegen*, p. 383.

Scott, J.P. and Marston, M.V. (1953) Nonadaptive behavior resulting from a series of defeats in fighting mice. *J. Abnorm. Soc. Psychol.*, 48: 417–428.

Seward, J.P. (1945) Aggressive behavior in the rat. I. General characteristics, age and sex differences. *J. Comp. Psychol.*, 38: 175–224.

Seward, J.P. (1946) Aggressive behavior in the rat. IV. Submission as determined by conditioning, extinction, and disuse. *J. Comp. Psychol.*, 39: 51–76.

Simon, N.G. and Gandelman, R. (1978) The estrogenic arousal of aggressive behavior in female mice. *Hormone Behav.*, 10: 118–127.

Södersten, P. (1972) Mounting behavior in the female rat during the estrous cycle, after ovariectomy, and after estrogen or testosterone administration. *Hormone Behav.*, 3: 307–320.

Södersten, P. (1973) Increased mounting behavior in the female rat following a single neonatal injection of testosterone propionate. *Hormone Behav.*, 4: 1–17.

Swanson, H.H. and van de Poll, N.E. (1983) Effects of an isolated or enriched environment after handling on sexual maturation and behaviour in male and female rats. *J. Reprod. Fertil.*, 69: 165–171.

Taylor, G.T. (1975) Male aggression in the presence of an oestrous female. *J. Comp. Physiol. Psychol.*, 89: 246–252.

Taylor, G.T. (1976) Influence of female's sexual cycle on aggressiveness in male rats. *J. Comp. Physiol. Psychol.*, 90: 740–746.

Tobet, S.A. and Baum, M.J. (1982) Implantation of dihydrotestosterone propionate into the lateral septum inhibits sexual receptivity in estrogen-primed, ovariectomized rats. *Neuroendocrinology*, 34: 333–338.

van de Poll, N.E. and van Dis, H. (1971) Sexual motivation and medial preoptic selfstimulation in male rats. *Psychon. Sci.*, 25: 137–138.

van de Poll, N.E. and van Dis, H. (1977) Hormone-induced lordosis and its relation to masculine sexual activity in male rats. *Hormone Behav.*, 8: 1–7.

van de Poll, N.E. and van Dis, H. (1979) The effect of medial preoptic-anterior hypothalamic lesions on bisexual behavior of the male rat. *Brain Res. Bull.*, 4: 505–511.

van de Poll, N.E., de Jonge, F., van Oyen, H.G., van Pelt, J. and de Bruin, J.P.C. (1981a) Failure to find sex differences in testosterone-activated aggression in two strains of rats. *Hormone Behav.*, 15: 94–105.

van de Poll, N.E., Swanson, H.H. and van Oyen, H.G. (1981b) Gonadal hormones and sex differences in aggression in rats. In: P.F. Brain and D. Benton (Eds.), *The Biology of Aggression*, Sijthoff and Noordhoff, Alphen a/d Rijn.

van de Poll, N.E., de Jonge, F., van Oyen, H.G. and van Pelt, J. (1982a) Aggressive behaviour in rats: Effects of winning or losing on subsequent aggressive interactions. *Behav. Proc.*, 7: 143–155.

van de Poll, N.E., Smeets, J., van Oyen, H.G. and van der Zwan, S.M. (1982b) Behavioral consequences of agonistic experience in rats: Sex differences and the effects of testosterone. *J. Comp. Physiol. Psychol.*, 96: 893–903.

van de Poll, N.E., van der Zwan, S.M., van Oyen, H.G. and Pater, J.H. (1982c) Sexual behavior in female rats born in all-female litters. *Behav. Brain Res.*, 103–109.

van de Poll, N.E., Bowden, N.J., van Oyen, H.G., de Jonge, F.H. and Swanson, H.H. (1983) Gonadal hormonal influences upon aggressive behavior in male and female rats. In: M. Segal (Ed.), *Psychopharmacology of Sexual Disorders*, John Libbey, London, in press.

Von Saal, F.S., Svare, B. and Gandelman, R. (1976) Time of neonatal androgen exposure influences length of testosterone treatment required to induce aggression in adult male and female mice. *Behav. Biol.*, 17: 391–397.

Waxenburg, S.E., Drellich, M.G. and Sutherland, A.M. (1959) The role of hormones in human behaviour. I. Changes in female sexuality after adrenalectomy. *J. Clin. Endocrinol. Metab.*, 19: 193–202.

Young, W.C. (1961) The hormones and mating behavior. In: W.C. Young (Ed.), *Sex and Internal Secretion, Vol. 11*, Williams and Wilkins, Baltimore, MD, pp. 1173–1239.

G.J. De Vries et al. (Eds.),
Progress in Brain Research, Vol. 61
© 1984 Elsevier Science Publishers B.V., Amsterdam

Comparison of Aggressive Behaviour Induced by Electrical Stimulation in the Hypothalamus of Male and Female Rats

MENNO R. KRUK, CORRIE E. VAN DER LAAN, JAN MOS, A.M. VAN DER POEL,
WOUT MEELIS and BEREND OLIVIER [1]

Department of Pharmacology, Sylvius Laboratories, University of Leiden, Wassenaarseweg 72, 2333 AL Leiden, and [1] Department of Pharmacology, Duphar B.V., P.O. Box 2, 1380 AA Weesp (The Netherlands)

INTRODUCTION

Sex differences in aggressive behaviour are present in many species. The genders often become aggressive in different ways or in different conditions (Moyer, 1968). Gonadectomy, or conversely treatment with sex hormones often profoundly affects some types of aggressive behaviour, especially intermale and territorial aggression. Since sex hormones do also change brain organization, sex differences in aggression may be attributed to differences within the brain. There is, however, little direct evidence of sex differences in the brain mechanisms involved in aggressive behaviour, mainly because there is little known about the brain mechanisms underlying aggressive behaviour per se. However, aggression induced by stimulation in the hypothalamus of rats has been extensively studied in our laboratory and its behavioural characteristics (Kruk et al., 1979; Koolhaas, 1978; Van der Poel et al., 1982), its localization in the brain (Kruk et al., 1983), its projections (Mos et al., 1982, 1983) and its excitability are well documented (Kruk et al., 1981). Moreover, the behaviour appears to be sensitive to androgen manipulations (Bermond et al., 1982). Therefore, it seems an excellent "model" to study brain mechanisms and sex differences in aggression.

Although it is clear that female rats are capable of becoming aggressive (Van de Poll et al., 1981, 1982; De Jonge and Van de Poll, 1984), aggression in rats is still considered to be a predominantly male activity. In principle, sex differences in aggression could be caused (1) by a complete absence of certain mechanisms within the brain of one of the sexes, (2) by differences in organization, activity and sensitivity and (3) by differences in the level of circulating sex hormones. Aggression induced by electrical stimulation in the hypothalamus offers a possibility to study such questions directly.

Hypothalamic stimulation induces a behaviour quite similar to so-called intermale aggression. Hypothalamic aggression in male rats is sensitive to manipulations of androgen levels (Bermond et al., 1982). Moreover, it is induced in an area which roughly coincides with the areas where levels of circulating sex hormones are regulated and where structural changes following ovariectomy and oestrogen treatment have been demonstrated (Carrer and Aoki, 1982; Kruk et al., 1983). In this study we have tried to induce aggression by stimulation in the hypothalamus of female as well as male rats and have compared behaviour, histology, and current intensity required to induce attacks, in the two sexes. In addition, we have tried to assess the effects of ovariectomy and subsequent oestradiol replacement on attack thresholds in female rats.

EXPERIMENTAL PROCEDURES

52 brown-eyed, beige-coloured female CPB/WE-zob rats derived from the Central Breeding Institute for Laboratory Animals (CPB-TNO, Zeist, The Netherlands) weighing between 250 and 300 g were used as experimental animals. Weight is an important factor in determining the topology and the outcome of fights. Therefore, the attack patterns displayed, and the wound patterns inflicted by these females were compared with those of a group of 20 males of the same strain and the same weight. The results of another group of 20 other males weighing between 320 and 400 g were included in the comparison of success rate and threshold current intensities. There are no significant differences between these two groups of males as regards these measures. The animals were kept on a reversed 14 h light/10 h dark day–night schedule, with lights off at 8.00 a.m. Prior to operation the animals were housed in groups of 6–8 in large macrolon cages situated in quiet rooms at 22°C and 75% relative humidity. During this period the animals were accustomed to handling. Following surgery the animals were housed individually. Male albino CPB/WU rats (Wistar random) were used as sparring partners for both male and female CPB/WE-zob rats. In all cases these partners were about 65% of the weight of their opponents.

Under Hypnorm® anaesthesia one or two bipolar stimulation electrodes were aimed unilaterally or bilaterally at a point corresponding with the −2.5 mm D.V., 1.5 mm M.L. and 5.5 mm A.P. coordinates of the atlas of König and Klippel (1963). For further details on surgical techniques and electrode construction see Kruk et al. (1978, 1979, 1983). Animals were allowed a postoperative period of 1 week.

Ovaries were removed under light ether anaesthesia. Oestrogen replacement was achieved by subcutaneous implantation in the neck region of 1 cm silastic tube 0.1 mm i.d. and 0.2 o.d. containing oestradiol benzoate kindly provided by Dr. J.T.M. Vreeburg of the Department of Endocrinology, Growth and Development, Erasmus University, Rotterdam, The Netherlands. The tubes had been soaked in saline for 24 h before implantation.

Partners were anaesthetized with ether following fights, and the places of the wounds on their bodies were scored on maps of the rat's body surface exemplified in Fig. 7.

During the first testing animals were stimulated in the presence of a male partner rat. Trains of symmetrical biphasic square-wave pulses of 0.2 msec and a phase interval of 12.5 msec were delivered by two Grass PSIU6 isolated constant-current sources driven by a Grass S88 stimulator. Current was on for 120 sec and off for 60 sec periodically. Initial current was set at 50 μA. In subsequent stimulation periods current intensity was increased by 50-μA steps until either an attack at the partner was induced, wild motor patterns precluded further testing, or an upper limit of 400 μA was reached. If possible, threshold current intensities for attack behaviour and switch-off — i.e., the interruption of stimulation for 1 sec by the animal itself by pressing a lever — were determined directly following the first testing. Switch-off is a behaviour which is induced in a much larger area in the brain than aggression and there is evidence to suggest that it is derived from the activation of a different neural substrate (Kruk and Van der Poel, 1980; Mos et al., 1983; Van der Poel et al., 1982). Therefore, thresholds for switch-off behaviour can be used as a control for the specificity of changes in attack thresholds. Thresholds were determined according to a modification of the up-and-down method of Dixon and Mood (1948) proposed by Wetherill (1966). In threshold determinations the rat is stimulated for 10 sec alternating with 50-sec intervals without stimulation. Thresholds determined by this method are by definition estimates of the current intensity inducing a behaviour in 50% of the stimulation trials. For further details on the procedure see Kruk et al. (1979, 1981) and Van der Poel et al. (1982).

After completion of the experiments, the rats were anaesthetized and perfused with saline followed by 4% formaldehyde. Coronal brain sections were stained according to the Klüver–Barrera method. Electrode localizations were projected on computer-plotted sections of the stereotaxic atlas of the rat hypothalamus by Kruk et al. (1983) and the anterior-posterior, medio-lateral and dorso-ventral coordinates of both the aggression-inducing electrodes and the "negative" electrodes were measured and stored in a computer dataset for further statistical evaluation. For details on histology, atlas and computer procedures see Kruk et al. (1983).

RESULTS

Success rate and localization

There is no significant difference in success rate of implantation between the sexes. Aggression was induced via 26 out of 52 implanted electrodes in females, via 9 out of 20 in the group of males of the same weight, and in 12 out of 20 in the group of heavier males. A success rate of implantation of about 50% is in agreement with our experience with more than 1000 implantations in males (Kruk et al., 1979, 1983; Mos et al., 1982, 1983). In Fig. 1 the localization of electrode placements inducing aggression in females (black triangles) is compared with the localization of a large series of electrode placements inducing aggression in male rats (open triangles). The localization of electrodes that did not induce aggressive behaviour in females is given in black diamonds, in males in open squares. In an earlier publication (Kruk et al., 1983) we proposed and successfully applied a method to discriminate between populations of electrode localizations in which different behavioural effects are induced. The analysis amounts to a sort of "averaging over space" which can be visualized on a computer-plotted stereotaxic atlas of the rat hypothalamus. With this method we are also able to delimit the areas where the chance to induce aggression in females is above 80% (Fig. 2, filled squares), between 80 and 50% (thick-walled squares), between 50 and 20% (intermediate-walled squares), and below 20% (thin-walled squares). The number of aggressive and non-aggressive electrode placements lying in each of the depicted discriminated areas can be used to compute and test the error rate of the analysis in a contingency table. This allocation matrix is highly significant (Table I). It seems that in both females (this analysis) and in males (Kruk et al., 1983) aggression-inducing electrode placements cluster in

TABLE I

ALLOCATION OF ELECTRODE PLACEMENTS TO AREAS WITH HIGH, MODERATE–HIGH, MODERATE–LOW AND LOW CHANCE TO INDUCE AGGRESSION IN FEMALE RATS

$\chi^2 = 15.5$, $df = 4$, $P = 0.004$. *P of cells < 0.05; **P of cell < 0.005. For details see Kruk et al. (1983).

Probability (P) to induce aggression	Actual behaviour induced	
	No aggression	Aggression
$1 \geq P > 0.8$	1	7**
$0.8 \geq P > 0.5$	4	5
$0.5 \geq P > 0.2$	12*	3
$0.2 \geq P > 0$	8*	1
Outlyers	0	1

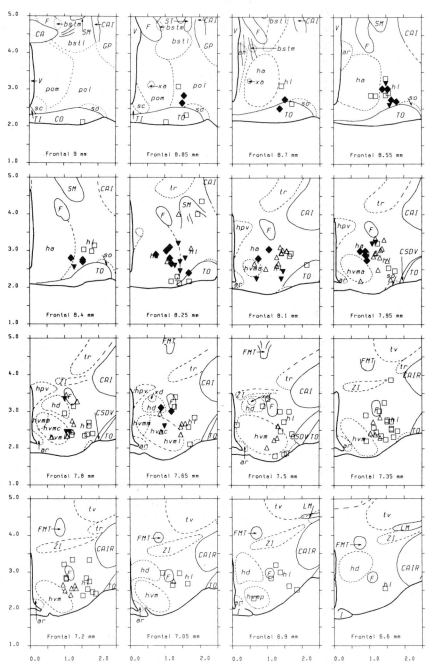

Fig. 1. Computer-assisted plotting of histology on an atlas of the hypothalamus of the rat. Abbreviations of names of structures according to König and Klippel (1963). Triangles, attack-inducing electrode localizations; squares and diamonds, no-attack-inducing electrode localizations; filled symbols, localizations in female rats; open symbols, localizations of a large previous series in male rats (see Kruk et al., 1983).

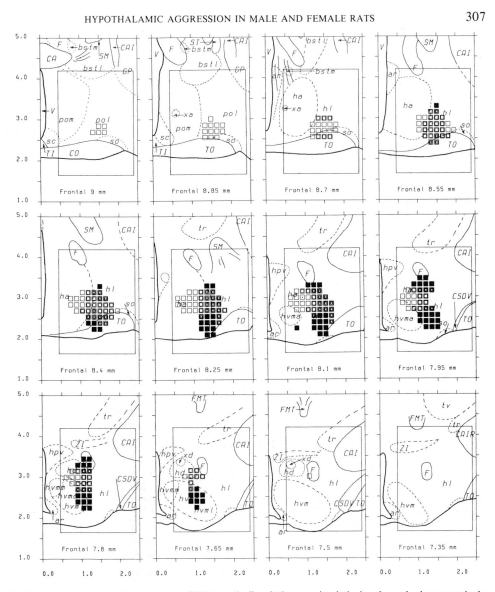

Fig. 2. Results of a discriminant analysis of 25 "negative" and 17 aggression-inducing electrode placements in the female rat's hypothalamus. Filled squares, a high probability to induce aggression; thin open squares, a low probability to induce aggression. Intermediate squares depict intermediate areas. Blank areas, electrode density too low to compute probabilities. See also Table I.

distinct areas. Due to their generally smaller skull size both positive and negative electrode placements in females cluster in the frontal part of the distribution of electrode placements in males (Fig. 1, open versus filled symbols). Within that frontal area, however, the "aggressive" area in females largely overlaps with the "aggressive" area in males. These results strongly suggest that stimulation-induced aggression in male and female rats is elicited in the same neural substrate.

Thresholds

Mean threshold values required to induce attack in 50% of the trials did not differ between male and female rats (Fig. 3). After an initial decrease, subsequent daily thresholds for attack behaviour become quite stable for periods of up to several months. In males ($n = 20$) as well as in females ($n = 20$) attack thresholds decrease to about 50% of their initial value (Fig. 3). This decrease is highly significant in males as well as in females (two-way Anova $F(4, 19) = 25.6$, $P < 0.00001$; $F(4, 19) = 32.9$, $P < 0.00001$ respectively). The main decrease is between the first and the second threshold determination. The differences between the second and third thresholds or subsequent thresholds are no longer statistically significant. Apparently there is no sex difference in the sensitivity of the hypothalamic substrate of aggression for activation by electrical stimulation.

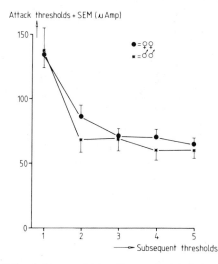

Fig. 3. Decrease of subsequent threshold current intensities required to induce attack behaviour in 20 males (asterisks) and in 20 females (filled circles).

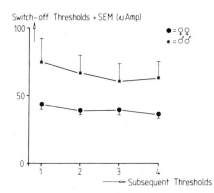

Fig. 4. Subsequent thresholds for switch-off behaviour in aggression-inducing electrode placements in 12 males (asterisks) and 12 females (filled circles).

In 24 of these electrode placements (12 in male rats, 12 in female rats) we determined both attack and switch-off thresholds. Switch-off thresholds decreased only 16% in the electrode placements, while the attack thresholds in this subgroup decreased the usual 50%. The decrease of switch-off thresholds is much smaller than the decrease in attack thresholds. Moreover, the former is only significant when males and females are taken together (two-way Anova $F(3, 23) = 3.0$, $P = 0.004$) and not when males and females are tested separately ($P = 0.18$ and $P = 0.08$ respectively). However, as is shown in Fig. 4, females have generally lower switch-off thresholds than males (difference: 27.0 μA, 95% confidence limits of the difference: from 11.2 to 42.8 μA, $F = 4.9$, $P < 0.0001$, Scheffé, 1959).

Types of attack and wound patterns

Hypothalamic aggression can take several forms at threshold current intensity (Fig. 5). These different forms are probably elicited in the same substrate (Kruk et al., 1983). In descending order of intensity of fighting we distinguish between attack jumps with or without a kick by the hind paws (A), a strong bite attack (C), a weak bite attack (D, not shown) and skin pulling (E). Clinch fights (F) are a very intense form of fighting in which the rats roll over the floor, while biting and kicking with hind paws. Clinch fights may either follow other forms of attack or may be started without preliminaries. In some electrode placements all of these attacks can be induced, in other electrodes only one or a few.

We compared these attack patterns in 20 female rats with the attack patterns of a group of 9 male rats of the same weight. Both in males and females all types of attacks are induced.

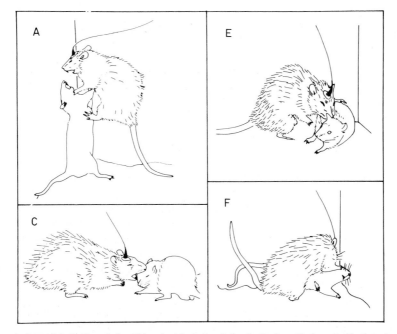

Fig. 5. Types of attack behaviour induced by electrical stimulation in the hypothalamus of both male and female rats. A, attack jump; C, bite attack; E, skin pulling; F, clinch fight.

Fig. 6 suggests that males display more often the more intense forms of attack such as attack jump (A) and clinch fight (F), while females seem to display more often the more gentle forms such as the weak bite (D) and skin pulling (E). However, only in the case of skin pulling these differences reach statistical significance ($\chi^2 = 4.4$, $df = 1$, $P = 0.04$). The prevalent attack in males and females is the strong bite (C) and skin pulling is relatively rare, even in most of the females that do display this attack now and then.

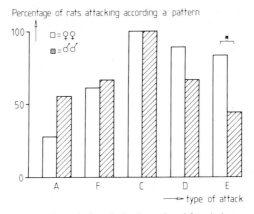

Fig. 6. Comparison of attack patterns in male (hatched columns) and female (open columns) rats. Percentage of rats displaying a particular attack pattern during the first 5 threshold determinations.

Further experiments have shown that during hypothalamic stimulation, rats do not distinguish between the sex of the opponent. Male rats attack both female and male opponents in the same way, and the same is true for female rats.

The distribution of wounds inflicted on male partners by females ($n = 20$) and by males ($n = 9$) of the same weight, during the first 5 threshold determinations is shown in Fig. 7. Both males and females inflict most of the wounds on the head (61.1, respectively 68.0%), quite a few on the upper back (21.4, respectively 14.3%) and very few on lower back, upper and lower belly, and forepaws. The sexes do not differ in the percentages of wounds inflicted in a particular area of the opponent (Mann–Whitney U test, $P > 0.10$ for all areas).

Ovariectomy and oestrogen replacement

The next question to be dealt with is whether threshold values for attack behaviour are dependent on levels of circulating ovarian hormones. Therefore, 4 females were ovariectomized and thresholds were determined before ovariectomy ($n = 2$), following ovariectomy ($n = 7$) and following oestrogen replacement ($n = 4$). In addition we have determined threshold values for switch-off behaviour in the same electrode placements in the same animals and on the same days. The data (Fig. 8) show an initial decrease in attack thresholds following ovariectomy (first 2 thresholds) which has disappeared after 3 weeks (the next remaining 5 thresholds before oestrogen replacement). Treatment with oestradiol benzoate does not affect threshold values. A two-way analysis of variance reveals a significant effect of treatment ($F(3, 12) = 2.4$, $P = 0.022$), which is largely due to the fact that the first 2 postovariectomy attack thresholds were somewhat lower than the rest. It seems that (1) in the long run ovariectomy does not affect thresholds for hypothalamic attack, and that (2) threshold

dorsal vtew   ventral vtew

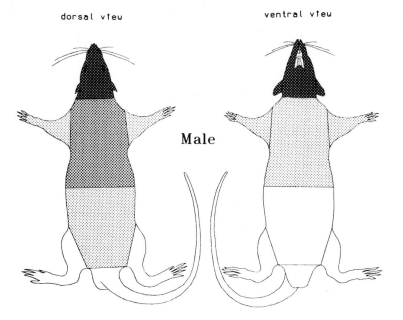

Male

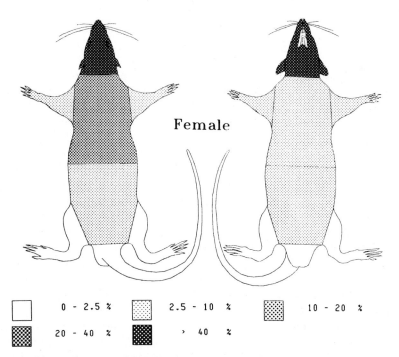

Female

| | 0 - 2.5 % | | 2.5 - 10 % | | 10 - 20 % |
| | 20 - 40 % | | > 40 % | | |

Fig. 7. Percentage of wounds on parts of the body of male opponents inflicted by 20 females (bottom) and 9 males (top) during the first 5 threshold determinations.

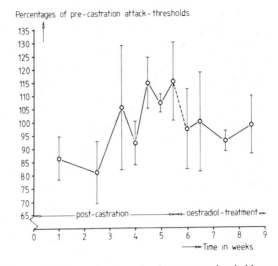

Fig. 8. Effects of ovariectomy and subsequent oestrogen replacement on threshold current intensities for attack in 4 female rats. Ordinate: mean percentage of pre-ovariectomy thresholds with standard deviation.

values in ovariectomized rats are not affected by oestrogen replacement. Neither ovariectomy nor oestrogen replacements resulted in changes in thresholds for switch-off behaviour (two-way Anova, $F(3, 12) = 1.185$, $P = 0.33$).

SUMMARY AND DISCUSSION

Our results demonstrate quite clearly that electrical stimulation in the hypothalamus elicits aggression in both male and female rats. It seems to be derived from the same neural systems and no sex differences could be detected in the sensitivity of these neural systems to stimulation. The present results give little support to the hypothesis that the organization of the hypothalamic substrate involved in these forms of aggression would be different between males and females. Slight differences were observed in the forms of attack behaviour induced by hypothalamic stimulation: males tend to show the more intense, females the weaker forms of attack. These differences may be due to hormonal differences of the animals, the males having normal levels of testosterone. One may hypothesize that females treated with testosterone would show attack behaviour of the same intensity as normal males and that castrated males would be similar to this group of females as in spontaneous aggression (cf. Van de Poll et al., 1981).

In spontaneous aggression, different environmental conditions are required to ascertain that males or females will behave aggressively. Comparisons of effects of drugs, hormones or brain manipulations on male and female aggression are therefore often confounded by an environmental or developmental variable which cannot easily be isolated. In contrast, hypothalamic aggression is a method to induce the *same* type of aggressive behaviour in the *same* environment with the *same* means. It seems, therefore, suited for further studies of sex differences in the effects of drugs, hormones and brain manipulations on aggressive behaviour.

Neither ovariectomy, nor subsequent oestrogen replacement affects thresholds for hypothalamic attack in a convincing way. This finding is in contrast with the effects of castration and testosterone replacement in male rats. In males a consistent increase in the threshold of hypothalamic aggression was witnessed following castration, whereas a subsequent testosterone treatment resulted in a return to precastration threshold levels (Bermond et al., 1982).

The fact that the neural substrate involved in these forms of aggression appears to be similar in males and females seems surprising in the view of the classical studies in mice, which demonstrate that the neonatal hormonal development is crucial for the performance of aggressive behaviour in adulthood. Testosterone would affect the sexual differentiation of brain areas underlying aggressive behaviour (Edwards, 1970). However, recent studies have shown that in rats the neonatal hormonal condition is less important for aggression in later life. Female rats are capable of showing the full repertoire of "male-type" aggression (Van de Poll et al., 1981; De Jonge and Van de Poll, 1984). Since both hypothalamic thresholds, as well as the forms of the aggressive acts elicited during stimulation are remarkably similar in both sexes, our findings seem to support the hypothesis that the "organizing" role of the neonatal hormonal condition could be less important for the performance of aggressive behaviour in rats than in mice.

It is not unlikely that this hypothalamic area is also involved in spontaneous aggression (Kruk and Van der Poel, 1980; Olivier, 1977). If so, one might speculate that sex differences in aggression derive from the facilitating effects of circulating *androgens* on brain mechanisms involved in aggression which are present in males and females alike. The precise neural mechanisms of this behavioural facilitation are not known.

REFERENCES

Bermond, B., Mos, J., Meelis, W., Van der Poel, A.M. and Kruk, M.R. (1982) Aggression induced by electrical stimulation of the hypothalamus: Effects of androgens. *Pharmacol. Biochem. Behav.*, 16: 41–45.

Carrer, H.F. and Aoki, A. (1982) Ultrastructural changes in the hypothalamic ventromedial nucleus of ovariectomized rats after estrogen treatment. *Brain Res.*, 240: 221–233.

De Jonge, F.H. and Van de Poll, N.E. (1984) Relationships between sexual and aggressive behavior in male and female rats: effects of gonadal hormones. In: G.J. De Vries, J.P.C. De Bruin, H.B.M. Uylings and M.A. Corner (Eds.), *Sex Differences in the Brain. The Relation between Structure and Function. Progress in Brain Research*, this volume, Ch. 17.

Dixon, W.J. and Mood, A.M. (1948) A method for obtaning and analyzing sensitivity data. *J. Am. Statist. Assoc.*, 43: 109–126.

Edwards, D.A. (1970) Post-neonatal androgenization and adult aggressive behaviour in female mice. *Physiol. Behav.*, 5: 465–467.

König, J.F.R. and Klippel, R.A. (1963) *The Rat Brain: A Stereotaxic Atlas of the Forebrain and Lower Parts of the Brain Stem*, Williams and Wilkins, Baltimore, MD.

Koolhaas, J.M. (1978) Hypothalamically induced intraspecific aggressive behaviour in the rat. *Exp. Brain Res.*, 32: 365–375.

Kruk, M.R. and Van der Poel, A.M. (1980) Is there evidence for a neural correlate of an aggressive behavioural system in the hypothalamus of the rat? In: P.S. McConnell et al. (Eds.), *The Adaptive Capabilities of the Nervous System, Progress in Brain Research, Vol. 53*, Elsevier, Amsterdam, pp. 385–390.

Kruk, M.R., Kuiper, P. and Meelis, W. (1978) An air pressure operated commutator system for electrical brain stimulation in a fighting rat. *Physiol. Behav.*, 21: 125–127.

Kruk, M.R., Van der Poel, A.M. and De Vos-Frerichs, T.P. (1979) The induction of aggressive behaviour by electrical stimulation in the hypothalamus of male rats. *Behaviour*, 70: 292–322.

Kruk, M.R., Meelis, W., Van der Poel, A.M. and Mos, J. (1981) Electrical stimulation as a tool to trace physio-
    logical properties of the hypothalamic network in aggression. In: P.F. Brain and D. Benton (Eds.), *The
    Biology of Aggression*, NATO Advanced Study Institute Series, Sijthoff and Noordhoff, Alphen aan de
    Rijn, pp. 383–395.
Kruk, M.R., Van der Poel, A.M., Meelis, W., Hermans, J., Mostert, P.G., Mos, J. and Lohman, A.H.M. (1983)
    Discriminant analysis of the localization of aggression-inducing electrode placements in the hypothalamus
    of male rats. *Brain Res.*, 260: 61–79.
Mos, J., Kruk, M.R., Van der Poel, A.M. and Meelis, W. (1982) Aggressive behaviour induced by electrical
    stimulation in the central gray of male rats. *Aggress. Behav.*, 8: 261–284.
Mos, J., Lammers, J.H.C.M., Van der Poel, A.M., Bermond, B., Meelis, W. and Kruk, M.R. (1983) Effects of
    midbrain central gray lesions on spontaneous and electrically induced aggression in the rat. *Aggress.
    Behav.*, 9: 133–155.
Moyer, K.E. (1968) Kinds of aggression and their physiological basis. *Comm. Behav. Biol.*, A2: 65–87.
Olivier, B. (1977) The ventromedial hypothalamus and aggressive behaviour in rats. *Aggress. Behav.*, 3: 47–56.
Scheffé, H. (1959) *The Analysis of Variance*, John Wiley, New York.
Siegel, S. (1956) *Non-Parametric Statistics for the Behavioural Sciences*, McGraw-Hill, New York.
Van de Poll, N.E., De Jonge, F.H., Van Oyen, H.G., Van Pelt, J. and De Bruin, J.P.C. (1981) Failure to find sex
    differences in testosterone activated aggression in two strains of rats. *Hormone Behav.*, 15: 94–105.
Van de Poll, N.E., Smeets, J., Van Oyen, H.G. and Van der Zwan, S.M. (1982) Behavioural consequences of
    agonistic experience in rats: Sex-differences and the effects of testosterone. *J. Comp. Physiol. Psychol.*,
    96: 893–903.
Van der Poel, A.M., Olivier, B., Mos, J., Kruk, M.R., Meelis, W. and Van Aken, J.H.M. (1982) Anti-aggressive
    effect of a new phenylpiperazine compound DU27716 on hypothalamically induced behavioural activities.
    Pharmacol. Biochem. Behav., 17: 147–153.
Wetherill, G.B. (1966) Sequential estimation of points on quantal response curves. In: G. Barrie and
    G.B. Wetherill (Eds.), *Sequential Methods in Statistics*, Methuen, London, pp. 162–179.

G.J. De Vries et al. (Eds.),
Progress in Brain Research, Vol. 61
© 1984   Elsevier Science Publishers B.V., Amsterdam

Hormonal Organization of Sex Differences in Play Fighting and Spatial Behavior

WILLIAM W. BEATTY

Department of Psychology, North Dakota State University, Fargo, ND 58105 (U.S.A.)

INTRODUCTION

Sex differences are known to exist in a variety of non-reproductive behaviors in mammals. Among such sexually dimorphic behaviors are: activity, reactions to various stimuli, certain components of the play behavior of juveniles, aggression, feeding and body weight regulation, as well as the learning of certain avoidance and maze problems. Depending on the particular behavior in question gonadal hormones may exert either a primarily organizational or a primarily activational effect or a combination of both on the magnitude of the sex differences (for general reviews see Beatty, 1979; or MacLusky and Naftolin, 1981; other reviews consider the influence of gonadal hormones on feeding: Nance, 1983; aggression: Brain 1981; and sensory function: Gandelman, 1983). The present review confines itself to the effects of gonadal hormones on sex differences in play and spatial behavior.

SOCIAL PLAY

Among the best studied of juvenile social behaviors is play fighting (sometimes called rough and tumble play). Play fighting often resembles intraspecific aggression among adults but lacks those components of adult agonistic behavior that are related to the communication of threat (Bekoff, 1974; Symons, 1974). In addition, biting and other responses that might seriously injure the opponent are partially inhibited in play fighting while dominance relationships are generally unstable (Aldis, 1975; but also see Panksepp, 1981). In some species there are explicit play signals (Symons, 1978). These occur in all sensory modalities and include distinctive vocalizations, movements and postures.

Play fighting is sexually dimorphic in a number of diverse species including humans, several species of great apes and old world monkeys as well as in ungulates, pinnipeds and rodents (see Mitchell, 1979; Fagen, 1981; Smith, 1982, for references). In all of these species, juvenile males engage in some components of play fighting more frequently than females. In contrast sex differences in play fighting are minimal in several canid and felid species (see Fagen, 1981), marmosets (Stevenson and Poole, 1982) as well as in the Northern grasshopper mouse, a predatory rodent (Davies and Kemble, 1983). The significance of sex differences in play patterns and of play in general for the development of adult behavior patterns remains a matter of conjecture (see Fagen, 1981; Smith, 1982). However, sex differences in play fighting are more common in group-living polygynous species that exhibit marked sexual dimorphism in body size and social roles and are less frequently seen in species that lack one or more of these differences between males and females.

Which of the factors mentioned above is most important is not at all clear. If play fighting fosters the development of predatory skills (e.g. Aldis, 1975; Vincent and Bekoff, 1978), then no sex difference would be anticipated in species in which both sexes are equally dependent on such skills. The apparent absence of sex differences in play fighting among terrestrial carnivores is consistent with this idea. However, Stockman et al. (1983) have recently reported sex differences in two components of social play (neckbite and standover) among juvenile ferrets. Since both male and female ferrets are equally dependent on hunting skill, this factor cannot be critical. Male ferrets are much larger than females, but physical dimorphism alone cannot explain the existence of sex differences in play fighting. If anything female golden hamsters are larger than males, but juvenile male hamsters nevertheless engage in more play fighting than females (Goldman and Swanson, 1975). Since both hamsters and ferrets are thought to lead largely solitary lives, living in social groups is not a necessary condition for the existence of sex differences in juvenile play fighting. Whatever its function in behavioral development play fighting is clearly pleasurable enough that young rats will learn a maze when rewarded with the opportunity to play with a conspecific (Humphreys and Einon, 1981).

HORMONAL CONTROL OF SEX DIFFERENCES IN PLAY

If the reasons for the evolution of sex differences in juvenile social play are unclear, the role of gonadal hormones in the control of sexually dimorphic play patterns is now well established, at least in rhesus monkeys (Goy, 1978) and Norway rats (Meaney and Stewart, 1981b). Males of both species engage in more play fighting than do females and this differentiation appears early in life under the organizational influences of testosterone (T) or its 5α-reduced metabolite, dihydrotestosterone (DHT).

Juvenile rhesus monkey males engage in and initiate more play fights than do females and most of their play fights involve bouts with other males. The sex difference is quite robust, appearing across widely varying conditions of social rearing early in life, including conditions of social isolation (see Mitchell, 1979). The sex difference in play fighting is little affected by the composition of the rearing group. Males and females reared in isosexual groups play fight about as frequently as animals of the same sex reared in heterosexual groups (Goldfoot et al., 1980).

Play fighting by rhesus females can be increased by prenatal exposure to TP or DHTP; the latter is at least as effective as T (Goy, 1978). Since neonatal castration has no effect on play fighting by juvenile males (Goy, 1978) and postnatal androgen treatment does not stimulate play fighting by females (Joslyn, 1973), the prenatal period evidently constitutes the most sensitive period for the organizational effects of androgens on the tissues governing sexually dimorphic play patterns in this species.

Sex differences in preadolescent play are well documented in humans. Boys play more roughly and more vigorously than girls. Qualitatively similar differences have been observed using a variety of different research techniques and in several different cultures (e.g., Whiting and Edwards, 1973; Maccoby and Jacklin, 1974; Di Pietro, 1981).

Studies with humans generally support the idea that gonadal hormones are important in the development of sexually dimorphic patterns of preadolescent play. For example, Ehrhardt and Baker (1974) reported that girls with congenital adrenal hyperplasia (CAH), a condition in which excess amounts of androgens are secreted by the adrenal cortex, were more masculine on a number of measures of preadolescent and adolescent social behavior than were their unaffected sisters or mothers. The CAH girls reported more intense energy expenditure and were more likely to be labeled tomboys by themselves and their mothers. They showed greater preference for boy playmates and functional clothes, but less interest in jewelry, dolls, and infant care. However, Slijper (1984) failed to replicate these differences.

Since the CAH syndrome involves adrenocortical insufficiency, it is reassuring to have confirmatory data, albeit from a single case. Money and Schwartz (1978) reported a case of a male child whose penis was accidentally ablated at 7 months of age during attempted circumcision. The child was surgically feminized and reared as a girl from 17 months of age. As far as could be told she adopted the feminine gender identity and sex role unambiguously, but also displayed long-lasting tomboyism, similar to that described in CAH girls. In contrast to these positive findings McGuire et al. (1975) did not find differences between CAH and control subjects in self-reported tomboyism. The reasons for this discrepancy are not clear.

Investigations of the play behavior of children exposed prenatally to exogenous estrogens and progestins have not revealed consistent changes (see Hines, 1982). Hence, while the data on humans are inconclusive, they are not inconsistent with the results of perinatal hormone manipulations in rhesus monkeys.

As is true of several primates, male rats engage in and initiate more play fights than females (Meaney and Stewart, 1981a). When exposed to a non-playful but active partner, males also solicit more play than females (Thor and Holloway, 1983). Play fighting in this species is most frequently observed in both sexes at 25–45 days of age (Meaney and Stewart, 1981a; Panksepp, 1981), declining precipitously after puberty. Although the sex difference in play fighting by juvenile rats is not as large in magnitude as in rhesus monkeys, it has been observed in both group and dyadic testing situations (Olioff and Stewart, 1978; Meaney and Stewart, 1981a; Thor and Holloway, 1982).

Organizational actions of testicular androgens appear to be responsible for the sex difference in play fighting in rats. If males are castrated shortly after birth their social play resembles that of females but, if castration is delayed until 10 days or more after birth, play fighting is already masculinized (Beatty et al., 1981; Meaney and Stewart, 1981b). The implication from these data, namely that activational effects of androgens are unimportant, is also supported by the lack of effect of TP injections during the juvenile period on play fighting (Meaney and Stewart, 1983). Ovarian hormones, in contrast, appear relatively unimportant for the development of social play of females since even neonatal ovariectomy is without effect (Meaney and Stewart, 1981b).

The mechanism by which androgens exert their organizational effect on play fighting in rats appears to involve a direct effect upon androgen-sensitive target tissues, presumably in the brain. In this respect play fighting in rats is quite different from sexually dimorphic patterns of sexual behavior in this species. In rats sexual differentiation of reproductive behavior, particularly the process of defeminization, is strongly dependent on the aromatization of T to E (see Baum, 1979; Goy and McEwen, 1980; Hutchison and Steimer, 1984; Södersten, 1984). For example, the capacity of female rats to display lordosis is suppressed by neonatal treatment with T or E, but DHT has little effect. In contrast, play fighting by juvenile female rats is induced by neonatal T or DHT injections, but E is without any significant effects (Meaney and Stewart, 1981b). Further, males that are treated with the aromatase inhibitor androst-1,4,6-triene-3,17-dione from birth to 10 days of age, i.e., the sensitive period for the organizational effects of testicular hormones, display just as much play fighting as do control males (Meaney and Stewart, 1981b). In contrast, neonatal exposure of male rat pups to the androgen antagonist, flutamide, during the first 10 days of postnatal life reduces play fighting to levels typical of control females (Meaney et al., 1983). Finally, male rats of the King–Holtzman strain that exhibit the androgen insensitivity syndrome (tfm) engage in play fighting only slightly more frequently than control females but significantly less than unaffected control males of the same strain (Meaney et al., 1983). The tfm animals have normal levels of gonadal hormones, a normal complement of estrogen receptors but greatly reduced numbers of androgen receptors (Attardi et al., 1976; Naess et al., 1976).

Taken together these data imply that hormonal stimulation of an androgen receptor mechanism during the first 10 days of postnatal life in the rat alters the course of development of brain tissues that are responsible for sex differences in play behavior that appear in the juvenile period. Insofar as it is possible at the present time to make comparative statements, sexual differentiation of play fighting appears to involve similar hormonal mechanisms in rats and primates. The details of the hormonal organization remain unclear. While T and DHT are equally effective in inducing play fighting in female rats and monkeys, male rats treated with the reductase inhibitor, testosterone 17β-carboxylic acid, engage in as much play fighting as do control males (Meaney and Stewart, 1981b). This finding is amenable to at least two interpretations: (1) the putative androgen receptor may not discriminate between T and DHT, and either hormone can act on it, or (2) DHT is normally the active organizing agent and a more potent treatment with a reductase inhibitor might have inhibited play when administered neonatally to males.

While most of the data favor the idea that an androgen receptor mechanism plays a major role in the organization of sex differences in play fighting, involvement of estrogens cannot be ruled out. Hines et al. (1982) reported that treatment with the synthetic estrogen diethylstilbestrol (DES) from day 16 of gestation to day 10 of postnatal life increased play fighting by female rats. Interpretation of these data is complicated, however, because Hines and her colleagues did not observe a difference in play fighting between untreated males and females under their testing conditions.

Other gonadal hormones may also play a role in sexual differentiation of social play. For instance, Birke and Sadler (1983) noted that neonatal exposure to medroxyprogesterone acetate (MPA) reduced play fighting in juvenile rats of both sexes. Since this progestin is anti-androgenic (see Wright et al., 1979), it is tempting to assume that this action of the hormone is responsible for its effects on play. Alternatively, since MPA affected play in both sexes, its effect may involve progestin receptors which are believed to exist in the brains of newborn rats (see MacLusky and Naftolin, 1981). The significance of progesterone in the sexual differentiation of play remains to be determined.

Glucocorticoids probably also play a role in the sexual differentiation of play. Neonatal treatment with corticosterone or dexamethasone within the first 9–10 days after birth suppresses play fighting in males, but not in females. The effective treatment does not alter plasma T levels so it presumably does not involve androgen receptors (Meaney et al., 1982). This conclusion is buttressed by the fact that glucocorticoid treatments that suppress play in juvenile males do not affect the masculine sexual behavior of the same animals in adulthood. As is true of T there appear to be no activational influences of corticosterone on play since concurrent treatment with corticosterone has no effect on play fighting in juvenile males (Meaney and Stewart, 1983).

BRAIN MECHANISMS CONTROLLING PLAY

At present it appears that a major determinant of the sex difference in play fighting is the induction of androgen receptors during the neonatal period by hormones of testicular origin. Presumably this organizational effect is directly upon CNS tissues although that assumption has not been tested. Androgen receptors are indeed to be found in various regions of the developing rat brain, especially in the hypothalamus and other parts of the limbic system (Lieberburg et al., 1980; Sheridan, 1981; Vito and Fox, 1982). In an attempt to provide basic information about the neurology of play we have studied the effects of lesioning various brain regions that are known to contain androgen receptors and have been implicated in the control of sexual or other sexually dimorphic social behaviors such as aggression. In all of our studies electrolytic lesions have been produced in weanling rats of both sexes. After recovery from surgery, the animals were placed into heterosexual groups of 6–8 and play fighting was studied for approximately 2 weeks. Of the brain areas studied, only lesions of the amygdala had differential effects on play fighting by males and females. Specifically these lesions depressed play fighting in males, but were without effect in females (Meaney et al., 1981).

Lesions in other brain areas did not have sex-dependent effects. Septal lesions increased play fighting in both males and females (Beatty et al., 1982) while lesions of the anterior or ventromedial hypothalamic areas reduced play fighting in both sexes (Beatty and Costello, 1983a). Lesions of the medial preoptic area did not affect play by males or females (Leedy et al., 1980; Beatty and Costello, 1983a).

How might the amygdala be involved in controlling play fighting? One possibility is by processing chemosensory information, a function which is important for copulatory behavior in the male hamster (Lehman et al., 1980). However, since neither olfactory bulbectomy (Beatty and Costello, 1983b) nor intranasal treatment with zinc sulfate (Thor and Holloway, 1982) have marked effects on play fighting, chemosensory stimuli are apparently of little importance in arousing play fighting.

A more daring interpretation of the role of the amydala in play fighting proposes that exposure to androgens during the neonatal period causes some change in development of the same region which is ultimately critical for the sex difference in play fighting. Nishizuka and Arai (1981a) have in fact described rather subtle sex differences in the organization of certain synapses in the amygdala and have shown that these sexually dimorphic features are dependent on the neonatal hormone environment. However, estrogens rather than androgens appear to be critical to the hormonal effects on the fine structure of the amygdala (Nishizuka and Arai, 1981b). More recently Meaney (personal communication) has measured both cytosol and nuclear androgen receptor number in several different regions of the developing rat brain, using a new exchange assay (McGinnis et al., 1983). Of considerable interest is the finding that nuclear androgen binding is greater in the amygdala of the male rat pup throughout the first 10 days of postnatal life than in the same region in the female. No sex differences in nuclear androgen receptor number were observed in hypothalamic, preoptic or septal area samples during the same age range. Cytosol androgen binding was similar in both sexes in all brain areas studied.

If androgenic action on the developing amygdala is critical to sexual differentiation of play fighting, exposing the amygdala of the female rat to androgens during the neonatal period should masculinize play fighting. Preliminary data (Meaney, personal communication) suggest that this is indeed the case. Bilateral T implants into the amygdala which were left in place from 2 to 10 days of age appeared to increase play fighting thus mimicking the effects of peripheral androgen injections. However, the concentration of hormone in this initial study (1 : 2 T : cholesterol) was rather high so the possibility of diffusion to other brain areas must be considered an important problem. Assuming that: (1) DHT implants in amygdala will prove to be effective in stimulating play fighting, and (2) hormone implants in other brain areas are ineffective, the idea that androgen-mediated organization of the developing amygdala is important for the emergence of sex differences in play fighting would be nicely supported.

Whether or not play fighting in rats can serve as a model system for studying the organizational influences of androgens on behavioral development in general as I once hoped now seems rather doubtful. Initially it appeared that masculine sexual differentiation could be separated into two processes: masculinization which required primarily androgens and defeminization which required estrogens. Further, certain species, notably ferrets and rhesus monkeys, seemed not to undergo the process of defeminization (see Baum, 1979). It is now clear that prenatal exposure to TP or DHTP causes some defeminization in female rhesus monkeys (Thornton and Goy, 1983). Furthermore, although there are sex differences in some components of the play of juvenile ferrets which can be modified by altering the pattern of exposure to gonadal hormones shortly after birth, it is already clear that hormonal influences on play fighting are quite different in the rat and the ferret. In particular, ovarian hormones seem to be involved in stimulating play in female ferrets (Stockman et al., 1983).

Finally, it is important to realize that treatments that are highly effective in masculinizing play fighting in juvenile animals do not necessarily result in masculinization of adult behaviors. For example, pseudohermaphroditic rhesus females whose juvenile play behavior was impressively masculinized have been disappointingly inept at displaying male copulatory behavior as adults (e.g., Phoenix and Chambers, 1982). Since these animals were reared in social isolation for much of their lives, their inadequate display of male sexual behavior may reflect only the differential influence of the rearing environment on play and sex. But that in itself is a critical conceptual point.

SEXUAL DIMORPHISM IN SPATIAL BEHAVIOR

Human studies

For a long time it has been recognized that human males generally outperform human females on a number of tasks that tap some aspect of visuospatial ability. While these differences are not large in magnitude (approximately 0.4 S.D.), they are quite reproducible, at least with adequate samples of adult Caucasians (Maccoby and Jacklin, 1974). McGee (1979) suggests that two separable factors are involved in the sex-related differences in human spatial behavior. The first, spatial visualization, is the ability to rotate mentally two- or three-dimensional objects when they are presented pictorially. The second, spatial orientation, is the "aptitude to remain unconfused by the changing orientations in which a spatial configuration may be presented" (McGee, 1979, p. 897). Various tasks, including map reading, perceptual maze learning as well as the Embedded Figures Test in which the person has to find a relatively simple form in a more complex geometric array are thought to measure spatial orientation.

While there is little disagreement about the existence of sex differences in various spatial tasks in some human populations, there is no basis for consensus about how to explain them (see Hines, 1982; McGee, 1979; Sherman, 1978, for various hypotheses). Part of the uncertainty arises because of two unsettled issues that are essentially descriptive. First, there is the question of whether the sex-related differences in spatial ability that are readily observable in adult Caucasians are also characteristic of other racial groups. For example, the evidence concerning sex-related differences in spatial abilities among blacks is contradictory (Schratz, 1978; Jahoda, 1980). Second, there is some dispute about the age at which the male advantage in spatial tasks first appears. Maccoby and Jacklin (1974) concluded that "male superiority on visual-spatial tasks is fairly consistently found in adolescence and adulthood, but not in childhood" (p. 351). However, in a number of studies a male advantage in spatial tasks has been reported even prior to adolescence (e.g., Keogh, 1971; Herman and Siegel, 1978). Particularly impressive in this regard is the finding (Roberts, 1971) that Caucasian males consistently outperformed females on the WISC Block Design Test for all age groups between 6 and 12 years. The study is important because the large sample (more than 7000 children) was carefully chosen to comprise 96% of a total probability sample of non-institutionalized U.S. children. In contrast, no significant differences were found among black children in this study.

The possibility that sex differences in spatial performance are only found in certain racial and ethnic groups and the belief that these differences do not appear until adolescence have sometimes been taken to support the view that the male advantage on visuospatial tasks is primarily the result of differential socio-cultural influences which encourage boys to participate and excel in spatial skills and discourage girls from engaging in such activities (see Sherman, 1978; Nash, 1979, for reviews of this position). Without minimizing the importance of socio-cultural influences it should be obvious that neither the age at which a sex-related difference is first discernable nor the fact that it is observed only in certain racial or ethnic groups (assuming this is true of sex differences in spatial behavior) is a persuasive argument either for or against a biological or a socio-cultural explanation of the observed dimorphism. Several biological mechanisms have been offered to explain sex differences in human spatial ability but none is convincingly supported by the available data.

One hypothesis states that there is a gene carried on the X chromosome with a major influence on spatial ability. This proposition has been tested by examining patterns of correlations for various family members (e.g., father–son, mother–son) on a variety of tests of spatial ability. Although an early study (Stafford, 1961) supported the idea of an X-linked recessive gene for spatial ability, more recent studies which have employed larger samples have failed to confirm the earlier work (see McGee, 1979, 1982; Vandenberg and Kuse, 1979, for reviews). Furthermore, the performance of women with Turner's syndrome on spatial tasks is at variance with the X-linked hypothesis. Because these individuals have only one X chromosome, their spatial behavior should resemble that of males. In fact, women with Turner's syndrome display a selective impairment in standard tests of spatial behavior (Money, 1964). However, Turner's syndrome is associated with ovarian dysgenesis and it is possible that the putative gene for spatial ability requires gonadal hormones for its expression.

In a more general sense the possibility that gonadal hormones might exert either organizational or activational influences upon human spatial behavior has also been considered. Prior to 1982 there was no evidence that females exposed to higher than normal levels of androgens, estrogens or progestins display enhanced spatial ability (see Reinisch et al., 1979; Hines, 1982, for reviews). For example, Baker and Ehrhardt (1974) and McGuire et al. (1975) reported that females with CAH did not differ from unaffected controls on several tests of spatial ability. But recently Resnick and Berenbaum (1982) have found evidence of superior performance on such tests in women with CAH. These workers employed a larger sample of subjects who were at least 12 years old at testing. They also studied tasks that are maximally sensitive to the sex difference in adult men and women.

Let us assume, for the moment, that enhanced spatial ability in CAH women is a reproducible effect and that it is the consequence of perinatal exposure to adrenal androgens. Do the androgens act directly or after aromatization to estrogens? The limited data favor the former alternative. For example, males with the androgen insensitivity syndrome tend to display the typically feminine pattern of higher verbal than performance IQ (Masica et al., 1969). In addition no consistent changes in spatial behavior have been observed in females whose mothers received estrogens and/or progestins during pregnancy (Reinisch et al., 1979; Hines, 1982). Similarly, Hines and Shipley (1983) found no evidence of enhanced spatial ability in the female offspring of mothers who had been given diethylstilbestrol (DES), a synthetic estrogen, for at least 5 months during pregnancy, although these women exhibited a more masculine pattern of performance on a dichotic listening task (see McGlone, 1980; Kimura and Harshman, 1984, for reviews).

Another approach is to attempt to correlate patterns of cognitive functioning in normal individuals to some index of hormone exposure. This approach allows the study of large samples but precludes separation of organizational and activational influences unless hormone levels are assayed. Peterson (1976) inferred hormone influence from various somatic measures (e.g., muscle, fat and pubic hair distribution) and found that adolescent females who were more androgynous in body appearance also exhibited better spatial visualization. If one assumes that these females in fact had greater exposure to androgens, then one might infer that androgens are involved in the usual male superiority on spatial tasks. However, Peterson also found that less "masculine" males (in terms of body appearance) did better on spatial tasks than their more stereotypically masculine counterparts. Using a larger sample Berenbaum and Resnick (1982) obtained qualitatively similar trends, but the relationships were not statistically significant.

In summary, while there is currently no evidence that decisively indicates that gonadal hormones play an important role in sex-related differences in human spatial behavior, recent findings support the hypothesis that perinatal exposure to androgens may be a factor. Most of the human studies necessarily employ patients with endocrine anomalies and, consequently, the samples are usually small. Since the magnitude of the sex difference is not very great, careful attention to task and age variables is important but larger samples may also be required to detect whatever hormonal influences exist.

Animal studies

Alternatively, one might try to find a suitable animal model of the sex differences in human spatial behavior. In rats there are sex differences in the learning of complex mazes such as the Lashley III or Hebb–Williams maze which are thought to reflect spatial ability. As might be expected from the human literature, males consistently learn more rapidly than females (see Beatty, 1979). The sex difference is not evident until after puberty (Krasnoff and Weston, 1976). But since gonadectomy in adulthood has little effect (Joseph et al., 1978), activational effects of gonadal hormones appear to be relatively unimportant.

Manipulating the neonatal hormone environment has consistent effects on maze learning in both sexes. Neonatal treatment with TP improves maze learning by female rats (Dawson et al., 1975; Stewart et al., 1975; Joseph et al., 1978), while neonatal castration increases the number of errors made by males (Dawson et al., 1975; Joseph et al., 1978). Thus, testicular androgens exert some sort of organizational effect which influences the sex difference in maze learning.

It is not yet clear whether or not organizational influence involves a direct effect of T, or another hormone, on an androgen receptor mechanism. The fact that neonatal treatment with the anti-androgen cyproterone acetate (CA) impairs performance by males is consistent with an androgen receptor mechanism (Joseph et al., 1978), but in the same study neonatal CA improved the performance of females. Furthermore, the observation that neonatal E treatment impaired rather than improved maze learning by males that had been neonatally castrated (Dawson et al., 1975) suggests that aromatization of T to E may be unimportant in the masculinization of performance in complex mazes. Unfortunately, there is no published experiment in which the effects of neonatal treatment with T, DHT and E have been compared under conditions where there is a sex difference in maze learning between normal males and females. Likewise, the influence of estrogen antagonists and aromatase and reductase inhibitors has not been studied. Until such basic information is available, the mechanism by which gonadal hormones influence the ability to learn complex mazes must remain obscure.

An equally important question is whether the sex difference in complex maze learning in rats actually represents a difference in spatial ability or, instead, is simply another manifestation of the well-known sex differences in activity and exploration (see Beatty, 1979). The latter possibility is quite plausible since the mazes that yield clear-cut sex differences resemble open fields with a few extra walls. It is easy to imagine that the higher levels of activity and/or exploration displayed by female rats could translate rather directly into an increase in the total number of "errors" in the maze learning task. Moreover, the pattern of organizational and activational influences of gonadal hormones on maze learning and open-field activity is very similar in rats.

Although there is probably no foolproof way of eliminating the influences of activity and exploration from a test of spatial ability in rats, the radial maze allows one to minimize their influence. This apparatus resembles a rimless wagon wheel (see Olton and Samuelson, 1976, Fig. 1). Since the arms are relatively long and the maze is elevated, the chances that individual differences in activity will be mistakenly reflected in error scores is reduced, especially if a choice is recorded only when the rat goes all the way to the end of the arm where the food cup is located. In the conventional testing procedure each arm is baited with food at the outset of the daily test session and the rat is tested until it visits every arm and finds all of the food. Since food is never replenished during the run, optimal performance entails visiting each arm only once. In the 8-arm version of the task, rats quickly acquire nearly perfect accuracy and maintain this level of performance indefinitely even if delays of as long as 4 h are imposed during the run (Beatty and Shavalia, 1980). In most experiments with rats the animals do not enter the arms in any particular order even after months of training. Furthermore, performance is equally accurate if the animals are forced to make their first 4 choices in a randomly determined order. Hence it is reasonable to describe the task as a test of working (i.e., short-term) memory for spatial information (see Olton, 1978, 1982).

Using the above-mentioned procedure, we have failed to observe consistent sex differences in performance although in some experiments the females performed somewhat more poorly than males. In contrast, Einon (1980) observed a slight, but significant difference in favor of the males. This sex difference occurred only if the animals were raised with conspecifics in an enriched environment from weaning until the time of testing. Using a 17-arm maze, Tees et al. (1981) also found that males performed more accurately than females, a difference which was larger in magnitude among dark-reared animals than in controls reared individually in standard laboratory cages. However, in two separate studies using a 17-arm maze Juraska (personal communication) has failed to find any evidence of sex differences in rats that were raised in enriched or restricted environments. In agreement with Einon (1980) environmental enrichment improved performance equally for both sexes. In summary, using the standard testing procedures, sex differences in the radial maze are small in magnitude and not readily reproduced. This is equally true of the 8- and 17-arm versions of the task. Since rats usually do not attain errorless performance in the larger maze, the failure to find consistent sex differences in the 8-arm maze cannot be simply the result of a ceiling effect.

We have recently modified the basic testing procedure in order to obtain information about possible sex differences in reference (i.e., long-term) as well as working memory. For each rat only 6 of the 8 arms were baited with food so that the baited and unbaited arms remained the same from day to day. Entries into these unbaited arms were considered as reference memory errors. Working memory errors were defined as before (i.e., re-entries into baited arms that had already been visited on that particular test day). Males made reliably fewer errors of both types than females (Fig. 1) and, surprisingly, the sex difference on working memory errors was of much greater magnitude than for reference memory errors. As yet we have no data concerning possible influences of gonadal hormones on this test of spatial behavior, but the magnitude of the sex difference encourages the view that this situation may provide a useful behavioral end point for such studies.

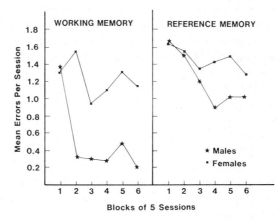

Fig. 1. Mean number of working and reference memory errors per session by adult male and female rats. Males made fewer working memory errors (re-entries into baited arms already visited that day) on blocks 2–6 and fewer reference memory errors (entries into arms that were never baited) on blocks 4 and 5.

Whether or not animal studies using the radial maze will provide a valid model of sex differences in human spatial behavior is an altogether different question. Jan Aadland, working in my laboratory, has recently tested college students in an 8-arm maze. The subjects were given a single test. Each arm of the maze contained a poker chip and the students were instructed that once a poker chip was removed from a particular arm it would not be replaced. Thus, the procedure was similar to the standard tests of working memory employed with animals. Since the major goal of the study was to determine the temporal span of accurate spatial memory for humans, delays ranging from zero to 168 h were imposed between the fourth and fifth choices. Adult humans typically enter adjacent arms in sequence if allowed to choose freely in this task so roughly half of the subjects were forced to enter 4 arms selected at random (forced choice condition). The remaining subjects were allowed to pattern their first 4 choices in any way they wished (free choice condition). As expected almost all subjects in the free choice condition chose 4 adjacent arms in sequence. Retention was better for subjects in the free choice condition, but for simplicity the results are averaged across free and forced choice conditions. The most striking result is the highly accurate memory, even at rather long delays under both conditions (Table I). Of greater interest in the present context is the consistent tendency for females to outperform males, a trend, which fell just short of statistical significance ($P < 0.06$).

TABLE I

RADIAL MAZE PERFORMANCE OF COLLEGE UNDERGRADUATES

Delay (h)	Mean percent correct (choices 5–8)	
	Males	Females
0	90.4	97.2
0.5	94.4	97.2
15	87.5	92.5
48	90.3	100
168	82.1	90.9

We must be wary of overinterpreting a single investigation and, under testing conditions which did not contain a reference memory component, no sex differences might have been expected based on our experiments with rats. However, these data may serve to underscore a major void in the literature on sex-related differences in human spatial behavior. There are not many data concerning sex-related differences in children and virtually no data on adults in tasks that require locomotion in space. What is true for the standard tests of spatial visualization and orientation cannot necessarily be generalized to other situations. For example, in studies with male patients suffering from unilateral damage in the posterior part of the right hemisphere Ratcliff and Newcomb (1973) observed deficits on a perceptual stylus maze, but not on a locomotor maze.

Clearly additional research with adult humans in spatial tasks that more closely resemble those employed with animals would be helpful in assessing the validity of animal models of sex differences. There are many questions that need to be resolved, but two issues seem particularly important. First of all, we need to discover what cognitive processes humans use to solve problems in spatial learning and memory in locomotor mazes and how these processes compare with those employed by animals to solve similar problems. Secondly, we need to determine how human performance in locomotor maze tasks is related to performance in the more traditional tests of spatial visualization and orientation.

ACKNOWLEDGEMENTS

The experimental work from my own laboratory was supported by Grant HD 12620 from NICHHD and Grant BNS-8201448 from NSF.

I am especially grateful to my colleagues Drs. Michael Meaney, Jane Stewart, Jan Juraska, Melissa Hines, Sheri Berenbaum and D.H. Thor who permitted me to cite their unpublished work.

REFERENCES

Aldis, O. (1975) *Play Fighting*, Academic Press, New York.

Attardi, B., Geller, L.N. and Ohno, S. (1976) Androgen and estrogen receptors in brain cytosol from male, female and Tfm mice. *Endocrinology*, 98: 864–874.

Baker, S.W. and Ehrhardt, A.A. (1974) Prenatal androgen, intelligence and cognitive sex differences. In: R.C. Friedman, R.M. Richart and R.L. Vande Wiele (Eds.), *Sex Differences in Behavior*, Wiley, New York, pp. 53–76.

Baum, M.J. (1979) Differentiation of coital behavior in mammals: A comparative analysis. *Neurosci. Biobehav. Rev.*, 3: 265–284.

Beatty, W.W. (1979) Gonadal hormones and sex differences in nonreproductive behaviors in rodents: Organizational and activational influences. *Hormone Behav.*, 12: 112–163.

Beatty, W.W. and Costello, K.C. (1983a) Medial hypothalamic lesions and play fighting in juvenile rats. *Physiol. Behav.*, 1: 141–145.

Beatty, W.W. and Costello, K.C. (1983b) Olfactory bulbectomy and play fighting in juvenile rats. *Physiol. Behav.*, 30: 525–528.

Beatty, W.W. and Shavalia, D.A. (1980) Spatial memory in rats: Time course of working memory and effect of anesthetics. *Behav. Neural Biol.*, 28: 454–462.

Beatty, W.W., Dodge, A.M., Traylor, K.L. and Meaney, M.J. (1981) Temporal boundary of the sensitive period for hormonal organization of social play in juvenile rats. *Physiol. Behav.*, 26: 241–243.

Beatty, W.W., Dodge, A.M., Traylor, K.L., Donegan, J.C. and Godding, P.R. (1982) Septal lesions increase play fighting in juvenile rats. *Physiol. Behav.*, 28: 649–652.

Bekoff, M. (1974) Social play and play-soliciting by canids. *Am. Zool.*, 14: 323–340.

Berenbaum, S.A. and Resnick, S. (1982) Somatic androgyny and cognitive abilities. *Develop. Psychol.*, 18: 418–423.

Birke, L.I.A. and Sadler, D. (1983) Progestin-induced changes in play behaviour of the prepubertal rat. *Physiol. Behav.*, 30: 341–347.

Brain, P.F. (1981) Hormones and aggression in infra-human vertebrates. In: P.F. Brain and D. Benton (Eds.), *The Biology of Aggression*, Sijthoff and Noordhoff, Alphen aan den Rijn, pp. 181–213.

Davies, V.A. and Kemble, E.D. (1983) Social play behaviours and insect predation in Northern grasshopper mice (*Onychomys leucogaster*). *Behav. Proc.*, 8: 197–204.

Dawson, J.L.M., Cheung, Y.M. and Law, R.T.S. (1975) Developmental effects of neonatal sex hormones on spatial and activity skills in the white rat. *Biol. Psychol.*, 3: 213–229.

Di Pietro, J.A. (1981) Rough and tumble play: A function of gender. *Develop. Psychol.*, 17: 50–58.

Ehrhardt, A.A. and Baker, S.W. (1974) Fetal androgens, human central nervous system differentiation, and behavior sex differences. In: R.C. Friedman, R.M. Richart and R.L. Vande Wiele (Eds.), *Sex Differences in Behavior*, Wiley, New York, pp. 33–52.

Einon, D. (1980) Spatial memory and response strategies in rats: Age, sex and rearing differences in performance. *Quart. J. Exp. Psychol.*, 32: 473–489.

Fagen, R. (1981) *Animal Play Behaviour*, Oxford University Press, Oxford.

Gandelman, R. (1983) Gonadal hormones and sensory function. *Neurosci. Biobehav. Rev.*, 7: 1–18.

Goldfoot, D.A., Walen, K., Collins, M. and Goy, R.W. (1980) Experience and the development of "gender roles" in male and female rhesus monkeys. Paper presented at Eastern Conference on Reproductive Behavior, New York.

Goldman, L. and Swanson, H.H. (1975) Developmental changes in pre-adult behavior in confined colonies of golden hamsters. *Develop. Psychobiol.*, 8: 137–150.

Goy, R.W. (1978) Development of play and mounting behaviour in female rhesus virilized prenatally with esters of testosterone or dihydrotestosterone. In: D.J. Chivers and J. Herbert (Eds.), *Recent Advances in Primatology, Vol. 1, Behaviour*, Academic Press, London, pp. 449–462.

Goy, R.W. and McEwen, B.S. (1980) *Sexual Differentiation of the Brain*, MIT Press, Cambridge.

Herman, J.F. and Siegel, A.W. (1978) The development of cognitive mapping of the large-scale environment. *J. Exp. Child Psychol.*, 26: 389–406.

Hines, M. (1982) Prenatal gonadal hormones and sex differences in human behavior. *Psychol. Bull.*, 92: 56–80.

Hines, M. and Shipley, C. (1983) Prenatal diethylstilbestrol (DES) exposure and sexually dimorphic cognitive abilities and cerebral lateralization. *Develop. Psychol.*, in press.

Hines, M., Dohler, K.D. and Gorski, R.A. (1982) Rough play in female rats following pre- and postnatal treatment with diethylstilbestrol or testosterone. Paper presented at the Conference on Reproductive Behavior, East Lansing.

Humphreys, A.P. and Einon, D.F. (1981) Play as a reinforcer for maze learning in juvenile rats. *Anim. Behav.*, 29: 259–270.

Hutchison, J.B. and Steimer, T. (1984) Androgen metabolism in the brain: behavioural correlates. In: G.J. De Vries, J.P.C. De Bruin, H.B.M. Uylings and M.A. Corner (Eds.), *Sex Differences in the Brain. The Relation between Structure and Function. Progress in Brain Research*, this volume, Ch. 2.

Jahoda, G. (1980) Sex and ethnic differences on a spatial-perceptual task. *Br. J. Psychol.*, 71: 425–431.

Joseph, R., Hess, S. and Birecree, E. (1978) Effect of hormone manipulations and exploration on sex differences in maze learning. *Behav. Biol.*, 24: 364–377.

Joslyn, W.D. (1973) Androgen-induced social dominance in infant female rhesus monkeys. *J. Child Psychol. Psychiat.*, 14: 137–145.

Keogh, B.K. (1971) Pattern copying under three conditions of an expanded spatial field. *Develop. Psychol.*, 4: 25–31.

Kimura, D. and Harshman, R.A. (1984) Sex differences in brain organization for verbal and non-verbal functions. In: G.J. De Vries, J.P.C. De Bruin, H.B.M. Uylings and M.A. Corner (Eds.), *Sex Differences in the Brain. The Relation between Structure and Function. Progress in Brain Research*, this volume, Ch. 27.

Krasnoff, A. and Weston, L.M. (1976) Puberal status and sex differences: Activity and maze behavior in rats. *Develop. Psychobiol.*, 9: 261–269.

Leedy, M.G., Vela, E.G., Popolow, A.B. and Gerall, A.A. (1980) Effect of prepuberal medial preoptic area lesions on male rat sexual behavior. *Physiol. Behav.*, 24: 341–346.

Lehman, M.N., Winans, S.S. and Powers, J.B. (1980) Medial nucleus of the amygdala mediates chemosensory control of male hamster sexual behavior. *Science*, 210: 557–560.

Lieberburg, I., MacLusky, N. and McEwen, B.S. (1980) Androgen receptors in the perinatal rat brain. *Brain Res.*, 190: 125–138.

Maccoby, E.E. and Jacklin, C.N. (1974) *The Psychology of Sex Differences*, Stanford University Press, Stanford, CA.

MacLusky, N.S. and Naftolin, F. (1981) Sexual differentiation of the nervous system. *Science*, 211: 1294–1303.

Masica, D.N., Money, J., Ehrhardt, A.A. and Lewis, V.G. (1969) IQ fetal sex hormones and cognitive patterns: Studies of the testicular feminizing syndrome of androgen insensitivity. *Johns Hopk. Med. J.*, 124: 34–43.

McGee, M.G. (1979) Human spatial abilities: Psychometric studies and environmental, genetic, hormonal, and neurological influences. *Psychol. Bull.*, 86: 889–918.

McGee, M.G. (1982) Spatial abilities: The influence of genetic factors. In: M. Potegal (Ed.), *Spatial Abilities: Development and Physiological Foundations*, Academic Press, New York, pp. 199–222.

McGinnis, M.Y., Davis, P.G., Meaney, M.J., Singer, M. and McEwen, B.S. (1983) An in vitro cytosol and nuclear exchange assay for androgen receptors in rat brain. *Brain Res.*, in press.

McGlone, J. (1980) Sex differences in human brain asymmetry: A critical survey. *Behav. Brain Sci.*, 3: 215–263.

McGuire, L.S., Ryan, K.O. and Omenn, G.S. (1975) Congenital adrenal hyperplasia. II. Cognitive and behavioral studies. *Behav. Genet.*, 5: 175–188.

Meaney, M.J. and Stewart, J. (1981a) A descriptive study of social development in the rat (*Rattus norvegicus*). *Anim. Behav.*, 29: 34–45.

Meaney, M.J. and Stewart, J. (1981b) Neonatal androgens influence the social play of prepubescent rats. *Hormone Behav.*, 15: 197–213.

Meaney, M.S. and Stewart, J. (1983) The influence of exogenous testosterone and corticosterone on the social behavior of prepubertal male rats. *Bull. Psychon. Soc.*, 21: 232–234.

Meaney, M.J., Dodge, A.M. and Beatty, W.W. (1981) Sex-dependent effects of amygdaloid lesions on the social play of prepubertal rats. *Physiol. Behav.*, 26: 467–472.

Meaney, M.J., Stewart, J. and Beatty, W.W. (1982) The influence of glucocorticoids during the neonatal period on the development of play fighting in Norway rat pups. *Hormone Behav.*, 16: 475–491.

Meaney, M.J., Stewart, J., Poulin, P. and McEwen, B.S. (1983) Sex differences in the social play of juvenile rats are mediated by the neonatal androgen receptor system. *Neuroendocrinology*, 37: 85–90.

Mitchell, G. (1979) *Behavioral Sex Differences in Nonhuman Primates*, Van Nostrand Rheinhold, New York.

Money, J. (1964) Two cytogenetic syndromes: Psychologic comparisons. 1. Intelligence and specific factor quotients. *J. Psychiat. Res.*, 2: 223–231.

Money, J. and Schwartz, M. (1978) Biosocial determinants of gender identity differentiation and development. In: J.B. Hutchinson (Ed.), *Biological Determinants of Sexual Behaviour*, Wiley, Chichester, pp. 765–784.

Naess, D., Haug, E., Attrramadal, A., Aakvaag, A., Hansson, V. and French, F. (1976) Androgen receptors in the anterior pituitary and central nervous system of the androgen "insensitive" (Tfm) rat: Correlation between receptor binding and effects of androgens on gonadotropin secretion. *Endocrinology*, 99: 1295–1303.

Nance, D.M. (1983) The developmental and neural determinants of estrogen on feeding in the rat: A theoretical perspective. *Neurosci. Biobehav. Rev.*, 7: 189–211.

Nash, S.C. (1979) Sex role as a mediator of intellectual functioning. In: M.A. Wittig and A.C. Petersen (Eds.), *Sex-Related Differences in Cognitive Functioning*, Academic Press, New York, pp. 263–302.

Nishizuka, M. and Arai, Y. (1981a) Sexual dimorphism in synaptic organization in the amygdala and its dependence on neonatal hormone environment. *Brain Res.*, 212: 31–38.

Nishizuka, M. and Arai, Y. (1981b) Organizational action of estrogen on synaptic pattern in the amygdala: Implication for sexual differentiation of the brain. *Brain Res.*, 213: 422–426.

Olioff, M. and Stewart, J. (1978) Sex differences in play behavior of prepubescent rats. *Physiol. Behav.*, 20: 113–115.

Olton, D.S. (1978) Characteristics of spatial memory. In: S.H. Hulse, H. Fowler and W.K. Honig (Eds.), *Cognitive Processes in Animal Behavior*, Lawrence Erlbaum, Hillsdale, pp. 342–373.

Olton, D.S. (1982) Spatially organized behaviors of animals: Behavioral and neurological studies. In: M. Potegal (Ed.), *Spatial Abilities: Development and Physiological Foundations*, Academic Press, New York, pp. 335–360.

Olton, D.S. and Samuelson, R.J. (1976) Remembrance of places passed: Spatial memory in rats. *J. Exp. Psychol.: Anim. Behav. Proc.*, 2: 97–116.

Panksepp, J. (1981) The ontogeny of play in rats. *Develop. Psychobiol.*, 14: 327–332.

Peterson, A.C. (1976) Physical androgyny and cognitive functioning in adolescence. *Develop. Psychol.*, 12: 524–533.

Phoenix, C.H. and Chambers, K.C. (1982) Sexual behavior in adult gonadectomized female pseudohermaphrodite, female, and male rhesus macaques (*Macaca mulatta*) treated with estradiol benzoate and testosterone propionate. *J. Comp. Physiol. Psychol.*, 96: 823–833.

Ratcliff, G. and Newcombe, F. (1973) Spatial orientation in man: Effects of left, right and bilateral posterior cerebral lesions. *J. Neurol. Neurosurg. Psychiat.*, 36: 448–454.

Reinisch, J.M., Gandelman, R. and Spiegel, F.C. (1979) Prenatal influences on cognitive abilities: Data from experimental animals and human genetic and endocrine syndromes. In: M.A. Wittig and A.C. Petersen (Eds.), *Sex-Related Differences in Cognitive Functioning*, Academic Press, New York, pp. 215–240.

Resnick, S. and Berenbaum, S.A. (1982) Cognitive functioning in individuals with congenital adrenal hyperplasia. *Behav. Genet.*, 12: 594–595.

Roberts, J. (1971) *Intellectual Development of Children by Demographic and Socioeconomic Factors*, DHEW Publ. No. HSM 72-1012, Series 11, No. 110, U.S. Government Printing Office, Washington, DC.

Schratz, M.M. (1978) A developmental investigation of sex differences in spatial (visual-analytic) and mathematical skills in three ethnic groups. *Develop. Psychol.*, 14: 263–267.

Sheridan, P.J. (1981) Unaromatized androgen is taken up by the neonatal rat brain: Two receptor systems for androgen. *Develop. Neurosci.*, 4: 46–54.

Sherman, J. (1978) *Sex-Related Cognitive Differences*, Thomas, Springfield, IL.

Slijper, F.M.E. (1984) Androgens and gender role behaviour in girls with congenital adrenal hyperplasia (CAH). In: G.J. De Vries, J.P.C. De Bruin, H.B.M. Uylings and M.A. Corner (Eds.), *Sex Differences in the Brain. The Relation between Structure and Function. Progress in Brain Research*, this volume, Ch. 26.

Smith, P.K. (1982) Does play matter? Functional and evolutionary aspects of animal and human play. *Behav. Brain Sci.*, 5: 139–184.

Södersten, P. (1984) Sexual differentiation: do males differ from females in behavioral sensitivity to gonadal hormones? In: G.J. De Vries, J.P.C. De Bruin, H.B.M. Uylings and M.A. Corner (Eds.), *Sex Differences in the Brain. The Relation between Structure and Function. Progress in Brain Research*, this volume, Ch. 15.

Stafford, R.E. (1961) Sex differences in spatial visualization as evidence of sex linked inheritance. *Percept. Motor Skills*, 13: 428.

Stevenson, M.F. and Poole, T.B. (1982) Playful interactions in family groups of the common marmoset (*Callithrix Jacchus Jacchus*), *Anim. Behav.*, 30: 886–900.

Stewart, J., Skvarenina, A. and Pottier, J. (1975) Effects of neonatal androgens on open field and maze learning in the prepubescent and adult rat. *Physiol. Behav.*, 14: 291–295.

Stockman, E.R., Baum, M.J., Gallagher, C.A. and Callaghan, R.S. (1983) Sexual differentiation of prepubertal play in the ferret. Presented at the Conference on Reproductive Behavior, Medford.

Symons, D. (1974) Aggressive play and communication in rhesus monkeys (*Macaca mulatta*). *Am. Zool.*, 14: 317–322.

Symons, D. (1978) *Play and Aggression, A Study of Rhesus Monkeys*, Columbia University Press, New York.

Tees, R.C., Midgley, G. and Nesbit, J.C. (1981) The effect of early visual experience on spatial maze learning in rats. *Develop. Psychobiol.*, 14: 425–438.

Thor, D.H. and Holloway Jr., W.R. (1982) Anosmia and play fighting in prepubescent male and female rats. *Physiol. Behav.*, 29: 281–285.

Thor, D.H. and Holloway Jr., W.R. (1983) Play soliciting behavior in juvenile male and female rats. *Anim. Learn. Behav.*, 11: 173–178.

Thornton, J.E. and Goy, R.W. (1983) Female sexual behavior of adult hermaphroditic rhesus. Paper presented at the Conference on Reproductive Behavior, Medford.

Vandenberg, S.G. and Kuse, A.R. (1979) Spatial ability: A critical review of the sex-linked major gene hypothesis. In: M.A. Wittig and A.C. Petersen (Eds.), *Sex-Related Differences in Cognitive Functioning*, Academic Press, New York, pp. 67–96.

Vincent, L.E. and Bekoff, M. (1978) Quantitative analyses of the ontogeny of predatory behaviour in coyotes (*Canis latrans*). *Anim. Behav.*, 26: 225–231.

Vito, C.C. and Fox, T.O. (1982) Androgen and estrogen receptors in the embryonic and neonatal rat brain. *Develop. Brain Res.*, 2: 97–110.

Whiting, B. and Edwards, C. (1973) A cross-cultural analysis of sex differences in the behavior of children aged three through eleven. *J. Soc. Psychol.*, 91: 177–178.

Wright, P.S., Stelmasiak, T., Black, D. and Sykes, D. (1979) Medroxy progesterone acetate and reproductive processes in male dogs. *Aust. Vet. J.*, 55: 437–438.

DISCUSSION

K.-D. DÖHLER: "Masculinization" of sexual behavior patterns is known to be controlled, in the rat, by estrogens. "Masculinization" of play behavior, as you demonstrated, is organized by androgens. Vom Saal (1983) has shown that organization of aggressive behavior is also under androgenic control. He even demonstrated that prenatal estrogens may actually interfere with androgen effects on organization of aggressive behavior in rats and mice. Since Vom Saal is not here, I want to be his advocate and point out that the term "masculinization" is very complex. Perinatal treatment with estrogens can stimulate masculinization (of sexual behavior patterns) and the same treatment can inhibit masculinization (of aggressive behavior).

H.H. SWANSON: How were the animals housed for the study of play behavior? If males and females lived together, how did you score male/female interactions?

W.W. BEATTY: Typically we house 6–8 rats/cage. About half are males and half are females. We scored only the frequency of play fighting and play initiation, without regard to the sex of the play partner. However, Meaney and Stewart (1979) have studied partner preference throughout development, and males tend to play with males, although this varies with age.

H.H. SWANSON: In the radial maze, females make more errors than males. If females are more active than males they might still finish in the same length of time. Did you measure how long they took?

W.W. BEATTY: We did not measure session time, so I cannot say for sure. However, most animals run the radial maze rather quickly. Further, the females showed much greater variability, especially in working memory errors, than did the males. That is, many females did fairly well for a few days and then made a large number of errors, performed well for a few days and so on. Males were more consistent in their performance from day to day.

S. BUTLER: It seems possible that what is a spatial task for rats may not be so for humans. The radial maze lends itself to verbal analysis by humans and this is a cognitive strategy which females may apply more readily or more successfully than males.

W.W. BEATTY: That is certainly possible. In addition all of the female students employed a strategy of entering 4 adjacent alleys during the first 4 choices while only 2/3 of the males used this strategy. Hence the males may have constructed a more difficult task for themselves.

E. KEMBLE: Do amygdaloid lesions reduce the play of males selectively or is the effect strictly quantitative?

W.W. BEATTY: We only counted the frequency of play, so I cannot really say. But females do play differently (more short play bouts) so it is a good question.

C.D. TORAN-ALLERAND: Do you have any idea where in the amygdala your "recreation" center might be, since this region is unusually rich in aromatase which one might think might produce significant amounts of estrogen.

W.W. BEATTY: Only 1–2% of testosterone is aromatized to estrogen, so there would still be plenty to interact with androgen receptors.

C.D. TORAN-ALLERAND: Synaptogenesis in amygdala in response to androgen has been recently shown by Nichizuka and Arai (1982) in amygdaloid transplants of females androgenized in oculo.

REFERENCES

Meaney, M.J. and Stewart, J. (1979) Environmental factors influencing the affiliative behavior of male and female rats (*Rattus norvegicus*). *Anim. Learn. Behav.*, 7: 397–405.

Nichizuka, M. and Arai, Y. (1982) Synapse formation in response to estrogen in the medial amygdala developing in the eye. *Proc. natl. Acad. Sci. (U.S.A.)*, 79: 7024–7026.

Vom Saal, F.S., Grant, W.M., McMullen, C.W. and Laves, K.S. (1983) High fetal estrogen concentrations: correlation with increased adult sexual performance and decreased aggression in male mice. *Science*, 220: 1306–1309.

G.J. De Vries et al. (Eds.),
Progress in Brain Research, Vol. 61
© 1984 Elsevier Science Publishers B.V., Amsterdam

Social Influences on Sex Differences in the Behaviour and Endocrine State of Talapoin Monkeys

E.B. KEVERNE, J.A. EBERHART, U. YODYINGYUAD and D.H. ABBOTT

Department of Anatomy, University of Cambridge, Cambridge CB2 3DY (Great Britain)

INTRODUCTION

The social environment is known to influence sexual behaviour in several mammalian species, either by a direct action on the expression of behaviour, or indirectly by modifying endocrine states. Thus in male mice, hamsters, rats, rabbits, the ram and the bull, the presentation of a sexually stimulating oestrous female may increase plasma levels of testosterone (Macrides et al., 1975; Katangole et al., 1971; Illius et al., 1976). Conversely, social stress and overcrowding can suppress gonadotrophin secretion (Bronson, 1973) and, in turn, reproductive behaviour in all these species and, many more besides. However, it is only when we examine group-living primates that the social environment becomes all important especially in relationship to sexual behaviour. Important, that is, not only for the ways in which the social environment restricts sexual behaviour, but also for the way it enhances its development, a feature exemplified by the now classical studies of Harlow (1969) on infant peer separation. Monkeys reared by their mothers in the absence of peers exhibit a severe impairment of their adult sexual behaviour (Harlow, 1969). Even in social environments where the peer group is numerically adequate, but consists of only males or only females, then the development of sexual interactions is such that foot clasp mounting in all female groups is enhanced, and suppressed in all male groups (Goldfoot and Wallen, 1978).

In the adult, the sexual behaviour of monkeys, apes and, indeed, man "himself" is not so strictly regulated by gonadal hormones as appears to be the case in most other mammalian species. Captive studies of several monkey species have shown females to be receptive at all times of their cycle (Keverne, 1976) and, in the chimpanzee, mating has been observed throughout 30% of the menstrual cycle (Tutin, 1980) despite the physical restrictions imposed by the changing dimensions of a sexual skin swelling. Other apes, such as the orangutan, have been observed to be prepared to mate on every day of the menstrual cycle (Nadler, 1977). Hence the view arose long ago (Beach, 1942) that the primate brain has become largely "emancipated" from the fluctuations in gonadal hormone levels. This view is further reported by more recent studies which illustrate the persistence of sexual motivation in male rhesus monkeys that have been castrated for some years (Phoenix et al., 1973), while ovarian hormones primarily influence female attractiveness rather than receptivity (Baum et al., 1977).

For group-living primates, the structure of the social group affects diverse aspects of an individual's behaviour. In many species, dominant males demand sexual prerogative so that the subordinate males will have limited access to attractive females and thus produce far fewer offspring. Likewise, high ranking females in many primate groups not only engage more frequently in sexual interactions than do low ranking females, but also give birth more often. It is therefore important to understand how a monkey's neuroendocrine system responds to the factors that shape and organise its society and determine its individual role in that society.

We have addressed this issue through long-term studies on the talapoin monkey (*Miopithecus talapoin*), which is the smallest cercopithecine primate having a weight range of 800–1500 g for adult females and 1200–2500 g for males. The talapoin's natural habitat is the rain forest of West Africa, where animals normally live in both single- and mixed-sex groups consisting of up to 80 animals. Our studies have taken place over 8 years on several experimental groups, consisting of 3–5 adult males (intact and castrate) and a similar number of females (intact and ovariectomised). The monkeys were observed for 50 min twice daily, with all animals being monitored continuously for sexual, aggressive and social interactions (see Dixson et al., 1975, for details of behavioural scoring). A minimum of 1000 min of observations was obtained for each treatment condition over a 3-week period. Plasma levels of testosterone, cortisol, prolactin, LH and progesterone were measured in blood samples taken twice weekly by femoral venipuncture under ketamine anaesthesia using radioimmunoassay (RIA) techniques described elsewhere (Yodyingyuad et al., 1982). The social status of each monkey was assessed from its interactions with others in the group, dominance being defined in terms of the direction of "spontaneous" aggression among them.

RELATIONSHIP BETWEEN SOCIAL RANK AND SEXUAL BEHAVIOUR IN MALES AND FEMALES

The distribution of sexual behaviour among males and females is strongly influenced by each of their hierarchies. Fig. 1a shows that for males in the group mounting of females is the exclusive prerogative of the dominant male. This "patterning" of sexual behaviour applies equally to other behaviours that are related to reproduction, with significant differences for ejaculations, inspects, looks and approaches to females, which all vary according to rank (Keverne et al., 1978a; Eberhart et al., 1980).

Like the males female talapoin monkeys also form a social hierarchy which can be assessed by the direction of aggressive encounters. Although aggressive behaviour among females is significantly less frequent than among males, social status has important consequences for many behaviours including sexual activity (Fig. 1b). Highest ranking females not only receive the most sexual attention, but they also solicit and approach males significantly more often than do the subordinate females.

The influence of the social environment on the sexual behaviour of males and females is therefore similar in its outcome, restricting reproductive activity to animals of higher social rank. Since moving into the social group itself entails changes in gonadal status, it is conceivable that such endocrine changes might in themselves account for this skewed distribution of sexual behaviours. A number of studies have shown that social variables can modify the effects of a given hormone on behaviour (Dixson and Herbert, 1977) or the hormone levels in individual monkeys (Rose et al., 1971, 1975). Our own studies on talapoin monkeys have shown that the dominant males tend to have higher levels of testosterone than subordinates (Eberhart et al., 1980) and that subordinate females are less likely to conceive or to show LH surges in response to positive oestrogen feedback (Keverne, 1979; Bowman et al., 1978). These studies illustrate a marked influence of the social hierarchy on gonadal hormones in both males and females, and lead to the question of whether or not such gonadal hormone changes represent the mechanism by which social group behaviours are regulated.

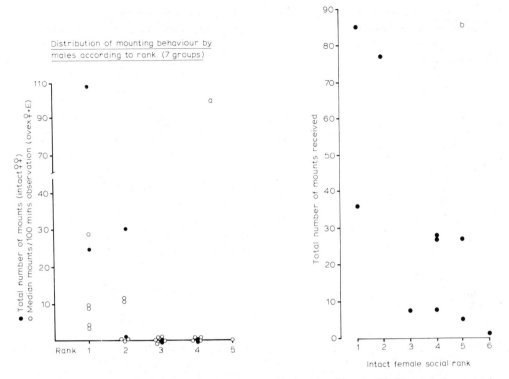

Fig. 1. Distribution of sexual behaviour according to rank of males (a) and females (b). Closed circles are total mounts during a 3-week period of observations for intact females and the males in their groups. Open circles (a) are medians for intact males per 100 min of observations with ovariectomised oestrogen-treated females. Data from intact males from 7 groups; data from intact females in only 2 of these groups.

DO GONADAL HORMONES DETERMINE THE SOCIAL HIERARCHY OR THE DISTRIBUTION OF SEXUAL BEHAVIOUR WITHIN IT?

To address this issue, males were castrated and females were ovariectomised in their respective groups and given hormone replacement therapy. In this way, gonadal hormone levels could be either maintained constant in all animals or selectively manipulated in specific individuals. Among dominant males, castration never completely eliminated their sexual interest in females and, although testosterone replacement "therapy" increased their sexual behaviour, subordinates never copulated even after high doses of testosterone (Fig. 2). Moreover, the administration of sufficient testosterone to produce supra-normal "physiological" levels in subordinate animals did not improve their status in the hierarchy (Dixson and Herbert, 1977). Among females, ovariectomy eliminated overt sexual interactions regardless of rank, but since the sexual skin swelling of females is dependent upon gonadal steroids, its absence would preclude such behaviour under any circumstances. Oestradiol replacement reinstated sexual behaviour only in high ranking females, and even selective oestrogen treatment of the lowest ranking female did not enhance her sexual interactions (Fig. 3). Hence, with only the lowest ranking female "attractive" in a group, sexual behaviour is not observed, although aggression of high ranking females towards those of lower rank increased (Fig. 3).

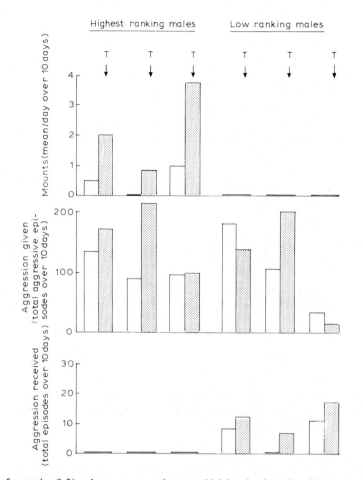

Fig. 2. Effect of castration (left) and testosterone replacement (right) to dominant ($n = 3$) and subordinate ($n = 3$) males. Testosterone enhances the sexual behaviour of dominant males but not subordinates, although the latter do receive more aggression.

Gonadal hormones appear, therefore, to be without any effect among either males or females in determining the hierarchical distribution of sexual behaviours within the group. It is the social hierarchy which is primarily influential in determining sexual behaviour and which can override the effects of the gonadal hormones.

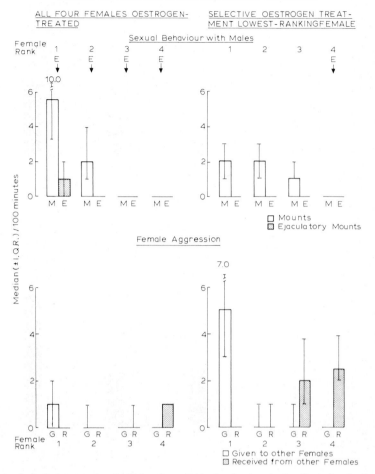

Fig. 3. Effects of ovariectomy and oestradiol replacement to dominant and subordinate females (*n* = 4). Oestradiol enhances the sexual behaviour of the two highest ranking but not of the two lowest ranking females. Selective oestrogen treatment of only the lowest ranking female does not enhance her sexual behaviour, but does enhance the aggression received (lower section). I.Q.R., inter-quarterile range.

MECHANISMS FOR DETERMINING HIERARCHICAL SOCIAL INFLUENCES ON SEXUAL BEHAVIOUR

If gonadal hormones do not form a major part of the mechanism whereby the distribution of sexual behaviour is restricted with respect to the social hierarchy, how can we account for these reproducible and enduring effects? In order to answer this question, it is necessary to look at behaviours other than sexual and to examine the strategies which dominant individuals adopt in order to inhibit the behaviour of subordinates.

Fig. 4 shows the aggressive behaviour of males directed towards those of lower rank when each group was with "attractive" oestrogen-treated females. In contrast to sexual behaviour there was no evidence that the highest ranking male in each group was necessarily the most aggressive. Not surprisingly, the highest ranking males in each group received the least

Male-Male Aggression: All Males with Females (E)

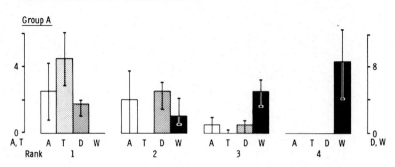

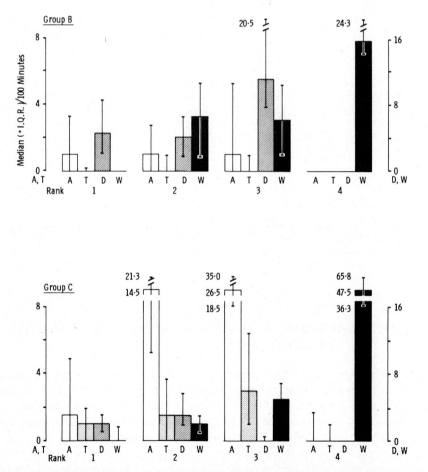

Fig. 4. Aggressive behaviour of males of differing social rank (ranks 1–4) during the time they have access to ovariectomised oestradiol-treated females (E). Data expressed as medians over a total of 1000 min of observation during a 3-week period. A, attack; T, threat; D, displace; W, withdrawn. (From Eberhart et al., 1980.)

aggression, whereas the lowest ranking males received most. Hence, although the highest-ranking male is clearly the "boss" a fact confirmed by the amount of visual monitoring he receives from all of the other males in the group (Keverne et al., 1978b), he keeps his subordinates under control through intermediaries. Such a strategy frees the dominant male from continuous monitoring of all males in the group and, by keeping the intermediary males under control, "aggression" can be indirectly exerted on subordinates through the hierarchical chain of "command". Moreover, such intimidation of subordinates as witnessed not only from the overt aggression they receive but also from their high levels of withdrawals from other males (Fig. 4), undoubtedly places them under considerable "stress". Hence, it is hardly surprising to find that once the social hierarchy has become firmly established, the stress hormones may fall in the dominant male and rise in the subordinates (Fig. 5). Thus, not only is the aggressive behaviour different among dominant and subordinate males, but their endocrine profiles differ accordingly (Eberhart et al., 1983b).

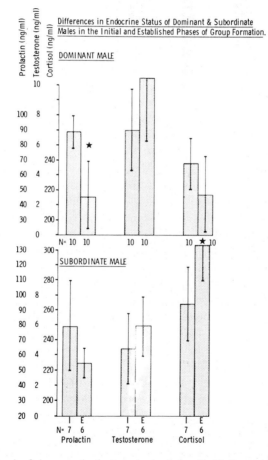

Fig. 5. Mean (± S.D.) levels of plasma prolactin, testosterone and cortisol in the most dominant and subordinate males of the group within the initial, I (first 3 months), and the established period, E (12 months later) of group formation. The females in the group were oestrogen treated in both cases. Prolactin fell in the dominant males while cortisol increased in the subordinates from I to E. (From Keverne et al., 1982.) *$P < 0.01$.

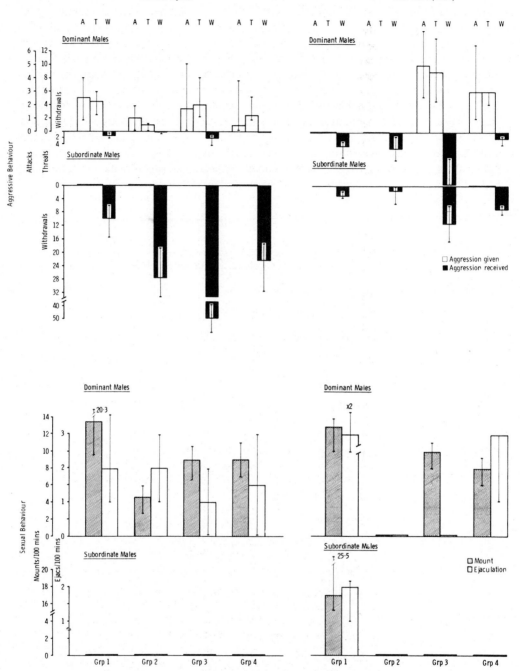

Fig. 6. Distribution of aggressive (above) and sexual (below) behaviour of dominant and subordinate males in 4 social groups, first with all males together (left), and subsequently each male separately (right), with the same females in both situations. A, attacks; T, threats; W, withdrawals from aggression. Although the aggressive behaviour which subordinates received when they are housed individually with females decreases (Anova $P < 0.001$) their sexual behaviour does not increase to that of former dominants (Anova $P < 0.001$).

Although aggressive behaviour among females is less frequent than among males, social status also has consequences for endocrine state as well as for many behaviours (Keverne et al., 1982). Solicits from the highest ranking females towards males are not only more frequent than from lower ranking females, but they are more likely to lead to a mount. Sequential analysis of behaviour has shown that, when females solicit low ranking males, aggression from other high ranking males rather than male mounting is the most likely consequence. However, the most likely behaviour to follow "solicitations" of low ranking females are solicits from a higher ranking female. In other words, the strategies adopted to restrict sexual activity in low ranking individuals tend to differ between males and females. Males are more likely to intimidate subordinates by the threat of impending aggression, preferably via an intermediary "agent", while females are more likely to prevent subordinate females from being mounted by themselves sexually soliciting the male's attention.

DOES CHRONIC SUBORDINATION HAVE CONSEQUENCES FOR SEXUAL BEHAVIOUR EVEN IN THE ABSENCE OF DOMINANTS?

If infrequent socio-sexual activity in subordinate males primarily reflects the constant threat of receiving aggression, then removing all other males from social groups should enhance the sexual behaviour of subordinates. This hypothesis was tested by allowing each male to interact with the oestrogen-treated females of his group in the absence of any other males (Eberhart et al., 1983a). With one exception, former subordinate males failed to display sexual behaviour even in the absence of other males (Fig. 6); this exceptional male received frequent solicits from females, and all his sexual behaviour was in fact initiated by the females. Males that had experienced long-term social dominance showed less mating when alone than when there were some subordinate males in their groups. The virtual absence of sexual behaviour in males that once had been socially subordinate cannot be accounted for in terms of current aggression. Subordinate males received less aggression (aggression from females was low) in the absence of other males than they did in their presence (Fig. 6 upper section). Moreover, the differences in socio-sexual behaviour between high vs. low status males cannot be attributed to differences in female sexual initiative since females in fact solicited former subordinates even more than former dominant males.

These differences in socio-sexual interactions of former dominant and subordinate males when alone with females also have distinct endocrine correlates. Subordinate males had higher cortisol levels under these conditions than did males that had experienced dominance. This difference disappeared when the animals were isolated. Prolactin levels were also higher in former subordinate than in former dominant males when left alone with females. Testosterone levels increased only in males that were sexually active at the time and were not significantly different between dominant or subordinate males when alone with females.

If infrequent sexual activity on the part of subordinate females reflects primarily the competition for male attention by dominant females, then removing all other females from the social group should enhance the sexual attention subordinate females receive. The hypothesis was tested by allowing each oestrogen-treated female to interact with males of her own group in the absence of other females. Unlike males, former subordinate females showed high levels of soliciting, which were successful in view of the fact that mounts and ejaculations were frequent (Fig. 7). Moreover, unlike the male situation, the stress hormones cortisol and prolactin were lower in subordinate females when alone within the male group than if other females were present too. Clearly, there are no endocrine or behavioural indications that females experience the same kind of "learned inadequacy" as do males under traumatic social situations.

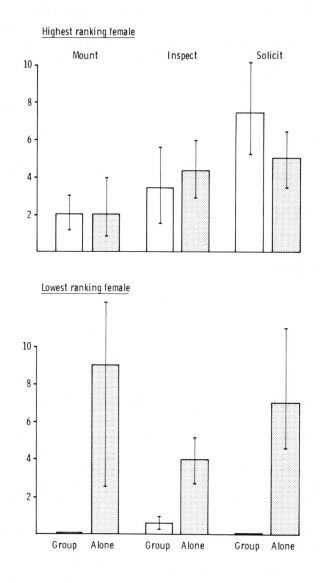

Fig. 7. Distribution of proceptive behaviour (solicits) and attractiveness (inspects and mounts by males) of dominant (above) and subordinate (below) females in the social group (group) and in the absence of other females (alone) when oestrogen treated. Although subordinates do not solicit and are not attractive to males in the group, the same hormonal treatment in the absence of other females markedly enhances these behaviours.

OPIATE RECEPTOR BLOCKADE, BEHAVIOUR AND ENDOCRINE STATE IN THE SOCIAL GROUP

The endocrine profiles that we observed in subordinate individuals, particularly the high prolactin and low LH (see above) suggest differences in activity of the brain's endorphin system (Blank et al., 1979; Ellingre et al., 1980). We have therefore begun to investigate the effects of interference with endogenous opiates on behaviour and endocrine responsiveness in social groups of monkeys (Meller et al., 1980; Fabre-Nys et al., 1982). High ranking males treated with the opiate antagonist naltrexone showed a significant reduction of sexual behaviour, a deficit that did not recover rapidly after withdrawal of the drug. Low ranking males did not show any enhancement of sexual behaviour on treatment with naltrexone. Opiate blockade did not alter aggression, but a consistent effect of the drug was a marked increase in grooming invitations and hence grooming received, irrespective of rank, in both males and in females.

In addition to its behavioural effects, naltrexone had marked effects on hormone levels, which occurred independently of social rank and were the same even in animals living in social isolation. In most males, cortisol, LH, testosterone and prolactin increased (Fig. 8). These endocrine changes appeared to occur independently of the behavioural effects of opiate blockade, since they appeared with the lowest dose of naltrexone ($250 \mu g/kg$) and were slow to develop (30 min) whereas the behavioural effects were observed within 5–10 min after drug administration. This separation of endocrine and behavioural effects of opiate receptor blockade is essential to our interpretation of how the endogenous opiates may influence or be influenced by behaviour.

Naltrexone administration to females, unlike males, does not appear to have any effects on their sexual behaviour. Neither solicits by nor mounts or inspects of females change under drug treatment, suggesting no change in their proceptivity or their attractiveness. Females (whether dominant or subordinate) approach males less frequently but this is probably a reflection of the increased time they spend grooming each other (Fabre-Nys et al., 1982). Moreover, naltrexone did not have the same effects on situationally induced endocrine changes in females as it did in males. Thus, cortisol increased significantly and consistently in females following opiate receptor blockade, although not so markedly as in males, and neither LH nor prolactin showed a significant or consistent increase in females (Fig. 8).

We have recently been measuring in the CSF 5HIAA (a metabolite of 5HT) and HVA (a metabolite of dopamine). A consistent finding has been the increased levels of 5HIAA seen in those male monkeys which on moving into the group become socially subordinate. Interestingly, a similar condition can be induced in non-subordinate monkeys living in social isolation by treatment with the opiate receptor blocker, naltrexone.

Hence, the data we have collected from monkeys living socially suggest that subordination has much in common at the behavioural, neuroendocrine and neural levels with non-subordinate monkeys treated with the opiate receptor blockers naloxone or naltrexone. In many respects this finding is counter-intuitive since the prediction might be for increased opiate activity in monkeys under social stress. However, we may be looking at a situation here in which chronic social subordination has functionally depleted the endogenous opiate system (possibly by down regulation of receptors) and the animals' coping ability.

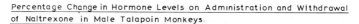

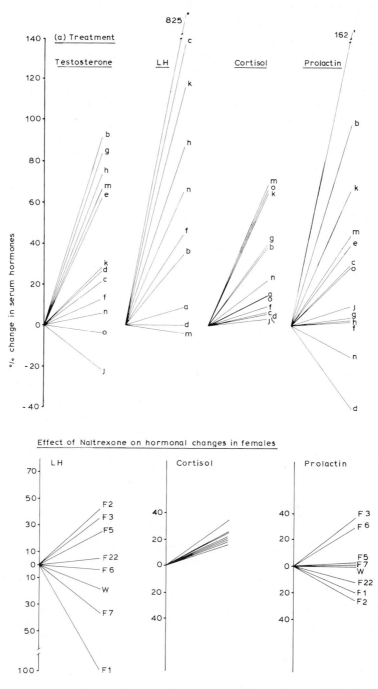

Fig. 8. Percentage change in hormone levels 1 h after naltrexone administration in individual male (above) and individual female (below) talapoin monkeys. Testosterone, cortisol and LH increase significantly in males, but only cortisol increased significantly in females. (From Meller et al., 1980 — male data.)

SEXUAL DIFFERENCES IN REPRODUCTIVE STRATEGIES
AND POSSIBLE NEURAL CORRELATES

It is clear from these studies that the social environment has an important influence on the expression and suppression of reproduction in both males and females: the dominant animals have the prerogative over mating behaviour in males while females of low rank fail to conceive. These laboratory findings appear to apply equally well to primates in the wild since numerous field reports draw attention to high ranking males being sexually more active (Carpenter, 1942; Hall, 1962; Bernstein, 1976; Harcourt and Stewart, 1977) and producing more offspring than low ranking males (Smith, 1981). Likewise, high ranking females in many free-ranging primate groups not only engage more frequently in sexual interactions, but also reproduce more often than do low ranking females (Drickamer, 1974; Abbott and Hearn, 1978; Dunbar, 1980).

Since moving into the social group itself entails a change in activity of the gonads, one cannot ignore the possibility that such endocrine changes can reinforce the social hierarchy. Pertinent to this question is the increase in testosterone seen solely in dominant males (Rose et al., 1975), as well as the suppression of cyclicity seen in subordinate females and their failure to show LH surges in response to oestrogen (Bowman et al., 1978). However, although the relationship between the social hierarchy and gonadal hormones may have important consequences for fertility, there is no evidence for differential effects of gonadal hormones on behaviour with respect to the hierarchy. Thus, testosterone treatment of castrated males increased sexual behaviour only in those individuals that were dominant, and in no case was there any change in the social hierarchy when a subordinate male selectively received testosterone treatment (Dixson and Herbert, 1977). Similarly, selective oestrogen treatment in females altered neither the sexual behaviour nor the social rank of the subordinate monkey.

Many behaviours other than sexual are also influenced according to the social hierarchy, in particular aggression. It is, in fact, a skillful deployment of aggressive tactics by high ranking males that achieves the suppression of sexual behaviour of subordinates. Such a constant threat of aggression increases visual monitoring by subordinates (Keverne et al., 1978b) and decreases their use of cage space and opportunities to interact with females (Keverne, 1979). Moreover, this unreciprocated aggression from which the subordinate males can neither escape nor control induces a state of "learned inadequacy" (Seligman, 1975). Even when given the uncontested opportunity for access to females they fail to mate in marked contrast to the sexual behaviour which they show in this situation prior to becoming subordinate. This impaired sexual drive together with elevated cortisol and prolactin levels indicates that the experience of long-term social subordination may have drastic consequences for a male's ability to handle a sexually demanding situation. In primate groups, such a mechanism would ensure reduced sexual behaviour in subordinate males, at least in the short term, hence providing a strategy which reinforces the social hierarchy without recourse to overt aggression.

Among females of the social group, the major strategy employed by dominant females to restrict the sexual activity of subordinates is quite different from that of males. Female–female aggression is relatively low but when subordinates solicit males, the dominant female either distracts male attention by counter-soliciting or, occasionally disrupts the interaction by threatening or mounting the female. When the competing dominant females are removed from the group, however, then subordinates show high levels of sexual behaviour and without any endocrine changes (e.g. in cortisol or prolactin) that are indicative of increased stress under these circumstances.

The brain mechanisms underlying these differential behavioural and endocrine responses in males and females are currently under investigation, and may involve the endorphin system. When dominant males are deprived of their endogenous opiates by administration of the opiate receptor blocker, naltrexone, they show reduced sexual behaviour despite increases in LH and testosterone, but they also show increases in the stress hormones cortisol and prolactin. The sexual behaviour of females is not inhibited by opiate receptor blockade, nor does LH or prolactin increase. Invitations to be groomed and grooming behaviour increase in both males and females (Fabre-Nys et al., 1982). One possible interpretation of these findings is that opiate receptor blockade might enhance the need for social attachment, which is fulfilled by the support and comfort of mutual grooming behaviour. Interestingly in the heterosexual groups compared with isosexual groups, huddling and grooming (affiliative behaviour) in males decrease markedly, while intrasexual aggression increases. This is not the case for females who show high levels of affiliative behaviour in the heterosexual group and very low levels of intrasexual aggression. The different effects which this drug has on sexual behaviour in males and females may reflect the different strategies the sexes adopt to inhibit sexual behaviour in subordinates. Since coping with a sexually demanding situation is an important determinant of male sexual behaviour, as exemplified by "learned inadequacy", then in males the removal of their "coping mechanism" by opiate receptor blockade would be expected to have marked repercussions for their sexual behaviour. The fact that females compete for male attention rather than aggressively suppress the behaviour of subordinates, taken together with the importance of their attractiveness for sexual interactions (a behaviourally passive condition which is obligatorily under the influence of ovarian hormones), emancipates their sexual behaviour, though possibly not their reproductive endocrinology, from the endogenous opiate system. That is not to say that there is a fundamental difference in the brain's opiate system between males and females, but that the different behavioural strategies adopted call this into play more in males than in females.

At the present time little more can be said of the neural mechanisms which underlie these differences in behaviour between dominant and subordinate individuals, or between males and females. A consideration of other experimental data involving opioids in a behavioural context is not particularly enlightening. They unfortunately suffer from the same methodological weaknesses which arise from the lack of specific μ or Δ opioid receptor agonists or antagonists. Hence the systemic administration of drugs such as naloxone or naltrexone effect both the β-endorphin and the enkephalin systems both peripherally and centrally. It is therefore not surprising that widespread actions of opiates have been reported as a consequence of using these drugs. These actions range from the implication of endogenous opiates in psychopathological processes, feeding behaviour, sexual behaviour, memory, social attachment, neuroendocrine regulation, to nociception and analgesia (reviewed in Fabre-Nys et al., 1982). Since it seems unlikely that specific opioid receptor blockers are going to become available in the short term, a more profitable approach might be the direct application of the less specific drugs currently available to discrete brain areas. Such an approach has recently been made in the context of sexual behaviour (lordosis) in the female rat (Sirinathsinghji et al., 1983). It was found that infusion of β-endorphin or the antagonist naloxone into the midbrain central grey aea of the female rat inhibited or promoted respectively the action of LHRH on lordosis. However, the lordosis response of the female rat is a rather specialised sexual reflex with no obvious counterpart in the monkey. Moreover, opiate receptor blockade in the rat facilitates sexual behaviour, while its effects are inhibitory to sexual behaviour in the monkey. Hence, until we have a direct measure of changes in or a means of manipulating specific parts of the opiate systems, the current interpretations of the data remain in the realms of speculation.

ACKNOWLEDGEMENTS

We are grateful to Helen Shiers and Kathy Batty for their excellent technical assistance with radioimmunoassays, and to the help and constructive criticism of our colleague Joe Herbert. The LH for iodination were prepared by Dr. L.E. Reichert and obtained through NIAMDD. The LH antiserum was supplied by Dr. G.D. Niswender. The prolactin standard was obtained from the MRC and the prolactin for iodination from Dr. P.S. Lowry. The prolactin antiserum was a gift from Dr. H. Friesen.

The work was supported by a programme grant from the Medical Research Council, a Marshall Scholarship to Jerry A. Eberhart, and a Girton Scholarship to U. Yodyingyuad.

REFERENCES

Abbott, D.H. and Hearn, J.P. (1978) Physical, hormonal and behavioural aspects of sexual development in the marmoset monkey, *Callithrix jacchus. J. Reprod. Fertil.* 53: 155–166.

Baum, M.J., Everitt, B.J., Herbert, J. and Keverne, E.B. (1977) Hormonal basis of proceptivity and receptivity in female primats. *Arch. Sex. Behav.*, 6: 173–192.

Beach, F.A. (1942) Central nervous mechanisms involved in the reproductive behaviour of vertebrates. *Psychol. Bull.*, 39: 200–226.

Bernstein, I.S. (1976) Dominance, aggression and reproduction in primate societies. *J. Theoret. Biol.*, 60: 459–472.

Blank, M.S., Panerai, A.E. and Friesen, H. (1979) Opioid peptides modulate luteinising hormone secretion during sexual maturation. *Science*, 203: 1129–1131.

Bowman, L.A., Dilley, S.R. and Keverne, E.B. (1978) Suppression of oestrogen-induced LH surges by social subordination in talapoin monkeys. *Nature (London)*, 275: 56–58.

Bronson, F.H. (1973) Establishment of social rank among grouped male mice: relative effects on circulating FSH, LH and corticosterone. *Physiol. Behav.*, 10: 947–951.

Carpenter, C.R. (1942) Sexual behaviour of free-ranging rhesus monkeys: (*Macaca mulatta*). I. Specimens, procedures and behavioural characteristics of estrus. *J. Comp. Psychol.*, 33: 113–142.

Dixson, A.F. and Herbert, J. (1977) Gonadal hormones and sexual behaviour in groups of adult talapoin monkeys (*Miopithecus talapoin*). *Hormone Behav.*, 8: 141–154.

Dixson, A.F., Scruton, D.M. and Herbert, J. (1975) Behaviour of the talapoin monkey (*Miopithecus talapoin*) (studied in groups in the laboratory). *J. Zool.*, 176: 177–210.

Drickamer, L.C. (1974) A ten-year summary of reproductive data from free-ranging *Macaca mulatta. Folia Primat.*, 21: 61–80.

Dunbar, R.I.M. (1980) Determinants and evolutionary consequences of dominance among female gelada baboons. *Behav. Ecol. Sociobiol.*, 7: 253–265.

Eberhart, J.A., Keverne, E.B. and Meller, R.E. (1980) Social influences on plasma testosterone levels in male talapoin monkeys. *Hormone Behav.*, 14: 247–266.

Eberhart, J.A., Keverne, E.B., Meller, R.E., and Yodyingyuad, U. (1983a) Socially induced learned helplessness inhibits sexual behaviour in male talapoin monkeys. *Science*, submitted.

Eberhart, J.A., Keverne, E.B. and Meller, R.E. (1983b) Social influences in circulating levels of cortisol and prolactin in male talapoin monkeys. *Physiol. Behav.*, 30: 361–369.

Ellingre, J., Mendelson, J.H. and Kuehnle, J.C. (1980) Effects of heroin and naltrexone on plasma prolactin levels in man. *Pharmacol. Biochem. Behav.*, 12: 163–165.

Fabre-Nys, C., Meller, R.E. and Keverne, E.B. (1982) Opiate antagonists stimulate affiliative behaviour in monkeys. *Pharmacol. Biochem. Behav.*, 16: 653–660.

Goldfoot, D.A. and Wallen, K. (1978) Development of gender role behaviours in heterosexual and isosexual groups of infant rhesus monkeys. In: D.J. Chivers and J. Herbert (Eds.), *Recent Advances in Primatology, Vol. 1*, Academic Press, New York, pp. 155–159.

Hall, K.R.L. (1962) Numerical data, maintenance activities and locomotion of the wild chaema baboon, *Papio ursinus. Proc. Zool. Soc.*, 139: 181–220.

Harcourt, S.A. and Stewart, K.J. (1977) Apes, sex and societies. *New Sci.*, 76: 160–162.

Harlow, H.F. (1969) Age-mate or peer affectional system. *Adv. Study Behav.*, 2: 333–383.

Illius, A.W., Haynes, M.B. and Lamming, G.E. (1976) Effects of ewe proximity on plasma testosterone levels and behaviour in the ram. *J. Reprod. Fertil.*, 48: 25–32.

Katangole, C.B., Naftolin, F. and Short, R.V. (1971) Relationship between blood levels of luteinising hormone and testosterone in bulls and the effects of social stimulation. *J. Endocrinol.*, 50: 457–466.

Keverne, E.B. (1976) Sexual receptivity and attractiveness in the female monkey. *Adv. Study Behav.*, 7: 155–200.

Keverne, E.B. (1979) Sexual and aggressive behaviour in social groups of talapoin monkeys. In: *Sex Hormones and Behaviour, CIBA Symposium 62* (new series), Excerpta Medica, Amsterdam, pp. 271–286.

Keverne, E.B., Meller, R.E. and Martinez-Arias, A.M. (1978a) Dominance, aggression and sexual behaviour in social groups of talapoin monkeys. In: D.J. Chivers and J. Herbert (Eds.), *Recent Advances in Primatology, Vol. 1*, Academic Press, New York, pp. 533–548.

Keverne, E.B., Leonard, R.A., Scruton, D.M. and Young, S.K. (1978b) Visual monitoring in social groups of talapoin monkeys (*Miopithecus talapoin*). *Anim. Behav.*, 26: 933–944.

Keverne, E.B., Eberhart, J.A. and Meller, R.E. (1982) Social influences on behaviour and neuroendocrine responsiveness of talapoin monkeys. *Scand. J. Psychol.*, Suppl. 1: 37–47.

Macrides, F., Bartke, A. and Dalterio, S. (1975) Strange females increase plasma testosterone levels in mice. *Science*, 189: 1104–1106.

Meller, R.E., Keverne, E.B. and Herbert, J. (1980) Behavioural and endocrine effects of naltrexone in male talapoin monkeys. *Pharmacol. Biochem. Behav.*, 13: 663–672.

Nadler, R.D. (1977) Sexual behaviour of captive orang-utans. *Arch. Sex. Behav.*, 6: 457–475.

Phoenix, C.H., Slob, A.K. and Goy, R.W. (1973) Effects of castration and replacement therapy on sexual behaviour of adult male rhesuses. *J. Comp. Physiol. Psychol.*, 84: 472–481.

Rose, R.M., Holaday, J.W. and Bernstein, I.S. (1971) Plasma testosterone, dominance rank and aggressive behaviour in male rhesus monkeys. *Nature (London)*, 231: 366–368.

Rose, R.M., Bernstein, I.S. and Gordon, T.P. (1975) Consequences of social conflict on plasma testosterone levels in rhesus monkeys. *Psychosom. Med.*, 37: 50–61.

Seligman, M.E.P. (1975) *Helplessness: On Depression, Development and Death*, W.H. Freeman, San Francisco, CA.

Sirinathsinghji, D.J.S., Whittington, P.E., Audsley, A. and Fraser, H.M. (1983) β-Endorphin regulates lordosis in female rats by modulating LHRH release. *Nature (London)*, 301: 62–64.

Smith, D.G. (1981) The association between rank and reproductive success of male rhesus monkeys. *Am. J. Primat.*, 1: 83–90.

Tutin, C.E.G. (1980) Reproductive behaviour of wild chimpanzees in the Gombe National Park, Tanzania. *J. Reprod. Fertil.*, Suppl. 28: 43–57.

Yodyingyuad, U., Eberhart, J.A. and Keverne, E.B. (1982) Effects of rank and novel females on behaviour and hormones in male talapoin monkeys. *Physiol. Behav.*, 28: 995–1005.

DISCUSSION

S.M. BREEDLOVE: I was interested in the submissive males who fail to display sexual behaviour even when the dominant males are removed. Do you know the composition of talapoin groups in the wild? I am wondering if, in natural situations, subordinate males leave mixed-sex groups in favor of all-male groups. Such males might thereby avoid what you term "learned inadequacy" and eventually become sexually active.

E.B. KEVERNE: I am afraid that in the talapoin monkey we do not have the feral observations to permit a direct answer to that question. However, I would predict exactly what you have said, and certainly for a number of primate species, subordinate males remain peripheral and form all-male groups. I used the term "learned inadequacy" in a descriptive way rather than wishing to imply anything permanent about the animals' future capabilities. I think that what we are seeing here is a short-term effect of chronic social subordination, which given the right environment would be reversible.

Th.M. JONES: I have a 3-part comment and a 2-part question. In the tree shrew, it is clear that stress causes involution of the testis so that, in fact, reproductive potential is dramatically reduced. In the red deer, manipulation of testosterone levels can dramatically alter social rank. In humans, despite the sensitivity of cortisol, growth hormone and prolactin to stress, no convincing studies have demonstrated an influence of stress on testosterone. Thus, are you willing to generalize your findings to other species? If so, how? In particular, why are we missing those sorts of relationships in humans?

E.B. KEVERNE: There is no denying the need to recognize that species differences are likely to occur especially when dealing with a concept like social dominance/subordination. It is quite likely that different aspects of behaviour may be important for achieving reproductive goals, even within a species, and I think I have demonstrated this for the talapoin monkey with the different strategies shown by the different sexes. However, when we consider man, then even determining hierarchies is difficult. While one individual may seek to achieve status in social life another may do so in academic life, another in recreational life and others in all three. It is first a matter of determining what that individual sees as important for status, before any sense can be made of human hierarchies, objective goals and lack of achievement caused by social pressures. Infertility in women and possibly impotence in men is associated with hyperprolactinaemia, but the ontogeny of this syndrome is little understood. I therefore feel it would be precipitous to say these sorts of relationships are missing in man; perhaps we simply have not investigated them in the right kind of way.

The other point you made about testosterone in red deer dramatically altering social rank draws our attention to the importance of hormones in the periphery as well as in the brain. Hard horn antlers and the shedding of "velvet" are dependent on testosterone, and since the antlers are the weaponry of social status, it is hardly surprising that changes in testosterone may affect rank. However, in the monkey, dominance is not dependent on body weight, canine size or any other somatic marker, so here we have a clear example of species differences.

R.G. DYER: You showed that LH secretion in subordinate females was not affected by treatment with the opiate antagonist naloxone. Could you give us more details of these experiments? In particular, were you assessing the effects of naloxone or LH surges or the pulsatile release associated with basal secretion?

E.B. KEVERNE: We have looked at both LH surges and pulsatile release of LH in females given naltrexone/ naloxone and it seems to be without effect on either. However, data in the human female have shown that the action of naloxone is most effective in LH release in the luteal phase of the cycle, and we have not yet examined these endocrine parameters in the monkey.

R.G. DYER: I asked my question because, as you know, there are some who hold the view that the LH control systems in rodents and primates are substantially different. However, your data are to some extent similar with some recent results we have obtained in rats subjected to the environmental stress of short-term starvation. Thus, when female rats are deprived of food for 72 h, ovulation will not occur. The block to LH release is not at the level of the pituitary or the LHRH-secreting nerve terminals in the median eminence. The failure to ovulate is a consequence of an inhibition of oestrogen to activate the LHRH-releasing system in the preoptic area. This model may be rather similar to the one you have just described. The difference is that treatment with naloxone overcomes the inhibition to LH release resulting from 3 days food deprivation.

E.B. KEVERNE: Certainly, the inhibitory action of endogenous opiates on reproductive function is intriguing and may represent a common pathway whereby environmental events, including the social environment, exert their influence. My prediction was that treatment of subordinate females would overcome the inhibition to LH release, and I was disappointed not to find this. However, we are dealing here with a chronic as opposed to acute situation, and I cannot say what might be happening at the receptor level. Moreover, the problem with naloxone is that it not only influences receptors of β-endorphin, but also those for the more diffusely organized enkephalin neurons. In a complex behavioural situation, therefore, it was perhaps simplistic to expect anything like a straightforward result.

G.J. De Vries et al. (Eds.),
Progress in Brain Research, Vol. 61
© 1984 Elsevier Science Publishers B.V., Amsterdam

Differentiation of Sexual Behaviour in Female Marmoset Monkeys: Effects of Neonatal Testosterone or a Male Co-Twin

DAVID H. ABBOTT*

MRC Reproductive Biology Unit, 37 Chalmers Street, Edinburgh, EH3 9EW (Great Britain)

INTRODUCTION

In mammals, testicular hormones during fetal or neonatal life "organise" the neural mechanisms which control sexual behaviour in the developing male brain (*rat*: Harris and Levine, 1962; *mouse*: Manning and McGill, 1974; *hamster*: Johnson, 1975; *guinea pig*: Phoenix et al., 1959; *dog*: Beach et al., 1972; *sheep*: Clarke, 1977; *rhesus monkey*: Goy, 1968; *man*: Money and Ehrhardt, 1972). In short-gestation species, such as the rat, the critical period for this organisational effect occurs mainly after birth (Grady et al., 1965), whereas it seemingly occurs before birth in long-gestation species, such as sheep, primates and man (Short, 1970; Goy and Resko, 1972; Money and Ehrhardt, 1972). As a consequence, females exposed to testicular hormones during early life can become behaviourally masculinised.

In this respect, the normal development of female marmoset monkeys (*Callithrix jacchus jacchus*), born as co-twins to males has long proved an enigma for theories of sexual differentiation (Short, 1970). The dizygotic twin embryos commonly produced by marmosets (Hearn et al., 1978) establish vascular anastomoses between their placental circulations within a few days of implantation (Benirschke and Layton, 1969; Wislocki, 1939) and share a single chorion by day 29 (J.P. Hearn, personal communication). Hence, male–female co-twins develop as XX/XY haematopoietic chimeras (Benirschke and Brownhill, 1962; Benirschke et al., 1962; Gengozian, 1964). However, females experiencing a similar pattern of fetal development in other mammalian species, i.e. co-joined to a male, become "inter-sex freemartins" (Marcum, 1974) suffering both from partial sex reversal of the gonads (Jost et al., 1972, 1973, 1975; Short et al., 1969) and from partial masculinisation of behaviour (Greene et al., 1979). The marmoset may have overcome such problems by developing mechanisms to protect female fetuses against the testicular secretions of their male co-twins during fetal life, as well as delaying some aspects of sexual differentiation, e.g. neural mechanisms controlling reproductive behaviour, until after birth. Abbott and Hearn (1979) have already provided evidence for the latter by demonstrating that testosterone given to neonatal female marmosets will indeed masculinise certain aspects of their sexual behaviour. Further support of this hypothesis comes from the observation that, in early life, male marmosets are only exposed to higher circulating testosterone concentrations than females during the first

* Present address, and reprint requests to: Dr. David H. Abbott, University of Cambridge, Department of Anatomy, Downing St., Cambridge CB2 3DY, Great Britain.

50–80 days after birth (Abbott and Hearn, 1978; Chambers, 1981), unlike other primates, including humans (Resko et al., 1973; Reyes et al., 1973; Takagi et al., 1977; Winter et al., 1976).

Since no other information has become available about the effects of early hormone exposure on the reproductive development of female marmoset monkeys, the purpose of this paper is twofold: (i) to further investigate the effects of neonatal testosterone treatment in female marmosets on (a) their subsequent fertility and ability to raise offspring and on (b) their behavioural interactions in dyadic sex tests, and (ii) to compare the sexual behaviour of females born as co-twins to males with that of females born as co-twins to females.

EXPERIMENTAL PROCEDURES

The common marmoset monkey is monogamous and normally lives in family groups. Its reproductive biology and colony management have been reported elsewhere (Hearn et al., 1975, 1978).

In the first experiment, 5 female marmosets were each subcutaneously implanted with 25 mg of testosterone (Organon Ltd.) between 1 and 4 days after birth, as previously described (Abbott and Hearn, 1979). This was equivalent to a daily dose of 3–10 mg/kg. The implants were removed 49–51 days later. The plasma concentrations of testosterone produced by the implants (approximately 100 ng/ml; Abbott and Hearn, 1979), were much higher than those found in normal males at this age (up to 13 ng/ml; Abbott and Hearn, 1978). The external genitalia of the females were permanently affected by this treatment, the clitoris becoming markedly enlarged, with scrotal-like folds developing below the pudendal pad. This genital change was maximal during testosterone treatment, when the external genitalia of the female neonates resembled those of adult males in miniature, and was still obvious in adulthood, though to a lesser degree. There was no effect on the ability of testosterone-treated or androgenised females to ovulate, however, since by puberty (400–600 days of age; Abbott and Hearn, 1978) plasma progesterone concentrations of greater than 10 ng/ml (indicative of ovulation: Harding et al., 1982) could be measured. Co-twin or triplet sisters of androgenised females were sham-operated at the same times, but no implants were inserted.

In the second experiment, 5 female marmosets born co-twins to males, and 5 females born co-twins to females, were selected for behavioural testing. Only the former were XX/XY haematopoietic chimeras (R. Speed, personal communication). 5 unrelated males were also used during the behavioural sex tests in both experiments.

Animals in both experiments were left with their families, which usually consisted of the parents and two sets of offspring, until puberty. The animals were then removed from their families and separated into peer groups (usually comprising 3 unrelated males and 3 unrelated females). The social hierarchy in every peer group was assessed by scoring the dominant-subordinate interactions between pairs of animals (Abbott, 1984; Abbott and Hearn, 1978). The dominant male and female within each peer group rapidly form a "pair-bond" and sexual behaviour is virtually monopolised by this pair (Abbott, 1984; Abbott and Hearn, 1978). Two of the 5 androgenised females became the dominant female in their peer groups.

Animals were intermittently removed from their peer groups in order to participate in dyadic sex tests during both experiments (Abbott, 1979; Abbott and Hearn, 1979). Each set of animals, e.g. androgenised females or females born as co-twins to males, was balanced with respect to their social status in the different peer groups. The animals were observed in all possible randomised combinations of unfamiliar pairs for 15 min at a time, in an exercise cage of 2.1 m $\times$ 2.4 m $\times$ 2.2 m. All observations were made through a one-way mirror between 09.30 and 16.30 h. The animals were then immediately returned to their peer groups and not observed in any further pair test for at least 2 h. In the first experiment, involving androgenised females, two series of sex tests were carried out, 1 month apart, so that each pair combination was observed twice. In the second experiment, involving females born as co-twins to males, only one series of sex tests was performed. No pregnant females were included in any sex tests.

Behaviour observed during sex tests was coded onto magnetic tape by means of a computerised keyboard (Abbott, 1979). The numbers of animals displaying each behaviour were compared by using Fisher's exact probability test (one-tailed; Siegel, 1956).

NEONATAL TESTOSTERONE TREATMENT IN FEMALE MARMOSET MONKEYS

Fertility

The two androgenised females which were dominant in their peer groups became pregnant for the first time between 530 and 730 days of age. Three of their pregnancies spontaneously aborted and about half of the offspring from their full-term pregnancies died before weaning. There was no apparent inhibition of lactation in androgenised females and no noticeable lack of maternal care in comparison with other equally young and inexperienced marmoset mothers.

Behaviour

The behavioural responses of normal males, normal females and androgenised females during the sex tests are illustrated in Fig. 1 and are shown in more detail in Figs. 2–4. More males than females displayed pursuit courtship, attempted mount, mount and pelvic thrusting, whereas more females than males displayed head turning, limb and body rigidity, crouching and accept-mount. Androgenised females exhibited components of both male and female sexual behaviour repertoires (Fig. 1). With behavioural components from the male sexual repertoire, there was no difference between the numbers of androgenised females and normal males displaying pursuit courtship, attempted mount and mount, although fewer androgenised females showed pelvic thrusting than normal males. More androgenised females were observed showing pursuit courtship and attempted mounts than normal females. With behavioural components from the female sexual repertoire, more androgenised females than normal males exhibited head turning and limb and body rigidity, while the only statistically significant difference between androgenised and normal females arose from fewer androgenised females accepting mounts.

Normal males showed pursuit courtship to other normal males, androgenised females and normal females (Fig. 2). However, fewer males continued to show sexual behaviour, e.g. mounting and pelvic thrusting, towards other males than to normal females and, interestingly, fewer males mounted and showed pelvic thrusts with androgenised females than with normal females. These differences in the distribution of male sexual behaviour were at least partly caused by the refusals of both androgenised females and other normal males to accept

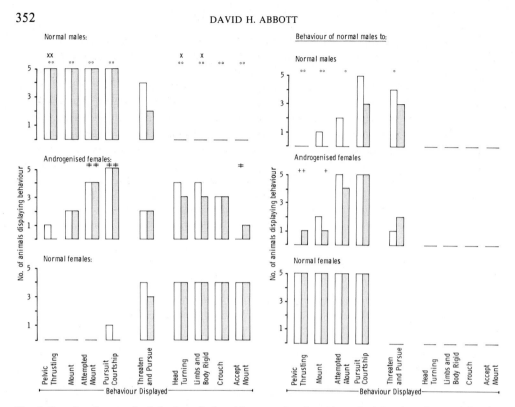

Fig. 1. Sexual and aggressive behaviour displayed by normal male, androgenised female and normal female marmosets during two series of 15-min sex tests (1st series: open bars; 2nd series: shaded bars). There was an interval of 1 month between the first and second series. Behavioural categories are modified from Abbott and Hearn (1979) and are described in Abbott (1979, 1983): "limbs and body rigid" is equivalent to the previous "lordosis" or "limbs and body motionless". Significant differences ($P < 0.05$) were found between (*) normal males and normal females, (X) normal males and androgenised females, and (∓) androgenised females and normal females (Fisher's exact probability test; one-tailed). These behavioural data summarise those illustrated in detail in Figs. 2–4.

Fig. 2. Sexual and aggressive behaviour displayed by normal male marmosets to other normal males, androgenised females and normal females during two series of 15-min sex tests (1st series: open bars; 2nd series: shaded bars). Significant differences ($P < 0.05$) were found between (*) behaviour displayed to other normal males and to normal females, and between (+) behaviour displayed to androgenised females and normal females (for details see Fig. 1 legend).

mount attempts by males, unlike the receptive responses of normal females. Notice that none of the males displayed any components of female sexual behaviour (Fig. 2). Males never threatened and pursued normal females, but they displayed this aggressive behaviour to androgenised females as well as to partners of their own sex.

Normal females displayed all components of the female sexual repertoire in response to normal males (Fig. 3), but only a few responded sexually to androgenised females. There was virtually no sexual response by normal females to other normal females, perhaps related to the large number of females which responded aggressively towards other normal females (Fig. 3). Noticeably, there was also a large number of normal females which threatened and pursued androgenised females in contrast to the lack of aggression directed towards normal males. A single normal female displayed some typically masculine courtship behaviour (Fig. 3).

The distribution of sexual and aggressive behaviour from androgenised females was different from that observed with either normal males or normal females (Fig. 4). Androgenised females exhibited behavioural components from both male and female sexual repertoires in response to any test partner, regardless of its sex or previous treatment. Not surprisingly then, there were no significant differences between the responses of androgenised females to normal males, normal females or other androgenised females. Androgenised females exhibited less persistent male sexual behaviour but, like normal males, pursuit courtship was frequently expressed towards any test partner. Rejection of most of their mount attempts was seemingly the major factor responsible for so few androgenised females displaying further male sexual behaviour, such as mounting and pelvic thrusting. On the other hand, one androgenised female did accept mounts from male partners. Finally, androgenised females directed the aggressive threaten and pursuit behaviour only towards normal females or other androgenised females, and never towards normal males (Fig. 4).

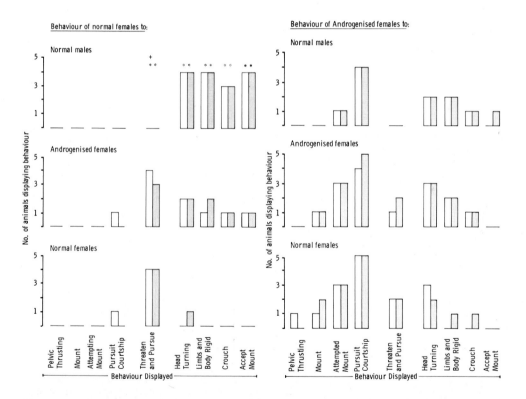

Fig. 3. Sexual and aggressive behaviour displayed by normal females to normal males, androgenised females and other normal females during two series of 15-min sex tests (1st series: open bars; 2nd series: shaded bars). Significant differences ($P < 0.05$) were found between (*) behaviour displayed to normal males and to normal females, and between (+) behaviour displayed to normal males and androgenised females (for details see Fig. 1 legend).

Fig. 4. Sexual and aggressive behaviour displayed by androgenised females to normal males, other androgenised females and normal females during two series of 15-min sex tests (1st series: open bars; 2nd series: shaded bars). For details see the legend under Fig. 1.

BEHAVIOUR OF FEMALES BORN AS CO-TWINS TO MALES COMPARED WITH FEMALES BORN AS CO-TWINS TO FEMALES

Fig. 5 summarises the behaviour shown by females in the third series of sex tests. The sexual behaviour of females born as co-twins to males was identical to that of females born as co-twins to females. All components of female sexual behaviour were observed. One female in both sets of animals displayed "masculine" pursuit courtship (Fig. 5). As with normal females in the previous two series of tests, more females born either as co-twins to males or as co-twins to females exhibited threaten and pursuit to other females than to males (data not presented).

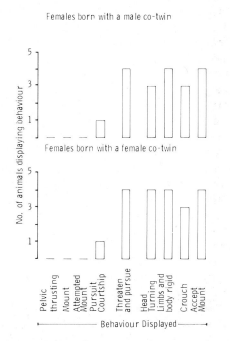

Fig. 5. Summary of sexual and aggressive behaviour patterns displayed by females born as co-twins to either males or females during a single series of 15-min sex tests. The sex tests involved all possible combinations of male–female, female–female and male–male pairs.

GENERAL DISCUSSION

This report, along with that of Abbott and Hearn (1979), amply demonstrates the effects of neonatal testosterone treatment on the sexual behaviour of female marmoset monkeys. Neonatally androgenised females were able to show all reasonably expected components of male sexual behaviour (except for intromission and ejaculation) and displayed a concomitant deficit in their female sexual repertoire, with a loss in their ability to accept mounts. These behavioural changes could well be attributable to the neonatal organisational effects of testosterone on the neural systems controlling sexual behaviour. It is unlikely that this abnormal sexual behaviour of androgenised females could have been caused by hormonal differences at the time of testing, because the pair tests were undertaken approximately 18–24 months after the testosterone treatment, at a time when the endogenous endocrine levels of androgenised and normal females did not differ significantly (Abbott, 1979; Abbott and Hearn, 1979). On the other hand, since neonatal androgenisation permanently altered the appearance of the female external genitalia and significantly increased the likelihood of these females initiating rough-and-tumble play with their female co-twin during infancy (Abbott and Hearn, 1979), it is thus conceivable that differential reactions of family members to androgenised females might also have played a part in the development of their (abnormal) sexual behaviour. Certainly in other primate species (Goy and Goldfoot, 1974; Wallen et al., 1981) including the human (Ehrhardt, 1978), the early social environment can have a powerful effect on subsequent adult sexual behaviour.

Androgenised female marmosets did not exhibit the same degree of male sexual behaviour as was shown by the normal males during sex tests. This behavioural difference might have been due to differences in circulating testosterone concentrations between androgenised females (< 1 ng/ml; Abbott and Hearn, 1979) and males (< 1–53 ng/ml; Abbott and Hearn, 1978). On the other hand, the negative responses of normal females to mounting attempts by androgenised females might have suppressed the expression of male sexual behaviour patterns in androgenised females. Certainly, normal females responded as aggressively to androgenised females as they did to each other, especially after sniffing the external genitalia or pelage (unpublished data). Such hostile behaviour would explain why, although all 5 androgenised females displayed pursuit courtship towards normal females, only two succeeded in actually mounting. This sort of negative response to mount attempts was also employed by males to dissuade other males from mounting them during the sex tests. During these tests, males attempted to copulate with any animal, regardless of sex or treatment, until they were either actively rejected or came into sniffing range of the pelage or external genitalia of the other test animal (unpublished data). It is, therefore, not clear whether male marmosets initially treat all unfamiliar animals as potential sexual mates, or whether their behaviour is in fact a form of social greeting. However, the behavioural testing of pairs of animals, in this case, may be a rather artificial situation because these monkeys normally live in groups in the wild and contact with strangers may mostly arise when groups converge. In previous studies of marmoset monkeys, or of their close relatives, the tamarin monkeys, unfamiliar animals (or "intruders") presented to established groups elicited scent marking and aggressive behaviour, but no sexual behaviour was reported (Epple, 1970, 1975, 1978; French and Snowdon, 1981). Nevertheless, copulations have been observed during group interactions involving common marmoset monkeys in the wild (Hubrecht, 1984).

When groups of unfamiliar marmosets are set up in the laboratory, their social hierarchy becomes established on the basis of the status of animals within each sex rather than between the sexes (Abbott, 1979, 1984; Abbott and Hearn, 1978). Aggressive and submissive interactions occur significantly more often between members of the same sex in the majority (67%) of groups (Abbott, 1979): only the highest-ranking male and highest-ranking female form a pair bond and reproduce, thus maintaining an exclusive monogamous reproductive system in this primate (Abbott, 1984). In other primates, such as the polygamous talapoin monkey (*Miopithecus talapoin*), similar social hierarchies restrict reproduction to high-ranking individuals, though not exclusively to one male and female (Keverne et al., 1984). In the sex tests of unfamiliar marmoset monkeys in this study, males and females threatened and pursued normal members of their own sex as well as androgenised females, whereas no such interactions occurred between normal males and females. Perhaps *both* males and females responded to androgenised females as members of their own sex's social hierarchy!

This response pattern was not fully reciprocated by androgenised females, however, because threaten-and-pursuit behaviour was shown only to normal females and other androgenised females but never to males.

There was some evidence of defeminization of sexual behaviour in neonatally androgenised female marmosets, because of their repeated refusal to accept mounts in sex tests, similar to normal males and unlike normal females. This resistance to male sexual behaviour was also seen when the peer groups were first set up (Abbott and Hearn, 1979). Nevertheless, when the peer groups were observed 3 months later, the two androgenised females which had become dominant in their groups had formed a pair bond with the dominant male and were showing completely normal female sexual behaviour. These two females, in fact, subsequently became pregnant and, although they lost some pregnancies and failed to wean almost half of their infants, they fared no worse in these respects than control females of the same age (Abbott, 1979). Whether they will ever become completely normal, experienced, mothers remains to be seen. Despite the apparently normal female behaviour displayed by androgenised females in established peer groups, their intermittent removal for sexual behaviour testing before and between pregnancies still revealed the "hidden" male components of their sexual behaviour repertoire, as well as their reluctance to accept mounts from unfamiliar males (these data formed part of the present study and are included in the figures). In human studies, where the available evidence for the role of hormones during early life in effecting sexual orientation is inconclusive (Ehrhardt, 1979a,b), it is interesting to speculate, in the light of the findings from marmosets, whether or not the adult social environment may obscure or even counteract any behavioural effects of early hormone exposure. The adult social environment certainly plays a powerful role in modulating the normal expression of sexual behaviour in non-human primates (Keverne et al., 1984).

The sensitivity of female marmosets to neonatal testosterone treatment, as demonstrated in the present study, may be due to the unusual embryology of this primate. In which case these findings may be unique and limited to the marmoset monkey and its close relatives. However, elevated circulating testosterone concentrations have also been found neonatally in male rhesus and pig-tailed macaques (Robinson and Bridson, 1978) and in newborn boys (Forest et al., 1973, 1974). Whether or not newborn female macaques or newborn girls are as sensitive to testosterone as are female marmosets remains to be determined. However, there is other recent evidence which suggests that hormonally induced differentiation of sexual behaviour in primates may not be solely restricted to early fetal life. In rhesus monkeys, although male fetuses experience higher circulating testosterone concentrations than females during early to midgestation (Resko et al., 1973), testosterone administered to pregnant mothers can nonetheless masculinise the behaviour of female fetuses well beyond this time (R.W. Goy, personal communication). It is therefore tempting to speculate that sexual differentiation of the primate brain may span more stages of development than are currently supposed.

ACKNOWLEDGEMENTS

I thank Prof. R.V. Short and J.P. Hearn for criticism of earlier drafts of the manuscript, Mr. F.J. Burden and Miss C. Malcolm for care and maintenance of the animals, Messrs. R. Overhill and R.P. Liles for preparation of the figures and Miss K. Cullum for typing the manuscript.

REFERENCES

Abbott, D.H. (1979) *The Sexual Development of the Common Marmoset Monkey, Callithrix jacchus jacchus*, Ph.D. thesis, University of Edinburgh.

Abbott, D.H. (1984) Behavioural and physiological suppression of fertility in subordinate marmoset monkeys. *Am. J. Primatol.*, 6:164–186.

Abbott, D.H. and Hearn, J.P. (1978) Physical, hormonal and behavioural aspects of sexual development in the marmoset monkey, *Callithrix jacchus. J. Reprod. Fertil.*, 53: 155–166.

Abbott, D.H. and Hearn, J.P. (1979) The effects of neonatal exposure to testosterone on the development of behaviour in female marmoset monkeys. In: *Sex, Hormones and Behaviour, Ciba Foundation Symposium 62 (New Series)*, Excerpta Medica, Amsterdam, pp. 299–316.

Beach, F.A., Kuehn, R.E., Sprague, R.H. and Anisko, J.J. (1972) Coital behaviour in dogs. XI. Effects of androgenic stimulation during development on masculine mating response in females. *Hormone Behav.*, 3: 143–168.

Benirschke, K. and Brownhill, L.E. (1962) Further observations on marrow chimerism in marmosets. *Cytogenetics*, 1: 245–257.

Benirschke, K. and Layton, W. (1969) An early twin blastocyst of the golden lion marmoset, *Leontocebus rosalia* L. *Folia Primatol.*, 10: 131–138.

Benirschke, K., Anderson, J.M. and Brownhill, L.E. (1962) Marrow chimerism in marmosets. *Science*, 138: 513–515.

Chambers, P.L. (1981) *The Endocrinology of Pregnancy in the Marmoset Monkey, Callithrix jacchus*, Ph.D. Thesis, University of Edinburgh.

Clarke, I.J. (1977) The sexual behaviour of pre-natally androgenised ewes observed in the field. *J. Reprod. Fertil.*, 49: 311–315.

Ehrhardt, A.A. (1979a) Psychosexual adjustment in adolescence in patients with congenital abnormalities of their sex organs. In: H.L. Vallet and I.H. Porter (Eds.), *Proc. Birth Defects Inst. Symp. VII on Genetic Mechanisms of Sexual Development*, Academic Press, New York, pp. 473–484.

Ehrhardt, A.A. (1979b) Psychosexual development: an examination of the role of prenatal hormones. In: *Sex, Hormones and Behaviour, Ciba Foundation Symposium 62 (New Series)*, Excerpta Medica, Amsterdam, pp. 41–50.

Epple, G. (1970) Quantitative studies on scent marking in the marmoset (*Callithrix jacchus*). *Folia Primatol.*, 13: 48–62.

Epple, G. (1975) The behaviour of marmoset monkeys. In: L.A. Rosenblum (Ed.), *Primate Behaviour*, Academic Press, New York, pp. 195–239.

Epple, G. (1978) Notes on the establishment and maintenance of the pair bond in *Saguinus fuscicollis*. In: D.G. Kleiman (Ed.), *The Biology and Conservation of the Callithrichidae*, Smithsonian Institution Press, Washington DC, pp. 231–238.

Forest, M.G., Cathiard, A.M. and Bertrand, J.A. (1973) Evidence of testicular activity in early infancy. *J. Clin. Endocrinol. Metab.*, 37: 148–151.

Forest, M.G., Sizonenko, P.C., Cathiard, A.M. and Bertrand, J. (1974) Hypophyso-gonadal function in humans during the first year of life. I. Evidence for testicular activity in early infancy. *J. Clin. Invest.*, 53: 819–828.

French, J.A. and Snowdon, C.T. (1981) Sexual dimorphism in responses to unfamiliar intruders in the tamarin, *Saguinus oedipus. Anim. Behav.*, 29: 822–829.

Gengozian, N., Batson, J.S. and Eide, P. (1964) Hematologic and cytogenetic evidence for chimerism in the marmoset, *Tamarinus nigricollis. Cytogenetics*, 3: 384–393.

Goy, R.W. (1968) Organising effects of androgen on the behaviour of rhesus monkeys. In: R.P. Michael (Ed.), *Endocrinology and Human Behaviour*, Oxford University Press, London, pp. 12–31.

Goy, R.W. and Goldfoot, D.A. (1974) Experiential and hormonal factors influencing development of sexual behaviour in the male rhesus monkey. In: *The Neurosciences Third Study Programme*, MIT Press, Massachusetts, pp. 571–581.

Goy, R.W. and Resko, J.A. (1972) Gonadal hormones and behaviour of normal and pseudo-hermaphroditic nonhuman female primates. *Recent Progr. Hormone Res.*, 28: 707–733.

Grady, K.L., Phoenix, C.H. and Young, W.C. (1965) Role of the developing rat testis in differentiation of the neural tissues mediating mating behaviour. *J. Comp. Physiol. Psychol.*, 59: 176–182.

Harding, R.D., Hulme, M.H., Lunn, S.F., Henderson, C. and Aitken, R.J. (1982) Plasma progesterone levels throughout the ovarian cycle of the common marmoset (*Callithrix jacchus*). *J. Med. Primatol*, 11: 43–51.

Harris, G.W. and Levine, S. (1962) Sexual differentiation of the brain and its experimental control. *J. Physiol. (London)*, 163: 42P–43P.

Hearn, J.P., Lunn, S.F., Burden, F.J. and Pilcher, M.M. (1975) Management of marmosets for biomedical research. *Lab. Anim.*, 9: 125–134.

Hearn, J.P., Abbott, D.H., Chambers, P.L., Hodges, J.K. and Lunn, S.F. (1978) Use of the common marmoset, *Callithrix jacchus*, in reproductive research. In: N. Gengozian and F.W. Dienhardt (Eds.), *Marmosets in Experimental Medicine, Primates in Medicine, Vol. 10*, Karger, Basel, pp. 40–49.

Hubrecht, R. (1984) Field observations on group size and composition of the common marmoset (*Callithrix jacchus jacchus*) at Tacapura, Brazil. *Primates*, 25: 13–21.

Johnson, W.A. (1975) Neonatal androgenic stimulation and adult sexual behaviour in male and female golden hamsters. *J. Comp. Physiol. Psychol.*, 89: 443–451.

Jost, A., Vigier, B. and Prepin, J. (1972) Freemartins in cattle: the first steps in organogenesis. *J. Reprod. Fertil.*, 29: 349–379.

Jost, A., Vigier, B., Prepin, J. and Perchellet, J.P. (1973) Studies on sex determination in mammals. *Recent Progr. Hormone Res.*, 29: 1–41.

Jost, A., Perchellet, J.P., Prepin, J. and Vigier, B. (1975) The prenatal development of bovin freemartins. In: R. Reinboth (Ed.), *Intersexuality in the Animal Kingdom*, Springer, Berlin, pp. 392–406.

Keverne, E.B., Eberhart, J.A., Yodyingyuad, U. and Abbott, D.H. (1984) Social influences on sex differences in the behaviour and endrocine state of talapoin monkeys. In: G.J. De Vries, J.P.C. De Bruin, H.B.M. Uylings, M.A. Corner (Eds.), *Sex Differences in the Brain. The Relation between Structure and Function. Progress in Brain Research*, this volume, Ch. 20.

Manning, A. and McGill, T.E. (1974) Neonatal androgen and sexual behaviour in female house mice. *Hormone Behav.*, 5: 19–31.

Marcum, J.B. (1974) The freemartin syndrome. *Anim. Breeding Abstr.*, 42: 227–242.

Money, J. and Ehrhardt, A.A. (1972) *Man and Woman, Boy and Girl: The Differentiation and Dimorphism of Gender Identity from Conception to Maturity*, The Johns Hopkins University Press, Baltimore, MD.

Phoenix, C.H., Goy, R.W., Gerall, A.A. and Young, W.C. (1959) Organising action of prenatally administered testosterone propionate on the tissues mediating mating behaviour in the female guinea pig. *Endocrinology*, 65: 369–382.

Resko, J.A., Malley, A., Begley, D. and Hess, D.L. (1973) Radioimmunoassay of testosterone during fetal development of the rhesus monkey. *Endocrinology*, 93: 156–161.

Reyes, F.I., Winter, J.S.D. and Faiman, C. (1973) Studies on human sexual development. I. Fetal gonadal and adrenal sex steroids. *J. Clin. Endocrinol. Metab.*, 38: 612–617.

Robinson, J.A. and Bridson, W.E. (1978) Neonatal hormone patterns in the macaque. I. Steroids. *Biol. Reprod.*, 19: 773–778.

Short, R.V. (1970) The bovine freemartin: a new look at an old problem. *Phil. Trans. Roy. Soc. Lond., Ser. B*, 259: 141–147.

Siegel, S. (1956) *Nonparametric Statistics for the Behavioural Sciences*, McGraw-Hill, New York.

Takagi, S., Yoshida, T., Tsubata, K., Ozaki, H., Fujii, T.K., Nomura, Y. and Sawada, M. (1977) Sex differences in fetal gonadotropins and androgens. *J. Steroid Biochem.*, 8: 609–620.

Wallen, K., Goldfoot, D.A. and Goy, R.W. (1981) Peer and maternal influences on the expression of foot-clasp mounting by juvenile male rhesus monkeys. *Develop. Psychobiol.*, 14: 299–309.

Winter, J.S.D., Hughes, I.A., Reyes, F.I. and Faiman, C. (1976) Pituitary-gonadal relations in infancy: 2. Patterns of serum gonadal steroid concentrations in man from birth to two years of age. *J. Clin. Endocrinol. Metab.*, 42: 679–686.

Wislocki, G.B. (1939) Observations on twinning in marmosets. *Am. J. Anat.*, 64: 445–483.

SEX DIFFERENCES IN THE HUMAN BRAIN

G.J. De Vries et al. (Eds.),
Progress in Brain Research, Vol. 61
© 1984 Elsevier Science Publishers B.V., Amsterdam

Sexual Differentiation of the Human Brain
A Historical Perspective

D.F. SWAAB and M.A. HOFMAN

Netherlands Institute for Brain Research, Meibergdreef 23, 1105 AZ Amsterdam (The Netherlands)

INTRODUCTION

Although Eve is supposed to have been the first to eat from the tree of wisdom, sex differences of the brain or higher functions have received only little attention in the ancient literature. It is not known whether Aristotle (384–322 B.C.) designated the period around the 9th week of gestation as the moment "upon which the fetus receives its soul" on the basis of the observation that this is the moment when rapid cerebral development begins (cf. Dobbing, 1970). This is unlikely, however, because of the sex difference that has been proposed in this process by Aristotle. The male fetus was supposed to receive its soul around the 40th day of gestation and the female around the 80th day of pregnancy. Since no such sex difference in brain development has even yet been observed, this suggests that a direct relationship between animation and the brain growth spurt was not in fact taken into consideration. Hippocrates the Greek (460–377 B.C.) estimated the moment at which the male and female become "animated" to be at 30 and 42 days of gestation, respectively (P.H. van Laer, personal communication, 1980). Thomas Aquinas (1225–1274), the Italian theologian and philosopher, adopted Aristotle's views without explicitly accounting for the remarkable sex difference as regards the moment of animation. The justification for believing that the female fetus was supposed to be animated at a later stage might, however, be deduced from his opinion that woman is a "mas occasionatus" (i.e. a man who has not reached his full destination) (*Summa Theologiae I*, 92, 1; J.A. Aertsen, personal communication, 1980).

The *mechanism* of sexual differentiation of the rest of the body has been the subject of much speculation ever since the time of Greek antiquity and was beautifully reviewed by Lesky (1950), Guthrie (1965) and Döhler and Gorski (1981). According to Democritus (± 420 B.C.) differentiation of the sexes would depend on whether the mother's or father's seed would preponderate, while Anaxagoras (± 500 B.C.) proposed that semen from the right testis produces male offspring, while semen from the left side gives rise to females. These notions have in the meantime not received any experimental support, in contrast to the option of Empedocles (± 460 B.C.), who claimed that a hot uterus would produce a male and a cold uterus a female fetus. It is now well known that the incubation temperature of the eggs in many Chelonians affects sexual differentiation. However, at higher temperatures it is the female of the species which is produced in greater abundance (Mrosovsky, 1982; Yntema and Mrosovsky, 1982; Morreale et al., 1982), just the opposite of the ancient Greek option.

Systematic observations concerning morphological sex differences in the human *brain*, on the other hand do not go back much further than a hundred years. In the course of the

19th century the interest in possible mascroscopic sex differences grew rapidly, while in the 20th century the mechanism of their possible origin received attention by an animal experimental approach. The insight that hormones were involved in the sexual differentiation of the reproductive organs, as pointed out by Bouin and Ancel (1903) was followed in the thirties by postulated sex differences in the pituitary (Pfeiffer, 1936), and at the end of the fifties by sex differences in the brain (Phoenix et al., 1959). These last authors showed that sex hormones had permanent effects upon behaviour, when given during early development. (These experiments can, however, partly be considered as a confirmation of those of Vera Dantchakoff, who reported in 1938 that prenatally androgenized guinea pigs showed increased masculine sexual behaviour in adulthood (cf. Dörner, 1981).) Until the 1960s animal experimental investigations were generally performed on male animals, so as "to avoid the troublesome variable of the female oestrous cycle" (cf. the publication "A cry for the liberation of the female rodent", Doty, 1974; De Jonge and Scholtens, 1983). However, a rapid increase in animal experimental data concerning sex differences has become noticeable in the literature over the last decades (e.g., this volume).

SEX DIFFERENCES IN MACROSCOPIC BRAIN MORPHOLOGY

The literature on macroscopic sex differences in the human brain is a remarkable mixture of scientific observations and cultural bias. The existence of comparatively minor and seemingly random morphological sex differences in the human brain, which were often used to "prove" female inferiority, has alternately been claimed and disclaimed. Thus, Huschke (1854) "showed" that the frontal lobe in the male is all of 1% larger than that of the female, leading him to the following sweeping statement: "Woman is a *Homo parietalis* and *interparietalis*, man a *Homo frontalis*, and the shape of the woman's brain is therefore more round than that of the man". * He further states that the central sulcus is straighter, more perpendicular and nearer to the front end in the female brain. Although it was admitted by Huschke that it is extremely difficult to recognize a difference in the convolutions due to sex, he nevertheless stated: "There is, however, no question that it does exist".** Mall (1909) proposed, therefore, in his critical review "that differences like those of Huschke are largely due to the personal equation of the investigator". Also the data presented by Retzius (1900) regarding proposed differences in the gyri and sulci associated with gender have been extensively criticized, e.g. by Karplus (1905), who wrote: "I will not go into the few sex differences of the brain as indicated by the authors, which after all are challenged by many. First considerably more material should also be collected here; I am so far not convinced that from the structure of the convolutions an inferiority of the female brain could be deduced". *** The observation of Meynert (1867) that in men, as contrasted with women, there is relatively more brain substance in front of the central sulcus than behind it, was discussed and criticized by anatomists such as Snell (1891) and Mall (1909). They began also to take differ-

---

* "Das Weib ist eine *Homo parietalis* und *interparietalis*, der Mann ein *Homo frontalis*, und das Weib hat deshalb auch ein runderes Gehirn als der Mann".

** "Es ist aber keine Frage dasz sie existieren".

*** "Auf die von den Autoren angegebenen einzelnen Geschlechtsmerkmale der Gehirne, die ja von vielen bestritten werden, will ich hier nicht näher eingehen. Auch hier muß zunächts viel mehr Material gesammelt werden; bisher bin ich nicht davon überzeugt dasz sich aus dem Furchenbild eine Inferiorität des weiblichen Gehirns ableiten liesse".

ences in age and body size into account, as more reliable measures related to sexual differences in brain form and size. In his major study, Mall (1909) concludes: "(...) that with the
methods at our disposal it is impossible to detect a relative difference in the weight or size of
the frontal lobe due to (...) sex and that probably none exists". In the final paragraph Mall
(1909) states: "Each claim for specific differences (in type of the brain) fails when carefully
tested, and the general claim that the brain type of woman is foetal or of simian type, is
largely an opinion without any scientific foundation. Until anatomists can point out specific
differences which can be weighed or measured, or until they can assort a mixed collection of
brains, their assertions regarding male and female types are of no scientific value".

That time may now have come, in view of the fact that Mall's opinion that "there is no
variation in either genu or splenium of the corpus callosum due to (...) sex" was recently
refuted by the investigation of De Lacoste-Utamsing and Holloway (1982), who by surface
measurements showed the female splenium of the corpus callosum to be larger and more
bulbous than its male counterpart. This is consistent with the hypothesis that the female
brain is less well lateralized, such as the trend found for the left temporal planum to be larger
in adult males than in females (Wada et al., 1975). In conclusion, the sex differences in
macroscopic appearance of the human brain which have been reported so far are relatively
small, and those which seem to be truly present are related to a sex difference in
lateralization. This is not exactly a novel notion, since such a difference was proposed as
early as 1880, by Crichton-Browne, who stated that "the tendency to symmetry in the two
brain halves of the cerebrum is stronger in women than in men".

SEX DIFFERENCES IN BRAIN WEIGHT

A sex difference in brain weight is a consistent finding in the literature and has been used
frequently to "prove" woman's inferiority. Although feminists of both the first wave (Suffra-
gettes) and the second wave (Women's lib) have pointed out such malpractices with fully
justifiable disapproval, distinguished women in both periods sometimes made comparable
mistakes in "proving" women's superiority. An early example can be found in the handbook
of *Pedagogical Anthropology* by Maria Montessori (1913). She was the first woman in Italy
to be conferred a doctor's degree in medicine, became a professor of Anthropology and
Hygiene at the University of Rome, and developed a pedagogical system that is still popular
in The Netherlands. Montessori (1870–1952) writes in her handbook: "Because, as you
know, there is a very widespread belief of long standing that is confirmed in the name of
science: that woman is biologically, in other words totally, inferior, that the volume of her
brain is condemned by nature to an inferiority against which nothing can prevail (...). Names
as famous as that of Lombroso, which are associated with the progress of positive science,
lend the weight of their authority to this form of condemnation! That the cerebral volume
should be considered in its relation to the stature is a familiar principle. Accordingly we find
that Manouvrier compares the brain with the mass of the whole body (...). He deduces from
them (...) "the index of sexual mass", (...) and calculates how much brain man would lose if he
were reduced to a mass having feminine limits. (...) Consequently the cerebral volume of
woman is superior to that of man! This is an anthropological superiority which is further
revealed in the more perfected form of the cranium, insomuch as woman has an absolutely
erect forehead and has no remaining traces of the supra-orbital arches (characteristics of
superiority in the species). Thus, we have a contradiction between existing anthropological

and social conditions: woman, whom anthropology regards as a being having the cranium of an almost superior race, continues to be relegated to an unquestioned social inferiority, from which it is not easy to raise her".

Also today, sex differences in one or another brain parameter are used to "prove" female inferiority, superiority or are simply denied ("the androgyne human being"), vide infra. The coinciding attention for sex differences in on the one hand neurobiological research of the last decades and, on the other hand, the second feministic wave have once again led to an intensification of criticism by women's lib concerning research on sexual dimorphism. It has been pointed out that especially in this period of economic recession the nature-nurture aspect of this topic might be used to confirm male domination as being "a biologically determined inevitability" (De Jonge and Scholtens, 1983; Van Manen and Oudshoorn, 1983). This fear may explain — without justifying it — why a similar line of specious reasoning is employed by certain feminist writers in order to claim some sort of "female superiority".

By way of illustration for such an inversion of the traditional bias, Germaine Greer (1972) may be quoted: "It was thought that the relative lightness of the female brain argued lesser mental powers, although it was pointed out that women have a heavier brain considered relatively to the total body weight (quod not; see below). In any case, brain weight is irrelevant, as was swiftly admitted when it was found to operate to male disadvantage. If the frontal lobes are to be considered as the seat of intelligence, then it must also be pointed out that the frontal area of the brain is more developed in women". (A reference for the latter observation was not given, although Huschke (1854) came to the opposite conclusion, and Mall (1909) could not find any sex difference.)

The fact that the two most quoted authors in this subchapter are women might be not simply the result of a biased selection on our part. Studies of sections of the human experimental literature indicate that female authors analyse sex differences comparatively more frequently than do their male counterparts (Harris, 1972). A sex difference in the interest in this particular topic also became apparent from the fact that 26 participants of the current Summer School (which forms the basis for the present book, eds.) were women, while the comparable rate of the previous Summer School — entitled "Chemical Transmission in the Brain" (1981) — was only 13 ($P < 0.05$, χ^2 test).

SEX DIFFERENCES IN RELATIVE BRAIN SIZE

Since the latter half of the 19th century it has been well known that the sex difference in absolute brain weight is already present at birth (Bischoff, 1880; Pfister, 1897). The recent literature is in full agreement with earlier findings, although the reported values vary widely (Table I). Selection of material which differs with respect to cause of death, time of birth, and nutritional condition, might account for discrepancies. Although, on the average, male neonates have larger brains than do their female counterparts, differences in neonatal body weight and height between the sexes are present as well (Bayley, 1956; Tanner et al., 1966; Dekaban and Sadowsky, 1978; Voigt and Pakkenberg, 1983). One must, therefore, consider the possibility that the sexual dimorphism in neonatal brain weight is simply a result of differences in stature. Indeed, Fig. 1 demonstrates that allometric scaling explains almost all the variance in neonatal brain weight. Female neonates will have brain weights which are similar to those in males of comparable body weight. In contrast to neonatal brain weight, the head circumference values at birth reveal a consistent sex difference of approximately 2–3% (Table I), for healthy subjects. Using the data of Voigt and Pakkenberg (1983) and of

TABLE I
SEXUAL DIMORPHISM IN MEAN NEONATAL BRAIN WEIGHT

Reference	Brain weight (g)		$\dfrac{Male-female}{female}$ (%)
	Male	Female	
Schultz et al., 1962	506	401	26.2
Chrzanowska and Kredowiecki, 1977	325	330	−1.5
Dekaban and Sadowsky, 1978	380	360	5.6
Voigt and Pakkenberg, 1983	448	372	20.4

SEXUAL DIMORPHISM IN MEAN NEONATAL HEAD CIRCUMFERENCE

Reference	Head circumference (cm)		$\dfrac{Male-female}{female}$ (%)
	Male	Female	
Eichorn and Bailey, 1962	35.66	34.47	3.4
Nellhaus, 1968	34.8	34.0	2.1
Meredith, 1971	34.9	34.4	1.5
Brandt, 1979	35.4	34.6	2.3

Dekaban and Sadowsky (1978), a similar degree of sexual dimorphism was found for neonatal body height (Fig. 2). When comparing differences between variables, it should be emphasized that it is important to take dimensional differences into account. Variations in linear measures, such as head circumference, simply cannot be compared directly with variations in volumetric parameters such as brain weight or volume.

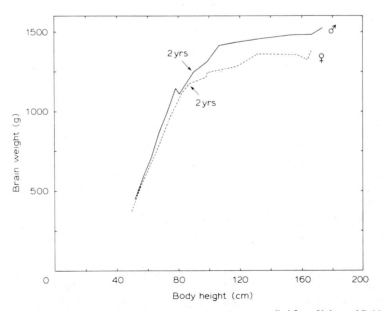

Fig. 1. Brain weight as a function of body height. Data have been compiled from Voigt and Pakkenberg (1983).

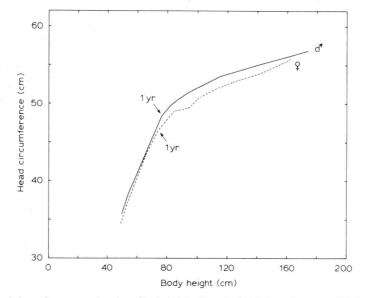

Fig. 2. Head circumference as a function of body height. Data for head circumference and body height have been compiled from Eichhorn and Bayley (1962) and Tanner et al. (1966), respectively.

TABLE II
SEXUAL DIMORPHISM IN MEAN ADULT BRAIN WEIGHT*

Reference	Brain weight (g)		$\dfrac{Male\text{–}female}{female}$ (%)
	Male	Female	
Rössle and Roulet, 1938	1357	1220	11.2
Pakkenberg and Voigt, 1964	1526	1366	11.7
Chrzanowska and Beben, 1973	1463	1312	11.5
Dekaban and Sadowsky, 1978	1450	1290	12.4

* Age: $18 < t < 30$ years.

SEXUAL DIMORPHISM IN MEAN ADULT HEAD CIRCUMFERENCE*

Reference	Head circumference (cm)		$\dfrac{Male\text{–}female}{female}$ (%)
	Male	Female	
Eichorn and Bailey, 1962	57.20	55.84	2.4
Nellhaus, 1968	56	55	1.8
Meredith, 1971	56.2	54.6	2.9

*Age: $t = 18$ years.

A sexual dimorphism in brain weight and head circumference is present also in adulthood (Table II); the quoted sources all show a lower brain weight and a smaller head circumference in adult females compared with adult males. This sexual dimorphism has often given rise to vehement and emotional reactions, that might be related to the direct relationship set forth in the literature between brain size and intellectual capacity. Thus Röse (1905), who investigated a number of German professors and soldiers concluded: "The professors have considerably larger heads than the officers. The regular professors have the largest heads, followed at only a very short distance by the other university teachers; extraordinary professors..." *. Bayerthal (1911) followed up these observations by the remarks: "One can at least become an ordinary professor of surgery and obstetrics with a minimum head circumference of 52–53 cm (...), but with a head circumference under 52 cm you cannot expect an intellectual performance of any significance, while under 50.5 cm no normal intelligence can be expected" **. In this connection he also makes the remark: "We do not have to ask for the head circumference of women of genius — they do not exist" ***.

In spite of such sweeping statements, it seems plausible to suppose that intelligence is determined in part by the amount of brain tissue in excess of that required for receiving sensory information and controlling muscle movements (Passingham, 1979; Hofman, 1982). The absolute brain size is, however, not the whole story since differences in body size must also be taken into account (Tobias, 1970; Jerison, 1973; Hofman, 1983). This means that the 11–12% difference in average adult human brain weights between the sexes might be a purely allometric phenomenon, as in neonates. However, a graphic representation (Figs. 1 and 2) reveals that this is not the case and that the sexual dimorphism in both brain weight and head circumference in postnatal life cannot be explained by differences in height. The sex difference in relative head circumference seems to disappear after the puberal growth spurt (Fig. 2). The sexual dimorphism in relative brain size, on the other hand, which does not appear until the brain has reached about 85% of its adult value, i.e., around the 2nd year of life, persists throughout life. It seems as if the rapid growth phase of the brain in males is slightly prolonged as compared with that of females, causing a larger brain weight relative to height. Whether or not this minor sexual dimorphism in average degree of encephalization in humans has any analogue in neural function cannot be answered at the moment.

FUNCTIONAL AND MICROSCOPICAL SEX DIFFERENCES

Evidence for the presence of functional sex differences in the human has accumulated over the last decades, e.g., for female superiority in certain verbal tasks and male superiority in spatial functioning (McGlone, 1980; Inglis and Lawson, 1981). Differences in sleep (Webb, 1982), lateralization e.g. of language (McGlone, 1980; Inglis and Lawson, 1981) have also been reported. A sex difference in lateralization of visual field accuracy was found already in 3- and 4-year-old children (Jones and Anuza, 1982). In addition, sex differences in cerebral organization for speech and praxic functions have emerged from retrospective studies of aphasic and apraxic patients (Kimura, 1983). In spite of such studies the possibility of a "hardware" basis in the brain for such functional sex differences has often been rejected vigorously throughout the years. The starting point and ideal of the author Couperus (1904–05) was the "androgynous human being", who supposedly possesses both male and female

---

* "Die Professoren haben bedeutend grössere Köpfe als die Offiziere. Die ordentlichen Professoren haben die grössten Köpfe mit ganz geringen Abständen folgen die übrigen Universitätslehrer: ausserordentliche Professoren...".

** "Man kan wenigstens bei einem Umfang des Kopfes von 52–53 cm noch ordentlicher Professor der Chirurgie und Geburtshilfe werden". (...) "doch werden wir beim erwachsenen Mann unter 52 cm keine bedeutende geistige Leistungen mehr zu erwarten haben, und unter 50.5 cm keine normale Intelligenz".

*** "Nach der Kopfgrösse genialer Weiber brauchen wir nicht zu fragen es gibt keine...".

characteristics in equal measure. This concept has been revived by the women's liberation movement during the few last decades, sometimes to the point of dogmatism, by which the very possibility of any sexual dimorphism whatsoever (even in the face of available experimental data and psychological observations) is flatly denied as far as brain function is concerned. Germaine Greer (1972), for example, states "(...) although sex hormones do enter the brain, (...) no correlation between that physiological fact and mental capacity or behaviour has ever been established". Indeed, macroscopically the similarities and not the differences between male and female human brains are the most striking, but functional sex differences do exist. Recent biochemical and microscopical observations throughout the animal kingdom, however, show that in the brain similar macroscopical structures may be built up from sexually dimorphic neurotransmitter systems, and may contain differences in synaptic termination patterns, regional cell size, density and number, and dendritic trees. Such differences could easily serve as the basis for functional sex differences (Ayoub et al., 1982; Swaab and Ter Borg, 1981; De Vries et al., 1981, 1983). Studies on the microscopical and chemical differentiation of the human brain have only recently been started, but the sex difference reported for the hypothalamic LHRH content in the human fetus (Siler-Khodr and Khodr, 1978) already supports the possible presence of such differences in the human brain.

A SEX DIFFERENCE IN THE HUMAN SUPRACHIASMATIC NUCLEUS?

We are currently investigating the human suprachiasmatic nucleus (SCN) for the possible presence of microscopical and chemical sex differences. The SCN is considered to be the "endogenous hypothalamic clock" (Mosko and Moore, 1978) which controls circadian rhythms such as the sleep-wake cycles (Bethea and Neill, 1980; Moore, 1982). In addition, the SCN plays an essential role in longer rhythmic phenomena such as the ovulation cycle (Brown-Grant and Raisman, 1977). These considerations together with the sex differences in rhythms (Davis, 1982; Webb, 1982) make this structure of special interest for the study of sex differences. Such differences have in fact been reported for the rat with respect to the size of the SCN (Gorski et al., 1978) and its synaptology (Güldner, 1982). Until recently, the very existence of the SCN in the *human* brain was questioned because it was difficult to visualize (e.g., Defendini and Zimmerman, 1978; for references see Lydic et al., 1980). The SCN contains vasopressinergic neurones, not only in the rat (Swaab et al., 1975) but also in the human brain (Dierickx and Vandesande, 1977), which now makes it much easier to visualize this structure. Such cells are present already at birth (Swaab and Ter Borg, 1981) and have been shown in the rat to innervate the periventricular nucleus, the organum vasculosum laminae terminalis (OVLT) and the dorsomedial hypothalamic nucleus (DMH) (Hoorneman and Buijs, 1982). These last two structures are implicated in the regulation of the oestrous cycle (Szentágothai et al., 1968; Wenger et al., 1979; Piva et al., 1982). Studies on the Brattleboro rat, which is homozygous for vasopressin deficiency, suggest that the vasopressinergic neurones of the SCN might be essential for a regular ovarian cycle (Boer et al., 1981). Interesting in this respect is also the observation that vasopressin inhibits sexual behaviour (Bohus, 1977; see reviews Södersten et al., 1983). The observation that homozygous Brattleboro rats maintain normal circadian rhythmicity (Peterson et al., 1980) does not mean that the vasopressinergic cells of the SCN are not normally essential in this respect. Plasticity in the developing brain is sometimes very impressive, so that other neuronal systems might take over the function of the absent vasopressin cells. This makes the Brattle-boro rat not the ideal model for investigating the possible functions of vasopressinergic cells in adulthood (Swaab, 1980). T. Partiman in our group was struck by a sex difference in the rostro-caudal diameter of this nucleus in the human brain. The diameter of the nucleus in women was 43% larger than that of men. The maximal area covered by vasopressinergic cells in the middle of the SCN was, however, 35% smaller in women. The overall volume, cell density and total cell number of the SCN, turned out to be virtually identical in both sexes, so that the difference is basically one of shape (D.F. Swaab, E. Fliers and T. Partiman, unpublished observation). This is — to our knowledge — the first transmitter-characterized system in the *human* brain for which a clear sex difference has been demonstrated. The functional implication of the SCN shape difference is still obscure.

EXOGENOUS SEX STEROIDS AND FURTHER RESEARCH

Although research on the possible effects of endogenous steroids on the developing brain is just starting, it is clear from psychometric studies that such substances, when administered during development, may cause permanent changes in human brain function. This is illustrated by the behavioral changes observed in children of pregnant women who were treated for impending abortion by the administration of sex hormones. Although this treatment is not effective in preventing abortion, it has nevertheless been used extensively, and appears to have induced behavioral changes in the children of these mothers (Reinisch and Karow, 1977; Reinisch, 1981; Reinisch and Sanders, 1984). In The Netherlands, DES (diethylstil-boestrol, an estrogen compound) turns out even to have been dispensed by mail order as a sex-stimulating compound! Developmental sequelae of such an abuse cannot easily be traced for obvious reasons.

If permanent morphological alterations in the human brain are indeed induced by sex hormones during development in a similar fashion as has been observed in animal experiments, the morphometric determination in later life of lasting changes in immunocytochemically identified neural systems might give information concerning the exposure of the fetus to steroids or other potentially deleterious chemicals. If this turns out to be the case, it would be all the more important to test, by means of similar methodology, the hypothesis that prenatal hormonal influences upon brain differentiation underlie such conditions as homosexuality, the Imperato–McGinley syndrome and transsexuality (e.g., Gooren, 1984; Meyer-Bahlburg, 1984). The next decades will tell us if this is a fruitful course to pursue.

SUMMARY AND CONCLUSIONS

Although Aristotle designated the moment at which the male fetus receives its "soul" as the 40th day of pregnancy as compared with day 80 for the female fetus, very little attention was paid in the ancient literature to the possibility that there existed gender differences either in structure or in functions of the brain.

In the course of the 19th century the interest in this topic grew rapidly. However, the literature on macroscopic sex differences of the human brain, was, and still is, a remarkable mixture of scientific observations and cultural bias. Those sex differences which seem to be really present, i.e. the larger splenium of the corpus callosum in women and the larger left temporal planum in men, involve sex differences in brain *lateralization*. Recent allometric calculations have revealed that the sex difference in average neonatal brain weight can be largely if not entirely explained by differences in body size. The lower brain weight of females as compared to males, particularly after the 2nd year of life, however, cannot be explained by differences in mean height. Whether or not this sexual dimorphism in encephalization during the postnatal life of humans has an analogue in neural function is not known.

Evidence for sex differences in brain function has accumulated over the last 30 years. From the animal experimental literature it can be extrapolated that similar appearing macroscopic brain structures may be built up from sexually dimorphic neurotransmitter systems. Differences between the sexes might also be present in synaptic termination patterns, regional cell size, density or number, and in dendritic arborization.

By way of example, some of our own observations on the human suprachiasmatic nucleus (SCN) are mentioned. Staining with antibodies raised to vasopressin enables morphometric studies on this "hypothalamic clock". These studies revealed that the SCN in women tends to be larger in its cranio-caudal diameter, while in men it has a larger maximal diameter in the middle of the nucleus. On the whole, however, neither the total volume nor the cell number of the SCN turned out to differ. This sexual dimorphism in the SCN shape is to our knowledge the first gender-linked difference in an identified neurotransmitter system that has been reported within the human brain.

The next decade will hopefully tell us whether or not the careful study of such transmitter systems is a fruitful way of obtaining information concerning the effects of endogenous or exogenous steroid hormones on the developing human brain.

ACKNOWLEDGEMENTS

We should like to thank Carla Calis and Rivka Ravid for their stimulating suggestions and W. Chen-Pelt, P.J. van Nieuwkoop and J. van der Velden for their secretarial assistance.

REFERENCES

Ayoub, D.M., Greenough, W.T. and Juraska, J.M. (1982) Sex differences in dendritic structure in the preoptic area of the juvenile macaque monkey brain. *Science*, 219: 197–198.

Bayerthal (1911) *Arch. Rassen- u. Gesellschaftsbiol.*, VIII.

Bayley, N. (1956) Growth curves of height and weight by age for boys and girls, scaled according to physical maturity. *J. Pediat.*, 48: 187–194.

Bethea, C.L. and Neill, J.D. (1980) Lesions of the suprachiasmatic nuclei abolish the cervically stimulated prolactin surges in the rat. *Endocrinology*, 107: 1–5.

Bischoff, T.L. (1880) *Das Hirngewicht des Menschen*, Neusser, Bonn, pp. 46–64.

Boer, K., Boer, G.J. and Swaab, D.F. (1981) Reproduction in Brattleboro rats with diabetes insipidus. *J. Reprod. Fertil.*, 61: 273–280.

Bohus, B. (1977) The influence of pituitary peptides on sexual behavior. In: H.-P. Klotz (Ed.), *Hormones et Sexualité, Problèmes Actuels d'Endocrinologie et de Nutrition*, Expansion Scientifique Française, Paris, pp. 235–246.

Bolk, L. (1918) *Hersenen en Cultuur*, 2nd Edn., Scheltema en Holkema, Amsterdam.

Bouin, P. and Ancel, P. (1903) Sur la signification de la glande interstitielle du testicule embryonnaire. *C.R. Soc. Biol.*, 55: 1682–1684.

Brandt, I. (1979) Perzentilkurven für das Kopfumfangswachstum. *Kinderarzt*, 2: 185–188.

Brown-Grant, K. and Raisman, G. (1977) Abnormalities in reproductive function associated with the destruction of the suprachiasmatic nuclei in female rats. *Proc. Roy. Soc. Lond. B*, 198: 279–296.

Chrzanowska, G. and Beben, A. (1973) Weight of the brain and body height in man between the ages of 20 and 89 years. *Folia Morphol. (Warsz.)*, 32: 391–406.

Chrzanowska, G. and Kredowiecki, A. (1977) Analyse der Frischgewichte 993 menschlicher Gehirne, *Ergebn. Exp. Med.*, 25: 161–172.

Couperus, L. (1904–05) *De Berg van Licht*, L.J. Veens Uitgeversmaatschappij, Amsterdam, 1973, pp. 26–27.

Crichton-Browne, J. (1880) On the weight of the brain and its component parts in the insane. *Brain*, 2: 42–67.

Dantchakoff, V. (1938) Rôles des hormones dans les manifestations des instincts sexuels. *C.R. Acad. Sci. (Paris)*, 206: 945–947.

Davis, F.C. (1982) Development of the suprachiasmatic nuclei and other circadian pacemakers. In: D.C. Klein (Ed.), *Melatonin Rhythm Generating System*, Karger, Basel, pp. 1–19.

Defendini, R. and Zimmerman, E.A. (1978) The magnocellular neurosecretory system of the mammalian hypothalamus. In: S. Reichlin, R.J. Baldessarini and J.B. Martin (Eds.), *The Hippocampus*, Raven Press, New York, pp. 137–154.

De Jonge, F. and Scholtens, J. (1983) Aangeboren of aangeleerd. *Wetensch. Samenl.*, 2: 13–21.

Dekaban, A.S. and Sadowsky, D. (1978) Changes in brain weights during the span of human life: relation of brain weights to body heights and body weights. *Ann. Neurol.*, 4: 345–356.

De Lacoste-Utamsing, C. and Holloway, R.L. (1982) Sexual dimorphism in the human corpus callosum. *Science*, 216: 1431–1432.

De Vries, G.J., Buijs, R.M. and Swaab, D.F. (1981) Ontogeny of the vasopressinergic neurons of the suprachiasmatic nucleus and their extrahypothalamic projections in the rat brain — presence of a sex difference in the lateral septum. *Brain Res.*, 218: 67–78.

De Vries, G.J., Best, W. and Sluiter, A.A. (1983) The influence of androgens on the development of a sex difference in the vasopressinergic innervation of the rat lateral septum. *Brain Res.*, 8: 377–380.

Dierickx, K. and Vandesande, F. (1977) Immunocytochemical localization of the vasopressinergic and the oxytocinergic neurons in the human hypothalamus. *Cell Tissue Res.*, 184: 15–27.

Dobbing, J. (1970) Undernutrition and the developing brain. The relevance of animal models to the human problem. *Am. J. Dis. Child.*, 120: 411–415.

Döhler, K.-D. and Gorski, R.A. (1981) Sexual differentiation of the brain: past, present and future. *BRI Bull.*, 5: 5–9.

Dörner, G. (1981) Sex hormones and neurotransmitters as mediators for sexual differentiation of the brain. *Endokrinologie*, 78: 129–138.

Doty, R.L. (1974) A cry for the liberation of the female rodent: courtship and copulation in rodentia. *Psychol. Bull.*, 81: 159–172.

Eichorn, D.H. and Bayley, N. (1962) Growth in head circumference from birth through young adulthood. *Child Develop.*, 33: 257–271.

Geschwind, N. and Levitsky, W. (1968) Human brain: left–right asymmetries in temporal speech region. *Science*, 161: 186–187.

Gooren, L. (1984) Sexual dimorphism and transsexuality: clinical observations. In: G.J. De Vries, J.P.C. De Bruin, H.B.M. Uylings and M.A. Corner (Eds.), *Sex Differences in the Brain. The Relation between Structure and Function. Progress in Brain Research*, this volume, Ch. 24.

Gorski, R.A., Gordon, J.H., Shryne, J.E. and Southam, A.M. (1978) Evidence for a morphological sex difference within the medial preoptic area of the rat brain. *Brain Res.*, 148: 333–346.

Greer, G. (1972) *The Female Eunuch*, Paladin, London, p. 99.

Gruenwald, P. and Minh, H.N. (1960) Evaluation of body and organ weights in perinatal pathology. I. Normal standards derived from autopsies. *Am. J. Clin. Pathol.*, 34: 247–253.

Güldner, F.-H. (1982) Sexual dimorphisms of axo-spine synapses and postsynaptic density material in the suprachiasmatic nucleus of the rat. *Neurosci. Lett.*, 28: 145–150.

Guthrie, W.K.C. (1965) *A History of Greek Philosophy, Vol. 2*, Cambridge University Press, Cambridge.

Harris, S.L. (1972) Who studies sex differences? *Am. Psychol.*, 27: 1077–1078.

Hofman, M.A. (1982) Encephalization in mammals in relation to the size of the cerebral cortex. *Brain Behav. Evol.*, 20: 84–96.

Hofman, M.A. (1983) Evolution of brain size in neonatal and adult placental mammals. A theoretical approach. *J. Theor. Biol.*, 105: 317–332.

Hoorneman, E.M.D. and Buijs, R.M. (1982) Vasopressin fiber pathways in the rat brain following suprachiasmatic nucleus lesioning. *Brain Res.*, 243: 235–241.

Huschke (1854) *Schädel, Hirn und Seele*, Jena, 1854 (cited in: Mall, 1909).

Inglis, J. and Lawson, J.S. (1981) Sex differences in the effects of unilateral brain damage on intelligence. *Science*, 212: 693–695.

Jerison, H.J. (1973) *Evolution of the Brain and Intelligence*, Academic Press, New York.

Jones, B. and Anuza, T. (1982) Sex differences in cerebral lateralization in 3- and 4-year-old children. *Neuropsychology*, 20: 347–350.

Karplus (1905) *Obersteiner's Arbeiten aus d. Neurol. Inst. XII*, Wien.

Kimura, D. (1983) Sex differences in cerebral organization for speech and praxic functions. *Can. J. Psychol.*, 37: 19–35.

Lesky, E. (1950) Die Zeugungs- und Vererbungslehren der Antike und ihr Nachwirken. In: *Abhandlungen der Geistes- und Sozialwissenschaftlichen Klasse, Vol. 19*, Akademie der Wissenschaften und der Literatur in Mainz, Wiesbaden, pp. 1225–1425.

Lydic, R., Schoene, W.C., Czeisler, C.A. and Moore-Ede, M.C. (1980) Suprachiasmatic region of the human hypothalamus: homolog to the primate circadian pacemaker? *Sleep*, 2: 355–361.

Mall, F.P. (1909) On several anatomical characters of the human brain, said to vary according to race and sex, with special reference to the weight of the frontal lobe. *Am. J. Anat.*, 9: 1–32.

McGlone, J. (1980) Sex differences in human brain asymmetry: a critical survey. *Behav. Brain Sci.*, 3: 215–263.

Meredith, H.V. (1971) Human head circumference from birth to early adulthood: racial, regional and sex comparisons. *Growth*, 35: 233–251.

Meyer-Bahlburg, H.F.L. (1984) Psychoendocrine research on sexual orientation. Current status and future options. In: G.J. De Vries, J.P.C. De Bruin, H.B.M. Uylings and M.A. Corner (Eds.), *Sex Differences in the Brain. The Relation between Structure and Function. Progress in Brain Research*, this volume, Ch. 23.

Meynert (1867) Das Gesamtgewicht und die Teilgewichte des Gehirns, etc., *Viertaljahrsschr. Psychiat.*, 1.

Montessori, M. (1913) *Pedagogical Anthropology*, William Heinemann, London.

Moore, R.Y. (1982) The suprachiasmatic nucleus and the organization of a circadian system. *Trends Neurosci.*, 5: 404–407.

Morreale, S.J., Ruiz, G.J., Spotila, J.R. and Standora, E.A. (1982) Temperature-dependent sex determination: current practices threaten conservation of sea turtles. *Science*, 216: 1245–1247.

Mosko, S. and Moore, R.Y. (1978) Neonatal suprachiasmatic nucleus ablation: absence of functional and morphological plasticity. *Proc. Natl. Acad. Sci. (U.S.A.)*, 75: 6243–6246.

Mrosovsky, N. (1982) Sex ratio bias in hatching sea turtles from artificially incubated eggs. *Biol. Conserv.*, 23: 309–314.

Nellhaus, G. (1968) Head circumference from birth to eighteen years. *Pediatrics*, 41: 106–114.

Pakkenberg, H. and Voigt, J. (1964) Brain weight of the Danes. *Acta Anat.*, 59: 297–307.

Passingham, R.E. (1979) Brain size and intelligence in man. *Brain Behav. Evol.*, 16: 253–270.

Peterson, G.M., Watkins, W.B. and Moore, R.Y. (1980) The suprachiasmatic hypothalamic nuclei of the rat. VI. Vasopressin neurons and circadian rhythmicity. *Behav. Neur. Biol.*, 29: 236–245.

Pfeiffer, C.A. (1936) Sexual differences of the hypophyses and their determination by the gonads. *Am. J. Anat.*, 58: 195–225.

Pfister, H. (1897) Das Hirngewicht im Kindesalter. *Arch. Kinderheilk.*, 23: 164–192.

Phoenix, Ch.H., Goy, R.W., Gerall, A.A. and Young, W.C. (1959) Organizing action of prenatally administered testosterone propionate on the tissues mediating mating behavior in the female guinea pig. *Endocrinology*, 65: 369–382.

Piva, F., Limonta, P. and Martini, L. (1982) Role of the organum vasculosum laminae terminalis in the control of gonadotrophin secretion in rats. *J. Endocrinol.*, 93: 355–364.

Reinisch, J.M. and Sanders, S.A. (1984) Prenatal gonadal steroidal influences on gender-related behavior. In: G.J. De Vries, J.P.C. De Bruin, H.B.M. Uylings and M.A Corner (Eds.), *Sex Differences in the Brain. The Relation between Structure and Function. Progress in Brain Research*, this volume, Ch. 25.

Reinisch, J.M. (1981) Prenatal exposure to synthetic progestins increases potential for aggression in humans. *Science*, 211: 1171–1173.

Reinisch, J.M. and Karow, W.G. (1977) Prenatal exposure to synthetic progestins and estrogens: effects on human development. *Arch. Sex. Behav.*, 6: 257–288.

Retzius (1900) *Biol. Untersuch.*, 9 (cited in: Mall, 1909).

Röse (1905) Archiv für Rassen- und Gesellschaftsbiologie, Vol. II. In: L. Bolk (Ed.), *Hersenen en Cultuur*, Scheltema en Holkema, Amsterdam, 1918, p. 19.

Rössle, R. and Roulet, F. (1938) *Mass und Zahl in der Pathologie*, Springer, Berlin.

Schultz, D.M., Giordano, D.A. and Schulz, D.H. (1962) Weights of organs of fetuses and infants. *Arch. Pathol.*, 74: 80–86.

Siler-Khodr, T.M. and Khodr, G.S. (1978) Studies in human fetal endocrinology. I. Luteinizing hormone-releasing factor content of the hypothalamus. *Am. J. Obstet. Gynecol.*, 130: 795–800.

Snell, O. (1891) Die Abhängigkeit des Hirngewichtes von dem Körpergewicht und den geistigen Fähigkeiten. *Arch. Psychiat. Nervenkr.*, 23: 436–446.

Södersten, P., Henning, M., Melin, P. and Ludin, S. (1983) Vasopressin alters female sexual behaviour by acting on the brain independently of alterations in blood pressure. *Nature (London)*, 301: 608–610.

Swaab, D.F. (1980) Neurohypophyseal hormones and their distribution in the brain. In: D. de Wied and P.A. van Keep (Eds.), *Hormones and the Brain*, MTP Press, Lancaster, pp. 87–100.

Swaab, D.F. and Ter Borg, J.P. (1981) Development of peptidergic systems in the rat brain. In: K. Elliott and J. Whelan (Eds.), *The Fetus and Independent Life, Ciba Foundation Symp. No. 86*, Pitman, London, pp. 271–294.

Swaab, D.F., Pool, C.W. and Nijveldt, F. (1975) Immunofluorescence of vasopressin and oxytocin in the rat hypothalamo-neurohypophyseal system. *J. Neur. Transm.*, 36: 195–215.

Szentágothai, J. Flerko, B., Mess, B. and Halasz, B. (1968) *Hypothalamic Control of the Anterior Pituitary.* Akadémiai Kiadó, Budapest.

Tanner, J.M., Whitehouse, R.H. and Takaishi, M. (1966) Standards from birth to maturity for height, weight, height velocity and weight velocity: British Children, 1965. *Arch. Dis. Childh.*, 41: 613–635.

Tobias, P.V. (1970) Brain size, grey matter and race — fact or fiction? *Am. J. Phys. Anthrop.*, 32: 3–26.

Van Manen, S. and Oudshoorn, N. (1983) Sociobiologie en feminisme. *Wetensch. Samenl.*, 2: 22–26.

Voigt, J. and Pakkenberg, H. (1983) Brain weight of Danish children: a forensic material. *Acta Anat.*, 116: 290–301.

Wada, J.A., Clarke, R.A. and Hamm, A. (1975) Cerebral hemisphere asymmetry in humans. Cortical speech zones in 100 adult and 100 infant brains. *Arch. Neurol.*, 32: 239–246.

Webb, W.B. (1982) Sleep in older persons: sleep structures of 50- to 60-year-old men and women. *J. Gerontol.*, 37: 581–586.

Wenger, T., Kerdelhue, B. and Halázs, B. (1979) Short-term effect of the lesion of the organum vasculosum of the lamina terminalis on hypothalamic LH-RH and serum LH, FSH and prolactin in adult female rats. *Neuroendocrinology*, 29: 276–280.

Yntema, C.L. and Mrosovsky, N. (1982) Critical periods and pivotal temperatures for sexual differentiation in loggerhead sea turtles. *Can. J. Zool.*, 60: 1012–1016.

DISCUSSION

M.A. CORNER: To what extent have individual differences *within* each sex been studied through the years, vis à vis the supposed sexually dimorphic brain measures?

D.F. SWAAB: In the more recent literature this is, of course, not such a problem because the statistics that are generally applied include manners for variation within the sex. But also in the old literature attention has been paid to this problem. Mall (1909) plotted all the individual data in his graphs. He failed to find sex differences and stated: "It is found, however, that portions of the brain vary greatly in different brains and that a very large number of records must be obtained before the norm will be found. For the present the crudeness of our method will not permit us to determine anatomical characters due to race, sex or genius and which, if they exist, are completely masked by the large number of individual variations".

J.C. KING: The outliné of vasopressin-positive cells corresponds well with that of tissue stained with cresyl violet?

D.F. SWAAB: In this (6-μm) sections it is impossible to see the boundaries of the SCN by means of a conventional staining (we used thionine for this purpose). Using cryostat (40-μm) sections, the anti-vasopressin staining appeared to coincide very well with the cytoarchitectural boundaries of the SCN.

J.C. KING: You are equating the SCN nucleus with that of vasopressin-immunopositive cells in the nucleus. Yet there is a ventral cell group that contains vasoactive intestinal polypeptide (VIP)-positive cells. Might not the relationship between VIP and vasopressin be different between the sexes rather than the shape of the SCN?

D.F. SWAAB: Indeed, the SCN contains many more transmitters than vasopressin alone, and it would be most interesting to study also the other peptides in this nucleus in relation to e.g. sex, age and dementia. However, we have not done that until now.

C.D. TORAN-ALLERAND: Studying gross anatomical differences is problematic, and without microscopical correlates such cases as the observed differences in the splenum of the corpus callosum are difficult to evaluate, since differences in fixation and length of fixation may produce significant differences in gross appearance.

D.F. SWAAB: Gross morphological sex differences can, of course, not be considered as the final answer to all questions. It should serve as a start to indicate those areas which might be of interest for further detailed and more sophisticated research (scanning the entire human brain, e.g. with an electron microscope, would be a less efficient procedure!). A sex difference appearing only after fixation, as hypothesized by you, is still a difference which could be due to physio-chemical sex differences in the brain. Also such differences have, of course, to be worked out by a multi-disciplinary approach.

REFERENCE

Mall, F.P. (1909) On several anatomical characters of the human brain, said to vary according to race and sex, with special reference to the weight of the frontal lobe. *Am. J. Anat.*, 9: 1–32.

G.J. De Vries et al. (Eds.),
Progress in Brain Research, Vol. 61
© 1984 Elsevier Science Publishers B.V., Amsterdam

Psychoendocrine Research on Sexual Orientation. Current Status and Future Options

HEINO F.L. MEYER-BAHLBURG

New York State Psychiatric Institute, and Department of Psychiatry, College of Physicians and Surgeons of Columbia University, 722 West 168th Street, New York, NY 10032 (U.S.A.)

INTRODUCTION

In his fourth letter to his relatives, written on December 23, 1862, the German lawyer and writer Ulrichs discussed the differentiation of the external genitalia in male and female embryos and the origin of genital intersexes. He then continued: "Why should it not be conceivable that nature, in its variability, takes a different approach in some individuals so that, with regard to the body, it lets the male "anlage" develop but not the female "anlage" while, with regard to the mind, it lets the female "anlage" develop in all its tendencies but not the male "anlage", thus allowing the "anlage" of femininity ("Muliebrität") to develop in terms of softness of character, occupational interests, mannerisms, and particularly, the direction of the sexual love drive toward men?" (Quoted in this author's translation from Hirschfeld, 1906, p. 132). Ulrichs then formulated his theory of homosexuality: "The sexual dualism which, in the "anlage", exists in each human individual without exception, is expressed in hermaphrodites and Uranians ("Uraniern", i.e., homosexuals) to a higher degree than in the usual man or woman. In the Uranian, it is expressed in a different way than in the hermaphrodite". As reformulated in his Memnon (Ulrichs, 1868, cited in Hirschfeld, 1906), "anima muliebris virili corpori innata" (the soul of a woman innate in a male body) has been the concept guiding biological explanations of homosexuality since then. In the most recent formulation of the theory, based on extensive neuroanatomic and neuroendocrine work in lower mammals, especially the rat, homosexuality is classified as a "central nervous pseudohermaphroditism" (Dörner, 1976) which refers to the differentiation of a predominantly feminine mating center in the brain of a genetic male individual and vice versa.

A basic assumption underlying this recent reformulation of the theory is the homology of the "homosexuality" of lower mammals and of human homosexual orientation. In the rat, the term "homosexuality" has been applied to the female-typical reflexive mating behavior of a genetic male in the presence of another genetic male, or the analogous situation for females. Human homosexual *orientation*, by contrast, refers to the degree of sexual responsiveness to members of the same sex as expressed in erotic attractions, sexual fantasies, and (not necessarily) actual sexual experiences. Homosexual *behavior* in humans is defined as any overt sexual behavior between partners of the same sex, regardless of their sexual orientation. Following Kinsey et al. (1948), sexual orientation is defined operationally on a rating scale continuum ranging from 0 (exclusive heterosexuality) to 6 (exclusive homosexuality) with the midpoint at 3, meaning equal sexual responsiveness to both males and females. This rating is usually based on interview material. In most psychoendocrine studies, subjects from both poles of the continuum are contrasted with regard to hormonal or other characteristics. The assessment of sexual orientation can be refined by direct measurement of genital arousal in response to sexual stimuli, i.e., by penile plethysmography in males (e.g., Abel and Blanchard, 1976) or corresponding vaginal measures in females (e.g., Heiman, 1978). Whereas mating behavior in the rat is highly stereotyped and reflexive, human sexual behavior is highly variable and to a considerable degree non-reflexive, so that the establishment of homologies even with respect to overt sexual behavior is very difficult (Meyer-Bahlburg, 1977). Moreover, the assessment of sexual orientation as introduced by Kinsey et al. (1948) relies strongly on representational processes such as fantasies and felt attractions, for which homologous behaviors in animals are difficult to establish. Beach (1979), in a detailed discussion of animal models for human sexuality, has pointed out that "commonality of descriptive terms as applied to different species does not guarantee identity of the concepts to which the terms apply. Model builders must evaluate interspecific similarities and differences and the *causes, mediating mechanisms* and *functional outcomes* of behavior". Beach then raised a number of critical issues that further cast doubts on the comparability of "homosexuality" in the rat and homosexual orientation of humans. At any rate, while research on rats can be heuristically useful, only human experimentation can establish whether or not (specific) hormones have anything to do with sexual orientation in humans.

The purpose of this paper is to review the existing data on endocrine abnormalities — both in the prenatal and adult stage — in homosexual individuals as well as the evidence concerning sexual orientation in individuals with prenatal hormone disorders. Finally, we will consider options for future research in the light of new developments in general and behavioral endocrinology.

HORMONAL STUDIES IN HOMOSEXUALITY

With the progressing clarification of the process of sexual differentiation and of the etiology of somatic intersexuality, research on sexual orientation initially centered on peripheral-somatic indications of intersexuality in homosexual individuals, with largely negative results. Primary and secondary sex characteristics — and later the sex chromosomes — were found to be normal in most homosexual individuals (e.g., Pritchard, 1962). Soon after the first sex hormones were identified and synthesized, treatment with sex-appropriate sex hormones was tried in a considerable number of homosexuals, yet this approach to changing homosexual orientation was abandoned as largely unsuccessful (for references, see Kinsey et al., 1953, p. 759). Nevertheless, the search for biological markers of intersexuality in homosexuals continued and followed the development of biochemical sex hormone assays, focusing first on urinary hormone excretion and later on blood hormone levels. The general rationale underlying these studies was derived from the well-known relationships of testosterone and other androgens to masculine body characteristics and, in animals, to certain aspects of masculine behavior, as well as from the analogous relationships of estrogens to feminine somatic and behavioral characteristics. Accordingly, the expectation was that male homosexuals would show a deficiency of testosterone and/or other androgens, and/or an excess of estrogens whereas female homosexuals would show the reverse. Other endocrine disorders were thought to be possibly associated with the sex hormone abnormalities as cause or consequence.

Studies of blood hormone levels in homosexual individuals were published from 1971 on. The early ones have been critically examined elsewhere (for males, see Meyer-Bahlburg, 1977; for females, Meyer-Bahlburg, 1979). Here, we present an updated summary.

Male homosexuals

Blood testosterone levels for male homosexuals (including 5 reports on homosexuals with gender identity disorder, i.e., transsexuals) have been reported in 27 studies. Excluding data on subjects with agonadism, castration, or current estrogen treatment, all of the available data can be summarized as follows.

The vast majority of male homosexuals investigated had testosterone levels within the normal range of male reference samples (which typically are unselected for sexual orientation). Gross deficiencies of testosterone levels were conspicuously rare, even in those few studies that reported statistically lower values for homosexuals compared to heterosexuals. Only 3 studies (Kolodny et al., 1971; Pillard et al., 1974; Starká et al., 1975) have reported significantly lower blood testosterone levels in homosexual than in heterosexual subjects. However, two of these studies lacked adequate control groups, while the third (Kolodny et al., 1971) seems to be confounded by the relatively high number of drug users in the homosexual group, given the fact that many psychotropic drugs can depress testosterone levels (Kolodny et al., 1979, pp. 321–351). By contrast, 20 studies [*] reported no systematic differences between homosexuals and controls, or among homosexuals with different Kinsey ratings. A particularly interesting report was published by Friedman et al. (1976), who described a pair of monozygotic twins (discordant for sexual orientation), both of whom had normal blood testosterone levels. Another two studies (Tourney and Hatfield, 1973; Brodie et al., 1974) even showed elevated levels of testosterone in homosexuals. Wilson and Fulford (1977, op. cit.) reported that bisexuals had higher testosterone levels than did heterosexuals or homosexuals, whereas the latter two groups did not significantly differ from each other. It is particularly noteworthy that decreased testosterone levels for homosexuals were not found in those studies that are methodologically the soundest, i.e., employed careful patient selection procedures and multiple blood samples per subject (e.g., Brodie et al., 1974; Parks et al., 1974; Newmark et al., 1979; Sanders et al., 1983, 1984a). The only two investigations (Migeon et al., 1968; Aiman and Boyar, 1982) that were concerned with the blood production rate of testosterone did not find a significant deviation from normal values. Three studies have been published concerning unbound plasma testosterone (i.e., the biologically active fraction). One of these (Doerr et al., 1976) found an elevated level in homosexuals, whereas the other two (both from Dörner's laboratory: Stahl et al., 1976; Rohde et al., 1977) reported a decrease in comparison with controls. No correlation could be demonstrated between the amount of circulating testosterone and the preferred role in sexual activity (i.e., active, passive, alternately active and passive) (Doerr et al., 1973), or the degree of effeminacy in non-sexual gender-role behavior (Pillard et al., 1974; Sanders et al., 1984a). Rohde et al. (1977), however, reported a (statistically non-significant) tendency to lower levels of unbound testosterone in effeminate as compared with non-effeminate homosexuals.

---

[*] Migeon et al., 1968; Birk et al., 1973; Doerr et al., 1973; Barlow et al., 1974; Parks et al., 1974; Dörner et al., 1975c; Stahl et al., 1976; Decourt, 1977; Friedman et al., 1977; James et al., 1977; Rohde et al., 1977; Wilson and Fulford, 1977; Halbreich et al., 1978; Livingstone et al., 1978; Newmark et al., 1979; Futterweit, 1980; Meyer et al., 1981; Aiman and Boyar, 1982; Gooren et al., 1983, 1984; Sanders et al., 1983, 1984a.

With regard to estrogen levels in homosexual men, Doerr et al. (1973, 1976) reported elevated plasma estradiol and estrone, whereas Newmark et al. (1979) showed elevated estradiol, but normal estrone levels. Although statistically significant, the differences in estrogen levels were not large: For instance, in both studies, the mean estradiol level of the homosexuals was about 25% above that of the heterosexuals. Friedman et al. (1977), however, found no difference at all in plasma estradiol and estrone levels between homosexual and heterosexual men, confirming their earlier report (Friedman et al., 1976) of comparable plasma estradiol levels in two homosexual and heterosexual twin brothers. Normal estradiol levels in homosexuals have also been found by Wilson and Fulford (1977), Futterweit (1980), and Sanders et al. (1984a). In addition, Aiman and Boyar (1982) reported that both the serum levels and the production rates of estradiol and of estrone in plasma were normal in male transsexuals. Thus, the weight of the evidence fails to support the notion that estrogen levels are elevated in male homosexuals or that their testosterone/estrogen ratio is decreased.

Data on gonadotropin levels in male homosexuals show similar variability. Three studies (Kolodny et al., 1972; Doerr et al., 1976; Rohde et al., 1977) found significant elevations of luteinizing hormone (LH) and one of these also of follicle-stimulating hormone (FSH) (Rohde et al., 1977; also several cases in Kolodny et al., 1972, had elevated FSH levels), whereas Newmark et al. (1979) reported significantly decreased FSH levels, but comparable LH levels. Ten studies (Brown et al., 1971; Parks et al., 1974; Tourney et al., 1975; Dörner et al., 1976; Friedman et al., 1977; Livingstone et al., 1978; Meyer et al., 1981; Aiman and Boyar, 1982; Gooren et al., 1984; Sanders et al., 1984a) did not find a systematic difference between homo- and heterosexual men. Halbreich et al. (1978) also failed to find significant differences in mean baseline FSH and LH levels, but reported significantly elevated day-to-day variations in FSH levels and a reversed LH-area/FSH-area ratio among homosexuals. ("Area" refers to the area under the curve for each hormone followed for 1 month.) Similarly, Boyar and Aiman (1982) studied the 24-h secretory pattern of LH along with the response to luteinizing hormone-releasing hormone (LHRH) in transsexual men, and found some aspect of LH and FSH secretory dynamics to be abnormal in 7 out of the 13 examined transsexuals. They concluded that "transsexualism may be associated with a neuroendocrine defect in the hypothalamus or pituitary that is characterized by high-frequency, high-amplitude pulsatile secretion of pituitary LH". (However, the fact that 5 of 8 subjects examined had low sperm counts and at least one a history of estrogen treatment suggests alternative interpretations.) Rohde et al. (1977) published considerably higher FSH (60%) and LH levels (48%) for a group of effeminate homosexuals, as compared with non-effeminate homosexuals, but a statistical test is lacking. The design of many of these studies leaves much to be desired, especially in terms of control group selection and sampling, but the conclusion is certainly justified that, as a group, male homosexuals show neither gross central understimulation or overstimulation of gonadotropin production or release, nor deficient negative feedback sensitivity of the hypothalamic–pituitary–gonadal axis. Nevertheless, findings such as the ones by Halbreich et al. (1978) and Boyar and Aiman (1982) still suggest the possibility of abnormalities in more subtle aspects of gonadotropin regulation.

A few investigators have been concerned with other hormones that are of interest in the area of sexual differentiation. For instance, Kolodny et al. (1972) reported an elevation of plasma prolactin levels in Kinsey-score-6 subjects, but this result was not confirmed in 3 other studies (Friedman and Frantz, 1977; Futterweit, 1980; Sanders et al., 1983). Thus, it is unlikely that prolactin, which has been implicated in the etiology of male sexual dysfunctions (e.g., Weizman et al., 1983), discriminates between adult homo- and heterosexual males.

Of particular interest seemed to be the finding by Friedman et al. (1976, op. cit.) that the blood level of androstenedione, a weak androgen usually of adrenal origin, was significantly higher in the homosexual than the heterosexual twin brother. Similarly, Friedman et al. (1977) described a significant elevation of androstenedione (along with cortisol) in their group of 20 homosexual men. They offered as the most likely explanation for the apparent alteration of adrenal functioning the fact that the homosexual group differs from heterosexual controls in emotional stress, since the homosexuals constitute a repressed minority group in a homophobic culture. However, 5 other studies (Tourney and Hatfield, 1973; Newmark et al., 1979; Meyer et al., 1981; Aiman and Boyar, 1982; Sanders et al., 1984b) failed to corroborate the findings by Friedman et al., and Aiman and Boyar (1982) reported the plasma production rate of androstenedione (studied in 4 transsexual men) to be normal as well. Moreover, Sanders et al. (1984b) were unable to demonstrate any differences between heterosexual men and homosexual men (both effeminate and non-effeminate) in dehydroepiandrosterone-sulfate or in cortisol. Thus, there is little support for a theory of stress-induced activation of adrenal hormone production in male homosexuals.

In summary, the available endocrine data on male homosexuals vs. heterosexuals make it seem highly unlikely that deviations in peripheral hormone levels or hormone production after puberty can be held responsible for the development of male homosexual orientation in general. Of course, this conclusion does not exclude the possibility that such endocrine irregularities may be a *contributing* factor in some homosexual men.

Female homosexuals

There are relatively few studies involving hormone measures on female homosexuals (including transsexuals). In addition to reports by Loraine et al. (1970, 1971) and by Griffiths et al. (1974) on urinary hormone levels in lesbian women who showed some elevation of testosterone excretion, there are 9 studies on plasma testosterone in homosexual women. Two of these are concerned with lesbian women and seven with transsexuals. Elevated plasma testosterone levels were found in about a third of the subjects in four of these studies (in lesbian women: Gartrell et al., 1977; in transsexuals: Fulmer, 1973; Jones and Samimy, 1973; Šipová and Starká, 1977). Futterweit's (1980) sample of 12 transsexual women included 5 patients with documented or suggested polycystic ovarian disease, i.e., with signs of hyperandrogenization such as hirsutism, and an additional 2 patients with borderline elevated values of serum testosterone in association with regular menses. On the other hand, 4 studies (in lesbian women: Downey et al., 1982; in transsexuals: Seyler et al., 1978; Meyer et al., 1981; Gooren et al., 1983, 1984) did not find differences in testosterone levels. Plasma androstenedione was reported as being normal in the only two studies that measured it (Meyer et al., 1981; Downey et al., 1982). Where estradiol was measured (in urine: Griffiths et al., 1974; in blood: Seyler et al., 1978; Meyer et al., 1981; Gooren et al., 1983, 1984), no differences between lesbian or transsexual subjects and controls were found. The only study concerning (urinary) estrone (Loraine et al., 1970, 1971) showed decreased excretion of this hormone.

Gonadotropins have been measured in only 3 investigations, with no differences reported in baseline plasma levels by Seyler et al. (1978) and by Gooren et al. (1984), whereas Loraine et al. (1970, 1971) found abnormally low urinary FSH in 1 and elevated LH excretion in 3 out of 4 subjects. Scattered reports on other hormones such as cortisol (Downey et al., 1982) or prolactin (Futterweit, 1980) did not show significant abnormalities.

We can conclude that the majority of adult female homosexuals appear to have testosterone and estrogen levels within the normal female range. However, there may be a significant subgroup — not more than a third of all subjects screened — with elevated testosterone levels. This finding has been replicated in 3 countries with considerable cultural differences (Great Britain, Czechoslovakia, and the United States), and has held up in studies with relatively larger sample sizes (Gartrell et al., 1977; Šipová and Starká, 1977). Whether the elevated testosterone levels seen in a subgroup of homosexual women (which still are far below the normal male range) have any causal significance with respect to homosexual behavior is yet unknown. Also, we do not know whether these data constitute artefacts of sampling, e.g., by the exclusion of endocrinopathies such as hirsutism or polycystic ovary syndrome from the normal but not from the homosexual samples. Elevated testosterone levels too could be due to artefacts of hormone assays, e.g., by the analysis of homo- and heterosexual subjects in separate batches or in non-blind procedures. Such important procedural details are frequently omitted from the published reports. Finally, hormone deviations may simply represent an adrenal endocrine response to the psychological situation of female homosexuals or career women who tend to be overrepresented in homosexual samples (see Purifoy and Koopmans, 1980, for data on an association of testosterone levels and professional roles in women).

THE PRENATAL HORMONE THEORY

During the past decade, the major focus of psychoendocrine theories of sexual orientation has shifted from the hormone situation in adulthood to the role of prenatal hormones. This approach is based on the vast amount of animal data demonstrating the influence of sex hormones on the sexual differentiation of brain and behavior in general and of mating behavior in particular. Currently, this theory enjoys widespread acceptance not only among biologists and physicians but also by behavioral scientists who are dissatisfied with the status of psychosocial explanations (e.g., Bell et al., 1981) and by behavior therapists frustrated by the low success rate of their methods in changing sexual orientation (e.g., MacCulloch and Waddington, 1981).

In an influential book, Dörner (1976, p. 116) formulated a "dual mating center" theory with the medial preoptic-anterior hypothalamic region being mainly involved in the regulation of male sexual behavior (in the rat: mounting, intromission, ejaculation) and the ventromedial nucleus in the regulation of female sexual behavior (lordosis). In the rat, the differentiation of these centers is under the control of perinatal hormones. If perinatal androgens are high, they will lead to the predominant organization of the male center; if androgens are low, the female center will predominate. Dörner assumes that these brain regions have a similar function in human beings, with predominance of the male or female center predisposing an individual for the corresponding sexual orientation. If the predominant differentiation of the female center occurs in a genetically and somatically male individual, he will be predisposed to homosexuality. If the male center develops in a genetically and somatically female individual, she will be predisposed to homosexuality. Bisexuality in either sex would represent the effects of intermediate levels of androgens in the fetus. In analogy to the terminology for disorders of *genital* differentiation, Dörner (1976) has labeled human homosexuality "central nervous pseudohermaphroditism".

Problems of the animal models

In relating the prenatal hormone theory of sexual orientation to human homosexuality, several major difficulties have arisen. One is the questionable homology of the copulatory behavior of animals and of human sexual orientation, as was mentioned in the introduction. Some progress has been made here insofar as a number of animal studies have shown that pre- or perinatal hormone treatment leads to a modification of preferences for male or female target animals (in terms of approach and/or proximity behavior) which conform to predictions from the prenatal hormone theory (e.g., in the rat: Meyerson and Lindström, 1973; Hetta and Meyerson, 1978; in the dog: Beach et al., 1977; in the rhesus monkey: Michael et al., 1972). Despite these superficial similarities of animal to sexual preferences, more research is needed in order to establish valid homologies.

A second problem with animal models is that they are not in full agreement with the prenatal hormone theory. Although the male rat fulfills the theoretical prediction that prenatal androgen deficiency in males leads to feminine sexual behavior (male "homosexuality") in the presence of normal plasma testosterone levels in adulthood, the same is not true with respect to the predictions about female rat "homosexuality". Rather than the predicted homosexuality in early androgen-exposed intact female rats (which is the typical condition of the human female homosexual), Dörner's (1976, p. 164, Table 16) own data show such "homosexuality" only after gonadectomy and testosterone administration in adulthood. If the experimental rats were left gonadally intact, they showed a very clear predominance of female sexual behavior, and only a slight increase in mounting. A similar problem arises with the scanty data which are available about the effects of pre- or perinatal hormone treatment on subhuman primates (cf. Abbott, 1984). So far, pertinent studies have been limited to prenatally androgenized female rhesus monkeys, where the expected effects of prenatal androgens on the development of sex-dimorphic social play behaviors in childhood were found (Goy and Resko, 1972). The same animals showed increased aggression (another hormone-influenced sex-dimorphic behavior) between 5 and 7 years of age but their mounting rate did not differ from control females, and only 1 animal out of 7 showed the full masculine copulatory sequence (Eaton et al., 1973). At the more mature age of 15–17 years, these monkeys gave little evidence of masculinization in their sex-behavioral responsiveness to testosterone (Phoenix and Chambers, 1982). Finally, at 16–18 years, they responded in the typical female manner when treated with estrogen and paired with males, although there were some minor differences from normal females in certain components of proceptive behavior (Phoenix et al., 1983). A more recent study of a new sample of prenatally androgenized female rhesus monkeys (Thornton and Goy, 1983) showed some degree of defeminization in the sexual interaction of these monkeys with males. Due to the small number of prenatally hormone-treated monkeys in these studies, the results have to be considered preliminary; however, none of the findings to date constitute unequivocal support for the prenatal hormone theory of sexual orientation.

A third problem for the prenatal hormone theory is the fact that in the animal studies, systematic manipulation of sex hormones in the pre- or perinatal stage of development results not only in shifts of sex-dimorphic behavior, and in structural changes in (some of) the underlying brain systems but also in corresponding alterations of the genitalia. In contrast, the typical human homosexual has normal gender-appropriate genitalia as well as normal gender-appropriate secondary sex characteristics.

Evidence from prenatal endocrine disorders

Bypassing the above-mentioned problems for the moment, the validity of the prenatal hormone theory for human sexual orientation can be tested by the study of individuals with known prenatal hormone abnormalities. Prenatally hypoandrogenized genetic males and hyperandrogenized genetic females both should show increased rates of homosexuality. Two categories of abnormal prenatal hormone conditions permit the study of such effects, namely, spontaneously occurring endocrine disorders (i.e., intersexes), and the offspring of sex-hormone-treated pregnancies. The few available data on intersexes have been reviewed in detail elsewhere (Meyer-Bahlburg, 1977, 1979) and will here be only briefly summarized and updated.

Prenatally hypoandrogenized genetic males, as represented for instance by the syndromes of complete (Masica et al., 1971) or partial (Money and Ogunro, 1974) androgen insensitivity, are usually found to be heterosexual relative to their sex of rearing and their resulting gender identity. Thus, the influence of social learning appears to override the effect of prenatal androgens, if any, on sexual orientation; however, the partial or complete insensitivity to androgens in adolescence and adulthood may also play a role. The number of genetic male intersexes studied in detail and long enough, is too small to permit a satisfactory resolution of these issues.

Concerning prenatal hyperandrogenization of genetic females, the model endocrine syndrome is congenital adrenal hyperplasia (CAH), in which an enzyme defect shifts the bulk of steroid hormone production by the adrenal from cortisol to androgens and other steroids. The earlier data (Lev-Ran, 1974; Ehrhardt and Baker, 1976[*]; Money and Daléry, 1976; Money and Schwartz, 1977) appeared to indicate an overriding influence of the sex of assignment and rearing and of the resulting gender identity on sexual orientation. The majority of CAH patients with onset of corrective medical treatment in infancy or early childhood were found to be heterosexual, and only a small minority bi- or homosexual. It is not known whether the frequency of the latter was increased above that in unselected women without CAH, since no adequate control data were available. Even in the most extreme patient group, however, consisting of CAH women whose medical treatment did not start until adolescence or adulthood and who experienced both pre- and postnatal virilization, homosexuals did not predominate (Ehrhardt et al., 1968). In a recent controlled follow-up study of the Hopkins sample of early-treated CAH women in comparison to women with androgen insensitivity or Müllerian duct aplasia, the CAH women had a significantly increased bisexuality in imagery and/or sexual experience although here also the majority were heterosexual (Money et al., 1984; Schwartz and Money, 1983). Although these results are compatible with the prenatal hormone theory, they are also open for a social-learning interpretation if one assumes that the awareness of the medical condition on the part of the parents or the patients may have influenced their psychosexual development. Not enough data are available to clarify this point.

Another intersex syndrome, 5a-reductase deficiency, has recently become of major interest in the discussion of sexual orientation. Genetic males with this syndrome are born with largely female-appearing external genitalia but start virilizing in puberty due to the onset of responsiveness to endogenous testosterone. It has been reported (Imperato-McGinley et al., 1979) that in childhood these individuals are reared and identified as females but develop

---

[*] Ehrhardt, A.A. and Baker, S.W. (1976) Prenatal androgen exposure and adolescent behavior. Paper presented at the International Congress of Sexology, Montréal, Québec, October 28–31, 1976.

a sexual orientation towards other females during adolescence and finally, in late adolescence/young adulthood, change their gender identity to male. It is doubtful, however, that the psychosexual development of these patients mainly reflects CNS effects of their sex hormones. Direct assessments of gender identity and sexual orientation have not been performed, and there are other unresolved conceptual and methodological issues in the published reports (Meyer-Bahlburg, 1982, pp. 684–687).

Evidence from offspring of hormone-treated pregnancies

Sex hormone administration was a widely employed form of treatment of at-risk pregnancies in the 1940s, '50s and '60s, with both progestogens and estrogens being used. Behavioral studies of the offspring rarely focused on sexual orientation. Tables I–IV summarize the few available pertinent psychosexual data including measures that are only indirectly related to sexual orientation.

In the light of animal-research results, progesterone-related progestogens should have a demasculinizing effect, if any, on males, whereas androgen-derived progestogens should have a masculinizing effect on females (Meyer-Bahlburg and Ehrhardt, 1980). Out of 4 available progestogen studies (Tables I and II), 3 show no increases in homosexuality or related variables. The data by Zussman et al. (1975*, 1977**) on progesterone-treated males indicate a slight decrease in heterosexual activity but this may reflect a psychosexual delay in this adolescent sample rather than increased homosexuality.

Pertinent data on prenatal *estrogen* exposure involve only diethylstilbestrol (DES). To understand the role of estrogens in the prenatal hormone theory, we have to make a brief excursion into current neuroendocrine formulations. In the sexual differentiation of the brain, two major pathways seem to be involved (McEwen, 1983), an androgenic one which mainly utilizes testosterone and/or dihydrotestosterone (DHT), and an estrogenic one which relies primarily on estradiol derived from testosterone by aromatization within the brain. Endogenous estradiol is believed to be largely inactivated before it reaches the fetal brain, in the rat by binding to α-fetoprotein (Plapinger and McEwen, 1978), in the rhesus monkey and, possibly, in man by placental conversion to the relatively ineffective estrone (Slikker et al., 1982). The (non-steroidal) synthetic estrogen DES is of particular interest since it bypasses both mechanisms and reaches the fetal brain in a biologically active form, where it exerts organizational effects similar to those of androgens after conversion in the brain to estrogens. Indeed, recent studies — as yet unreplicated — indicate that pre- or perinatally administered DES (a) alters sex-dimorphic social play during childhood in female rats (Hines et al., 1982b), (b) increases masculine mounting behavior and decreases feminine lordosis in adult female guinea pigs (Hines et al., 1982a) and (c) leads to decreased mounting and intromission behavior in adult male rats (Monroe and Silva, 1982***), a "paradoxical" effect well known

---

* Zussman, J.U., Zussman, P.P. and Dalton, K. (1975) Post-pubertal effects of prenatal administration of progesterone. Paper presented at the Meeting of the Society for Research in Child Development, Denver, CO, April 1975.

** Zussman, J.U., Zussman, P.P. and Dalton, K. (1977) Effects of prenatal progesterone on adolescent cognitive and social development. Paper presented at the Third Annual Meeting of the International Academy of Sex Research, Bloomington, IL, 1977.

*** Monroe, J.A. and Silva, D.A. (1982) Effects of neonatal diethylstilbestrol (DES) on adult male rats' sexual behavior. Paper presented at the 90th Annual Convention of the American Psychological Association, Washington, DC, August 22–27, 1982.

TABLE I

SEXUAL ORIENTATION AFTER PRENATAL PROGESTOGENS: MALES

Author(s), year, country	Exogenous hormones	N	Source	Age (years) Mean	Range	Interview variable	Ex vs. Co	P*
Zussman et al., 1975**, 1977***, Great Britain	Progesterone	18	Hospital; practice. Chart-identified: treated for toxemic pregnancy		16–19	Daydreaming about females / Dating	Ex < Co / Ex < Co	<0.05 / <0.05
	(Co)	17	Same as above; normal or toxemic pregnancies		16–19	Thinking about marriage and family life	Ex < Co	<0.01
Kester et al., 1980, U.S.A.	Progesterone	10	Private clinic. Chart-identified	20.5	19–24	Fantasy: Excl. hetsex. / Predom. hetsex. / Ambisex.	6 vs. 6 / 1 vs. 3 / 3 vs. 1	N.S.
	(Co)	10	(Same as above)	20.9	19–24	Behavior: Excl. hetsex. / Predom. hetsex.	8 vs. 9 / 2 vs. 1	N.S.
	Other progestogens	13	Private clinic. Chart-identified	21.5	19–24	Fantasy: Excl. hetsex. / Predom. hetsex. / Ambisex. / Predom. hosex. / Excl. hosex.	10 vs. 11 / 1 vs. 1 / 1 vs. 0 / 1 vs. 0 / 0 vs. 1	N.S.
	(Co)	13	(Same as above)	21.8	19–24	Behavior: Excl. hetsex. / Excl. hosex.	12 vs. 12 / 1 vs. 1	N.S.

Ex, exposed to exogenous hormones, prenatally; Co, unexposed controls.

* P values are based on various scale-appropriate statistical tests.

** Zussman, J.U., Zussman, P.P. and Dalton, K. (1975) Post-pubertal effects of prenatal administration of progesterone. Paper presented at the Meeting of the Society for Research in Child Development, Denver, CO, April 1975.

*** Zussman, J.U., Zussman, P.P. and Dalton, K. (1977) Effects of prenatal progesterone on adolescent cognitive and social development. Paper presented at the Third Annual Meeting of the International Academy of Sex Research, Bloomington, IL, 1977.

TABLE II

SEXUAL ORIENTATION AFTER PRENATAL PROGESTOGENS: FEMALES

Author(s), year, country	Exogenous hormones	Sample characteristics		Age (years)		Interview variable	Results	
		N	Source	Mean	Range		Ex vs. Co	P**
Zussman et al., 1975***, 1977†, Great Britain	Progesterone	12	Hospital; practice. Chart-identified: treated for toxemic pregnancy		16–19	Daydreaming about males Dating		N.S. N.S.
	(Co)	12	Same as above; normal or toxemic pregnancies		16–19	Thinking about marriage and family life		N.S.
Money and Mathews, 1982, U.S.A.	Masculinizing progestogens	12*	Chart-identified on basis of genital masculinization after hormone exposure (except 1 unmasculinized hormone-exposed sister)	19 (median)	16–27	Married or hetsex. dating (mother's or subject's report)	(All married or dating)	—
		6*	Subgroup of above, interviewed in person			Bi- or homosexual imagery	(None)	—
						Bi- or homosexual activity	(None)	—

Ex, exposed to exogenous hormones, prenatally; Co, unexposed controls.
* No controls.
** P values are based on various scale-appropriate statistical tests.
*** See footnote ** to Table I.
† See footnote *** to Table I.

from studies employing high-dose steroidal estrogens instead of DES (e.g., Levine and Mullins, 1964). Döhler and coworkers (1982) have reported structural sequelae of perinatal DES administration in the preoptic area of the female rat brain. Another recent study has found that prenatal DES exposure leads to abnormal gonadotropin secretion in infant rhesus monkeys (Fuller et al., 1981), suggesting direct organizational effects of prenatal DES on sex-dimorphic areas of the primate brain.

To date, 3 behavioral studies have been published concerning prenatally DES-exposed human males (Table III), none of which showed a significant effect on heterosexual development. Two of the 3 published studies on prenatal DES effects in human females (Table IV) report only marriage rates, in which variable there is no difference between DES-treated women and controls. The third study, which comes from our own group (Ehrhardt et al., 1984), shows a significant increase of bi- and homosexuality among DES-exposed women as compared to two control groups.

In summary, the evidence from intersex patients as well as from offspring of hormone-treated pregnancies, suggests that prenatal hormones contribute to, but do not actually determine, the development of sexual orientation in individuals with abnormal sex hormone histories. None of the available studies permit us to fully exclude a confounding of the prenatal hormone factor with putative social factors. Further improvements of research methods and replications of the results on independent samples are needed.

Potential indicators of prenatal endocrine disorders in homosexuals

In applying the prenatal hormone theory of sexual orientation to the study of homosexual women and men, one has to search for functional indicators of prenatal hormone abnormalities, since there are usually no genital symptoms of intersexuality. Two phenomena are of interest here: the positive estrogen feedback effect on LH and the sex dimorphism of hepatic steroid metabolism.

The positive feedback effect on LH

The positive feedback effect on LH is the phenomenon that leads to ovulation in women. The estrogen levels rise in the follicular phase of the menstrual cycle and elicit an LH surge which triggers ovulation. The same effect can be achieved by administration of estrogens. In human males, rising estrogen levels typically suppress LH (negative feedback), but a positive feedback effect is occasionally found (Dörner et al., 1975b). Adult female rats also respond to increasing levels of estrogens with a surge of LH. This response to estrogens cannot be elicited when the rats have been neonatally androgenized, and it also cannot be elicited in male rats castrated in adulthood (Neill, 1972) although some data (Dörner et al., 1975a) indicate that the difference is more quantitative than absolute.

It follows from the prenatal hormone theory that homosexual men should show a stronger feedback effect on LH than heterosexual men. This has in fact been demonstrated by Dörner's group in 3 investigations (Dörner et al., 1972, 1975c, 1976) using a single intravenous injection of estrogens. As a group, gonadally intact homosexual men showed a positive feedback effect (after an initial decrease of LH), whereas intact heterosexual men did not. In comparison to normal women, however, the response of the homosexual men to the injection

TABLE III

SEXUAL ORIENTATION AFTER PRENATAL DES: MALES

Author(s), year, country	Exogenous hormones	Sample characteristics				Interview variable	Results	
		N	Source	Age (years)			Ex vs. Co	P*
				Mean	Range			
Yalom et al., 1973, U.S.A.	DES + progesterone	20	Clinic. Chart-identified: treated for diabetic pregnancy. Non-diabetic subjects	16	16–17	Heterosexual development (rank order: 1 = most hetsex.)	Ex > Co (i.e. Ex are less hetsex. developed)	N.S.
	(Co)	22	From diabetic and non-diabetic pregnancies; mostly volunteers; a few chart-identified. Non-diabetic subjects	16?	16?			
Beral and Colwell, 1981, Great Britain	DES + ethisterone	25	Chart-identified: treated for diabetic pregnancy	27.0		Married or living as married (general practitioner's report)	8/25 vs. 13/21	<0.10
	(Co)	21	Same as above, untreated	26.8				
Kester et al., 1980, U.S.A.	DES + progesterone	21	Private clinic. Chart-identified	25.8	24–29	Fantasy: Excl. hetsex. Predom. hetsex. Ambisex. Excl. hosex.	15 vs. 14 4 vs. 2 1 vs. 5 1 vs. 0	N.S.
	(Co)	21	(Same as above)	26.0	24–29	Behavior: Excl. hetsex. Predom. hetsex. Ambisex. Excl. hosex.	20 vs. 16 0 vs. 3 0 vs. 1 1 vs. 0	N.S.
	DES	17	Private clinic. Chart-identified	25.6	18–30	Fantasy: Excl. hetsex. Predom. hetsex. Ambisex.	13 vs. 13 3 vs. 2 1 vs. 1	N.S.
	(Co)	16	(Same as above)	26.0	18–30	Behavior: Excl. hetsex. Ambisex.	15 vs. 16 1 vs. 0	N.S.

Ex, exposed to exogenous hormones, prenatally; Co, unexposed controls.
* P values are based on various scale-appropriate statistical tests.

TABLE IV

SEXUAL ORIENTATION AFTER PRENATAL DES: FEMALES

Author(s), year, country	Exogenous hormones	Sample characteristics		Age (years)		Interview variable	Results		
		N	Source	Mean	Range		Ex vs. Co	P**
Beral and Colwell, 1981, Great Britain	DES + ethisterone	18	Chart-identified: treated for diabetic pregnancy	27.0		Married (general practitioner's report)	13/18 vs. 15/21	N.S.
	(Co)	21	Same as above, untreated	27.0				
Hines, 1981, 1982, U.S.A.	DES (+ progestogens in 7)	25	DES screening clinic	24.8	14.9–29.7	Married at time of study	9/25 vs. 5/25	N.S.
	(Co)	25	Sisters of above	24.1	14.6–47.2			
Ehrhardt et al., 1984, U.S.A.	DES (+ progestogens in 5)	30	DES screening clinic.	25.1		Kinsey scales, past 12 months:*		
	(Co)	30	Women with abnormal Pap smear	26.0		hosex. imagery	Ex > Co	0.094
						hosex relations	Ex > Co	0.017
						hosex. responsiveness	Ex > Co	0.044
						Kinsey scales, life-long:		
						hosex. relations	Ex > Co	0.018
						hosex. responsiveness	Ex > Co	0.004
	DES	12	(Subgroup of above)	24.5		Kinsey scales, past 12 months:*		
	(Co)	12	Sisters of above	23.6		hosex. imagery	(Ex > Co)	N.S.
						hosex. relations	(Ex > Co)	N.S.
						hosex. responsiveness	Ex > Co	0.032
						Kinsey scales, life-long:		
						hosex. relations	(Ex > Co)	N.S.
						hosex. responsiveness	Ex > Co	0.016

Ex, exposed to exogenous hormones, prenatally; Co, unexposed controls.

* Global ratings only; for the statistical results on the individual components, see the original article.

** P values are based on various scale-appropriate statistical tests.

was delayed for 24 h and was weaker. Dörner et al. (1976) studied the same phenomenon in 4 genetic female transsexuals, 3 of which were homosexually oriented and had oligomenorrhea or hypomenorrhea. They showed only a weak (2 cases) or moderate (1 case) positive feedback action on LH after a single intravenous injection of estrogen. However, in the fourth of the female transsexual subjects (who had bisexual behavior and normal menstruation) a normal female positive estrogen feedback effect could be evoked. Goh et al. (1980) found a suppressive effect of estrogen administration on LH secretion for 7 h in castrated male transsexuals, with a significant LH rebound above baseline observed in 24 patients at 16–22 h post injection.

The changing responsiveness of gonadotropins to LHRH, after estrogen priming, has also been studied directly. The results concerning sex differences in normal humans were essentially similar to those of the earlier procedures (in females, Keye and Jaffe, 1975; Young and Jaffe, 1976; in males, D'Agata et al., 1976; Dhont et al., 1976; Lasley et al., 1976). However, a positive estrogen feedback effect on LH can be found in both intact and castrated men if blood estradiol levels are brought up to those of women around midcycle, and if these levels are maintained for 4–5 days (Barbarino et al., 1982, 1983). Using the LHRH test, Seyler et al. (1978) studied 9 female transsexuals after 7 days of daily DES administration (2 mg/day). A significantly abnormal intermediate response more similar to the male than to the female controls was found; the individual effects of the DES treatment ranged from a moderate increase to a decline of LH. A careful replication attempt by Gooren et al. (1984) using estradiol benzoate (4.5 µg/kg/12 h) for 5 days, failed to find the expected difference in the LH responsiveness to LHRH between 6 intact genetic female transsexuals and 6 heterosexual women; the LH response to LHRH was even significantly greater in the transsexuals. In 6 male transsexuals, the LH response to LHRH prior to estrogen administration was similar to those of the two female groups before treatment (on day 5 of their menstrual cycle), with an LH peak at 30 min after LHRH administration. After 5 days of estrogen priming, however, the overall LH responsiveness to LHRH of these men had become reduced, in contrast to the finding in females, although now the peak of the LH response to LHRH was delayed, as it was in the two female groups. Unfortunately, there was no male control group. The small sample sizes and the differences in priming procedures make definitive conclusions from these inconsistent results impossible at the present time. It is important to note that also the previously mentioned findings of enhanced variability of gonadotropin levels in homosexual men by Halbreich et al. (1978) and Boyar and Aiman (1982) have been considered as possibly related to abnormal prenatal hormone conditions.

There are two major difficulties with this research approach that need to be resolved. One is that it is unlikely that LH regulation in humans reflects prenatal hormonal conditions to any marked extent. In contrast to lower mammals, the gonadotropin regulation of non-human primates shows only a slight influence of prenatal hormones and depends largely on concurrent sex hormone levels in adolescence and adulthood (Karsch et al., 1973; Steiner et al., 1976). Thus, spontaneous variations of endogenous steroid levels in the circulation as well as the treatment with exogenous sex hormones, which is pursued by many transsexuals, are likely to affect gonadotropin regulation. Moreover, as in the case of rhesus monkeys (Steiner et al., 1976), experiments with varying priming hormone dosages and durations may be needed to demonstrate any prenatal hormone effects. The other difficulty is that it is doubtful, at least in humans, that LH dynamics are necessarily correlated with sexual orientation. For instance, two studies of gonadally intact genetic males with the complete syndrome of androgen insensitivity have shown that the LH response to estrogen in this syndrome is typically masculine rather than feminine, i.e., LH is suppressed rather than increased after estrogen priming (Van Look et al., 1977; Aono et al., 1978). Nevertheless, these patients typically have a female gender identity and a feminine heterosexual orientation (toward males), in contrast to their male-like LH dynamics.

Sex dimorphism of hepatic steroid metabolism

A consistently found hormonal difference between homosexual and heterosexual males concerns the ratio between the two androgen metabolites, androsterone and etiocholanolone, as measured in the urine. Three available studies (Margolese, 1970; Evans, 1972; Margolese and Janiger, 1973) have shown a significant decrease — i.e., towards the ratio values typical for females — in homosexuals, particularly in those individuals with Kinsey scores of 5 and 6. A fourth report (Tourney and Hatfield, 1973) showed a slight, but statistically insignificant, difference in the same direction. These findings may assume considerable importance for the prenatal hormone theory of sexual orientation when seen in the context of recent animal research which established the existence of a hypothalamo–pituitary–liver axis (Gustafsson et al., 1983). In the rat, neonatal androgen "imprints" the level and the androgen responsiveness of certain sex-dependent enzymes in the adult period. If an analogous prenatal androgen effect underlies sexually dimorphic patterns of hepatic steroid metabolism in humans, which is not known at present, the androsterone/etiocholanolone ratio of homosexual men may constitute a sign of a prenatal/perinatal hormonal abnormality (provided, of course, that postnatal confounding factors such as sex-hormone abnormalities, drug intake, or disease states can be ruled out).

PROMISING OPTIONS FOR FUTURE RESEARCH

If the postnatal hormone theory is by and large untenable and the prenatal hormone theory presents so many serious problems, why do we not abandon the psychoendocrine approach altogether in favor of a social-learning theory of sexual orientation? A number of arguments favor a further pursuit of the psychoendocrine approach. One of these is the fact that throughout the mammalian class there appear to be marked similarities in the anatomical structures of the genitals as well as of sex-behavior-related brain regions and in the role of sex hormones in the differentiation and development of these structures. It appears unlikely that such brain regions as the preoptic area or the ventromedial nucleus in humans should fundamentally differ from those in subhuman mammals. A second argument is that the available data on patients with prenatal hormone abnormalities — in spite of some methodological shortcomings — implicate prenatal hormones as an important contributing factor. Currently, these findings cannot be adequately explained as a reflection of social-learning influences upon sexual orientation. Prenatal hormone influences are also suggested by the literature on the positive estrogen feedback effect on LH, and on the urinary androsterone/etiocholanolone ratio in homosexual individuals. Finally, the social-learning theory of sexual orientation (e.g., Thompson and McCandless, 1976; Bell et al., 1981) is no more compelling than is the psychoendocrine theory, and although an interesting alternative, it too is fraught with conceptual and methodological problems. In all likelihood, a comprehensive theory combining both endocrine and social factors will turn out to best reflect the empirical data.

If we therefore do not abandon the psychoendocrine approach, which avenues of research seem most fruitful? First of all, we have to take seriously the fact that in the vast majority of cases, homosexuality cannot be explained by intersexuality of sex chromosomes, gonads, genitals, or secondary sex characteristics. This implies that the biological factors, if any, involved in the development of homosexuality directly influence the structural and/or functional sex dimorphism of the brain without markedly affecting peripheral hormone levels or peripheral hormone utilization at the time of genital differentiation. Abnormalities of gonadal hormone production or of systemic androgen levels in the fetus would have to occur after genital differentiation is completed, do not markedly affect the later prenatal growth of penis or clitoris, and are not reflected in the gonadal sex hormone levels in adulthood. It seems unlikely that an endogenous systemic endocrine disorder would show such a time course. One could speculate that abnormalities of estrogen metabolism in the feto-placental unit might remove the protection of the fetal brain from biologically active estradiol which then would affect brain differentiation without influencing genital differentiation; however, no such abnormalities are currently known. Since temporary endocrine abnormalities can be achieved by precise experimental manipulation in animals, one has to look for potential exogenous agents which might lead to an analogous interference with fetal gonadal hormones in humans. Among these are maternal hormone abnormalities, maternal psycho-tropic drug intake, and severe stress. Importantly, there is now a rat model available which demonstrates that severe stress leading to reduced testosterone blood levels (in males) and brain aromatase activity (in both sexes), results later in behavioral demasculinization (Ward, 1977; Weisz et al., 1982). In humans, an association between homosexual orientation and prenatal stress has been suggested for males (Dörner et al., 1980, 1983).

A different model for psychoendocrine factors in the development of homosexuality is the new concept that certain endocrine-based peripheral disorders may involve mainly a tissue-specific instead of a general systemic increase in the production of biologically potent androgens. For instance, local production of DHT appears to underlie the pathogenesis of benign prostatic hyperplasia in men where alterations of peripheral androgen levels occur in prostatic tissue while only hints of these events can be found in the circulation (Morimoto et al., 1980). Another interesting example has been reported by Horton et al. (1982) in a recent study of 25 women with idiopathic hirsutism. They found that the mean plasma $3a$-diol glucuronide was increased 15-fold above normal, being elevated in all but a single mild case, whereas other plasma androgens were only moderately increased or not at all. Additional findings led the authors to conclude that excessive $3a$-diol glucuronide formation in these patients took place primarily in the skin. The important point here is that the mechanism underlying idiopathic hirsutism does not seem to be a major systemic abnormality of the pituitary-gonadal system but relatively tissue-specific major alterations of androgen metabolism. It seems at least feasible that there may be similar processes limited to CNS tissues (which, like skin, are of ectodermal origin).

In the search for psychoneuroendocrine mechanisms that are largely limited to the brain, it is helpful to recall how complex the processes involved in genital differentiation in fact are, with at least 3 different hormones participating. Testosterone itself effects the differentiation of the Wolffian ducts and, in puberty, promotes penile growth. Yet, for it to influence the prenatal differentiation of the external genitalia, testosterone must first be metabolized into dihydrotestosterone (DHT). This latter process is impaired in the $5a$-reductase deficiency syndrome, while responsiveness to both testosterone and DHT is impaired or lacking in the androgen insensitivity syndromes. In addition, the anti-Müllerian hormone is necessary for the completion of male differentiation by causing the regression of the Müllerian ducts; if anti-Müllerian hormone is absent or if its receptors are insensitive to it, internal intersexuality is the consequence.

Similarly, the theory of the androgen-dependent sexual differentiation of brain and behavior has undergone modifications (McEwen, 1983) which offer new possibilities for psychoendocrine approaches to the development of sexual orientation. The most important of these conceptual improvements is the recognition of the existence of several metabolic pathways for testosterone in the brain. The two most important pathways currently recognized are (1) the testosterone/DHT/$3a$-diol pathway (involving the enzymes, $5a$-reductase and $3a$-hydroxysteroid dehydrogenase, along with *androgen* receptors); and (2) the testosterone/19-hydroxytestosterone/estradiol pathway (involving the enzyme, steroid aromatase, along with *estrogen* receptors). The existence of these pathways and receptors has been demonstrated in fetal and adult stages in a variety of mammalian species including the human, for both males and females (see Martini, 1982, for references).

Particularly relevant to our discussion are data showing the behavioral specificity which is associated with these pathways. According to McEwen (1983), "defeminization" (namely, "the suppression of traits such as feminine sexual behavior and the ability to ovulate, through testosterone action during a specific period of pre- or postnatal development") always appears to involve the aromatization pathway (however, defeminization may not exist in some species such as the ferret or the rhesus monkey). "Masculinization" (namely, "the enhancement of traits such as male sexual and aggressive behavior") on the other hand is more variable with respect to the pathway(s) used: in rats, masculinization seems to be achieved by a combination of both the aromatization and the androgen pathway; in guinea pigs and rhesus monkeys, $5a$-DHT is an effective masculinizing agent; while in hamsters, estrogens masculinize. An important implication of these research results is that it is now conceivable that there are specific variations or abnormalities of pathways underlying a certain sex-dimorphic behavior, independent of mechanisms underlying peripheral sex dimorphism, and possibly even independent of other sex-dimorphic brain systems and related behaviors. Pathway abnormalities may be thought to result among other things from genetically based variations of specific enzymes or minor localized brain lesions.

Which of these metabolic pathways may underlie human sexual orientation? In this regard, the human endocrine models are of particular interest. For instance, if it can be conclusively demonstrated that sexual orientation is masculinized (at least to some degree) in genetic females with CAH and demasculinized in genetic males with androgen insensitivity, this would imply a role for prenatal androgens in the development of sexual orientation but would not distinguish between the androgen and estrogen pathways. If genetic males with $5a$-reductase deficiency are really reared and identified as females throughout childhood but nevertheless become sexually oriented toward females in adolescence, that would speak against a decisive role of DHT in the masculinization of sexual orientation but would not distinguish between an influence of testosterone itself and of testosterone aromatized to estradiol. If our findings of increased masculinization of sexual orientation in genetic females with DES exposure can be replicated, that would make the estrogen pathway the most likely underlying mechanism of sexual orientation (unless prenatal DES effects involve brain cell lesions, a possibility raised by the studies of Brawer and Sonnenschein (1975) and Brawer et al. (1978)).

The large number of hypothetical neuroendocrine mechanisms that must be considered in the search for an explanation of homosexuality makes it unlikely that a single mechanism underlies all forms of homosexuality. The great variability of sex-dimorphic and, more specifically, cross-gender behavior patterns in homosexual individuals already makes a universal hormonal mechanism very unlikely and requires at the very least an assumption of the modification of hormonal effects by social learning. Since social learning itself cannot be assumed to be a unitary mechanism, this assumption simply emphasizes the necessity of multifactorial explanations in this field. It could be that the intersex rationale applies, at best, only to a subgroup of homosexuals (e.g., the patients with peripheral intersexuality). In that case, the history of the psychoendocrine theory of homosexuality would resemble other once popular unifactorial theories of medicine — compare, for instance, the role of hypothyroidism or of Cushing's syndrome in the theory of obesity: once seen as a homogeneous disease entity, obesity is now understood to derive from a multitude of biological and psychological conditions. If one wants to draw lessons from the endocrine research on genital intersexuality, an endocrine basis of homosexuality — even if valid only for a subgroup of homosexuals — is likely to be multifactorial in itself.

ACKNOWLEDGMENTS

This work was supported in part by U.S.P.H.S. research grants MH-34635 (NIMH) and Y01-CN-00711 (NCI).

Dorothy A. Lewis and Patricia A. Connolly provided secretarial assistance.

REFERENCES

Abbott, D.H. (1984) Differentiation of sexual behaviour in female marmoset monkeys: effects of neonatal testosterone or a male co-twin. In: G.J. De Vries, J.P.C. De Bruin, H.B.M. Uylings and M.A. Corner (Eds.), *Sex Differences in the Brain. The Relation between Structure and Function. Progress in Brain Research*, this volume, Ch. 21.

Abel, G.G. and Blanchard, E.B. (1976) The measurement and generation of sexual arousal. In: M. Hersen, R. Eisler and P.M. Miller (Eds.), *Progress in Behavior Modification, Vol. II*, Academic Press, New York, pp. 99–136.

Aiman, J. and Boyar, R. (1982) Testicular function in transsexual men. *Arch. Sex. Behav.*, 11: 171–179.

Aono, T., Miyake, A., Kinugasa, T., Kurachi, K. and Matsumoto, K. (1978) Absence of positive feedback of oestrogen on LH release in patients with testicular feminization syndrome. *Acta Endocrinol.*, 87: 259–267.

Barbarino, A., De Marinis, L., Mancini, A., Giustacchini, M. and Alcini, A.E. (1982) Biphasic effect of estradiol on luteinizing hormone response to gonadotropin-releasing hormone in castrated men. *Metabolism*, 31: 755–758.

Barbarino, A., De Marinis, L. and Mancini, A. (1983) Estradiol modulation of basal and gonadotropin-releasing hormone-induced gonadotropin release in intact and castrated men. *Neuroendocrinology*, 36: 105–111.

Barlow, D.H., Abel, G.G., Blanchard, E.B. and Mavissakalian, M. (1974) Plasma testosterone levels and male homosexuality: A failure to replicate. *Arch. Sex. Behav.*, 3: 571–575.

Beach, F.A. (1979) Animal models for human sexuality. In: *Sex, Hormones and Behaviour, Ciba Foundation Symposium 62 (new series)*, Excerpta Medica, Amsterdam, pp. 113–143.

Beach, F.A., Johnson, A.I., Anisko, J.J. and Dunbar, I.F. (1977) Hormonal control of sexual attraction in pseudohermaphroditic female dogs. *J. Comp. Physiol. Psychol.*, 91: 711–715.

Bell, A.P., Weinberg, M.S. and Hammersmith, S.K. (1981) *Sexual Preference. Its Development in Men and Women*. Indiana University Press, Bloomington, IN.

Beral, V. and Colwell, L. (1981) Randomised trial of high doses of stilboestrol and ethisterone therapy in pregnancy — long-term follow-up of the children. *J. Epidemiol. Community Health*, 35: 155–160.

Birk, L., Williams, G.H., Chasin, M. and Rose, L.I. (1973) Serum testosterone levels in homosexual men. *New Engl. J. Med.*, 289: 1236–1238.

Boyar, R. and Aiman, J. (1982) The 24-hour secretory pattern of LH and the response to LHRH in transsexual men. *Arch. Sex. Behav.*, 11: 157–169.

Brawer, J.R. and Sonnenschein, C. (1975) Cytopathological effects of estradiol on the arcuate nucleus of the female rat. A possible mechanism for pituitary tumorigenesis. *Am. J. Anat.*, 144: 57–87.

Brawer, J.R., Naftolin, F., Martin, J.B. and Sonnenschein, C. (1978) Effects of a single injection of estradiol valerate on the hypothalamic arcuate nucleus and on reproductive function in the female rat. *Endocrinology*, 103: 501–512.

Brodie, H.K.H., Gartrell, N., Doering, C. and Rhue, T. (1974) Plasma testosterone levels in heterosexual and homosexual men. *Am. J. Psychiat.*, 131: 82–83.

Brown, G.M., Zajac, A.S. and Steiner, B.W. (1971) Solid phase human luteinizing hormone (HLH) radioimmunoassay (RIA): Findings in intact and castrated transsexuals (Abstract). *Clin. Res.*, 19: 770.

D'Agata, R., Gulizia, S., Andó, S., Vitale, G. and Polosa, P. (1976) Effect of oestradiol on gonadotrophin release induced by LHRH in men. *Clin. Endocrinol.*, 5: 393–397.

Decourt, J. (1977) Sur 91 cas d'homosexualité masculine: étude morphologique et hormonale. In: H.-P. Klotz (Ed.), *Hormones et Sexualité, Probl. Actuels Endocrinol. Nutr., Vol. 21:* 219–230.

Dhont, M., De Gezelle, H. and Van de Kerckhove, D. (1976) Modulation of pituitary responsiveness to exogenous LHRH by an oestrogenic and an anti-oestrogenic compound in the normal male. *Clin. Endocrinol.*, 5: 175–180.

Doerr, P., Kockott, G., Vogt, H.J., Pirke, K.M. and Dittmar, F. (1973) Plasma testosterone, estradiol, and semen analysis in male homosexuals. *Arch. Gen. Psychiat.*, 29: 829–833.

Doerr, P., Pirke, K.M., Kockott, G. and Dittmar, F. (1976) Further studies on sex hormones in male homosexuals. *Arch. Gen. Psychiat.*, 33: 611–614.

Döhler, K.-D., Hines, M., Coquelin, A., Davis, F., Shryne, J.E. and Gorski, R.A. (1982) Pre- and postnatal influence of diethylstilboestrol on differentiation of the sexually dimorphic nucleus in the preoptic area of the female rat brain. *Neuroendocrinol. Lett.*, 4: 361–365.

Dörner, G. (1968) Hormonal induction and prevention of female homosexuality. *J. Endocrinol.*, 42: 163–164.

Dörner, G. (1976) *Hormones and Brain Differentiation*, Elsevier, Amsterdam.

Dörner, G., Rohde, W. and Krell, L. (1972) Auslösung eines positiven Östrogen-Feedback-Effekt bei homosexuellen Männern. *Endokrinologie*, 60: 297–301.

Dörner, G., Götz, F. and Rohde, W. (1975a) On the evocability of a positive oestrogen feedback action on LH secretion in female and male rats. *Endokrinologie*, 66: 369–372.

Dörner, G., Rohde, W. and Schnorr, D. (1975b) Evocability of a slight positive oestrogen feedback action on LH secretion in castrated and oestrogen-primed men. *Endokrinologie*, 66: 373–376.

Dörner, G., Rohde, W., Stahl, F., Krell, L. and Masius, W.-G. (1975c) A neuroendocrine predisposition for homosexuality in men. *Arch. Sex. Behav.*, 4: 1–8.

Dörner, G., Rohde, W., Seidel, K., Haas, W. and Schott, G. (1976) On the evocability of a positive oestrogen feedback action on LH secretion in transsexual men and women. *Endokrinologie*, 67: 20–25.

Dörner, G., Geier, Th., Ahrens, L., Krell, L., Münx, G., Sieler, H., Kittner, E. and Müller, H. (1980) Prenatal stress as possible aetiogenetic factor of homosexuality in human males. *Endokrinologie*, 75: 365–368.

Dörner, G., Schenk, B., Schmiedel, B. and Ahrens, L. (1983) Stressful events in prenatal life of bi- and homosexual men. *Exp. Clin. Endocrinol.*, 81: 83–87.

Downey, J., Becker, J.V., Ehrhardt, A.A., Schiffman, M., Abel, G.G. and Dyrenfurth, I. (1982) Behavioral, psychophysiological, and hormonal correlates in lesbian and heterosexual women. In: *Abstracts, International Academy of Sex Research, 8th Annual Meeting, Copenhagen, Denmark, August 22–26, 1982*, p. 9.

Eaton, G.G., Goy, R.W. and Phoenix, C.H. (1973) Effects of testosterone treatment in adulthood on sexual behavior of female pseudohermaphrodite rhesus monkeys. *Nature (New Biol.)*, 242: 119–120.

Ehrhardt, A.A., Evers, K. and Money, J. (1968) Influence of androgen and some aspects of sexually dimorphic behavior in women with the late-treated adrenogenital syndrome. *Johns Hopk. Med. J.*, 123: 115–122.

Ehrhardt, A.A., Meyer-Bahlburg, H.F.L., Rosen, L.R., Feldman, J.F., Veridiano, N.P., Zimmerman, I. and McEwen, B.S. (1984) Sexual orientation after prenatal exposure to exogenous estrogen. *Arch. Sex. Behav.*, in press.

Evans, R.B. (1972) Physical and biochemical characteristics of homosexual men. *J. Consult. Clin. Psychol.*, 39: 140–147.

Friedman, R.C. and Frantz, A.G. (1977) Plasma prolactin levels in male homosexuals. *Hormone Behav.*, 9: 19–22.

Friedman, R.C., Wollesen, F. and Tendler, R. (1976) Psychological development and blood levels of sex steroids in male identical twins of divergent sexual orientation. *J. Nerv. Ment. Dis.*, 163: 282–288.

Friedman, R.C., Dyrenfurth, I., Linkie, D., Tendler, R. and Fleiss, J.L. (1977) Hormones and sexual orientation in men. *Am. J. Psychiat.*, 134: 571–572.

Fuller, G.B., Yates, D.E., Helton, E.D. and Hobson, W.C. (1981) Diethylstilbestrol reversal of gonadotropin patterns in infant rhesus monkeys. *J. Steroid Biochem.*, 15: 497–500.

Fulmer, G.P. (1973) Testosterone levels and female-to-male transsexualism. *Arch. Sex. Behav.*, 2: 399–400.

Futterweit, W. (1980) Endocrine management of transsexual. Hormonal profiles of serum prolactin, testosterone, and estradiol. *N.Y. State J. Med.*, 80: 1260–1264.

Gartrell, N.K., Loriaux, D.L. and Chase, T.N. (1977) Plasma testosterone in homosexual and heterosexual women. *Am. J. Psychiat.*, 134: 1117–1119.

Goh, H.H., Chew, P.C.T., Karim, S.M.M. and Ratnam, S.S. (1980) Control of gonadotrophin secretion by steroid hormones in castrated male transsexuals. I. Effects of oestradiol infusion on plasma levels of follicle-stimulating hormone and luteinizing hormone. *Clin. Endocrinol.*, 12: 165–175.

Gooren, L.J.G., van Kessel, H. and Harmsen-Louman, W. (1983) Gonadotropin response to estrogen administration in transsexuality (Abstract). *Neuroendocrinol. Lett.*, 5: 130.

Gooren, L.J.G., Rao, B.R., van Kessel, H. and Harmsen-Louman, W. (1984) Estrogen positive feedback on LH secretion in transsexuality. *Psychoneuroendocrinology*, in press.

Goy, R.W. and Resko, J.A. (1972) Gonadal hormones and behavior of normal and pseudohermaphroditic nonhuman female primates. *Recent Progr. Hormone Res.*, 28: 707–733.

Griffiths, P.D., Merry, J., Browning, M.C.K., Eisinger, A.J., Huntsman, R.G., Lord, E.J.A., Polani, P.E., Tanner, J.M. and Whitehouse, R.H. (1974) Homosexual women: An endocrine and psychological study. *J. Endocrinol.*, 63: 549–556.

Gustafsson, J.-Å., Mode, A., Norstedt, G. and Skett, P. (1983) Sex steroid induced changes in hepatic enzymes. *Annu. Rev. Physiol.*, 45: 51–60.

Halbreich, U., Segal, S. and Chowers, I. (1978) Day-to-day variations in serum levels of follicle-stimulating hormone and luteinizing hormone in homosexual males. *Biol. Psychiat.*, 13: 541–549.

Heiman, J.R. (1978) Uses of psychophysiology in the assessment and treatment of sexual dysfunction. In: J. LoPiccolo and L. LoPiccolo (Eds.), *Handbook of Sex Therapy*, Plenum, New York, pp. 123–125.

Hetta, J. and Meyerson, B.J. (1978) Sexual motivation in the male rat. A methodological study of sex-specific orientation and the effects of gonadal hormones. *Acta Physiol. Scand.*, Suppl., 453: 1–68.

Hines, M. (1981) *Prenatal Diethylstilbestrol (DES) Exposure, Human Sexually Dimorphic Behavior and Cerebral Lateralization*, Doctoral dissertation, University of California, Los Angeles, 1981, Dissertation Abstracts International, 42: 423B (University Microfilms No. 81-13858).

Hines, M. (1982) Prenatal gonadal hormones and sex differences in human behavior. *Psychol. Bull.*, 92: 56–80.

Hines, M., Alsum, P., Gorski, R.A. and Goy, R.W. (1982a) Prenatal exposure to estrogen masculinizes and defeminizes behavior in the guinea pig (Abstract). *Abstr. Soc. Neurosci.*, 8: 196.

Hines, M., Döhler, K.-D. and Gorski, R.A. (1982b) Rough play in female rats following pre- and postnatal treatment with diethylstilbestrol or testosterone. In: *Abstracts, Fourteenth Conference on Reproductive Behavior, East Lansing, MI, June 6–9, 1982*, p. 66.

Hirschfeld, M. (1906) Vom Wesen der Liebe. Zugleich ein Beitrag zur Lösung der Frage der Bisexualität. *Jahrb. Sex. Zwischenstufen*, 8: 1–284.

Horton, R., Hawks, D. and Lobo, R. (1982) 3-alpha,17-beta-Androstanediol glucuronide in plasma. A marker of androgen action in idiopathic hirsutism. *J. Clin. Invest.*, 69: 1203–1206.

Imperato-McGinley, J., Peterson, R.E., Gautier, T. and Sturla, E. (1979) Androgens and the evolution of male-gender identity among male pseudohermaphrodites with 5a-reductase deficiency. *New Engl. J. Med.*, 300: 1233–1237.

James, S., Carter, R.A. and Orwin, A. (1977) Significance of androgen levels in the aetiology and treatment of homosexuality. *Psychol. Med.*, 7: 427–429.

Jones, J.R. and Samimy, J. (1973) Plasma testosterone levels and female transsexualism. *Arch. Sex. Behav.*, 2: 251–256.

Karsch, F.J., Dierschke, D.J. and Knobil, E. (1973) Sexual differentiation of pituitary function: apparent difference between primates and rodents. *Science*, 179: 484–486.

Kester, P., Green, R., Finch, S.J. and Williams, K. (1980) Prenatal 'female hormone' administration and psychosexual development in human males. *Psychoneuroendocrinology*, 5: 269–285.

Keye Jr., W.R. and Jaffe, R.B. (1975) Strength-duration characteristics of estrogen effects on gonadotropin response to gonadotropin-releasing hormone in women. I. Effects of varying duration of estradiol administration. *J. Clin. Endocrinol. Metab.*, 41: 1003–1008.

Kinsey, A.C., Pomeroy, W.B. and Martin, C.E. (1948) *Sexual Behavior in the Human Male*, Saunders, Philadelphia, PA.

Kinsey, A.C., Pomeroy, W.B., Martin, C.E. and Gebhard, P.H. (1953) *Sexual Behavior in the Human Female*, Saunders, Philadelphia, PA.

Kolodny, R.C., Masters, W.H., Hendryx, J. and Toro, G. (1971) Plasma testosterone and semen analysis in male homosexuals. *New Engl. J. Med.*, 285: 1170–1174.

Kolodny, R.C., Jacobs, L.S., Masters, W.H., Toro, G. and Daughaday, W.H. (1972) Plasma gonadotrophins and prolactin in male homosexuals. *Lancet*, 2: 18–20.

Kolodny, R.C., Masters, W.H. and Johnson, V.E. (1979) *Textbook of Sexual Medicine*, Little, Brown, Boston, MA.

Lasley, B.L., Wang, C.F. and Yen, S.S.C. (1976) Assessment of the functional capacity of the gonadotropins in men: effect of estrogen and clomiphene. *J. Clin. Endocrinol. Metab.*, 43: 182–189.

Levine, S. and Mullins Jr., R. (1964) Estrogen administered neonatally affects adult sexual behavior in male and female rats. *Science*, 144: 185–187.

Lev-Ran, A. (1974) Sexuality and education levels of women with late-treated adrenogenital syndrome. *Arch. Sex. Behav.*, 3: 27–32.

Livingstone, I.R., Sagel, J., Distiller, L.A., Morley, J. and Katz, M. (1978) The effect of luteinizing hormone releasing hormone (LRH) on pituitary gonadotropins in male homosexuals. *Hormone Metab. Res.*, 10: 248–249.

Loraine, J.A., Ismail, A.A.A., Adamopoulos, D.A. and Dove, G.A. (1970) Endocrine function in male and female homosexuals. *Br. Med. J.*, 4: 406–408.

Loraine, J.A., Adamopoulos, D.A., Kirkham, K.E., Ismail, A.A.A. and Dove, G.A. (1971) Patterns of hormone excretion in male and female homosexuals. *Nature (London)*, 234: 552–555.

MacCulloch, M.J. and Waddington, J.L. (1981) Neuroendocrine mechanisms and the aetiology of male and female homosexuality. *Br. J. Psychiat.*, 139: 341–345.

Margolese, M.S. (1970) Homosexuality: A new endocrine correlate. *Hormone Behav.*, 1: 151–155.

Margolese, M.S. and Janiger, O. (1973) Androsterone/etiocholanolone ratios in male homosexuals. *Br. Med. J.*, 3: 207–210.

Martini, L. (1982) The 5a-reduction of testosterone in the neuroendocrine structures. Biochemical and physiological implications. *Endocrine Rev.*, 3: 1–25.

Masica, D.N., Money, J. and Ehrhardt, A.A. (1971) Fetal feminization and female gender identity in the testicular feminizing syndrome of androgen insensitivity. *Arch. Sex. Behav.*, 1: 131–142.

McEwen, B.S. (1983) Gonadal steroid influences on brain development and sexual differentiation. In: R.O. Greep (Ed.), *Reproductive Physiology IV, International Review of Physiology, Vol. 27*, University Park Press, Baltimore, MD.

Meyer III, W.J., Finkelstein, J.W., Stuart, C.A., Webb, A., Smith, E.R., Payer, A.F. and Walker, P.A. (1981) Physical and hormonal evaluation of transsexual patients during hormonal therapy. *Arch. Sex. Behav.*, 10: 347–356.

Meyer-Bahlburg, H.F.L. (1977) Sex hormones and male homosexuality in comparative perspective. *Arch. Sex. Behav.*, 6: 297–325.

Meyer-Bahlburg, H.F.L. (1979) Sex hormones and female homosexuality: a critical examination. *Arch. Sex. Behav.*, 8: 101–119.

Meyer-Bahlburg, H.F.L. (1982) Hormones and psychosexual differentiation: Implications for the management of intersexuality, homosexuality and transsexuality. *Clin. Endocrinol. Metab.*, 11: 681–701.

Meyer-Bahlburg, H.F.L. and Ehrhardt, A.A. (1980) Neurobehavioral effects of prenatal origin: Sex hormones. In: R.H. Schwarz and S.J. Yaffe (Eds.), *Drugs and Chemical Risks to the Fetus and Newborn*, Alan R. Liss, New York, pp. 93–107.

Meyerson, B.J. and Lindström, L.H. (1973) Sexual motivation in the female rat. A methodological study applied to the investigation of estradiol benzoate. *Acta Physiol. Scand.*, Suppl., 389: 1–80.

Michael, R.P., Zumpe, D., Keverne, E.B. and Bonsall, R.W. (1972) Neuroendocrine factors in the control of primate behavior. *Recent Progr. Hormone Res.*, 28: 665–706.

Migeon, C.J., Rivarola, M.A. and Forest, M.G. (1968) Studies of androgens in transsexual subjects: Effects of estrogen therapy. *Johns Hopk. Med. J.*, 123: 128–133.

Money, J. and Daléry, J. (1976) Iatrogenic homosexuality: Gender identity in seven 46,XX chromosomal females with hyperadrenocortical hermaphroditism born with a penis, three reared as boys, four reared as girls. *J. Homosex.*, 1: 357–371.

Money, J. and Mathews, D. (1982) Prenatal exposure to virilizing progestins: An adult follow-up study of twelve women. *Arch. Sex. Behav.*, 11: 73–83.

Money, J. and Ogunro, C. (1974) Behavioral sexology: Ten cases of genetic male intersexuality with impaired prenatal and pubertal androgenization. *Arch. Sex. Behav.*, 3: 181–205.

Money, J. and Schwartz, M. (1977) Dating, romantic and nonromantic friendships, and sexuality in 17 early-treated adrenogenital females, aged 16–25. In: P.A. Lee, L.P. Plotnick, A.A. Kowarski and C.J. Migeon (Eds.), *Congenital Adrenal Hyperplasia*, University Park Press, Baltimore, MD, pp. 419–431.

Money, J., Schwartz, M. and Lewis, V.G. (1984) Adult erotosexual status and fetal hormonal masculinization and demasculinization: 46,XX congenital virilizing adrenal hyperplasia (CVAH) and 46,XY androgen insensitivity syndrome (AIS) compared. *Psychoneuroendocrinology*, in press.

Morimoto, I., Edmiston, A. and Horton, R. (1980) Alteration in the metabolism of DHT in elderly men with prostate hyperplasia. *J. Clin. Invest.*, 66: 612–615.

Neill, J.D. (1972) Sexual differences in the hypothalamic regulation of prolactin secretions. *Endocrinology*, 90: 1154–1159.

Newmark, S.R., Rose, L.I., Todd, R., Birk, L. and Naftolin, F. (1979) Gonadotropin, estradiol, and testosterone profiles in homosexual men. *Am. J. Psychiat.*, 136: 767–771.

Parks, G.A., Korth-Schütz, S., Penny, R., Hilding, R.F., Dumars, K.W., Frasier, S.D. and New, M.I. (1974) Variation in pituitary-gonadal function in adolescent male homosexuals and heterosexuals. *J. Clin. Endocrinol. Metab.*, 39: 796–801.

Phoenix, C.H. and Chambers, K.C. (1982) Sexual behavior in adult gonadectomized female pseudohermaphrodite, female, and male rhesus macaques (*Macaca mulatta*) treated with estradiol benzoate and testosterone propionate. *J. Comp. Physiol. Psychol.*, 96: 823–833.

Phoenix, C.H., Jensen, J.N. and Chambers, K.C. (1983) Female sexual behavior displayed by androgenized female rhesus macaques. *Hormone Behav.*, 17: 146–151.

Pillard, R.C., Rose, R.M. and Sherwood, M. (1974) Plasma testosterone levels in homosexual men. *Arch. Sex. Behav.*, 3: 453–458.

Plapinger, L. and McEwen, B.S. (1978) Gonadal steroid–brain interactions in sexual differentiation. In: J.B. Hutchison (Ed.), *Biological Determinants of Sexual Behaviour*, John Wiley, New York, pp. 153–218.

Pritchard, M. (1962) Homosexuality and genetic sex. *J. Ment. Sci.*, 108: 616–623.

Purifoy, F.E. and Koopmans, L.H. (1980) Androstenedione, testosterone, and free testosterone concentrations in women of various occupations. *Soc. Biol.*, 26: 179–188.

Rohde, W., Stahl, F. and Dörner, G. (1977) Plasma basal levels of FSH, LH and testosterone in homosexual men. *Endokrinologie*, 70: 241–248.

Sanders, R., Langevin, R. and Bain, J. (1983) Hormones and human sexuality (Abstract). *Neuroendocrinol. Lett.*, 5: 129.

Sanders, R.M., Bain, J. and Langevin, R. (1984a) Peripheral sex hormones, homosexuality, and gender identity. In: R. Langevin (Ed.), *Erotic Preference, Gender Identity, and Aggression in Men*, Erlbaum, Hillsdale, NJ, pp. 227–247.

Sanders, R.M., Bain, J. and Langevin, R. (1984b) Adrenal hormones and established sexuality in the adult human male. *Psychoneuroendocrinology*, in press.

Schwartz, M.F. and Money, J. (1983) Dating, romance and sexuality in young adult adrenogenital females (Abstract). *Neuroendocrinol. Lett.*, 5: 132.

Seyler, L.E., Canalis, E., Spare, S. and Reichlin, S. (1978) Abnormal gonadotropin secretory responses to LRH in transsexual women after diethylstilbestrol priming. *J. Clin. Endocrinol. Metab.*, 47: 176–183.

Šipová, I. and Starká, L. (1977) Plasma testosterone values in transsexual women. *Arch. Sex. Behav.*, 6: 477–481.

Slikker Jr., W., Hill, D.E. and Young, J.F. (1982) Comparison of the transplacental pharmacokinetics of 17β-estradiol and diethylstilbestrol in the subhuman primate. *J. Pharmacol. Exp. Ther.*, 221: 173–182.

Stahl, F., Dörner, G., Ahrens, L. and Graudenz, W. (1976) Significantly decreased apparently free testosterone levels in plasma of male homosexuals. *Endokrinologie*, 68: 115–117 (cited in Dörner, 1976, p. 264).

Starká, L., Šipová, I. and Hynie, J. (1975) Plasma testosterone in male transsexuals and homosexuals. *J. Sex. Res.*, 11: 134–138.

Steiner, R.A., Clifton, D.K., Spies, H.G. and Resko, J.A. (1976) Sexual differentiation and feedback control of luteinizing hormone secretion in the rhesus monkey. *Biol. Reprod.*, 15: 206–212.

Thompson, N.L. and McCandless, B.R. (1976) The homosexual orientation and its antecedents. In: A. Davids (Ed.), *Child Personality and Psychopathology: Current Topics, Vol. 3*, Wiley, New York, pp. 157–197.

Thornton, J.E. and Goy, R.W. (1983) Female sexual behavior of adult hermaphroditic rhesus (Abstract). In: *Program and Abstracts, Conference on Reproductive Behavior, June 4–7, 1983, Tufts University, Medford, MA*, p. 21

Tourney, G. and Hatfield, L.M. (1973) Androgen metabolism in schizophrenics, homosexuals, and normal controls. *Biol. Psychiat.*, 6: 23–36.

Tourney, G., Petrilli, A.J. and Hatfield, L.M. (1975) Hormonal relationships in homosexual men. *Am. J. Psychiat.*, 132: 288–290.

Van Look, P.F.A., Hunter, W.M., Corker, C.S. and Baird, D.T. (1977) Failure of positive feedback in normal men and subjects with testicular feminization. *Clin. Endocrinol.*, 7: 353–366.

Ward, I.L. (1977) Exogenous androgen activates female behavior in noncopulating, prenatally stressed male rats. *J. Comp. Physiol. Psychol.*, 91: 465–471.

Weisz, J., Brown, B.L. and Ward, I.L. (1982) Maternal stress decreases steroid aromatase activity in brains of male and female rat fetuses. *Neuroendocrinology*, 35: 374–379.

Weizman, R., Weizman, A., Levi, J., Gura, V., Zevin, D., Maoz, B., Wijsenbeek, H. and Ben David, M. (1983) Sexual dysfunction associated with hyperprolactinemia in males and females undergoing hemodialysis. *Psychosom. Med.*, 45: 259–269.

Wilson, G.D. and Fulford, K.W.M. (1977) Sexual behaviour, personality and hormonal characteristics of hetero-sexual, homosexual and bisexual men. In: M. Cook and G. Wilson (Eds.), *Love and Attraction*, Pergamon, Oxford, pp. 387–394.

Yalom, I.D., Green, R. and Fisk, N. (1973) Prenatal exposure to female hormones. *Arch. Gen. Psychiat.*, 28: 554–561.

Young, J.R. and Jaffe, R.B. (1976) Strength-duration characteristics of estrogen effects on gonadotropin response to gonadotropin-releasing hormone in women. II. Effects of varying concentrations of estradiol. *J. Clin. Endocrinol. Metab.*, 42: 432–442.

DISCUSSION

R.A. GORSKI: I had thought that transsexuals were often considered different than homosexuals, in fact that this is an important factor in decisions whether or not to perform the required surgery. Yet you have grouped them with homosexuals. Can you comment on this?

H.F.L. MEYER-BAHLBURG: There are three reasons why I have grouped together homosexual and trans-sexual individuals in this discussion. (1) Compared to their genital and gonadal sex (before surgical treatment), almost all transsexuals have a homosexual orientation. (2) Retrospective surveys show significant cross-gender childhood behavior in about two thirds of homosexual males and females. This cross-gender behavior is similar to, although often not as marked as that found in the histories of transsexuals. Prospective studies of pre-teenage boys with gender identity disorders show that many of them become homosexual, some transsexual. (3) A number of markedly effeminate homosexual males have become transsexuals in adulthood. Conversely, quite a few self-declared transsexuals have changed into well-adjusted homosexuals (without hormones and surgery). Thus, in terms of psychological development, there seems to be a wide overlap between homosexual and trans-sexual individuals, involving largely identical aspects of sex-dimorphic behavior. Since there is only one broad endocrine theory of sex-dimorphic behavior, we assume that it would underly both homosexual and transsexual development, if at all valid for the human case. Obviously, there must be some additional explanation for the fact that some individuals become homosexual only and others homosexual-plus-transsexual. This would be a question of degree of the biological factor or due to more specific psychosocial influences.

R.A. GORSKI: Has the incidence of homosexuality increased recently?

H.F.L. MEYER-BAHLBURG: Since the original Kinsey studies were published in 1948 and 1953, no other surveys have been conducted that are methodologically comparable. We have no way of evaluating whether there is a genuine change in the prevalence of various types of sexual orientation.

H.H. SWANSON: Did prenatally DES-treated females showing bisexual fantasies exhibit the tomboy syndrome?

H.F.L. MEYER-BAHLBURG: The respective data analysis is currently in progress. Our preliminary impression is that in DES-exposed females maternal behavior and related variables are reduced while tomboyish behavior is not particularly enhanced. The specific relationship of these behaviors to bisexuality has not yet been analyzed.

G.J. De Vries et al. (Eds.),
Progress in Brain Research, Vol. 61
© 1984 Elsevier Science Publishers B.V., Amsterdam

Sexual Dimorphism and Transsexuality: Clinical Observations

L.J.G. GOOREN

*Division of Endocrinology, Academic Hospital of the Vrije Universiteit, P.O. Box 7057, 1007 MB Amsterdam
(The Netherlands)*

DEFINITION OF TRANSSEXUALITY

Transsexuality is an incongruence between the biological sex and the self-declared gender identity. In the sexual differentiation of the transsexual, as manifested by the chromosomal pattern, the gonads, secondary sex characteristics and hormone levels, no abnormalities can be found. Nevertheless there is a persistent and non-suppressible and compelling feeling to belong to the opposite sex. Attempts to resolve this conflict by psychotherapeutic means, directed toward reconciling the gender identity with the anatomy have consistently failed, perhaps in part because to the transsexual such a therapeutic objective fails to recognize the legitimacy of his/her own feelings (Money and Erhardt, 1972). To the transsexual the problem does not lie with the *self-identity*, but rather with the *body* that does not match properly, so that motivation to attempt to change one's self-identity is lacking. On the contrary, transsexuals regard themselves as integrated personalities and view any attempts to tamper with a part of their personality as any other person would: as an unacceptable assault on one's dignity and integrity.

The finding of one, rather isolated area of disharmony without evidence of gross psychiatric illness had led many researchers to believe that biological factors must be involved in the etiology of transsexuality. Most transsexuals themselves are convinced that some unfortunate biological error has trapped them in a body of the wrong gender.

The attraction of the theory of a biological origin is also in part of a politico-social nature, since it would very likely be advantageous in the validation of the transsexual status and it would facilitate its acceptance by society and its legal institutions. If the specific biological factor(s) predisposing to transsexuality could be identified, transsexuals would receive the attention of the medical profession and of the public similar to that generally given to cases of (pseudo)hermaphroditism. If a psychogenetic (cultural, educational) mechanism is found, many believe that transsexuals would be held responsible for their identity, which could be changed or at least curbed, if they were sufficiently motivated. In other words: biology is supposed to be unescapable, whereas psychology is a matter of will.

Sexual differentiation in animals and man has been extensively investigated and has been thoroughly reviewed in an issue of *Science* (Naftolin and Butz, 1981). Human differentiation was reviewed by Meyer-Bahlburg (1982). On the basis of their extensive experience with gender reassignment in cases of (pseudo)hermaphroditism, Money et al. (1955) defended the idea that gender identity in the human is undifferentiated at birth and formed by subsequent sex assignment and rearing in the first years of life, irrespective of internal and external somatic characteristics: "Differentiation as masculine or feminine is the product of various experiences of growing up". This concept was challenged by the report of Imperato-McGinley et al. (1979) on a successful reversal of gender identity during puberty of boys suffering from 5α-reductase deficiency. They concluded that androgen exposure has a more profound effect on gender identity than does sex of rearing. Several investigators, however, have called attention to the poor documentation of sociosexual factors in their study (Meyer-Bahlburg, 1982). In addition a report of an abnormal gonadotrophin response to luteinizing hormone-releasing hormone (LHRH) in transsexual women after diethylstilbestrol priming (Seyler et al., 1978) was contradicted by Wiesen and Futterweit (1983), who found a normal plasma gonadotrophin response to LHRH after diethylstilbestrol priming in transsexual women.

In Europe Dörner and coworkers have contributed a great deal to this research, using a rat experimental model to substantiate their human observations. Noting an unusually high incidence of homosexuality in men born during the stressful years of World War II, Dörner (1980) hypothesized that maternal stress during pregnancy presents an etiological factor in the development of homosexuality and transsexuality, in his view two deviations, resulting from a common defect: the insufficient androgenization of the brain. The pathophysiological mechanism would presumably work via maternal adrenal hormones, which, after passing the placenta, could influence the proper sexual differentiation of the brain by interfering with neurotransmitters and sex hormones. Dörner (1976, 1980) proposed that the positive feedback action of estrogens on luteinizing hormone (LH) secretion presents a method for evaluating male versus female differentiation of the brain in adulthood: present in heterosexual women, but absent in their counterparts i.e. heterosexual men; present in homo/transsexual males, but attenuated or absent in homo/transsexual females (Dörner et al., 1975). Dörner (1976) reported intravenous administration of 20 mg of conjugated estrogens to 19 homosexual and 2 transsexual males. When measuring LH levels, it was found that, in contrast to heterosexual and bisexual men, LH levels in transsexual and homosexual men rose 20–25% above pretreatment values when measured 48–72 h after the estrogen administration. On the basis of these observations, Dörner has made far-reaching recommendations as to the prevention of homosexuality and transsexuality in the human. On the basis of his findings that (a) sex-specific brain differentiation occurs between the fourth and seventh months of fetal life; (b) genetic sex can be determined from amniotic fluid cells; and (c) testosterone levels in the amniotic fluid of male fetuses are higher than those in females, Dörner arrives at the conclusion that a genuine prophylaxis is possible now. "Preventive therapy of disturbances of sexual differentiation is possible by administration of androgen to genetic male fetuses with clear evidence of androgen deficiency during critical differentiation periods" (Dörner, 1980, 1981). Caution to accept this seems justified for the following reason: Dörner designed rat studies, translating observations of human sexuality into concepts of animal experimentation and then he extrapolated the findings back to the human again. Dörner (1976, 1980) treated female rats both perinatally and postpubertally with testosterone and orchidectomized male rats neonatally and treated them peripubertally with testosterone. It was shown that the female rat mounted the male rat, which displayed lordosis. In his view "a total sex hormone dependent inversion of sexual behavior" was demonstrated. The design of this animal experiment, however, has inconsistencies, which invalidate its extrapolation to human sexual behavior. Human homosexual acts generally take place between two homosexuals, in his view suffering from an identical degree of insufficient androgenization of the brain. Dörner failed to demonstrate what type of sex behavior is displayed by two hormonally identically manipulated rats. This experiment clearly does not reflect the human situation. A further point of criticism voiced by Meyer-Bahlburg (1982) is the ambiguous genital morphology of endocrine-manipulated animals in this type of experiment, as opposed to the normally developed genitalia in human homosexuals and transsexuals.

ANIMAL MODELS?

The following will be a further discussion of the difficulties of using animal models to study human homosexuality and transsexuality. A valid animal model may in fact prove to be an impossible goal. Transsexuality could merely reflect the underlying behavioral predisposition that leads to the self-perception of a male or female identity. Observation of *behavior*, as in animal experimentation, does not always provide information relevant to human gender identity problems. Often the behavior does not reflect the gender identity. Many transsexuals, in an attempt to suppress gender dysphoria will for some time conform to the heterosexual gender role expected by society, until it becomes too difficult to continue. Further, some male-to-female transsexuals have relationships with females, which appear heterosexual to the observer. These are often continued after gender reassignment and would then be considered lesbian, whereas formerly they would have been perceived as heterosexual. Many male-to-female transsexuals, looking for male sexual partners, experiment in a male homosexual milieu. This, according to them, is mutually disappointing: Their desire to be recognized as a female and the denial of their male sexual functioning will not be appreciated by male homosexual partners, who by nature of their sexual orientation are looking for male partners. Female transsexuals have relationships almost exclusively with females, often started before gender reassignment treatment. Both partners, when questioned about the nature of their relationship, always identify it as heterosexual, even prior to gender reassignment.

Another point of endless confusion in observational studies is the femininity found in male transsexuals and in some male homosexuals on one hand and the masculinity in female transsexuals and lesbians on the other hand. This high degree of similarity to an observer without an attempt to investigate their motivation or intention has led researchers (Dörner, 1980) to believe that there exists a continuum from the male transsexual to the very effeminate male homosexual and on the other end of the scale from the masculine lesbian to the female transsexual.

A homosexual, be it male or female, enjoys sex only with someone of the own sex. Whether the role assumed by that person is active or passive, a good part of that person's pleasure comes from the physical functioning of his/her sexual organs. A transsexual, on the other hand, can have no pleasure from the natural function of his/her sexual organs, because the transsexual sees his/her sexual organs with distaste, as they are *not* the organs they desire to have. They may be capable of functioning in a normal manner, but even if they admit to a transitory sexual pleasure, their real and deepest personal reaction will be one of disgust, because emotionally they are not fulfilling their "natural" role. This, in my view, constitutes the core difference between homosexuality and transsexuality. It is therefore misleading to rely on observation alone, without an in-depth interview regarding the subjective meaning and the intention of the observed behavior. This is a serious obstacle in designing appropriate animal models of human transsexuality and probably to a lesser extent of homosexuality.

BIOLOGICAL DATA COLLECTED IN TRANSSEXUALS

Between January 1975 and April 1983 we have examined 322 cases at our clinic. Psychological criteria for the diagnosis followed those of the Harry Benjamin International Gender Dysphoria Association. A history was presented of rejection of their originally assigned gender role, together with a strong repugnance of their own genital functioning. Each had an unalterable and compulsive desire to assume the anatomical characteristics of the other sex to correct their "misformed" bodies to match their gender identity.

The group consisted of 240 male-to-female transsexuals and 82 female-to-male transsexuals. This ratio of 3 : 1 is consistent with other reports in the literature.

While the data of the histories of these subjects were primarily collected to provide proper endocrine treatment and not to evaluate the etiology of transsexuality, some observations are of interest. First, based on the interviews with the transsexuals and 15 parents of transsexuals, no pattern of stress during pregnancy was noted which would distinguish this group from the general population. Second, parental rearing of a child opposite to the biological sex was only found in 2 cases of this group. No support was provided, therefore, for theories of maternal stress on the fetus or of early life experiences in the etiology of transsexuality.

It was noteworthy that many transsexuals indicated an early feeling of being "different" from their peers. However, in most cases it took a considerable amount of life experience and testing to identify the basis of this difference. Many had to hear about the existence of transsexuality before recognizing their identity with it. This perspective emphasizes the difficulty of simplifying the etiology of this entity. Conclusions based on any one point in their life history or based on mere observations, as is done in animal studies, could obviously be misleading.

The chromosomal pattern in the subjects was consistent with the anatomical sex, with the exception of one male-to-female transsexual in whom an XXY configuration was found. The clinical characteristics of Klinefelter's syndrome were also present. Since the incidence of Klinefelter's syndrome is 1 : 1500 in The Netherlands, it was not unlikely to find a case in our population.

Interestingly, 6 subjects had twin siblings, 3 of which were monozygotic and the other 3 dizygotic, as indicated by blood group typing. Two of the monozygotic pairs were female and one was male. Of the dizygotic twins 2 pairs were both males, while in the other pair one was female, and the other male. The male in this pair was transsexual. In 5 pairs the other twin was interviewed as to sexual identity, but for 1 case only circumstantial evidence was available. In all cases the twin of the transsexual subject was heterosexual. This could provide evidence that genetic factors do not play a role in the etiology, and seems to cast doubt on Dörner's (1981) contention that maternal stress is an important factor in the etiology of transsexuality.

Furthermore we have observed 1 case of a female, afflicted with a severe form of congenital adrenal hyperplasia, who at birth was erroneously assigned to the male sex and reared as a male to the age of 4. She was diagnosed as a female, following which a clitorectomy was performed and glucocorticoid treatment was given. This gender reassignment at 4 proved to be unsuccessful: at age 22, "she" demanded to return to the male role, for which appropriate treatment was provided.

Of the 322 cases, 260 were examined without any previous (self) medication. In all these cases normal basal levels of LH, FSH, prolactin, testosterone and estradiol were found (Tables I and II). In 42 male transsexuals the response of LH/FSH to 100 μg LHRH and of TSH and prolactin to 200 μg TRH was studied. Results were comparable in all cases to those found in control males (Table I). 15 female-to-male transsexuals recorded for 2–3 months their basal body temperature in order to study their menstrual cycles. In no case were abnormalities detected (Table II). 12 male-to-female transsexuals and 6 female-to-male transsexuals had procreated, which reflects an integrity of their reproductive system.

TABLE I

HORMONAL DATA IN MALE-TO-FEMALE TRANSSEXUALS

(expressed as mean values ± S.D.)

	Male-to-female trans (n = 140)		Control males (n = 42)
Basal LH (U/l)	5.8 ± 2.1	N.S.	5.3 ± 2.6
Basal FSH (U/l)	3.8 ± 1.2	N.S.	4.1 ± 1.3
Basal prolactin (U/l)	0.21 ± 0.11	N.S.	0.18 ± 0.12
Basal testosterone (nmoles/l)	17.1 ± 4.9	N.S.	15.8 ± 5.0
Basal estradiol (nmoles/l)	0.11 ± 0.03	N.S.	0.10 ± 0.03
	(n = 42)		(n = 30)
Response to 100 μg LHRH (0–90 min) and to 200 μg TRH (0–60 min) calculated as area under the response curve			
LH response (U/l × min)	7.5 ± 2.0	N.S.	7.0 ± 2.1
FSH response (U/l × min)	2.1 ± 0.6	N.S.	2.4 ± 0.8
Prolactin response (U/l × min)	6.9 ± 1.9	N.S.	5.9 ± 2.0
	(n = 6)		(n = 6)
Response to naloxone infusion 2 mg/h for 4 h			
LH response (U/l × min)	2.4 ± 0.4	N.S.	2.6 ± 0.5

Statistical analysis: Wilcoxon's rank sum test.

In 6 female-to-male transsexuals and 6 male-to-female transsexuals the response of LH to serial administration of 4.5 μg estradiol benzoate/kg twice daily for 5 days was studied. In all female-to-male transsexuals an unequivocal positive estrogen feedback was found of the same magnitude as in control heterosexual females (Table II).

In none of the male-to-female transsexuals undergoing the same test protocol, in contrast, were any signs of an estrogen-positive feedback found.

In order to test whether or not opioid neurotransmitters are involved in the biology of transsexuality, 6 male-to-female transsexuals underwent an infusion of the opioid receptor antagonist naloxone (2 mg/h for 4 h) and LH levels were measured. No distinction between this group and a group of 7 heterosexual infertility patients (normal LH/FSH, testosterone and estradiol levels) could be made.

TABLE II

BIOLOGICAL DATA IN FEMALE-TO-MALE TRANSSEXUALS

(expressed as mean values ± S.D.)

	Female-to-male trans (n = 44)		Control female (n = 18)
Days 5–8 of the cycle			
Basal LH (U/l)	4.2 ± 1.2	N.S.	4.3 ± 1.4
Basal FSH (U/l)	3.9 ± 1.0	N.S.	4.1 ± 1.2
Basal prolactin (U/l)	0.21 ± 0.08	N.S.	0.17 ± 0.09
Basal testosterone (nmoles/l)	1.9 ± 0.3	N.S.	1.7 ± 0.4
Basal estradiol (nmoles/l)	0.12 ± 0.02	N.S.	0.11 ± 0.02
	(n = 15)		(n = 12)
Menstrual cycle analysis			
Follicular phase (days)	14.2 ± 2.0	N.S.	13.9 ± 2.1
Luteal phase (days)	13.7 ± 0.5	N.S.	14.1 ± 0.7
Total length (days)	27.9 ± 2.1	N.S.	28.0 ± 2.1
	(n = 6)		(n = 6)
Response to administration of $E_2B/9$ µg/kg/day *for 5 days expressed as area under the curve*			
LH response (U/l × days)	4.6 ± 1.2	N.S.	3.9 ± 1.2
FSH response (U/l × days)	2.0 ± 1.0	N.S.	1.8 ± 0.8
	(n = 6)		(n = 6)
Response to 100 µg LHRH before and after E_2B administration			
Before: LH (U/l × min)	3.6 ± 1.9	N.S.	3.2 ± 1.6
After: LH (U/l × min)	5.9 ± 2.0	N.S.	5.7 ± 1.9

Statistical analysis: Wilcoxon's rank sum test.

CONCLUSIONS

The phenomenon of transsexuality discloses that biological sexual differentiation is not necessarily concordant with the subjectively experienced gender identity. It appears that the formation of gender identity is a developmental process with potential mishaps between anatomy and gender identity. Since it is now well documented that genetic and hormonal factors govern sexual differentiation it is reasonable to implicate such biological factors in the etiology of transsexuality. To date, however, human studies have provided little evidence for biological factors. Our data, collected by history taking, physical examination and genetic plus hormonal studies have failed to reveal any difference between the male-to-female trans-sexual and heterosexual male, on one hand, and the female-to-male transsexual and the heterosexual female, on the other hand. Other reports in the literature on this subject are far from conclusive. Reports of a reduced positive feedback after diethylstilbestrol priming in transsexual women are disconcordant (Seyler et al., 1978; Wiesen and Futterweit, 1983). Observations of Dörner (1976, 1980) relating to the possible existence of a positive estrogen feedback in homo/transsexual men lack proper experimental design and interpretation of results. The definition of estrogen-positive feedback requires that LH levels rise upon administration of estrogens, resulting in an elevation of circulating estrogen levels for a sufficient duration. In Dörner's design a single, high dose of estrogen was administered and no information is provided on estrogen levels on subsequent days. Furthermore the observed LH rise is of a magnitude similar to that found in men by other authors following discontinuation of estrogen administration and then considered to be merely a rebound LH rise (Sherins and Loriaux; 1973; Kjeld et al., 1979).

To date, no solid evidence has been presented for a biological substrate of human gender identity disturbances. In terms of psychiatry the relative monosymptomatology of the gender problem in transsexuals is impressive. Transsexuals cannot be diagnosed as grossly mentally disturbed. The lack of psychiatric symptoms concurrent with gender dysphoria makes it attractive to think of a biological origin. The substrate must then be found in other than the presently known genetic and hormonal factors, which influence sexual differentiation.

In this context the observations of Money et al. (1955) and Erhardt et al. (1968) are not to be disregarded. These authors demonstrated that the gender of rearing, evidenced by parental affirmation of the child's gender, is pivotal in the developing gender identity.

Presently evidence is accumulating that gender role behavior (to be distinguished from gender identity) is affected by prenatal endocrine influences (Erhardt and Meyer-Bahlburg, 1981).

In conclusion: no solid evidence exists at the moment linking biological factors with human transsexuality. However gender role behavior may be influenced by biological factors. The distinction between transsexuality and gender role behavior is essential. As proposed in the introduction the applicability of animal models to the study of human transsexuality is doubtful.

ACKNOWLEDGEMENT

Throughout the described experiments there has been a close and pleasant collaboration with Mrs. W. Harmsen-Louman, who is thanked for technical and secretarial assistance.

REFERENCES

Dörner, G. (1976) *Hormones and Brain Differentiation*, Elsevier/North-Holland, Amsterdam, p. 272.

Dörner, G. (1980) Sexual differentiation of the brain. *Vitam. Hormones*, 38: 325–381.

Dörner, G. (1981) Sex hormones and neurotransmitters as mediators for sexual differentiation of the brain. *Endokrinologie*, 78: 129–138.

Dörner, G., Götz, F. and Rohde, W. (1975) On the evocability of a positive estrogen feedback action on LH secretion in female and male rats. *Endokrinologie*, 66: 369–372.

Erhardt, A.A. and Meyer-Bahlburg, H.F.L. (1981) Effects of prenatal sex hormones on gender-related behavior. *Science*, 211: 1312–1318.

Erhardt, A.A., Evers, K. and Money, J. (1968) Influence of androgen and some aspects of sexually dimorphic behavior in women with the late treated adrenogenital syndrome. *Johns Hopk. Med. J.*, 123: 115–122.

Imperato-McGinley, J., Peterson, R.E., Gautier, T. and Sturla, E. (1979) Androgens and the evolution of male gender identity among male pseudohermaphroditism with 5a-reductase deficiency. *New. Engl. J. Med.*, 300: 1233–1237.

Kjeld, J.M., Puat, C.M., Kaufman, B., Loizou, S., Vlotides, J., Gwee, H.M., Kahn, F., Sood, R. and Joplin, G.F. (1979) Effects of norgestrel and ethinyloestradiol ingestion on serum levels of sex hormones and gonadotrophin levels in man. *Clin. Endocrinol.*, 11: 497–504.

Meyer-Bahlburg, H.F.L. (1982) Hormones and psychosexual differentiation: implications for the management of intersexuality, homosexuality and transsexuality. *Clin. Endocrinol. Metab.*, 11: 681–701.

Money, J. and Erhardt, A.A. (1972) *Man and Woman, Boy and Girl*, Johns Hopkins University Press, Baltimore, MD.

Money, J., Hampson, J.G. and Hampson, J.L. (1955) Hermaphroditism: recommendations concerning assignment of sex, change of sex and psychological management. *Bull. Johns Hopk. Hosp.*, 98: 43–57.

Naftolin, F. and Butz, E. (Eds.) (1981) Sexual dimorphism. *Science*, 211: 1261–1324.

Seyler Jr., L.E., Canalis, E., Spare, S. and Reichlin, S. (1978) Abnormal gonadotropin response to LRH in transsexual women after diethylstilbestrol priming. *J. Clin. Endocrinol. Metab.*, 47: 176–183.

Sherins, R.J. and Loriaux, D.L. (1973) Studies on the role of sex steroids in the feedback regulation of LH and FSH concentrations in men. *J. Clin. Endocrinol. Metab.*, 36: 886–893.

Wiesen, M. and Futterweit, W. (1983) Normal plasma gonadotropin response to gonadotropin-releasing hormone after diethylstilbestrol priming in transsexual women. *J. Clin. Endocrinol. Metab.*, 57: 197–199.

G.J. De Vries et al. (Eds.),
Progress in Brain Research, Vol. 61
© 1984 Elsevier Science Publishers B.V., Amsterdam

Prenatal Gonadal Steroidal Influences on Gender-Related Behavior

JUNE MACHOVER REINISCH and STEPHANIE A. SANDERS

*The Kinsey Institute for Research in Sex, Gender, and Reproduction,
and Department of Psychology, Indiana University, Bloomington, IN 47405 (U.S.A.)*

INTRODUCTION

In this chapter we will be concentrating on the influence of prenatal exposure to steroid hormones on the behavioral development of humans. In order to provide a foundation for the necessarily non-experimentally derived data on the effects of prenatal hormone exposure in humans, a brief review of the process of sexual differentiation and comments on laboratory animal experiments that provide support for the conclusions of the human studies will be presented. Since several detailed reviews have been published during the past decade (Reinisch, 1974, 1983; Naftolin and Butz, 1981; Reinisch and Sanders, 1983), an exhaustive treatment would be redundant. Instead, this paper will describe the highlights and concentrate on relevant findings from our laboratory.

SEXUAL DEVELOPMENT AND DIFFERENTIATION

A primary role of steroid hormones during early development is the establishment of morphological sex differences which provide the foundation for sex differences of behavior. The process of sexual development begins with the sex difference of the chromosomes established at conception. The gonosomes are comprised of an X from the mother and a Y from the father in the male, and an X from each parent in the female. The second factor is genetically induced differentiation of the undifferentiated gonads. The process of testicular development is initiated at approximately 6 weeks post conception in males while ovarian development does not begin in earnest until the 16th week following conception. The third sex difference is hormonal. Testes produce high levels of fetal testosterone beginning at approximately 8 weeks post conception (Sitteri and Wilson, 1974), while the ovary appears to remain quiescent during the period critical for differentiation of the sexes.

The last four events in the prenatal psychobiological sequence of development from conception to the expression of behavioral sex differences are all hormonally induced. The presence (in males) or absence (in females) of testosterone, leads to the differentiation of the internal genitalia from two sets of mesonephric ducts present in both sexes. The external genitalia are formed from identical anlagen mediated by similar hormonal action. The sixth difference between the sexes to be sequentially differentiated is hormonally induced in various areas of the brain (see Gorski, 1984, for details). Sex differentiation of the brain appears to follow a pattern similar to that of the external genitalia in that the same area of tissue is hormonally masculinized by the presence of testosterone or becomes feminized by the absence of such hormonal stimulation.

The demonstration that brains of male and female mammals, from rodents to primates, exhibit hormonally mediated differences in neurotransmitter levels, neural connections, and cell nuclear volume, strongly suggests that similar sexual dimorphism of structure and function exists in human brains as well. Moreover, it is reasonable to assume that morphological and physiological differences between male and female brains have some relationship to the development of the behavioral sex differences, which also appear to be hormonally induced.

SEX DIFFERENCES IN BEHAVIOR

Just as with the genitalia and the brain, exposure to androgen during the prenatal era identified as critical for sexual differentiation, masculinizes juvenile, adolescent and adult behavior. The relative absence of steroid hormone exposure results in feminization regardless of genetic sex. Data collected during the past 25 years on a wide variety of species have demonstrated that, whether sexual differentiation primarily occurs neonatally, as in such short-gestation mammals as rats and mice, or prenatally, as in long-gestation mammals like guinea pigs and rhesus monkeys, the principle holds that exposure to androgen during early critical periods of development is essential for masculinization of behavior. In this regard, it is important to note that in some species, such as rats, only androgens which can be aromatized to estrogen are capable of causing masculinization of brain and behavior as well as activating male-like frequencies of behavior in adulthood. However, in many other species including the guinea pig, rhesus monkey and probably humans, androgens such as dihydrotestosterone which do not aromatize to estrogen, are also capable of producing all these effects. In other words, in many species estrogen may not be crucial to male sexual differentiation and activation of masculine behavior.

STUDIES OF HUMAN BEHAVIOR

Before discussing some of the relevant research on the biological bases of the development of sex differences in human behavior, it is necessary to address several pragmatic and theoretical issues essential for interpreting the findings from studies of human subjects. First, it is important to emphasize that true experimental design is precluded when studying potentially harmful prenatal interventions in humans. Therefore, our confidence in the conclusions from the following human "experiments of nature" or quasi-experiments derives from the consistency between them and the observations from laboratory animal experiments designed with random assignment to treatment and control conditions (Reinisch and Gandelman, 1978). A second note of caution for interpreting the results of the studies to be discussed relates to the fact that behavioral differences between the sexes are quantitative and not qualitative in their expression. That is, differences between males and females reside in differential frequencies of exhibition of behaviors rather than in whether or not a particular behavior is expressed.

Finally, based upon both theory and empirical evidence, masculinity and femininity are no longer considered opposite poles of a unidimensional scale. The unidimensional model implies that the more masculine an individual, the less feminine he or she must be; conversely higher femininity, by definition, is associated with lower masculinity. Instead, masculinity and femininity are now conceptualized as independent or semi-independent traits (Whalen, 1974; Reinisch, 1976; Reinisch and Sanders, 1983). This orthogonal or oblique model of psychobehavioral gender states that some individuals of either sex have the potential for exhibiting high frequencies of both masculine and feminine behavior. Such individuals have been categorized as androgynous (Bem, 1974; Spence and Helmreich, 1978). According to this paradigm, individuals may be characterized as high masculine/low feminine or high feminine/low masculine and would therefore be categorized as masculine or feminine, respectively, in gender role. Some individuals are designated as undifferentiated when they exhibit low levels of behaviors which are characteristically seen at high frequencies in either males or females. This scheme applies equally well to categorizing non-human mammals as well as human subjects.

CLINICAL ENDOCRINE SYNDROMES

The initial evaluations of the effects of prenatal hormone exposure on the development of gender-related behavior in human subjects enlisted patients presenting genetic endocrine syndromes. These subjects' developmental histories parallel in some important respects the experiments conducted with laboratory animals. Adrenogenital syndrome is a genetically induced condition the effects of which are similar to animal experiments exposing genetic females to androgen during critical periods of development. The two major differences derive from the source of androgenic stimulation, which is adrenal in these patients instead of gonadal, and the etiology of the hormonal excess which is genetic rather than exogenous in origin. Like animal counterparts, females with adrenogenital syndrome are born with masculinized external genitalia. If left untreated, girls will continue to virilize due to the continuing androgenic steroid hormone production, experiencing precocious puberty with concomitant short stature. Males born with this syndrome have normal-appearing genitalia at birth but also evidence early puberty and short stature if untreated. Treatment consists of lifetime administration of corticosteroids to replace the missing cortisol unavailable due to the lack of an essential enzyme in the process of cortisol synthesis. The enzymatic deficiency secondarily results in the excess production of adrenal androgens.

A series of evaluations of groups of female patients with adrenogenital syndrome at Johns Hopkins (Ehrhardt et al., 1968a,b) and Buffalo (Ehrhardt and Baker, 1974; Baker and Ehrhardt, 1974) revealed clear evidence of masculinization of behavior. Briefly, in a study that compared 17 female adrenogenital patients with 11 unaffected sisters (Ehrhardt and Baker, 1974), the patients were described by themselves and others as more tomboyish for longer durations and as exhibiting higher levels of intense energy expenditure. They reported a higher preference for male playmates, utilitarian rather than frilly clothing, and boys' toys during childhood with a concomitant lower interest in dolls. Further, they demonstrated a lower interest in pregnancy, motherhood and maternal behavior, and expressed more sex role ambivalence. There was an interesting non-significant trend for girls with adrenogenital syndrome to be more likely to instigate fights within the family. These differences between the affected subjects and their unaffected sister-controls can be interpreted as indicating masculinization and/or defeminization of behavior.

Androgen insensitivity syndrome is a genetic/endocrine disorder in humans mimicking the laboratory animal experiments which deprive genetic males of androgen during the periods critical for sexual differentiation of the genitalia, brain, and behavior. Due to an inability of the cells of the body to utilize the normal levels of testosterone produced by the normally differentiated testes, males presenting this syndrome are born with normal-appearing female external genitalia and experience a feminizing puberty stimulated by the normal levels of testicular estrogen. As would be expected from the findings in androgen-deprived male laboratory animals, behaviorally these patients have been shown to be more feminine than matched controls on many of the same dimensions listed in the above study of female adrenogenital syndrome subjects (Money et al., 1968).

EXOGENOUSLY HORMONE-EXPOSED SUBJECTS

The next studies of human subjects to be reviewed are more similar on one dimension to the studies of experimental animals than to the patients with genetic/endocrine syndromes: That is, the hormonal intervention derives from an exogenous source rather than from a genetic anomaly. As a result there are no progressive effects of exposure after birth as are found in the genetic syndromes and, therefore, no postnatal hormonal treatment is necessary. On the other hand, in another respect exogenously exposed individuals are less parallel to the animal subjects in that the hormones administered to pregnant women are not identical in action to testosterone or adrenal androgens. The major class of hormones used for treatment of at-risk pregnancy have strong gestogenic action. They are primarily synthetic hormones with oral potency. Since 1961, those used for pregnancy maintenance are progesterone-based synthetics such as hydroxyprogesterone caproate or medroxyprogesterone acetate. However, until their virilizing influence on the genitalia of exposed female fetuses was identified in the early 1960s (Jacobson, 1961; Wilkins, 1960), several strong synthetic progestins based upon androgen were administered. One of the most prescribed was Norlutin (19-nor-17a-ethynyltestosterone). Similar androgen-based progestins are still the major hormonal component of most birth-control pills.

Consideration of an additional complexity should be taken into account when interpreting the results of studies with prenatally hormone-exposed humans as subjects: Treatment regimens during pregnancy are rarely simple or consistent both within a subject or across subjects. In some pregnancies, several different kinds of progestins were administered; while in others some estrogen had been combined with the progestin. In many cases, dosage, timing and duration of hormone exposure are not even consistent among patients within the same medical practice. Despite the vicissitudes of treatment, a startling consistency has been demonstrated between the laboratory animal experiments and the quasi-experimental studies of hormone-exposed humans.

Androgen-based and progesterone-based synthetic progestins

Girls exposed to androgen-based synthetic progestins when compared to matched controls (Money and Ehrhardt, 1972) were shown to exhibit a pattern of responses similar to those described for female patients with adrenogenital syndrome. That is, the exposure to synthetic progestins with virilizing potential appeared to have a masculinizing effect on the behaviors reported in interviews with subjects and mothers. Similarly, in a study from our laboratory, it was found that male and female offspring of mothers treated during pregnancy with androgen-based and/or progesterone-based synthetic progestins (in some cases administered in combination with low levels of estrogen) when compared to unexposed brothers and sisters were more "self-sufficient", "self-assured", "independent", and "individualistic" as measured by a standardized personality questionnaire (Reinisch, 1977). These results can be interpreted as evidence of the masculinizing effect of prenatal exposure to synthetic progestins since, in general, males achieve significantly higher scores than females on all four of these dimensions (Cattell and Cattell, 1975).

In a second evaluation including 8 progestin-exposed males and 17 progestin-exposed females who were each compared to a same sex unexposed sibling on a test which measures aggression potential, exogenously hormone-exposed subjects, regardless of genetic sex, chose significantly more physically aggressive responses to hypothetical moderate-level conflict situations (Reinisch, 1981). This finding is consistent with the expectation that synthetic progestins have virilizing potential (Reinisch, 1983) and thus masculinize prenatally exposed individuals, since males at most ages choose more physically aggressive responses on this measure than do females (Leifer and Roberts, 1971; Reinisch and Sanders, 1984; Sanders and Reinisch, in preparation).

One study has introduced data not supportive of the putative masculinizing action of one progesterone-based synthetic progestin which appeared to have virilizing potential in our studies. Although there were no significant differences between the 13 boys exposed to medroxyprogesterone acetate (MPA) prenatally and their unexposed matched controls (Meyer-Bahlburg et al., 1977), the 15 girls evaluated appeared to be feminized in clothing preference, with a statistically non-significant trend reported toward less likelihood of being characterized as a "tomboy" on a long-term basis (Ehrhardt et al., 1977). One possible explanation both for the small number of differences found, and even the direction of the effects may be the low-dose short-duration hormone treatment regimens administered during many of these subjects' gestations as compared to the exposure experienced by subjects tested in our laboratory. Only additional evaluations of larger groups of prenatally progestin-exposed individuals will help to clarify the role of dose, timing, and duration of exposure as well as the possible differences in effect of the various synthetic progestins.

Sub-asymptotic prenatal androgen stimulation

The finding of increased levels of masculine behavior in males in two of the studies cited above was unexpected since experiments evaluating the effects of prenatal exposure to testosterone in rhesus monkeys (Goy et al., 1977) had revealed no evidence of such an effect on the male. However, data do exist for humans which lend some support to the possibility that if hormones with androgenic potential are added to the normal amounts present during prenatal critical periods of sexual differentiation, male development might be additionally virilized. When 9 boys with adrenogenital syndrome were compared to their unaffected brothers, they evidenced significantly "more frequently a high energy-expenditure level in sports and rough outdoor activities on a long-term basis" (Ehrhardt and Baker, 1974). This increase in an aspect of behavior which has been identified as normally higher in human males than females during childhood, indicates that males exposed prenatally to increased levels of adrenal androgen may have even higher levels of masculine response than males exposed to normal concentrations of hormones.

Providing additional support for this unexpected finding are data recently collected in our laboratory from a group of 10 males exposed prenatally to the testosterone-based synthetic progestin 19NET as compared to their brothers whose gestations were untreated. Preliminary analyses have revealed increased masculine response on a variety of sexually dimorphic psychological parameters. These parameters include personality dimensions, mental abilities, masculinity/femininity, self-esteem, and attitudes toward work and family. A further unanticipated finding was that although similar results were found for sister pairs, the effects appear to be much stronger in males. This outcome is similar to that for the brother and sister pairs in which prenatal exposure to synthetic progestins was found to increase potential for aggression (Reinisch, 1981).

In an attempt to understand this tentatively identified phenomenon of enhanced masculinization of males as a result of increased prenatal exposure to hormones with androgenic potential, support for the hypothesis that human males normally do not exhibit the full expression of their potential masculine genotype will be explored. First, there is no doubt that testosterone produced by the fetal or neonatal testes is responsible for the masculine differentiation of the genitalia, hypothalamus and behavior in mammals. The likelihood of the human male fitting this same pattern is supported by the fact that it has been incontrovertibly demonstrated that the testes of human male fetuses are capable of producing testosterone as early as the eighth week post conception (Sitteri and Wilson, 1974) and that this ability continues to rise to a maximum level at approximately 20 weeks, after which it declines until parturition (Abramovich, 1974; Diez D'Aux and Murphy, 1974; Reyes et al., 1974; Taylor et al., 1974). This period from 8 to 20 weeks post conception encompasses both the era considered critical for the sexual differentiation of the internal and external genitalia and the critical period of brain differentiation which most likely occurs in the latter part of this interval. The levels of testosterone appear to be asymptotic for morphologic genital differentiation since the only overlap between the sexes occurs under pathological conditions (e.g. androgen insensitivity syndrome or $5a$-reductase deficiency — Rubin et al., 1981).

In the expression of behavioral sex differences, however, there is considerable overlap between males and females (Fig. 1A). In fact, the quantitative differences in frequency of

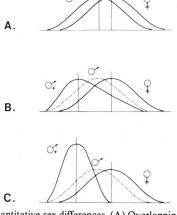

Fig. 1. Phenotypic expression of quantitative sex differences. (A) Overlapping normal distributions representing the result of normal prenatal hormonal environmental conditions. B and C represent the possible effects of elevated levels of androgen on the male distribution of behavior. (B) The range remains the same, but the distribution is skewed. (C) The distribution is normal, but the kurtosis is affected. The result of the alterations in the distributions reflected in B and C is an increase of the mean difference between the sexes.

occurrence or level of exhibition of behaviors which are expressed dimorphically between the sexes are in general very small (Maccoby and Jacklin, 1974). Our data and those on males with adrenogenital syndrome suggest that if more testosterone were normally available to males during the period in which the human brain is differentiated, the magnitude of behavioral differences between the sexes would be much greater (Fig. 1B and C). Thus, it follows that human males may normally be subject to sub-asymptotic prenatal androgen stimulation in relation to the sexual differentiation of brain and behavior. Based upon the foregoing assumptions, the existence of levels of androgen which are not high enough to generate the fullest possible expression of the *behavioral* genotype although stimulating full expression of the *morphological* genotype, might hypothetically be due not only to relatively low plasma levels but also reflect differing demands of neural vs. somatic cells and/or greater difficulty of testosterone in reaching CNS tissue.

A second question relates to how an alteration in the environment, exemplified here by an elevation of androgen levels, would change the expression of the genotype — higher frequencies and/or more extreme levels of masculine behavior. If we assume that the full range of the male behavioral genotype is expressed by the population of phenotypic males, then there are at least two ways that additional androgen might affect the distribution of masculine behavior so that the resulting difference between the means of males and females would be augmented. The first possibility is an alteration in the skewness of the distribution (Fig. 1B). In this case, the endpoints of the range of the distribution would remain the same; but the actual frequency distribution of males within the range would be shifted reflecting the fact that more individuals are exhibiting increased levels of masculine response. The second influence might be on the variance (Fig. 1C) so that additional androgen would result in decreased variability, moving the distribution toward the masculine pole of the continuum. The symmetry of the distribution would not be affected here, only the kurtosis would be altered. Both these possibilities are supported in part by the fact that a wide range of individual differences in testosterone concentrations has been identified in human fetal amniotic fluid at the same period of gestation (Warne et al., 1977), indicating that there are large differences among males with regard to the amount of androgen to which each is exposed during development. Whatever the mechanism, it appears from our limited data that the possibility exists that the human male is naturally exposed to levels of androgen prenatally which are below asymptote. This would result in lower levels of masculine behavior than the genotype might ultimately permit, consequently yielding smaller behavioral differences between the sexes than would be the case if more androgen were available.

Behavioral development and prenatal estrogen exposure

The possible influence of prenatal exposure to estrogen in humans is of particular interest because of its role in masculine brain organization of rats and several other species (see above; Goy and McEwen, 1980). Diethylstilbestrol (DES), a non-steroidal estrogen with 5 times the potency of estradiol when taken orally, was used extensively as an hormonal support for at-risk pregnancy until 1975 when the United States Federal Drug Administration banned its use during pregnancy because a relationship between prenatal exposure and adenocarcinoma of the vagina had been revealed. More recently, teratogenic effects on prenatally exposed male genitalia have been identified as well. Although the findings in rats might lead to the expectation that prenatal exposure to estrogen would virilize human females and have little effect on males, the preponderance of the limited evidence available points to a feminizing or demasculinizing influence. A study of 16-year-old boys whose diabetic mothers had been treated with DES and progestins during pregnancy showed decreased "assertiveness, aggressiveness, athletic skill and grace", and performance on the Embedded Figures test (Yalom et al., 1973). In our evaluation of personality in males and females exposed to DES the exposed males and females received scores indicating that they were "more group-oriented" (less individualistic) and more group-dependent (less self-sufficient) than their unexposed siblings (Reinisch, 1977). Scores like these are more characteristic of girls than boys and indicate feminization or demasculinization of response. Most recently, in a preliminary analysis of 13 pairs of brothers, one of whom in each pair was prenatally exposed to DES, it appeared that the exposed males demonstrated aspects of brain laterality more representative of females than males who have been tested on the Witelson Dichhaptic Shapes test (Witelson, 1974). One contradictory note derives from the data reported in this volume by Meyer-Bahlburg (1984) suggesting that girls exposed to DES prenatally may exhibit a less heterosexual orientation than controls. Additional evaluations of human subjects whose gestations have been treated with either non-steroidal or steroidal estrogens are necessary to clarify the long-term influence of these hormones on behavioral development.

PRENATAL HORMONE ENVIRONMENT AND BEHAVIORAL DEVELOPMENT

This selective review of studies has evaluated the effects of prenatal exposure to hormones on behavioral development in humans. An attempt was made to reveal the parallels between the quasi-experimental human studies and the animal experiments on hormone exposure and alterations of brain and subsequent behavior. It can be concluded from the studies presented here that although the data are sparse, there is adequate evidence to suggest that exposure to steroid hormones during gestation does affect human behavioral development in a manner generally consistent with that demonstrated experimentally in laboratory animals. It follows, based upon the concordance of evidence between the laboratory animal and human studies of behavioral alteration in response to critical period exposure to steroids, that the human brain is likely to undergo a process of sexual differentiation similar to that of other mammals. Sex differences in human brain morphology have been identified (e.g., deLacoste-Utamsing and Holloway, 1982), awaited only is definitive empirical evidence of the role hormones play in brain differentiation.

ACKNOWLEDGEMENTS

Supported in part by the National Institute of Child Health and Human Development (HD 17655) to JMR.

We would also like to acknowledge the editorial assistance of C.S. Kaufman, R. Beasley, L.A. Rosenblum and K.A. Lanyi and graphics of M. Blizzard.

REFERENCES

Abramovich, R.D. (1974) Human sexual differentiation — in utero influences. *J. Obstet. Gynaecol. Br. Commonw.*, 81: 448–453.

Baker, S.W. and Ehrhardt, A.A. (1974) Prenatal androgen, intelligence and cognitive sex differences. In: R.C. Friedman, R.M. Richart and R.L. Vande Wiele (Eds.), *Sex Differences in Behavior*, John Wiley, New York, pp. 53–84.

Bem, S.L. (1974) The measurement of psychological androgyny. *J. Consult. Clin. Psychol.*, 42: 155–162.

Cattell, R.B. and Cattell, M.D.L. (1975) *Handbook for the Jr.–Sr. High School Personality Questionnaire "HSPQ"*, Institute for Personality and Ability Testing, Champaign, IL.

deLacoste-Utamsing, C. and Holloway, R.L. (1982) Sexual dimorphism in the human corpus callosum. *Science*, 216: 1431–1432.

Diez D'Aux, R.C. and Murphy, B.E.P. (1974) Androgens in the human fetus. *J. Ster. Biochem.*, 5: 207–210.

Ehrhardt, A.A. and Baker, S.W. (1974) Fetal androgens, human central nervous system differentiation, and behavioral sex differences. In: R.C. Friedman, R.M. Richart and R.L. Vande Wiele (Eds.), *Sex Differences in Behavior*, John Wiley, New York, pp. 33–51.

Ehrhardt, A.A. and Meyer-Bahlburg, H.F.L. (1981) Effects of prenatal sex hormones on gender-related behavior. *Science*, 211: 1312–1318.

Ehrhardt, A.A., Epstein, R. and Money, J. (1968a) Fetal androgens and female gender identity in the early-treated adrenogenital syndrome. *Johns Hopk. Med. J.*, 122: 160–167.

Ehrhardt, A.A., Evers, K. and Money, J. (1968b) Influence of androgen and some aspects of sexually dimorphic behavior in women with the late-treated adrenogenital syndrome. *Johns Hopk. Med. J.*, 115–122.

Ehrhardt, A.A., Grisanti, G.C. and Meyer-Bahlburg, H.F.L. (1977) Prenatal exposure to medroxyprogesterone acetate (MPA) in girls. *Psychoneuroendocrinology*, 2: 391–398.

Gorski, R.A. (1984) Critical role for the medial preoptic area in the sexual differentiation of the brain. In: G.J. De Vries, J.P.C. De Bruin, H.B.M. Uylings and M.A. Corner (Eds.), *Sex Differences in the Brain. The Relation between Structure and Function. Progress in Brain Research*, this volume, Ch. 7.

Goy, R.W. and McEwen, B. (1980) *Sexual Differentiation of the Brain*, MIT Press, Cambridge, MA.

Goy, R.W., Wolf, J.E. and Eisele, S.G. (1977) Experimental female hermaphroditism in rhesus monkeys: anatomical and psychological characteristics. In: J. Money and H. Musaph (Eds.), *Handbook of Sexology*, Elsevier/North-Holland Biomedical Press, Amsterdam, pp. 139–156.

Jacobson, B.D. (1961) Abortion: its prediction and management. Clinical experience with norlutin. *Fertil. Steril.*, 12: 474–485.

Leifer, A.D. and Roberts, D.F. (1971) *Children's Responses to Television Violence*, Institute for Communication Research, Standford, CA.

Maccoby, E.E. and Jacklin, C.N. (1974) *The Psychology of Sex Differences*, Stanford University Press, Stanford, CA.

Meyer-Bahlburg, H.F.L. (1984) Psychoendocrine research on sexual orientation. Current status and future options. In: G.J. De Vries, J.P.C. De Bruin, H.B.M. Uylings and M.A. Corner (Eds.), *Sex Differences in the Brain. The Relation between Structure and Function. Progress in Brain Research*, this volume, Ch. 23.

Meyer-Bahlburg, H.F.L., Grisanti, G.C. and Ehrhardt, A.A. (1977) Prenatal effects of sex hormones on human male behavior: medroxyprogesterone acetate (MPA). *Psychoneuroendocrinology*, 2: 383–390.

Money, J. and Ehrhardt, A.A. (1972) *Man and Woman, Boy and Girl*, Johns Hopkins Press, Baltimore, MD.

Money, J., Ehrhardt, A.A. and Masica, D.N. (1968) Fetal feminization induced by androgen insensitivity in the testicular feminization syndrome: effects on marriage and maternalism. *Johns Hopk. Med. J.*, 123: 105–114.

Reinisch, J.M. (1974) Fetal hormones, the brain, and human sex differences: a heuristic and integrative review of the literature. *Arch. Sex Behav.*, 3: 51–90.

Reinisch, J.M. (1976) Effects of prenatal hormone exposure on physical and psychological development in humans and animals: with a note on the state of the field. In: E.J. Sacher (Ed.), *Hormones, Behavior, and Psychopathology*, Raven, New York, pp. 69–94.

Reinisch, J.M. (1977) Prenatal exposure of human foetuses to synthetic progestin and oestrogen affects personality. *Nature (London)*, 266: 561–562.

Reinisch, J.M. (1981) Prenatal exposure to synthetic progestins increases potential for aggression in humans. *Nature (London)*, 211: 1171–1173.

Reinisch, J.M. (1983) Influence of early exposure to steroid hormones on behavioral development. In: W. Everaerd, C.B. Hindley, A. Bot and J.J. van der Werff ten Bosch (Eds.), *Development in Adolescence: Psychological, Social and Biological Aspects*. Martinus Nijhoff, Boston, MA.

Reinisch, J.M. and Gandelman, R. (1978) Human research in behavioral endocrinology: methodological and theoretical considerations. In: G. Dorner and M. Kawakami (Eds.), *Hormones and Brain Development*, Elsevier/North-Holland Biomedical Press, Amsterdam, pp. 77–86.

Reinisch, J.M. and Sanders, S.A. (1983) Hormonal influences on sexual development and behavior. In: Mark F. Schwartz, A.S. Moraczewski and J.A. Monteleone (Eds.), *Sex and Gender — A Theological and Scientific Inquiry*, The Pope John XXIII Medical-Moral Research and Education Center, St. Louis, MO.

Reyes, F.I., Boroditsky, R.S., Winter, J.S.D. and Faiman, C. (1974) Studies on human sexual development. II. Fetal and maternal serum gonadotropin and sex steroid concentrations. *J. Clin. Endocrinol. Metab.*, 38: 612–617.

Rubin, R.T., Reinisch, J.M. and Haskett, R.F. (1981) Postnatal gonadal steroid effects of human behavior. *Science*, 211: 1318–1324.

Sanders, S.A. and Reinisch, J.M. (in preparation) Sex-role correlates and hierarchy of aggressive response to hypothetical conflict situations.

Sitteri, P. and Wilson, J.D. (1974) Testosterone formation and metabolism during male sexual differentiation in the human embryo. *J. Clin. Endocrinol. Metab.*, 38: 113–125.

Spence, J.T. and Helmreich, R.L. (1978) *Masculinity and Femininity: their Psychological Dimensions, Correlates and Antecedents*, University of Texas Press, Austin, TX.

Taylor, T., Coutts, J.R. and MacNaughton, M.C. (1974) Human foetal synthesis of testosterone from perfused progesterone. *J. Endocrinol.*, 60: 321–326.

Warne, G.L., Faiman, C.M., Reyes, F.I. and Winter J.S. (1977) Studies on human sexual development. V. Concentrations of testosterone 17-hydroxyprogesterone, and progesterone in human amniotic fluid throughout gestation. *J. Clin. Endocrinol. Metab.*, 44: 934–938.

Whalen, R.E. (1974) Sexual differentiation: models, methods, and mechanisms. In: R.C. Friedman, R.M. Richart and R.L. Vande Wiele (Eds.), *Sex Differences in Behavior*, John Wiley, New York.

Wilkins, L. (1960) Masculinization of female fetus due to use of orally given progestins. *J. Am. Med. Assoc.*, 172: 1028–1032.

Witelson, S. (1974) Hemispheric specialization for linguistic and non-linguistic tactual perception using a dichotomous stimulation technique. *Cortex*, 10: 3–7.

Yalom, I.D., Green, R. and Fisk, N. (1973) Prenatal exposure to female hormones: effect on psychosexual development in boys. *Arch. Gen. Psychiat.*, 28: 554–561.

G.J. De Vries et al. (Eds.),
Progress in Brain Research, Vol. 61
© 1984   Elsevier Science Publishers B.V., Amsterdam

Androgens and Gender Role Behaviour in Girls with Congenital Adrenal Hyperplasia (CAH)

FROUKJE M.E. SLIJPER

Department of Child Psychiatry, Sophia Children's Hospital, Gordelweg 160, Rotterdam (The Netherlands)

INTRODUCTION

In the literature (Ehrhardt et al., 1968; Ehrhardt and Baker, 1974) the difference in gender role behaviour between congenital adrenal hyperplasia (CAH) girls and control girls is described as "tomboy" behaviour, by which is meant: expression of physical energy in outdoor games and sports; preference for playing with boys and boy's toys rather than with girls and girl's toys; little interest in marriage, pregnancy, motherhood and caring for young children; a preference for casual clothes (particularly trousers) and a minimal interest in jewelry, makeup and different hairstyles; the wish to be a boy rather than a girl. It is not made clear by the authors how many of these criteria are required in order to be called a "tomboy".

The explanation for tomboy behaviour is sought by Ehrhardt et al. in the prenatal action of the male hormone. According to these authors, the male hormone has an "imprinting effect on the central nervous system", which gives rise to tomboy behaviour. They find evidence for this hypothesis in rough-and-tumble play, which occurs more frequently in the male than in the female in both rhesus monkeys and small children. Young et al. (1965) found that female rhesus monkeys whose mother had received androgen injections in pregnancy exhibited rough-and-tumble play which resembled that of male control monkeys. In both CAH girls and CAH boys Ehrhardt and Baker (1974) found that the "vigorous muscular energy expenditure and intense interest in athletic sports" was greater than in brothers and sisters of CAH children.

The question remains, to what extent are the results of animal experiments relevant for human behaviour? In the first place, tomboy behaviour in girls with excessive male hormone could, in principle, also be attributable to the way in which the parents experience the child's deviant genitalia. CAH girls are born with genitalia resembling those of a boy. Experiments have shown that parents often exhibit significant different behaviour towards a baby who is dressed as a boy and has a boy's name than towards the same baby dressed as a girl and with a girl's name (e.g. Will et al., 1976). Even immediately after delivery Out and Vierhout (1983) found that mothers exhibited significantly more emotional involvement (in handling, smiling, verbally responding to the baby) with a son than with a daughter. At any rate, the deviant genitalia can create doubts in the parents about the child's sex. Secondly, CAH is a chronic sickness. The girls with the salt-loss variant of CAH especially — there are two forms of CAH, with and without salt loss — are frequently and often seriously ill during their first years of life. They experience frequent hospitalizations, checkups, etc. Moreover, these children have to undergo at least two genitalia operations (one immediately after birth and another in adulthood to correct the vagina). Furthermore, all of them have to take hydrocortisone throughout their lives. It is known of chronically sick children that they tend to react to a feeling of insufficiency with compensatory behaviour of a self-assured and bustling kind (Tavormina et al., 1976). One also frequently finds an anxiety for the future in these children which expresses itself in a low level of interest in marriage, motherhood and caring for small children (Schowalter, 1979).

OBSERVATIONS ON CAH CHILDREN

On the basis of the aforementioned problem definitions we decided to compare CAH girls with chronically ill girls in gender role behaviour. Diabetes mellitus as type of chronic illness seems to be the best match for CAH. The sample of CAH girls consisted of 10 girls with the salt-loss variant of CAH and 12 girls with the non-salt-loss variant. The total group of CAH girls ($n = 25$) was compared with a group of healthy girls ($n = 61$), a group of diabetic girls ($n = 26$) and a group of sisters of CAH children ($n = 10$). Similarly CAH boys ($n = 19$) were compared with healthy boys ($n = 56$), with boys suffering from diabetes ($n = 22$) and with brothers of CAH children ($n = 21$). The age range of all groups is from 7 to 17 years.

To measure the gender role behaviour of CAH girls an instrument was recently developed by myself — the Sophia test — which is based on the aspects of gender role behaviour distinguished by Ehrhardt et al. (Slijper, 1983). The values attached by the healthy children to outdoor play, indoor play, playing with boys, girls, dolls and cars, marriage etc. were measured. The children were asked to draw a person and to answer the question: "If I could have chosen between being born a girl or a boy I would have chosen...". The Sophia test was given to a control group of healthy schoolchildren in primary and secondary education (ages 7–17 years).

The purpose of this study of the control group was to construct a scale on which boys were distinguished from girls. The principle for computing the gender score was based on the differences between the number of girls and the number of boys giving a particular response. A higher gender score means more "girlishness" (Fig. 1). The parents of sick children (CAH and diabetes) were interviewed using precoded questions about the children's psychosexual

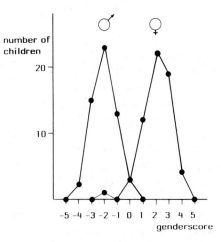

Fig. 1. Distribution of frequencies of control boys ($n = 56$) and girls ($n = 61$) on the Sophia test.

TABLE I

MEAN GENDER SCORE, STANDARD DEVIATION AND SAMPLE SIZE
FOR CONTROL CHILDREN, CHILDREN WITH DIABETES, SICK CHILDREN (CAH + DIABETES)
AND BROTHERS/SISTERS OF CAH CHILDREN, BY SEX

	Boys			Girls		
	Mean score	S.D.	n	Mean score	S.D.	n
Control	− 2.0	1.0	56	+ 2.2	1.1	61
CAH	− 1.6	0.8	19	+ 1.0	1.2	25
Diabetes	− 1.4	1.1	22	+ 1.7	1.0	26
Sick	− 1.5	1.0	41	+ 1.4	1.1	41
Brother/sister CAH	− 1.5	1.5	21	+ 2.2	1.0	10

TABLE II

MEAN GENDER SCORES OF CAH CHILDREN BY SEX AND VARIANT
OF CAH (SALT-LOSS/NON-SALT-LOSS), SAMPLE SIZE, STANDARD DEVIATION,
AND P VALUE ACCORDING TO STUDENT's t TEST

	Variant	n	Mean score	S.D.	P
CAH ♀	Salt-loss	13	0.3	13.2	< 0.001
	Non-salt-loss	11	1.9	5.0	
CAH ♂	Salt-loss	13	− 1.4	10.0	N.S.
	Non-salt-loss	6	− 1.6	4.2	

and psychosocial development. Medical data were also collected, e.g. on the degree of virilization prior to the genitalia operation.

The study showed the following:

Sick girls (both CAH and diabetes) score significantly more towards the boyish side on the Sophia test (see Table I). Thus, the effect on gender role behaviour is not necessarily explained by hormonal action alone; *being sick plays a role.*

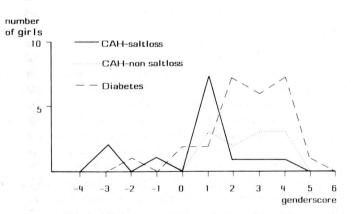

Fig. 2. Frequency distribution of the gender score for CAH salt-loss (*n* = 13), CAH non-salt-loss (*n* = 11) and diabetic girls (*n* = 26).

The CAH girls score significantly more to the boyish side than the diabetic girls (Table I); thus, there is also a specific CAH effect in girls. Closer examination of the data revealed that the *specific CAH effect is fully accounted for by the group of girls with the salt-loss variant of CAH* (Table II); with CAH girls with the non-salt-loss variant scoring about the same as diabetic girls (Fig. 2).

Analysis of variances (ANOVA) of the interview variables revealed that two groups of variables may be linked to the difference between salt-loss and non-salt-loss CAH girls: (a) a group of variables which indicate the seriousness of the CAH as a sickness, salt-loss CAH girls are more seriously ill than non-salt-loss CAH girls; (b) a group of variables which express parents' doubts about the sex of the child, with doubts occurring in the case of salt-loss girls but not in the case of non-salt-loss girls.

In the group of girls with the salt-loss variant of CAH, those girls score most towards the boyish side who were originally registered as boys. These, however, are not the children who are most virilized; the objective degree of virilization does not correlate with the gender score.

CAH and diabetic boys score significantly more towards the girlish side on the Sophia test. Thus, being sick causes boys to score more towards the girlish side.

CAH girls do not differ from control girls in their appreciation of fighting, romping, wild play and outdoor play. However, more parents of a CAH daughter (80%) than of a diabetic daughter (50%) consider that their child is extremely fond of romping.

Diabetic girls differ from control girls in their appreciation of fighting (significantly more positive). CAH boys and diabetic boys differ from control boys in their appreciation of romping with father (significantly more negative). So chronically ill children seem to have more problems with aggressive behaviour than healthy children.

Tomboy behaviour in CAH girls as described by Ehrhardt et al. was not found in the study. It was found, however, that CAH girls differed from diabetic and control girls with respect to the following: (i) appreciation of playing with cars (significantly more positive); (ii) expression of the wish to have been born a boy (significantly more frequent); and (iii) drawing of a man/boy as human figure (significantly more frequent). It is possible that parents' doubts about the sex of their child unconsciously (Daléry et al., 1982) generate doubt and uncertainty in the child about its true sex. This hypothesis points more in the direction of gender identity problems. The first requirement in dealing with these problems is therefore the prevention of doubt on the part of the parents about their child's sex.

CONCLUDING REMARKS

Although it is impossible to separate the influence of androgen hormones from that of psychosocial factors on behaviour, most studies have not even considered environmental influences. Reinisch (1981), for example, found that females and males who were exposed during gestation to synthetic progestins showed a significantly higher potential for physical aggression than did their sex-matched unexposed siblings. However, the higher potential for physical aggression might also be attributed to the mother's fear of losing the baby (progestin is a treatment for imminent abortion). In our study, CAH boys and girls were not different from control children in their "appreciation" of fighting. Diabetic girls, however, showed a significantly more positive appreciation of fighting as compared to control girls. From our study, therefore, it seems more plausible that activation of aggression is related to sickness (e.g. physical interventions, hospitalizations etc.) rather than to prenatal hormonal factors.

A problem in comparing results of different studies is often the difference in method; Reinisch asked her children to react verbally on conflict situations, whereas we asked our children to give verbally their appreciation of fighting! In contrast to Reinisch (1981) Ehrhardt asserts that male sex hormone is not related to aggressive behaviour in the true sense but rather to rough-and-tumble play (Ehrhardt and Money, 1967; Ehrhardt et al., 1968; Ehrhardt and Baker, 1974). Indeed, CAH children and progestin-exposed girls exhibited more romping behaviour in our study than did control children of the same sex.

In our study there is no difference between CAH and normal girls as regards the appreciation of romping. However, more parents of CAH daughters than of diabetic daughters considered that their child is extremely fond of romping. Moreover, there is no difference in gender score between the group of CAH girls of which the parents consider their daughters fond of romping and the group of CAH girls of which the parents do not consider their daughters fond of romping.

The evaluation of the child's behaviour by parents is, therefore, not always the same as the evaluation of the behaviour by the child herself (Ehrhardt interviewed only the parents of CAH girls). As regards romping in boys: our study revealed an opposite result, with CAH and diabetic boys responding more negatively to romping behaviour than control boys. Again our study indicates a relation between romping behaviour and illness in general. Both Money et al. (1955), Money and Ehrhardt (1972) and Ehrhardt and Baker (1974) suppose that only the gender role behaviour of CAH girls is affected, not the gender identity. Our research suggests that there is uncertainty in CAH girls about their gender identity. The instability of the gender identity seems, in turn, to be related to the doubts of the parents about the child's sex.

In conclusion, the hypothesis that behaviour is masculinized by exposure to androgen hormones during early stages of development cannot be supported by this study. Psychosocial factors such as the child being sick, and parents' doubts about the sex of the child seem to have more influence on gender rol behaviour than does androgenic hormone action (i.e. degree of virilization).

REFERENCES

Daléry, J., François, R. and de Villard, R. (1982) Les androgènes de la période fœtale jouent-ils un rôle dans l'identification sexuelle de la fille avec hyperplasie surrénale congénitale? *Arch. Franç. Pédiat.*, 39: 659–662.

Ehrhardt, A.A. and Baker, S.W. (1974) Fetal androgens, human central nervous system differentiation, and behavior sex differences. In: R.C. Friedman, R.M. Richart and R.L. van the Wiele (Eds.), *Sex Differences in Behavior*, Wiley, New York, pp. 33–52.

Ehrhardt, A.A. and Money, J. (1967) Progestin-induced hermaphroditism: I.Q. and psychosexual identity in the study of ten girls. *J. Sex. Res.*, 3: 83–100.

Ehrhardt, A.A., Epstein, R. and Money, J. (1968) Fetal androgens and female gender identity in the early-treated adrenogenital syndrome. *Johns Hopk. Med. J.*, 122: 165–167.

Money, J. and Ehrhardt, A.A. (1972) *Man and Woman, Boy and Girl: the Differentiation and Dimorphism of Gender Identity from Conception to Maturity*, Johns Hopkins University Press, Baltimore, MD.

Money, J., Hampson, J.G. and Hampson, J.L. (1955) Hermaphroditism: recommendations concerning assignment of sex, change of sex and psychological management. *Bull. Johns Hopk. Hosp.*, 98: 43–57.

Out, J.J. and Vierhout, M.E. (1983) *Elective Induction of Labor: A Prospective Obstetrical and Psychological Investigation*, Doctoral Thesis, Dept. of Medical Psychology, Erasmus University Rotterdam, Pasmans, The Hague.

Reinisch, J.M. (1981) Prenatal exposure to synthetic progestins increases potential for aggression in humans. *Science*, 211: 1171–1174.

Schowalter, J.E. (1979) The chronically ill child. In: J.D. Noshpitz (Ed.), *Basic Handbook of Child Psychiatry, Vol. 1*, Basic Books, New York, pp. 432–436.

Slijper, F.M.E. (1983) *Gender Role Behaviour in Girls with Congenital Adrenal Hyperplasia*, Doctoral Thesis, Dept. of Child Psychiatry, Erasmus University Rotterdam.

Tavormina, J.B., Kastner, L.S., Slater, P.M. and Watt, S.L. (1976) Chronically deviant population?. *J. Abnorm. Child Psychol.*, 4: 99–111.

Will, J.A., Self, P.A. and Datan, N. (1976) Maternal behavior and perceived sex of infant. *Am. J. Orthopsychiat.*, 46: 135–140.

Young, W.C., Goy, R.W. and Phoenix, C.H. (1965) Hormones and sexual behavior. In: J. Money (Ed.), *Sex Research, New Developments*, Holt, New York.

G.J. De Vries et al. (Eds.),
Progress in Brain Research, Vol. 61
© 1984 Elsevier Science Publishers B.V., Amsterdam

Sex Differences in Brain Organization for Verbal and Non-Verbal Functions

DOREEN KIMURA and RICHARD A. HARSHMAN

Department of Psychology, University of Western Ontario, London, Ont. (Canada)

INTRODUCTION

Although it is widely accepted that there are sex differences in brain organization related to sexual and parenting behaviours, there is a curious resistance to the idea that the brains of men and women may also differ in ways which affect behaviour outside the narrow reproductive sphere. Thus, well-established sex differences in performance on certain spatial and verbal tasks (Maccoby and Jacklin, 1974) have been repeatedly (sometimes vociferously) interpreted as reflecting sex differences only in early experience, training and social expectations. While we do not deny the importance of such social–environmental influences on male–female behaviours, it also seems reasonable to assume that substantial components of some problem-solving behaviours depend on mechanisms built into the genetic plan of each individual, and that such plans may differ in certain systematic ways between men and women.

Apart from its intrinsic interest, the study of sex differences in brain organization is important because it contributes to the broader question of individual differences in brain organization and abilities. By studying normal variations in brain structure, along with their functional consequences, we can identify functional units more clearly, and perhaps begin to understand how particular biological characteristics constrain or enhance particular functional abilities. Thus when differences in neuropsychological function can be related to salient "marker" characteristics of the individual such as gender or handedness, we can implicitly study the effects of brain variation by comparing appropriate sex or handedness subgroup means.

Studies on intellectual differences between men and women, on the one hand, and the studies on sex differences in brain organization, on the other, are typically done by different researchers, often with different goals and in different settings. Ultimately, however, these two lines of investigation must converge on an integrated understanding of human sex differences. In this paper, we will focus primarily on sex differences in brain organization, and only occasionally attempt to link our results to data on ability differences. We will suggest that the neuropsychological data point to the conclusion that there are indeed sex differences in brain organization, but that the pattern of these differences may be more complex than previously suspected.

The human brain is known to be functionally asymmetrical, in that some verbal functions are typically subserved by the left cerebral hemisphere, whereas some perceptual-spatial functions depend more on the right hemisphere (see Milner, 1974). Previous studies on sex differences in brain organization were concerned primarily with the question of whether or not the degree and/or nature of such asymmetry differed between men and women. These have been reviewed elsewhere (for reviews see: Bryden, 1979, 1982; Harshman and Remington, 1976; McGlone, 1980). The two major sources of evidence have been the different effects of damage to one or other hemisphere in male and female neurological patients (Inglis and Lawson, 1981; Lansdell, 1962; McGlone, 1978), and differences between normal males and females in the perceptual asymmetries assumed to reflect cerebral asymmetry of processing (Harshman et al., 1983; Kimura, 1969; Lake and Bryden, 1976).

The most common method for assessing cerebral lateralization of function in normal persons is the auditory dichotic method. When two different words are presented simultaneously to the two ears, the words arriving at the right ear tend to be reported more accurately than those arriving at the left ear. Because of the predominance of the crossed auditory pathways, the right-ear advantage was assumed to reflect the specialized role of the opposite (left) hemisphere for speech functions (Kimura, 1961). Melodic patterns, in contrast, are generally identified better from the left ear (Kimura, 1964), consistent with the demonstrated importance of the right temporal lobe for processing melodies (Milner, 1962). The visual analogue of this phenomenon usually employs the brief presentation of material, by means of a tachistoscope, to either left cr right visual field, so that the initial input is restricted to one hemisphere of the brain. Under these conditions, and paralleling the dichotic studies, verbal material is reported more accurately from the right visual field, whereas certain types of non-verbal processing are done more accurately from the left visual field (Kimura, 1966; see Bryden, 1982, for a recent review).

Sex differences which may occur in the appearance or degree of such perceptual asymmetries could potentially imply that there are sex differences in the pattern of functional brain asymmetry. These studies have been extensively reviewed elsewhere (Bryden, 1979, 1982; McGlone, 1980), and will only be summarized here. The majority of dichotic studies, in which the sex of the subject was explicitly investigated, have found no significant influence of sex. Harshman et al. (1983) argue, however, that this may be due to the use of small sample sizes, i.e. that the sex effect is modest, and that since there is considerable within-sex variation as well, a large sample is necessary in order to obtain a statistically significant difference. Several larger-sample comparisons have been presented (Bryden, 1979; Harshman et al., 1983) which have found that the right-ear superiority for verbal material is larger and occurs significantly more often in males than in females. The usual interpretation of this finding is that functional brain asymmetry is more marked in males than in females. As we shall argue below, such an interpretation is probably too sweeping. Sex differences in asymmetry for one type of function do not necessarily imply that similar sex differences will be found for other functions (for further arguments on this see Harshman and Remington, 1976; Harshman et al., 1983).

There are very few data on sex differences in non-verbal dichotic lateralization. Several samples studied by Piazza (1980), however, and data from two different samples of Harshman, Hampson, Lundy and Berenbaum (personal communication), indicate that females show *greater* asymmetry than males for melodic patterns or environmental sounds. Taken together with the verbal dichotic results, this would seem to indicate a more complex sex difference in brain patterning than is usually supposed: one sex (males) would appear to be more asymmetrically organized for auditory verbal tasks, with the other sex (females) being more asymmetrically organized for auditory non-verbal tasks. An alternative interpretation, however, is that women have a general tendency to preferentially process auditory material from the left channel, thus reducing the right-ear effect for verbal material, but enhancing the left-ear effect for melodies and environmental sounds.

Studies employing tachistoscopic visual presentation generally show a less consistent reflection of cerebral asymmetry than do dichotic studies, perhaps because this technique is more subject to the complicating effects of extraneous factors such as reading habits (Bryden, 1982). Nevertheless, when sex differences in visual field asymmetry appear, they again suggest that females show less asymmetry in perception (see reviews by Bryden, 1982; McGlone, 1980).

Caution is necessary in interpreting male–female differences involving perceptual asymmetry, since such differences could arise even when males and females did not differ in brain asymmetry. For example, males and females might differ in the part of a given hemisphere (anterior or posterior) which is specialized for processing the stimuli (Kimura, 1983). Alternatively, they might differ in their approach to a given task, such that if females used a more verbal method of encoding and recalling tachistoscopically presented "non-verbal" stimuli, they would show reduced left-field superiorities. Of course, these behavioural differences might still reflect a sex difference in brain organization, but the interpretation of differences in perceptual asymmetry as reflecting differences in brain asymmetry is clearly not the only possible one.

Another possible factor contributing to sex-linked differences involves the commissural connections between hemispheres. For example, deLacoste-Utamsing and Holloway (1982) have recently reported that the posterior half of the corpus callosum is thicker in females than in males. In functional terms, assuming this means more fibre connections between the posterior part of the hemispheres, it is possible that verbal stimuli presented to the left field or ear and exciting the right hemisphere may, by means of efficient callosal transmission, be more readily processed by the left hemisphere in females than in males. This could reduce the asymmetry perceptually apparent between ears or visual fields in females, without necessarily implying a lesser degree of brain asymmetry. Lansdell and Davie's (1972) report that the presence of a massa intermedia (connecting the thalami) is associated with altered levels of non-verbal function in males but not females, further underscores the possibility that anatomical facts do not in themselves provide the final functional story. In this context, the lesser anatomical asymmetry in the posterior temporal region of the female cerebral cortex (Wada et al., 1975), acquires significance because we can relate it to a functional correlate, the apparently lesser role of this region in speech functions in females (Kimura, 1983; and see below).

In contrast to studies which investigate perceptual asymmetries, the evidence from one type of motor asymmetry, hand preference, does not favour a more asymmetrical brain organization in males. Thus, not only do females show a higher incidence of right-hand preference than males, but within right-handers, females show a stronger favouring of the right hand than do males (Annett, 1980). Assuming that hand preference is less dependent than are perceptual functions on the posterior systems (where asymmetry may possibly be attenuated by increased callosal fibres), one might expect motor asymmetry patterns to be stronger in females than are perceptual asymmetry patterns.

Evidence from neurological cases for lesser functional asymmetry of brain organization in females is not extensive. Early reports by Lansdell and Urbach (1965) suggested that differential effects of left and right temporal lobectomy on verbal and non-verbal intelligence respectively, appeared in males but not in females. Lansdell and Urbach used as a measure the discrepancy between scores on the verbal IQ and performance IQ scales of the Wechsler Adult Intelligence Scale (WAIS) (Wechsler, 1955). This measure has subsequently been used in other confirmatory studies (Inglis and Lawson, 1981; McGlone, 1978), since it reduces the problems of comparing across individuals with quite disparate IQ levels. It is unfortunately ambiguous, however, since a significant discrepancy between the two scales may exist within a variety of patterns: one scale is depressed, while the other is not (usually assumed to be the case); both scales are depressed but one more than the other; or one scale is enhanced and the other is unaffected or depressed. All such patterns might indicate sex differences in brain organization, but the nature of such organization would not be the same in each case. Given the already heterogeneous nature of the verbal and performance scales, a measure which merely contrasts those scales is likely to be minimally informative. Much more convincing (but very difficult to achieve), would be a comparison of unilaterally lesioned patients with a matched control group, on the verbal and performance tests separately. McGlone (1980) attempted to do this but the high mean IQ of her normal control group makes the comparison with the patient group difficult to interpret. The problems of what constitutes an appropriate control group are discussed later in the paper in the section on intelligence test data.

Other attempts to make inferences about lateralization of verbal or non-verbal function have employed direct comparisons of the scores of males and females after unilateral damage (Kimura, 1983; McGlone, 1978), but it has been pointed out (Kimura, 1983) that this kind of comparison does not rule out the possibility that some part of the differences observed in such comparisons may be due to enhancement of abilities above the normal in one of the groups.

In addition, recent data on patients have revealed another important but complicating factor of differential intrahemispheric functional organization (Kimura, 1983); i.e. that the left anterior region is of particular importance for speech function in females. Previous reports of a lack of significant intellectual decrement in females with unilateral lesions may therefore have to be re-interpreted, in that the critical anterior region may simply have been unaffected in many of the cases included.

When, to all the above difficulties of interpretation, is added the complication of differing subject samples across studies (in age, etiology, etc.), it is perhaps not surprising that few unequivocal conclusions concerning the lateralization of verbal or non-verbal composite intelligence functions are currently possible. Some data will be presented in the present paper which it is hoped may reduce some of the ambiguity inherent in both the normal and the neurological studies. First, a short review of the findings relating incidence of aphasia and apraxia to locus of lesion within the hemisphere will be presented, followed by a more detailed description of the effects of unilateral lesions on verbal and non-verbal intelligence tests in non-aphasic patients. Finally, an in-depth consideration of data from our studies on manual asymmetry in normal subjects will be undertaken.

SEX DIFFERENCES IN INTRAHEMISPHERIC ORGANIZATION

The incidence of aphasia has been reported to be higher after left-hemisphere damage in males than in females (McGlone, 1977; Kimura, 1980). Although this finding has been interpreted as indicating a more bilateral organization of speech functions in women than in men (McGlone, 1977), a crucial factor underlying this sex difference appears to be a differential organization of speech functions within the left hemisphere (Kimura, 1983). In females, speech appears to be critically dependent on the left anterior cerebral region, with left posterior damage rarely producing aphasia; in contrast, aphasia in males is produced equally often from anterior or posterior damage (Table I). An equivalent statement can be made for

TABLE I

INCIDENCE OF APHASIA AND APRAXIA
IN RESTRICTED LEFT-HEMISPHERE LESIONS

Site of damage	Incidence of aphasia		
	Total sample	Aphasic (N)	Non-aphasic (N)
Anterior lesions			
Males	15	6 (40%)	9
Females	13	8 (62%)	5
Posterior lesions			
Males	34	14 (41%)	20
Females	19	2 (11%)	17

χ^2 (sex $\times$ locus $\times$ aphasia) = 5.6006, df = 1, P < 0.02

	Incidence of manual apraxia		
	Total sample	Apraxic (N)	Non-apraxic (N)
Anterior lesions			
Males	12	3 (25%)	9
Females	10	6 (60%)	4
Posterior lesions			
Males	31	13 (42%)	18
Females	17	1 (6%)	16

χ^2 (sex $\times$ locus $\times$ apraxia) = 9.3431, df = 1, P < 0.01

manual apraxia, a disorder of movement in which, although the limb is mobile, specified movements cannot be produced or imitated (Liepmann, 1908; Kimura and Archibald, 1974). Since, with our population of vascular accidents, restricted brain damage more often affects the posterior than the anterior regions, it is probable that the lower incidence of aphasia in females with left-hemisphere damage is related simply to the relative sparing of the critical anterior region (Kimura, 1983). This finding also has relevance for the comparison of other test results after unilateral damage in males and females, as will be discussed in the following section on word fluency.

Oral word fluency

The influence of differential intrahemispheric organization between males and females can be seen on a verbal task which measures word fluency. Word fluency is usually defined as the ability to generate words within a specified category or under particular constraints (usually, beginning with a particular letter) (Thurstone and Thurstone, 1941), and is often reported to be superior in females (see Maccoby, 1966). Damage to the left anterior or central regions of the brain impairs performance on both an oral (Benton, 1968) and a written (Jones-Gotman and Milner, 1977; Milner, 1967) version of word fluency.

Data for one version of this task, the generating of as many "d" words as possible in 60 sec *, are shown in Table II. It can be seen that left-hemisphere damage, even in non-aphasic patients, depresses performance on this task. Consistent with the earlier reports (Benton, 1968; Milner, 1967), this is particularly true of left anterior damage. However, the

TABLE II
ORAL FLUENCY IN PATIENTS WITH RESTRICTED LESIONS
(number of "d" words/min)

	N	Left damage	(S.D.)	N	Right damage	(S.D.)	P *
Anterior lesions	15	4.9	(4.6)	13	10.1	(5.1)	< 0.02
(non-aphasics)	9	7.0	(4.7)				
Posterior lesions	37	8.6	(6.5)	21	12.8	(4.6)	< 0.01
(non-aphasics)	28	10.9	(5.8)				
Anterior, female	7	4.0	(4.5)	5	10.8	(2.3)	< 0.01
(non-aphasics)	3	8.0	(3.6)				
Anterior, male	8	5.6	(4.9)	8	9.6	(6.4)	N.S.
(non-aphasics)	6	6.5	(5.5)				
Posterior, female	16	11.4	(6.2)	12	13.2	(5.1)	N.S.
(non-aphasics)	14	13.0	(4.8)				
Posterior, male	21	6.5	(6.1)	9	12.2	(4.1)	< 0.01
(non-aphasics)	14	8.9	(6.1)				

* All comparisons are based on two-tailed t tests.

consequences of left anterior damage in females are more evident inasmuch as left posterior damage has a relatively mild effect on oral fluency in females (as compared with right-hemisphere damage). Overall, it indeed appears that women perform better at this task than do men but one must caution that the differential effects of anterior and posterior damage in this patient sample, make this result difficult to interpret. However, there is no suggestion that right-hemisphere damage results in lower scores in women than in men, i.e., that oral word fluency is more bilaterally organized in women. This is somewhat at variance with a recent report that in women injection of sodium amytal into the right hemisphere was as disruptive of word fluency as injection into the left hemisphere, whereas for men performance was impaired only after injection into the left hemisphere (McGlone and Fox, 1982). We do not see such a pattern in the data of Table II, where a mild deficit after right anterior damage is present in both males and females. One can only conjecture that either the cases chosen for the amytal study were atypical (the sample was small and of course highly selected, consisting of 5 males and 6 females), or that the amytal injection somehow affected the critical functional regions to differing degrees in the two sexes.

Our oral fluency data after lesions are thus in fair agreement with the findings for aphasia and apraxia, in as much as they indicate that anterior-posterior locus in the left hemisphere interacts with the sex of the subject, and in providing little evidence for more bilateral organization in females than in males. However, an examination of other verbal tasks suggests a somewhat different organization. This will appear in the analysis of intelligence test data described below.

* The collection of oral fluency data was a joint project of J. McGlone and D. Kimura. In addition, D. Kimura carried out the patient classifications, and was responsible for the data analysis reported in this paper.

EFFECTS OF UNILATERAL LESIONS ON VERBAL
AND NON-VERBAL INTELLIGENCE

One of the chief difficulties in making inferences about hemispheric specialization of function from IQ data is the uncertainty about what constitutes an appropriate comparison group. Comparison of patients who have suffered unilateral lesions through strokes or tumours with normals of equivalent age is rarely satisfactory, even when the normals are only average in intelligence. This is because normal subjects and unilaterally lesioned patients are likely to be different in ways other than the presence of CNS damage, and these variables might affect various components of the IQ differently. For example, the general health of a neurological patient is likely to be poorer than an ambulatory normal, and this will affect performance on a variety of tests (particularly timed tests). In addition, patients, but not normals, are likely to be on some kind of medication, and normal subjects are not selected from the community in the same way as patients. The first author had fortuitously been involved in a research project studying the effects of carotid endarterectomy on intellectual performance *, and had thereby collected IQ data on a group of patients who had minimal CNS disturbance. These were 36 patients (18 males, 18 females) who, despite transient ischaemic attacks, showed no residual neurological signs nor any infarcts which were visible on a CT scan. For the reasons outlined above, these made ideal control patients, especially because whatever selection factors operated to bring patients to this institution were the same as in our unilateral lesion group. 24 of the 36 subsequently underwent carotid endarterectomy. The data for these 36 patients before surgery is used as the control data, against which to compare the effects of residual unilateral lesions in non-aphasic patients, about two-thirds of whom suffered from strokes.

The mean age of the control group (64.0 years) was significantly higher than for the patient group (47.7 years), but age corrections are standard on the Wechsler Adult Intelligence Scales (Wechsler, 1955), which formed the data base. The verbal and performance scale IQ data on these two major groupings (control, unilateral lesion) are presented in Table III. It is apparent that the control group means are very near the estimated IQ levels

TABLE III

IQ DATA * ON PATIENTS WITH UNILATERAL PATHOLOGY COMPARED WITH CONTROLS

	N	Verbal IQ *	(S.D.)	Performance IQ *	(S.D.)
Control patients	36	101.7		104.0	
Females	18	100.9	(10.4)	103.6	(13.3)
Males	18	102.4	(11.5)	104.4	(9.2)
Non-aphasic patients with unilateral lesions	270	100.0		95.5 †	
Left lesions, female	62	99.6	(11.9)	99.4	(13.7)
Left lesions, males	72	96.8 **	(15.2)	97.5 ***	(14.1)
Right lesions, female	63	98.8	(13.4)	94.1 ***	(14.0)
Right lesions, males	73	104.6	(15.0)	91.5 †	(18.5)

* These scores have a built-in age adjustment.
** $P < 0.05$ compared with like-sex control score, one-tailed test.
*** $P < 0.01$ compared with like-sex control score, one-tailed test.
† $P < 0.001$ compared with like-sex control score, one-tailed test.

* That study was done in collaboration with Dr. G. Ferguson, Dr. V. Hachinski, and Mr. Joe Casey.

for North American normals (Mattarazzo, 1972). All comparisons between lesioned patients and normal controls are tested for significance with one-tailed *t* tests, with the rejection region placed in the tail corresponding to impaired performance in the patient sample. Because the variance of the patient group was often significantly larger than that of the controls, the normal pooled-variance *t* test was not employed. Instead, a separate-variance version of the *t* test was used (see Nie et al., 1975) which provides a more sensitive test of differences when variances are highly unequal.

The unilateral lesion group (disregarding for the moment the side of lesion and the sex of the patient), is quite similar to the control group in verbal IQ, but is significantly inferior in performance IQ. This is compatible with a wealth of literature suggesting that the non-verbal "fluid" intellectual abilities are generally more affected by central nervous system damage than are the more overlearned verbal abilities (Hebb, 1942). Of course, the mean IQ values obtained in any neurological sample will vary greatly depending on etiology, socio-economic status, whether or not aphasic patients are included, etc. The patients in the present series were chosen almost exclusively on the basis of a unilateral lesion, but only data from non-aphasic patients are presented, since the verbal IQ was not administered to aphasics.

This general picture of depressed performance IQ and unaffected verbal IQ changes, however, when we examine the effects of the side of the lesion, and the sex of the subject. These data are also shown in Table III, where the unilateral lesion group as a whole is broken down into left- and right-sided lesions, males and females. Left-sided lesions in our sample have the effect of slightly reducing both verbal and non-verbal intelligence, and this is despite the fact that aphasic patients are excluded. Were they included, all scores would decline still further. Curiously, this global depression after left-sided damage is significant only for males. It suggests that some aspects of "non-verbal" task performance may be mediated by the left hemisphere in males, a possibility that will be pursued in the following section in which we view the subtests in more detail.

Right-sided lesions, in contrast, impair only the non-verbal skills, or the performance IQ, and this is true for both males and females, though perhaps not to an equivalent degree. Specifically, depression of the overall verbal IQ in females with right-hemisphere lesions, is small and is not statistically significant, in contrast to earlier findings (McGlone, 1980). The normal control group in the McGlone study, however, had an IQ well above average. Thus, the suggestion (Kimura, 1983) that the higher verbal IQ found after right-hemisphere lesions in males than in females does not permit the unequivocal inference that the verbal IQ is depressed in the females, is pertinent here.

It is perhaps pertinent to note that we also see, in Table III, the usual larger verbal-minus-performance discrepancy in males after right-hemisphere lesions than in females, and this sex difference is significant, confirming earlier reports. However, this discrepancy difference fails to reveal some of the more interesting findings which emerge when we compare our patient groups with appropriate controls, and in the past, this type of comparison has sometimes led to inappropriate conclusions. As it happens, even the verbal and performance IQ scores themselves are probably too conglomerate to be maximally informative, but some interesting selective effects are seen when we examine the subtests, particularly of the verbal scale.

Verbal subtests

Table IV shows a breakdown by subtests of the *age-corrected* scaled scores of the verbal scale (Wechsler, 1955, 1958). It will be recalled that left-sided damage in males affected the overall verbal IQ, but examination of the subtest scores indicates that this effect is particu-

TABLE IV

WAIS VERBAL IQ SUBTESTS, AGE-CORRECTED SCORES

	Controls		Left lesions (non-aphasics)				Right lesions			
	Females	Males	Females		Males		Females		Males	
	$(\bar{X})$	$(\bar{X})$	$\bar{X}$	P	$\bar{X}$	P	$\bar{X}$	P	$\bar{X}$	P
Comprehension	10.33	10.41	9.82	0.27	9.57	0.14	10.02	0.35	11.25	0.87
Arithmetic	9.94	11.29	9.15	0.12	10.33	0.11	9.32	0.17	10.81	0.26
Similarities	9.72	9.71	10.08	0.68	9.44	0.38	9.81	0.54	10.21	0.73
Digit span	11.50	11.47	10.60	0.10	8.76**	0.000	10.05*	0.02	10.74	0.12
Vocabulary	11.44	10.71	10.44*	0.015	9.20*	0.015	10.09**	0.005	10.91	0.63

"Information" subtest was not included because it had not been routinely administered to the control group. All P values are based on one-tailed t tests comparing each patient group with like-sex controls.

  * $P < 0.05$.
 ** $P < 0.01$.

larly marked for two of these tests — Vocabulary and Digit Span. In females, these same tests tend to be affected by left-sided lesions, despite the fact that the overall verbal IQ was not significantly impaired. While it is not completely clear what functions are measured by the digit span and vocabulary tasks, both might be thought to involve aspects of verbal memory; this suggests that it might be interesting, in future studies, to compare male and female patterns of impairment on other memory tests, such as the Wechsler Memory Scale. However, vocabulary and digit span are not at all synonymous, since the former test requires a definition of words, and thus seems to tap long-term "semantic" memory, whereas the latter test requires the repeating back of number sequences, and thus would depend heavily on immediate memory span. Since these two quite different verbal abilities were both affected by left-sided damage, whereas other verbal tests (such as Similarities, which requires finding a common characteristic between two named items), showed little or no effect (in this non-aphasic sample), a search for specific verbal functions might prove to be more informative than the composite-score approach in defining the functions of brain regions.

Of equal interest is the finding that in females, Vocabulary and Digit Span not only were the tests most sensitive to left-hemisphere damage, but also were the most impaired by right-hemisphere damage, when compared with the female control group. Furthermore, the females' bilateral pattern of impairment differs significantly from the more unilateral pattern exhibited by the males: both vocabulary and digit span show a highly significant sex-by-side interaction when a two-way analysis of variance is used to compare the means of the 4 clinical subgroups. Since this latter comparison does not involve the control subjects, it could not be attributed to unrepresentatively high female control scores on these tests, and thus it further strengthens the inference that the functions underlying these two subtests are differently represented in male and female brains.

It should be emphasized that the claim being made here for bilaterality of representation in females for some of the verbal subtest functions is *not* based on a lack of impairment after left-hemisphere damage. Rather, it is based on a significant decrement in performance after both left- and right-hemisphere damage. Thus, the question whether critical brain regions (e.g., anterior) remain undamaged in females as compared with males, does not enter into this picture. Further analyses comparing the effects of more restricted lesions on verbal and non-verbal subtests will of course be carried out in future, when a sufficient sample size has been achieved to lend reliability to the data.

432

Performance subtests

Table V shows the data for the performance IQ subtests. It will be recalled from Table III that right-hemisphere lesions affected the performance IQ in both males and females, and this effect appears from Table V data to be general across all subtests.

TABLE V

WAIS PERFORMANCE IQ SUBTESTS, AGE-CORRECTED SCORES

| | Controls | | Left lesions (non-aphasics) | | | | Right lesions | | | |
| | Females | Males | Females | | Males | | Females | | Males | |
	$(\bar{X})$	$(\bar{X})$	$\bar{X}$	P	$\bar{X}$	P	$\bar{X}$	P	$\bar{X}$	P
Pict. complet.	10.56	11.0	9.89	0.14	10.15	0.07	9.33*	0.03	9.58**	0.01
Block des.	10.17	10.59	10.19	0.51	9.92	0.21	9.05	0.06	8.03**	0.005
Pict. arrang.	10.39	10.63	9.29	0.12	9.58	0.06	9.00	0.07	8.60**	0.005
Obj. assemb.	10.00	10.00	9.97	0.49	9.43	0.17	8.77	0.10	7.74**	0.001

"Digit Symbol" subtest is not included because it was not routinely administered to the control group. All P values are based on one-tailed t tests comparing each patient group with like-sex controls.
* $P < 0.05$.
** $P < 0.01$.

In males, left-hemisphere lesions also impair performance IQ (Table III), but when results are broken down into the subtests, all comparisons with controls are non-significant, due perhaps to the lower reliability of the individual subtest scores. Comparisons are therefore risky, so we will only note that there are fairly consistent trends suggesting impairment in males and, to a lesser extent, in females as well: in every case but one the left-lesioned subjects perform below the level of the same-sex controls. These performance scale data suggest less selective deficits after unilateral lesions than do the verbal data. There is no indication that females are more bilaterally organized for the performance functions measured; in fact, if anything, these data would suggest that males were more bilaterally organized for these tasks. One must caution, however, that when the 4 clinical means are compared by two-way analysis of variance, none of the performance IQ subtests show sex-by-side interactions even approaching significance ($P > 0.35$ in all cases), so that there is little statistical support for inferences of sex differences on these tasks. We should note, also, that WAIS "performance" tasks are not particularly good measures of spatial ability. They are almost certainly cognitively complex or "impure", and thus might involve both hemispheres because several different lateralized functions are required for correct solution.

In summary, the intelligence subtests differ from basic speech, praxic and fluency functions in that the former do not show the same clear hemispheric asymmetry of control in either males or females as emerges in a task like oral word fluency (Table II). Rather, verbal tasks like vocabulary and digit span, although clearly affected by left-hemisphere damage, are also impaired, in females, by right-hemisphere damage. For "non-verbal" tests such as picture arrangement and picture completion no indication has been found that females are more bilaterally organized than males. Taken together, the data indicate that a much more focussed analysis of both "verbal" and "non-verbal" functions is required, before one can conclude that such functions are more asymmetrically represented in male than in female brains.

ASYMMETRY IN HAND MOVEMENTS

The phenomenon of hand preference, which is almost universal amongst humans, and apparently exists also for some animal species (Warren et al., 1967), is considered another reflection of asymmetric hemispheric control of behaviour. The actual neural mechanism that determines which hand will be preferred for many daily activities is unknown, though it has been suggested that it may be related to the systems underlying manual praxis (Kimura and Humphreys, 1981). Generally, the incidence of mixed or left-handedness is higher in males than in females (Annett, 1970), and even within right-handers, females are more strongly right-handed on certain manual skill tasks than are males (Annett, 1980). It will be recalled (Table I) that some manual skills, subsumed under the general label "praxis", are critically dependent on the left hemisphere. If hand preference were to some extent based on manual praxis control, it might explain why females are highly asymmetrical in hand preference, since they show a very sharp asymmetry in praxic control, with performance severely depressed after left anterior lesions and essentially unaffected after right anterior lesions (Kimura, 1983).

Manual and oral movement control systems are very closely tied to speech control in both males and females (Kimura, 1982), and so one might expect any motor manifestations of speech in normal persons to be lateralized as well. Certain hand movements which occur during speaking might thus be expected to be just as asymmetrical in females as in males. When people speak, they make more hand movements than when silently engrossed in a non-motor problem-solving task, and moreover, during speaking, a unique kind of movement described as a "free movement" (Kimura, 1973) occurs with great frequency. This is a movement — typically called a "gesture" — in which the hand and/or arm moves through space without either touching any object, or coming to rest. Such free movements can be contrasted with another major category, self-touching movements, which are not unique to speech, that is, they happen also when people are not speaking. Right-handers, with presumed left-hemisphere speech representation, make more of the free movements with the right hand than with the left (Table VI). However, no significant sex differences have been found in the magnitude of this right-hand effect, even when we combine the data from all three of the studies reported in Kimura (1973). A proportional measure ($R/R + L$) of right-hand movements to total movements is used, such that the larger the number, the greater the right-hand preference. Right-handed females show a greater tendency than right-handed males to prefer the right hand, for both of the activities recorded, but the difference between sexes is not significant. The male–female difference in hand bias in the present study remains fairly constant across the two types of activity. In a replication of this study in natural conversational settings (Dalby et al., 1980), essentially the same results were obtained except

TABLE VI

SPONTANEOUS HAND MOVEMENTS DURING SPEAKING

	N	Number of free movements			Number of self-contacts		
		Left mean	Right mean	$\dfrac{R}{R+L}$	Left mean	Right mean	$\dfrac{R}{R+L}$
Females	33	1.2	4.9	0.80	3.5	4.2	0.55
Males	32	1.2	3.2	0.73	4.7	3.7	0.44
F − M				0.07			0.11

that males showed a non-significant trend for greater right-hand preference than did females. However, because it was a naturalistic study, no specification could be made that nothing be held in either hand, that the environment be symmetrical, etc., which are possibly important determinants of which hand will move. In general, then, the right-hand bias for gesturing while speaking is no more marked in males than in females, in contrast to the studies reviewed (above) on perceptual asymmetry.

There is another way in which manual asymmetry may shed light on sex differences in brain organization, and that is, that hand use preference may shift with the degree of verbal or non-verbal processing required on a task. Thus the basic right-hand preference which may be dependent on left-hemisphere praxic control, can be modulated by which hemisphere is primary in directing a task. In a pilot study of asymmetry in directed hand movements during problem solving, Kilbreath (1979) compared the degree of right-hand preference exhibited by normal persons during tasks which varied along the verbal–non-verbal dimension. On the assumption that verbal tasks would engage the left hemisphere more than would spatial tasks, Kilbreath compared the hand movements made in manipulation of plastic letters during a verbal task (anagrams), with those made during the assembling of pieces on a two-dimensional non-verbal task (jig-saw puzzle) and on a presumptively more strongly spatial non-verbal task (soma cube). She found that the degree of right-hand preference did decline overall from the verbal to the spatial task (Table VII), with females again showing a general

TABLE VII

MEAN NUMBER OF LEFT AND RIGHT HAND MOVEMENTS ON 3 TASKS *

	Left hand	Right hand	$\dfrac{R}{R+L}$
Females (N = 10)			
Anagrams	13.4	39.9	0.75
Jigsaw puzzle	25.9	57.2	0.69
Soma cube	21.1	41.6	0.66
Males (N = 10)			
Anagrams	16.4	35.0	0.68
Jigsaw puzzle	24.0	51.2	0.68
Soma cubes	25.9	39.7	0.61

* Modified from Kilbreath (1979).

trend to prefer the right hand more than did the males. Moreover, the right-hand preference declined equivalently (or the left-hand preference increased equivalently) in males and females, from the verbal to the spatial tasks. Thus the presumptively increasing involvement of the right hemisphere from the verbal to the spatial tasks was reflected in a shift to left-hand usage in both sexes, and suggested that the shift in cerebral hemispheric control during these tasks was roughly equivalent in females and in males, at least by the time it manifested itself in overt motor control.

This study was promising, but the sample sizes were small, and the changes in hand preference from one task to another were difficult to interpret because the manipulanda varied greatly. Moreover, the hand movements were not described or scored in detail, and there was no unequivocally "neutral" task (i.e., one in which one could plausibly assume the absence of any hemispheric bias) included in the planning. Consequently, a more thorough study along the same lines, but which solved some of these methodological problems, was done by Hampson and Kimura (1984). The same manipulanda were used for all verbal and non-verbal tasks — 1-in. cubes. In most tasks, 25 of these cubes had to be arranged in a 5 × 5 pattern, with the tasks ranging from a highly verbal pattern (crossword puzzle) to a highly spatial task (construction of a design which had to be imaginally rotated from a model). There was also a "neutral" baseline task to enable the measurement of shifts from neutral in either a left-hand or a right-hand preference direction.

Subjects again showed an overall right-hand preference, but also showed a leftward shift for non-verbal tasks and a rightward shift for verbal tasks (Fig. 1). Again, no significant sex differences were evident in these shifts. We do not, however, rule out the possibility that sex differences in such shifts may occur. Our own IQ data, for example, might predict that a vocabulary-related task would be less likely to produce a shift in hand usage in females than in males, because it appears to depend on both hemispheres to a greater degree than in males.

In general, it appears that if one studies normal motor asymmetry, as compared to studies on perceptual asymmetry, the right-hand preference which generally obtains is as great for

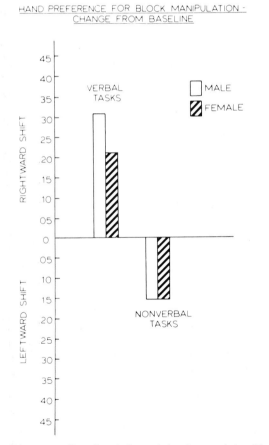

Fig. 1. Shifts in hand usage from a neutral baseline, during verbal and non-verbal problem-solving (modified from Hampson and Kimura, 1984).

females as for males, in agreement with Annett (1980). The shifts in hand usage during problem-solving tasks, because they are assumed to reflect differential involvement of right or left hemispheres, provide information different from hand preference per se. Such shifts have not as yet shown significant differences between males and females.

CONCLUSIONS

Our study confirms that there are undoubtedly sex differences in brain organization for a variety of human abilities. However, these sex differences cannot be depicted simply in terms of male brains tending to be more asymmetrically organized than female brains. Our data indicate that females are just as asymmetrically organized as males for systems controlling speech and related motor praxic function, as well as on other verbal functions such as oral fluency. If anything, females appear to possess somewhat more focally organized systems within the left hemisphere for such functions than do males. However, for other verbal tasks (in our study, vocabulary and digit span), there appear to be sex differences of another kind; these tasks are affected by damage to *either* hemisphere in females, but are affected only by left-hemisphere damage in males. We do not know what the precise functional requirements of these two tasks are, but they apparently differ from basic speech tasks used to test aphasia and from oral word fluency. Such findings must direct us to look at human abilities less globally, at least in relation to neuropsychological systems, than we have done in the past.

Of special interest for the bilateral vs. unilateral argument is the trend for some non-verbal functions to be impaired by both right- and left-hemisphere damage in males. The performance IQ was significantly impaired after left-hemisphere damage in males (in non-aphasic patients), which raises the possibility that there are abilities in each sex which are bilaterally represented, but that the nature of these diffusely represented abilities is not the same in males and females. Such an interpretation would certainly be consonant with the rather different evolutionary history of men and women. Alternative interpretations of the performance IQ data in terms of task complexity or "impurity", however, need also to be considered.

The reader should note that we have not discussed the possibility that functions which are not affected by damage to either hemisphere are also more diffusely represented in the brain, an inference which has commonly been made in the past. This is certainly a logically acceptable conclusion, but it needs to be adopted more cautiously, since there are plausible alternative explanations, e.g. that the critical brain regions for the task in question happen to be minimally affected in most of the cases sampled, or that the function is so heterogeneous ("impure") that it partakes of several definable neural systems operating in each hemisphere, etc. Were there in fact functions which are not significantly changed by even extensive damage to either hemisphere, it would be reasonable to conclude that their organization is not only diffuse but also highly redundant. While such abilities may exist, it is difficult at present to conceptualize their organization, or to see what function such redundancy would serve, given that some very important abilities are quite focally organized. Nevertheless, this possibility cannot be ruled out.

Our study, taken together with previous work, strongly suggests that we need to look at sex differences in brain organization for abilities in a much more refined way than we have in the past. "Verbal" and "non-verbal" are imprecise tags for a conglomerate of abilities each of which can be quite differently affected, even by loosely defined damage to one or other hemisphere of the brain. A more precise delineation is needed of the type of function involved, and to a significant extent, the kind of analysis we have presented here, in terms of differential hemispheric effects on different tests, is one avenue to making such a delineation. At the same time, it is important to emphasize that a more focussed neuroanatomical approach than we have presented in this paper, is also desirable. Preliminary analyses indicate that even crude anterior-posterior classifications yield sex differences in brain organization, at least as reliable and interesting as left hemisphere–right hemisphere comparisons. Although a finer-grained neuroanatomical analysis was beyond the scope of this paper, the relative precision with which brain lesions in living humans can now be defined will unquestionably add greatly to our information on human sex differences in the future. Thus we regard the findings of the present study as merely scratching the surface of a very exciting field of research, which, however fraught with methodological difficulties, will undoubtedly be productive of new insights into brain–behaviour relations.

SUMMARY

Some evidence bearing on sex differences in functional brain asymmetry is reviewed, and some new data presented. It is suggested on the basis of clinical data, that basic speech and praxic motor function are at least as unilaterally (and probably even more focally) organized in women as in men. Some additional verbal functions also follow this pattern, e.g. word fluency, but others (e.g. vocabulary) do not. Instead, the latter appear to be more bilaterally represented in females than in males. "Non-verbal" intellectual functions, perhaps because they are assessed by less pure tests, do not show such striking patterns but there is a suggestion that these also may be somewhat bilaterally organized, in both sexes. When brain organization is assessed by non-clinical methods, perceptual asymmetries are sometimes less striking in females than in males, whereas motor asymmetries appear similar in both sexes. In general, it appears that a more focussed approach to the study of sex differences in brain organization, both in terms of specificity of function examined, and in specificity of neuroanatomical locus, will provide better answers to the questions of individual differences in brain organization.

ACKNOWLEDGEMENTS

This research was supported by grants to D. Kimura from the Natural Sciences and Engineering Research Council and from the Medical Research Council, Ottawa, Canada, and to Richard Harshman from the Natural Sciences and Engineering Research Council.

We are grateful to Elizabeth Hampson for comments on the manuscript, and to Rob Faust and Gary Wood for assistance in data analysis.

REFERENCES

Annett, M. (1970) The growth of manual preference and speed. *Br. J. Psychol.*, 61: 545–558.
Annett, M. (1980) Sex differences in laterality — meaningfulness versus reliability. *Behav. Brain Sci.*, 3: 227–228.
Benton, A. (1968) Differential behavioural effects in frontal lobe disease. *Neuropsychologia*, 6: 53–60.

Bryden, M.P. (1979) Evidence for sex-related differences in cerebral organization. In: M. Wittig and A.C. Peterson (Eds.), *Sex-Related Differences in Cognitive Functioning*, Academic Press, New York, pp. 121–143.

Bryden, M.P. (1982) *Laterality: Functional Asymmetry in the Intact Brain*, Academic Press, New York, 315 pp.

Dalby, J.T., Gibson, D., Grossi, V. and Schneider, R.D. (1980) Lateralized hand gesture during speech. *J. Mot. Behav.*, 12: 292–297.

deLacoste-Utamsing, C. and Holloway, R.L. (1982) Sexual dimorphism in the human corpus callosum. *Science*, 216: 1431–1432.

Hampson, E. and Kimura, D. (1984) Hand movement asymmetries during verbal and nonverbal tasks. *Can. J. Psychol.*, 38: 102–125.

Harshman, R.A. and Remington, R. (1976) Sex, language and the brain. Part I. A review of the literature on adult sex differences in lateralization. *UCLA Working Papers Phonet.*, 31: 86–103 (Univ. Microfilms, Ann Arbor, No. 10,085).

Harshman, R.A., Remington, R. and Krashen, S.D. (1983) Sex, language and the brain. Part II. Evidence from dichotic listening for adult sex differences in verbal lateralization. *Dept. Psychol. Res. Bull.*, No. 588, Univ. Western Ontario, London, Canada.

Hebb, D.O. (1942) The effect of early and late brain injury upon test scores, and the nature of normal adult intelligence. *Proc. Am. Phil. Soc.*, 85: 275–292.

Inglis, J. and Lawson, J.S. (1981) Sex differences in the effects of unilateral brain damage on intelligence. *Science*, 212: 693–695.

Jones-Gotman, M. and Milner, B. (1977) Design fluency: the invention of nonsense drawings after focal cortical lesions. *Neuropsychologia*, 15: 653–674.

Kilbreath, M. (1979) Task-related motor asymmetries in males and females. Unpublished B.A. thesis, Univ. Western Ontario, London, Canada.

Kimura, D. (1961) Cerebral dominance and the perception of verbal stimuli. *Can J. Psychol.*, 15: 166–171.

Kimura, D. (1964) Left–right differences in the perception of melodies. *Quart. J. Exp. Psychol.*, 14: 355–358.

Kimura, D. (1966) Dual functional asymmetry of the brain in visual perception. *Neuropsychologia*, 4: 275–285.

Kimura, D. (1969) Spatial localization in left and right visual fields. *Can. J. Psychol.*, 23: 445–448.

Kimura, D. (1973) Manual activity during speaking. I. Right-handers. *Neuropsychologia*, 11: 45–50.

Kimura, D. (1980) Sex differences in intrahemispheric organization of speech. *Behav. Brain Sci.*, 3: 240–241.

Kimura, D. (1982) Left-hemisphere control of oral and brachial movements and their relation to communication. *Phil. Trans. Roy. Soc. London*, B298: 135–149.

Kimura, D. (1983) Sex differences in cerebral organization for speech and praxic function. *Can. J. Psychol.*, 37: 19–35.

Kimura, D. and Archibald, Y. (1974) Motor functions of the left hemisphere. *Brain*, 97: 337–350.

Kimura, D. and Humphrys, A. (1981) A comparison of left- and right-arm movements during speaking. *Neuropsychologia*, 19: 807–812.

Lake, D. and Bryden, M.P. (1976) Handedness and sex differences in hemispheric asymmetry. *Brain Lang.*, 3: 266–282.

Lansdell, H. (1962) A sex difference in effect of temporal-lobe neurosurgery on design preference. *Nature (London)*, 194: 852–854.

Lansdell, H. and Davie, J.C. (1972) Massa intermedia: possible relation to intelligence. *Neuropsychologia*, 10: 207–210.

Lansdell, H. and Urbach, N. (1965) Sex differences in personality measures related to size and side of temporal lobe ablations. In: *Proc. 73rd Annual Convention Am. Psychol. Assoc., Chicago, IL*, APA Inc., Washington, DC, pp. 113–114.

Liepmann, H. (1908) *Drei Aufsätze aus dem Apraxie Gebiet*, Karger, Berlin.

Maccoby, E.E. (1966) *The Development of Sex Differences*, Stanford University Press, Stanford, CA.

Maccoby, E.E. and Jacklin, C.N. (1974) *The Psychology of Sex Differences*, Stanford University Press, Stanford, CA.

Mattarazzo, J.D. (1972) *Wechsler's Measurement and Appraisal of Adult Intelligence*, 5th Edn., Williams and Wilkins, Baltimore, MD.

McGlone, J. (1977) Sex differences in the cerebral organization of verbal functions in patients with unilateral brain lesions. *Brain*, 100: 775–793.

McGlone, J. (1978) Sex differences in functional brain asymmetry. *Cortex*, 14: 122–128.

McGlone, J. (1980) Sex differences in human brain asymmetry: a critical survey. *Behav. Brain Sci.*, 3: 215–263.

McGlone, J. and Fox, A.J. (1982) Evidence from sodium amytal studies of greater asymmetry of verbal representation in men compared to women. In: H. Akimoto, H. Katzamatsuri, M. Seino and A. Ward (Eds.), *Advances in Epileptology: XIIIth Epil. Int. Symp.*, Raven, New York, pp. 389–391.

Milner, B. (1962) Laterality effects in audition. In: V.B. Mountcastle (Ed.), *Interhemispheric Relations and Cerebral Dominance*, Johns Hopkins, Baltimore, MD, pp. 177–195.

Milner, B. (1967) Brain mechanisms suggested by studies of temporal lobes. In: C.H. Millikan and F.L. Darley (Eds.), *Brain Mechanisms Underlying Speech and Language*, Grune and Stratton, New York, pp. 122–132.

Milner, B. (1974) Hemispheric specialization: scope and limits. In: F.O. Schmitt and F.G. Worden (Eds.), *The Neurosciences, 3rd Study Program*, MIT, Cambridge, MA, pp. 75–89.

Nie, N.H., Hull, C.H., Jenkins, J.G., Steinbrenner, K. and Bent, D.H. (1975) *Statistical Package for the Social Sciences*, McGraw-Hill, New York.

Piazza, D.M. (1980) The influence of sex and handedness in the hemispheric specialization of verbal and nonverbal tasks. *Neuropsychologia*, 18: 163–176.

Thurstone, L.L. and Thurstone, T.G. (1941) *Factorial Studies of Intelligence*, University of Chicago Press, Chicago, IL.

Wada, J.A., Clarke, R. and Hamm, A. (1975) Cerebral hemispheric asymmetry in humans. Cortical speech zones in 100 adult and 100 infant brains. *Arch. Neurol.*, 32: 239–246.

Warren, J.M., Abplanalp, J.M. and Warren, H.B. (1967) The development of handedness in cats and rhesus monkeys. In: H.W. Stevenson (Ed.), *Early Behavior: Comparative and Developmental Approaches*, Wiley, New York.

Wechsler, D. (1955) *Wechsler Adult Intelligence Scale* (Manual), Psychol. Corp., New York.

Wechsler, D. (1958) *The Measurement and Appraisal of Adult Intelligence*, Williams and Wilkins, Baltimore, MD.

DISCUSSION

D.F. SWAAB: How, exactly, did you check the borders of the lesions in your patients? Only by CT scan? And if so, how well does it work? Or was pathology done later and, if so, how well did the borders match with those in the CT scans?

D. KIMURA: All available information was used on each patient to localize the lesions, including at least two of: neurological examination (hemiparesis, visual field defects, etc.), EEG, angiogram, brain scan and CT scan (in the last 5–6 years). We have no post-mortem pathology, in part because the patients typically survive up to several years after we have seen them, and so the correlation with our data would be difficult to make. Where there was any doubt from the clinical history, angiogram or CT scan whether the lesion was anterior or posterior to the Rolandic fissure, the neuroradiologist was consulted. Even if errors had been made, which I doubt, it is unclear how they could be made with a systematic bias. I should perhaps have pointed out that all localization was done without regard to our test data, and indeed was carried out without any particular hypothesis in mind. The test data are entirely retrospective.

H.B.M. UYLINGS: Can you specify the distribution of ages in the groups you analysed, and do you have data on the effect of hemisphere lesions in the developmental period of males and females?

D. KIMURA: I have not included, and we rarely see, patients under age 15. Most of the patients are vascular accidents, and the next most common pathology is tumours. The age range is about 20–70, but the mean age is near 50, and the vast majority of patients is over 40. It would of course be of interest to know what happens in children, but we have no such information at present.

S. BUTLER: Your distinction between anterior and posterior areas corresponds with the historical boundary between receptive and expressive "areas". The fact that you are not using these terms suggests that you do not accept their validity.

D. KIMURA: The classification into anterior and posterior lesions was not done with regard to looking at aphasia, nor indeed at any other symptom. Our patients were selected for study on the basis of unilateral damage, not for aphasic symptomatology, and the lesion localization (of which anterior-posterior is one crude part) was done without any reference to our test data, and indeed was finally done only in the last couple of years, long after the patients were seen by us. It is true that I do not use the terms "expressive" and "receptive", but I think these terms have fallen out favour even with aphasiologists. However, our aphasia screening test, which is used to classify our patients, is an abbreviation of a test developed by Schuell, and it samples typical basic speech functions sampled by most aphasia tests. However, you are correct in assuming that I do not find the terms "expressive" and "receptive" useful.

R.A. GORSKI: When after the lesion do you see your patients, and do you see any indication of a sex difference in "recovery"?

D. KIMURA: We typically see patients between a week and 2 weeks after admission; their admission to our hospital, which is a university hospital, is usually at least several days after onset of symptoms, which are initially treated at a local hospital. This does mean, nevertheless, that we are seeing patients about 2 weeks after the onset of symptoms, presumably too soon for any major recovery to occur. I have not systematically looked at recovery of aphasia to compare men and women, but my general impression is that although women are aphasic less often, their aphasia is quite severe. This is also borne out by their scores on aphasia testing (Kimura, 1983).

R.A. GORSKI: Dr. M. Hines (1982) has reported an effect of prenatal exposure to DES on the dichotic listening test in which these women were in the male direction compared with their sisters. Since many of us here are interested in possible hormonal effects, I was wondering whether clinicians pay attention to hormonal variables (e.g. prenatal hormone exposure, onset of menses, regularity of cycles, etc.) or indeed, whether they should?

D. KIMURA: Probably they should, but I am not certain how good the information is on these factors. What is available on our patients in the medical charts is of course available to us, but I suspect that not very much attention is paid to hormonal factors in the neurological examination or history, unless there is some indication for doing so. Our sample is mixed, but my impression is that most of them have not had significant medical problems until the few years or months preceding their admission for neurological symptoms. If one sought out patients with known perinatal abnormalities in hormonal environment, one might of course see some different effects.

W.W. BEATTY: Could you reconcile your results and conclusions with the earlier studies of McGlone?

D. KIMURA: There are no major discrepancies between Dr. McGlone's data and my own. Indeed, as a former student and collaborator of mine, Dr. McGlone saw some of the patients on whom I presented data, and her patient sample up to 1983 is a subset of mine. I thus confirm her report that aphasia is less frequent in women than in men, after unilateral left-hemisphere damage. My interpretation of the data is, however, slightly different from her earlier conclusions, in that I infer that speech is not bilaterally organized in women, but more focally organized within the left hemisphere. Consequently, left-hemisphere lesions less often affect the critical area in women than in men, in whom either anterior or posterior damage may result in aphasia. I believe that Dr. McGlone now accepts this alternative interpretation, at least for basic speech functions.

   As far as the IQ data in non-aphasic patients are concerned, again, our facts are quite similar, as they should be, with overlapping samples. However, I have been very concerned about the problems of choosing an appropriate control group against which to measure IQ changes. Consequently, my conclusions have been perhaps more conservative than Dr. McGlone's, but remember that we do find some support for a verbal intellectual deficit in women with right-hemisphere damage, but only on specific tests.

E. FRIDE: In view of the relationship between verbal and motor functions, which you pointed out, do you think that studies on asymmetries in animals, and possible manipulations and pathologies of these asymmetries in animals, are of any use as a model for human (abnormal) lateralization?

D. KIMURA: Yes, I do think the animal work on brain asymmetry has great potential relevance for human asymmetry. It is quite unlikely that significant functional asymmetry began in an evolutionary sense only with humans, and animal studies should therefore be instructive. We do not know precisely what the parallel will be, but one intriguing study done a few years ago by Webster (1977) at Carleton University in Ottawa on cats suggested that if the two hemispheres were defined as being ipsilateral or contralateral to the preferred paw, there were some significant differences between them in the solution of certain visual discrimination tasks. Many more animal studies are now being carried out than before and a very recent review of these has been done by Dr. Terry Robinson at Ann Arbor, MI.

REFERENCES

Hines, M. (1982) Prenatal gonadal hormones and sex differences in human behavior. *Psychol. Bull.*, 92: 56–80.

Kimura, D. (1983) Sex differences in cerebral organization for speech and praxic function. *Can. J. Psychol.*, 37: 19–35.

McGlone, J. (1980) Sex differences in human brain asymmetry: a critical survey. *Behav. Brain Sci.*, 3: 215–263.

Webster, W.G. (1977) Hemispheric asymmetry in cats. In: S.R. Hanrad, R.W. Doty, L.W. Goldstein, J. Jaynes and G. Krauthamer (Eds.), Academic Press, New York, pp. 471–484.

G.J. De Vries et al. (Eds.),
Progress in Brain Research, Vol. 61
© 1984 Elsevier Science Publishers B.V., Amsterdam

Sex Differences in Human Cerebral Function

STUART BUTLER

Department of Anatomy, Medical School, Birmingham University, Birmingham (Great Britain)

INTRODUCTION

Psychometric studies have revealed a number of statistically significant differences between male and female populations with respect to cognitive ability and hand preference. Females appear on the whole to be more strongly right-handed than males. They use the right hand more consistently for unimanual tasks and the incidence of left-handedness is lower (Barnsley and Rabinovitch, 1970; Bakan, 1971; Annett, 1972, 1973; Newcombe et al., 1975; Hicks and Kinsbourne, 1976). Females also tend to be more articulate and fluent in speech than males (Herzberg and Lepkin, 1954; Hutt, 1972). In childhood they usually learn to speak earlier (Morley, 1957), have larger vocabularies (Nelson, 1973), use complex grammatical constructions sooner (Horgan, 1976) and are better readers (Gates, 1961). By contrast males tend to excell at non-verbal tasks which depend upon the ability to visualise spatial relationships — the rod and frame test, embedded figures, visual and tactual mazes, map reading, sense of direction and mechanical skills (see Harris, 1978, for review).

The nature and extent of these sex differences is not entirely clear (McGlone, 1980, for review). There have been negative findings and methodological difficulties, particularly with regard to the assessment of handedness. The stronger preference of females for using the right hand is not accompanied by greater speed or precision in its use (Kimura and Vanderwolf, 1970; Kimura and Davidson, 1975). Neither does their advantage in verbal expression extend to other aspects of the use of language such as verbal reasoning (Hutt, 1972). Nevertheless wherever sex differences are reported, they are almost always in the direction of stronger right-handedness and superior verbal skills in females, and superior spatial ability in males.

SEX DIFFERENCES IN CEREBRAL HEMISPHERE FUNCTIONS

It is well established, from the effects of unilateral cerebral lesions and from studies of split brain patients, that the left cerebral hemisphere normally controls speech and other verbal processes whereas spatial ability is critically dependent upon the right hemisphere (see for reviews: Hecean and Albert, 1978; Nebes, 1978; Kimura and Harshman, 1984). In addition, of course, the left hemisphere is also responsible for motor control of the right hand. Accordingly, many authors have speculated that sex differences in hand preference and cognitive ability are due either to variations on this pattern of hemispheric specialisation, or to the readiness with which the cognitive strategies of the two sides of the brain are deployed (see e.g. Bryden, 1978; Galin et al., 1978).

It is not at all obvious from the psychometric findings what form such differences in hemispheric specialisation might take. For example, one might postulate that the left hemisphere is in some way better developed in females and that the reverse is true in males. Or, that the left hemisphere is assisted by areas of the right cortex which enable females to excel in verbal skills at the expense of visuospatial skills, while the reverse occurs in males. However, the effects of unilateral cerebral lesions on cognitive abilities fail to support such simple hypotheses. After left hemisphere stroke, or unilateral surgical intervention for the removal of space occupying lesions, men are more impaired than women on tests of verbal function (Edwards et al., 1976; Messerli et al., 1976; Inglis et al., 1982; Basso et al., 1982). After right-hemisphere damage, too, impairment in the performance of certain spatially guided tasks seems to be greater in males than in females (Lansdell, 1968; McGlone, 1977). If these findings are substantiated, it will mean that males rely on the left hemisphere for certain verbal functions and on the right hemisphere for spatial skills to a greater extent than do females, i.e., functional asymmetry is more marked in the male than in the female brain (McGlone, 1977, 1978, 1980; Harris, 1978; Bryden, 1979).

It is hard to see why greater differentiation of hemispheric function in the men should lead the sexes to excel in skills which depend upon opposite sides of the brain. Actually, this conclusion may be premature, for there are also negative findings on the question of relative impairment, especially when the lesion is situated in the right hemisphere (Lansdell, 1968; McGlone and Kertez, 1973; Benton et al., 1975; Edwards et al., 1976). It could be that the "asymmetry" model is altogether too general. Indeed, sex differences in recovery from brain damage have so far been reported only for tasks which make demands on motor as opposed to cognitive or perceptual skills (McGlone, 1980; Basso et al., 1982), just as sex differences in verbal ability occur in fluency but not in reasoning (Hutt, 1972; also Benbow and Benbow, 1984).

A further problem in interpreting recovery from unilateral brain damage, especially in the case of cerebrovascular accident, lies in the fact that the sexes and the hemispheres differ in their vulnerability to vascular occlusion. The differences are of a type that might lead artefactually to the impression of greater asymmetry in males, particularly for verbal function. In principle, the circle of Willis should protect the forebrain against failure of any of its major arterial inputs, the carotid and basilar arteries. In reality, there is a high incidence of abnormality in its posterior components, the middle and posterior cerebral and posterior communicating arteries, particularly on the left side, with the effect that stroke more commonly affects the left hemisphere than the right. In addition, the arterial tree is more often occluded at its larger branches in males than in females, with the effect that areas of cerebral ischaemia are usually more extensive in males (Sinderman et al., 1970; Kaste and Waltimo, 1976). This factor alone would cause greater functional impairments in men and so give rise to the impression that functions were more strictly lateralised than in women.

These and further sex differences in the vulnerability of the cerebral blood supply (Hutchinson and Acheson, 1975; Cope and Roach, 1977) make it necessary to exert caution in drawing conclusions from psychological studies of stroke victims and possibly also of patients with cerebral tumours in whom the vascular supply may be secondarily affected. We are therefore obliged to turn for corroborative evidence to non-invasive studies on the normal brain. Although there are four main sources of such information — split-field tachistoscopy, dichotic listening, electroencephalography (EEG) and positron emission tomography — this article will restrict itself to the contribution of EEG studies.

SEX DIFFERENCES IN EEG "ACTIVATION"

The suppression of the alpha rhythm during cerebral activity was one of the earliest phenomena to be described in human electroencephalography (Berger, 1929; Adrian and Matthews, 1934). During the last decade considerable attention has been directed to the pattern of EEG suppression which occurs during types of mental activity which supposedly engage the cognitive specialisation of one cerebral hemisphere. The early studies established that the power of the EEG at the frequency of the alpha rhythm was reduced over the left hemisphere during tasks which required verbal or mathematical thinking, but over the right hemisphere during spatial tasks (Morgan et al., 1971; Galin and Ornstein, 1972; Butler and Glass, 1974a). Similar asymmetries were noted in other EEG phenomena (e.g. Butler and Glass, 1971, 1974b; Wood et al., 1971; Morrell and Salamy, 1971; Matsumiya et al., 1972). Since then, an extensive literature has reported the use of these phenomena in order to investigate asymmetries in cerebral function. The field has not been without its crop of negative results (among them: Provins and Cunliffe, 1972; Rebert and Mahoney, 1978; Gevins et al., 1979) and methodological problems (Gevins et al., 1979). Although EEG asymmetries have sometimes been sought and interpreted uncritically, a detailed evaluation of methodological issues is beyond the scope of the present chapter (see review Donchin et al., 1977).

Advantage has been taken of task-induced asymmetries in the alpha rhythm by a number of investigators to study sex differences in cerebral function. In describing this literature, I shall refer to "activation" of one hemisphere during mental activity. By this I shall mean that the amplitude of the alpha rhythm is reduced more on that side than on the other side of the brain, relative to the "baseline" levels recorded during a specific reference period, e.g. relaxed wakefulness.

Tucker (1976) studied the scalp distribution of the alpha rhythm in right-handed men and women during the performance of two visuospatial tasks (recognition of Mooney faces and embedded figures) and during the vocabulary test of the Wechsler Adult Intelligence Scale. The average amplitude of the alpha rhythm at the various electrode sites was similar in males and females for all tasks, although the degree of right hemisphere activation was positively correlated with performance scores in the males on the faces task. A study by Rebert and Mahoney (1978), in which the tasks were tests of reaction time to verbal and pattern stimuli, also failed to reveal any significant sex differences in average amplitudes on either task, possibly because the pattern recognition task designed to engage the right hemisphere was so difficult that it encouraged subjects to adopt an analytical (i.e. verbal) strategy for its solution. Other investigations have similarly failed to reveal sex differences in the EEG during mental activity (Ornstein et al., 1980; Haynes and Moore, 1981a,b; Galin et al., 1982).

Haynes and Moore (1981b) observed that females had alpha rhythm of lower amplitude over the left hemisphere during the performance of two verbal tasks than did males and they interpreted this to mean that the left hemisphere was more actively engaged in their women subjects. This might appear to be at variance both with those who find no sex differences in clinical studies and with those who infer that males are the more dependent of the two sexes on the left hemisphere for verbal skills. However, the relative level of alpha activity over the two sides of the brain is not informative when taken in isolation in this way, i.e., in the absence of any control to show that the degree of asymmetry is not constant across all test situations. Other investigators have in fact revealed sex differences in overall EEG asymmetry which appear to be independent of mental activity, but in the direction of higher amplitude alpha rhythm over the left hemisphere in females (Ray et al., 1976; Rebert and Mahoney, 1978; Trotman and Hammond, 1979).

The necessary controls for baseline asymmetry were present in 5 EEG studies which did find sex differences in hemispheric activity (Glass et al., 1975; Ray et al., 1976; Tucker, 1976; Trotman and Hammond, 1979; Ray et al., 1981). Glass et al. (1975) found that left-hemisphere activation during mental arithmetic was more marked in males than in females. The recordings were made from occipital regions and the activation was referred to baseline recordings made while the subjects relaxed with their eyes closed. Ray et al. (1976) compared EEG power at alpha frequencies recorded from left and right temporal regions in 6 subjects of each sex while they performed a number of putative left-hemisphere (adding, counting verbs, making sentences) and right-hemisphere tasks (listening to music, visualising scenes). The two left : right power ratios remained unchanged during the two groups of tasks in the females, but in the males changed in the predicted direction. In a subsequent study on much larger groups, Ray et al. (1981) again found sex differences, but this time the EEG asymmetry during two spatial imagery tasks was contrasted with baseline measures taken at rest. Alpha asymmetry was significantly correlated with task performance in males of high spatial ability, but not in males of low spatial ability, or in females. Trotman and Hammond (1979) measured alpha power over left and right temporal regions in 5 males and 5 females during the performance of 3 tasks which were designed to engage each hemisphere preferentially. They found left hemisphere activation in the men during verbal tasks but in the women the left : right alpha power distribution remained unchanged from "baseline" values.

THE ASYMMETRICAL BRAIN: MEN vs. WOMEN

From the above survey it appears that electroencephalographers and clinical psychologists are equally divided on the question of whether or not male brains tend to greater asymmetry than do female brains. Unfortunately, it is not possible to reconcile the different results in terms of differences in technique, either with respect to the EEG measures and electrode placements or the tasks employed in the various investigations. However, many of these studies employed such small numbers of subjects (often fewer than 10 of each sex), that the reliability of the conclusions with respect to the general population is questionable.

Another potentially important factor concerns the manner in which subjects switch between the cognitive strategies of left and right hemispheres (Bryden, 1978; Galin et al., 1978). If the task is either too easy or too difficult the strategy adopted may not be the symbolic or spatial form of thinking best suited to its solution. EEG asymmetries provide only a measure of hemispheric activation and not a direct indication of functional specialisation, and are therefore liable to be misleading if subjects adopt left-hemisphere analytical strategies for the solution of nominally spatial problems and vice versa. Earle and Pickus (1982) looked at the alpha power over left and right parietal regions in 8 subjects of each sex, both while they were at rest and during the performance of mental arithmetic tasks of various degrees of difficulty. Alpha asymmetry developed in both groups: in men, it appeared only during the more difficult tasks; by contrast in women it was present during the easier tasks but not the more difficult ones. Whatever cognitive strategies were being used by the majority of women in this study, they evidently no longer relied exclusively on the left hemisphere for the most difficult tasks.

This finding raises a general problem with all such studies on the normally functioning brain. It is naive to describe any task as involving only one hemisphere. In clinical practice a patient may fail a language task completely after damage to Wernicke's area alone but of course many additional areas of the brain are necessary for its successful performance by a normal subject. In other words the speech areas are necessary but not sufficient for performance of language tasks. However hard the investigator using EEG or divided sensory field techniques tries to keep his verbal tasks free of imagery, or his spatial tasks resistant to verbal solution, a complex pattern of verbal and visual associations is likely to be evoked in the subject. This will presumably reveal itself in the EEG as a complex pattern of alpha suppression. Even when the experimenter is successful in presenting a task which places the predominant load on one hemisphere, individual differences are likely to persist in the application of verbal and spatial strategies to the same problem. The significance of such considerations is that sex differences in cerebral function might exist in the *readiness to deploy* the major cognitive strategies of one or other hemisphere, rather than in the degree of lateralisation of the underlying mechanisms themselves. The EEG findings to date do not enable us to distinguish between these possibilities, and indeed it may prove difficult to do so because alpha asymmetry measures the lateralisation of activity rather than functional specialisation per se.

To summarise thus far: EEG studies of lateralisation are divided on the question of simple sex differences. As in the clinical investigations with which we began, there are reports that the male brain is functionally more asymmetric than the female, and there are negative findings. The balance of opinion seems to favour the former position, especially since there are no valid reports of greater asymmetry in females. We have emphasised the additional complication that it may be difficult to distinguish sexual dimorphism with respect to the *organisation* of cerebral function from sex dimorphism with respect to the *readiness* to resort to particular cognitive strategies.

The EEG studies do not appear to be vulnerable to false positive findings of sex differences in the way that vascular factors may distort the clinical studies. On the other hand, they may well fail to detect any sex differences that exist if the tasks employed failed to engage one hemisphere predominantly. The study of Earle and Pickus (1982) demonstrated how EEG asymmetry may be missed if the task difficulty is inappropriate. The design and presentation of the task, the location of the electrodes, and the method of quantifying the EEG may have similar effects. These considerations lead to the view that the available evidence best fits a model of greater asymmetry of function in males. (At least, in right-handed subjects whose familial tendencies toward left-handedness have not been controlled for.) The idea of greater asymmetry in males is consistent with the views put forward by Levy (1974) concerning the neurological basis of sex differences in ability. She envisaged males as having strictly lateralised verbal and spatial functions, while in females verbal functions have encroached upon the capacities of the right hemisphere to the disadvantage of spatial abilities.

INTERACTION OF BRAIN ASYMMETRY WITH HAND PREFERENCE

We began by noting that females differed from males in hand preference as well as in cognitive and expressive functions. None of the EEG studies which we have considered so far controlled for handedness beyond, in some cases, selecting only right-handed subjects. There is reason to believe that sex differences in the asymmetry of cognitive activity may interact with handedness, not only with overt hand preference but also with a familial predisposition for left-handedness among right-handed subjects.

Saunders et al. (1982) report that strongly left-handed males tend to perform better on spatial tasks than right-handed males, but that strongly left-handed females do worse than right-handed females on such tests. In other words, the normal pattern of sex differences seen in right-handed subjects is exaggerated in left-handers (at least in those in whom the trait is strongly expressed). Yeo and Cohen (1983) found that right-handers who had left-handed relatives performed less well on spatial tasks than those who did not have left-handers in the family. The males without left-handed relatives were impaired on a hidden figures test but not on a task involving the mental rotation of three-dimensional shapes. The reverse occurred in the females and it is interesting to note that in EEG studies the mental rotation task has been reported to elicit activation of the left hemisphere rather than the right despite its apparently spatial nature (Ornstein et al., 1980).

Overt vs. familial handedness

One of the earliest EEG studies of sex differences in lateralisation (Davidson et al., 1976) also observed what seemed like an interaction with handedness, though the numbers of subjects were too small to be conclusive. The alpha asymmetries induced during the performance of various tasks including talking and whistling, were measured in 9 males and 5 females. Using the whistling task as a point of reference, talking caused less alpha activation over the left hemisphere in both sexes, and the effect was most marked in the 5 males and 4 females without any close left-handed relatives. Self-induced affective states were accompanied by greater right-hemisphere activation in females than males, but it is unclear how sex differences in the emotional responsiveness of the cerebral cortex fit into the verbal–visuospatial dichotomy. If this result were replicated in a large group, it would raise serious doubts as to whether the verbal–visuospatial dimension is sufficient, or even appropriate for understanding gender differences in hemispheric specialisation.

A larger study, carried out by Galin et al. (1982) on 45 males and 45 females, also revealed an interaction between sex and overt handedness. In right-handers, recordings from both parietal and central regions showed the expected differences in alpha distribution during writing and block design, but not during other putatively left-hemisphere tasks such as reading and speaking. In left-handers, the main effect was weak and reversed and the variance was high, suggesting that cerebral organisation in this group was more heterogeneous than in the right-handers. Sex differences emerged only in the form of an interaction with handedness. That is to say, left-hemisphere suppression of alpha activity during writing, using the bilateral distribution during block design as the point of reference, became reversed most often in left-handed females. Taking both sexes together, such reversal occurred in 10% of all right-handers and 36% of all left-handers but in 46% of left-handed females.

Recent studies in our own laboratory (Butler et al., 1982) have confirmed that lateralisation is different in right-handed subjects with and without left-handed close relatives. Moreover, the sexes are differently affected. We measured the EEG from left and right parietal regions while 48 right-handed subjects relaxed, or carried out mental arithmetic (serial subtraction) and a face recognition task. The subjects were divided into 4 equal groups: males and females, with and without left-handed relatives. The males, taken together, showed the expected EEG activation of the left hemisphere during arithmetic and of the right hemisphere during the facial recognition tasks (Table I). In the females the suppression of alpha rhythm was greater over the left than over the right hemisphere on both tasks, although the asymmetry did not reach statistical significance in either case. Presented in this way, the data are consistent with the previously discussed findings of greater tendencies towards asymmetries in males.

Pooling the data from males and females according to familial handedness, EEG activation was greater over the left hemisphere during both of the tasks in subjects having no left-handed relatives (Table II). By contrast, subjects with left-handed relatives showed symmetrical suppression of alpha amplitude during arithmetic but right hemisphere activation during the faces task. These observations suggest a complex interaction between sex and handedness and indeed, the sexes did behave differently when grouped on the basis of familial handedness (Fig. 1). The left hemisphere was activated during arithmetic chiefly in those males without any left-handed relatives, while the right hemisphere was activated on the facial recognition task chiefly in those who did have left-handed relatives. Among the females asymmetric suppression of alpha rhythm occurred only in those without left-handed relatives and took the form of left-hemisphere activation on both tasks.

TABLE I

TASK-DEPENDENT ALPHA POWER SUPPRESSION ACCORDING TO GENDER

Tasks	Males (N = 24)		Females (N = 24)	
	P3	P4	P3	P4
Mental arithmetic	2.39	2.03	3.10	2.85
Face recognition	0.58	1.0	1.49	1.08
Analysis of variance				
Tasks × hemispheres	$F = 4.61, P < 0.05$		$F = 0.18$, N.S.	

Suppression of alpha power (arbitrary units) relative to baseline levels at rest, recorded from left (P3) and right (P4) parietal regions. Data from 12 subjects with and 12 subjects without left-handed relatives have been pooled in each gender group.

TABLE II

TASK-DEPENDENT ALPHA POWER SUPPRESSION ACCORDING TO FAMILIAL HANDEDNESS

Tasks	Males and females with left-handed relatives (N = 24)		Males and females without left-handed relatives (N = 24)	
	P3	P4	P3	P4
Mental arithmetic	2.60	2.01	2.84	2.88
Face recognition	1.31	0.64	0.77	1.44
Analysis of variance				
Hemispheres	$F = 9.61, P < 0.01$		$F = 1.50$, N.S.	
Tasks × hemispheres	$F = 0.06$, N.S.		$F = 4.62, P < 0.05$	

Suppression of alpha power (arbitrary units) relative to baseline levels recorded at rest over left (P3) and right (P4) parietal regions during the performance of mental arithmetic and face recognition. Data from 12 men and 12 women in each familial handedness group.

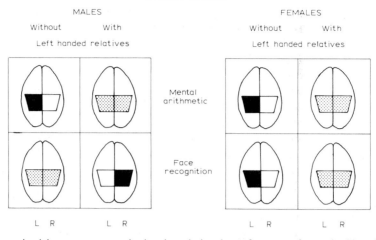

Fig. 1. Changes in alpha power over parietal regions during the performance of mental arithmetic and facial recognition as a function of gender and familial handedness. In each case the changes are referred to the power recorded during relaxed wakefulness. Solid black indicates the activated hemisphere, i.e. that alpha rhythm was suppressed more over that parietal region than the other during the task. Grey stipple indicates that the alpha rhythm was suppressed equally over both halves of the brain during the task.

Assuming the findings from these subjects are typical of the population at large, and that our two tasks are representative of those which call upon lateralised functions, we can characterise the pattern of sex and familial handedness effects in the following way: the use of left-hemisphere strategies for the solution of verbal /numerical problems is strongly expressed only when there is no left handedness in the family; females with this background are inclined to apply predominantly left-hemisphere strategies even to spatial problems; people with left-handed relatives do not have a strong tendency to use the cognitive strategies of one hemisphere more than the other except for males, who are inclined to use the right hemisphere preferentially for spatial problems.

The existence of such variations on the classical pattern of cerebral dominance is supported by the observation that the normal superiority for the recall of verbal material flashed to the right visual field is absent in right-handed subjects who have close left-handed relatives (Hines and Satz, 1971). Of course, it is well known that the lateralisation of language is often obscured or reversed in overt left-handers (Zangwill, 1960; Lansdell, 1962; Branch et al., 1964; Warrington and Pratt, 1973) and in this group too it depends on whether or not the left-handedness is a family trait (Zurif and Bryden, 1969; Lishman and McKeekan, 1977; McKeever and Van Deventer, 1977).

From a methodological point of view, the interaction between sex and familial handedness may go some way to explaining the discrepancies among EEG and other assessments of functional asymmetry. Only 5 investigations, only two of them being EEG studies, appear to have controlled for familial left-handedness among right-handed subjects, although its role as a possible confounding variable has been evident for more than a decade.

Our own study and that of Davidson et al. (1976) are in accord in finding that the left hemisphere is relatively more active during verbal/numeric thinking in both males and females without left-handed relatives, but the studies do not overlap in other respects. It is difficult to compare our results with those of Galin et al. (1982) because they were concerned only with overt handedness. However, like their left-handed females, the right-handed women with left-handed relatives in our own study were the ones who showed the smallest task-dependent asymmetries. Unfortunately, the psychometric studies pointing toward an interaction between handedness and sex (Saunders et al., 1982; Yeo and Cohen, 1983) have nothing to say about the asymmetry of the underlying neurological mechanisms. Accordingly, the data base is as yet too tenuous to justify erecting theoretical models. It is particularly important to establish whether or not the cortical representation of spatial functions is affected by gender and familial handedness in a different way than the representation of verbal/numeric functions, as appears to be the case in our work.

Such effects would implicate a strong genetic element in programming individual differences involving the cerebral organisation of spatial and linguistic activity. If sex were the only significant factor, gender role could conceivably be sufficient to account for changes in hemispheric specialisation through differences in the repertoire of acquired skills. If, however, sex differences in the functional organisation of the cortex take different forms according to the handedness of family members, one has to conclude that experience alone cannot be responsible. This general conclusion is supported to some extent by observations that sex differences in cerebral asymmetry are already present at an early age (Ingram, 1975; Kimura, 1967; Nagafuchi, 1970; Piazza, 1977; Ruoff et al., 1981).

Annett's (1973) "Right Shift Factor" theory of the inheritance of handedness and language lateralisation appears to lead to the prediction that females, who as a group are more strongly right-handed than males, have brains which are functionally more asymmetrical than males. As we have seen, this is not supported by either the clinical or EEG literature if a contrast is made between "right-handed" males and females without any consideration of the strength of manual preference. All studies which report any difference find the male brain more asymmetrical. A more appropriate test would be a contrast between subjects with and without left-handed relatives, because the right-shift factor would presumably be more prevalent among the latter irrespective of their sex. It is interesting to note that in the study of Butler et al. (1982) the subjects without left-handed relatives show stronger left-hemisphere activation on the verbal/numeric test than do those with left-handed relatives, regardless of gender (Fig. 1). This is important because it reveals that the data are not in conflict with Annett's model, as the greater brain asymmetry in the males when all are pooled together at first suggests.

The problem of distinguishing functional asymmetry from flexibility of cognitive strategies has already been mentioned in relation to sex differences. The same problem clearly applies to individual differences associated with familial handedness. Although a tendency toward right- rather than left-hemisphere EEG activation appears to be conferred by both familial left-handedness and by being male, it is as yet still obscure whether these two factors affect the lability of cognitive strategy, the degree of lateralisation, and other aspects of the organisation of cerebral function in a similar fashion.

REFERENCES

Adrian, E.D. and Matthews, B.H.C. (1934) The Berger rhythm: potential changes from the occipital lobes in man. *Brain*, 57: 355–385.

Annett, M. (1972) The distribution of manual asymmetry. *Br. J. Psychol.*, 63: 545–558.

Annett, M. (1973) Handedness in families. *Ann. Hum. Genet.*, 37: 93–105.

Bakan, P. (1971) Handedness and birth order. *Nature (London)*, 229: 195.

Barnsley, R. and Rabinovitch, A. (1970) Handedness proficiency versus stated preference. *Percept. Mot. Skills*, 30: 343–362.

Basso, A., Cupitani, E. and Monaschini, S. (1982) Sex differences in recovery from aphasia. *Cortex*, 18: 469–475.

Benbow, C.P. and Benbow, R.M. (1984) Biological correlates of high mathematical reasoning ability. In: G.J. De Vries, J.P.C. De Bruin, H.B.M. Uylings and M.A. Corner (Eds.), *Sex Differences in the Brain. The Relation between Structure and Function. Progress in Brain Research*, this volume, Ch. 30.

Benton, A., Hannay, H. and Varney, N. (1975) Visual perception of line direction in patients with unilateral brain disease. *Neurology*, 25: 907–910.

Berger, H. (1929) Über das Electronenkephalogramm des Menschen. *Arch. Psychiat. Nervenkr.*, 87: 527–570.

Branch, C., Milner, B. and Rasmussen, T. (1964) Intracarotid amytol for the lateralisation of cerebral speech dominance. *J. Neurosurg.*, 21: 399–405.

Bryden, M. (1978) Strategy effects in the assessment of hemispheric asymmetry. In: G. Underwood (Ed.), *Strategies of Information Processing*, Academic Press, New York, pp. 117–149.

Butler, S.R. and Glass, A. (1971) Interhemispheric asymmetry of contingent negative variation during numeric operations. *Electroenceph. Clin. Neurophysiol.*, 30: 366 (abstr.).

Butler, S.R. and Glass, A. (1974a) Asymmetries in the electroencephalogram associated with cerebral dominance. *Electroenceph. Clin. Neurophysiol.*, 36: 481–491.

Butler, S.R. and Glass, A. (1974b) Asymmetries in the contingent negative variation over left and right hemispheres while subjects await numeric information. *Biol. Psychol.*, 2: 1–16.

Butler, S.R., Glass, A. and Carter, J.C. (1982) Influence of sex and familial handedness on alpha asymmetry during cognitive activity. *Electroenceph. Clin. Neurophysiol.*, 54: 51P (abstr.). Full report in *Biol. Psychol.*, in press.

Carter, R.L., Hohenegger, M.K. and Satz, P. (1982) Aphasia and speech organisation in children. *Science*, 218: 797–799.

Cope, D. and Roach, M. (1977) Effects of high static pressures on human cerebral arteries in vivo. *Stroke*, 8: 254–257.

Davidson, R., Schwartz, G., Pugash, E. and Bromfield, E. (1976) Sex differences in patterns of EEG asymmetry. *Biol. Psychol.*, 4: 119–138.

Donchin, E., Kutas, M. and McCarthy, G. (1977) Electrocortical indices of hemispheric utilization. In: S. Harnad, R. Doty, L. Goldstein, J. Jaynes and G. Drauthamer (Eds.), *Lateralisation in the Nervous System*, Academic Press, New York.

Earle, J.B.B. and Pickus, A.A. (1982) The effect of sex and task difficulty on EEG alpha activity in association with arithmetic. *Biol. Psychol.*, 15: 1–14.

Edwards, S., Ellams, J. and Thompson, J. (1976) Language and intelligence in dysphasia: are they related? *Br. J. Disord. Commun.*, 11: 83–114.

Galin, D. and Ornstein, R. (1972) Lateral specialisation of cognitive mode: an EEG study. *Psychophysiology*, 9: 412–418.

Galin, D., Johnstone, J. and Herron, J. (1978) Effects of task difficulty on EEG measure of cerebral engagement. *Neuropsychologia*, 16: 461–472.

Galin, D., Ornstein, R., Herron, J. and Johnstone, J. (1982) Sex and handedness differences in EEG measures of hemispheric specialisation. *Brain Lang.*, 16: 19–55.

Gates, A.I. (1961) Sex differences in reading ability. *Elem. School. J.*, 61: 431–434.

Gevins, A., Zeitlin, G., Doyle, J., Yingling, C., Schaffer, R., Callaway, E. and Yeager, C. (1979) Electroencephalogram correlates of higher cortical function. *Science*, 203–655.

Glass, A., Butler, S.R. and Allen, D. (1975) Sex differences in the functional specialisation of the cerebral hemispheres. *Proc. 10th Int. Congr. Anatom.*, 204.

Harris, L.J. (1978) Sex differences in spatial ability: possible environmental, genetic and neurological factors. In: M. Kinsbourne (Ed.), *Asymmetrical Functions of the Brain*, Cambridge University Press, Cambridge, pp. 405–522.

Haynes, W.O. and Moore, W.H. (1981a) Sentence, imagery and recall: An electroencephalographic evaluation of hemispheric processing in males and females. *Cortex*, 17: 49–62.

Haynes, W.O. and Moore, W.H.J. (1981b) Recognition and recall: an electroencephalographic investigation of hemispheric alpha asymmetries for males and females on perceptual and retrieval tasks. *Percept. Mot. Skills*, 53: 283–290.

Hecean, H. and Albert, M.L. (1978) *Human Neuropsychology*, Wiley, New York.

Herzberg, F. and Lepkin, M.A. (1954) A study of sex differences on the Primary Mental Abilities Test. *Educ. Psychol. Meas.*, 14: 687–689.

Hicks, R. and Kinsbourne, M. (1976) Human handedness: a partial cross-fostering study. *Science*, 192: 908–910.

Hines, D. and Satz, P. (1971) Superiority of right visual half fields in right-handedness for recall of digits presented at varying rates. *Neuropsychologia*, 9: 21–25.

Horgan, D. (1976) Sex differences in language development. Cited by Harris (1978).

Hutchinson, E.C. and Acheson, E. (1975) Strokes. Natural history, pathology and surgical treatment. In: E.C. Hutchinson and E. Acheson (Eds.), *Major Problems in Neurology*, Vol. 4, Saunders, London,

Hutt, C. (1972) *Males and Females*, Penguin, Middlesex.

Inglis, J., Ruckner, M., Lawson, J.S., MacLean, A.W. and Monga, T.N. (1982) Sex differences in the cognitive effects of unilateral brain damage. *Cortex*, 18: 277–286.

Ingram, D. (1975) Cerebral speech lateralisation in young children. *Neuropsychologia*, 13: 103–105.

Kaste, M. and Waltimo, O. (1976) Prognosis of patients with middle cerebral artery occlusion. *Stroke*, 482–485.

Kimura, D. (1967) Functional asymmetry of the brain in dichotic listening. *Cortex*, 3: 163–178.

Kimura, D. and Davidson, W. (1975) Right arm superiority for tapping with distal and proximal joints. *J. Hum. Mov. Stud.*, 1: 199–202.

Kimura, D. and Harshman, R.A. (1984) Sex differences in brain organization for verbal and non-verbal functions. In: G.J. De Vries, J.P.C. De Bruin, H.B.M. Uylings and M.A. Corner (Eds.), *Sex Differences in the Brain. The Relation between Structure and Function. Progress in Brain Research*, this volume, Ch. 27.

Kimura, D. and Vanderwolf, C. (1970) The relation between hand preference and the programme of individual finger movement by left and right hands. *Brain*, 93: 769–774.

Lansdell, H. (1962) Laterality of verbal intelligence in the brain. *Science*, 135: 922–923.

Lansdell, H. (1968) The use of factor scores from the Wechsler–Bellevue Scale of Intelligence in assessing patients with temporal lobe removals. *Cortex*, 4: 257–268.

Levy, J. (1974) Psychobiological implications of bilateral asymmetry. In: S.J. Dimond and J.G. Beaumont (Eds.), *Hemisphere Function in the Human Brain*, Elek Science, London, Ch. 6.

Lishman, W.A. and McKeekan, E.R. (1977) Hand preference patterns in psychiatric patients. *Br. J. Psychiat.*, 129: 158–166.

Matsumiya, Y., Tagliasco, V., Lombroso, C.T. and Goodglass, H. (1972) Auditory evoked responses: meaningfulness of stimuli and interhemispheric asymmetry. *Science*, 175: 790–792.

McGlone, J. (1977) Sex differences in the cerebral organisation of verbal functions in patients with unilateral brain lesions. *Brain*, 100: 775–793.

McGlone, J. (1978) Sex differences in functional brain asymmetry. *Cortex*, 14: 122–128.

McGlone, J. (1980) Sex differences in human brain asymmetry: a critical survey. *Behav. Brain Sci.*, 3: 215–263.

McGlone, J. and Kertez, A. (1973) Sex differences in cerebral processing of visuospatial tasks. *Cortex*, 9: 313–320.

McKeever, W.F. and Van Deventer, A.D. (1977) Visual and auditory language processing asymmetries: influences of handedness, familiar sinistrality and sex. *Cortex*, 13: 225–241.

Messerli, P., Tissot, A. and Rodriguez, J. (1976) Recovery from aphasia: some factors and prognosis. In: Y. Lebrun and R. Hoops (Eds.), *Recovery in Aphasics*, Swets and Zeitlinger, Amsterdam, pp. 124–135.

Morgan, A.H., McDonald, P.J. and Macdonald, H. (1971) Differences in bilateral alpha activity as a function of experimental tasks, with a note on lateral eye movements and hypnotizability. *Neuropsychologia*, 9: 459–469.

Morley, M.E. (1957) *The Development and Disorders of Speech in Childhood*, Livingstone, London.

Morrell, L.K. and Salamy, J.G. (1971) Hemispheric asymmetry of electrocortical responses to speech stimuli. *Science*, 174: 164–166.

Nagafuchi, M. (1970) Development of dichotic and monaural hearing abilities in young children. *Acta Otolaryngol.*, 69: 409–414.

Nebes, R.D. (1978) Direct examination of cognitive function in the right and left hemispheres. In: M. Kinsbourne (Ed.), *Asymmetrical Function of the Brain*, Cambridge University Press, Cambridge, pp. 99–140.

Nelson, K. (1973) Structure and strategy in learning to talk. *Monogr. Soc. Res. Child Develop.*, 38: (1,2).

Newcombe, F., Ratcliffe, G., Carrivick, P., Hionns, R., Harison, G. and Gibson, J. (1975) Hand preference and IQ in a group of Oxfordshire villages. *Ann. Hum. Biol.*, 2: 235–242.

Ornstein, R., Johnstone, J., Herron, J. and Swencionis, C. (1980) Differential right hemisphere engagement in visuospatial tasks. *Neuropsychologia*, 18: 49–64.

Piazza, D. (1977) Cerebral lateralisation in young children as measured by dichotic listening and finger tapping tasks. *Neuropsychologia*, 15: 417–426.

Provins, K.A. and Cunliffe, P. (1972) The relationship between EEG activity and handedness. *Cortex*, 8: 136–146.

Ray, W., Morrell, M., Frediani, A. and Tucker, D. (1976) Sex differences and lateral specialisation of hemispheric functioning. *Neuropsychologia*, 14: 391–394.

Ray, W.J., Newcombe, N., Semon, J. and Cole, P.M. (1981) Spatial ability, sex differences and EEG functioning. *Neuropsychologia*, 19: 719–722.

Rebert, C. and Mahoney, R. (1978) Functional cerebral asymmetry and performance III: Reaction time as a function of task, hand, sex and EEG asymmetry. *Psychophysiology*, 15: 9–16.

Ruoff, P., Doer, R.H., Fuller, P., Martin, D. and Ruoff, L.O. (1981) Motor and cognitive interactions during lateralised cerebral functions in children. An EEG study. *Cortex*, 17: 5–18.

Saunders, B., Wilson, J.R. and Vandenberg, S.G. (1982) Handedness and optical ability. *Cortex*, 18: 79–90.

Sinderman, F., Bechinger, D. and Dichgans, J. (1970) Occlusions of the internal carotid artery compared with those of the middle cerebral artery. *Brain*, 93: 199–220.

Trotman, S.C.A. and Hammond, G.R. (1979) Sex differences in task depedent EEG asymmetries. *Psychophysiology*, 16: 429–431.

Tucker, D. (1976) Sex differences in hemispheric specialisation for synthetic visuospatial functions. *Neuropsychologia*, 14: 447–454.

Warrington, E.K. and Pratt, R.T. (1973) Language laterality in left handers assessed by unilateral E.C.T. *Neuropsychologia*, 11: 423–428.

Wood, C.C., Goff, W.R. and Day, R.S. (1971) Auditory evoked potentials during speech perception. *Science*, 173: 1248–1251.

Yeo, R.A. and Cohen, D.B. (1983) Familial sinistrality and sex differences in cognitive abilities. *Cortex*, 19: 125–130.

Zangwill, O. (1960) *Cerebral Dominance and its Relation to Psychological Function*, Thomas, Springfield, IL.

Zurif, E.B. and Bryden, M.P. (1969) Familial handedness and left–right difference in auditory and visual perception. *Neuropsychologia*, 7: 179–187.

DISCUSSION

R.A. GORSKI: Would it be of advantage in determining a possible role of sex to study ambidextrous individuals — if there are truly ambidextrous individuals?

S. BUTLER: If ambidextrous subjects were in some way "neutral" with respect to manual preferences, I suppose this group would provide the opportunity to examine the sex difference, independent of handedness. Unfortunately, there are methodological difficulties in defining handedness and one certainly cannot identify an ambidextrous group. At best, such people lie somewhere on a unimodal distribution and vary according to the measure you take.

J.M. REINISCH: Do you consider handedness and footedness in your categorization of subjects?

S. BUTLER: There are reports that crossed handedness and eyedness are associated with learning difficulties, as is left-handedness itself. However, there are many failures to replicate this observation and, because of the 50% decussation in the human visual pathway, it is hard to see any association between eyedness and lateral cerebral function.

E. FRIDE: Since it has been observed in the "animal literature" that neonatal handling affects paw reference, is there any evidence that (perinatal) environmental conditions affect laterality in humans?

S. BUTLER: There is an indication that some cases of left-handedness are associated with birth difficulty. I am not aware of any studies linking the status of lateralization to psychological stress on the mother before birth or on the individual post partum.

H.H. SWANSON: Is it true that if left-handed children are forced to use their right hand, this may cause them to stutter, and is this more serious in boys than in girls?

S. BUTLER: During this century the practice of forcing children to write with their right hand has declined and it certainly seems to make sense not to override the neurologically direct expression of lateralized motor skills. However, the formal evidence that such forced use is harmful is not strong.

R.A. GORSKI: I wanted to reinforce your statement that lesion studies actually investigate the functional capacity of the undamaged brain. Given the growing evidence of dynamic morphological plasticity in the adult brain and the possible role gonadal hormones play in this process, it could be that apparent sex differences may be manifestations of this process rather than of an inherent difference in the lesioned tissue.

S. BUTLER: I think we know little about hormonal influences on sex differences in lateralization. With regard to the logical difficulties with lesion studies, I do not wish to diminish their importance in this field. The point is that you need corroborative evidence using a different approach to validate the conclusions.

G.J. De Vries et al. (Eds.),
Progress in Brain Research, Vol. 61
© 1984   Elsevier Science Publishers B.V., Amsterdam

Sex Differences in Visual Half-Field Superiority as a Function of Responding Hand and Motor Demands

GABRIELE HEISTER*

Universität Konstanz, Fachgruppe Psychologie, D-7750 Konstanz (F.R.G.)

INTRODUCTION

With respect to sex differences in cerebral lateralization of cognitive functions, several very controversial positions are to be found in the literature. Whereas Buffery and Gray (1972) assume that language function matures earlier and becomes more strongly localized in the left hemisphere in women than in men, and visual spatial function matures earlier and becomes more strongly localized in the right hemisphere of women, other authors (e.g. Bryden, 1979; McGlone, 1980) have concluded that the male brain is more asymmetrical in all functions than the female brain. Kimura (1983) and Kimura and Harshman (1984), however, suggest that these differences in lateralization are actually based upon a sex difference in the intrahemispheric anatomical localization of specific functions. Fairweather (1982) concluded that with respect to split (visual) field studies, few positive findings are on record as far as sex differences in degree of cerebral lateralization are concerned. In his review, 103 out of 129 experiments failed to demonstrate significant differences between men and women (but see Bradshaw and Gates, 1978; McKeever and Hoff, 1982; Barry, 1981; Pring, 1981). Most neuroanatomical and clinical studies, on the other hand, point towards the existence of sex differences (cf. McGlone, 1980). These discrepancies probably result from theoretical as well as methodological problems.

Poffenberger (1912) was the first to investigate cerebral organization using the divided visual field paradigm, in combination with the registration of unimanual latencies on the basis of the then available knowledge about the optic nerve fibre decussation. Reaction times have been recently favoured as a dependent variable in visual half-field studies, since it is a more sensitive measure than accuracy (i.e. hit rate) for detecting cerebral asymmetries and intrahemispheric transmission (Moscovitch, 1973; Day, 1977, 1979; Landis et al., 1979; Babkoff et al., 1980; McKeever and Hoff, 1982). Reaction times are especially useful to register in investigations of right-hemisphere language capabilities, since the interpretation of hit rates involves an essential ambiguity. That is, one does not know whether a right-field superiority is because stimuli from the left visual field had to be processed primarily in the right hemisphere (which is inferior to the left hemisphere, or whether the relatively poor left-

---

* Present address: Universität Tübingen, Physiologische Psychologie, Außenstelle Weißenau, Rasthalde 3, D-7980 Ravensburg, F.R.G.

field performance is due to a necessity for the information to be transferred to the left hemisphere (before it can be effectively dealt with) for processing.

Initially, only simple reaction times, e.g. reactions to the onset of lateralized light flashes, were recorded, and these gave consistent results for the interhemispheric transmission time (for review see Bashore, 1981). More recently, many cognitive experiments (viz., choice reactions to verbal or visual/spatial stimuli) have been carried out in which asymmetry of performance has been noted (for review see Beaumont, 1982). Such asymmetry suggests differential hemispheric processing, the working hypothesis being that reaction times to right-field stimulation will be faster for both hands than to left-field stimulation if the left hemisphere alone processes the pertinent information in dextral individuals. If, on the other hand, both hemispheres can process verbal information equally well, one will expect faster right-hand reactions to right visual field stimulation than to left-field stimulation but also faster left-hand reactions to left than to right visual field stimulation, and the field difference should be stable and amount to a few milliseconds. In such cognitive divided visual field studies, however, the reaction time differences are usually far too large and variable to be explicable by interhemispheric transmission (see Cohen, 1982). Therefore, we assume that one of the underlying assumptions of this paradigm is not justified. In particular, the "static" concept of cerebral lateralization for cognitive processing as expressed in the dichotomic models of hemispheric specialization "verbal vs. spatial", "analytic vs. holistic", "sequential vs. parallel" etc., and the independence of stimulus processing from motor processes might be questionable.

Kinsbourne has proposed a more dynamic concept of cerebral functional asymmetry (e.g. Kinsbourne and Hicks, 1978). The underlying assumption is that if two cerebral foci of activity work at the same time, e.g., speaking and finger tapping of the right hand, interference might result since these two functions are localized within the same hemisphere. Until now, many authors have been able to demonstrate a language-related lateralized interference effect using the so-called dual task or time-sharing paradigm, i.e., they obtained a decrement in the performance of tapping with the right hand as compared with the left hand, with concurrent speaking, and as compared with a base rate of tapping without a concomitant verbal task (e.g. Lomas and Kimura, 1976; Sussman, 1982). Other experiments (e.g. Hellige and Cox, 1976; Kinsbourne, 1970) showed that the addition of a verbal memory task to a divided visual field study, e.g., memorizing a list of words and processing visually presented stimuli at the same time, may lead to an increase of field superiority or (under more difficult conditions) to a decrease of asymmetry such that, for example, an initial right-field superiority disappears. A study of Rizzolatti et al. (1979) demonstrated an effect of concomitant verbal tasks on simple reaction times (reactions to lateralized light flashes).

We presume, on the basis of these experiments, that already in a divided visual field study without a concurrent task the processing hemisphere might be "aroused" not only by certain cognitive aspects of the task but also by the motor processes related to the response. In neuropsychological experiments (e.g., divided visual field studies) cognitive and motor aspects of a task are usually confounded, even in electrophysiological studies where the subjects often have to react or answer vocally in order to stay awake and concentrated during the experiment. If it is true that, within the same experiment, cognitive and motor processes can interfere with each other intrahemispherically, this would be an explanation for some of the differences in experimental results (among them those concerning sex differences). We therefore examined the presence of interference of visual, cognitive and motor processes in divided visual field studies.

EVIDENCE FOR INTERFERENCE OF COGNITIVE AND MOTOR PROCESSES

Three experiments were conducted which were identical with respect to procedure, stimuli and processing requirements, only the mode of reply being different. These experiments consisted of 40 practice trials and 120 experimental slides presented tachistoscopically to 32 subjects (16 male, 16 female). Altogether 96 subjects took part in this investigation. All were unambiguously right-handed (without any close left-handed relatives) and were native speakers of German. They all had normal or corrected to normal vision when tested with a Bausch and Lomb "vision tester" (this is important in order to not disadvantage female subjects in our sample who, more often than the male subjects preferred having poor eye sight to wearing eye-glasses).

In all slides either a 3-letter word (noun) or a 3-letter meaningless syllable (consonant–vowel–consonant string) was presented vertically (see Heister et al., 1983). Half of the words and half of the syllables were "high" familiar (i.e., frequently used in the German language) and the other half "low" familiar (i.e., rare words and regular but seldom used syllables). The stimuli were located 2.5° either on the right or left side from a fixation point viewed by the subjects, who sat with their heads in a head-and-chin rest. Each stimulus appeared once in the right and once in the left visual field. A warning signal was followed immediately by the presentation of the slide for 125 msec. The subjects had to decide as fast and as accurately as possible whether the letter sequence was a German word or a non-word (lexical decision), and then to press the appropriate button with the index or middle finger of one hand. The answer key was located laterally in either the right or the left, the use of hand and buttons being balanced across subjects. The demands of motor processing were varied by asking the subjects in the first experiment to press the button once for every answer (Heister et al., 1983), in the second experiment by pressing twice, and in the third experiment by pressing 3 times (Heister, 1984). Reaction time was recorded for the first press of the button on each trial.

The one-press experiment

The men in this experiment were aged 20–35 years ($\overline{X} = 23.9$), the women 19–30 ($\overline{X} = 22.9$). Mean median correct reaction times were computed for both subject groups to right and left visual field presentation of the different stimulus categories. All subjects reacted faster to words than to syllables and faster to high than to low familiar material. The results showed, furthermore, a significant sex difference in reaction time asymmetry (see Fig. 1). Men showed a significant field × hand interaction, i.e. a right visual field superiority when reacting with their right hands and a left-field superiority when reacting with their left hands. Women did not show such an asymmetry. Both men and women showed a non-significant left-field superiority in processing low familiar meaningless syllables. However, there was a significant right-field superiority in processing high and low familiar words and high familiar non-words. The latter was expected for verbal material and lexical decisions because of the well documented *left* hemispheric superiority for language processing (see e.g. Kimura and Harshman, 1984).

The sex difference in asymmetry is difficult to interpret. With respect to Kinsbourne's more dynamic concept of cerebral lateralization one might suggest that reacting with one hand might stimulate the contralateral hemisphere for men, while for women there might be a tendency towards an intrahemispheric interference effect i.e., in this context, longer reaction

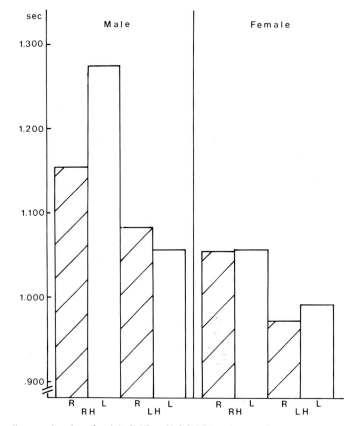

Fig. 1. Mean median reaction times for right (RH) and left (LH) hand responding men and women to right (R) and left (L) field stimulation (high and low familiar words and syllables combined) in the one-press experiment.

times for the direct neuronal pathway compared to the indirect pathway. Women showed such a pattern (faster right-hand reactions to left-field stimulation, and faster left-hand reactions to right-field stimulation) already in the second half of the one-press experiment (see Heister et al., 1983). A further increase of demands on motor reaction might result in an "interference effect" for men and, possibly, an increase of this effect in women. If, on the other hand, motor and cognitive processes were unrelated (as is generally assumed in visual half-field studies) the result should be the same in experiments with increased demands on motor processes. This would result in there being no significant difference in the direction of reaction time asymmetry between the experiments, since this asymmetry would be an indicator of the cerebral locus of processing only. In order to answer this question, an experiment which involved pressing a button *twice* was performed. With respect to the above-mentioned "interference hypothesis" one would now expect either a breakdown or a shift of asymmetry for right-hand-reacting men, since the asymmetry they showed in the one-press experiment was already extremely large, and either a reduction or a further increase of asymmetry for left-hand-reacting men. For women, if anything, one would expect an increase of the asymmetry in the reversed direction.

The two-press experiment

Subjects in this experiment had to react by pressing the button twice instead of once for every answer, thus increasing the "motor component". A comparable sample of subjects (16 men aged 20–43 years ($\bar{X} = 24.2$) and 16 women aged 19–36 years ($\bar{X} = 24.9$)) participated in this experiment. The latency data revealed only a small right-field superiority, so that the main effect for field fell far short of statistical significance (see Fig. 2). The interaction between visual field and "familiarity" was significant ($F(1, 28) = 4.06$, $P = 0.05$). For highly familiar stimuli reactions were 50 msec faster with right-field than with left-field presentations, whereas for low familiar stimuli the reaction times for left-field versus right-field presentation did not differ significantly.

The interaction between field, familiarity, meaningfulness and sex just failed to reach significance ($F(1, 28) = 4.03$, $P = 0.0545$). This result nevertheless shows the tendency to process low familiar syllables in a left-field superior fashion, a result which here reached significance only for the females, as shown by a separate analysis of variance ($F(1, 14) = 5.29$, $P < 0.05$). No other interactions with field were significant.

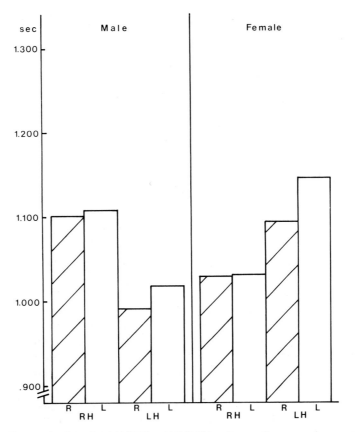

Fig. 2. Mean median reaction times for right (RH) and left (LH) hand responding men and women to right (R) and left (L) field stimulation (high and low familiar words and syllables combined) in the two-press experiment.

The results are as expected from the "interference hypothesis". With an increase of motor demands we predicted a reduction of the field superiority or even a switch of field superiority to the reversed direction. This took place for men. While in the first experiment the right-hand reactions were 128 msec faster to right-field stimulation, now these reactions were only 7 msec faster; and while in the first experiment left-hand reactions were faster with left-field presentations, the direction of asymmetry switched with 2 times button pressing to a right-field superiority (cf. Figs. 1 and 2). And for females there was a tendency for the right-field superiority of left-hand reactions to increase, whereas right-hand reactions did not show the usual field asymmetry.

The three-press experiment

32 new subjects participated: 16 women aged 19–32 years ($\bar{X} = 23.9$) and 16 men aged 21–35 years ($\bar{X} = 25.1$). These subjects showed similar results with respect to the stimulus categories as in the other two experiments. With respect to the asymmetry of reaction time, however, not only was there an overall right-field superiority but also a significant interaction between field, sex and hand ($F(1, 28) = 4.90$, $P < 0.05$) (see Fig. 3). This expresses the fact that all groups reacted faster to right-field presentations except the men who had been

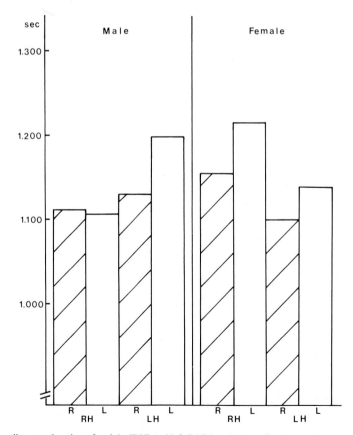

Fig. 3. Mean median reaction times for right (RH) and left (LH) hand responding men and women to right (R) and left (L) field stimulation (high and low familiar words and syllables combined) in the three-press experiment.

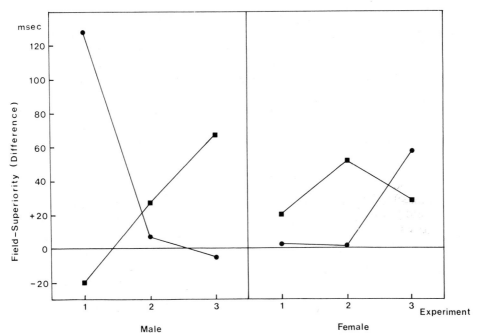

Fig. 4. Field superiority (difference left–right) for right (circles) and left hand (squares) responding men and women in the one-press, the two-press and the three-press experiments.

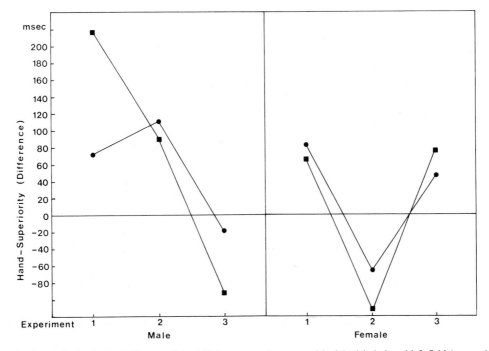

Fig. 5. Hand superiority (difference right–left) for men and women with right (circles) and left field (squares) presentations in the one-press, the two-press and the three-press experiments.

required to react with their right hand. They were left-field superior so that the interaction between field and hand was significant for them, $F(1, 14) = 5.88$, $P < 0.05$. Both right- and left-hand-reacting women were right-field superior, $F(1, 14) = 6.38$, $P < 0.05$, but this superiority had now become somewhat larger for right-handed than for left-handed responses (see Fig. 3).

Comparison of the three experiments

A common analysis of variance was performed for the reaction time data of all 3 experiments in order to detect possible differences between their results. The main effects for field and hand did not reach statistical significance but, overall, females tended to react faster than males (28 msec) and to be more accurate in making lexical decisions. That the women in our study did not perform more slowly than the men (cf. Welford, 1980) may be due to the control for visual acuity, and partially to the possibly higher verbal abilities of female students and university employees than of male ones. In the overall data (i.e., men and women combined) left-handed reactions were carried out 39 msec faster than right-handed reactions, a trend which is consistent with other studies concerned with verbal processing (e.g., Klatzky and Atkinson, 1971; Rizzolatti et al., 1971; Gross, 1972; Shanon, 1979). Although the difference between right- and left-handed reactions was not significant, it might express a tendency towards a generalized "cognitive/motor interference" since, if anything, one would expect faster right-hand reactions by right-handed subjects.

The main effects for "familiarity", "meaningfulness", and their interaction were highly significant ($P < 0.0001$), indicating that: (1) high familiar linguistic material is processed faster than low familiar material; (ii) words are processed faster than syllables; and (iii) high familiar words are processed the fastest of all. More interesting in this context are the effects for the factor field and related interactions. The main effect for field was highly significant ($F(1, 84) = 11.57$, $P = 0.001$), indicating that the expected overall right-field superiority was indeed obtained for these lexical decisions (see Fig. 4). A right-field superiority was also obtained for both right-handed reactions and left-handed reactions (31 and 27 msec faster, respectively) and for men and women (32 and 26 msec faster, respectively). Only for male subjects were significant interactions found between field and "familiarity" ($F(1, 42) = 4.01$, $P = 0.05$) and between field and "meaningfulness" ($F(1, 42) = 4.70$, $P < 0.05$). These results demonstrate that, in men, it is not a general hemispheric dominance for verbal processing or linguistic stimuli which underlies the data, but that there are differences in hemispheric superiority which depend upon certain semantic aspects of the linguistic stimuli. Because of these differences, the results cannot be explained as an effect of general orienting of attention, which would predict an overall field superiority irrespective of the different aspects of the verbal stimuli. The significant interaction between field, familiarity and meaningfulness ($F(1, 84) = 4.45$, $P < 0.05$) expresses the fact that low familiar meaningless syllables were processed faster when presented in the left than in the right visual field. This result is "new" in the sense that ours is the first visual half-field study in which familiarity was controlled not only for words but also for meaningless syllables. It might be seen as an indicator of right hemispheric processing of low familiar meaningless syllables which are less "language-like" stimuli in this context.

One of the most interesting results of this investigation was the shift of cerebral asymmetry between the different answer conditions, expressed in the significant interaction for field, hand and experimental condition ($F(2, 84) = 3.32$, $P < 0.05$). Another important finding was the existence of sex differences in the influence of motor processes on cognitive processing, as expressed in the significant interaction of field, sex, hand and condition ($F(2, 84) = 4.94$, $P < 0.01$). This result is mainly due, first of all, to the right-handed reactions for which the interaction between field, sex, and condition was significant ($F(2, 42) = 3.56$, $P < 0.05$) and, secondly, to male subjects for whom the interaction between field, hand and condition was significant ($F(2, 42) = 6.65$, $P < 0.005$). These results express the change in (direction of) asymmetry as a function of the increase of motor requirements in the task (see Fig. 4).

CONCLUDING REMARKS

The comparison of these 3 experiments, which involved identical cognitive tasks but made different demands on motor processes for the reaction, showed on the whole the well documented right-field superiority for verbal stimuli (i.e., left hemispheric specialization for linguistic processing). The interactions between hand, field and answer condition, however, show that not only the stimulus categories but also the hand used in responding and the motor requirements for the answer had a significant effect on reaction time asymmetry. An increase of motor demands led to a significant dominance shift for right- and left-hand-reacting men but not for women (see Fig. 4). In general, the females tended to have a lower right-field superiority than did the males, which is consistent with other findings (e.g., Bradshaw and Gates, 1978) but, additionally, our results demonstrate that a simple explanation, e.g., "males are more asymmetric than females", is not sufficient. In our study women not only "started" with a different pattern of asymmetry from men in the single press experiment, but also the influence of the increase of motor demands is different for them. Whereas for men it led to a reversal in the direction of asymmetry, in women the direction remained the same; however they did show changes in degree of asymmetry. If one combines the overall field differences for right- and left-hand reactions in women, an almost linear increase of right-field superiority — from a small superiority when pressing once, to a large superiority when pressing 3 times — was obtained (see Fig. 4, right panel), although the reaction times appear to become slightly longer. Low and Rebert (1978), using central stimulus presentation and single hand reactions or mixed bimanual reaction to verbs, obtained the result that females showed a "paradoxical" hand asymmetry, i.e., slower right-hand reactions to verbal stimuli (especially under difficult task conditions: shorter stimulus duration). Our results are similar in the sense that an interference effect is expressed in the reaction time data. While subjects in our study showed only a small tendency towards overall faster left-hand reactions, a significant lateralized interference effect took place for males (a shift in field asymmetry for right- and left-hand responses), dependent upon the difficulty of motor reactions related to the answer. Females, however, showed a tendency towards a lateralized interference effect ("paradoxical field asymmetry") in the single answer condition and, remarkably, the largest overall right-field superiority under the most difficult answering condition (see Fig. 4).

Using different methods, Low and Rebert (1978) came to the same result as Kimura (1983), viz., that women differ from men in left intrahemispheric coordination of language-related areas and motor regions. The present study suggests that cognitive/motor interference may take place in either hemisphere in both men and women. The most interesting result is that the sex difference in cognitive/motor interference seems to be due to a "phase shift", i.e., interference in male subjects occurs under more difficult conditions. If one compares the field differences for females in experiments 1 and 2 with the results for males in experiments 2 and 3 (see Fig. 4) they show strong similarities, in particular with respect to the direction of change in field asymmetry. The same holds for a comparison of hand differences (see Fig. 5). These results suggest that, for women, the interference effect takes place already under less "difficult" conditions, although they were generally superior to the men in speed and correctness of responses.

These results cannot be accounted for by the "classical" view which regards senso-cognitive and motoric processing as being unrelated, so that the time required for motor processing can be neglected. Since the reversal effect was obtained only for men, one can postulate that sex differences found in lateralization studies, as well as inconsistent results in the visual half-field studies are partly due to differences in motor influences.

Increases in or reversal of asymmetry cannot be explained on the basis of the classical reaction-time model since, according to that view, the field differences (which express only the interhemispheric transmission time) should be very small and stable. Based on the assumption, however, that the stimuli are processed by the hemisphere to which they are directly projected (and there is ample evidence for right-hemispheric abilities in processing simple nouns; for review see Searleman, 1977) our results become explicable as effects of a relative increase or decrease of intrahemispheric processing speed, resulting from the interaction of a difficult cognitive task with the more or less difficult demands on motor preprogramming.

In conclusion: the increase of motor demands had a dramatic effect on the asymmetry of reaction times (interference effect) of male subjects, but no significant effect on asymmetry in females. Our experimental results cannot be interpreted as implicating only language lateralization. Our findings seem to be pertinent to the theory of hemispheric lateralization since, in contrast to the classical stable dichotomies theory, they support a more dynamic view of hemispheric processing. A difficulty with Kinsbourne's concept is that it can explain nearly every conceivable change in asymmetry, and thus allows only a few precise predictions, but its merit compared with the classical static concepts of hemispheric processing is, that it is so far the only concept which accounts for the experimentally demonstrated changes in asymmetry at all. A divided visual field study should be seen as a kind of "dual task", which consists of possibly interfering visuo-cognitive and motor-cognitive processes (i.e. the response). We think that interference is possible, since motor processes seem to begin in speeded reactions more than a full second prior to the recorded movement (see Richer et al., 1983).

It is clear that further research — preferably using a within-subjects design, plus comparison of verbal and visual spatial processing — should aim at clarifying the conditions under which such interference is to be found, and why gender differences are involved. The present study was at least able to show that motor demands which are put upon reactions in a divided visual field study may have a considerable influence on reaction time asymmetry, and that this effect is often different for men and women. Sex differences, therefore, presumably depend upon the fact that the interference effect manifests itself more readily in women than in men. Sex differences in cerebral asymmetry seem to be more complicated than has been supposed in earlier studies (see also, e.g., Kimura and Harshman, 1984) and it may be postulated that sex differences found in lateralization studies — even in those evoked potential studies where some kind of reaction is required on the part of the subject — are in fact due, at least in part, to differences in intrahemispheric *motor* influences.

ACKNOWLEDGEMENTS

I should like to thank Christa Kolbert for the permission to use her familiarity normed stimuli, Prof. R.B. Freeman for the opportunity to use the tachistoscope which was financed by the Deutsche Forschungsgemeinschaft, Dr. P. Schroeder-Heister for checking the data, Prof. D. Vorberg for valuable discussions, Dr. H.B.M. Uylings and Dr. M.A. Corner for many helpful comments and suggestions on an earlier version of this paper, and Stella Lewis for checking the English.

REFERENCES

Babkoff, H., Ben-Uriah, Y. and Eliashar, S. (1980) Grammatical decision time and visual hemifield stimulation. *Cortex*, 16: 575–586.

Barry, C. (1981) Hemispheric asymmetry in lexical access and phonological encoding. *Neuropsychologia*, 19: 473–478.

Bashore, T.R. (1981) Vocal and manual reaction time estimates of interhemispheric transmission time. *Psychol. Bull.*, 89: 352–368.

Beaumont, J.G. (Ed.) (1982) *Divided Visual Field Studies of Cerebral Organisation*, Academic Press, London.

Bradshaw, J.L.and Gates, E.A. (1978) Visual field differences in verbal tasks: Effects of task familiarity and sex of subject. *Brain Lang.*, 5: 166–187.

Bryden, M.P. (1979) Evidence for sex-related differences in cerebral organization. In: M.A. Wittig and A.C. Petersen (Eds.), *Sex Related Differences in Cognitive Functioning*, Academic Press, New York, pp. 121–143.

Buffery, A.W.H. and Gray, J.A. (1972) Sex differences in the development of spatial and linguistic skills. In: C. Ounsted and D.C. Taylor (Eds.), *Gender Differences: their Ontogeny and Significance*, Churchill-Livingstone. Edinburgh, pp. 123–157.

Cohen, G. (1982) Theoretical interpretations of lateral asymmetries. In: J.G. Beaumont (Ed.), *Divided Visual Field Studies of Cerebral Organisation*, Academic Press, London, pp. 87–111.

Day, J. (1977) Right-hemisphere language processing in normal right handers. *J. Exp. Psychol.: Hum. Percept. Perform.*, 3: 518–528.

Day, J. (1979) Visual half-field word recognition as a function of syntactic class and imageability. *Neuropsychologia*, 17: 515–519.

Fairweather, H. (1982) Sex differences: little reason for females to play midfield. In: J.G. Beaumont (Ed.), *Divided Visual Field Studies of Cerebral Organisation*, Academic Press, London, pp. 148–194.

Gross, M.M. (1972) Hemispheric specialization for processing of visually presented verbal and spatial stimuli. *Percept. Psychophys.*, 12: 357–363.

Heister, G. (1984) Sex differences and cognitive/motor interference with visual half-field stimulation. *Neuropsychologia*, 22: 205–214.

Heister, G., Kolbert, C. and Hofmeister, K. (1983) Sex differences and asymmetry of lexical processing: Effects of responding hand, stimulus familiarity and intra-experimental experience. *Int. J. Neurosci.*, 21: 1–14.

Hellige, J.B. and Cox, P.J. (1976) Effects of concurrent verbal memory on recognition of stimuli from the left and right visual fields. *J. Exp. Psychol.: Human Percept. Perform.*, 2: 210–221.

Kimura, D. (1983) Sex differences in cerebral organization for speech and praxic functions. *Can. J. Psychol.*, 37: 19–35.

Kimura, D. and Harshman, R.A. (1984) Sex differences in brain organization for verbal and non-verbal functions. In: G.J. De Vries, J.P.C. De Bruin, H.B.M. Uylings and M.A. Corner (Eds.), *Sex Differences in the Brain. The Relation between Structure and Function. Progress in Brain Research*, this volume, Ch. 27.

Kinsbourne, M. (1970) The cerebral basis of lateral asymmetries in attention. *Acta Psychol.*, 33: 193–201.

Kinsbourne, M. and Hicks, R.E. (1978) Functional cerebral space: A model for overflow, transfer and interference effects in human performance. In: J. Requin (Ed.), *Attention and Performance, Vol. VII*, Erlbaum, Hillsdale, NJ, pp. 345–362.

Klatzky, R.L. and Atkinson, R.C. (1971) Specialization of the cerebral hemispheres in scanning for information in short-term memory. *Percept. Psychophys.*, 10: 335–338.

Landis, T., Assal, G. and Perret, E. (1979) Opposite cerebral hemispheric superiority for visual associative processing of emotional facial expressions and objects. *Nature (London)*, 278: 739–740.

Lomas, J. and Kimura, D. (1976) Intrahemispheric interaction between speaking and sequential manual activity. *Neuropsychologia*, 14: 23–33.

Low, D.W. and Rebert, C.S. (1978) Sex differences in cognitive/motor overload in reaction time tasks. *Neuropsychologia*, 16: 611–616.

McGlone, J. (1980) Sex differences in human brain asymmetry: A critical survey. *Behav. Brain Sci.*, 3: 215–263.

McKeever, W. and Hoff, A. (1982) Familial sinistrality, sex, and laterality differences in naming and lexical latencies of right-handers. *Brain Lang.*, 17: 225–239.

Moscovitch, M. (1973) Language and cerebral hemispheres: Reaction time studies and their implications for models of cerebral dominance. In: P. Pliner, L. Krames and T. Alloway (Eds.), *Communication and Affect: Language and Thought*, Academic Press, New York, pp. 89–126.

Poffenberger, A.T. (1912) Reaction time to retinal stimulation with special reference to the time lost in conduction through nerve centers. *Arch. Psychol.*, 23: 1–73.

Pring, T.R. (1981) The effect of stimulus size and exposure duration on visual field asymmetries. *Cortex*, 17: 227–240.

Richer, F., Silverman, C. and Beatty, J. (1983) Response selection and initiation in speeded reactions: A pupillometric analysis. *J. Exp. Psychol. Human Percept. Perform.*, 9: 360–370.

Rizzolatti, G., Umilta, C. and Berlucchi, G. (1971) Opposite superiorities of the right and left cerebral hemispheres in discriminative reaction time to physiognomical and alphabetical material. *Brain*, 94: 431–442.

Rizzolatti, G., Bertoloni, G. and Buchtel, H.A. (1979) Interference of concomitant motor and verbal tasks on simple reaction time: A hemispheric difference. *Neuropsychologia*, 17: 323–330.

Searleman, A. (1977) A review of right hemisphere linguistic capabilities. *Psychol. Bull.*, 84: 503–528.

Shanon, B. (1979) Lateralization effects in lexical decision tasks. *Brain Lang.*, 8: 380–387.

Sussman, H. (1982) Contrastive patterns of intrahemispheric interference to verbal and spatial concurrent tasks in right-handed, left-handed and stuttering populations. *Neuropsychologia*, 20: 675–684.

Welford, A.T. (1980) Relationships between reaction time and fatigue, stress, age and sex. In: A.T. Welford (Ed.), *Reaction Times*, Academic Press, New York, pp. 321–354.

G.J. De Vries et al. (Eds.),
Progress in Brain Research, Vol. 61
© 1984   Elsevier Science Publishers B.V., Amsterdam

Biological Correlates
of High Mathematical Reasoning Ability *

CAMILLA PERSSON BENBOW and ROBERT M. BENBOW

The Johns Hopkins University, Baltimore, MD 21218 (U.S.A.)

INTRODUCTION

The Study of Mathematically Precocious Youth (SMPY) has gathered extensive data showing that large sex differences in mathematical reasoning ability which favor males, exist before age 13. In this paper we evaluate some of the major "environmental" hypotheses that have been proposed to account for this difference. We will conclude that these "environmental" hypotheses need to be reformulated in order to account for the findings with our population of intellectually talented youths. While it is possible to adapt these exclusively environmental hypotheses to fit our data, we propose to take an alternative approach, which involves both environmental and biological causes for the observed sex difference.

It has long been obvious that certain sex differences, such as those in height, weight, and onset of puberty are largely determined by endogenous factors. No doubt these differences are also accentuated by the environment. Nevertheless, few deny that biological factors strongly contribute to these obvious sex differences. We now wish to propose that a combination of exogenous and endogenous factors also determines the sex difference in mathematical reasoning ability. In support of this hypothesis we present some new findings on possible biological correlates of extremely high mathematical and verbal abilities.

We recognize that any hypothesis involving biological differences between males and females will prove to be unpopular and controversial (see Tomizuka and Tobias, 1981; Stage and Karplus, 1981; Chipman, 1981; Egelman et al., 1981; Moran, 1981; Luchins and Luchins, 1981; Kelly, 1981; Benbow and Stanley, 1981). The scientific method, however, does not always allow one to take the most socially or politically expedient approach. In our opinion the evidence supporting a possible role for biological factors is sufficiently strong to merit serious consideration. We want to emphasize, however, that we are only proposing an hypothesis, not a proven theory.

The data presented in this chapter were obtained at the Study of Mathematically Precocious Youth (SMPY) and the Center for the Advancement of Academically Talented Youth (CTY). SMPY was founded at Johns Hopkins University in 1971 by Julian C. Stanley with the express purpose of identifying and educationally facilitating intellectually advanced students. In 1979 at Johns Hopkins he also helped create CTY, which carries on the tradition

* We wish to dedicate this chapter to Julian C. Stanley on the occasion of his 65th birthday. We also thank Lola L. Minor and Pamela J. Hines for helpful comments. This work was supported by grants from the Spencer and Donner Foundations.

of talent searches and academic programs for academically talented students. The programs created by Julian Stanley have received well-deserved international recognition. Without his foresight, creative ideas, and dedication, the findings presented in this chapter, many of which he contributed to, could not have been made.

SEX DIFFERENCES IN MATHEMATICAL REASONING ABILITY BEFORE AGE 13

The SMPY talent searches

It is well documented that there are large sex differences in mathematical ability and achievement favoring males (Bieri et al., 1958; Very, 1967; Garai and Scheinfeld, 1968; Glennon and Callahan, 1968; Suydam and Weaver, 1970; Backman, 1972; Wilson, 1972; Fennema, 1974; Keating, 1974; Maccoby and Jacklin, 1974; National Assessment of Educational Progress, 1975; Ernest, 1976; Fox, 1976; Fox et al., 1980). In the United States these differences have been found after puberty when the mathematics curriculum becomes more abstract. Sex differences favoring males, however, are not consistent across all mathematical abilities. Boys excel in tasks requiring mathematical reasoning ability, whereas girls excel in computation (Fennema, 1974). Moreover, no differences were seen in ability to apply knowledge that has already been learned.

Before 1980 the generally accepted explanation for these differences was the differential course-taking hypothesis of Fennema and Sherman (1977). They postulated that males developed more advanced mathematical reasoning abilities because males enrolled in more advanced mathematics courses, especially higher level courses, than females. This hypothesis has often been used to discount as sociological artifacts the sex differences found in mathematical ability (e.g., Wise et al., 1979).

In 1980 Benbow and Stanley presented data collected over an 8-year period by the Study of Mathematically Precocious Youth (SMPY), which could not be accounted for by the differential course-taking hypothesis. They showed that large sex differences in mathematical reasoning ability were observed in pre-adolescent students with essentially identical formal educational experiences.

These findings were based on data obtained from SMPY's mathematics talent searches conducted in 1972, 1973, 1974, 1976, 1978 and 1979 and involved 9927 intellectually gifted junior high-school students, who were between 12 and 14 years of age. Students attending schools in the Middle Atlantic Region of the United States were eligible to participate in an SMPY talent search if they scored in the upper 5% (1972), 2% (1973 and 1974), or 3% (1976, 1978 and 1979) in mathematical ability on the national norms of a standardized achievement test administered in the regular testing program of the students' schools. Thus, both male and female talent-search participants were selected by equal criteria for high mathematical ability before entering. Girls comprised 43% of the participants in these searches.

As part of the talent search, these students took the College Board Scholastic Aptitude Test's mathematics (SAT-M) and verbal (SAT-V) sections. These tests normally measure developed mathematical and verbal reasoning abilities, respectively, and are designed for above-average 12th-graders (Donlon and Angoff, 1971). Most of the students in our study, however, were in the middle of the seventh grade and were less than age 13. Few had received formal opportunities to develop their abilities in algebra and beyond (Benbow and Stanley,

1982a,b). Our rationale was that most of these young students were demonstrably unfamiliar with mathematics from algebra onward, yet were able to score highly. This could presumably occur only by the use of extraordinary mathematical reasoning ability. As an example of this, we have established that a majority of the students in the top 10% of our talent-search students (i.e., the top 0.3% of the general population in ability) did not even know Algebra I completely. Yet they scored far higher than most high-school students exposed to algebra and geometry. Thus, we conclude that the SAT-M must function far more at an analytical reasoning level for our SMPY testees than it does for high-school juniors and seniors who have already studied abstract mathematics for several years. We define this talent as mathematical reasoning ability.

The results from the 6 talent searches are shown in Table I. Most students scored high on both the SAT-M and SAT-V. There were no important sex differences in verbal test scores. This is consistent with the findings for high-school students, who also do not show sex differences favoring girls in this specific ability (ATP, 1981). In contrast, Maccoby and Jacklin (1974) concluded that there is a fairly well-established sex difference in verbal ability favoring girls. It is approximately 0.25 S.D. in magnitude.

A large sex difference in mathematical reasoning ability was, however, observed in every talent search. On the average, the boys scored about 0.5 S.D. better than the girls did. Moreover, there were indications that the greatest disparity between the boys and girls was in the upper ranges of mathematical reasoning ability. For example, in SAT-M scores of over 500 (average score of college-bound 12th-grade males) boys outnumbered girls more than 2 to 1 (1817 boys versus 675 girls in all 6 talent searches). It should be noted that the boys' SAT-M scores had a greater variance than the girls. This obviously relates to finding many more high-scoring boys than girls. Why boys tend to be more variable than girls has been addressed by Eysenck and Kamin (1981).

These results were limited by the fact that only selected, mathematically able, highly motivated students were tested. Also, too few cases of extremely high-scoring students were obtained to conclude whether greater differences exist at the high end of the scoring scale of the SAT-M.

Sex differences in mathematical reasoning ability among the most gifted

In 1980 two new talent-search programs were developed. The first was a modification of the original talent-search procedure. As previously, any seventh grader or student of typical seventh-grade age in a higher grade in the Middle Atlantic area of the United States could participate in the 1980, 1981, and 1982 annual talent searches, which were conducted by Johns Hopkins' Center for the Advancement of Academically Talented Youth (CTY). The major change was that not only mathematically able students but also students in the top 3% in verbal or in overall ability were allowed to participate. Thus, we had a more general sample of intellectually talented students. These searches also had equal representation by sex. Despite these modifications, the mean sex difference remained constant at 30 points favoring males among 19 883 boys and 19 937 girls (see Table I and Benbow and Stanley, 1983a). As previously, no important sex differences in mean SAT-V scores nor in the distribution of SAT-V scores were found.

It is not the mean difference in SAT-M scores, however, that should be emphasized. Rather, the ratios of high-scoring boys to girls are of major importance. The ratio of boys to girls scoring ≥ 500 SAT-M (493 was the SAT-M mean of 1982–83 college-bound 12th-grade males) was 2.1 to 1 (based on 5325 cases); at ≥ 600 SAT-M (80th percentile of 12th-

CAMILLA PERSSON BENBOW, ROBERT M. BENBOW

TABLE I

SAT PERFORMANCE BY SEX OF 12–14 YEAR OLDS IN A TALENT SEARCH

Talent-search date	Grade	Number		SAT-M scores* (mean (S.D.))		SAT-V scores (mean (S.D.))	
		Boys	Girls	Boys	Girls	Boys	Girls
March 1972	7	90	77	460 (104)	423 (75)		
	8+	133	96	528 (105)	458 (88)		
January 1973	7	135	88	495 (85)	440 (66)	385 (71)	374 (74)
	8+	286	158	551 (85)	511 (63)	431 (89)	442 (83)
January 1974	7	372	222	473 (85)	440 (68)		
	8+	556	369	540 (82)	503 (72)		
December 1976	7	495	356	455 (84)	421 (64)	370 (73)	368 (70)
	8**	12	10	598 (126)	482 (83)	487 (129)	390 (61)
January 1978	7 and 8**	1549	1249	448 (87)	413 (71)	375 (80)	372 (78)
January 1979	7 and 8**	2046	1628	436 (87)	404 (77)	370 (76)	370 (77)
January 1980, 1981, 1982	7 and 8**	19832	19937	416 (87)	386 (74)	367 (77)	365 (76)

Ratios of high-scoring talent-search boys vs. girls

	SAT-M ≥ 500	SAT-M ≥ 600	SAT-M ≥ 700
1972–1979	2.0:1	—	—
1980–1982	2.1:1	4.1:1	12.9:1***

* All sex differences on SAT-M were significant by a two-sided t test, mostly at the $P < 0.001$ level.

** The few 8th-graders in this sample had been accelerated by 1 year in their education.

*** This ratio is obtained from the special national talent rearch described on p. 470.

grade males) the ratio was 4.1 to 1 for the 806 students scoring that highly (Benbow and Stanley, 1983a). These ratios were similar to those reported in Benbow and Stanley (1980), but are based on a much larger and more general data base.

Scoring 700 or more on the SAT-M before age 13 is a rare occurrence. We estimate that students who reach this criterion (the 95th percentile of college-bound 12th-grade males) before their 13th birthday comprise the top 1 in 10 000 of their age group. Because of the rarity of such students, a special nationwide talent search was created in November 1980 in order to locate and educationally facilitate such students (Stanley, 1983). As of August 1983, the number of boys identified was 258 and the number of girls, 20; a 12.9 to 1 ratio (Benbow and Stanley, 1983a). This high ratio of boys to girls was found even though the available evidence suggested that essentially equal numbers of boys and girls took the SAT.

In summary, the total number of students tested in the Johns Hopkins regional talent searches and reported so far is 49 747 (9 927 in the initial study plus 39 820 in the later study). Preliminary reports from the 1983 CTY Talent Search based on some 15 000 cases yield essentially identical results. In the 10 Middle Atlantic regional talent searches from 1972 through 1983, therefore, we have tested about 65 000 students. In this large sample it is abundantly clear that *far* more boys than girls (chiefly, 12 year olds) scored high in SAT-M, even though girls were matched with boys by ability, age, grade, and talent-search entry.

Consequences of sex differences in mathematical reasoning

In view of the large sex differences in mathematical reasoning ability observed before age 13, it seemed important to examine the consequences of this difference. Benbow and Stanley (1982a) have carried out a longitudinal study for a subset of the talent-search participants in their 1980 study. These were the students in the 1972, 1973, and 1974 talent searches who as seventh or eighth graders scored at least 370 on SAT-V or 390 on SAT-M. These scores were equivalent to the average scores of a national sample of high-school females. Their development during the 4 or 5 years after participation in the talent search (usually during high

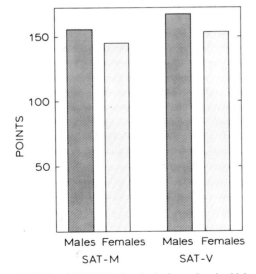

Fig. 1. Improvement on SAT-M and SAT-V during the junior and senior high-school years for SMPY's mathematically talented students by sex.

school) was investigated. It was found that the sex difference in mathematical reasoning ability persisted and was related to subsequent sex differences in mathematics and science achievement (Benbow and Stanley, 1982a, 1983d). Both the verbal and mathematical reasoning abilities of males developed to a more advanced level than those of females during this time. Males improved their scores on SAT-M an average of 10 points more than females (the mean difference went from 40 to 50 points). On the SAT-V, however, the boys also improved their mean score by at least 10 points more than females (see Fig. 1). Moreover, sex differences in achievement during high school favoring males, which were related to and predicted by the initial sex difference on SAT-M, were found in: participation in mathematics and science, performance on the SAT-M 5 years later, and performance on mathematics and science achievement and Advanced Placement Program examinations. The sex difference favoring males in science achievement test scores are shown in Fig. 2. The overall sex difference was slightly greater than 0.5 S.D. in biology and chemistry and approximately 1 S.D. in physics. Although the boys scored better than the girls on standardized tests of mathematics knowledge, it was of interest that SMPY females received better grades in their mathematics courses than SMPY males did (Benbow and Stanley, 1982a).

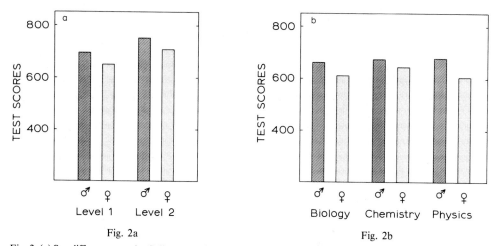

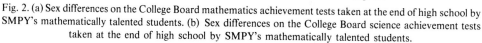

Fig. 2a   Fig. 2b

Fig. 2. (a) Sex differences on the College Board mathematics achievement tests taken at the end of high school by SMPY's mathematically talented students. (b) Sex differences on the College Board science achievement tests taken at the end of high school by SMPY's mathematically talented students.

In summary, we have shown that sex differences in mathematical reasoning ability can be found at an early age (before puberty) among intellectually talented students. Moreover, these differences persist over a number of years and are related to subsequent differences in mathematics and science achievement.

SOCIAL AND ENVIRONMENTAL HYPOTHESES

A large number of environmental and sociological hypotheses have been proposed to account for sex differences in mathematical reasoning ability in the general population. In this review, which is not meant to be exhaustive, we consider the major hypotheses, which, for convenience, we have grouped into 4 broad categories: differential course-taking hypothesis, masculine identification hypotheses, social reinforcement hypotheses, and the impact of socializers hypotheses. Each category will be evaluated to determine the extent to which it can account for the sex differences found in the SMPY population. We recognize that it is not possible to do full justice to the complexity of the environmental hypotheses in the limited space available, and apologize in advance for any oversimplification we may have introduced.

Differential course-taking hypothesis

Fennema and Sherman (1977) postulated that sex differences in mathematical reasoning ability are observed in high school because boys take more high-school mathematics courses than girls. It is often called the differential course-taking hypothesis. Because SMPY boys did take slightly more mathematics in high school than SMPY girls, this might appear to be the reason why the boys improved more in their mathematical reasoning ability in high school. The boys, however, also improved more in their verbal reasoning ability, in spite of the fact that girls traditionally take more verbal courses in high school. More importantly, the differential course-taking hypothesis cannot explain why there is a large sex difference on SAT-M before high school. In addition, as we will show, differential course-taking does not even adequately account for the increase in the sex difference in high school. Firstly, the initial sex difference on SAT-M was found in the seventh grade *before* differential course-taking took effect, as is evident from the normal curriculum available to seventh graders and from the students' reports (Benbow and Stanley, 1982b). Secondly, an equal percentage of SMPY girls and boys took mathematics in high school straight up to the 12th grade, when the SATs are normally taken. SMPY boys did take about one semester more of mathematics than did SMPY girls. This difference, however, was due to the larger number of SMPY boys than girls taking calculus: calculus was completed after the SAT-M was taken and calculus items do not appear on the SAT-M. Finally, the best predictor of high school SAT-M score was talent search SAT-M, not the number of semesters of mathematics taken in high school, which accounted for little additional variance (Benbow, 1981). Clearly, the differential course-taking hypothesis does not explain either the ability difference found in this population or the increase in the ability difference during high school. The converse was, however, supported. The students who took calculus in high school had significantly higher initial mathematical and verbal reasoning abilities than students not selecting to take this course (Benbow and Stanley, 1982a).

The masculine identification and social reinforcement hypotheses

The masculine identification hypothesis has been proposed to account for sex differences in mathematical achievement and perhaps also in aptitude (extensively reviewed in Fox et al., 1979). It is based on the postulate that it is necessary for one to identify psychologically with a male in order to have strong interest and ability in mathematics. We have not specifically tested this hypothesis for our population since Fox et al. (1979) in their review of the literature found contradictory results and thus rejected the masculine identification hypothesis.

Fox et al. (1979), however, presented "stronger" evidence to support the social reinforcement hypothesis. In essence, this hypothesis states that sex-related differences in mathematical achievement are, at least in part, the result of differential social conditioning and expectations for boys and girls. "The evidence shows that male prejudice against girls competing in mathematics does exist and the girls believe it exists. The perception of mathematics as a domain restricted to males may create a conflict for mathematically able girls between academic achievement and popularity, leading to reduced course-taking in mathematics" (Fox et al., 1979, p. 324). Furthermore, these investigators concluded that "differences in mathematics course-taking and ability seem to be less a function of biology and identification with a masculine role than of socialization forces (i.e., self-confidence with respect to mathematics, different career interests, and therefore, different perception of the usefulness of mathematics)" (Fox et al., 1979, pp. 324–325).

The socializer hypotheses

Meece et al. (1982) also reviewed the literature describing how socialization might account for the observed sex differences in mathematics. Specifically, they addressed the impact of "socializers" (i.e., individuals who influence the socialization process of children). Their hypothesis states that the "attitudes of teachers, parents, and counselors often reflect cultural stereotypes regarding not only the alleged natural superiority of boys' mathematical abilities but also the different utility of mathematical skills for boys and girls... By embracing these views, socializers could undermine girls' confidence, their motivation to perform well, and their actual learning in mathematics" (p. 327). They postulate that there are 3 main processes by which this takes place: (1) because male and female adults exhibit different attitudes and behaviors toward mathematics, they create differences among minors through their influence as role models; (2) society has different expectations of boys and girls, which are indirectly and directly communicated; and (3) parents and other socializing agents encourage different activities and provide different toys for their children on the basis of sex, which may train different skills and interests. In their comprehensive review of the literature, Meece et al. (1982) found strong support for their hypothesis. The authors also found support for the related hypothesis that student attitudes toward mathematics and math anxiety (both variables favoring boys) were another source of sex differences.

Finally, in a related study of scientists, Benbow and Stanley (1983d) found in their literature review that the typical personality traits associated with scientists are more frequently held by males than females. Females and males in the same field, however, tend to be quite similar. There may be some differences in the way parents treat males and females, and parental evaluation may be more important to females than to males.

The studies on which these environmental and sociological hypotheses are based generally used students of average ability. Undoubtedly, these environmental and sociological factors are important in determining sex differences in mathematics in the average population. Do these hypotheses apply, however, to the students of superior intellectual ability whom we have studied?

SOCIALIZATION HYPOTHESES AND SMPY

The validity of these hypotheses has been evaluated for the high-ability population studied by Benbow and Stanley (1980). No substantial differences were found in attitudes towards mathematics and the sciences (biology, chemistry, and physics) of these high-ability pre-adolescent boys and girls nor in their backgrounds (Benbow and Stanley, 1982b). Differences are predicted by the socialization hypotheses. Moreover, when these same students were studied 5 years later (after high school), few sex differences in attitudes were found. SMPY boys and girls reported liking mathematics, biology, chemistry, and science at that time. We found no substantial sex differences in their attitudes except perhaps towards physics (Benbow and Stanley, 1982a, 1983d). This was further exemplified by the fact that slightly more girls than boys were planning to major specifically in the mathematical sciences in college. In addition, SMPY females received better grades in their high school mathematics classes than did SMPY males. Moreover, reported attitudes toward mathematics had little relationship with subsequent achievement in mathematics. For example, attitudes toward mathematics at approximately ages 13 and 18 could predict neither the number of semesters of mathematics taken, SAT-M score in high school, nor the high-school mathematics achievement test score (Benbow, 1981; Benbow and Stanley, 1982a).

Relevant in this connection is the finding of Benbow and Stanley (1982a) that high-aptitude girls may participate in mathematics less than high-aptitude boys, not because they like it less, but perhaps because they like verbal areas (especially English) to a greater extent than do boys.

SMPY students do not suffer from "math anxiety". A student with math anxiety would not enter a mathematics competition such as SMPYs. Additionally, the students with whom we deal are all in the top 3% of intellectual ability with a demonstrated aptitude for mathematics and above-average performance in their mathematics classes. Thus, the math anxiety hypothesis is not appropriate for this population.

Fox et al. (1982) have investigated the family backgrounds of SMPY talent-search participants. They found few differences between male and female participants. In particular, few indications of differential training or encouragement of boys and girls were discovered. It is noteworthy that the study of Fox et al. was carried out by researchers who are not part of SMPY and who favor an environmental hypothesis.

It is of particular interest that the sex difference on SAT-M did not increase substantially during the 5 years of high school. The strong well-documented socialization pressures during junior and senior high school have remarkably little effect on sex differences in SAT-M scores. For socialization alone to account for our results, it becomes necessary to hypothesize ad hoc that mainly early socialization experiences significantly influence mathematical reasoning ability as measured by the SAT-M.

We urge caution when generalizing from the results of our limited study of highly able students. For example, it is possible that the variables measured were inadequate indicators of attitudes toward mathematics (i.e., mathematics liking, importance of mathematics for future job, and having rated mathematics as a favorite course in high school) since Fennema and Sherman (1976) have demonstrated that attitude toward mathematics involves several distinct components. Furthermore, the reason for not finding any substantial differences in the socializing experiences of our high-aptitude boys and girls may be because it was not possible to detect subtle social influences that affect a child from birth. Of course, our findings are limited to highly able students. Yet another important variable to be considered is the difference in toys that boys and girls play with. Our precocious boys may have more frequently played with toys that enhance their reasoning abilities than our girls did. Nevertheless, it is not entirely clear how differences in socialization experiences of boys and girls could affect the mathematical reasoning ability of girls so adversely and significantly, yet at the same time have no detectable effect on their reported attitudes toward mathematics, taking of mathematics courses during the pre-SAT years, and mathematics course grades. We are currently examining these hypotheses.

In summary, it appears that the main environmental hypotheses that have been proposed to account for sex differences in mathematical reasoning ability do not explain the results obtained for our high-aptitude group. Although large sex differences in mathematical reasoning ability before age 13 were found, few differences in the relevant socialization of the participants have been discovered. Thus, a reconceptualization of the commonly proposed environmental hypotheses is necessary in order to account for our data.

Rather than attempting to reformulate the environmental hypotheses, we propose to ask if other factors might also contribute to sex differences in mathematical reasoning ability. We do not dispute the fact that environmental influences contribute greatly to mathematical achievement and even to measures of mathematical reasoning ability. Instead, we wish to ask if endogenous factors may also contribute to the large sex difference we have observed.

Mathematical ability and spatial ability

It has been proposed that spatial ability is related to mathematical aptitude (Smith, 1964; Sherman, 1967, 1977; Maccoby and Jacklin, 1974; Harris, 1978; McGee, 1979). Since there is a well-documented sex difference in spatial ability favoring males (see, for example, Maccoby and Jacklin, 1974, for a review), it has been proposed that sex differences in spatial ability can account for the sex difference in mathematical performance (i.e., Sherman, 1967). The results of testing this hypothesis are somewhat mixed, however. Armstrong (1981) did not find that sex differences in mathematics achievement were related to sex differences in spatial ability. Moreover, Becker (1978) found that the three-way interaction of spatial ability, sex, and item performance on the SAT-M was not significant for the seventh-graders in a SMPY mathematics talent search. Her conclusion was that among SMPY students there was no difference in performance from item to item on the SAT-M according to sex and spatial ability. Spatial ability was found, however, to be related to superior performance on the SAT-M as a whole. Becker's results could have been confounded by the spatial ability test used, which had a large verbal component. Thus, the girls may have solved the test using a verbal strategy (McCall, 1955; Sherman, 1974; Benbow, 1978). Alternatively, mathematically precocious girls may require higher spatial ability than mathematically precocious boys in order to perform as well on the SAT-M (Cohn, 1977).

Two studies by Fennema and Sherman (as cited in Sherman, 1977) have, however, found evidence that sex differences in mathematical ability could be attributed in part to sex differences in spatial ability. More recently, Burnett et al. (1979) found that the sex difference on SAT-M was no longer significant after controlling for spatial ability among a college sample. Finally, McGee (1979) concluded that "sex differences in various aspects of perceptual-cognitive functioning (e.g., mathematics and field independence) are a secondary consequence of differences with respect to spatial visualization and spatial orientation abilities" (p. 909).

In view of the results above, the possibility that mathematical reasoning ability and spatial ability are related deserves to be seriously considered. This may also be true for the SMPY population for an additional reason. In a separate study, the most precocious students that SMPY had identified using the SAT-M and SAT-V were tested with a battery of cognitive tests (Benbow et al., 1983b). Two factors accounted for their superior performance: a verbal and a spatial factor. Therefore, spatial ability may be influencing the test performance of mathematically precocious individuals. Moreover, sex differences in spatial ability favoring males were observed in this population (Benbow et al., 1983b).

There might not, however, be a direct link between the two factors (i.e., that spatial ability positively influences mathematical reasoning ability). Instead, these two mental abilities may simply involve similar cognitive processes. For example, both may rely on processes best performed by the right hemisphere of the brain. Thus, the close relationship may indicate that both abilities depend upon similar problem-solving strategies.

The possibility that there is either a connection or a parallel between mathematical reasoning ability and spatial ability is of great interest. A large amount of research has been performed on biological factors that may cause or influence spatial ability. We will review these in the following pages and attempt to relate them to mathematical reasoning ability.

BIOLOGICAL HYPOTHESES FOR SEX DIFFERENCES

Sex-linked gene hypothesis

O'Connor (1943) has proposed that spatial ability is controlled by a recessive sex-linked gene and that this may be the cause of the sex difference in spatial ability favoring males. He, and subsequently several other investigators (Stafford, 1961; Corah, 1965; Hartlage, 1970; Bock and Kolakowski, 1973; Yen, 1975), have reported a pattern of familial correlations that suggest the involvement of a recessive sex-linked gene. Vandenberg and Kuse (1979), however, performed a comprehensive literature review of the topic. They found several contradictory results and therefore did not support O'Connor's theory. They concluded that spatial ability showed a developmental trend, an influence from sex hormones, and might be an autosomal gene with reduced penetrance in women. That spatial ability is under some genetic influence has been clearly demonstrated by several studies (DeFries et al., 1978, 1979; McGee, 1979). This also seems to be the case for the SMPY population (Benbow et al., 1983c).

Laterality studies

Another frequently proposed theory to explain the existence of sex-related differences in spatial ability is that men and women have the left and right hemispheres of the brain lateralized differently. Clinical and experimental data indicate that the left cerebral hemisphere is specialized for language processing and the right cerebral hemisphere is specialized for spatial processing (see Springer and Deutsch, 1981; Bryden, 1982, for comprehensive reviews). Although the evidence that has been presented is not without some methodological problems, it does appear that males have greater right hemisphere specialization than females (see Bryden, 1979; McGee, 1979; McGlone, 1980; Springer and Deutsch, 1981, for reviews) as Levy (1972) proposed. Both Butler (1984) and Kimura and Harshman (1984) have investigated the possibility that males are more lateralized than females. This finding may account for some of the sex differences in spatial ability. Much further research, however, needs to be conducted before any firm conclusions can be drawn.

Hormonal hypotheses

Many researchers have postulated that the different male and female hormones, androgens and estrogens respectively, produce sex-related differences in spatial ability. Petersen (1979) in her review of these studies found little support for the hypothesis that females excel on simple repetitive tasks and males at tasks that require perceptual restructuring because of sex hormones. There is, however, some support for the contention that high body androgenization is associated with low spatial scores among males and with high spatial scores among females (Broverman et al., 1964; Petersen, 1976). Thus, it may be the estrogen–androgen balance rather than the absolute level of androgen that affects spatial ability. This hypothesis states that the estrogen–androgen ratio is optimal and as a result spatial abilities the highest among males low in androgen and among females high in androgen (see Nyborg, 1984).

Sexual maturation is obviously dependent upon sex hormones. Waber (1977) found that late maturing children exhibit better spatial ability than children who mature early. She relates this finding to brain specialization: at the onset of puberty, there is a major reorganization of brain functioning (see Waber, 1979, for a review). Since girls enter puberty earlier than boys, their spatial abilities would tend to be less well developed at that point than in boys. Moreover, males who mature relatively early are perhaps more androgenous than males who mature later (Broverman et al., 1964). Thus, the influence of sex hormones on spatial ability may be through their effect on maturation, which in turn influences the degree to which a person becomes androgenized.

This is also consistent with the findings of Levy (1969) who found that spatial ability depended upon the degree of lateralization of the cerebral hemisphere of the brain. In 1976 she proposed that the degree of lateralization was determined by a gene which is under the influence of the sex hormones. Not entirely consistent with this hypothesis, however, is the fact that degree of lateralization may be established by birth or soon thereafter (Bryden, 1979, for a review). Petersen (1979) has also presented evidence that is difficult to reconcile with this position.

Also to be considered are the possible effects of hormones on the brain during early development. In their review, Reinisch et al. (1979) have concluded that: "(1) prenatal exposure to excess estrogen or to no hormone at all may have a negative influence on the development of spatial-perceptual skills but not on overall measures of intelligence, such as IQ; (2) progesterone exposure may enhance numerical ability; (3) exposure to either exogenously introduced synthetic or naturally occurring progestins may augment school achievement; and (4) the absence or excess of sex chromosomes may have an effect on cognitive abilities and measures of general intelligence in some individuals". Moreover, Geschwind and Behan (1982) postulated that exposure to an increased level of testosterone in a developing fetus has, as one effect, the slowing down of neuronal development of the left hemisphere. As a result, the right hemisphere would become relatively more dominant. Such a connection would perhaps contribute to sex differences in spatial ability. Similarly, Levy and Gur (1980) proposed that high levels of fetal sex hormones (as are found in males) promote the expression of cerebral lateralization and selectively enhance the maturational rate and cognitive capacity of the right hemisphere.

Mathematical reasoning ability: biological correlates

As mentioned above, mathematical reasoning ability appears to be related to spatial ability. Can the various biological explanations for the sex difference in spatial ability apply to mathematical reasoning ability? Little research of this type with mathematical reasoning ability has been done. Only one study has specifically dealt with the way biological factors affect mathematical reasoning ability. Stafford (1972) has shown that there is a genetic component to mathematical reasoning ability, and suggested that the pattern of familial correlations fit the sex-linked recessive gene model fairly well. Since this model was subsequently shown to be invalid for spatial ability, however, it obviously may not apply for mathematical reasoning ability either.

We have chosen to make the assumption, which seems reasonable although by no means proven, that the hypotheses that have been investigated for spatial ability also may apply to mathematical reasoning ability. We have begun to test some of these hypotheses for the abilities to reason mathematically and verbally among the intellectually precocious students identified by SMPY and the Center for the Advancement of Academically Talented Youths (CTY) at Johns Hopkins. Our findings suggest that there are certain specific physiological correlates of extremely high mathematical and verbal reasoning abilities.

PHYSIOLOGICAL CORRELATES OF EXTREME ABILITY

When Julian Stanley and I first published our finding of sex differences in mathematical reasoning ability (Benbow and Stanley, 1980) much controversy was generated over the role of "nature" versus "nurture" in determining high intelligence. This had led us to search for other biological differences, in addition to sex, which correlate with extreme intellectual precocity. Presently, we have found three such correlates: left-handedness, immune disorders, and myopia. Some of our findings relate to possible biological origins for sex differences in cognitive abilities. We again wish to emphasize that this is only our working hypothesis, not a proven theory.

Two organizations at Johns Hopkins, SMPY and CTY, conduct annual national talent searches for pre-adolescents who are *extremely* precocious in their mathematical and verbal reasoning abilities, respectively. The criterion for extreme mathematical precocity is a score of at least 700 on SAT-M prior to age 13. Similarly, the criterion for extreme verbal precocity is a score of 630 or more on SAT-V prior to age 13. Both scores are equivalent to the 95th percentile of above-average 17–18-year-old males. We estimate that selected students comprise the top 1 in 10 000 of their age group. As of August 1983, we had identified 278 mathematically precocious students and 165 verbally precocious students. Our work on physiological correlates of extreme mathematical and verbal precocity is being performed on this sample. The work is still in progress (August 1983), so the frequencies reported here will be slightly different from those in the final report (Benbow, manuscript in preparation).

Handedness and intellectual precocity

Each student was first asked to report his handedness to us and then later to complete the Edinburgh Handedness Inventory of Oldfield (1971). Students were also requested to report whether their natural parents and siblings considered themselves to be left- or right-handed. Ambidexterity was also assessed. Results from the inventory and from the self-report measure were in excellent agreement. Since our comparison studies dealt with self-report data, we will not present the data obtained from the inventory here.

Between 7 and 10% of the general population report that they are left-handed. Approximately twice as many mathematically and verbally precocious Caucasian students than Caucasian students in the general population considered themselves to be strongly left-handed ($P < 0.01$). Many were ambidextrous. When we included such individuals, 19.3% of the mathematically precocious students were either left-handed or ambidextrous and 21.2% of the verbally precocious students (see Table II).

The degree of left-handedness and ambidexterity for the parents and siblings of these students are also shown in Table II. It is clear that the rate is lower among them than among the index cases but still higher than for the general population. Approximately 31% of the

TABLE II

PHYSIOLOGICAL CHARACTERISTICS OF EXTREMELY PRECOCIOUS STUDENTS, THEIR FAMILIES, AND 3 COMPARISON GROUPS

	630 SAT-V students	700 SAT-M students	630 SAT-V and 700 SAT-M students	Fathers	Mothers	Brothers	Sisters	Low-scoring talent-search students (SAT ≤ 540)	Students scoring ≥ 370 SAT-V or ≥ 390 SAT-M	Students scoring 2 SAT-M + SAT-V ≥ 1330
Number	115	218	34	364	364	223	212	191	271	162
Percent left-handed	15.4 (M = 24.0* / F = 7.4)	15.1	13.8	9.9	9.5	13.8	11.5	9.5 (M = 10.8 / F = 8.4)	10.7	15.7
Percent ambidextrous	5.8 (M = 0* / F = 11.1)	4.2	0	0.7	0.4	4.2	2.3	2.1 (M = 3.6 / F = 0.9)	3.7	1.8
Percent having symptomatic atopic disease	54.2 (M = 62.7 / F = 46.4)	56.5	53.8	34.3	36.8	47.1	32.1	35.1 (M = 38 / F = 33)	—	—
Mean severity rating of symptomatic atopic disease**	4.5 (M = 4.4 / F = 4.5)	4.4	4.2	4.6	4.7	4.6	4.8	4.9 (M = 4.8 / F = 4.9)	—	—
Percent myopic	75.5 (M = 71.4 / F = 79.6)	52.8	72.0	60.0	53.6	41.2	38.1	19.9 (M = 15.5 / F = 23.4)	—	—
Mean age for onset of myopia	8.4 (M = 9.3 / F = 7.5)	9.1	9.3	17.1	14.1	10.3	10.1	9.5 (M = 10.1 / F = 9.2)	—	—
Percent entering puberty before 12.5 years	31.6 (M = 18.5* / F = 43.3)	18.4	14.3	14.8	42.4	—	—	31.6 (M = 20.2* / F = 41.1)	—	—

* Sex difference between proportions was significant.

** 3, infrequently recurring problem, no longer recurs; 4, mild recurring problem; 5, moderate recurring problem; 6, severe recurring problem.

left-handed or right-handed students had a sibling or parent who was also left-handed. Thus, left-handedness appears to be a familial trait of these precocious students.

In a comparison study handedness responses were obtained from 3 independently selected samples. The first sample, which was least able, was comprised of seventh-grade students scoring least well in the 1983 Hopkins Regional Talent Search conducted by CTY. The combined SAT scores of this group were less than or equal to 540, which means that the students were scoring slightly above chance on the SAT. They must, nevertheless, still be considered gifted since only the top 3% in ability can participate in the Hopkins regional talent searches. Out of a sample of 465 students, 191 returned a questionnaire to us. We could see no logical reason for assuming that the non-respondents would differ from the respondents on the questions, such as handedness. Among such students, 9.5% were left-handed and 2.1% reported that they had equal facility with both hands (see Table II). The second sample consisted of students who had scored as a seventh or eighth grader at least 370 on SAT-V or 390 on SAT-M in 1972 or 1973. They were surveyed when they were approximately 23 years old. Among such students 10.7% reported that they were left-handed and 3.7% that they were ambidextrous (see Table II). The third sample of students were selected from the 1976 talent search and consisted of those seventh-grade students who met the following criterion: $2SAT\text{-}M + SAT\text{-}V \geq 1330$. The top one-third of the talent-search participants met this criterion. In this group, which was the most able of the three comparison samples, 15.7% were left-handed and 1.8% ambidextrous. Since the different ability groups demonstrated a progressively higher degree of left-handedness, it appears that this trait is more frequent among extremely intellectually able students.

Immune disorders and intellectual precocity

The work of Geschwind at Harvard suggested that we should ask whether intellectually precocious students are more likely to suffer from immune disorders than individuals in the general population. Geschwind and Behan (1982) have shown that left-handers in the general population are more likely than right-handers to suffer from immune disorders, learning disabilities, and migraine headaches. Testosterone exposure in utero was proposed to explain this fact. Geschwind and Behan postulated that exposure to increased levels of testosterone as a developing fetus has two effects. "Testosterone slows neuronal development of the left hemisphere, while simultaneously affecting immune development, and thus favoring later immune disorders" (p. 5100). Retarding growth of the left hemisphere would make the right hemisphere relatively stronger and would increase the chance of becoming left-handed. We thus decided to investigate whether mathematically or verbally precocious individuals suffered from immune disorders.

Because there may be a difference between medical definitions of allergies and notions held by the general population, a rather sophisticated allergy and immune disorder questionnaire was mailed to both the students and their parents. This questionnaire was provided by Dr. Franklin Adkinson, who is a specialist in immune disorders at Johns Hopkins University. We found that approximately 56 and 54% of mathematically and verbally precocious students, respectively, suffered from symptomatic atopic disease (allergies of various kinds). By contrast, in the general population of the United States 10% suffer from this affliction (Stites et al., 1982). The percentage of parents and siblings having allergies was significantly lower ($P < 0.01$, see Table II). The severity ratings for the mathematically and verbally precocious, however, did not greatly differ from their parents' and siblings' (see Table II).

As a comparison, the allergy questionnaire was completed by 191 students in the first comparison group described above (i.e., the same age individuals scoring less than 540 on total SAT). Approximately 35% of those individuals reported having symptomatic atopic disease (see Table II). This is much less than for the extremely precocious students ($P <$ 0.01), but the severity rating that they gave was slightly higher. It should be emphasized that this control group is also gifted, though less so than our most precocious group. Thus, our data suggest that symptomatic atopic disease may be a physiological correlate of extreme intellectual precocity.

Myopia, blood type and intellectual precocity

Over the past 10 years we have noted that many of our most gifted students wore glasses. These observations coupled with the work of Karlsson (1973, 1975) led us to investigate the possibility that extremely precocious students might tend to be myopic. We found that 53% of the mathematically precocious students were myopic and 75% of the verbally precocious students were myopic (see Table II), while less than 5% were farsighted. For the lowest-in-ability comparison group only 20% were myopic. In the general population approximately 15% of high-school students are myopic (Karlsson, 1975). Clearly, these are substantial differences. The mean age of onset of myopia was 9.1 for the mathematically precocious, 8.4 for the verbally precocious, and 9.5 for the lowest-in-ability comparison group (see Table II). The siblings of the extremely precocious were about 50% less likely to be myopic. Although this is a fascinating finding, we have as yet been unable to think of a plausible mechanism relating myopia to extreme intellectual precocity.

Although it has been reported that blood type related to social class in England (Beardmore and Karimi-Booshehri, 1983), we found no such relationship in our sample. Thus, blood type did *not* relate to intellectual precocity in our study.

BIOLOGICAL CORRELATES OF MATHEMATICAL REASONING ABILITY

In this section we will attempt to relate our findings of biological correlates of extreme mathematical reasoning ability to the sex difference in this trait. The major biologically based hypotheses will be evaluated and we shall propose our own working hypothesis.

Sex differences in left-handedness and symptomatic atopic disease would be interesting. Unfortunately, because such a small number of females had scores that qualified them for the mathematically most precocious group, sex differences could not be investigated among that group. For the students qualifying for the verbally precocious group, there was essentially equal representation by sex. Among such students there were sex differences in the percentage of left-handers and in the percentage with symptomatic atopic disease (see Table II). These differences were significant ($P < 0.05$), however, only for the left-handedness data. For the comparison group, sex differences were also found, which were not large or significant.

How do these findings on immune disorders and left-handedness relate to brain dominance? Familial left-handers (i.e., those who have a close relative, such as a parent or uncle who are left-handed) tend to be more bilateralized in their cognitive functions (McGee, 1979; Springer and Deutsch, 1981; Bryden, 1982). That is, the typical pattern of left-hemisphere dominance for language and right-hemisphere dominance for spatial tasks is not always found. Since our students, who have demonstrably superior skills in mathematical and verbal reasoning as well as in spatial ability (Benbow et al., 1983b), are more likely to be left-handed or come from families with left-handers, we *postulate* that bilateralization is related to their superior abilities. Similar findings have been reported by Burnett et al. (1982) for spatial ability for a college population. If this is the case, however, it is difficult to reconcile with the hypothesis that boys generally score better than girls on spatial tasks because males tend to exhibit greater specialization of their right and left hemispheres or are more lateralized (Levy, 1972). We are currently measuring brain dominance patterns of our verbally and mathematically precocious youths using a computer simulation of a tachisto-scope for a verbal and a spatial task in order to resolve this issue.

Since most of our extremely intellectually precocious students did not appear to have entered puberty by the time they took the SAT at approximately age 12.5 (see Table II), our work may be relevant to the hormonal hypotheses proposed by Broverman et al. (1964) and Waber (1977). Because our students have developed superior intellectual abilities and sex differences prior to puberty, it is likely that other factors contribute to the sex differences in our data at age 12.5. We postulate that the onset of puberty may relate to the increase in the sex difference we observe during adolescence. Our data indicate that precocious boys do enter puberty significantly ($P < 0.01$) later than precocious girls (see Table II).

The point we wish to emphasize, however, is that the sex differences we observe were evident before the onset of obvious puberty. It is important to stress that our indicators of entering puberty were not refined, since we could not ask students in the SMPY and CTY programs overly sensitive questions or examine them medically. Our principal indicator for entering puberty was onset of menses for girls and the beginning of voice change for boys. Nevertheless, both the ages of our students and their responses indicate that most had either not entered puberty or had not been in it a very long time. In this context it is of interest that two studies have found sex differences in mathematical reasoning ability even among 7 year olds and among 9 year olds (NAEP, 1975; Dougherty et al., 1980). Clearly, these youths have not entered puberty. Finally, the work of Petersen (1979) is difficult to reconcile with the hypothesis on the effect of timing of puberty.

Of the major biologically based hypotheses to account for differences in intellectual ability, only those dealing with early hormonal exposure are readily reconciled with our data. This does not imply that the other hypotheses are invalid. Each may still be correct for the populations studied, as was also true for the environmental hypotheses discussed earlier. A reformulation of these hypotheses is necessary, however, to account for the data gathered by SMPY and CTY.

We propose the following unifying hypothesis, which is consistent with our results, but needs much further work to validate. Our hypothesis is an extension of the hypothesis proposed by Geschwind and Behan (1982), in which exposure of the developing brain to testosterone is a major factor. It owes certain features to the biopsychosocial hypothesis of Petersen (1981). The environment and the interaction between environment *and* physiological structures are of key significance, however.

Geschwind and Behan (1982) proposed that exposure to increased levels of testosterone in the developing fetus retards neuronal development of the left hemisphere. This implies that the developing individual would have a (relatively) stronger right hemisphere. Because the left hemisphere, which is better at language processing, does not dominate over the right hemisphere, which is specialized for non-verbal problem-solving tasks (e.g., spatial problems), such an individual would have a greater chance at developing his/her spatial or mathematical reasoning abilities through environmental interactions. By contrast, an individual with a dominant left hemisphere would rely more on his left hemisphere and would attempt to solve problems using a verbal approach. Such initial biases are then accentuated by the environment, which shapes the development of cognitive abilities. In our hypothesis, sex differences occur because males are more likely than females to be exposed to increased levels of testosterone. Males are indeed more likely than females to be left-handed or to suffer from immune disorders, which would be consistent with this hypothesis. Moreover, the two consequences of fetal exposure to an increased level of testosterone, as predicted by Geschwind and Behan, were in fact found for mathematically precocious youths. This would be necessary in order to validate our model.

It is not yet clear how extreme verbal precocity fits into this picture. We are not certain what aspects of verbal reasoning ability are tested by the SAT-V, although the ability to form analogies is clearly one. Dimond and Beaumont (1974) used analogical as one adjective to describe the thought processes exhibited by the right hemisphere. Thus, it may be that verbal reasoning as measured by the SAT-V is dependent upon right hemisphere thought processes.

SUMMARY

We conclude that large sex differences in mathematical reasoning ability are found prior to puberty among intellectually advanced students. This difference could predict subsequent sex differences in achievement in mathematics and science. Since few differences were found in the backgrounds and attitudes of the boys and girls tested, it is unlikely that simple environmental hypotheses can entirely explain our data. In addition, some of our findings on physiological correlates of extreme precocity are difficult to reconcile with most of the biologically oriented hypotheses that have been proposed to account for sex differences in cognitive functioning. We have proposed a single unifying hypothesis to account for sex differences observed by us.

Because there are well-documented differences in the environment as well as in the biology of boys and girls, we propose that it is a combination of *both* of these factors that cause the sex difference in mathematical reasoning ability.

REFERENCES

Admissions Testing Program (1981) *National Report on College-Bound Senior*, Educational Testing Service, Princeton, NJ.

Armstrong, J.M. (1981) Achievement and participation of women in mathematics: Results of two national surveys. *J. Res. Math. Educ.*, 12: 356–372.

Backman, M.E. (1972) Patterns of mental abilities: Ethnic, socioeconomic, and sex differences. *Am. Educ. Res. J.*, 9: 1–12.

Beardmore, J.A. and Karimi-Booshehri, F. (1983) ABO genes are differentially distributed in socio-economic groups in England. *Nature (London)*, 303: 522–524.

Becker, B.J. (1978) *The Relationship of Spatial Ability to Sex Differences in the Performance of Mathematically Precocious Youths on the Mathematical Sections of the Scholastic Aptitude Test*, Master's Thesis, The Johns Hopkins University, Baltimore, MD.

Benbow, C.P. (1978) *Sex-Related Differences in Spatial Ability*, Master's Thesis, The Johns Hopkins University, Baltimore, MD.

Benbow, C.P. (1981) Development of superior mathematical ability during adolescence, Unpublished Doctoral Dissertation, The Johns Hopkins University, Baltimore, MD.

Benbow, C.P. and Stanley, J.C. (1980) Sex differences in mathematical ability: Fact or artifact? *Science*, 210: 1262–1264.

Benbow, C.P. and Stanley, J.C. (1981) Mathematical ability: Is sex a factor? *Science*, 212: 118, 121.

Benbow, C.P. and Stanley, J.C. (1982a) Consequences in high school and college of sex differences in mathematical reasoning ability: A longitudinal perspective. *Am. Educ. Res. J.*, 19: 598–622.

Benbow, C.P. and Stanley, J.C. (1982b) Intellectually talented boys and girls: Educational profiles. *Gifted Child Quart.*, 26: 82–88.

Benbow, C.P. and Stanley, J.C. (1983a) Sex differences in mathematical reasoning ability: More facts. *Science*, 222: 1029–1031.

Benbow, C.P., Stanley, J.C., Zonderman, A.B. and Kirk, M.K. (1983b) Structure of intelligence of intellectually precocious children and of their parents. *Intelligence*, 7: 129–152.

Benbow, C.P., Zonderman, A. and Stanley, J.C. (1983c) Assortative marriage and the familiality of cognitive abilities in families of extremely gifted students. *Intelligence*, 7: 153–161.

Benbow, C.P. and Stanley, J.C. (1983d) Gender and the science major. In: M.W. Steinkamp and M.L. Maehr (Eds.), *Women in Science*, JAI Press, Greenwich, CT, in press.

Bieri, J., Bradburn, W. and Galinsky, M. (1958) Sex differences in perceptual behavior. *J. Personal.*, 26: 1–12.

Bock, R.D. and Kolakowski, D. (1973) Further evidence of sex-linked major gene influence on human spatial visualizing ability. *Am. J. Hum. Genet.*, 25: 1–14.

Broverman, D.M., Broverman, I.K., Vogel, W., Palmer, R.D. and Klaiber, E.L. (1964) The automatization cognitive style and physical development. *Child Develop.*, 35: 1343–1359.

Bryden, M.P. (1979) Evidence for sex-related differences in cerebral organization. In: M. Wittig and A.C. Petersen (Eds.), *Sex-Related Differences in Cognitive Functioning: Developmental Issues*, Academic Press, New York.

Bryden, M.P. (1982) *Laterality: Functional Asymmetry in the Intact Brain*, Academic Press, New York.

Burnett, S.A., Lane, D.M. and Dratt, L.M. (1979) Spatial visualization and sex differences in quantitative ability. *Intelligence*, 3: 345–354.

Burnett, S.A., Lane, D.M. and Dratt, L.M. (1982) Spatial ability and handedness. *Intelligence*, 6: 57–68.

Butler, S. (1984) Sex differences in human cerebral function. In: G.J. De Vries, J.P.C. De Bruin, H.B.M. Uylings and M.A. Corner (Eds.), *Sex Differences in the Brain. The Relation between Structure and Function. Progress in Brain Research*, this volume, Ch. 28.

Chipman, S. (1981) Mathematical ability: Is sex a factor? *Science*, 212: 114–115.

Cohn, S.J. (1977) Cognitive characteristics of the top-scoring participants in SMPY's 1976 talent search. *Gifted Child Quart.*, 22: 416–421.

Corah, N.L. (1965) Differentiation in children and their parents. *J. Personal.*, 33: 300–308.

DeFries, J.C., Ashton, G.C., Johnson, R.C., Kuse, A.R., McClearn, G.E., Mi, M.P., Rashad, M.N., Vandenberg, S.G. and Wilson, J.R. (1978) The Hawaii Family Study of Cognition: A reply. *Behav. Genet.*, 8: 281–288.

DeFries, J.C., Johnson, R.C., Kuse, A.R., McClearn, G.E., Polovina, J., Vandenberg, S.G. and Wilson, J.R. (1979) Familial resemblance for specific cognitive abilities. *Behav. Genet.*, 9: 23–43.

Dimond, S. and Beaumont, J.G. (Eds.) (1974) *Hemisphere Function in the Human Brain*, Wiley, New York.

Donlon, T.F. and Angoff, W.M. (1971) The Scholastic Aptitude Test. In: W.M. Angoff (Ed.), *The College Board Admissions Testing Program*, College Entrance Examination Board, Princeton, NJ.

Dougherty, K., Herbert, M., Edenhart-Pepe, M. and Small, A. (1980) Sex-related differences in mathematics, grades 2–5, unpublished manuscript.

Egelman, E., Alper, J., Leibowitz, L., Beckwith, J., Levine, R. and Leeds, A. (1981) Mathematical ability: Is sex a factor? *Science*, 212: 115.

Ernest, J. (1976) Mathematics and sex. *Am. Math. Monthly*, 83: 595–612.

Eysenck, H. and Kamin, L. (1981) *The Intelligence Controversy*, Wiley, New York.

Fennema, E. (1974) Mathematics learning and the sexes: A review. *J. Res. Math. Educ.*, 5: 126–139.

Fennema, E. and Sherman, J.A. (1976) Fennema–Sherman mathematics attitudes scales: Instruments designed to measure attitudes toward the learning of mathematics by females and males. *Catalog Selected Docum. Psychol.*, 6: 31–32.

Fennema, E. and Sherman, J.A. (1977) Sex-related differences in mathematics achievement, spatial visualization, and sociocultural factors. *Am. Educ. Res. J.*, 14: 51–71.

Fox, L.H. (1976) Sex differences in mathematical precocity: Bridging the gap. In: D.P. Keating, *Intellectual Talent: Research and Development*, The Johns Hopkins University Press, Baltimore, MD, pp. 183–214.

Fox, L.H., Tobin, D. and Brody, L. (1979) Sex-role socialization and achievement in mathematics. In: M.A. Wittig and A.C. Petersen (Eds.), *Sex-Related Differences in Cognitive Functioning: Developmental Issues*, Academic Press, New York, pp. 303–332.

Fox, L.H., Brody, L. and Tobin, D. (1980) *Women and the Mathematical Mystique*, The Johns Hopkins University Press, Baltimore, MD.

Fox, L.H., Brody, L. and Tobin, D. (1982) The study of social processes that inhibit or enhance the development of competence and interest in mathematics among highly able young women. Report to the National Institute of Education.

Garai, J.E. and Scheinfeld, A. (1968) Sex differences in mental and behavioral traits. *Genet. Psychol. Monogr.*, 77: 169–229.

Geschwind, N. and Behan, P. (1982) Left-handedness: Association with immune disease, migraine, and developmental learning disorder. *Proc. Natl. Acad. Sci. (U.S.A.)*, 79: 5097–5100.

Glennon, V.J. and Callahan, L.G. (1968) *A Guide to Current Research: Elementary School Mathematics*, Association for Supervisional Curriculum Development, Washington, DC.

Harris, L.J. (1978) Sex differences in spatial ability: Possible environmental, genetic, and neurologic factors. In: M. Kinsbourne (Ed.), *Asymmetrical Function of the Brain*, Cambridge University Press, Cambridge, pp. 405–522.

Hartlage, L.C. (1970) Sex-linked inheritance of spatial ability: *Percept. Mot. Skills*, 3: 610.

Karlsson, J.L. (1973) Genetic relationship between giftedness and myopia. *Hereditas*, 73.

Karlsson, J.L. (1975) Influence of the myopia gene on brain development. *Clin. Genet.*, 8: 314–318.

Keating, D.P. (1974) The study of mathematically precocious youth. In: J.C. Stanley, D.P. Keating and L.H. Fox (Eds.), *Mathematical Talent: Discovery, Description, and Development*, The Johns Hopkins University Press, Baltimore, MD, pp. 23–47.

Kelly, A. (1981) Mathematical ability: Is sex a factor? *Science*, 212: 118.

Kimura, D. and Harshman, R.A. (1984) Sex differences in brain organization for verbal and non-verbal functions. In: G.J. De Vries, J.P.C. De Bruin, H.B.M. Uylings and M.A. Corner (Eds.), *Sex Differences in the Brain. The Relation between Structure and Function. Progress in Brain Research*, this volume, Ch. 27.

Levy, J. (1972) Lateral specialization of the human brain: Behavioral manifestations and possible evolutionary basis. In: J.A. Kliger (Ed.), *The Biology of Behavior*, Oregon State University Press, Corvallis, OR.

Levy, J. (1976) Cerebral lateralization and spatial ability. *Behav. Genet.*, 6: 171–188.

Levy, J. and Gur, R.C. (1980) Individual differences in psychoneurological organization. In: J. Herron (Ed.), *Neuropsychology of Left-Handedness*, Academic Press, New York, pp. 199–210.

Luchins, E.H. and Luchins, A.S. (1981) Mathematical ability: Is sex a factor? *Science*, 212: 115–118.

Maccoby, E.C. and Jacklin, C.N. (1974) *The Psychology of Sex Differences*, Stanford University Press, Stanford, CA.

McCall, J.R. (1955) *Sex Differences in Intelligence: A Comparative Factor Study*, The Catholic University of America Press, Washington, DC.

McGee, M.G. (1979) Human spatial abilities: Psychometric studies and environmental, genetic, hormonal, and neurological influences. *Psychol. Bull.*, 86: 889–918.

McGlone, J. (1980) Sex differences in human brain organization: A critical survey. *Behav. Brain Sci.*, 3: 215–227.

Meece, J.L., Parson, J.E., Kaczala, C.M., Goff, S.B. and Futterman, R. (1982) Sex differences in math achievement: Toward a model of academic choice. *Psychol. Bull.*, 91: 324–348.

Moran, D.J. (1981) Mathematical ability: Is sex a factor? *Science*, 212: 115.

National Assessment of Educational Progress (1975) Males dominate in educational success. *NAEP Newslett.*, 8/5: insert.

Nyborg, H. (1984) Performance and intelligence in hormonally different groups. In: G.J. De Vries, J.P.C. De Bruin, H.B.M. Uylings and M.A. Corner (Eds.), *Sex Differences in the Brain. The Relation between Structure and Function. Progress in Brain Research*, this volume, Ch. 31.

O'Connor, J. (1943) *Structural Visualization*, Human Engineering Laboratory, Boston, MA.

Oldfield, R.C. (1971) The assessment and analysis of handedness: The Edinburgh Inventory. *Neuropsychologica*, 9: 97–113.

Petersen, A.C. (1976) Physical androgeny and cognitive functioning in adolescence. *Develop. Psychol.*, 12: 524–533.

Petersen, A.C. (1979) Hormones and cognitive functioning in normal development. In: M. Wittig and A.C. Petersen (Eds.), *Sex-Related Differences in Cognitive Functioning: Developmental Issues*, Academic Press, New York, pp. 189–214.

Petersen, A.C. (1981) Sex differences in performance on spatial tasks: Biopsychosocial influences. In: A. Ansara, N. Geschwind, A. Galaburda, M. Albert and N. Gartrell (Eds.), *Sex Differences in Dyslexia*, The Orton Dyslexia Society, Towson, MD, pp. 41–54.

Reinisch, J.M., Gandelman, R. and Spegel, F.S. (1979) Prenatal influences on cognitive abilities: Data from experimental animals and human and endocrine syndromes. In: M. Wittig and A.C. Petersen (Eds.), *Sex-Related Differences in Cognitive Functioning: Developmental Issues*, Academic Press, New York, pp. 215–240.

Sherman, J.A. (1967) The problem of sex differences in space perception and aspects of individual functioning. *Psychol. Rev.*, 74: 290–299.

Sherman, J.A. (1974) Field articulation, sex, spatial visualization, dependency, practice, laterality of the brain, and birth order. *Percept. Mot. Skills*, 38: 1223–1235.

Sherman, J.A. (1977) Effects of biological factors on sex-related differences in mathematical achievement. In: *Women and Mathematics: Research Perspectives for Change*, NIE Papers in Education and Work, No. 8.

Smith, I.M. (1964) *Spatial Ability*, University of London Press, London.

Springer, S.P. and Deutsch, G. (1981) *Left Brain, Right Brain*, Freeman, San Francisco, CA.

Stafford, R.E. (1961) Sex differences in spatial visualization as evidence of sex-linked inheritance. *Percept. Mot. Skills*, 13: 428.

Stafford, R.E. (1972) Heredity and environmental components in quantitative reasoning. *Rev. Educ. Res.*, 42: 183–201.

Stage, E. and Karplus, R. (1981) Mathematical ability: Is sex a factor? *Science*, 212: 114.

Stanley, J.C. (1983) Searches under way for youths *exceptionally* talented mathematically *or* verbally. *Roeper Rev.*, in press.

Stites, D.P., Stobo, J.D., Fudenberg, H.H. and Wells, J.V. (1982) *Basic and Clinical Immunology*, 4th Edn., Lange Medical Publications, Los Altos, CA.

Suydam, M.N. and Weaver, J.F. (1970) *Individualized Instruction*, Research Utilization Branch, U.S. Office of Education, Publication of the Interpretive Study of Research and Development in Elementary School Mathematics.

Tomizuka, C. and Tobias, S. (1981) Mathematical ability: Is sex a factor? *Science*, 212: 114.

Vandenberg, S.G. and Kuse, A.R. (1979) Spatial ability: A critical review of the sex-linked major gene hypothesis. In: M. Wittig and A.C. Petersen (Eds.), *Sex-Related Differences in Cognitive Functioning: Developmental Issues*, Academic Press, New York, pp. 67–96.

Very, P.S. (1967) Differential factor structures in mathematical ability. *Genet. Psychol. Monogr.*, 75: 169–207.

Waber, D.P. (1977) Sex differences in mental abilities, hemispheric lateralization, and rate of physical growth at adolescence. *Develop. Psychol.*, 13: 29–38.

Waber, D.P. (1979) Cognitive abilities and sex-related variations in the maturation of cerebral cortical functions. In: M. Wittig and A.C. Petersen (Eds.), *Sex-Related Differences in Cognitive Functioning: Developmental Issues*, Academic Press, New York, pp. 161–186.

Wilson, J.W. (1972) *Patterns of Mathematics Achievement in Grade 11: Z Population*, National Longitudinal Study of Mathematical Abilities, Report No. 17, School Mathematics Study Group, Stanford, CA.

Wise, L.L., Steel, L. and MacDonald, C. (1979) *Origins and Career Consequences of Sex Differences in Mathematics Achievement*, American Institutes for Research, Palo Alto, CA.

Yen, W.M. (1975) Sex-linked major gene influences on selected types of spatial performance. *Behav. Genet.*, 5: 281–298.

DISCUSSION

G.J. DE VRIES: You demonstrated that precocity in mathematical reasoning ability goes more often with myopia and allergy than the normal group. Should this precocity be seen as a pathological state? To be more exact, does it often go together with, e.g., disturbances in speech?

C.P. BENBOW: Mathematical precocity appears along with some advanced verbal ability. Our mathematically precocious students are also precocious verbally, but to a lesser degree. In terms of achievement in higher level mathematics, verbal ability is very important. It seems that only those of our students who have extreme mathematical *and* verbal precocity do well in very high level mathematics.

E. BRENNER: Did you try to correlate the sex differences in mathematical ability with the choice of hobbies?

C.P. BENBOW: There clearly are differences in the toys that male and female children play with. As of yet nobody has shown that there is a causal link between toys played with and ability. It is also not clear why boys play with certain toys and girls with others. Our retrospective studies of the backgrounds of our students seem to indicate remarkably similar treatment by the parents of their boys and girls. A further study is in progress of the exact toys played with by our students as children.

J.M. REINISCH: Does the space-form blindness reported in patients with Turner's syndrome (45XO) relate to the sex-linked recessive gene hypothesis of mathematical ability?

C.P. BENBOW: The sex-linked recessive gene hypothesis for the sex difference in spatial ability is generally not accepted any longer as a viable explanation (see Vandenberg and Kuse, 1979, for a review). Part of the evidence not supporting this hypothesis comes from the Turner syndrome patients. Since this hypothesis is no longer accepted for spatial ability, I doubt that it is viable for mathematical reasoning ability.

A.P. SFIKAKIS: There is a great variation in the hormone profile in girls because of the estrous cycle while this profile is steady in boys. Were there any menstruating girls in the 12-year-old group and did these variations in the 17-year-old girls have any influence when compared to boys?

C.P. BENBOW: We discovered a sex difference in mathematical reasoning ability among 12 year olds. Some of the girls had begun to menstruate by then, but certainly not most. The girls who had begun to menstruate had not done so for very long. Moreover, our boys had a larger variance of their SAT-M scores in our measure for mathematical reasoning ability than had our girls. Therefore, I doubt that the hormone cycle is an important determinant of the sex difference at age 12. Perhaps it relates to the even larger difference at age 17. We do not have any data to address this point.

B. MEYERSON: Could the sex difference between males and females be due to different rates in developing the mathematical ability? What I mean is this:

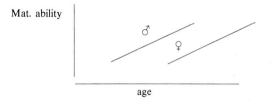

C.P. BENBOW: Yes, there could be a sex difference in the rates of development of mathematical reasoning ability. Our data indicate, however, that there is a difference in the slopes of the two lines representing developmental growth. The lines for boys and girls are not parallel. The boys appear to be developing their mathematical reasoning ability at a faster rate than the girls.

W.W. BEATTY: In the U.S.A. there has been much recent concern about the quality of education, especially in science and math. Further math and science achievement may be correlated with success in an increasingly technical society. Could you comment on the implications of your work for math and science education, particularly of young women?

C.P. BENBOW: Julian Stanley and I showed that there are many more males than females who can reason extremely well mathematically. This is group data and they are not applicable to any one individual. Thus, they cannot be used to counsel any single person. Our data do, however, tell us that it is likely that many more boys than girls will be successful in their pursuit of degrees or careers in quantitatively oriented sciences.

J.M. REINISCH: Are there any studies of the poorest or least precocious mathematics students? Since males are considered to be more variable in general, might there not be an overrepresentation of males in this group as well?

C.P. BENBOW: It has been established that there are more learning disabled boys than girls. Thus, this would seem likely.

H.H. SWANSON: Is there anything in which girls are better than boys?

C.P. BENBOW: Other studies have shown that girls are better at verbal tasks than males (e.g., Maccoby and Jacklin, 1974). In our sample, however, girls were not better in verbal reasoning ability than the boys.

H.H. SWANSON: Have any similar studies been made in other countries than the U.S.A.?

C.P. BENBOW: Allison Kelly (1978) studied sex differences in mathematical ability in several different countries. Within each country there was a sex difference in mathematics favoring males. Girls of one country, however, were better in some cases than boys of a different country.

REFERENCES

Kelly, A. (1978) *Girls and Science: International Study of Sex Differences in School Science Achievement*, Almqvist and Wiksell, Stockholm.

Maccoby, E.C. and Jacklin, C.N. (1974) *The Psychology of Sex Differences*, Stanford University Press, Stanford, CA.

Vandenberg, S.G. and Kuse, A.R. (1979) Spatial ability: a critical review of the sex-linked major gene hypothesis. In: M. Wittig and A.C. Petersen (Eds.), *Sex-Related Differences in Cognitive Functioning: Developmental Issues*, Academic Press, New York, pp. 67–96.

G.J. De Vries et al. (Eds.),
Progress in Brain Research, Vol. 61
© 1984   Elsevier Science Publishers B.V., Amsterdam

Performance and Intelligence in Hormonally Different Groups

H. NYBORG

Institute of Psychology, University of Aarhus, Risskov (Denmark)

INTRODUCTION

Males and females differ with respect to both performance and intelligence (for review, see Garai and Scheinfeld, 1968; Maccoby and Jacklin, 1974; Hoyenga and Hoyenga, 1979). Compared to women, men tend to be more assertive (e.g. to behave more independently and self-reliantly), aggressive, and to show high physical energy expenditure (e.g. they demonstrate a preference for "rough-and-tumble" outdoor play and "chasing behavior" in childhood and show more athletic interests in adulthood). Prepubertal play patterns are typically instrumental and object-oriented in boys, while many girls behave in some respects as though they rehearsed a later maternal role. General IQ scores do not differ markedly between men and women but certain subscores and IQ factors tend to do so. Men tend to outperform women on difficult spatial tasks, whereas women generally outperform men on certain types of verbal tasks. Men typically score higher on performance IQ than on verbal IQ, whereas the opposite is true for women. The differences in performance and intelligence between men and women are summarized in Table I.

These commonly observed sex differences have been explained in several ways. "Environmentalists" with a preference for "tabula rasa" models propose that sex differences appear because boys and girls are reared differently. Such workers typically use concepts like "reinforcement", "training", and "imitation", or assume that careless transfer of now inadequate cultural stereotypes can explain their observations. "Genetically oriented" researchers, on the other hand, often resort to less one-sided but sometimes very complex genetic models. A number of "interactionist" paradigms have also seen the light of day (see Hoyenga and Hoyenga, 1979, for review of theories). Unfortunately, neither nurture nor nature or combination models have succeeded in indicating whether specific environmental or genetic factors may be attributed a causal status with respect to the origin of gender differences. Furthermore, the mediating mechanisms have not been identified.

We have also looked for causal factors and their "route of impact" on sex-related personality and intellectual development in genetically abnormal groups. We examined the hypothesis that various karyotypes predispose for abnormal personality and intellectual development. However, after 10 years of work with persons of karyotypes 45,X; 47,XXY and 47,XYY and their normal controls, we could find neither a simple relationship between sex chromosome complement and performance, nor could any existing genetic or environmentalistic hypothesis be supported (Nielsen et al., 1977; Nyborg and Nielsen, 1979, 1981a,b). Some of our data led, in fact, to a rejection of the prominent X-linked, recessive

TABLE I

COMMONLY OBSERVED SEX DIFFERENCES IN GENDER IDENTITY, GENDER ROLE PERFORMANCE, AND INTELLECTUAL PERFORMANCE

| | Gender identity | Assertiveness, independence, self-reliance | Level of aggression | Physical energy expenditure | Prepubertal play preference | | Maternal interests | Spatial ability | Verbal ability | Verbal (V) — performance (P) score relationship |
					Objects	Persons				
Men	Masculine	+	+	+	+	÷	÷	+	÷	P > V
Women	Feminine	÷	÷	÷	÷	+	+	÷	+	V > P

+, high "normal"; ÷, low "normal".

gene theory for spatial ability (O'Connor, 1943; Stafford, 1961). We, therefore, reanalyzed our data, taking into account the fact that the groups were not only genetically abnormal but also abnormal hormonally. Thus, women with Turner's syndrome (i.e. lack of X-chromosome material) produce only minute amounts of sex hormones as their gonads develop improperly, and such women also perform poorly on spatial tasks and in mathematics. The reanalysis unexpectedly showed that Turner's women who had been treated with cyclic estrogen and gestagen for a period ranging from 3 months to 2 years performed at a normal female spatial ability level. In contrast, those who either received no hormone therapy at all or received this treatment for many years (8 years on the average) showed extremely low spatial ability in a number of spatial tasks (Nyborg and Nielsen, 1981a). These observations, the findings of Broverman et al. (1964, 1968) and of Petersen (1976), and the fact that other groups with abnormal sex hormone levels show deviant spatial ability suggest that sex hormones influence spatial ability. Therefore we began to pay more attention to the relationship between gonadal hormones and spatial problem-solving ability. We soon found several lines of evidence for such relations. Firstly, spatial ability apparently varies with the menstrual cycle (Klaiber et al., 1974; Dor-Shav, 1976). Secondly, the development of spatial ability may be related to early and late pubertal maturation (Waber, 1976, 1977a,b; but see also Petersen, 1976). Thirdly, using bodily or gender role criteria, individuals at the extremes of sexual polarity exhibit opposite levels of spatial ability. Thus, masculine men and feminine women show low spatial ability while androgynous men and women show high spatial ability (Maccoby and Jacklin, 1974; Hoyenga and Hoyenga, 1979). Fourthly, there is little difference between the sexes with respect to spatial abilities during the long prepubertal period during which the sexes are much alike as far as plasma hormone values are concerned, but in puberty a significant gender difference in spatial ability suddenly appears shortly before the time when plasma hormone levels differ maximally. Finally, spatial ability differences remain fairly stable throughout adulthood, just as do the sex hormone differences. We interpreted these relationships in terms of an ability-specific hormonal "optimal estrogen range" (OER) model (Nyborg, 1983). Furthermore, a growing body of recent evidence supports the notion that also gender role performance is under the influence of sex hormones. For example, human studies as well as animal studies indicate that dominance, assertiveness, aggression and parental behavior may depend on the pattern of prenatal hormone exposure (for review, see Hoyenga and Hoyenga, 1979). These and other observations recently led to a revision of our OER model in order to account for the general covariant pattern of development of personality and intellectual characteristics in men and women seen in Table I.

Both models are based on the fact that males are normally exposed both prenatally, perinatally and postpubertally to more circulating testosterone (T) than are women, whereas women are exposed to higher concentrations of 17β-estradiol (E_2). According to the general covariance (GC) model, circulating T and E_2 act as intervening variables coordinating the development of the gender-related traits seen in Table I. Thus, we assume these two factors to explain concerted prototypic development of the male and female gender pattern of personality and intelligence, in addition to differentiating the body sexually. Stated in its most radical form, the basic tenet of the GC model is that all gender-related characteristics — whether mental or somatic — develop harmoniously as a primary function of circulating sex hormones. Logically, then, adequate hormonal manipulation might be able to overrule whatever gender-differentiating power the sex chromosome complement may have on the phenotype. Furthermore, social impact is considered secondary to gonadal hormone effects. The GC model makes a distinction between the biochemically conditioned development of gender-related characteristics and their phenotypical expressions; the former is a function of sex hormones while the latter can be inhibited or facilitated by various environmental means that may act via the sex hormones among other mechanisms.

The present paper has two aims: (1) to perform a comparative analysis of gender-related characteristics in hormonally different groups, and (2) to see to what extent the outcome of the comparison can be predicted by the GC model. Material concerning gender role and intellectual performance of persons with various hormonal disturbances and different karyotypes was collected and compared in order to see whether the male and the female patterns indicated in Table I vary with the hormones or with the karyotypes. Persons with a history of "normal male hormone exposure", along with individuals who were exposed to more circulating T than was usual for people with their chromosomal make-up, were pooled in a so-called "T/E" group, and compared to an "E/T" group consisting of persons with a history of "normal female hormone exposure", along with individuals having been exposed to more circulating E_2 than was usual for their chromosomal make-up.

LITERATURE, DATA AND METHODOLOGICAL PROBLEMS

Subjects

Data for inclusion in the comparative analysis were compiled from the literature and from the author's own files on the following 9 hormonally atypical groups (see Table II): (1) individuals with the adrenogenital syndrome (karyotype 46,XX and 46,XY: Money and Lewis, 1966; Ehrhardt and Money, 1967; Ehrhardt et al., 1968a,b; Lewis et al., 1968; Money and Ehrhardt, 1968, 1972; Ehrhardt, 1973, 1975; Perlman, 1973; Baker and Ehrhardt, 1974; Ehrhardt and Baker, 1974, 1975; Lev-Ran, 1974; McGuire and Omen, 1975; Money and Daléry, 1975; Money and Schwartz, 1975; Solomon and Schoen, 1975; Reinisch, 1976; Reinisch et al., 1979), (2) persons with progestin priming early in life (46,XX and 46,XY: Ehrhardt and Money, 1967; Money and Ehrhardt, 1968, 1972; Reinisch, 1976, 1977; Reinisch and Karow, 1977; Reinisch and Gandelman, 1978), (3) men with two Y chromosomes (47,XYY: Nielsen, 1969; Owen, 1972; Nielsen and Christensen, 1974; Nöel et al., 1974; Witkin et al., 1976; Nyborg and Nielsen, 1981b), (4) women with three X chromosomes (47,XXX: Kidd et al., 1963; Tennes et al., 1975), (5) men with two X chromosomes (47,XXY: Nielsen, 1969; Money and Ehrhardt, 1972; Theilgaard, 1972; Witkin et al., 1976), (6) men with protein deficiency leading to kwashiorkor syndrome (46,XY: Dawson, 1966, 1972), (7) individuals insensitive to androgen (46, XY: Money et al., 1968; Masica et al., 1969; Money and Ehrhardt, 1972; Perlman, 1973; Money and Ogunro, 1974), (8) individuals with estrogen priming early in life (46,XX and 46,XY: Dalton, 1968, 1976, 1981; Yalom et al., 1973; Zussman et al., 1975; Ehrhardt et al., 1977; Meyer-Bahlburg et al., 1977; Reinisch, 1977), and (9) women lacking some X chromosome material (45,X or mosaics: Schaffer, 1962; Money, 1964; Money and Alexander, 1966; Ehrhardt et al., 1970; Theilgaard, 1972; Nielsen et al., 1977; Baekgaard et al., 1978; Nyborg and Nielsen, 1979, 1981a). For general discussion of hormone–behavior relationships, see Reinisch (1976), Meyer-Bahlburg and Ehrhardt (1977), Ehrhardt and Meyer-Bahlburg (1979), Hoyenga and Hoyenga (1979) and Nyborg (1983).

These groups were categorized in accordance with whether they had a history of "usual high" or an "unusual high" (i.e. hypernormal) hormone level of T (the T/E group) for either endogenous (e.g. adrenogenital syndrome) or exogenous reasons (e.g. due to the effect on the fetus of androgen treatment of the pregnant woman), or of "usual high" or an "unusual high"

TABLE II

HORMONALLY ABNORMAL GROUPS CONSIDERED IN THE PAPER

Group*	Karyotype	Origin of anomaly	Hormonal deviation	Phenotype	Treatment
1. Adrenogenital syndrome (congenital adrenal hyperplasia)	46,XX 46,XY	Autosomal, recessive	Excessive adrenal androgenic output, pre- and postnatally	Virilized Normal	Cortisone ± surgery Cortisone
2. Prenatal progestin induction	46,XX 46,XY	Androgenic hormone treatment of mother during pregnancy	Prenatal androgen priming	Virilized Further masculinized	Surgery None
3. Men with double-Y chromosomes	47,XYY	Non-disjunction during meiosis in the father	Perhaps increased androgen levels and/or abnormal metabolism	Tall, masculine	—
4. Women with triple-X chromosomes	47,XXX	Non-disjunction during meiosis	Sometimes early menopause and menstrual irregularities	Delayed development	—
5. Men with double-X chromosomes (Klinefelter's syndrome)	47,XXY	Non-disjunction during meiosis	Low androgen output	Tall, small testes, feminized	Hormone therapy
6. Men with kwashiorkor syndrome	46,XY	Severe protein deficiency causing liver damage etc.	Elevated plasma estrogen values	Feminized	—
7. Androgen-insensitive persons	46,XY	X-linked, recessive	Receptors insensitive to androgen	Tall, little pubic hair, no internal sex organs, distinctively feminine	—
8. Prenatal estrogen induction	46,XX 46,XY	Estrogenic hormone treatment of mother during pregnancy	Prenatal estrogen priming	Normal Shorter, some genitally abnormal	—
9. Women lacking X-chromosome material (Turner's syndrome)	45,X and mosaics	Non-disjunction or other loss of X-chromosome material	Very low plasma hormone values	Short and sexually infantile	Hormone therapy

* For literature sources, refer to the text.

level of E_2 (the E/T group) relative to their chromosomal sex. Groups with hormonal variations within a physiologically more normal range were also included in the study. These non-clinical individuals were categorized hormonally according to their bodily appearance, because heavy masculinization depends on ample plasma T and feminization on the presence of E_2.

A number of important reservations must be made about the present survey. There is little consensus about how to define gender variables, and no metric scale exists for their measurement. The various authors' definitions of the variables were accepted on face value in the comparative analysis, as were the various approaches by which they chose to study them. Obviously, experimental studies of the effects of sex hormone variations in humans are not feasible for ethical reasons. The survey relies therefore mainly on the outcome of relatively few, small-scale clinical studies typically including less than 50 subjects each. Most of the observations reported here reached statistical significance, but in some cases positive trends in the direction expected from the results of other studies were accepted as well even if not tested for statistical significance because of too few subjects or because the measuring scale or the test applied precluded quantitative treatment. A further problem with some studies of prepubertal children is that they take the absence of significant hormone–intelligence relationships to mean that sex hormones do not influence intelligence. This conclusion is unwarranted, because the usual sex differences in intelligence typically do not appear before puberty anyhow. Other factors that tend to obscure hormone–behavior relationships if not taken into consideration are: that some children are more sensitive to hormone treatment than others as seen in differences in genital development; that treated individuals may be pooled despite different time of onset and length of treatment, and that dosage and type of hormones applied differed; and that prenatal sex hormone effects may differ radically from postnatal effects. Furthermore, it is the exception rather than the rule that details of medical treatment are given and that plasma sex hormone values were measured, especially in the early studies. But even if exact measures were at hand, they would probably tell only a small part of the story about the relationship between circulating sex hormone values and their biological effects, because plasma sex hormones may be bound, aromatized or degraded long or shortly before action. It can, accordingly, be misleading to draw conclusions from plasma values to central effects. In order to solve these problems via studies of hormonally abnormal individuals, we need large-scale, internationally coordinated, cross-disciplinary studies, in which the researchers use identical methods.

GENDER ROLE PERFORMANCE AND INTELLIGENCE

The T/E group is characterized by a masculine or an androgynous gender identity (see Table III). In general, T/E individuals show high self-reliance and physical energy expenditure but are not particularly aggressive. They appear to be object-oriented rather than person-oriented, and to show relatively little maternal interests. This characterization applies regardless of sex chromosomal make-up. Table IV indicates that the general IQ is variable in the T/E group, in that both high and low IQs are compatible with a T/E balance. With the exception of the first two masculine groups, spatial ability was high, and performance IQ scores were equal to or better than verbal IQ scores. Verbal ability was also variable between the groups. No systematic relationship between chromosomal gender and phenotypic traits was observed.

TABLE III

PERSONALITY CHARACTERISTICS IN THE TESTOSTERONE/ESTROGEN (T/E) GROUPS

| Groups | | | | Gender role performance | | | | | |
Characteristics	Chromosomal sex	Genital sex	Gender identity	Assertiveness, independence, self-reliance	Level of aggression	Physical energy expenditure	Prepubertal play preference Objects	Persons	Maternal interests
Men with extra Y material	47,XYY	♂	Masculine	?	+ +*	+ +	+	÷ ÷	÷ ÷
"Masculine" men**	46,XY	♂	Masculine	+ +	+ +	+ +	+ +	÷ ÷	÷ ÷
Adrenogenital syndrome	46,XX	♀ or mixed	Androgynous	+ +	+	+ +	+ +	÷ ÷	÷ ÷
	46,XY	♂	Masculine	+	+	+ +	+	÷	÷
Prenatal progestin induction	46,XX	♀ or mixed	Androgynous	+ +	+ +	+ +	+ +	÷ ÷	÷ ÷
	46,XY	♂	Masculine	+	+	+	+	÷	÷
"Normal" men	46,XY	♂	Masculine	+	+	+	+	÷	÷
Androgynous men	46,XY	♂	Androgynous	+ +	+	+	+ +	÷ ÷	÷
Androgynous women	46,XX	♀	Androgynous	+ +	+	+	+ +	÷ ÷	÷ ÷

+ +, unusually high for their sex; +, high "normal"; ÷, low "normal"; ÷ ÷, unusually low for their sex; ?, not determined or disputable.
* Perhaps impulsive rather than aggressive.
** For definition, see Broverman et al. (1964); Petersen (1976); for discussion, see Maccoby and Jacklin (1974); Hoyenga and Hoyenga (1979).

TABLE IV

INTELLECTUAL CHARACTERISTICS IN THE TESTOSTERONE/ESTROGEN (T/E) GROUPS

| Characteristics | Groups | | | Intellectual performance | | | Verbal (V) — performance (P) score relationship |
	Chromosomal sex	Genital sex	Gender identity	General IQ	Spatial ability	Verbal ability	
Men with extra Y material	47,XYY	♂	Masculine	÷÷	÷÷	÷÷	?
"Masculine" men *	46,XY	♂	Masculine	+	÷÷	++	V > P
Adrenogenital syndrome	46,XX	♀ or mixed	Androgynous	++	++	++	P = V**
	46,XY	♂	Masculine	++	++	++	P = V**
Prenatal progestin induction	46,XX	♀ or mixed	Androgynous	++	++	+	P = V
	46,XY	♂	Masculine	++	+	+	P > V
"Normal" men	46,XY	♂	Masculine	+	+	÷	P > V
Androgynous men	46,XY	♂	Androgynous	+	++	+	P > V
Androgynous women	46,XX	♀	Androgynous	+	++	+	P > V

+ +, unusually high for their sex; +, high "normal"; ÷, low "normal"; ÷ ÷, unusually low for their sex; ?, not determined or disputable.
* See ** in Table III.
** However, very high IQ range: V > P.

TABLE V

PERSONALITY CHARACTERISTICS IN THE ESTROGEN/TESTOSTERONE (E/T) GROUPS

| Groups | | | Gender identity | Gender role performance | | | | | |
| Characteristics | Chromosomal sex | Genital sex | | Assertiveness, independence, self-reliance | Level of aggression | Physical energy expenditure | Prepubertal play preference | | Maternal interests |
							Objects	Persons	
"Normal" women	46,XX	♀	Feminine	÷	÷	÷	÷	+	+
"Feminine" women *	46,XX	♀	Feminine	÷ ÷	÷ ÷	÷ ÷	÷ ÷	+ +	+ +
Women with triple-X syndrome	47,XXX	♀	Feminine	÷ ÷	?	?	?	?	?
Men with Klinefelter's syndrome	47,XXY	♂	Demasculinized	÷ ÷	?	÷ ÷	?	?	?
Men with kwashiorkor syndrome	46,XY	♂	Demasculinized	?	÷ ÷	÷ ÷	?	?	?
Androgen-insensitive persons	46,XY	♀	Feminine	÷ ÷	÷ ÷	÷ ÷	÷ ÷	+ +	+ +
Prenatal estrogen induction	46,XX / 46,XY	♀ / ♂	Feminine / Demasculinized	÷ / ÷ ÷	÷ ÷ / ÷ ÷	÷ / ÷ ÷	÷ / ÷ ÷	+ + / + +	+ / ?
Women with Turner's syndrome	45,X and mosaics	♀	Feminine	÷ ÷	÷ ÷	÷ ÷	÷ ÷	+ +	+ +

+ +, unusually high for their sex; +, high "normal"; ÷, low "normal"; ÷ ÷, unusually low for their sex; ?, not determined or disputable.
* See ** in Table III.

TABLE VI

INTELLECTUAL CHARACTERISTICS IN THE ESTROGEN/TESTOSTERONE (E/T) GROUPS

| Groups | | | Gender identity | Intellectual performance | | | Verbal (V) — Performance (P) score relationship |
Characteristics	Chromosomal sex	Genital sex		General IQ	Spatial ability	Verbal ability	
"Normal" women	46,XX	♀	Feminine	+	÷	+	V > P
"Feminine" women	46,XX	♀	Feminine	+	÷ ÷	?	?
Women with triple-X syndrome	47,XXX	♀	Feminine	÷ ÷	?	?	?
Men with Klinefelter's syndrome	47,XXY	♂	Demasculinized	÷ ÷	÷ ÷	÷ ÷	?
Men with kwashiorkor syndrome	46,XY	♂	Demasculinized	÷ ÷	÷ ÷	+ +	V > P
Androgen-insensitive persons	46,XY	♀	Feminine	+	÷	+	V > P
Prenatal estrogen induction	46,XX	♀	Feminine	+	÷	+	V > P
	46,XY	♂	Demasculinized	+	÷ ÷	+ +	V > P
Women with Turner's syndrome	45,X and mosaics	♀	Feminine	+	÷ ÷	+	V > P

+ +, unusually high for their sex; +, high "normal"; ÷ low "normal"; ÷ ÷, unusually low for their sex; ?, not determined or disputable.

In the E/T group a "feminine" or a demasculinized gender identity predominates (see Table V). Self-reliance tends to be low, as do aggression and physical energy expenditure. Object play preference is low, while preference for playing with dolls and other "girlish" toys tends to go together with maternal interests in the E/T group. There is a downward trend in spatial ability in the E/T groups, whereas verbal IQ scores tend to exceed performance IQ scores (see Table VI).

THE GENERAL COVARIANCE MODEL FOR GENDER DEVELOPMENT

The major pattern that emerges from the findings is that the majority of T/E individuals exhibited the male gender repertoire, whereas most E/T individuals had the female gender repertoire. These observations support the main predictions of the GC model, namely that sex hormones act as the primary determinants of whether a prototypic male, female, or mixed mental development will take place, whereas the karyotype is a poor predictor of gender development. I believe that the observations point to the need for a re-evaluation of research into gender differences, calling for an analysis that is based neither on traditional environmentalist nor on available genetic theories. Such an analysis should be able to specify and quantify the major factors responsible for gender differentiation; primarily those biochemical variables that can account for the fact that gender-related traits show continuous, overlapping distributions that tend to cluster around the male and the female prototypic developmental pathways (summarized in Table I) despite considerable environmental and genetic variation. Any new analysis must account for the causal chain of the biochemical variables, for stability as well as for flexibility in gender development, and should have individuals rather than statistical group means as its target. Finally, a new analysis has to address the problem why gender differences appear at all.

The GC model is conceived in accordance with these requirements, but may be too simple to meet them fully. The GC hypothesis views sex hormones as the fingers on the physiological switchboard for gender differentiation. More specifically, the GC model assigns to sex hormones the ultimate biochemical responsibility for producing not only gender-related differences in sensory modality priorities, but also in interests, cognitive style, gender role differences, physical energy expenditure, androgenization of the muscles and fat distribution, and in other gender-related somatic characteristics. All these traits would depend on whether or not the sex hormones were present at the right place, and at the right time, and in the right amount.

But what is the right place, right time, and the right amount for sex hormone actions? How can biochemical signals be translated into gender-specific behavioral patterns, and what is the purpose of this translation? Which mechanisms mediate the processes, and what specific endogenous and exogenous factors influence the hormonal systems? What keeps the system in balance and how great is its flexibility? Unfortunately, there are no satisfactory answers to these vital questions today, but systematizing the fragments of relevant information already available may enable us to formulate testable hypotheses.

Only those aspects of the GC model which are relevant for understanding how the gender repertoires described in this paper became a reality will be discussed.

The right place

Let us assume that the sites of sex hormone uptake in the brain correspond to their site of biological action. High uptake of sex hormones occurs in the preoptic-hypothalamic and the limbic systems (McEwen, 1976). This is especially interesting from a cognitive point of view, because it might indicate that traditional explanations for gender-related differences in verbal–spatial ability based upon left–right brain lateralization fail to incorporate an important cortical-*subcortical* dimension. However, there are also sex hormone receptors in other parts of the brain, and our knowledge about their significance depends to a large extent on our techniques for detecting the effects of uptake of circulating gonadal hormones in these areas. Furthermore, sex hormones interact both peripherally with each other, and centrally with neurotransmitters (Dörner, 1978), where they also influence pre- and postsynaptic membrane characteristics (Moss and Dudley, 1984). E_2 is biologically very active in the cell nucleus, whereas T seems effective in the nucleus only if aromatized to E_2. According to the GC model, E_2 is the most important hormone for gender-related actions in the central nervous system.

The right time

The GC model allows some tentative inferences to be made about when and how sex hormones exert their effects on phenotypical characteristics. Gender role traits such as physical energy expenditure, aggression and "nurturant" behavior appear long before puberty (e.g. Brindley et al., 1973), and can accordingly be ascribed to relatively permanent, prenatal organizational actions of sex hormones which do not need pubertal activation. In contrast, gender differences in the intellectual pattern do not usually appear before puberty, and probably they depend on pubertal activation in addition to early organizational effects.

The right amount

Peaks in T levels occur prenatally as well as perinatally in boys. Thereafter, differences are scarcely detectable in plasma sex hormone levels between boys and girls during the pre-pubertal period using current radioimmunoassay techniques. After puberty, however, boys produce about 10 times more T than do girls, whereas girls have about 3 times more plasma E_2 than do boys (moreover, their E_2 levels vary with the menstrual cycle). The GC model supposes that these average values result in the typical male or female gender repertoires. However, in order to account for individual variations in prototypic development, the GC model is designed explicitly as a person-specific, threshold model. Thus, the effect of E_2 is assumed to be curvilinearly related to spatial ability as illustrated in Fig. 1. Letters A–D and E–H in Fig. 1 signify two groups of individuals who are differently sensitized to sex hormones (and/or have a different brain organization) during the pertinent period. Letters A, B, C, and D represent in this case males who had been prenatally primed with T, and who therefore are relatively insensitive to their comparatively low levels of circulating E_2, and who scored just below their optimum level for spatial ability. The GC model assumes that a further increase in E_2 will enhance their spatial ability, and will influence their gender role performance and their body development in an androgynous direction. This explanation can account for covariant personality, intellectual, and somatic development. The curvilinear relationship shown in Fig. 1 predicts that increases in E_2 above the optimum level will inhibit the expression of spatial ability. This can explain the low spatial ability and the gender

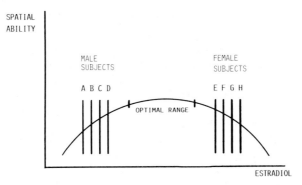

Fig. 1. The "optimal estrogen range" (OER) model for hormone-spatial ability relationship. (Modified from Nyborg, 1983.)

development both in demasculinized men with Klinefelter's syndrome and in men suffering from the kwashiorkor syndrome. These same principles may also explain what happens in distinctively "masculine" men, i.e. they aromatize part of their high plasma T to E_2 centrally and thereby exceed the optimal E_2 range, while at the same time being bodily androgenized, perhaps by direct action of T on somatic tissues (for details, see Nyborg, 1983). Letters E, F, G, and H here represent females who have relatively high plasma E_2 values and who are situated somewhat below their optimum level for spatial ability. The GC model predicts that a prolonged decrease in their E_2 levels will enhance their spatial ability, influence their gender performance in an androgynous direction, and enable T to androgenize their body while not being much antagonized peripherally by E_2. A transient decrease in their E_2 levels will also temporarily enhance their spatial ability, but will not influence their gender identity or body markedly, thus explaining why spatial ability is high in the estrogen-low phases of the menstrual cycle. On the other hand, a further increase in E_2 would lead to even more repressed spatial ability, in addition to feminizing their performance and their bodies. Thus, a curvilinear model can explain why spatial ability is optimal when gender identity and gender role performance are most alike in the two sexes, and why spatial ability will be low both in distinctively feminine women and in masculine men. The model also provides a basis for understanding the behavioral status of various hormonally deviant groups. Furthermore, the model explains some observations in Tables III, IV, V, and VI, that apparently run counter to what would have been expected from a simple T/E versus E/T classification of subjects. This points to important methodological constraints in traditional studies of gender differences. Identical changes in plasma sex hormone levels may lead to facilitation of personality and intellectual parameters in one subject but to inhibition of these same parameters in another subject. The GC model is person-specific and this makes it more useful than traditional dichotomic group mean approaches by allowing for individual evaluation of quantitative variation on the biochemical as well as on the behavioral side.

Mediating mechanisms

The GC model assumes at least 3 interrelated avenues for the effects of sex hormones: (1) by prenatal priming of sensitivity to pubertal sex hormones, (2) by early permanent "organizational" effects on developing neural tissues, and (3) by transient "activational" effects on the functioning of the mature nervous tissues. With regard to prenatal effects, Döhler and Hancke (1978) have suggested that absence of E_2 in the fetus will leave its brain sexually undifferentiated, that a moderate amount of E_2 will feminize its brain, and that large amounts of E_2 lead to masculinization (see Döhler et al., 1984). Massive amounts of E_2, however, have a neurotoxic effect leading to a less differentiated status of brain tissues. It is likely that E_2 exerts some of its growth-promoting effects on neural tissues (Toran-Allerand, 1976). This can partly explain gender-typing of the brain by "organizing" the specific neuronal circuits that are believed to be essential for the appearance of gender-related behavior. As E_2 influences genomic expression it modulates the production of proteins considered essential for neural development, so that the effects of E_2 in the central nervous system may show up long after the hormone itself has disappeared.

Sex hormones may also have rapid effects within the central nervous system. For example, E_2 alters the metabolism of neurotransmitters and also influences their actions by changing pre- and/or postsynaptic membrane characteristics (see Hutchison and Steimer, 1984; Moss and Dudley, 1984). Much more needs to be learned about antagonistic and agonistic effects of sex hormones on the CNS, but promising advances have already been made, as a number of chapters in this book testify.

Hormone–behavior translation

Like genes, hormones cannot produce behavior directly. The GC model states, in accordance with Hoyenga and Hoyenga (1979), that sex hormones promote gender-related tendencies to experience and to behave relatively consistently in different situations. Such tendencies have appeared in the past under names such as "drives", "subconscious motives", "traits", and "sex-stereotyped behavioral response patterns". According to the GC model, sex hormones color perceptions so that men and women put a different emphasis on given aspects of the surroundings, as with gender-related focus of interests. More specifically, the GC model assigns the sex hormones the biochemical responsibility for inducing gender-related differences in the way sounds and visual information are processed by the brain (e.g. McGuinness, 1974, 1976; McGuinness and Lewis, 1976). Gonadal hormones also influence whether visual or somatosensory information will be taken as a primary reference for determining the perception of the upright in a visual-vestibular (-somesthetic) conflict situation such as the rod-and-frame task (Nyborg, 1977; Nyborg and Nielsen, 1981a). Sex hormones can promote gender differences by the way perceptual input (verbal-communicative, social, or visuo-spatial information) is handled intellectually. In this way different tasks may be differentially rewarding to men and women, and may reinforce the expression of gender differences. However, the GC model also assumes that sex hormones can influence even more subtle behavioral patterns, such as toy preferences, and parents learn readily which toys their child prefers most, and act in accordance with this knowledge. It follows from the GC model that differential gonadal hormone conditioning is the prime mechanism for conservation of social institutions that guarantee, for better or for worse, the continuation of gender-related differences in child rearing. Obviously, this notion runs directly against prevailing environmentalist explanations of gender differences. According to the GC model, we are neither "tabula rasa" abstractions thrown helplessly at the forces of sex-typing, nor are we predetermined biological beings developing our genetic potentials in a cultural vacuum. We are more specialized than behaviorists believe, but less specialized than radical adherents to instinct theory claim. According to the GC model, sex hormones mediate behavioral readiness to perceive and respond in certain ways. Sex hormone-conditioned responses can, of course, be either positively or negatively reinforced according to cultural prescriptions.

Stability–flexibility of the development of prototypic gender patterns

The GC model assigns to the sex hormones the role of being important mediators between the organism and its environment. Although genes are crucial for sex hormone production, it is now generally acknowledged that sex hormone production is also influenced markedly by environmental factors such as nutrition, stress, experience of social pressure (dominance–submission), and the presence of sexually attractive partners. Adaptability of hormonal production to environmental requirements is secured in this way. A dynamic balance between genetic and environmental factors is essential for adequate gender behavior to appear. It is of interest to know whether certain gender-related parameters remain stable when environmentally induced changes in sex hormone parameters occur. If gender role performance is geared mainly by the prenatal "organizational" effect, then it will show only limited flexibility to environmental impacts. On the other hand, intellectual differences that also require pubertal "activation" can be expected to show greater flexibility to environmentally induced postpubertal hormonal changes.

The "why" of hormonal actions

It is of interest to speculate whether any evolutionary advantages might be associated with having sex hormones bear the major responsibility for gender-linked brain differences. It is generally acknowledged that the sexual mode of reproduction confers an evolutionary advantage in the form of increased genetic variability. The different gender roles must have been subjected to different selective pressures through time. Perhaps the constellation of a feminine behavioral repertoire (a low level of aggression and physical energy expenditure, a "preference for persons" and for early rehearsal of a maternal role, combined with high communicative skills) has optimized the reproductive success of women faced with successive child births, feeding and rearing of their offspring in primitive times. Perhaps the constellation of a "male" behavioral repertoire (independent, energetic, a certain amount of aggression, and high spatial ability) conferred men with an advantage in hunting and warfare, while not being unduly distracted by maternal interests. Thus, the gender roles mediated by sex hormones may have had survival value in primitive societies, and may thereby have become built into human behavior. According to the GC model, the genetic potentiality for developing male, female, or mixed behavioral repertoires exists in both sexes, and the phenotypic actualization of these potentials depends primarily on the kind of sex hormone signals available to the physiological switchboard.

REFERENCES

Baekgaard, W., Nyborg, H. and Nielsen, J. (1978) Neuroticism and extraversion in Turner's syndrome. *J. Abnorm. Psychol.*, 87: 583–586.

Baker, S.W. and Ehrhardt, A.A. (1974) Prenatal androgen, intelligence, and cognitive sex differences. In: R.C. Friedman, R.M. Richart and R.L. Vande Wiele (Eds.), *Sex Differences in Behavior*, Wiley, New York, pp. 53–76.

Brindley, C., Clarke, P., Hutt, C., Robinson, I. and Wethli, E. (1973) Sex differences in the activities and social interactions of nursery school children. In: R.P. Michael and J.H. Crook (Eds.), *Comparative Ecology and Behaviour of Primates*, Academic Press, London, pp. 799–828.

Broverman, D.M., Broverman, I.K., Vogel, W., Palmer, R.D. and Klaiber, E.L. (1964) The automatization cognitive style and physical development. *Child. Develop.*, 35: 1343–1359.

Broverman, D.M., Klaiber, E.L., Kobayashi, Y. and Vogel, W. (1968) Roles of activation and inhibition in sex differences in cognitive abilities. *Psychol. Rev.*, 75: 23–50.

Dalton, K. (1968) Ante-natal progesterone and intelligence. *Br. J. Psychol.*, 114: 1377–1382.

Dalton, K. (1976) Prenatal progesterone and educational attainments. *Br. J. Psychiat.*, 129: 438–442.

Dalton, K. (1981) The effect of progesterone and progestogens on the foetus. *Neuropharmacology*, 20: 1267–1269.

Dawson, J.L.M. (1966) Kwashiorkor, gynaecomastia, and feminization processes. *J. Trop. Med. Hyg.*, 69: 175–179.

Dawson, J.L.M. (1972) Effects of sex hormones on cognitive styles in rats and men. *Behav. Genet.*, 2: 21–42.

Döhler, K.-D. and Hancke, J.L. (1978) Thoughts on the mechanism of sexual brain differentiation. In: G. Dörner and M. Kawakami (Eds.), *Hormones and Brain Development*, Elsevier/North-Holland, Amsterdam, pp. 153–158.

Döhler, K.D., Hancke, J.L., Srivastava, S.S., Hofmann, C., Shrine, J.E. and Gorski, R.A. (1984) Participation of estrogens in female sexual differentiation of the brain; neuroanatomical, neuroendocrine and behavioral evidence. In: G.J. De Vries, J.P.C. De Bruin, H.B.M. Uylings and M.A. Corner (Eds.), *Sex Differences in the Brain. The Relation between Structure and Function. Progress in Brain Research*, this volume, Ch. 5.

Dörner, G. (1978) Hormones, brain development and fundamental processes of life. In: G. Dörner and M. Kawakami (Eds.), *Hormones and Brain Development*, Elsevier/North-Holland, Amsterdam, pp. 13–25.

Dor-Shav, N.K. (1976) In search of pre-menstrual tension: Note on sex-differences in psychological differentiation as a function of cyclical physiological changes. *Percept. Mot. Skills*, 42: 1139–1142.

Ehrhardt, A.A. (1973) Maternalism in fetal hormonal and related syndromes. In: J. Zubin and J. Money (Eds.), *Contemporary Sexual Behavior: Critical Issues in the 1970's*, Johns Hopkins University Press, Baltimore, MD, pp. 99–115.

Ehrhardt, A.A. (1975) Prenatal hormonal exposure and psychosexual differentiation. In: E.J. Sachar (Ed.), *Topics in Psychoendocrinology*, Grune and Stratton, New York, pp. 67–82.

Ehrhardt, A.A. and Baker, S.W. (1974) Fetal androgens, human central nervous system differentiation, and behavior sex differences. In: R.C. Friedman, R.M. Richart and R.L. Vande Wiele (Eds.), *Sex Differences in Behavior*, Wiley, New York, pp. 33–51.

Ehrhardt, A.A. and Baker, S.W. (1975) Males and females with congenital adrenal hyperplasia: A family study of intelligence and gender-related behavior. In: P.E. Lee, L.P. Plotnich, A.A. Kowarski and C.J. Migeon (Eds.), *Congenital Adrenal Hyperplasia*, University Park Press, Baltimore, MD, pp. 447–461.

Ehrhardt, A.A. and Meyer-Bahlburg, H.F.L. (1979) Psychosexual development: An examination of the role of prenatal hormones. In: *Sex, Hormones and Behaviour, Ciba Foundation Symposium 62 (New Series)*, Excerpta Medica, Amsterdam, pp. 41–57.

Ehrhardt, A.A. and Money, J. (1967) Progestin-induced hermaphroditism: I.Q. and psychosexual identity in a study of ten girls. *J. Sex Res.*, 3: 83–100.

Ehrhardt, A.A., Epstein, R. and Money, J. (1968a) Fetal androgens and female gender identity in the early-treated adrenogenital syndrome. *Johns Hopk. Med. J.*, 122: 160–167.

Ehrhardt, A.A., Evers, K. and Money, J. (1968b) Influence of androgen and some aspects of sexually dimorphic behavior in women with the late treated adrenogenital syndrome. *Johns Hopk. Med. J.*, 123: 115–122.

Ehrhardt, A.A., Greenberg, N. and Money, J. (1970) Female gender identity and absence of fetal gonadal hormones: Turner's syndrome. *Johns Hopk. Med. J.*, 126: 237–248.

Ehrhardt, A.A., Grisanti, G.C. and Meyer-Bahlburg, H.F.L. (1977) Prenatal exposure to medroxyprogesterone acetate (MPA) in girls. *Psychoneuroendocrinology*, 2: 391–398.

Garai, J.E. and Scheinfeld, A. (1968) Sex differences in mental and behavioral traits. *Genet. Psychol. Monogr.*, 77: 169–299.

Hoyenga, K.B. and Hoyenga, K.T. (1979) *The Question of Sex Differences*, Little, Brown and Co., Boston, MA.

Hutchison, J.B. and Steimer, Th. (1984) Androgen metabolism in the brain: behavioural correlates. In: G.J. De Vries, J.P.C. De Bruin, H.B.M. Uylings and M.A. Corner (Eds.), *Sex Differences in the Brain. The Relation between Structure and Function. Progress in Brain Research*, this volume, Ch. 2.

Kidd, C., Knox, R.S. and Month, D.I. (1963) A psychiatric investigation of triple-X syndrome females. *Br. J. Psychiat.*, 109: 90–94.

Klaiber, E.L., Broverman, D.M., Vogel, W. and Kobayashi, Y. (1974) Rhythms in plasma MAO activity, EEG, and behavior during the menstrual cycle. In: M. Ferin, F. Halverg, R.M. Richart and Vande Wiele (Eds.), *Biorhythms and Human Reproduction*, Wiley, New York.

Lev-Ran, A. (1974) Sexuality and educational levels of women with the late-treated adrenogenital syndrome. *Arch. Sex. Behav.*, 3: 27–32.

Lewis, V.G., Money, J. and Epstein, R. (1968) Concordance of verbal and nonverbal ability in the adrenogenital syndrome. *Johns Hopk. Med. J.*, 122: 192–195.

Maccoby, E.E. and Jacklin, C.N. (1974) *The Psychology of Sex Differences*, Stanford University Press, Stanford, CA.

Masica, D.N., Money, J., Ehrhardt, A.A. and Lewis, V.G. (1969) I.Q., fetal sex hormones and cognitive patterns: Studies in the testicular feminizing syndrome of androgen insensitivity. *Johns Hopk. Med. J.*, 124: 34–43.

McEwen, B.S. (1976) Interactions between hormones and nerve tissue. *Sci. Am.*, 7: 48–58.

McGuinness, D. (1974) Equating individual differences for auditory input. *Psychophysiology*, 11:113–120.

McGuinness, D. (1976) Away from a unisex psychology: individual differences in visual sensory and perceptual processes. *Perception*, 5: 279–294.

McGuinness, D. and Lewis, I. (1976) Sex differences in visual persistence: Experiments on the Ganzfeld and afterimages. *Perception*, 5: 295–301.

McGuire, L. and Omen, G. (1975) Congenital adrenal hyperplasia. I. Family studies of IQ. *Behav. Genet.*, 2: 165–174.

Meyer-Bahlburg, H.F.L. and Ehrhardt, A.A. (1977) Effects of prenatal hormone treatment on mental abilities. In: R. Gemme and C.C. Wheeler (Eds.), *Progress in Sexology*, Plenum, New York, pp. 85–92.

Meyer-Bahlburg, H.F.L., Grisanti, G.C. and Ehrhardt, A.A. (1977) Prenatal effects of sex hormones on human male behavior: Medroxyprogesterone acetate (MPA). *Psychoneuroendocrinology*, 2: 383–390.

Money, J. (1964) Two Cytogenetic syndromes: Psychologic comparisons. 1. Intelligence and specific-factor quotients. *J. Psychiat. Res.*, 2: 223–231.

Money, J. and Alexander, D. (1966) Turner's syndrome: Further demonstration of the presence of specific cognitional deficiencies. *J. Med. Genet.*, 3: 47–48.

Money, J. and Daléry, J. (1975) Hyperadrenocortical 46,XX hermaphroditism with penile urethra: Psychological studies in seven cases, three reared as boys, four as girls. In: P.E. Lee, L.P. Plotnick, A.A. Kowarski and C.J. Migeon (Eds.), *Congenital Adrenal Hyperplasia*, University Park Press, Baltimore, MD, pp. 433–446.

Money, J. and Ehrhardt, A.A. (1968) Prenatal hormone exposure. Possible effects on behavior in man. In: R.P. Michael (Ed.), *Endocrinology and Human Behaviour*, Oxford University Press, London, pp. 32–48.

Money, J. and Ehrhardt, A.A. (1972) *Man and Woman, Boy and Girl*, Johns Hopkins University Press, Baltimore, MD, pp. 95–116.

Money, J. and Lewis, V. (1966) IQ, genetics and accelerated growth: Adrenogenital syndrome. *Bull. Johns Hopk. Hosp.*, 118: 365–373.

Money, J. and Ogunro, C. (1974) Behavioral sexology: Ten cases of genetic male intersexuality with impaired prenatal and pubertal androgenization. *Arch. Sex. Behav.*, 3: 181–205.

Money, J. and Schwartz, M. (1975) Dating, romantic and non-romantic friendships, and sexuality in 17 early-treated adrenogenital females, aged 16–25. In: P.E. Lee, L.P. Plotnick, A.A. Kowarski and C.J. Migeon (Eds.), *Congenital Adrenal Hyperplasia*, University Park Press, Baltimore, MD, pp. 433–446.

Money, J., Ehrhardt, A.A. and Masica, D.N. (1968) Fetal feminization induced by androgen insensitivity in the testicular feminizing syndrome: Effect on marriage and maternalism. *Johns Hopk. Med. J.*, 123: 105–114.

Moss, R.L. and Dudley, C.A. (1984) Molecular aspects of the interaction between estrogen and the membrane excitability of hypothalamic nerve cells. In: G.J. De Vries, J.P.C. De Bruin, H.B.M. Uylings and M.A. Corner (Eds.), *Sex Differences in the Brain. The Relation between Structure and Function. Progress in Brain Research*, this volume, Ch. 1.

Nielsen, J. (1969) *Klinefelter's Syndrome and the XYY Syndrome: A Genetical, Endocrinological and Psychiatric–Psychological Study of 33 Hypogonadal Male Patients and 2 Patients with Karyotype 47,XYY*, Munksgaard, Copenhagen, pp. 70–99.

Nielsen, J. and Christensen, A.-L. (1974) Thirty-five males with double Y chromosome. *J. Psychol. Med.*, 4: 38–47.

Nielsen, J., Nyborg, H. and Dahl, H. (1977) Turner's syndrome. A psychiatric–psychological study of 45 women with Turner's syndrome, compared with their sisters and women with normal karyotypes, growth retardation and primary amenorrhoea. *Acta Jutlandica, Med. Ser.*, 21: 101–151.

Nöel, D.R., Duport, J.P., Revil, D., Dussuyer, I. and Quack, B. (1974) The XYY syndrome: Reality or myth? *Clin. Genet.*, 5: 387–394.

Nyborg, H. (1977) *The Rod-and-Frame Test and the Field Dependence Dimension: Some Methodological, Conceptual, and Developmental Considerations*, Dansk Psykologisk Forlag, Copenhagen, pp. 92–132.

Nyborg, H. (1983) Spatial ability in men and women: Review and new theory. *Advances in Human Research and Therapy*, Vol. 5, Monography Series, Pergamon, London, pp. 39–140.

Nyborg, H. and Nielsen, J. (1979) Aberracioni chromosomiche e performance cognitiva. IV. Mancato sviluppo di strategie di soluzione del conflitto ottico-vestibolare, in relazione all'età, in ragazze con sindrome di Turner. In: M. Cesa-Bianchi and M. Poli (Eds.), *Aspetti Biosociali della Sviluppo: Un Approccio Inter-disciplinare, Vol. I, Problemi Medico-Biologici,* F. Angeli, Milan, pp. 77–90.

Nyborg, H. and Nielsen, J. (1981a) Sex hormone treatment and spatial ability in women with Turner's syndrome. In: W. Schmid and J. Nielsen (Eds.), *Human Behavior and Genetics,* Elsevier/North-Holland, Amsterdam, pp. 167–182.

Nyborg, H. and Nielsen, J. (1981b) Spatial ability of men with karyotype 47,XXY, 47,XYY, or normal controls. In: W. Schmid and J. Nielsen (Eds.), *Human Behavior and Genetics,* Elsevier/North-Holland, Amsterdam, pp. 97–106.

O'Connor, J. (1943) *Structural Visualization,* Human Engineering Laboratory, Boston, MA.

Owen, D.R. (1972) The 47,XYY male: A review, *Psychol. Bull.,* 78: 209–233.

Perlman, S.M. (1973) Cognitive abilities of children with hormone abnormalities: Screening by psychoeducational tests. *J. Learn. Disabil.,* 6: 21–29.

Petersen, A.C. (1976) Physical androgyny and cognitive functioning in adolescence. *Develop. Psychol.,* 12: 524–533.

Reinisch, J.M. (1976) Effects of prenatal hormone exposure on physical and psychological development in humans and animals: With a note on the state of the field. In: E.J. Sachar (Ed.), *Hormones, Behavior, and Psychopathology,* Raven, New York, pp. 69–94.

Reinisch, J.M. (1977) Prenatal exposure of human foetuses to synthetic progestin and oestrogen affects personality. *Nature (London),* 266: 561–562.

Reinisch, J.M. and Gandelman, R. (1978) Human research in behavioral endocrinology: Methodological and theoretical considerations. In: G. Dörner and M. Kawakami (Eds.), *Hormones and Brain Development,* Elsevier/North-Holland, Amsterdam, pp. 77–86.

Reinisch, J.M. and Karow, W.G. (1977) Prenatal exposure to synthetic progestins and estrogens: Effects on human development. *Arch. Sex. Behav.,* 6: 257–288.

Reinisch, J.M., Gandelman, R. and Spiegel, F.S. (1979) Prenatal influences on cognitive abilities: Data from experimental animals and human genetic and endocrine syndromes. In: M.A. Wittig and A.C. Petersen (Eds.), *Sex-Related Differences in Cognitive Functioning,* Academic Press, New York, pp. 215–239.

Shaffer, J.W. (1962) A specific cognitive deficit observed in gonadal aplasia (Turner's syndrome). *J. Clin. Psychol.,* 18: 403–406.

Solomon, I.L. and Schoen, E.J. (1975) Blood testosterone values in patients with congenital virilizing adrenal hyperplasia. In: P.E. Lee, L.P. Plotnick, A.A. Kowarski and C.J. Migeon (Eds.), *Congenital Adrenal Hyperplasia,* University Park Press, Baltimore, MD, pp. 163–172.

Stafford, R.E. (1961) Sex differences in spatial visualization as evidence of sex-linked inheritance. *Percept. Mot. Skills,* 13: 428.

Theilgaard, A. (1972) Cognitive style and gender role. *Dan. Med. Bull.,* 19: 276–282.

Toran-Allerand, C.D. (1976) Sex steroids and the development of the newborn mouse hypothalamus and preoptic area in vitro: Implications for sexual differentiation. *Brain Res.,* 106: 407–412.

Waber, D.P. (1976) Sex differences in cognition: A function of maturation rate? *Science,* 192: 572–573.

Waber, D.P. (1977a) Sex differences in mental abilities, hemispheric lateralization, and rate of physical growth at adolescence. *Develop. Psychol.,* 13: 29–38.

Waber, D.P. (1977b) Biological substrates of field dependence: Implication of the sex differences. *Psychol. Bull.,* 84: 1076–1087.

Witkin, H.A., Mednick, S.A., Schulsinger, R., Bakkestroem, E., Christiansen, K.O., Goodenough, D.R., Hirsch-horn, K., Lundsteen, C., Owen, D.R., Philip, J., Rubin, D.B. and Stocking, M. (1976) Criminality in XYY and XXY men. *Science,* 193: 547–555.

Yalom, I.D., Green, R. and Fisk, N. (1973) Prenatal exposure to female hormones: Effect on psychosexual development in boys. *Arch. Gen. Psychiat.,* 28: 554–561.

Zussman, J.U., Zussman, P.P. and Dalton, K. (1975) Prenatal administration of progesterone. Paper presented at the meeting of the Society for Research in Child Development, Denver, April (In: Dalton, 1976, 1981).

Subject Index